# MONEY AND BANKING

## A MARKET-ORIENTED APPROACH

### Second Edition

# MONEY AND BANKING

## A MARKET-ORIENTED APPROACH

### Second Edition

■

IVAN C. JOHNSON
*California State University, Northridge*

WILLIAM W. ROBERTS
*California State University, Northridge*

**THE DRYDEN PRESS**

Chicago  New York  Philadelphia  San Francisco  Montreal  Toronto
London  Sydney  Tokyo  Mexico City  Rio de Janeiro  Madrid

**Acquisitions Editor:**  Elizabeth Widdicombe
**Project Editor:**  Rebecca Ryan
**Managing Editor:**  Jane Perkins
**Design Director:**  Alan Wendt
**Design Supervisor:**  Jeanne Calabrese
**Production Manager:**  Mary Jarvis
**Permissions Editor:**  Doris Milligan

**Text and Cover Designer:**  Margery Dole
**Copy Editor:**  Susan Thornton
**Compositor:**  York Graphic Services
**Text Type:**  10/12 Garamond

**Library of Congress Cataloging in Publication Data**

Johnson, Ivan C.
    Money and banking.

    Includes bibliographies and index.
    1. Money.    2. Banks and banking.    3. Financial
institutions.    I. Roberts, William W.    II. Title.
HG221.J667   1985        332.1        84-13711
ISBN 0-03-001222-8

Printed in the United States of America
678-016-9876543

Address orders:
383 Madison Avenue
New York, NY 10017

Address editorial correspondence:
One Salt Creek Lane
Hinsdale, IL 60521

CBS College Publishing
The Dryden Press
Holt, Rinehart and Winston
Saunders College Publishing

*To our wives, Elizabeth and Gail,*

*and in memory of BENEDICT J. PEDROTTI   1928–1984*
*Chairman of the Department of Economics*
*California State University, Northridge   1973–1984*

# THE DRYDEN PRESS SERIES IN ECONOMICS

Asch and Seneca
**Government and the Marketplace**

Breit and Elzinga
**The Antitrust Casebook**

Breit and Ransom
**The Academic Scribblers, Revised Edition**

Campbell and Campbell
**An Introduction to Money and Banking,**
*Fifth Edition*

Dolan
**Basic Economics,** *Third Edition*

Dolan
**Basic Macroeconomics,** *Third Edition*

Dolan
**Basic Microeconomics,** *Third Edition*

Heertje, Rushing, and Skidmore
**Economics**

Hyman
**Public Finance**

Johnson and Roberts
**Money and Banking: A Market-Oriented
Approach,** *Second Edition*

Kidwell and Peterson
**Financial Institutions, Markets, and
Money,** *Second Edition*

Leftwich and Eckert
**The Price System and Resource
Allocation,** *Ninth Edition*

Lindsay
**Applied Price Theory**

Morley
**Inflation and Unemployment,**
*Second Edition*

Morley
**Macroeconomics**

Nicholson
**Intermediate Microeconomics and Its
Application,** *Third Edition*

Nicholson
**Microeconomic Theory: Basic Principles
and Extensions,** *Third Edition*

Pappas and Hirschey
**Fundamentals of Managerial Economics,**
*Second Edition*

Pappas, Brigham, and Hirschey
**Managerial Economics,** *Fourth Edition*

Poindexter
**Macroeconomics,** *Second Edition*

Puth
**American Economic History**

Richardson
**Urban Economics**

Welch and Welch
**Economics: Theory and Practice**

# PREFACE

The first edition of *Money and Banking: A Market-Oriented Approach* was written to incorporate the institutional changes that had been brought about by the passage of the Depository Institutions Deregulation and Monetary Control Act of 1980. That legislation promised to affect the financial system in the United States almost as much as the banking act that was passed in the aftermath of the Great Depression. We now know that this important legislation was not to be the final word on changing the financial system. Since the publication of the first edition, many changes have occurred within the institutional framework. The Monetary Control Act of 1980 has been amended by the Garn-St. Germain Act of 1982 and the money supply definitions have been replaced. Other institutional developments and policy changes have made a second edition imperative. The response of those instructors who adopted the first edition has been most encouraging, and we hope that this second edition will make their task of keeping abreast of developments that much easier.

## Intended Market

*Money and Banking: A Market-Oriented Approach* is intended for undergraduate use. It should provide the student with an accurate picture of forces that continually operate in financial markets and show how financial institutions influence resource allocation in the aggregate economy. It also explains how the monetary authorities operating in these markets are able to influence macroeconomic variables such as aggregate output, unemployment, and the general price level.

Although money and banking courses are essentially economics courses, this text is also designed to accommodate the wide spectrum of business students that these courses often serve. For example, the discussion of microeconomic aspects of the financial markets and their relation to the aggregate economy is conducted in the language of the contemporary business world. Thus, while the emphasis is on economics, a course based on this book can easily be integrated into a sequence of business courses.

## Features of the Text

Today, the ambivalent state of monetary theory continues to present a problem for the writing of money and banking books. Many authors choose to approach the subject by dogmatically propounding one basic theory. Others neglect the model differences and emphasize the policy similarities by collapsing the macroeconomic discussion into one all-purpose model (usually *IS-LM* curves). In *Money and Banking,* we have tried to avoid either extreme. The discussion is focused and straightforward—yet sophisticated enough to give the reader a flavor of current monetary controversy.

**Use of both Neoclassical and Keynesian models**  This book describes two distinct models: a neoclassical system that emphasizes the effect of the money supply and monetary conditions in the input markets, and a Keynesian system that emphasizes the effect of the money supply and monetary conditions on aggregate demand. This approach gives the reader a broad understanding of monetary economics. It includes the theoretical underpinnings of monetarism and supply-side economics, as well as the less dogmatic policy prescriptions of the Keynesian and neoclassical models.

**Use of Real and Nominal Values**  Throughout the discussion of economic theory, we have maintained a distinction between real and nominal values by using lower-case letters for real variables and upper-case letters for nominal values. We have designated the more familiar *IS-LM* curves as *is-lm* curves to emphasize that the model refers to *real* money supplies, *real* outputs, and *real* interest rates. We have found this a helpful teaching device and recommend it for classroom use. Because the distinction between real and nominal variables is crucial to a discussion of money and banking, we have deliberately given more coverage to the topic.

**Integration of Theory and Policy**  Instead of treating monetary theory and policy separately, as most texts, our approach integrates them into a coherent whole. The policies that can be derived from neoclassical theory are presented with the development of the neoclassical theory, while the policies that can be derived from the Keynesian theory are presented with the development of that theory. This allows the student to see monetary and fiscal policies as the implication of theory, not a separate problem.

*International Coverage*  Many of the financial problems that the United States has faced in recent years have been the result of this country's position in international affairs. Too often this subject is covered in a separate section of a text. Recognizing the importance of international coverage, we have included the international aspects of financial institutions throughout the discussion.

## New in This Edition

The following features are new to the second edition of *Money and Banking*:

- The institutional discussion has been completely updated to reflect the changes that have taken place since the first edition. This update includes the provisions of the Garn-St. Germain Act of 1982. (Throughout Part I)

- Reflecting the convergence in function of the various depository institutions, the thrifts have been fully incorporated into the discussion of commercial banking. Discussion of the thrifts now precedes the development of the money multipliers. (Chapters 8–12)

- The post-1982 definitions of the money supply have been used throughout, and newly included accounts (money market deposit and the super NOW) are fully explained. (Chapters 1 and 12)

- All statistical material has been updated.

- The explanation of the neoclassical, Keynesian, and monetarist approaches has been expanded into a new chapter. (Chapter 15)

- Policy impacts of the Keynesian system have been consolidated into the development of the theory. (Chapters 21 and 22)

- Post-1980 policy changes of the Federal Reserve System are discussed, including the move away from the use of M1 as a monetary target. (Chapter 23)

## Pedagogy and Ancillaries

This book is a comprehensive survey of money and banking that may be used in its entirety. Alternatively, selections may be used for shorter courses. The various chapter combinations for courses of different length and content are suggested in the *Instructor's Manual.* A complete teaching package includes textbook, *Instructor's Manual,* and *Study Guide.*

Each text chapter is divided into sections and ends with a summary of the material covered, a list of key terms, and a selection of discussion questions. The book concludes with a complete glossary of terms. The

*Instructor's Manual* contains brief outlines of lecture material (pointing out the distinguishing features of the textbook coverage), a test bank of examination questions, and suggested answers for the end-of-chapter questions. The *Study Guide* includes chapter outlines, multiple-choice and true-false questions, numerical problems, and a programmed guide to the salient points covered in each chapter.

## Acknowledgments

In writing both editions of this book we have incurred many debts. We wish to thank all of our teachers, both professors and students, who have managed over the years to provide a better understanding of the role of money and banking in the economy. For giving invaluable assistance by reviewing the new edition, we wish to thank Jeffrey S. Bader, LaFayette College; Robert C. Connolly, The University of North Carolina, Greensboro; H. Stephen Gardner, Baylor University; Beverly Hadaway, The University of Texas, Austin; Kenneth R. Kentosh, Franklin University; R. Keith Miller, Pennsylvania State University, Beaver; and Herbert Witt, University of San Francisco.

We are indebted to those reviewers who commented upon the first edition. These are: James Barth, George Washington University; John Buehler, University of Arizona; Timothy Gallagher, Syracuse University; John Hambelton, San Diego State University; John Harrington, Seton Hall University; David Lindsey, Board of Governors of the Federal Reserve System; Morgan Lynge, University of Illinois; Robert McGee, Florida State University; Nick Noble, Miami University; Douglas Pearce, University of Missouri-Columbia; M. Ray Perryman, Baylor University; John Rea, Oklahoma State University; David Roberts, University of Miami; Marjorie Stanley, Texas Christian University; Joseph Stellaccio, Ball State University; and Ronald Teigen, University of Michigan.

Also, we would like to thank our colleagues at California State University, Northridge, for all the help and advice they have given us. Once again we would particularly like to thank Sol Buchalter, who knows more about commercial banks than he ever told us. It is necessary, however, to absolve all but ourselves of responsibility for any error of fact or defect in presentation that remains.

Finally, we wish to thank all our friends at The Dryden Press, without whose help this book would never have been written.

Ivan C. Johnson
William W. Roberts
California State University
Northridge

# CONTENTS

## I MONEY AND FINANCIAL INSTITUTIONS 1

CHAPTER ONE
**INTRODUCTION** 2

THE ORIGINS OF MONEY IN THE UNITED STATES 4
MONEY IN THE UNITED STATES TODAY 6
THE DEFINITIONS OF THE MONEY SUPPLY 10
HELPING TO UNDERSTAND THE MONETARY SYSTEM 15

CHAPTER TWO
**MONEY AND ITS USES** 20

THE THEORY OF EXCHANGE 22
THE PLACE OF MONEY IN THE THEORY OF EXCHANGE 24
CHOOSING A MEDIUM OF EXCHANGE 26
MONEY AS A UNIT OF ACCOUNT 27
MONEY AS A STORE OF VALUE 28
MONEY PRICES, INFORMATION, AND COMPARATIVE
ADVANTAGE 30

CHAPTER THREE
**THE QUANTITY OF MONEY—A PREVIEW OF
MONETARY THEORY** 36

MARKET INTERACTION 38
MEASUREMENT AND AGGREGATION 38

THE EQUATION OF EXCHANGE   40
THE MONEY SUPPLY   40
THE FINANCIAL SECTOR AND NOMINAL OUTPUT   49


CHAPTER FOUR
**MONETARY STANDARDS**   66

COMMODITY STANDARDS   68
MONOMETALLISM—THE CASE OF THE GOLD STANDARD   68
BIMETALLISM—THE UNITED STATES' FIRST COMMODITY
STANDARD   81
SYMMETALLISM AND THE COMPOSITE COMMODITY STANDARD   90
PAPER STANDARDS   91
*APPENDIX 4A THE QUANTITY OF MONEY UNDER A GOLD STANDARD
WITH PAPER AND BANK MONEY*   94


CHAPTER FIVE
**INTEREST RATES AND MARKET ACTIVITY**   98

INTEREST RATES AS MARKET PRICES   100
INTEREST RATES IN FINANCIAL MARKETS   104
PRICE CHANGES AND WEALTH DISTRIBUTION   109
PRESENT AND FUTURE VALUES   112
INTEREST RATES AND COMMODITY PRICES   114


CHAPTER SIX
**CREDIT INSTRUMENTS AND THEIR MARKETS**   120

CREDIT INSTRUMENTS   121
TYPES OF CREDIT INSTRUMENTS   122
THE PRICE OF CREDIT INSTRUMENTS AND THE NOMINAL
RATE OF INTEREST   131


CHAPTER SEVEN
**CREDIT INSTRUMENTS ISSUED BY THE
UNITED STATES TREASURY**   142

THE PRIMARY MARKET FOR TREASURY BILLS   145
THE SECONDARY MARKET FOR TREASURY BILLS   148
THE MARKETS FOR TREASURY NOTES AND BONDS   149
CREDIT MARKET INTERACTION   150
THE TERM STRUCTURE OF INTEREST RATES   152

CHAPTER EIGHT
**FINANCIAL INTERMEDIATION AND
COMMERCIAL BANKING    162**

THE ROLE OF FINANCIAL INTERMEDIARIES    164
THE FUNDAMENTAL PROBLEM OF FINANCIAL
INTERMEDIATION    166
COMMERCIAL BANK ASSETS    170
COMMERCIAL BANK LIABILITIES    177


CHAPTER NINE
**COMMERCIAL BANK MANAGEMENT    188**

RESERVE REQUIREMENTS    190
THE CLEARING AND COLLECTION OF CHECKS    195
THEORIES OF BANKING    204
BANK ASSET MANAGEMENT    206
BANK LIABILITY MANAGEMENT    215
THE INTERACTION OF ASSET AND LIABILITY MANAGEMENT    221


CHAPTER TEN
**THE REGULATION OF BANKS AND
BANKING ACTIVITY    226**

THE REGULATORS    229
COMPETITIVE REGULATION    231
ENTRY INTO BANKING    234
EXIT FROM BANKING    245


CHAPTER ELEVEN
**NONBANK FINANCIAL INTERMEDIARIES    258**

THRIFT INSTITUTIONS    263
CONTRACTUAL SAVINGS INSTITUTIONS    271
FINANCE COMPANIES    277
INVESTMENT COMPANIES    279
MISCELLANEOUS NONBANK FINANCIAL INSTITUTIONS    280


CHAPTER TWELVE
**THE MONEY SUPPLY AND THE MULTIPLE
EXPANSION OF DEPOSITS    284**

NONBANK FINANCIAL INTERMEDIARIES IN THE MULTIPLE
EXPANSION PROCESS    288

TRANSACTIONS ACCOUNTS   294
MONEY MULTIPLIERS AND THE MARKET   301
THE GURLEY-SHAW HYPOTHESIS   307


CHAPTER THIRTEEN
**CENTRAL BANKING**   314

CENTRAL BANKING IN THE UNITED STATES BEFORE 1913   316
THE STRUCTURE OF THE FEDERAL RESERVE   317
INDEPENDENCE OF THE FEDERAL RESERVE   320
MONETARY MANAGEMENT   322


CHAPTER FOURTEEN
**THE MONETARY BASE AND MONETARY CONTROL**   342

MONETARY CONTROL   344
THE FEDERAL RESERVE BALANCE SHEET   346
THE MONETARY BASE   348
FINANCING GOVERNMENT EXPENDITURE   360
FOREIGN EXCHANGE MARKET INTERVENTION   364


**II   MONETARY THEORY AND POLICY**   369


CHAPTER FIFTEEN
**INTRODUCTION TO MONETARY THEORY AND POLICY**   370

ECONOMIC MODELS   372
MONETARISM AND MONETARY THEORY   379


CHAPTER SIXTEEN
**THE MONEY MARKET IN THE NEOCLASSICAL SYSTEM**   384

THE EQUATION OF EXCHANGE   385
THE CAMBRIDGE EQUATION   386
THE NAIVE QUANTITY THEORY OF MONEY   388
THE MODERN QUANTITY THEORY OF MONEY   394
THE MODERN QUANTITY THEORY AND CAMBRIDGE $k$   401

CHAPTER SEVENTEEN
**THE SUPPLY SIDE**   408

THE SUPPLY OF OUTPUT   410
THE LABOR MARKET   411
EQUILIBRIUM IN THE LABOR MARKET   422
UNEMPLOYMENT IN A NEOCLASSICAL SYSTEM   422
EXPECTATIONS: RATIONAL OR ADAPTIVE   428
AGGREGATE OUTPUT IN THE NEOCLASSICAL SYSTEM   430


CHAPTER EIGHTEEN
**THE PRODUCT MARKET IN THE
NEOCLASSICAL SYSTEM**   436

PRODUCT MARKET EQUILIBRIUM   438
FISCAL POLICY   448
THE FOREIGN SECTOR   454
INDIRECT EFFECTS OF FISCAL POLICY
ON AGGREGATE OUTPUT   455


CHAPTER NINETEEN
**MONETARY POLICY IN THE NEOCLASSICAL SYSTEM**   460

MONETARY POLICY IN AN ECONOMY WHERE WAGE FLEXIBILITY
ASSURES FULL EMPLOYMENT   462
MONETARY POLICY IN AN ECONOMY WITH UNEMPLOYMENT   465
MONETARY TARGETS   468
MONETARY POLICY AND NOMINAL INTEREST RATES   472
THE INTEREST RATE TARGET AND FISCAL POLICY   474
THE FOREIGN SECTOR   476
RULES VERSUS AUTHORITIES   481


CHAPTER TWENTY
**THE PRODUCT MARKET IN THE KEYNESIAN SYSTEM**   486

PRODUCT MARKET EQUILIBRIUM   489
COMPONENTS OF AGGREGATE DEMAND   491
INTEREST-INDUCED CHANGES IN AGGREGATE DEMAND
AND THE *is* CURVE   497
STABILITY IN THE PRODUCT MARKET   498


CHAPTER TWENTY-ONE
**THE MONEY MARKET IN THE KEYNESIAN SYSTEM**   504

THE DEMAND FOR REAL MONEY BALANCES   506
EQUILIBRIUM IN THE MONEY MARKET   511

EXPECTED PRICE CHANGES AND THE *lm* CURVE    514
EQUILIBRIUM IN THE KEYNESIAN SYSTEM    515
INFLATION IN THE KEYNESIAN SYSTEM    520
THE PHILLIPS CURVE    522


CHAPTER TWENTY-TWO
**MONETARY AND FISCAL POLICIES IN
THE KEYNESIAN SYSTEM**    528

FISCAL POLICY    530
MONETARY POLICY    534
EFFECTIVENESS OF MONETARY AND FISCAL POLICIES    536
MONETARISM AND THE *is-lm* CURVE ELASTICITIES    544
REAL BALANCE EFFECTS IN THE *is* CURVE    544
STABILIZATION POLICY    546


CHAPTER TWENTY-THREE
**THE CONDUCT OF MONETARY POLICY**    556

THE BASIC CONFLICT: RULES VERSUS AUTHORITIES    559
CONFLICT: MONETARY AGGREGATES OR INTEREST RATES    560
THE ROLE OF TARGETS AND INDICATORS    564
MONETARY POLICY FOLLOWING WORLD WAR II    566
MONETARY POLICY IN THE 1950s: DOMESTIC    568
MONETARY POLICY POST–WORLD WAR II:
INTERNATIONAL PAYMENTS    569
MONETARY POLICY IN THE 1960s: DOMESTIC    576
MONETARY POLICY IN THE 1970s: DOMESTIC    579
A SHIFT TOWARD MONETARISM    583
MONETARY POLICY INTO THE 1980s    584

GLOSSARY    593

INDEX    606

# I

## MONEY
## AND FINANCIAL
## INSTITUTIONS

# CHAPTER ONE

# INTRODUCTION

*Money has a functional definition, but the monetary authorities in the United States have established several operational definitions for statistical and policy purposes. The most important are money supply 1 (M1) and money supply 2 (M2).*

M oney appears to be the focus of many of mankind's most contradictory emotions. It has been desired almost universally, but at the same time it has been vilified as "filthy lucre" and as "the root of all evil." Although some religions have condemned money, others have attributed spiritual significance to it. Utopian societies have been established with the express purpose of rejecting its use, but the same societies often have created money supplies of their own.

Close examination of the condemnations of money usually reveals, however, that it is wealth, the possession of wealth, and the love of wealth that is being condemned, and not the particular substance that is being used in exchange (whatever form that substance might take). For example, the Bible does not say that money is the root of all evil, but that the love of money is the root of all evil (*see* 1 Timothy 6:10). Nonetheless, even well-known economists have shown a remarkable ambivalence on the subject. In explaining money's role as the prime mover in economic development, classical economist John Stuart Mill simultaneously extolled the benefits of using money and dismissed money itself as "an insignificant thing."

Although the significance of money can be downplayed by viewing it as a veil behind which the exchanging of goods and services takes place, it has been found more productive to investigate the disruptive role that money can play in the flow of goods and services being exchanged. Most of the problems of modern economies—including inflation, recession, and low rates of economic growth—can be attributed at least partially to mismanagement of the money supply in one way or another. Today, the significance of money is not denied. Its *existence* is thought significant because it facilitates trade to an extent impossible under a barter system, and more important for policy purposes, the *quantity* and the *rate of change of the quantity* of money are thought to be major determinants of output, employment, and prices. However, realization that changes in the money supply can lead to changes in the economy has led the public to express fears about *who* controls the money supply. Such fears have run the gamut from believing simply that central bankers *cannot* control the money supply, to fears that the money supply is being manipulated by "Wall Street," "the gnomes of Zurich," or even demonic influences within the central banks.

## THE ORIGINS OF MONEY IN THE UNITED STATES

The United States dollar was not defined until the Coinage Act of 1792, but this was by no means the beginning of the use of money in North America. Before the Europeans came, *wampum* (consisting of blue, black, and white beads usually strung on thread) was commonly used in exchange. When the Europeans immigrated, they added their own currencies to the money supply. The earliest immigrants used the currency of their native countries, but later immigrants of all nationalities used all of the currencies. Obviously, the amount of currency transported to North America was limited by the wealth of the immigrants, but also it was limited by the laws of some of the countries (for example, England) forbidding the export of coin. Many of the currencies were in very short supply, so to overcome the difficulties of exchange, the immigrants improvised by adding certain commodities to the circulation. Corn, tobacco, beaver skins, pins, wheat, and barley were commonly used as money. These commodities were accepted in exchange, not because they were wanted for their own sake, but because it was known that others would accept them in exchange for other goods.

Among the currencies imported from Europe, one was in much larger supply than all the others. This was the Spanish currency. Its presence led to the adoption of the dollar unit by the United States and also prescribed the size and content of the first United States coins. The Spanish currency included a silver coin known as a *dólar.* As with the first United States currency, the Spanish dollar was *full-bodied.* This means that if the coin is melted down, the metal contained in the coin sells in the commodity market for an amount equal to the face value of the coin. This is not the case with the coins we use today. When the value of the metal contained in a coin is below its face value, the coin is said to be a *token coin.*

Because the Spanish dollar was full-bodied, the problem of supplying small change was a simple one. A half-dollar was made by cutting a dollar

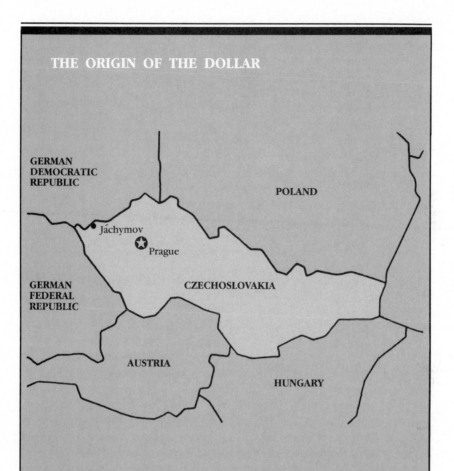

## THE ORIGIN OF THE DOLLAR

GERMAN
DEMOCRATIC
REPUBLIC

POLAND

Jáchymov

Prague

GERMAN
FEDERAL
REPUBLIC

CZECHOSLOVAKIA

AUSTRIA

HUNGARY

The word *dollar* is from the Spanish pronunciation of the German word *thaler*, which is itself an abbreviation of *Joachimsthaler*, which means "from the valley of St. Joachim." This is a reference to Joachimsthal, Bohemia—which is now the town of Jáchymov, Czechoslovakia—where a silver strike was made in 1516.

Coins were struck from the Joachimsthaler silver, and the name *Joachimsthaler*, later abbreviated to *thaler*, came to be used throughout Europe to indicate the coins that were of the same size and silver content as the 1516 coins. When the Spanish came to North America, they brought their own versions of the Bohemian thalers, which they called dólares.

When the United States created its own currency the government simply chose to copy these Spanish coins.

coin in half. Each half then would have an amount of silver that would sell in the commodity market for 50¢. Similarly, a quarter-dollar could be made by cutting the dollar coin into four equal parts. Quarters then were cut in half to make two *reales* (in Spanish) or two *bits* (in English). Spanish dollars were called "pieces of eight" because each of them could be cut into eight reales or bits. Even though this system is no longer used, calling a quarter "two bits" has survived.

Cutting the coins was not easy, and the inaccuracies yielded bits of unequal size. The large bits, known as "long bits," were valued at 15¢, and the small bits, known as "short bits," were valued at 10¢. When a bit was cut in half, the two pieces (called *picayunes*) were each valued at 6½¢. When the United States minted its own currency, the practice of cutting up coins to make change was discontinued, but the small coins (called *subsidiary coins*) still contained the same proportion of silver as before. It was also decided to divide the dollar according to the decimal system rather than to use the eighths and sixteenths of the Spanish system or the more complicated British system.

## MONEY IN THE UNITED STATES TODAY

What is used as money in the United States today is very different from the full-bodied coins of 1792, when the dollar was defined as a given weight of silver or of gold. Today we use token coins, which are not used in accordance with the value of the metal they contain but are accepted in exchange at face value because it is expected that everyone else will accept them at face value. Moreover, the coins that we use constitute a very minor part of the quantity of money used in exchange. Many payments are made by using paper currency and by writing orders (called *checks, negotiable orders of withdrawal,* or *share drafts*) to financial institutions, instructing them to move funds from one account to another. As the payments mechanism has become more complicated, the proportion of the money supply held in the form of coins has decreased greatly.

### Coins

All the coins we use today are tokens. They are metal discs with numbers stamped on them. The smallest coin is the penny, which is a copper-colored disc with "one cent" stamped on it. The 5¢ coin is made of a nickel alloy. It is called a *nickel* because it was the first coin in the system to contain nickel. It was designed as a token coin to replace a much smaller full-bodied coin called a *half-dime.* Dimes (10¢), quarters (25¢), and half-dollars (50¢) are tokens made from discs of nickel and copper that are sandwiched together. Coins made in this way are called *clad coins.* Dollar coins are rarely used today (outside of casinos). There are two types in circulation, but

## THE DOLLAR SYMBOL

The symbol for the dollar did not originate in the United States. Contrary to popular belief, the symbol has nothing to do with the initials of the United States being superimposed one on the other. The symbol was used prior to 1776 both in the American colonies and in Mexico. When the United States defined the dollar in 1792 (as a given weight of silver and a given weight of gold), the symbol was already well established.

There are in fact two competing theories of the symbol's origin. One is that it is a representation of a drawing that appears on the face of the Spanish silver dollar. On that coin the pillars of Hercules are drawn wrapped in the Spanish colors:

The other theory is that the symbol developed from the use of $P^s$ for *pesos* in Mexico. The development of the symbol has been traced through the following stages:

The word *peso,* adopted by Mexico and many other Latin American countries as the name for their monetary unit, is an apt description of a full-bodied coin. The word *peso* means "weight," and a full-bodied coin is a given weight of the metal.

*Source:* Cajori, Florian. "History of Mathematical Notation," *The Numismatist,* August 1929. Reprinted with permission of *The Numismatist,* the official publication of the American Numismatic Association, P.O. Box 2366, Colorado Springs, CO 80901.

neither of them currently is being manufactured by the Mint. The large *Eisenhower dollar* is a token coin the same size as the original full-bodied dollar of 1792. The smaller *Susan B. Anthony dollar* is a clad coin made of nickel alloy and copper that was intended as a replacement for the more costly paper dollar. Although paper dollars are relatively cheap to print, they are costly in that they frequently must be replaced. However, the costs at the Mint are seldom a factor in people's tastes and preferences. The Susan B. Anthony dollar was received with little enthusiasm by the general public.

The milling on the edge of all coins except the penny and the nickel has continued since the time when they were full-bodied coins. The milling prevented silver coins from being clipped. Clipping or shaving metal from the edge of full-bodied coins was a profitable business, so that accepting coins at face value was extremely risky until milling was introduced in the seventeenth century. Without milling, exchanges had to be made by weight, a practice that defeated the purpose of having coins at all.

## Paper Money

The paper money we use is issued by the Federal Reserve System, the central bank of the United States. Some paper money not issued by the Federal Reserve still circulates, but officially this type of money is retired. It still circulates because what is used as money is the result of usage, not law. The retired notes still circulating were issued by the United States Treasury. They include silver certificates, which at one time were redeemable for a given weight of silver, and United States Notes or "greenbacks," which were never redeemable for either gold or silver. As with the coins, paper money in use today is accepted at face value because it is expected that everyone will accept it as such. The pieces of paper do *not* represent any metal. Just as full-bodied coins have been replaced by token coins, so the type of paper money that was redeemable for a given weight of gold or silver has been replaced by irredeemable paper.

The Federal Reserve issues paper currency in denominations of $1, $2, $5, $10, $20, $50, and $100, and in the past has issued currency in the denominations of $500, $1000, $5000, and $10,000. The notes are printed by the United States Treasury for the Federal Reserve System, and each of the 12 Federal Reserve District Banks puts its own notes into circulation after printing serial numbers on them. The notes from each district can be identified by the name of the district bank, the number of the district (*see* the map of the districts in Chapter 13), and the letter of the alphabet corresponding to the number of the district (*see* Figure 1.1). The serial number on each note starts with the letter of the alphabet that corresponds to the number of the district that has issued the note. For example, the note shown in Figure 1.1 was issued by the Federal Reserve Bank of Boston; therefore, the serial number begins with the first letter of the alphabet.

*Figure 1.1*
**A Federal Reserve Note**

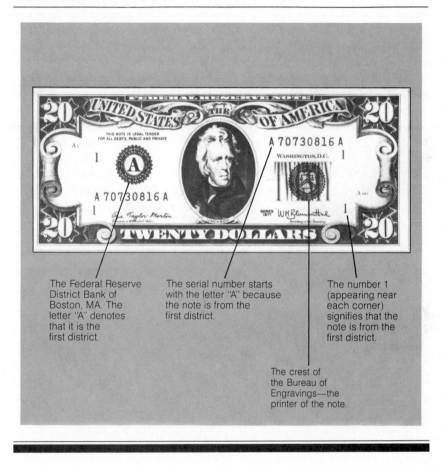

Although the Federal Reserve tries to control the total quantity of the money supply, the proportion of the money supply held in any particular form (coins, paper, or deposits) is set by public demand rather than by official policy. Individuals choose the proportion of their wealth they wish to hold in a particular monetary form according to the type of transactions they wish to make.

The statement "This Note Is Legal Tender for All Debts Public and Private" is printed on the face of all Federal Reserve notes (*see* Figure 1.1). Contrary to popular belief, this statement is not what makes currency acceptable as money. The legal tender laws refer only to the legal rights of people in situations where the offer of money to pay a debt is not accepted. If someone owing money offers to pay in legal tender and *actually produces the money* but payment is refused for some legal reason (for example, some dispute over the amount owed, or the recipient's fear that accepting the money will affect his or her legal rights), then there are three legal effects. First, any pledge securing the debt (for example, a mortgage) is extinguished; second, interest can no longer be charged on the debt; third, if the creditors later sue for the amount that has been offered, they must pay the court costs. Although it is *customary* to pay by check, producing a check does not produce the money because the payment is always conditional on the check's being honored by the bank.

## Accounts in Depository Institutions

Although most transactions are made by using currency, by far the highest *value* of transactions is made by checks or other drafts on accounts in depository institutions (that is, accounts in commercial banks, savings and loan associations, mutual savings banks, and credit unions). It must be emphasized, however, that the accounts are the money, not the checks or drafts used to transfer the funds from one account to another. The checks or drafts cannot be considered money because the receipt of such a check or draft does not signify that a person has been paid. Only when a check or draft clears (when the funds are actually transferred from one account to another) has payment been made.

Until the 1970s, commercial banks were alone among financial intermediaries in being allowed to hold accounts on which checks were written. This meant that the thrift institutions had no part in the administration of the money supply (apart from using currency, payments could only be made through the commercial banking system). After a brief experiment in the 1970s restricted chiefly to the New England states, the Monetary Control Act of 1980 made it possible for payments to be made throughout the United States by using checkable deposits in all depository institutions. The radical change in the payments system revolutionized banking and necessitated changes in the way that monetary policy is conducted. It even necessitated changes in the way that money is defined.

## THE DEFINITIONS OF THE MONEY SUPPLY

Modern economic theory considers the quantity of money and the rate of change of the quantity of money as important determinants of how an economy functions. The quantity of money is thought to have important effects on the level of aggregate output, the levels of employment and unemployment, and the rates of inflation and deflation. For this reason, it is necessary to determine exactly how much money is in the economy. The quantity of

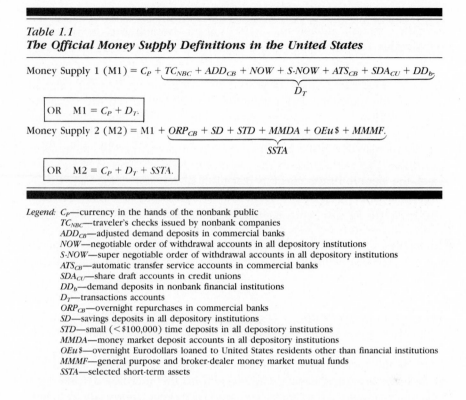

*Table 1.1*
**The Official Money Supply Definitions in the United States**

Money Supply 1 (M1) = $C_P + \underbrace{TC_{NBC} + ADD_{CB} + NOW + S\text{-}NOW + ATS_{CB} + SDA_{CU} + DD_b}_{D_T}$,

$$\boxed{\text{OR} \quad M1 = C_P + D_T.}$$

Money Supply 2 (M2) = $M1 + \underbrace{ORP_{CB} + SD + STD + MMDA + OEu\$ + MMMF}_{SSTA}$.

$$\boxed{\text{OR} \quad M2 = C_P + D_T + SSTA.}$$

*Legend:* $C_P$—currency in the hands of the nonbank public
  $TC_{NBC}$—traveler's checks issued by nonbank companies
  $ADD_{CB}$—adjusted demand deposits in commercial banks
  $NOW$—negotiable order of withdrawal accounts in all depository institutions
  $S\text{-}NOW$—super negotiable order of withdrawal accounts in all depository institutions
  $ATS_{CB}$—automatic transfer service accounts in commercial banks
  $SDA_{CU}$—share draft accounts in credit unions
  $DD_b$—demand deposits in nonbank financial institutions
  $D_T$—transactions accounts
  $ORP_{CB}$—overnight repurchases in commercial banks
  $SD$—savings deposits in all depository institutions
  $STD$—small ($<\$100,000$) time deposits in all depository institutions
  $MMDA$—money market deposit accounts in all depository institutions
  $OEu\$$—overnight Eurodollars loaned to United States residents other than financial institutions
  $MMMF$—general purpose and broker-dealer money market mutual funds
  $SSTA$—selected short-term assets

money cannot be counted, however, until the money supply has been defined. Economists differ on what should or should not be counted. To accommodate these different opinions, the Federal Reserve publishes several different measures. These measures are numbered M1, M2, M3, and so on. The current definitions of the first two are summarized in Table 1.1. These definitions, apart from some slight modification resulting from the Garn–St. Germain Act of 1982, are those adopted in 1980 in response to the changes in the payments system.

## Money Supply 1 (M1)

*Money supply 1* is the Federal Reserve's estimate of what they think is actually being used as a means of payment. It includes the currency in the hands of the nonbank public, the traveler's checks issued by nonbank companies, and the accounts in depository institutions that can be used in payment.

***Currency in the Hands of the Nonbank Public.*** Currency in the hands of the nonbank public includes all of the coin and paper money that is held outside the commercial banks, the Federal Reserve District Banks, and the Treasury. The amount is also adjusted (downwards) to allow for the estimated amount of vault cash held by thrift institutions to service their transactions accounts.

***Traveler's Checks Issued by Nonbank Companies.***   Traveler's checks are used like currency and are therefore included among the means of exchange. However, it is not so obvious why the definition includes only those traveler's checks issued by the nonbank companies. Many traveler's checks are issued by banks, and these too are obviously part of the means of exchange. The explanation is that when a traveler's check is issued by a bank, the amount of the check is placed in an account in the bank that is already counted as part of the means of exchange. To count traveler's checks issued by the banks would, therefore, entail counting this money twice. The same is not true with the traveler's checks issued by nonbank companies. The funds used to purchase nonbank-issued traveler's checks are not placed in demand deposits. Therefore the traveler's checks themselves must be counted.

***Transactions Accounts in Depository Institutions.***   Transactions accounts in depository institutions are either in commercial banks or thrift institutions. The *adjusted demand deposits in commercial banks* are defined as the total amount of demand deposits in commercial banks (all noninterest-bearing checking accounts) *minus* the interbank deposits (the accounts that commercial banks have with each other), *minus* the commercial bank deposits that are owned by foreign commercial banks, and *minus* the demand deposits of the United States Treasury and its agencies.

*Negotiable order of withdrawal accounts* (NOW accounts) in all depository institutions are checking accounts that bear interest. The written orders used in payment are called *negotiable orders of withdrawal* for the rather legalistic reason that the law forbids the payment of interest on checking accounts. NOW accounts pay interest, but the rates paid are subject to a maximum set by the Depository Institutions Deregulation Committee. *Super negotiable order of withdrawal accounts* (Super NOW accounts), which were first authorized in the Garn–St. Germain Act of 1982, are like ordinary NOW accounts except that they require a minimum initial and maintained balance of $1000 and have unregulated, market-determined interest rates. Super NOW accounts do not have a specified maturity period, but the depository institutions holding them reserve the right to require seven days notice before a withdrawal.

*Automatic transfer service accounts* (ATS accounts) in commercial banks offer a service that is essentially the same as a NOW account, but the mechanism is slightly different. In the case of the ATS account, there are actually two accounts: a checking account that does not bear interest and a savings account that does not have checks. When a check is written on the checking account, the funds are automatically transferred from the savings account (where they are earning interest) into the checking account so that the check can clear.

Share draft accounts are the NOW accounts of the credit unions. They are interest-bearing accounts, but they are also checkable. However, as with NOW accounts, for legal reasons the words *share draft* have been substituted for the written order that is, in all but name, a check. *Demand deposits in nonbank financial institutions* are noninterest-bearing checking accounts that are held in any financial institutions other than a commercial bank. These are restricted to savings and loan associations and mutual savings banks, and they do not exist in all parts of the country.

The total amount of transactions accounts is adjusted downwards to allow for the estimated amount of demand deposits held in commercial banks by thrift institutions to service their transactions accounts.

## Money Suppy 2 (M2)

*Money Supply 2* is a much broader definition of the money supply, encompassing both the means of exchange and certain highly liquid assets that can be converted easily into a means of payment. We shall refer to the highly liquid assets included in M2 as "Selected short-term assets" (SSTA). Owners of such assets who wish to spend them can first change the assets for some of the means of exchange and then spend the means of exchange. For example, a passbook savings account is not part of the means of exchange (unless it is an ATS account), but the account's funds can be withdrawn and then spent. Obviously, everything that can be sold is to some extent liquid, but the items under discussion are different in that they can be exchanged for the means of exchange with a minimum of delay and usually with no loss from their nominal value.

Money supply 2 includes all of the items included in money supply 1 *plus* all savings accounts (other than the ATS accounts already included in M1) and all small time deposits (those in amounts less than $100,000) in all depository institutions, all overnight repurchases in commercial banks, all money market deposit accounts, certain overnight Eurodollars, and the amounts that are held in general purpose and broker-dealer money market mutual funds.

**Savings Accounts and Small Time Deposits.** Savings accounts are passbook accounts that bear interest (apart from ATS accounts). Money can be placed in them at any time and, subject to a short delay specified at the time the accounts are opened, funds can be withdrawn at any time. Small time deposits differ from savings accounts in that funds will be withdrawn at a particular time in the future. In most time deposits, funds are placed in the accounts at a particular time and withdrawn at a particular time. In what are called *open-account time deposits,* the funds are placed in the accounts at any time but withdrawn at some particular time. (These are accounts for travel funds, Christmas clubs, and the like.) Financial institutions impose penalties if the funds are withdrawn before the specified date.

**Money Market Deposit Accounts.**  The Garn–St. Germain Act of 1982 authorized *money market deposit accounts* so that the depository institutions would be able to compete effectively with the money market mutual funds. The accounts are federally insured and pay unregulated interest rates. Like Super NOW accounts, they require minimal initial and maintained average balances of $1000, but they have limited transactions features. Unlimited personal withdrawals are allowed, but preauthorized, automatic, or telephone transfers are restricted to six per month.

**Overnight Repurchases.**  *Overnight repurchases* are funds that are deposited in commercial banks, but not in the form of deposits; instead the banks invest the funds for the depositor. The funds are invested one day at a time, and the interest on the investment accrues to the depositor. If the depositor wishes to leave the funds invested for an additional day, the repurchase is "rolled over" for one more 24-hour period. If the depositor wishes to spend the funds, the repurchase is not rolled over, and the funds reappear as an ordinary deposit that can be spent. Commercial banks perform this service for certain large corporations in order to keep control of the depositors' funds. However, a depositor who has an overnight repurchase does have control over a highly liquid asset, and because it is expected that the depositor will behave as though the asset were part of the means of exchange, the amount of these repurchases is included in money supply 2.

**Overnight Eurodollars.**  Outside the United States, there is an active market for United States dollars. They are lent and borrowed by those who wish to do business with the United States and those who simply prefer to do business with the security that that particular currency gives them. Even though many of these funds are not in Europe, they are referred to as *Eurodollars.* Some United States dollars are placed in banks outside the United States on a day-to-day basis. The fact that the funds can be placed in these banks on one day and withdrawn on the next means that they are a very liquid asset. They are called *overnight* Eurodollars and are included in the definition of money supply 2 whenever they are placed there by United States residents other than financial institutions. Not all banks outside the United States are capable of accepting dollars on a day-to-day basis for United States residents. Most of the overnight Eurodollars included in money supply 2 are in banks situated either in the Caribbean or in London; however, it is impossible for the United States authorities to acquire reliable information about Eurodollars in any bank other than one that reports to the Federal Reserve. Thus, the overnight Eurodollars included in the definition of money supply 2 are those in the Caribbean and London branches of United States banks.

***Money Market Mutual Funds.***   General purpose and broker-dealer money market mutual funds are included in the definition of money supply 2. They are of such high liquidity that there was some debate at the Federal Reserve over whether or not they should be included in money supply 1. Funds placed here are invested in certain highly liquid money market instruments but also can be transferred out to a third party by writing an order that is very similar to a check. There are restrictions on the minimum amount of such an order (usually $500), but there is no mistaking the fact that the funds are used as a means of exchange. The decision to exclude the money market mutual funds from money supply 1 was based on the fact that the number of transactions made was no greater than the number of transactions made with savings accounts and time deposits. The money market mutual funds included in money supply 2 do not include those funds in which the investors are wholly institutions (the institutional money market mutual funds).

***Consolidation Components in M2.***   As defined here, money supply 2 would involve some double counting. Many of the depository institutions that hold accounts included in the definition also hold reserves for these accounts either in vault cash or in demand deposits at commercial banks. Just as the estimated amounts of vault cash and demand deposits held by thrift institutions to service their transactions accounts are subtracted from the amount of currency held by the nonbank public and from the total amount of transactions accounts, so the estimated amounts of vault cash and demand deposits held by the thrift institutions to service their savings and time deposits are subtracted from M2 as a consolidation component.

The quantities of money supply 1 and money supply 2 are shown in Table 1.2. The table shows the upward trend in both quantities and the relative size of M1 to M2.

## HELPING TO UNDERSTAND
## THE MONETARY SYSTEM

This book is written with the intention of providing insight into the workings of the monetary system in the United States. It is aimed chiefly at students who have had some introduction to the principles of economics.

Part I begins with a general discussion about the significance of having a money supply and explains how money serves as a medium of exchange, a

Table 1.2
**The Quantities of Money Supply 1 and Money Supply 2**

| Date | M1 in Billions | M2 in Billions |
|---|---|---|
| Jan. 1982 | $453.4 | $1848.8 |
| Feb. 1982 | 437.1 | 1842.4 |
| Mar. 1982 | 440.0 | 1861.5 |
| Apr. 1982 | 455.4 | 1886.9 |
| May 1982 | 445.1 | 1888.9 |
| June 1982 | 450.5 | 1906.3 |
| July 1982 | 454.1 | 1925.2 |
| Aug. 1982 | 454.0 | 1939.4 |
| Sept. 1982 | 460.5 | 1951.3 |
| Oct. 1982 | 470.2 | 1972.1 |
| Nov. 1982 | 478.5 | 1987.2 |
| Dec. 1982 | 491.0 | 1964.5 |
| Jan. 1983 | 489.7 | 2018.3 |
| Feb. 1983 | 487.7 | 2042.5 |
| Mar. 1983 | 489.2 | 2066.0 |
| Apr. 1983 | 504.4 | 2088.8 |
| May 1983 | 499.8 | 2093.9 |
| June 1983 | 508.3 | 2114.0 |
| July 1983 | 514.7 | 2127.8 |
| Aug. 1983 | 511.6 | 2129.2 |
| Sept. 1983 | 514.1 | 2137.1 |
| Oct. 1983 | 519.5 | 2161.0 |
| Nov. 1983 | 523.8 | 2174.4 |
| Dec. 1983 | 535.3 | 2191.4 |

*Source:* Board of Governors of the Federal Reserve, *Federal Reserve Bulletin,* Washington D.C., Tables A13, A14, A15, various issues.

store of value, and a unit of account. Money's place in the exchange system is explained. The advantages to having a monetary system as opposed to relying on a system of barter are pointed out. The use of money and the financial system for transferring goods and services from one person to another are explained, as is the way in which lending and borrowing of money has the effect of reallocating goods and services through time.

Part I is also concerned with how the money supply is created and how the monetary authorities (the Federal Reserve and the Treasury) influence the amount of money in existence. The role of commercial banks and nonbank financial intermediaries is explained. The student will find out how most of the money supply is created by the commercial banking system and how the supply is affected by the operations of nonbank financial intermediaries. The way in which the Federal Reserve is able to control the money supply through its influence over the commercial banks is also explained. Although the discussion is couched in terms of the particular institutions of the United States, much of it can be generalized to explain the workings of most economic systems. The historical facts, however, are restricted almost exclusively to the United States.

Part II differs considerably from Part I in that it attempts to provide the monetary theories on which modern monetary policy is based. Because it cannot be claimed that the monetary authorities are the adherents of any particular monetary theory, it is necessary to describe what the different theories are. Once the various theories are understood, it is possible to use them to explain the implications of the monetary policies that actually are carried out by the Federal Reserve. Although there are numerous monetary theories, they can be classified into two groups: those that depend on the neoclassical theory and those that depend on Keynesian theory. Both types are explained, and the implications of various monetary policies are investigated as they can be deduced from each model.

Part II does not aim at making a distinction between the models to judge one of them correct and the other false. Rather, the aim is to show that the economy can be explained by using either model. It is shown how the neoclassical theory starts on the supply side. The level of employment, together with the capital stock of buildings and machines, determines the level of real output in the economy. The money supply is then seen as a key determinant of the price level at which the level of real output is sold. The Keynesian type of model, on the other hand, is shown to be demand-oriented. In this type of model the level of output is produced in response to an expected level of aggregate demand. The money supply is then seen to have an effect on the economy through its effect on the level of aggregate demand. If the level of aggregate demand can be increased, the level of production will be increased, and the level of employment will be increased.

## Key Terms

| | |
|---|---|
| currency | NOW accounts |
| full-bodied money | share draft accounts |
| token coins | ATS accounts |
| Federal Reserve Notes | money supply 2 |
| checking accounts | overnight repurchases |
| money supply 1 | Eurodollars |
| adjusted demand deposits | money market mutual funds |

## Questions

1. In what way can it be said that the monetary system in the United States was merely an imitation of the Spanish system?

2. How have recent changes in payments practices in the United States led to changes in the definition of money?

3. What is the difference between NOW and ATS accounts?

4. What is the difference between money supply 1 and money supply 2?

## Additional Readings

Barnard, Billings D. "How the Federal Reserve Creates and Destroys Currency." *Voice*. Federal Reserve Bank of Dallas (February 1978): 12–14.

*A brief description of how currency is put into and taken out of circulation by Federal Reserve District Banks.*

Einzig, Paul. *Primitive Money, In Its Ethnological, Historical and Economic Aspects*. 2d ed. Oxford: Pergamon Press, 1966.

*A classic book on the origins and uses of primitive monies.*

Friedman, Milton, and Anna J. Schwartz. *Monetary Statistics of the United States.* New York: National Bureau of Economic Research, Columbia University Press, 1970.

*Chapters 2 and 3 contain an interesting discussion on the selection of a statistical definition for the money supply.*

Simpson, Thomas D. "The Redefined Monetary Aggregates." *Federal Reserve Bulletin*. Washington, D.C.: Board of Governors of the Federal Reserve (February 1980): 97–114.

*Although this article was written before the passage of the Garn–St. Germain Act of 1982, it contains a comprehensive comparison of the old and new definitions used by the Federal Reserve, along with the rationale for the changes.*

# CHAPTER TWO

## MONEY AND ITS USES

*Money is used as a medium of exchange, a unit of account, and a store of value. Although we commonly use governmentally provided money, money will arise without government intervention as a means of reducing transactions costs. This reduction in costs helps us realize the gains from specialization along the lines of comparative advantage.*

Although it is easy to see what is used as money in a particular economy (for example, the dollar is used in the United States), it is more difficult to find a general definition for money. *Money* only has a functional definition; that is, it can be defined only by its uses. The simple question "What is money?" is difficult to answer, but the easier question "How is money used?" has more than one answer. Money is generally considered to have three separate uses. It is used as a:

1.  *Medium of exchange*—it is what we use as a means of payment whenever we make purchases or pay debts.

2.  *Unit of account*—the unit of money adopted in a particular country is usually used to express prices, such as, one dollar for a loaf of bread, 30 francs for a pound of cheese, or 4000 yen for a brush.

3.  *Store of value*—this does not mean, of course, that money is the *only* store of value. In fact, during periods of inflation (that is, when prices expressed in units of money are continually rising), money is a rather poor store of value. Nevertheless, the value we receive in income can be stored in money until we want to exchange it for goods and services.

Money's primary function is as a medium of exchange. Although most countries use their medium of exchange as their unit of account and as a store of value, some countries do not. The British, for example, maintain a unit of account (the *guinea*) that has not existed as a medium of exchange for over a century. Also, George Washington, while using dollars in exchange, continued to use British pounds as his unit of account.

Using the primary function of money, we arrive at its commonly accepted definition:

> Money is *anything* that is commonly accepted as a means of payment for goods and services or the discharge of debts.

Given this definition, the physical form of money is of little consequence, as long as people accept it as a means of payment. Whether people accept wampum or green cheese, or krugerrands or greenbacks makes little difference. The sole criterion is common usage.

## THE THEORY OF EXCHANGE

Money is the commonly used medium of exchange. The benefits from its use rest with the gains from exchange. The use of money acts to lower transactions costs. This lowering of costs facilitates the gains from reallocating existing goods to higher-valued uses and reallocating the means of production toward increased output.

The basis for making exchanges of goods and services is the same as the basis for making any economic decision. An individual compares the additional benefits that the action is expected to produce to the additional costs that are expected to be incurred. If the expected additional benefits outweigh the expected additional costs, the action will be taken. With exchange decisions made in this way, the process of exchange will allocate goods and services away from those parties who place a lower value on the goods and services to the parties who place a higher value on the goods and services. By forgoing goods and services that are considered to be of lower value in exchange for goods and services more highly valued, gains are expected to be realized from the exchange. In fact, the basic principle underlying voluntary exchange is that both parties expect to gain from the exchange. If both parties did not expect to gain from the exchange, they would not undertake the actions that would bring about the exchange.

The exchanges that are made every day are based on the same type of comparison of expected additional benefits to expected additional costs. For example, if you do not expect the benefits from acquiring this textbook to outweigh the benefits you can acquire from the alternative goods and services you can purchase, you will not exchange your labor services (or those of your parents) for this book. Similarly, the publisher of this book will not offer it in exchange for those labor services unless the expected benefits outweigh the expected benefits from the use of the resources in other activities. Both parties in the exchange expect to benefit.

## Comparative Advantage

Individuals gain in the exchange process because they place different values on goods and services.

One of the reasons that people place different relative values on goods and services and gain from exchange is that individuals have different abilities to produce those goods and services. Some are more proficient in producing agricultural goods; others are relatively more productive with manufactured goods. This kind of difference brings about specialization in market economies. People tend to specialize in those activities in which they are relatively more productive.

Two important aspects of the production process are the concepts of opportunity costs and comparative advantage. The *opportunity cost* of producing a good or service is the value of the benefits *forgone* by *not* undertaking the next best alternative. The concept of comparative advantage flows directly from a consideration of opportunity costs. A *comparative advantage* in the production of a good is having the ability to produce that good at a lower opportunity cost than others in the market. Once opportunity costs are determined, the comparative (or relative) advantages of the individuals in the economy are also determined. If the costs of making exchanges are sufficiently small, individuals will be induced to specialize in those activities in which they have a comparative advantage.

Comparative advantage is indicated by having a lower opportunity cost in production relative to other individuals in the market. When the members of an economy are induced to produce those goods and services in which they have a comparative advantage, the economy will be utilizing the lowest cost producers in each production activity. However, this form of specialization requires exchange so that people have some variety in consumption. If exchange costs are sufficiently high, individuals will be induced to forgo the benefits from exchange so as not to incur the exchange costs. This will result in some parties producing goods and services for themselves that could have been produced at a lower opportunity cost by others.

When transactions costs are sufficiently low to make exchange feasible, individuals will be given the incentive through market activity to specialize in the production of those goods in which they have a comparative advantage. With a lower opportunity cost in the production of a good, an individual can offer the good for sale to others for less than it would cost them to produce the good. In exchange, individuals receive goods and services that would cost them more to produce. With goods being offered for exchange by their lowest cost producers, the members of an economy can acquire goods for less forgone output than it would cost them to produce the goods themselves.

Not only does society gain by having the goods and services available at a lower cost, but more goods and services will be made available. Specialization along the lines of comparative advantages leads to increased total output. By utilizing the lowest opportunity cost producers in each activity, less forgone alternative output is incurred in each production process. Thus, with specialization and exchange, the same amount of resources will be able to produce more goods and services.

These gains in output are directly attributable to the specialization that is possible because of the possibility of making exchanges. Thus, for these gains to be made it is essential that exchanges be made, and the exchanges will be made only if the exchange process is sufficiently low cost. It is clear that the mere existence of money holds a central place in the development of an economy. The significance of money in this process is revealed in its ability to reduce drastically the costs of making exchanges. The use of money as a medium of exchange is one of the causes of the degree of specialization the economy can achieve and hence is responsible for the increase in production that results from that specialization. In a barter economy the cost of exchanges is very high, with the result that specialization will be greatly curtailed. In a money economy, exchanges are encouraged by their low cost; greater specialization and great gains to both the economy and the individuals in that economy result.

## THE PLACE OF MONEY IN THE THEORY OF EXCHANGE

In most economies today, the money supply is provided by government action. This was not always the case, and it is certainly not the *origin* of money. Money arises in an exchange economy without government interference simply because it is useful. Money reduces the transactions costs inherent in exchange.

### *Transactions Costs*

Unfortunately, the making of exchanges between two parties is not simply determined from a comparison of the expected benefits and costs of the actual goods and services transferred. The process of making exchanges is complicated by the fact that there are costs involved in making exchanges. These costs are referred to as *transactions costs.* Transactions costs include the costs of bringing the parties and goods together physically so that the exchange can take place, and the costs of bargaining and obtaining information on the most beneficial exchanges to make. Any time that the transactions costs faced by the potential buyer or seller are greater than the expected gain from the exchange, that party will not make the exchange. Transactions costs reduce the amount of exchange activity taking place within an economy by reducing the net gains realized from making exchanges.

If the costs involved in making transactions could be reduced, more mutually beneficial exchanges would take place and the economy would realize the benefits from those exchanges. One development that tends to reduce transactions costs is the development of *central markets.* By setting up a common marketplace, a swap meet, a county fair, or a shopping center, the costs of searching the market to find someone willing to make an exchange are reduced. This induces more individuals to make exchanges, and the benefits from those exchanges are realized. Of course, individuals will make the exchanges only if they expect to benefit from the exchange, and a central market will be provided only if benefits are expected from providing the service. If rent is charged for space in the central market, the person setting up the market extracts some of the gains that are being realized from the exchanges.

Money has a role in the exchange process similar to the role of a central market. A commonly accepted medium of exchange greatly reduces one of the main transactions costs involved in exchanges: the cost of finding someone who has what you want and at the same time wants what you have sufficiently to make the exchange. This is known as the *double coincidence of wants.* Finding this double coincidence requires the use of time, energy, and resources in searching the market. With the existence of many different goods, these costs can be very high.

In a *barter economy,* goods would be exchanged directly for other goods. Suppose, for example, that you have strawberries and wish to exchange some for walnuts in a barter system. Although it is possible that you *might* find someone with walnuts who will exchange them for strawberries, it is more likely that those who have walnuts wish to exchange them for a third commodity, such as cucumbers. At this point, it becomes a problem of finding someone with cucumbers who wants strawberries, but the people with cucumbers might want something else, such as bread. Eventually, you might find someone who has bread and wants strawberries. This would make it possible to exchange the strawberries for the bread, the bread for the cucumbers, and the cucumbers for the walnuts that you desire.

In a *monetary economy* a commonly accepted medium of exchange is used in the process of making exchanges. If an economy has a money system, the process of finding a double coincidence of wants is much less costly. Although it is still necessary in a monetary economy to find a double coincidence of wants, the searching of the market is greatly reduced. A person having strawberries and wanting walnuts will simply look for someone who wants strawberries and has money to pay for them and will then take the money to someone who has walnuts and is prepared to sell them for money. The strawberries can be exchanged for the walnuts by selling the strawberries for money and using the money to purchase the desired walnuts.

By drastically easing the problem of finding a double coincidence of wants, using money as a medium of exchange reduces transactions costs and enables a realization of more of the gains from exchange.

## CHOOSING A MEDIUM OF EXCHANGE

Given that the advantages of having a medium of exchange are obvious, it is not surprising that an exchange economy functioning on a true barter system does not exist. However, the choice of certain commodities that have been used as money is surprising. A list of items used in colonial America reveals some strange choices. Apart from the various European currencies brought over by immigrants, the list includes corn, beaver skins, tobacco, musket balls, wheat, rye, barley, peas, and dried fish.

From an inspection of commodities that have been used as money, anthropologists have compiled a list of desirable properties for commodity money. But none of these properties, however desirable, can be considered essential. For every property listed, a commodity money can be named as a counterexample. The desirable properties usually listed are:

1. *Durable*—the substance withstands the wear and tear of being passed around in exchange.

2. *Divisible*—it can be divided easily into equal parts when making larger or smaller purchases.

3. *Portable*—it can be carried easily to make purchases in different locations.

4. *Standardized and recognizable*—individuals will know what they are receiving in exchanges.

Counterexamples, however, abound. Roman soldiers were paid in salt (the origin of the word *salary*), a substance that is far from durable, particularly in a wet climate. Many African peoples have used livestock as money, and this can hardly be considered divisible. Half a cow is a very different commodity from a whole (live) cow and is certainly less durable. The famous stone money on the Yap islands in Micronesia (large millstones, some of which are six feet in diameter) cannot be considered portable. Yap residents do not consider them divisible, as they only trade them whole. The tobacco used by the American colonists was easily recognized, but it could never be standardized so that equal quantities by weight could represent equal value.

Each of these desirable properties refers to the basic cost of using commodities as a means of exchange. For example, if the chosen commodity is not durable, the money will wear out very rapidly and will be costly to replace. If the commodity is not divisible, making small payments will be costly or impossible. If the commodity is not portable (that is, it is very expensive to move), its use as money will be very expensive. If the commodity is neither standardized nor recognizable, transactions will be very costly as each transaction will require that the commodity be assayed and weighed before use.

The superiority of the precious metals over most commodities is immediately apparent. Gold and silver are durable, can be cut into various sizes, are valuable enough that small pieces can be used in everyday exchanges, and are easily recognizable. Governments took a role in monetary affairs by certifying the weights of these metals in coins. A coin was nothing more than an officially certified and imprinted quantity of a metal for use in exchange.

Whenever the public is free to choose the commodity it will use as money, it will choose the commodity that to the individuals in the public is the least costly method of achieving the same level of benefits. (Coins, for example, are heavy, costly to use, and often fail to circulate. See box, page 29.) Over time, as production processes change and the types of exchanges change, the relative costs of using different commodities will change. This will result in changes in what is used as money.

## MONEY AS A UNIT OF ACCOUNT

Although no developed economy has ever been a barter economy where no medium of exchange is used, it is nonetheless instructive to imagine such a system. Rather than being bought with money, each good or service would be exchanged directly for other goods and services. Goods would not have one price expressed in money, but many relative prices, each expressed in terms of all other goods and services. A *relative price* is the number of units of a good that must be forgone to purchase another good.

The information expressed in relative prices is valuable for making exchanges, but the information would be very costly to obtain in a barter economy. If there are only two goods in an economy, say, strawberries and walnuts, then just one relative price will give all the information on values used in exchanges. Once the price of strawberries in terms of walnuts is known, the price of walnuts in terms of strawberries is the reciprocal of that number and gives no more information. The price of strawberries in terms of strawberries and the price of walnuts in terms of walnuts are both equal to one, and this relationship also gives no new information.

If the economy had a monetary system, and there were, therefore, money prices, the relative prices could easily be derived from the money prices. With the price of strawberries at 18¢ apiece and the price of walnuts at 3¢ apiece, it takes six walnuts to buy one strawberry.

The relative price of strawberries in terms of walnuts

$$= \frac{\text{money price of strawberries}}{\text{money price of walnuts}} = \frac{18¢}{3¢} = 6.$$

In the case of only two goods, there are two money prices (one for each good) and one relative price. However, if we increase the number of goods under consideration, the number of relative prices increases much

*Table 2.1*
**Relative and Money Prices for Four Goods**

| Price of | In Terms of | | | | |
| --- | --- | --- | --- | --- | --- |
| | **Strawberries** | **Walnuts** | **Cucumbers** | **Bread** | **Money** |
| Strawberries | 1 | 6 | ½ | ¼ | 18¢ |
| Walnuts | ⅙ | 1 | ¹/₁₂ | ¹/₂₄ | 3¢ |
| Cucumbers | 2 | 12 | 1 | ½ | 36¢ |
| Bread | 4 | 24 | 2 | 1 | 72¢ |

more rapidly than the number of money prices. For example, Table 2.1 shows the relative prices and money prices for four goods.

Obviously, there is one money price for each good, but there are six different relative prices, where the price of each good is expressed in terms of the other goods (remembering that each relative price will have a reciprocal that will also appear in the table). In general, if there are $n$ goods, there are

$$\frac{n(n-1)}{2}$$

relative prices. Using the four goods in Table 2.1, there are

$$\frac{4(4-1)}{2} = 6$$

relative prices. If there are 1000 goods in the economy, the number of relative prices is

$$\frac{1000(1000-1)}{2} = 499,500.$$

In a barter economy with 1000 goods, there would be 499,500 relative prices, but this same information is in the 1000 money prices used in a money economy. Using money as a unit of account greatly economizes on the number of prices that have to be stated without losing any information. Search costs, in a money economy, are thus going to be much lower than they would be in a barter economy.

## MONEY AS A STORE OF VALUE

A problem that arises in the process of making exchanges is the timing of exchanges. A person with a quantity of strawberries may desire to acquire cucumbers at some time in the future. As both of these goods are perishable, the exchange will be very difficult in the absence of money. The strawberries would spoil if held until the cucumbers were wanted, or if the exchange were made immediately, the cucumbers would spoil before they were

## HOW MUCH OF OUR CURRENCY LIES UNUSED IN THE BEDROOMS OF AMERICA?

Every night, all across America, people empty the loose change from their pockets and purses into some receptacle or other in their bedrooms. Every bedroom seems to contain an ashtray or a fraternity mug filled with coins. A few people pick up their coins in the morning, but most of them don't. Some keep them for a vacation, or a night on the town, or give them to children or grandchildren, but most of the coins simply lie there as inflation cuts into their worth.

According to the United States Mint (the branch of the Treasury that makes the coins), 172 billion pennies have been produced since 1959, but it has been estimated that only about 40 billion are still in circulation. The higher the face value of a coin the more likely it is to remain in circulation, but the story is similar when it comes to nickels, dimes, and even quarters. Some 17.2 billion nickels have been minted since 1956, and about 7.2 billion are in circulation. 22.5 billion dimes have been minted since 1965, but 14.1 billion are in circulation. 18.7 billion quarters have been minted since 1965, but 11.1 billion are in circulation. The unused coins have a face value of $4,260,000,000!

The "missing" coins are not a problem for the Treasury—it makes a profit on every coin it makes. The penny, which since 1982 has been 97% zinc, is manufactured for a cost of 0.6 of a cent, but its full face value is credited to the Treasury. Each penny thus profits the Treasury 0.4 cents. Each nickel (25% nickel and 75% copper) profits the Treasury 2.5 cents, each dime 8.3 cents, and each quarter 22.3 cents.

*Source:* From an article by Penny Pagano in the *Los Angeles Times*, Saturday, March 10, 1984.

wanted. Such problems are much reduced by using money as a store of value. By exchanging the strawberries for units of money now (that is, selling them), the money can be stored until such time as the cucumbers are wanted, when the money can be exchanged for them (that is, buying them).

Money does not necessarily solve the timing problem entirely. If the economy suffers from inflation (the general level of money prices continues to rise), the value of money will decline. If strawberries are sold and the money is kept for the future purchase of cucumbers, the longer the wait, the fewer the number of cucumbers that can be purchased with the money. In such a situation, money is a poor store of value, and some other good that retains its value will be generally used instead. Value is better stored in a good whose price is rising.

If prices are stable, money is a very useful store of value. It retains its purchasing power. If prices are falling, a unit of money will have an increasing purchasing power over time, thus making it a more preferred store of value. If, however, prices are rising generally, there are better ways of storing value than in the form of money.

It is surprising, however, the extent to which people will hold money even in the most extreme cases of inflation. As prices rise more rapidly, people tend to decrease their money balances and try to hold them for a shorter time, but they hold on to a money system with great tenacity. In the German Weimar Republic, when the money supply doubled every week and caused what is known as *hyperinflation,*[1] people still used money as a means of exchange, and so it retained its use as a store of value at least long enough for workers to rush their pay packets to local stores to buy goods.

## MONEY PRICES, INFORMATION, AND COMPARATIVE ADVANTAGE

In any economy the gains from specialization are generated by individuals producing those goods in which they have a comparative advantage. A difficulty in realizing the gains lies in determining those activities in which one has a comparative advantage. In a money economy, the information contained in the money prices of goods and services tells individuals where they have a comparative advantage relative to the rest of the producers in the market. The incentive to specialize is primarily perceived by the individual through the income that can be earned in each activity.

Suppose, for example, that during any given day you could perform either four units of accounting services *or* eight units of computer services and that both activities were considered to be equally burdensome or pleasant. From this information it is clear that your opportunity cost of providing one unit of accounting services is two units of computing services (assuming that these are the only activities available). However, this information on your opportunity cost is not sufficient to determine your comparative advantage. Where your comparative advantage *relative to the rest of the market* lies is determined by the opportunity cost of accounting services relative to computing services revealed by market activity. If the market is

---

[1] The word *hyperinflation* is generally used to describe those situations in which the general price level is increasing extremely rapidly, usually at rates in excess of 50 percent per month.

willing to pay $30 per unit of accounting services and only $10 per unit of computing services, the market-revealed opportunity cost of one unit of accounting is three units of computing services. Since your opportunity cost of one unit of accounting is only two units of computing services, you have a comparative advantage relative to the rest of the producers in the market in accounting as opposed to computing. This information is directly revealed in the incomes that are available. By providing accounting services at $30 per unit, your income would be $120 per day. If you provided computing services instead at the market price of $10 per unit, your daily income would only be $80.

As market conditions change, the relative prices of various types of goods and services will likely change, and where one's comparative advantage relative to the rest of the market lies may also change. Suppose, for example, that as a result of recent increases in graduations of accounting majors, an increase that alters the quantity of market producers, the price of accounting services falls relative to the price of computing services. As a result of the changing market conditions, the price of accounting services has declined to $20 per unit, whereas the price of computing services has risen to $12 per unit. With the same ability, indicated above, of being able to provide either four units of accounting services or eight units of computing services, your income in accounting would decline to $80 per day. However, your income from providing computing services would increase to $96 per day. Relative to the rest of the producers now in the market, your comparative advantage would have shifted away from the area of accounting into the activity of providing computing services.

It is the market that reveals to individuals where their comparative advantages are relative to the other producers. This information is contained in relative prices, which are easily obtained in a money economy. When individuals move into the activity that generates the highest income for them, their response represents, in a market economy, a movement into the production of the goods and services in which they have a comparative advantage.

## Changing Money Prices and Market Information

Prices are constantly changing, even in an economy in which the average price level is fairly constant. Market forces, through the interaction of supplies and demands, cause relative prices to change. If the average price level is changing, these same market forces will likely cause the various money prices to change at different rates, and so relative prices will change. Money plays an important role in transmitting this relative price information, and many important decisions are made on the basis of relative prices.

An increase in the amount of money in an economy will have its impact on general economic activity through changing supplies and demands for various goods and services. The additional money may have its

## MONEY CONSTRAINED—WAGE AND PRICE CONTROLS

If the use of money is constrained, money may no longer serve to provide market information on relative prices. With constrained use, money may no longer facilitate the exchange process. The usual constraint placed on the use of money is controls on prices.

Suppose that government officials observe that prices are generally rising. In response they may act to prevent the rise by fixing the money prices of some goods and services. The price control may be designed to protect a specific good or to prevent a general erosion of wage earners' purchasing power. What the officials are saying is, You may use money any way you wish, *except* that you may not use more than a specified amount to purchase something (say a basket of walnuts or a basket of strawberries). This constraint is called either an *incomes policy* or *wage and price controls.*

With price controls, money prices can no longer adjust to convey new information concerning the relative values of different goods and services. If the money prices of walnuts and strawberries are prevented from rising while other prices rise, the government's policy will have altered the relative prices of walnuts and strawberries in terms of other goods. By artificially holding the money price of some goods down while other prices rise, the relative prices of the controlled goods will fall. This will result in the movement of resources away from producing the controlled goods. Output of the price controlled goods will decline, further aggravating the problem.

In the government's attempt to "protect" a specific market by decreeing that prices cannot rise, the government may destroy the market altogether.

When constraints are placed on the use of money, individuals will move away from the use of money to realize mutually beneficial exchanges. Price controls imposed by government will encourage barter transactions, even with the accompanying higher transactions costs.

impact transmitted to general economic activity by increasing the amount of lending activity and so initially influence investment decisions, such as demand for new plant and equipment. Alternatively, the additional money simply may be spent directly in buying goods and services and thus directly affect the supplies and demands in the markets for specific goods. Whatever the transmission mechanism from the change in the amount of money available to general economic activity, it is highly unlikely that *all* supplies and demands will be affected equally such that all prices are affected equally. Relative prices will change and this will have an effect on the allocation of resources.

Suppose, for example, that the increase in the amount of money available initially results in additional spending on investment in computers and on computer services. With the increased demand for computing services, their price will rise relative to the price of accounting services, and resources will move away from accounting activity into computer activity. The impact will then be transmitted through changing market prices to other areas of the economy. For example, the reallocation of resources out of accounting into computing will result in the reduction of the supply of accounting services, and the price of accounting services will rise.

As general economic activity is being altered as the result of changes in the amount of money available, the information contained in money prices will change and some relative prices will change. However, for both accounting and computing services to continue to be produced in significant quantities, the ratio of accounting prices to computer service prices must remain in a particular range. If computing service prices rise to $1000 per unit, while accounting services prices remain at $20 per unit, few people would still have a market incentive to continue to provide accounting services. To continue providing an incentive for both services to be produced, unconstrained market forces will act to keep the relative price of accounting services high enough to induce the supply of the market-desired quantity.

As we consider the ways in which the average price level changes in the economy, we must always remember that allocations of resources will always be changing in response to changes in relative prices.

## SUMMARY

Money has a functional definition; it is whatever is used as a means of exchange. Different types of money have been used throughout history. This is a result of the changes in their costs associated with their durability, divisibility, portability, standardization, and recognizability.

The benefits from the use of money derive from its ability to reduce the costs of making exchanges. By serving as a medium of exchange, money facilitates the finding of the double coincidence of wants necessary to make exchanges possible. By serving as a unit of account, money transmits the information of the relative prices of goods and services to potential buyers and sellers. By serving as a store of value, money eases the problem of making exchanges through time.

Each of the basic functions of money serves to reduce the costs of making exchanges and induces the economy to realize a greater proportion of the potential gains that are available through exchange. When money reduces the costs of making exchanges, the economy benefits in three ways:

1. Exchanges reallocate the existing set of goods and services to those individuals who place a higher value on the goods and services received.

2. The reduction in the costs of making exchanges releases from the exchange process resources that can be used to produce additional goods and services.

3. With the costs of specialization reduced, the economy will be induced toward a greater level of specialization and an increased output that results when individuals produce along the lines of their comparative advantage.

## Key Terms

money
medium of exchange
unit of account
store of value
transactions costs

double coincidence of wants
comparative advantage
opportunity cost
relative price
specialization

## Questions

1. "Since gold is divisible, durable, portable, standardized, and recognizable, gold is money." Evaluate.

2. "Paper money has a lower cost in use than do gold coins." Evaluate. What about production costs?

3. Explain how durability is related to money's function as a store of value.

4. "No one can have the comparative advantage in the production of all goods." Evaluate.

5. Explain why some firms may resort to barter trades during periods of wage and price controls.

## Additional Readings

Alchian, Armen A. "Why Money?" *Journal of Money, Credit and Banking* 9 (February 1977): 133–140.

*An analysis of how ignorance leads to the use of money along with the use of specialized middlemen and how cost considerations enter into determining what will be used as money.*

Brunner, Karl, and Allan H. Meltzer. "The Uses of Money: Money in the Theory of an Exchange Economy." *American Economic Review* 61 (December 1971): 784–805.

*A coverage of the role of money in the exchange process and the importance of transactions costs in the use of money.*

Pryor, Frederic L. "The Origins of Money." *Journal of Money, Credit and Banking* 9 (August 1977): 391–409.

*A readable discussion of various propositions on the origins of money, including an empirical test of those propositions.*

# CHAPTER THREE

# THE QUANTITY OF MONEY—
# A PREVIEW OF MONETARY THEORY

*The authorities change the quantity of money in attempts to alter employment, output, the rate of change in prices or the foreign exchange value of the dollar. Theories of how the quantity of money affects the economy can be seen through the equation of exchange, $MV = Py$.*

A major theme of monetary theory today is the importance of changes in the quantity of money on the economy. Although some early economists emphasized the benefits of having a medium of exchange by explaining how money "lubricates the wheels of barter," even they were aware of the influence that the quantity of money has on the functioning of an economy. There are many opinions as to *how* the quantity of money affects an economy, but no one has suggested that it is an insignificant-relationship.

The differences of opinion arise from a consideration of how various markets in the economy interact. An economy obviously consists of a great number of markets. Predictions that can be made about the outcomes of various particular policy actions, such as increases in the money supply, are based on an analysis of the interactions and the extent of the interactions between various markets. A change in the conditions in one market will have an impact on many other markets, and it is impossible to consider all possible impacts on each and every market. Thus, in analyzing policies, it is crucial which impacts are deemed important and which can be safely ignored.

## MARKET INTERACTION

All markets are related. Whenever you demand a good, you must offer to supply some other good. For example, when you demand bread, you offer in exchange to sell (supply) some of your money holdings. In order to acquire (demand) money holdings you may have supplied labor services. Actions in one market will have an impact on other markets.[1] Analysis of economic activity hinges on the extent and importance of the market interactions assumed.

*Microeconomics* deals with the behavior of small units in small markets. Often, one market is analyzed in isolation from other markets. When the markets are small, the interactions between the markets will be minimal. The repercussions of actions in one market on other markets are broadly spread and may not even be measurable. Analysis of one market or set of markets in isolation is known as *partial equilibrium analysis.*

Much of monetary theory does not lend itself to simple, partial equilibrium analysis. It is macroeconomic in nature. *Macroeconomics* deals with large-scale economic phenomena. The assumption that the interactions between markets are sufficiently small to be ignored is not tenable. However, the analysis of the interactions resulting from, say, changes in monetary conditions can be conducted with a limited number of markets, where groups of similar markets have been combined into aggregate markets. For example, the markets for the goods and services produced in the economy can be aggregated into a product market. The markets for different types of labor services can be combined into an aggregate labor market, and the markets for the various types of assets considered to function as money can be aggregated into a money market. These markets are so large that it is impossible to discuss any of them in isolation. Yet, with only three markets it is reasonably easy to follow the analysis. A change in one of these markets will have an effect that can be traced on the other markets. The money market in particular cannot be discussed apart from the other markets. Money is unique in that it does not actually have a market of its own but appears as the medium of exchange in all other markets. Thus, monetary changes can be considered only in relation to the other markets.

## MEASUREMENT AND AGGREGATION

Economic activity is conducted in many diverse markets. Thousands of different goods and services are produced, and thousands of different prices are charged. Since it would be extremely difficult to evaluate the effect of an

---

[1] The relationship between markets is known as *Walras' law of markets.* This law states that the sum of values of the excess demands in all commodity and asset markets must sum to equal zero. In an economy with two goods, $A$ and $B$, with prices $P_A$ and $P_B$, and with quantity supplied of $A$ and demanded of $B$ indicated by $Q_A^S$ and $Q_B^D$, this law is:

$$P_A(Q_A^D - Q_A^S) = P_B(Q_B^D - Q_B^S).$$

increase in the supply of money on each of the markets in the economy, the information that we have about the various markets is combined into a small number of variables. For example, an *aggregate* measure of outputs is generated by adding together the outputs of many different markets, and a general price level is measured in a *price index,* which is a specific average of many prices in the economy.

For example, a price index is an aggregate variable that measures the average price of a set of goods. Changes in this aggregate variable do not inform us of changes in the price of a specific good or changes in relative prices. An increase in a price index does not mean that the price of a specific good, say of gasoline, has increased. Nor does an increase in the price of gasoline necessarily mean that the price index will also increase (other prices may have declined). Likewise, from a measure of aggregate output it cannot be discerned what happened in the market for a particular good or service. Because aggregate output has increased, it does not follow, for example, that output in the automotive industry has increased.

Great caution must be exercised in the interpretation of any aggregate data. In many cases, the *method of aggregation* is as important as the information that is aggregated.

## THE EQUATION OF EXCHANGE

The interaction between the money market and the aggregate market for output (the product market) can be summarized in the *equation of exchange.*

$$MV = Py, \tag{3.1}$$

where $M$ is the money supply, $V$ is the velocity of circulation, $P$ is the general price level, and $y$ is output of final goods and services.

In the analysis of general economic conditions it is desirable to distinguish unambiguously between values measured in current prices and values measured in constant prices. Throughout our discussion, capital letters are used to denote the *nominal variables,* measured in current dollar prices. Lowercase letters are used for *real variables,* measured in constant dollar prices. Thus, for example, where $y$ is real output, $Y$ is nominal output measured in current prices.

The equation of exchange is a defined relationship between the supply of money, a stock variable, and the level of output, a flow variable. A *stock variable* is measured *at a point in time.* Money, capital, inventory, and the labor force are examples of stock variables. A *flow variable* is measured *over a period of time.* Output, income, and labor services are examples of flow variables. Output is produced over, say, a year. Labor services are provided over an hour, a day, or a week.

The equation of exchange shows how adjustments in the financial sector (affecting either the money supply or the velocity of circulation or both) must be reflected in the market for final output. The relationships defined in the equation of exchange and any interpretation of the market interactions rely on the aggregated information measured in the variables $M$, $V$, and $Py$.

## THE MONEY SUPPLY

As $M$ is a stock variable, a certain amount exists and is owned by individuals in the economy at a point in time. If $M$ is to be related to the flow of output over a period of time, it is necessary to determine when the money supply is measured. The supply of money at the beginning of a period is likely to differ from the period-ending money supply. Also, any changes in the stock of money existing at different points of time during the period will have an impact on economic conditions. To account for the differences that exist in the supply of money over a period of time the average of the daily figures for the money supply over the period for which the flow of output is measured is used. Over the year 1983, for example, the average stock of money supply 1 (M1) in the United States was $507.8 billion. Over this period, M1 grew at an annual compound rate of 9 percent. For the same period, the average stock of money supply 2 (M2) was $2112.1 billion, and it grew at an annual compound rate of 11.5 percent.[2]

## The Flow of Output (Py)

The flow of aggregate output for an economy is measured by its *gross national product (GNP)*. This is the sum of the market values of all newly produced final goods and services over some period of time, usually a year. For an economy with $n$ final goods and services, GNP is given by

$$GNP = \sum_{i=1}^{n} p_i q_i = p_1 q_1 + p_2 q_2 + \cdots + p_{50} q_{50} + \cdots + p_n q_n, \quad (3.2)$$

where $p_i$ is the market price of the $i^{th}$ good or service and $q_i$ is the quantity of final output of that good or service.

In any interpretation of the benefits of a change in GNP or the policies that might lead to a change in GNP, it is important to realize what is being measured. GNP only measures a specific set of output and does not include some goods and services. Only "final" goods and services are included. Intermediary goods that are used in the production of final goods and services during the year are not included. If these intermediary goods were counted, they would necessitate a double counting: once as output of the good and a second time as the intermediary good adds to the value of the final good. However, intermediary goods left at the end of the year that have not been used in the production of final goods are counted. Individuals benefit from the production of goods for personal consumption at home. However, the value of output produced for oneself is not included. When you bake bread for your own use, the value of the labor services used to combine the flour and other ingredients is not included. If the same bread had been purchased in a store, the labor services of the baker would have been included. A simple shift in the way in which goods and services are produced can alter the measured aggregate output without an actual change in the amounts of goods and services produced.

***Gross National Income.*** GNP is used as a measure of economic activity because it represents the additional goods and services being made available for use over a period of time. GNP is also used as a measure of economic activity because it serves to measure the newly acquired ability of the members of an economy to buy those newly produced goods and services. The market value of all final goods and services produced by an economy during a period of time is equal to the amount of income generated during the same period. Thus, *gross national product is equal to gross national income.*

---

[2] *Economic Report of the President.* February 1984: 291.

## THE CONSUMER PRICE INDEX—CPI

*The consumer price index* (CPI) is this country's most widely used measure of price changes. The CPI is also used to deflate nominal variables to derive real variables and has a direct impact on income payments through escalator clauses in various contracts. Over 8.5 million workers (in 1978) were covered by collective bargaining contracts with escalator clauses based on the CPI. Over 50 million people, made up of those who are in the federal civil service, receive social security payments, or receive food stamps, have their incomes directly impacted by CPI changes. It has been estimated that a 1 percent increase in prices as measured by the CPI can, through these escalator clauses, increase income payments by about $1 billion.

The CPI is often referred to as a *cost of living index*. However, the CPI does not actually measure the cost of living. It only measures the price of a set commodity bundle determined in a survey of actual purchases of a specific group of individuals during a one- to two-year period. To the extent that individuals either are not consuming a bundle of goods and services similar to that of the survey group or have altered their consumption pattern since the survey because of changes in relative prices, changes in purchasing power, or changes in tastes and preferences, the actual cost of living will differ from that measured in the CPI.

If, for example, the price of beef rises faster than the price of chicken, individuals will typically substitute chicken for the now relatively more expensive beef and the typical commodity bundle will contain relatively more chicken. This change in the actual set of goods and services consumed will make the CPI misleading as an indicator of changes in the average price of the goods and services consumed.

Total income for an economy is the total payment made for the services of the factors of production used in producing the output: land, labor, capital, and entrepreneurial activity. Wages and salaries are paid for labor services; rents are paid for land and capital; entrepreneurs receive the residual payments (positive or negative) as profits or losses. The market value of final output can be divided into the payments made to the various factors of production. When payments for the use of land, labor, and capital used in the production of the final good (either directly or indirectly through inter-

In an attempt to make the CPI a more accurate indicator of the average price level of the goods and services actually consumed, the CPI has been revised periodically from its initial publication in 1919. The set of goods and services in the bundle was revised in 1940, 1946, 1953, and 1964. The most recent revision occurred in 1978. Prior to 1978 the price index was based on the consumption pattern of only urban wage earners and clerical workers. This narrow definition covers only about 40 percent of the population. It is still published as CPI-W. Since 1978 the Bureau of Labor Statistics has published a broader index for all urban consumers based on a Consumer Expenditure Survey conducted in 1972–1973. This index (published as CPI-U) covers about 80 percent of the population and includes the consumption patterns of the unemployed and those not in the labor force.

The percentage distribution of the goods and services included in the CPI market basket in different periods is given below.

### Percentage Distribution of CPI Market Basket—Major Groups

|  | 1963 (survey period 1960–1961) | 1977 (survey period 1972–1973) | |
| --- | --- | --- | --- |
|  | Old CPI | CPI-W | CPI-U |
| Food and Alcoholic Beverages | 25.2 | 20.5 | 18.8 |
| Housing | 34.9 | 40.7 | 43.9 |
| Apparel | 10.6 | 5.8 | 5.8 |
| Transportation | 14.0 | 20.2 | 18.0 |
| Medical Care | 5.7 | 4.5 | 5.0 |
| Entertainment | 3.9 | 3.9 | 4.1 |
| Personal Care | 2.8 | 1.8 | 1.8 |
| Other | 2.9 | 2.6 | 2.6 |

Source: U.S. Bureau of Labor Statistics. Consumer Price Index: Concepts and Content over the Years, May 1978.

mediary inputs) have been totaled, any remaining value is the amount earned or lost by the input of entrepreneurial ability. When this total income is measured in current market prices, the income figure is *nominal income* ($Y$). Since nominal income is identically equal to the nominal value of aggregate output, both are denoted by the symbol ($Y$).

The measure of nominal aggregate output is composed of two distinct components: the prices of the goods and services produced, and the quantities of the goods and services produced. If all money prices double, but the quantity of goods and services does not change, nominal income, $Y$, doubles. Similarly, if the quantities of goods and services double without the money prices changing, the measure of nominal income, $Y$, doubles. These two $Y$s, however, are very different and must be distinguished.

## The Price Index (P)

A price index is a measure that is used in an attempt to distinguish between price changes and quantity changes. A price index is really a measure of the level of money prices, but as we shall see, it is used to calculate *estimates* of *real* variables from *nominal* variables.

The price indexes that are most commonly used are the *Consumer Price Index* (CPI), the *Producer Price Index* (PPI), and the *GNP deflator*. The CPI measures the level of prices of the goods and services purchased by a typical consumer. (*See* box, pages 42–43.) The PPI (formerly the *Wholesale Price Index*) measures the level of prices for finished and semifinished goods and raw materials purchased by business firms. The *GNP deflator* is a measure of the level of prices of all goods and services included in GNP. Although each of these price indexes is calculated on a different set of goods and services, they are all weighted averages of money prices.

Unlike nominal income, which is directly measured, price indexes and real income cannot be directly observed and measured. Since all money prices are unlikely to change at the same rate, the use of different sets of goods and services will yield different measures of the price level and, when used to calculate real output, will yield different estimates of real output. In interpreting changes in real income, the price index used and the method of calculating that price index are as important as the actual estimate of real income generated.

## Calculating a Price Index

Assume that an economy produces two goods, wine and cheese, and the quantities and prices of these goods in two different years are those recorded in Table 3.1. In this simplified economy, all price and quantity information can be evaluated easily: the output of wine fell by 25 percent, cheese output increased by 50 percent, the price of wine fell by 25 percent, and the price of cheese doubled. However, for an economy with more goods and services, the entire set of information becomes very cumbersome, and some aggregate measure is used to consolidate the information.

For our simplified economy we have the aggregate observations for nominal GNP of

$$Y_1 = \$4 \times 100 + \$1 \times 100 = \$500$$
$$\text{and } Y_2 = \$3 \times 75 + \$2 \times 150 = \$525,$$

*Table 3.1*
**Price and Quantity Observations in Two Different Years**

|  | Year 1 | | Year 2 | |
|---|---|---|---|---|
|  | Wine (bottles) | Cheese (pounds) | Wine (bottles) | Cheese (pounds) |
| Quantity | 100 | 100 | 75 | 150 |
| Price | $4 | $1 | $3 | $2 |

where $Y_i$ is nominal GNP in Year i. The nominal value of GNP increased by $25 over the period, but our problem is to decide to what extent it is possible to consider this change one of quantity or one of price.

The observed data can be combined in various ways to give us a price index. One method is to define a commodity bundle and determine the number of units of money required to purchase that bundle in the different years. This is the method used to calculate the consumer price index. What goes into the bundle is of great importance, as very different results can arise from the same information.

The commodity bundle used to calculate a price index usually is based on a survey of actual consumption for that economy. The basic procedure is as follows:

1. Select a base year (a year from which the calculations are to be made).

2. Select a commodity bundle. This will usually consist of the relative quantities of goods and services consumed in the base year.

3. Calculate the number of units of money required to purchase the commodity bundle in the base year and in other years for which the price index is to be calculated.

4. Calculate the price index for any specific year by dividing the price of the commodity bundle for that specific year by the price of the commodity bundle for the base year. Some indexes use this number alone; others multiply it by 100. (Thus, the price index for the base year is either 1 or 100.)

If in our example Year 1 is selected as the base year and the commodity bundle is defined as one bottle of wine and one pound of cheese (Bundle 1), then

$$\text{Price of Bundle 1 (Year 1)} = \$4 \times 1 + \$1 \times 1 = \$5$$

$$\text{and Price of Bundle 1 (Year 2)} = \$3 \times 1 + \$2 \times 1 = \$5.$$

With this calculation, the price indexes for this economy are $P_1 = 1$ and $P_2 = 1$. This price index reveals that the "average" price remained constant.

***An Alternative Calculation.***   Alternatively, Year 2 could have been selected as the base year. The commodity bundle representing the quantities purchased in that year would then be one bottle of wine and two pounds of cheese (Bundle 2). The alternative, price-index ($\tilde{P}_i$) calculations would be

$$\text{Price of Bundle 2 (Year 1)} = \$4 \times 1 + \$1 \times 2 = \$6$$

$$\text{and Price of Bundle 2 (Year 2)} = \$3 \times 1 + \$2 \times 2 = \$7.$$

The price indexes are then: $\tilde{P}_1 = \$6/\$7 = 0.857$ and $\tilde{P}_2 = \$7/\$7 = 1$, which shows that the average price rose from Year 1 to Year 2.

Obviously, widely divergent results can be achieved by selecting different commodity bundles. Using Bundle 1, the price level remained constant, but using Bundle 2, the price level rose by more than 14 percent.

Great care must be taken in choosing the most representative bundle for the calculations. The *index number problem* is choosing a bundle of commodities that allows us to discern accurately whether changes in the money value of goods sold represent changes in prices only, changes in quantities only, or changes in both at the same time. Fortunately, the problem is not as drastic as the observations for our two-commodity case. When the commodities remain in roughly the same usage from year to year and prices move generally in the same direction, the information conveyed by different price indexes usually will be the same or very similar.

Figure 3.1 shows the annualized rates of change in two different consumption price indexes from 1979 through 1983. The CPI-W uses a constant commodity bundle to determine the price index. The implicit deflator for personal consumption expenditure is computed in a different (equally acceptable) manner. Essentially, the commodity bundle is selected for the current year, the real value of that bundle is determined using base year prices, and the implicit deflator is then computed as a residual.[3] As can be seen in Figure 3.1, both indexes reveal the same general information regarding trends in the movement of consumption prices. However, outside the general trend, significant differences are apparent.

---

[3]A price index for year $n$ is computed by using the following formula:

$$P_n = \frac{\sum\limits_{i=1}^{m} P_i^c Q_i^d}{\sum\limits_{i=1}^{m} P_i^a Q_i^b} \times 100.$$

The summation ($i$) runs over the number of commodities used to compute the price index. The superscripts indicate the year used to compute the price or quantity. If past quantity weights are used (as in the CPI), then $a$, $b$, and $d$ represent the base year and $c$ is the current year ($n$). If current weights are used, as in the GNP implicit price deflator, then $a$ is the base year and $b$, $c$, and $d$ represent the current year.

*Figure 3.1*
**Annualized Rates of Change in Consumption Price Indices,
Implicit Deflator for Personnel Consumption Expenditure
(PCE) and the CPI-W, 1970–1984**

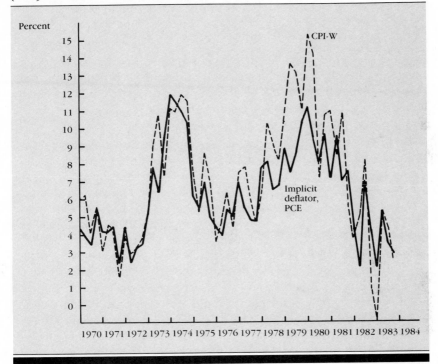

*Source:* The growth rates (% change in index $= 4[(ln (\text{index}_t) - ln(\text{index}_{t-i})]$ are computed from quarterly data given in *Business Statistics, 1979 edition,* pp. 75–78, 204, 205, and 260, and *Survey of Current Business,* July 1981, 82, 83, May 1979, March 1980, and Dec. 1981, Tables s1 and s2, U.S. Department of Commerce.

## The Level of Real Income (y)

Now that we have a measure of prices, it is possible to make the distinction between real and nominal output. In addition to being used as an indicator of price changes, the price index is used to convert (deflate) nominal valued variables into real variables. Deflating nominal values into real values accounts for the changing value of the dollar, and the real value measures an item in terms of a dollar with constant purchasing power.

In general, the relationship between a real and nominal variable is given in Equation 3.3.[4]

---

[4]Variables such as income, wealth, wage payments, and interest payments are deflated to real values by dividing by an appropriate price index. This method of conversion, however, only applies to stock and flow variables; it does not apply to ratios, such as the interest rate. (*See* "Real and Nominal Interest Rates," Chapter 5, page 106).

$$\text{Real variable (Year i)} = \frac{\text{Nominal variable (Year i)}}{\text{Price index (Year i)}} \qquad (3.3)$$

Thus, the relationship between nominal GNP ($Y$) and real GNP ($y$)[5] is given by:

$$y = \frac{Y}{P} \qquad \text{or} \qquad Y = Py.$$

In our example of a simplified, two-good economy (given in Table 3.1), we have observations on the nominal level of output for two different years. However, with the price indexes that we have calculated, it is possible to derive the real output figures. Using the price indexes calculated with Year 1 as the base year, we have

$$y_1 = \frac{Y_1}{P_1} = \frac{\$500}{1} = \$500$$

$$\text{and } y_2 = \frac{Y_2}{P_2} = \frac{\$525}{1} = \$525.$$

This calculation indicates that the quantity of goods produced in this economy, measured in constant dollars, has increased by $25.

Alternatively, by using the price indexes calculated by using Year 2 as the base year, we have

$$\tilde{y}_1 = \frac{Y_1}{\tilde{P}_1} = \frac{\$500}{0.857} = \$583.33$$

$$\text{and } \tilde{y}_2 = \frac{Y_2}{\tilde{P}_2} = \frac{\$525}{1} = \$525.$$

In this case we would say that output in real terms fell by $58.33 over the two years.

Using the same basic information, it is possible to calculate two distinct price indexes that can be used to produce two distinct measures of real income. Unfortunately, there is no clear answer to the question of which price index is the "correct" measure of the price change. Anyone evaluating economic conditions is likely to use a different collection of goods and services to calculate a price index, and is therefore likely to calculate a different amount of real income from any nominal income. Fortunately, economic conditions usually do not change as drastically as those in our example, so the information generated from price indexes is reasonably similar.

---

[5] Real GNP is usually calculated by dividing nominal GNP by the "GNP deflator." The GNP deflator is a price index calculated by using the goods and services that are included in GNP. It includes more goods and services than the CPI.

## The Velocity of Circulation (V)

With knowledge of the money supply and the value of nominal income, it is now possible to calculate the fourth variable in the equation of exchange, the velocity of circulation. Over any period of time, the amount of newly produced goods and services, measured in nominal terms, is purchased by using the currently available stock of money. The relationship between the average quantity of money and the nominal level of output during the period is the velocity of circulation. The *velocity of circulation* measures the number of times the stock of money is used (or turns over) in purchasing the goods and services during the period. The velocity of circulation thus can be calculated by dividing nominal GNP by the stock of money.

$$V = \frac{\text{Nominal } GNP}{M} \tag{3.4}$$

Because the velocity of circulation is defined this way, the *equation of exchange* is purely *definitional in nature.* The nominal money supply multiplied by the velocity of circulation is defined as being equal to the price level times the level of real output.[6]

$$MV = Py.$$

If nominal income is \$100 and the stock of money is \$5, then $V$ is 20. On average, each dollar of the money supply was spent 20 times buying final goods and services. This does not mean that *every* dollar was spent 20 times. One dollar may have been spent 100 times and the four other dollars not at all in buying final goods and services.

The velocity of circulation obviously depends on the particular definition of the money supply that is being used. There is a different velocity of circulation for every money supply definition:

$$V_1 = \frac{Y}{M1}, \qquad V_2 = \frac{Y}{M2},$$

and so on. Figure 3.2 shows the velocity of circulation since 1970 for the two commonly used definitions of the supply of money.

## THE FINANCIAL SECTOR AND NOMINAL OUTPUT

The equation of exchange gives us a useful indication of the possible relationships between the financial sector of the economy and the current market value of output, nominal income. $M$ multiplied by $V$, and $P$ multiplied by

---

[6]Alternatively, this may be viewed as follows: The percentage change in $M$ plus the percentage change in $V$ is equal to the percentage change in $P$ plus the percentage change in $y$. If $M$ increases by 3 percent and $V$ increases by 1 percent with a 2 percent increase in $y$, then the price index must have increased by 2 percent.

*Figure 3.2*
**Velocities of Circulation, 1970–1984**

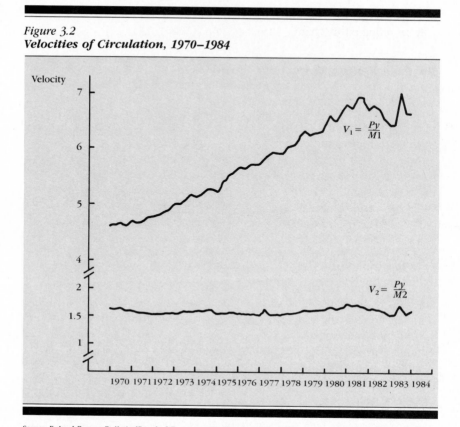

Source: *Federal Reserve Bulletin* (Board of Governors, Washington, D.C.); *Economic Report of the President* (U.S. Government Printing Office, Washington, D.C.); *Monetary Trends* (Federal Reserve Bank of St. Louis); *National Economic Trends* (Federal Reserve Bank of St. Louis).

$y$ are both definitions of the level of expenditure. As $P$ multiplied by $y$ states nominal GNP according to the two components, price and output, $M$ multiplied by $V$ indicates the activity of the financial sector.

The quantity of money available consists primarily of deposit liabilities of financial intermediaries, such as commercial banks and thrift institutions. In large part, this quantity of money is channeled through the economic system by the financial institutions. The activities of the various financial institutions thus can be represented either in $M$ or in $V$.

For example, with $M$ defined as M1, the activity of commercial banks and the thrift institutions directly related to transactions types of deposits is captured in M1; whereas their activity directly related to savings and other longer-term deposits is related through their impact on the velocity of circulation. When the definition of the money supply is broadened to M2, the activity of these financial institutions directly related to savings and small time deposits is shifted out of $V$ and into the measure of $M$. The actions of the financial sector will be revealed in changes in $M$ and $V$, and the impact will be reflected in changes in prices and output.

## Positive Versus Normative Economics

The actual measurement of economic variables and the placement of the variables in the equation of exchange can provide a useful description of the state of the economy. The implementation of any sound monetary policy, however, requires more than mere description. Some indication of the interrelationships between the economic variables is also required. Various monetary theories are designed to explain the interrelationships between the variables, and these theories are useful in answering questions such as, what will result if the money supply increases, and what monetary action will lead to an increase in real output? The area of economics that describes economic activity and the relationships between economic variables is positive economics. *Positive economics* describes what *is* and what the result of specific actions *will be.*

The major contribution of economists has been to explain the interrelationships that exist in the economy. A major segment of positive economic analysis is the use of different theories to *predict* what the results of specific policy actions will be. However, great care must be exercised when we move from positive economics and mere descriptions of what is. Explaining that a particular result is the result of some specific policy is dramatically different from deciding that the particular result is desirable and should be achieved. *Normative economics* is the area of economics devoted to the decisions regarding what *should be.* All normative decisions depend on the value judgments of individuals making the decisions. Therefore, as the goals set for monetary policy are the result of normative decisions, they involve value judgments made by decision makers.

Clearly, positive and normative economics are interrelated. The predictions of positive economic analysis are useful in selecting the appropriate policy actions that are likely to achieve the results selected by the normative decisions. Also, positive economics is helpful in indicating whether or not a desired goal can be achieved and what other results (some of which might be undesirable) are likely to occur.

## The Normative Decisions

The primary goal of United States economic policy in general, and monetary policy in particular, is to improve the level of economic well-being. This goal is extremely broad. To clarify the results considered desirable, certain traditional normative goals have been set by Congress. The Employment Act of 1946 stated that it was the responsibility of the federal government, with the assistance of the private sector and state and local governments, to "promote maximum employment, production and purchasing power." This act was amended and expanded by the Full Employment and Balanced Growth Act of 1978 (known as the Humphrey-Hawkins Act), which was passed:

> to assert the responsibility of the Federal Government to use all practicable programs and policies to promote full employment, production, and real income, balanced growth, adequate productivity growth, proper attention to national priorities, and reasonable price stability.

Though the monetary authority, the Federal Reserve, is an independent agency of the government, it shares in this responsibility and attempts to achieve the goals through monetary policy (through adjustments in the money supply or through changes in monetary conditions).

The Employment Act of 1946 as amended in 1978 still leaves the normative goals broadly stated and does not indicate what trade-offs should be made when the normative goals prove to be incompatible. The traditional normative goals of monetary policy are usually related to specific concerns over full employment, price stability, economic growth, and balance of payments.

## Full Employment

An individual is considered *unemployed* if actively seeking employment at the going wage rate but being unable to obtain a job. Full employment means that enough jobs and job openings exist that everyone actively seeking employment at the going wage rate has a job or could be offered one. At various times, the economy is considered fully employed even though a specified percentage of the labor force is unemployed.

Full employment is established as one of the normative goals of economic policy because the unemployment that exists when the economy is not fully employed imposes costs both on specific individuals and on the entire economy. The unemployed bear a large part of these costs. Typically, they are unable to pay for as many goods and services as they could if they were employed. Also, some suffer a psychic cost through reduced self-esteem. The employed also bear some of the direct cost on individuals through additional taxes to pay for social welfare to the unemployed.

The cost of unemployment, however, is not simply a redistribution of goods and services between the employed and the unemployed. The cost to the economy as a whole is a reduction in output. As the level of employment decreases, the level of real output decreases. When there is unemployment, the level of newly produced goods and services made available for current use is less than it would be at full employment.

Unemployment means that an underutilization of labor leads to a reduction in output below the potential level of output. The potential level of output is the amount of goods and services that can be produced with full

3  THE QUANTITY OF MONEY—A PREVIEW OF MONETARY THEORY

"I used to do just medicine, but lately I've been moving into economics."

utilization of the labor force and the other factors of production (land and capital). If there is full employment in the labor market and full utilization of land and capital, the aggregate level of output is at the potential output for the economy. If there is unemployment, the level of output is lower than the potential level.

In the short run, with the amount of land and capital in fixed supply, the level of real output and the level of employment move together. Thus, it is possible either to observe the level of unemployment directly by counting the number of people seeking work at the going wage rate, or to discern the level of unemployment indirectly through measures of the level of real output achieved by the economy.

**The Use of Monetary Policy.**  The close relationship between unemployment and the level of real output presents two ways that monetary policy can be used to alter the level of unemployment. Action might be taken to affect the labor market directly, thereby inducing an expansion in employment. Or policy might be designed to generate an increase in output directly, thereby requiring the employment of additional labor to produce the additional output.

There is a great difference of opinion as to how changing the level of output and employment should be attempted. One group of theorists believes that monetary policy should be used on the supply side of the economy. By utilizing monetary policy in the attempt to raise the price level ($P$) and thereby reduce the real wage ($w = W/P$), the real cost of labor would be reduced and firms would be induced to employ more labor. This would result in an increase in output.

Alternatively, another group believes that monetary policy should be used to change the demand for real output. By using monetary policy to reduce interest rates, the demand for additional capital goods (machines, houses, cars, and the like) could be increased. As producers attempt to supply the goods to satisfy this additional demand, more labor would be employed to cause a reduction in unemployment.

Regardless of the way in which theorists believe the economy functions, the normative goals are broadly established by acts of Congress. The Humphrey-Hawkins Act set 1983 *targets* to be achieved by economic policies. For employment, the Humphrey-Hawkins Act called for an overall unemployment rate of 4 percent and an unemployment rate of 3 percent for those 20 years of age and over. Following a dramatic rise starting in mid-1981 to well over 10 percent, the overall unemployment rate declined throughout 1983 to end the year at just over 8 percent.

Legislating a target is different from achieving a goal, and it is questionable whether or not these goals can be achieved at the same time as some of the other goals in the act. The president of the United States has been given the authority to change these target unemployment rates as economic conditions change.

## Price Stability

Price adjustments are an everyday feature of market-oriented economies. Changes in supply and demand cause continual changes in money prices. For example, housing prices may increase and electronic calculator prices may decrease as a result of changing production conditions and population growth. These changes should not be confused with inflation or deflation: They are changes in the *relative* prices of goods and services. Market conditions can cause the average price of a large collection of goods and services to rise, but this still does not constitute inflation. Inflation and deflation are continuous, ongoing processes. *Inflation* is defined as a continuous rise in the average price of goods and services, and *deflation* is defined as a continuous fall in the average price of goods and services.

The normative concern over price stability is primarily related to the costs associated with continuous increases or decreases in the general price level. Certainly, changes in the relative prices of goods and services present problems for members of an economy. However, the effects of relative price changes are primarily distributive in nature. Some people gain when the relative price of their output increases, and others lose as the relative price of their output declines. Both relative price changes and the instability of relative prices impose costs on the economy as people incur the costs of shifting out of one activity into another. Relative prices, however, are not directly under the control of government agencies. These relative price changes and their associated costs are part of the market process of allocating and reallocating goods, services, and productive resources into those activities considered most beneficial.

Economic policy is concerned primarily with the impacts of a changing *general* level of prices. The costs of inflation fall on individuals and on the economy as a whole. The costs to the individual are chiefly the result of the redistribution of income and wealth that inflation imposes. If a person receives an income fixed in dollars at, say, $100 per week, the purchasing power of that income will be eroded as the price level rises. If prices double, the individual only will be able to buy half of what was bought before prices rose. Not all incomes are fixed in dollar terms. When prices rise, not only does the person buying the goods and services pay more, but also the person selling the goods and services receives more. The problem is that not all prices move together. Incomes rise at different rates and people have different increases or decreases in their purchasing power as the price level changes. The costs that inflation imposes in such an arbitrary way may cause the monetary authority to try to control the inflation to avoid the redistribution.

One technique used by some countries is the indexation of money payments to reduce the redistributive effects. *Indexation* is the tying of monetary payments to changes in some price index. (*See* insert on Indexation, page 56). If incomes are indexed, a person with a fixed income of $100 per week would have that money income doubled to $200 per week if prices doubled. Thus, the individual would maintain a fairly constant purchasing power.

The costs to the economy as a whole arise from the fact that inflation interferes with the economy's ability to produce goods and services. With continuous rises in prices, people will try to predict the rates of change in prices. To the extent that the price rises are anticipated, individuals will use productive resources to preserve their purchasing power. For example, if prices in money terms were expected to rise by 10 percent over the next day, it is likely that many individuals would forgo working for at least part of today in order to spend their money on goods and services before the price rise took place. Although the price rises are rarely that drastic, we can be assured that some resources would be expended in the effort to avoid a reduction in purchasing power. Also, as prices rise, individuals will spend time and effort to bargain for higher wages and salaries. Apart from time spent in bargaining, the bargaining will require that effort be made to predict how prices will change so it can be included in wage and salary contracts.

## INDEXATION

*Indexation* is a method of linking the number of units of money in a payment to some specific measure of average prices. It is an attempt to reduce the costs associated with inflation by protecting individual purchasing power. By indexing monetary incomes, some of the redistributive effects associated with inflation would be reduced. Also, since an individual's purchasing power is protected, fewer resources would have to be used to make adjustments out of monetary assets.

Complete indexation would index all wage contracts all deposits with financial institutions, insurance policies and payments, loans and loan payments, pensions, taxes, and other payments. With indexation, the monetary payments would automatically be adjusted for some measured change in average prices. For example, if a wage contract called for an hourly wage rate of $7.00 and it was determined that prices had increased by 50 percent, the wage payment would be $10.50 per hour ( $7.00 × 1.5 ).

Historically, indexation has had rather limited use. The People's Republic of China indexed bank deposits in 1955. It has also been used recently in Finland, Israel, and France. The most recent widespread use of indexation has been in Brazil since 1965. After indexation Brazil's rate of increase in average prices declined dramatically and the rate of growth of output increased. Whether or not this was the result of the indexation, however, is unclear. In the United States the use of indexation has been limited to *cost of living allowances* (*COLAs*) in wage contracts and some variable interest rate loans.

Wherever effort is spent in avoiding the costs of inflation, resources are diverted away from the production of goods and services that would have taken place if the price level had been stable. The change in the use of resources imposes a cost on society as a whole in the form of forgone output. If it is possible to reduce and stabilize the rate of inflation, fewer resources will be used in the attempt to preserve the purchasing power that would have been eroded away through inflation. Also, the costs of a capricious redistribution of wealth and income will be avoided.

***The Use of Monetary Policy.*** Economic theories based on the equation of exchange ($MV = Py$) relate the general level of prices to activities in the

Complete indexation would also index tax receipts, and this would have a significant impact on an economy. Without indexation, a general increase in prices and incomes would shift individuals into higher tax brackets. Thus, the government's share of the goods and services produced would increase as the prices increased. With the indexation of tax receipts, the government would only acquire an ability to obtain more goods and services if the output of real goods and services increased. This might generate an incentive for the government to increase its efforts to control inflation as the benefit the government currently reaps from inflation would have been removed.

The principal arguments against indexation are that it would be both difficult and costly to implement. First, as all prices do not move together and the changes in some prices are more important to some individuals than to others, it is not clear what measure of price changes would be appropriate. Second, it is not clear how existing contracts should be treated. Most of the current contracts were made with some anticipated rate of inflation in mind, so an indexation of these contracts would generate a significant redistribution of wealth. If mortgage contracts taken out in the early 1960s were indexed, individuals would be paying interest in excess of 10 percent on contracts that initially called for only 4–5 percent. Also, by enabling us to "live with inflation," indexation might reduce the incentive to find a cure for the problem.[1]

---

[1] For additional information on indexation, *see* Jai-Hoon Yang, "The Case for and against Indexation: An Attempt at Perspective." *Federal Reserve Bank of St. Louis Review* (October 1974): 2–11.

financial sector of the economy. However, there are strong differences of opinion as to exactly how the price level is formed and what can be used to change it. Some economists relate the general price level directly to the quantity of money, but others relate the general price level to the level of aggregate demand for output. This difference of opinion has led to differences in belief about how monetary policy should be conducted to relieve the problem of inflation.

One group of theorists believes that the rate of increase in prices should be abated directly by reducing the rate of growth in the money stock. They argue that if there is less money available, the upward pressure on prices will be reduced. Alternatively, other theorists believe that the problem of rising prices should be attacked through aggregate demand. They argue that if interest rates are increased, aggregate demand will reduce, and the pressure on prices will be diminished.

Subject to modification by the president of the United States, the Humphrey-Hawkins Act calls for policies designed to reduce the rate of inflation to 3 percent by 1983 and zero by 1988. There is great skepticism about whether this policy on inflation is compatible with the policy that has been set for unemployment. Prices, as measured by the implicit price deflator for GNP, rose during 1983 at an annual rate of 4.2 percent.

## Growth

As a concern of monetary policy, growth is usually not given the same attention as unemployment and inflation. This is probably because the benefits of growth are long run, although the costs of unemployment and inflation are immediate and obvious. *Growth* is defined as an increase over time in the level of real output per person.

The benefit of growth is an increase in the total output that can be distributed to the members of an economy. In the long run, it is only possible to improve the level of economic well-being by increasing the amount of goods and services that are available per person. Some gains in the short run may be realized by redistributing goods to those groups considered more deserving (for instance, through welfare payments). However, the gains to one group come at a cost imposed on another group. Only with more goods and services would it be possible to distribute the goods and services to make everyone better off.

With increased attention being given to supply-side economics, growth is now being given increased attention. Growth in real output per capita results from increased productivity per worker. This increased productivity can result from improvement in the skills of the labor force, increases in the capital stock (plant and equipment), or improved technology. With more capital per worker and improved technology, a given labor force would be able to produce a greater level of real output.

***The Use of Monetary Policy.*** Monetary policy can be useful in stimulating growth by inducing producers to increase their capital stock and invest in research and development. By utilizing monetary policies designed to lower interest rates and reduce the charge for borrowing funds (in real terms), firms can be induced to invest in additional capital and improved technology. Growth also can be stimulated by monetary policies designed to stabilize prices and general economic conditions. This would reduce some of the uncertainty over future economic conditions and would make producers more willing to undertake longer-term investment projects.

## Balance of Payments

The balance of payments consideration of United States economic policy is the problem of maintaining the purchasing power and the stability of the purchasing power of the dollar in foreign markets. This is a concern over the exchange rate. An *exchange rate* is the price of a currency in terms of a foreign currency. The exchange rate for the dollar in terms of British pounds (£) is the number of pounds sterling that can be acquired with one dollar. The published exchange rate is often expressed as the number of dollars it takes to buy one unit of foreign currency. For example, the exchange rate is usually published as $2 = £1, which is the dollar price of a pound sterling. The corresponding pound price of the dollar is £½ = $1.

The concern over the level of economic well-being associated with exchange rates is related to the gains from international trade. Just as individuals benefit by acquiring goods from lower-opportunity-cost producers, so it is possible for the members of an economy to gain through the exchange of goods produced domestically at a lower opportunity cost for goods and services produced abroad at a lower opportunity cost. The United States, for example, trades wheat and agricultural products for electronic and other manufactured goods produced abroad.

Like domestic trade, international trade is conducted in monetary units. Thus, the purchase of goods and services from foreign countries requires that dollars be exchanged for various foreign currencies, and the purchase by foreign residents of United States goods requires that the foreign currencies be used to purchase dollars. The exchanges of dollars for foreign currencies occur on the *foreign exchange market.*

As is the case with any instability in prices, a lack of stability in the exchange rate will generate uncertainty concerning the benefits to be realized from international trade. The lack of a stable exchange rate is likely to disrupt the international flow of goods and the benefits from that flow. Although it is possible to shift the risk of a change in the exchange rate to another party willing to assume the risk by contracting for delivery of foreign currency in the future at a price established today, this forward market transaction also imposes additional transactions costs that could be avoided, or at least reduced, with exchange rate stability.

A change in the level of the exchange rate also has an impact on the distribution of the benefits from international trade. If, for example, the value of the dollar in terms of foreign currencies declines, foreign goods will cost United States residents more dollars. Consumers of imported goods would find these goods more expensive. However, exporters would find it easier to sell their goods (the price in foreign currencies would have declined), and producers of export goods, in general, would gain.

Perhaps just as important as the direct costs of transactions and the distributional effects is the bearing that the exchange rate has on the prestige of a country in international markets. If the exchange rate is high or rising, it is considered indicative of a strong economy. A low or falling exchange rate is considered an indication of a weak economy.

It may seem strange to call a concern over the exchange rate a concern over the balance of payments. However, payments balance and the exchange rate are determined in the same foreign exchange market. There are many different measures of payments balance used to extract information from exchange markets. For the United States, *international payments* are balanced when the number of dollars supplied to the foreign exchange market by United States residents to purchase foreign currency is equal to the demand for those dollars by foreign residents. When such a balance is reached, there is no pressure for the current exchange rate to change. Other measures of payments balance (such as the balance of merchandise trade) are used in attempts to discern what pressures are being placed on the foreign exchange market to cause the rate to adjust.

***The Foreign Exchange Market.***   The foreign exchange market is shown in Figure 3.3, where the exchange rate ($e$) is the number of pounds it takes to buy one dollar. Dollars are supplied to the foreign exchange market when residents of the United States desire to purchase goods and services or financial assets in foreign countries. Dollars are demanded from the foreign exchange market when residents of foreign countries desire to purchase goods and services or financial assets in the United States.

As the exchange rate ($e$) rises, more pounds can be bought with a dollar and, therefore, a dollar can be converted into more goods and services or financial assets in Britain. The ability of the dollar to buy more goods in Britain when the exchange rate rises is reflected by an increase in the quantity of dollars supplied to the foreign exchange market and is shown in the upward-sloping supply curve in Figure 3.3.[7] Similarly, as the exchange rate ($e$) increases, it will take more pounds to buy a dollar, and residents of Britain will find goods and services and financial assets in the United States more expensive. Thus, the quantity of dollars demanded by the British from the foreign exchange market will decline as the exchange rate rises. This is indicated by the downward-sloping demand curve in Figure 3.3.

If the exchange rate were at $e^*$ in Figure 3.3, the supply of dollars would be equal to the demand for dollars, payments with respect to the British would balance, and no pressure would be exerted on the exchange rate to change. In a *floating exchange rate system* (used for international payments since mid-1973), the exchange rate is allowed to adjust to market forces. With a floating exchange rate, market forces will result in the exchange rate $e^*$.

---

[7]Actually, it is the total expenditure on goods, services, and financial assets that determines the demand and supply of currency. Thus, the elasticity of demand for foreign goods with respect to the exchange rate is important. This analysis assumes that these demands are elastic.

*Figure 3.3*
**The Foreign Exchange Market**

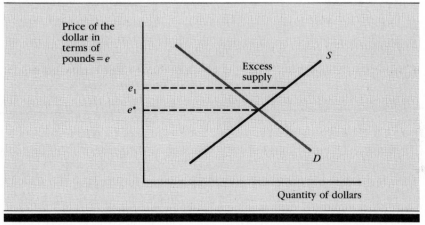

If the exchange rate were at $e_1$, there would be an excess supply of dollars on the foreign exchange market, and the United States would have a balance of payments deficit with respect to the British. The excess supply of dollars would put pressure on the value of the dollar to fall until the exchange rate stood at $e^*$ and payments balanced.

***The Use of Monetary Policy.*** Since 1973, when the exchange rate was allowed to float in response to market pressures, the monetary authority has generally intervened in the foreign exchange market to maintain orderly conditions. If, for example, the exchange rate were declining too rapidly, the monetary authority might step into the market and buy up some of the excess supply of dollars to reduce the pressure on the exchange rate to fall. This purchase of dollars by the monetary authority could be made with past accumulated holdings of foreign currency or, perhaps, with foreign currency borrowed from foreign monetary authorities. By temporarily reducing the excess supply of dollars on the foreign exchange market, the monetary authority might be able to smooth the market adjustments in the exchange rate and generate increased stability in the foreign exchange rate.

The monetary authority also could try to alter the level of the market-determined exchange rate by changing domestic monetary conditions. For example, if the monetary authority could influence the domestic price level, it could make goods and services in the United States cheaper for the British at any exchange rate by lowering domestic prices. This would cause the demand for dollars on the foreign exchange market to increase and the supply of dollars to decrease. The market forces would then drive the exchange rate ($e$) up to a higher level. This type of action on domestic economic conditions could also be used to maintain an exchange rate at the existing level in the face of market pressures for the exchange rate to decline.

## The Quantity Theories of Money

When economists explain what the result of money supply changes on the economy will be, they are giving, directly or indirectly, what is known as a *quantity theory of money.* There are many theories of this kind; not just one theory can be called *the* quantity theory of money. The various theories may even involve different channels for the analysis of the impact of changes in the money supply on economic conditions. For example, the money supply may be assumed to affect the price level initially or it may have its initial impact through changes in interest rates and the incentive to invest. Each of these theories may be more or less complicated, but it can be summarized by using the equation of exchange, $MV = Py$. The equation itself should not be confused with the theory. The equation is an identity and is true by definition. The theories, on the other hand, make statements about how some of the variables in the equation will behave when the money supply is changed.

As an example, if we knew that the velocity of circulation remained unchanged when the money supply changed (an inspection of Figure 3.2 shows that at least $V_2$ has remained fairly constant for an extended period), and if we assume that the level of real output would be unaffected by money supply changes, then we would have a theory that stated that prices vary in direct proportion to the money supply ($M_2$):

$$M_2 \uparrow \overline{V}_2 = P \uparrow \overline{y}.$$

If money supply 2 is increased, prices will increase in the same proportion. A doubling of money supply 2 will lead to a doubling of the average level of money prices; a cut in money supply 2 will lead to a reduction in the price index.

This version of the quantity theory of money is often called the *naive quantity theory of money,* but there is nothing particularly naive about it. Such a theory requires a sophisticated analysis of the economy to explain why the level of real output is unaffected by money supply changes. One possible explanation offered by some theorists is that output depends on employment and employment depends upon the real wage rate. If the monetary authority increases the money supply, the immediate result will be an increase in prices; but if prices rise, money wages are likely to be bid up in the same proportion. This would result in real wages, employment, and output remaining constant as the money supply was increased. If the velocity of circulation remained constant, this would mean that prices would rise in proportion to the money supply.

Theorists who believe that the naive theory might be true when prices are rising often do not believe it to be true in cases when prices are falling. This is because of the belief that money wages do not fall easily. If prices fall, they may well fall relative to wages, and this will result in real wages rising. Firms would thus be induced to employ less labor, and the result would then be that price reductions would be accompanied by output reductions:

$$M_2 \downarrow \overline{V}_2 = P \downarrow y \downarrow.$$

Obviously, many alternative theories can be derived with alternative explanations of how output might react to money supply changes. If we retain the assumption that the velocity of circulation remains constant, the effect on prices can be inferred once the effect of changes in the money supply on output is known.

One alternative theory states that money supply changes have a direct impact on output, and the changes in output induce employment and price changes. In this theory, an increase in the money supply leads to an increase in the level of expenditure on goods and services; and this increase in the demand for output leads producers to increase their output and hire more employees. The amount of the price change will then reflect the extent to which the money supply change is not reflected in a proportionate increase in output.

Until we have derived more detailed theories of how aggregate output is affected by money supply changes, we cannot know precisely the relationship between the money supply and the price level. It does seem, however, that we can rely on a much weaker assertion: that prices and money supplies tend to move in the same direction. Historically, there has never been a sustained increase in the money supply that has not led to increases in prices, and there have never been sustained increases in prices that have not been accompanied by increases in the money supply.

## SUMMARY

The primary goal of United States monetary policy is to improve our economic well-being. By altering either the quantity of money available or the conditions in specific financial markets, monetary policy attempts to deal with the specific problems of unemployment, inflation, growth of output, and balance of payments.

Aggregate economic variables are used both to evaluate the results of past policies and to discern potential problem areas. These aggregate variables, however, should be used with some caution because aggregation of large amounts of data can hide or even lose important information.

The results of any policy decision will depend on the interactions between various markets in the economy, so analysis of markets and how they interact is undertaken in an attempt to predict the outcome of the policies. These predictions are important in the normative process of monetary policy decision making.

The interaction between the financial sector and current aggregate output is shown in the equation of exchange, $MV = Py$. Even though this equation is purely definitional, the equation indicates that adjustments in the financial sector that affect the level of expenditure ($M$ multiplied by $V$) must be reflected in the nominal value of aggregate output ($P$ multiplied by $y$). By making various assumptions about how the variables in this equation behave, quantity theories of money can be derived. Such discussions are a large part of the theory section of this book.

## Key Terms

aggregation
price index
equation of exchange
nominal variable
real variable
stock variable
flow variable
gross national product (GNP)

velocity of circulation
positive economics
normative economics
unemployment
inflation
indexation
exchange rate
quantity theory of money

## Questions

1. What is the cost of inflation to the economy as a whole? Does a redistribution of income impose a cost on the economy? How?

2. How do the impacts of a once-and-for-all rise in average prices differ from the impacts of inflation?

3. You are given the following observations for an economy:

|  | Year 1 | | Year 2 | |
|---|---|---|---|---|
|  | Price | Quantity | Price | Quantity |
| Books | $10 | 50 | $15 | 25 |
| Bread | $0.50 | 50 | $0.30 | 300 |

Has output increased from Year 1 to Year 2? What has happened to the average price level?

4. Since the index number problem is known, why do we continue to use aggregate measures of economic activity?

5. Explain how markets interact. How could an increase in the price of wheat in Kansas have an impact on the price of tea in China?

Why, when the market is small, can the market interactions be ignored?

6. What is the equation of exchange? How does this equation differ from the quantity theories of money that are derived from it?

## Additional Readings

A wide variety of current statistical information is published regularly in: *Economic Report of the President,* which, along with the *Annual Report of the Council of Economic Advisors,* is transmitted annually to Congress in January, U.S. Government Printing Office, Washington, D.C.; *Federal Reserve Bulletin,* published monthly by the Board of Governors of the Federal Reserve, Washington, D.C.; and the *Survey of Current Business,* published monthly by the Bureau of Economic Analysis, U.S. Department of Commerce, U.S. Government Printing Office, Washington, D.C. In addition, these government publications also contain useful articles interpreting those data along with analysis of economic conditions.

Carlozzi, Nicholas. "Pegs and Floats: The Changing Face of the Foreign Exchange Market." *Business Review.* Federal Reserve Bank of Philadelphia (May–June 1980): 13–23.

*A review of how different nations manage their foreign exchange rates.*

Jester, John J. "Coping With Unemployment." *Business Review.* Federal Reserve Bank of Philadelphia (January–February 1977): 3–12.

*A discussion of the unemployment rate and what it may or may not indicate.*

Leisner, Thelma, and Marvyn King, eds. *Indexing for Inflation.* London: Heineman Educational Books Ltd., 1975.

*Proceedings of a conference held in England in 1975. Although the discussion concerned the United Kingdom, it is an excellent survey of the problems involved in instituting a general system of indexation in an inflationary period.*

Morgenstern, Oskar. *National Income Statistics.* San Francisco: Cato Institute, 1979.

*A critique of macroeconomic aggregation concerned with the meaningfulness, accuracy, and interpretation of available data.*

# CHAPTER FOUR

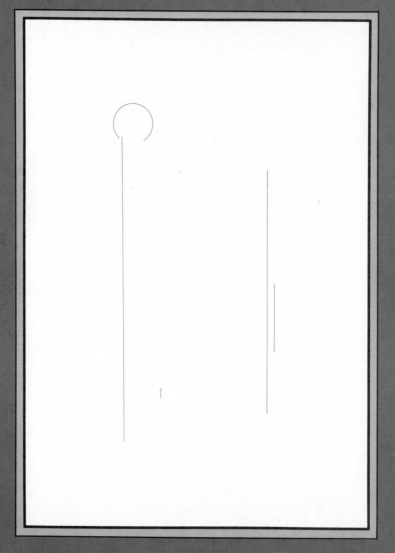

# MONETARY STANDARDS

*The money supply in an economy is established either as an automatic system based on some commodity such as gold or silver or as a managed system controlled by a monetary authority. Historically, the United States has used bimetallism (gold and silver together), monometallism (gold alone), and a managed paper system controlled by the Federal Reserve.*

Money predates the institution of government. As soon as economies evolved from individual self-sufficiency into interdependent exchange economies, the advantage of having a means of exchange became apparent. Even after governments were established, they did not immediately take up the powers of money creation. Their involvement with the money supply usually was limited to the verification of weights and measures. The seal of a government, or the face of a monarch, on a coin did not make that coin money; it merely certified the weight and fineness of the coin.[1] The means of exchange was not something imposed by government but originated in the individual choices of the buyers and the sellers in market economies.

As was explained in Chapter 2, buyers and sellers tended to select commodities that were durable, divisible, portable, standardized, and recognizable. When the unit of money is defined as a given quantity of a commodity and that commodity is used for redemption of the monetary unit, the

---

[1] The fineness of a coin refers to its percentage purity. If a gold coin is 0.9 fine, it is 90 percent pure gold. When the United States adopted 0.9 fine coins in 1837, the dollar was defined as 23.22 grains of *pure* gold (a grain is ¹⁄₄₈₀ of a troy ounce). The coins actually weighed 25.8 grains per dollar (0.05375 troy ounces).

monetary standard is a *commodity standard*. Even if there are circulating media other than full-bodied coins, so long as all token money and paper money in the system is redeemable in a particular commodity, then that commodity is the standard. Whenever a monetary system is set up so that the quantity of money is controlled by a government or other monetary authority *without regard* to its redeemability in a standard commodity, the system is said to be a *paper standard*.

## COMMODITY STANDARDS

There are three basic types of commodity standards that can be established, though history so far has afforded us examples of only the first two. The three standards are: *monometallism* (in which the money is redeemable in one metal only), *bimetallism* (in which money is redeemable in either of two metals), and the *composite commodity standard* (in which the money is redeemable in fixed proportions of several commodities). When the composite commodity money is defined in terms of metals only and each coin contains the metals in fixed proportion, the standard is known as *symmetallism*.

The automatic adjustment in the quantity of money that takes place when commodity standards are used is a market phenomenon. People can be expected to take advantage of a situation where they find the same commodity being sold at two different prices. If people find out they can buy a commodity cheaply and sell it immediately at a higher price, they can reasonably be expected to do so until the price differential is eliminated. This phenomenon is called *arbitrage*. The result of the arbitrage that takes place in the commodities in which the money supply is redeemable is referred to as Gresham's law.[2] *Gresham's law* states that the commodity or commodities in which the money supply is redeemable will always flow to where their value is the highest. In cases when the money supply is redeemable in metals only, Gresham's law is: Monetary metal always flows to where its value is the highest.

## MONOMETALLISM—THE CASE OF THE GOLD STANDARD

Apart from the gold standard used during the Byzantine Empire (A.D. 330–1453), silver standards have a longer history than gold standards. The gold standard is, however, more famous and is often looked back on as having produced the most stable monetary system. Although gold was used as *part* of the monetary system in the United States since 1792, the gold standard

---

[2]Gresham's law is named after Sir Thomas Gresham (*see* "Sir Thomas Gresham and His Law," page 69).

## SIR THOMAS GRESHAM AND HIS LAW

Sir Thomas Gresham was an English textile merchant who represented King Edward VI, Queen Mary I, and Queen Elizabeth I in Antwerp. His "representation" consisted mainly of borrowing money to help a depleted treasury (and occasionally smuggling the borrowed bullion back to England). Gresham is famous, however, for something he never said!

He is usually said to have told Queen Elizabeth that "bad money drives out good"—an expression that economists find difficult to use because of the kind of value judgment involved in deciding what is good money and what is bad money.

To his credit, Gresham did not express his views in this way. Nineteenth-century propagandists coined the phrase but attributed it to Gresham, who was known to have explained to Queen Elizabeth how the debasing of the currency by Henry VIII had caused people to take gold out of England.

Henry VIII had steadily reduced the silver content of the silver coinage. Coins that before 1543 had been 92.5 percent pure silver were reduced by 1545 to 33⅓ percent pure silver without their face value being reduced. This meant that the gold coins and heavier silver coins had a higher value for hoarding and for foreign trade, so that by the time Elizabeth came to the throne, only the debased silver coins were in circulation.

In a letter to Elizabeth, written in 1558, Gresham said:

> Ytt may pleasse your majesty to understande, thatt . . . the Kinges majesty, your latte ffather, in abasinge his quoyne . . . was the occasion thatt all your ffine goold was convayed ought of this your realme.[1]

The phenomenon of full-bodied money supplies being affected by monetary metal flowing to where its value is the highest was well known before Gresham ever wrote this letter. It was described by Aristophanes, explained by Oresme and Copernicus, and, as the thirteenth-century Chinese scholar Ma Duan Lin revealed, was fully understood by the Chinese monetary authorities in the tenth century.

Source: Bettman Archive

---

[1] Burgon, John William. *The Life and Times of Sir Thomas Gresham,* vol. 1. N.Y.: Burt Franklin Research and Source Work Series no. 123: 484.

was only used for about 50 years, starting in 1879 (the date known as *Resumption*[3]). During that period the United States dollar was defined as 23.22 grains of pure gold. This set the official price per troy ounce of gold at $20.67.[4]

## Requirements for a Monometallic System

*Monometallism* tends to stabilize prices both domestically and internationally if the following five requirements are met.

1.  The unit of account is defined as a given weight of the standard metal. This establishes an official price for the metal at which the authorities are pledged to buy and sell the metal.

2.  Interconvertibility is maintained for all kinds of money used in the system and the standard metal. This means that all paper money and bank money (bank deposits and bank notes issued) must be exchanged on demand for the standard metal.

3.  There must be free coinage. This means that whenever a quantity of the standard metal is presented to the authorities, usually at a mint, it must be made into coins on demand. After 1879, for example, anyone who presented 23.22 grains of pure gold to the United States mint would be paid $1. The word *free* is used in the sense of "freedom," not in the sense of "costless." Usually, monetary authorities have charged for converting standard metal into coin. A charge levied sufficient to cover the cost of conversion is called *brassage.* If the charge is greater than the cost of conversion, it is called *seigniorage* (meaning a profit for the seignior or king, the earliest monetary authority).

4.  There must be free melting of coins. If ever the standard metal is found to have a higher valued use than money, the public must be free to melt down the coins and to sell the standard metal in the commodity market.

5.  There must be free import and export of the standard metal. Whenever the standard metal has a higher value in some foreign country (either as a commodity or as money), the public must be free to take it to that country. Similarly, if the standard metal has a higher value here than elsewhere, the public must be able to bring it to this country.

---

[3] It may seem odd that the beginning of a new system should be referred to as *Resumption,* but the word signifies the resumption of redeemability of the paper money. Redemption in both gold and silver had been used before but had been suspended for the duration of the Civil War.

[4] There are 480 grains per troy ounce. Thus, 480 grains per ounce divided by 23.22 grains per dollar equals $20.67 per troy ounce.

The freedom to melt coins and the ability to have the standard metal coined allow for the flow of the metal between its use as a commodity and its use as money. This creates a tie between commodity markets and the quantity of money available and serves to create the automatic adjustments in the quantity of money that exist with commodity standards. The freedom to import or export the standard metal ties together the international markets. Interconvertibility for all forms of money and redeemability in the standard metal cause the quantity of the standard metal available for monetary use to impose a limit on the money supply. (A description of how monometallism works even when the public uses deposits and paper money in exchange is given in Appendix 4A.)

## *The Domestic Stabilization of Prices*

Even though the official price of gold is fixed by the monetary authority, this does not mean that commodity prices and the commodity price of gold cannot fluctuate when supply and demand change. However, arbitrage and the workings of Gresham's law will always ensure that the commodity price of gold will adjust to the official price. If the commodity market price of gold should rise above the official price, the public will react by exchanging its money for gold and selling that gold in the commodity market.

In Figure 4.1, the supply and demand conditions are such that the commodity price of gold is above the official price of $20.67 an ounce. Attracted by the price differential, people would find it profitable to redeem money for gold and sell that gold in the commodity market, or, what amounts to the same thing, would melt the coins and sell the metal in the commodity market. The amount of gold represented by *ab* would be supplied to the commodity market out of monetary use, and the commodity price of gold then would be bid down to the official price.

The significance of this for the economy is not the stabilization of the commodity price of gold, but what happens to the money supply. The excess demand for gold represented by *ab* reduces the money supply as the gold is taken from the money supply to be sold in the commodity market. Using the simplest possible connection between the general price level and the money supply, this reduction means that the general price level falls,[5]

$$M \downarrow V = P \downarrow y.$$

This adjustment in the supply of money is part of the automatic adjustment mechanism of a commodity standard that tends to stabilize the price level. If economic conditions change such that the price level rises, it is likely that the commodity price of gold will rise along with the other goods and services. The rise in the commodity price of gold will then cause a flow of gold

---

[5] This relationship uses the naive quantity theory of money that assumes that the velocity of circulation remains constant and that real output does not respond to changes in the supply of money.

*Figure 4.1*
**The Commodity Market for Gold: The Effect when the Commodity Price of Gold Rises above the Official Price**

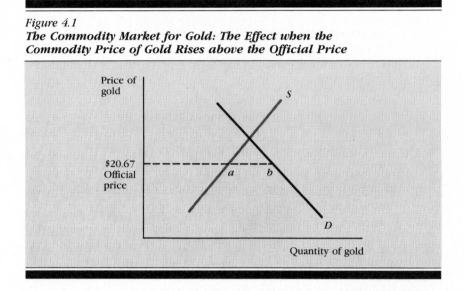

out of monetary use into use as a commodity, and the money supply will decline. With the decline in the money supply, the upward pressure on the money prices of goods and services will be reduced and the price level will tend to remain relatively constant.

This automatic stabilization also works when the commodity price of gold falls below the official price. As shown in Figure 4.2, if the commodity price of gold falls below the official price, the public will react by buying gold at the lower price in the commodity market and presenting it to the mint for coinage into money. The amount of gold represented by *cd* in Figure 4.2 will be taken from the commodity market, and the money supply will increase as the gold is used for monetary purposes. Again, using the simplest relationship between the money supply and the price level, the increase in the supply of money will result in an increase in the general price level,

$$M \uparrow V = P \uparrow y.$$

As long as the commodity price of gold moves in the same direction as the general price level, there is a built-in mechanism for correcting the money supply in the face of inflation or deflation. In inflation the commodity price of gold rises with the price level, but the automatic reaction of the system will shift gold out of monetary use into its higher valued use as a commodity, and the money supply will decline. This will tend to lower the price level. Similarly, during deflation, as the commodity price of gold falls with the price level, gold will be shifted out of its use as a commodity into its higher valued use as money. The money supply will increase, which will tend to increase the general price level or, at least, to reduce the decline in

*Figure 4.2*
**The Commodity Market for Gold: The Effect when the Commodity Price of Gold Falls below the Official Price**

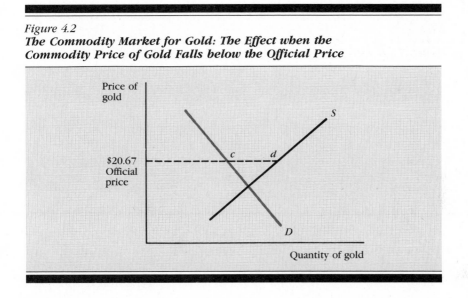

the price level. Thus, there is a tendency to stabilize the general price level without the interference of any monetary authority.

## The International Stabilization of Prices

So long as countries allow the free import and export of gold, there will also be price stability among countries on the gold standard such that the same quantity of gold by weight in each country will purchase the same quantity of goods and services in each country. If two countries have price levels such that the same amount of gold can buy different amounts of goods, the gold will be taken from the country with the higher prices to buy goods in the country with lower prices.

Figure 4.3 shows what would happen if the United States and Britain were both on gold standards, but the prices, in terms of gold weight, were different. If the United States has higher prices, then, following Gresham's law, gold will be taken from the United States to purchase goods in Britain. Goods will then be transported to the United States, where they can be sold at higher prices. Two forces on prices will bring the price levels in the two countries closer. First, increased demand for goods in Britain will force British prices up, and the increased supply of goods in the United States will force their prices down. Second, there will be a flow of gold from the United States to Britain. This will decrease the money supply in the United States and increase the money supply in Britain. Allowing, of course, for the transportation costs of both goods and gold, prices in the two countries eventually will be stabilized.

*Figure 4.3*
**The Gold Standard: The International Stabilization of Prices**

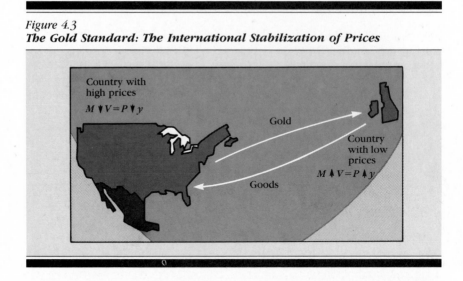

Under such a system, balance of international payments would be a matter of great simplicity. A fixed exchange rate between the monetary units of the two countries would be established as soon as each country defined its currency as a weight of gold. If the United States defined the dollar as 23.22 grains of gold, and Britain defined the pound as 116.1 grains of gold, then the exchange rate would be $5 = £1 (5 times 23.22 equals 116.1). If the forces of supply and demand in the foreign exchange market cause the exchange rate to deviate by more than the transportation costs of gold between the two countries from the exchange rate of $5 = £1, then arbitrage in the markets for gold would cause a gold flow until $5 again exchanged for £1. There would be no excess supply or excess demand for dollars to exchange for pounds on the foreign exchange market at the exchange rate of $5 = £1. If, for example, an excess supply of dollars (a balance of payments deficit) did arise at the exchange rate of $5 = £1, the dollars simply could be redeemed for gold and the gold transported to Britain; when the gold was presented at the British mint, the dollars would effectively be converted into pounds at the rate (adjusted for the transportation costs) of $5 for £1.

International payments would be made in gold, and any individual wishing to spend money in another country could simply take the coins from his or her country and present them to the mint in the other country to be made into the coins of that country. In many cases, the coins of one country circulated in other countries for use in exchange by weight. In 1834, for example, the United States passed a law allowing the domestic use of full-bodied gold coins of Britain, Portugal, Brazil, Spain, Mexico, and Colombia.

## The Problems with the Gold Standard

Clearly, the smooth operation of the gold standard depends on the flexibility of prices. Money supplies adjust when there are differences in prices, either between the commodity price and the official price of gold or between the price levels in different countries. The adjustments in the money supplies, however, are *intended* to cause changes in prices. If prices could not change, the system could not possibly work. Also, if domestic prices do not all change in the same direction and by the same proportion, serious disruptions in an economy can occur.

One problem with the gold standard was that when prices fell, they did not always fall in the same proportion. In particular, money wages did not tend to fall at the same rate as the prices of other goods and services. Therefore, the result of a decrease in the money supply was a reduction in commodity prices but an *increase* in real wages. This effect caused unemployment and a reduction in real output in the economy.

Given a choice between maintaining the gold standard with consequent unemployment whenever the money supply is reduced and abandoning the standard in order to maintain full employment, countries have chosen to abandon the system. A lack of price flexibility in a country could well make the gold standard politically unacceptable.

Despite the much-lauded price stability brought about by the gold standard, there is, unfortunately, a flaw here too. The system does *not* stabilize all prices; it only stabilizes the price of gold. The system works in such a way that the commodity price of gold is kept at the official price established by the authorities. It is possible for a country to suffer severe inflation even while maintaining a gold standard.

If a cheap source of gold is discovered, there will be a "gold rush." People will purchase the cheap gold or simply mine it or pan it and then exercise their right to free coinage. The newly discovered gold will be added to the money supply and prices will rise. Prices will continue to rise until the cost of the newly discovered gold is up to the official price of gold. If a large, easily attainable supply of gold is discovered, as in the case of the United States gold rush of 1849, the money supply, and hence the price level, could increase by a very large amount. Figure 4.4 shows the wholesale price index for 1848–1853. The index clearly shows the influence of the newly discovered gold. The money supply was increased, and the price level rose.

The gold standard also poses some problems with international payments. Since the supply of gold is finite, there might be a problem with the limited availability of liquid assets in the form of gold to finance an expansion of international trade. More important, through international payments the money supplies of the gold standard countries are linked. The benefits of the fixed and stable foreign exchange rates are realized, but this comes at a cost in terms of a loss of control over domestic economic conditions. An

*Figure 4.4*
**Wholesale Prices after the United States Gold Rush of 1849**

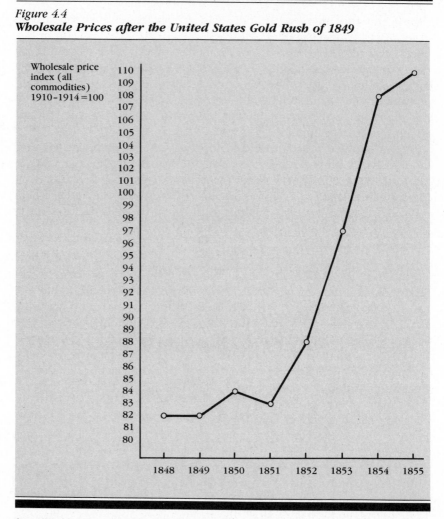

Source: United States Bureau of the Census. *Historical Statistics of the United States, Colonial Times to 1970,* Part I (1975): 205.

inflation that develops in one country will be transmitted as the gold flows to the other countries with lower prices. Countries may choose to abandon the gold standard to insulate their domestic economic conditions from prevailing conditions abroad. The general breakdown of the gold standard in the 1930s was the result of countries attempting (many of them too late) to insulate themselves from what was going on in other countries.

## The Gold Exchange Standard

A *gold exchange standard* links the nonredeemable paper money of a gold-less country to the money of a gold standard country. This system allows countries without a monetary stock of gold the advantage of the price stability associated with a gold standard. Also, this system has the advantage of not interfering in any way with the money supply of the country on the gold standard.

Perhaps the best example of this system is the one established by the Philippines in 1903 linking the peso to the United States dollar. The dollar at that time was defined as a weight of gold. The Philippines, having little gold, defined their unit as the equivalent of 50 United States cents. The system then stabilized Filipino prices to United States prices, and as long as the United States remained on the gold standard, prices in the Philippines behaved as though that country were on the gold standard also.

The key to the operation of the gold exchange standard is the establishment of what is called a *gold standard fund.* This is kept partly as a bank account in the gold standard country and partly as domestic currency held in a vault in the gold exchange standard country. The fund is then used exclusively for maintaining price stability between the two countries. In the case of the Philippines, part of the gold standard fund was kept as a dollar account in a New York bank and part was kept as Filipino pesos in a bank vault in Manila. The part of the gold exchange fund kept in the home country is kept out of circulation and is not part of the home country's money supply. The part of the fund kept as a bank deposit in the gold standard country is part of that country's money supply.

Control of the system rested with the Filipino treasurer, who stood ready at all times to exchange pesos for dollars at the rate of two to one. Whenever anyone made a deposit of one dollar into the account in the United States, the Filipino treasurer would give that person two Filipino pesos. As the pesos were spent in the Philippines, the money supply would increase.

Figure 4.5 shows what would happen if prices in the Philippines rose above those in the United States. With prices in the United States relatively low, it would pay to purchase goods in the United States and ship them to the Philippines for sale at the higher prices. In order to purchase these United States goods, Filipinos would acquire United States dollars by presenting pesos to the treasurer. The pesos presented for exchange would then be placed into the vault and taken out of circulation, while the purchasers would be credited with United States dollars in the account in the United States. The dollars would then be spent in the United States and would remain as part of the United States money supply. The money supply in the United States would not be affected, but the money supply in the Philippines would be reduced. This reduction in the money supply would cause Filipino prices to fall. The fall in prices would continue until it was no

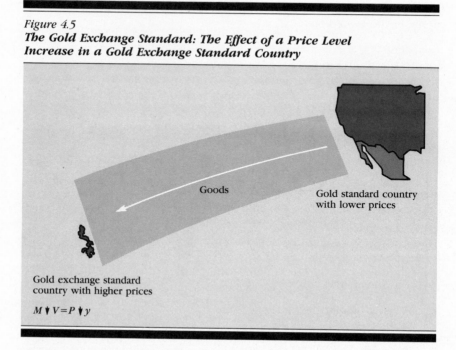

*Figure 4.5*
**The Gold Exchange Standard: The Effect of a Price Level Increase in a Gold Exchange Standard Country**

Goods

Gold standard country with lower prices

Gold exchange standard country with higher prices

$M \downarrow V = P \downarrow y$

longer profitable to purchase goods in the United States and ship them to the Philippines. The higher Filipino prices would continue to fall until the Filipino price level was only separated from the United States price level by the transportation costs of the goods.

Similarly, if prices in the Philippines should fall below those in the United States, the process would be reversed. Goods would be shipped to the United States and sold for United States dollars. These dollars would be deposited in the Filipino bank account in the United States, and an equivalent amount of pesos released from the vault in the Philippines. The result would be that Filipino prices would rise, as the money supply increased. In this way, the purchasing power of the peso would remain at 50 United States cents.

The Philippines would not, of course, be restricted to trading only with the United States. If they wished to purchase goods in a third country, they could do so by exchanging pesos for dollars and using the dollars to exchange for gold, which could then be used to buy goods in any other country.

In this system all monetary adjustments are made in the money supply and the price level of the country that has no gold. The money supply and the price level of the gold standard country are not affected by any changes because the bank account of the goldless country is no different from an ordinary bank account in the gold standard country. Money transferred into or out of the Filipino bank account in New York did not affect the money supply in the United States.

## The Bretton Woods System

After the demise of the gold standard during the 1930s, a modified gold exchange standard was adopted. This evolved into the *Bretton Woods system* (named after Bretton Woods, New Hampshire, the town where the conference establishing the system was held), which was utilized for international payments until mid-1973. This modified gold exchange standard allowed for the benefits of a fixed exchange rate between foreign currencies and also allowed countries in the short run to insulate their domestic money supplies from adjusting in response to international payment flows.

For domestic purposes, the monetary standard was a nonredeemable paper standard. Thus, the monetary authority was given control over the domestic money supply without regard to its redeemability in a standard metal. The direct tie between the quantity of money available and the monetary gold stock was broken.[6] Unlike in a gold standard, a flow of gold to make international payments no longer automatically required a change in the domestic money supply.

For international payments, exchange rates were pegged to the dollar. The dollar was defined in terms of gold ( $35 per troy ounce) and foreign currencies were given a *par value* in terms of the gold content of the dollar. This set the exchange rate. For example, in 1947 the British pound was defined as equal in value to $4.03.

In the short run the *pegged exchange rate* could be maintained even in the face of a balance of payments deficit or surplus through the use of official reserves. For international payments, official reserves consisted of gold, official holdings of foreign currencies, and the reserve position with the International Monetary Fund (IMF). This fund was established to coordinate foreign exchange transactions. Countries were assigned quotas to be paid into the fund in gold or United States dollars (25 percent) and in their domestic currency (75 percent). They could then borrow foreign currencies against these deposits for use in making accommodating payments when faced with a balance of payments deficit.

Suppose that foreign exchange market conditions for the dollar, relative to the British pound, would result in an excess demand for the dollar at the exchange rate $\bar{e}$. This is shown in Figure 4.6. This excess demand for dollars is an excess supply of pounds. The United States would have a balance of payments surplus relative to Britain, and Britain would have a balance of payments deficit relative to the United States. Britain could act to

---

[6]The United States continued to maintain the facade of a tie between gold and money by requiring the Federal Reserve to hold gold certificates in proportion to its liabilities until 1968. This, however, did not effectively restrict the quantity of money available. (*See* Chapter 14.)

*Figure 4.6*
**The Foreign Exchange Market: Dollars for Pounds**

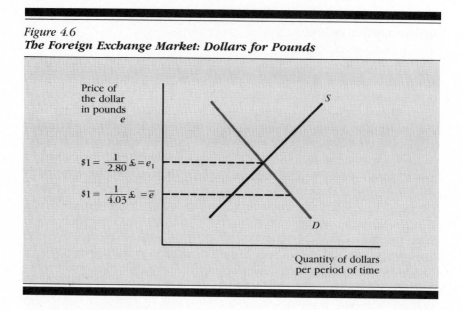

maintain the pegged exchange rate of $\bar{e}$ by utilizing some of its official reserves to buy up the excess supply of pounds.

Under the gold standard, this balance of payments deficit would involve a gold flow from Britain to the United States that would automatically increase the money supply in the United States and decrease the money supply in Britain. By causing a change in the price levels and other economic conditions in both countries, the supply of dollars on the foreign exchange market would increase as United States residents sought to buy the now cheaper goods in Britain, and the demand for dollars would decline as British residents found United States goods to be more expensive. The supply and demand would continue to shift in the face of the gold flow and the changes in the money supplies until the foreign exchange market balanced at the exchange rate $\bar{e}$.

Under the Bretton Woods system, gold or other official reserves would flow from Britain to the United States.[7] However, with a nonredeemable paper standard, the flow of official reserves would not force a decline in the British money supply and an increase in the United States money supply. Thus, each country's money supply could be insulated in the short run from changes caused by international payments. With no forced automatic adjustment in domestic conditions, however, the balance of payments disequilibrium at $\bar{e}$ would continue.

---

[7] Flows of official reserves were only required when the exchange rate was being pushed outside of a narrow band. The exchange rate was allowed to float within ± 1 percent of the par value. In 1971 the band was widened to ± 2¼ percent.

Britain could continue to maintain the exchange rate $\bar{e}$ as long as it had sufficient official reserves to buy up the continuing excess supply of pounds. As official reserves would decline to accommodate the continuing balance of payments deficit, sooner or later some adjustment would have to be made. Britain could alter domestic conditions along the lines of the automatic adjustments of the gold standard. By shifting domestic conditions, the supply and demand for the dollar in terms of the pound could be changed and the exchange market brought into equilibrium at the exchange rate $\bar{e}$. Domestic conditions would then be adjusted in response to changes in foreign economic conditions. Alternatively, the pegged exchange rate simply could be changed to the market clearing exchanging rate. This would require a devaluation of the pound. A balance of payments deficit for Britain similar to that shown in Figure 4.6 occurred in the late 1940s, and Britain devalued the pound in 1949 to $2.80 = £1$.

The Bretton Woods system gave countries short-term insulation from changes in economic conditions abroad. Also, with the ability to alter the pegged exchange rate, adjustments in response to an imbalance in international payments could be made by changing the exchange rate. In general, however, countries were reluctant to change the exchange rate. A continual adjustment in the pegged rates would eliminate the stability in exchange rates for the system. Also, exchange rate changes would benefit those speculators who had purchased the currency that was being increased in value.

The Bretton Woods system relies on the availability of official reserves. Problems with the distribution and short supply of official reserves in the 1960s resulted in the IMF's creation of a new form of reserves, *special drawing rights* (*SDRs*). Initially, SDRs were paper gold designed for use in international payments in a manner similar to the use of gold. For payments purposes, an SDR was defined as a weight in gold. In 1974 the SDR was redefined to be a "basket of currencies." The initial distribution of SDRs was made by the IMF in 1970. Problems with the availability of official reserves continued to plague the system into the 1970s and, with the lack of a mechanism to alter directly the value of the dollar, the system was abandoned in mid-1973 in favor of a floating exchange rate system.

## BIMETALLISM—THE UNITED STATES' FIRST COMMODITY STANDARD

Historically, monetary units have often been defined in terms of more than one metal. The most common such system has been a definition involving both silver and gold, and this was the system originally adopted by the United States Congress in 1792. When a monetary unit is defined as a given weight of either of two metals, *with free coinage of both,* the system is called *bimetallism.*

## Requirements for a Bimetallic System

The rules for establishing a bimetallic system are exactly the same as the rules for establishing a monometallic system except, of course, for the actual definition of the unit.

1.   The unit of money must be defined as a given weight of silver and also as a given weight of gold. To use the example of the bimetallic system established by the United States in the Coinage Act of 1792, the dollar was defined as being either 371.25 grains of pure silver[8] or 24.75 grains of pure gold.[9]

2.   There must be interconvertibility of all kinds of money. This means that any paper money or bank money in the system could be converted to silver or gold at a fixed rate.[10] Also, it was possible to convert silver to gold at a fixed rate derived from the two definitions of the unit. This ratio was known as the *mint ratio,* and it is very important for understanding bimetallism. Using the example of the United States standard in 1792, the mint ratio was 15:1 (i.e., 371.25/24.75 = 15). Fifteen ounces of silver was considered equivalent to one ounce of gold.

3.   There must be free coinage of both silver and gold.

4.   There must be free melting of both silver and gold.

5.   There must be free import and export of both silver and gold.

## The Workings of a Bimetallic System

The logic behind the operation of the bimetallic system is exactly the same as that behind monometallism. The less-abundant gold was used for large denomination coins, and the silver was used for smaller denominations.

Just as the free market for gold controls the gold standard, so the markets for gold and silver control the bimetallic standard. The quantity of money is limited by the public's willingness to buy and sell the gold and silver in the commodity markets, a willingness governed by how the commodity prices of gold and silver fluctuate in relation to their official prices. If it is profitable to melt coins and to sell the gold or silver as commodities, the

---

[8] This definition was derived from an estimate of the weight and fineness of Spanish silver dollars already in circulation. It was estimated that on average Spanish silver dollars weighed 416 grams and were 1485/1664 fine (that is, they were 89.24 percent pure silver).

[9] This definition was arrived at by finding the Spanish silver dollar price of gold at the time. It was found that one silver dollar would buy 27.0 grains of 22 carat gold (gold that was 22/24 pure); 24.75 is exactly 22/24 of 27.0.

[10] It should be remembered, however, that in 1792 bank notes were little known and bank deposits were unknown.

money supply will be automatically reduced, and prices will fall. Whenever the commodity prices of gold and silver are below the official prices, the public will have gold and silver coined into money, the money supply will rise, and prices will increase.

It would seem that the adoption of a bimetallic system would lead to price stability, again by the operation of Gresham's law. If the general price level rose, gold and silver would have a higher value as commodities than as coins, and the money supply would be reduced and the inflation checked. If the general price level started to fall, gold and silver would have a higher valued use as money than as commodities, so the money supply would increase and the deflation would be checked. Unfortunately, there is a very serious problem with bimetallism, one that caused the system to self-destruct. Historically, this problem has been more significant than any problems associated with the smooth operation of monometallic systems.

## The Breakdown of Bimetallism

The problem with bimetallism stems from the fact that the system has one more fixed point than monometallism. By defining the unit of account in terms of two different metals, the ratio at which the two metals exchange (the mint ratio) has also been defined. This means that by trying to maintain the official price of both metals, the system will also attempt to keep the *relative* price of gold to silver fixed. It is, however, most unlikely that the relative price of gold to silver in the commodity market will remain fixed. Thus, one of the metals is likely to have a higher valued use as a commodity and the other as money. The operation of Gresham's law will ensure that only one of the metals will remain as money while the other is sold as a commodity. If the system is to operate smoothly, the official mint ratio must be the same as the relative price of gold to silver in the commodity market *and* the same as the mint ratios in other countries.

Before the passage of the Coinage Act of 1792, there was great discussion in the Congress concerning the correct mint ratio to adopt. From their letters, it is clear that both Thomas Jefferson and Alexander Hamilton understood the problems involved with the definition. Though they did not mention Gresham's law by name, they knew of its operation. If the mint ratio were not the same as the ratio at which silver and gold traded in the commodity market, one of the metals would have a higher value as a commodity, and the system would break down.

In the Coinage Act of 1792, the mint ratio was set by defining the gold dollar according to the commodity price of gold in terms of Spanish silver dollars. This put the ratio at 15:1, and at the outset the system ran smoothly. Trouble soon came, however, when France readopted a bimetallic system in 1796. France had been on an inconvertible paper standard for a number of years, but when it returned to the commodity standard again it chose the mint ratio that had been used when it last had a bimetallic standard rather

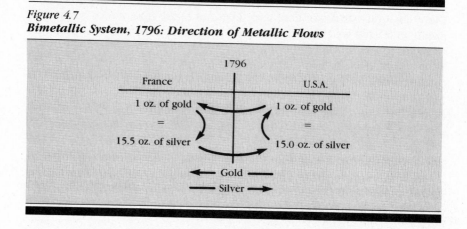

*Figure 4.7*
**Bimetallic System, 1796: Direction of Metallic Flows**

than the ratio at which the two metals exchanged in 1796. France established a mint ratio of 15.5 : 1. As Figure 4.7 shows, it would be profitable to take gold to France and exchange it for silver to take to the United States.

An ounce of gold in France could be exchanged for 15.5 ounces of silver. When transported to the United States, only 15 ounces of silver would be required to buy an ounce of gold. Each time this transaction was made, there would be half an ounce of silver remaining, and so long as the transactions costs were less than 3⅓ percent ( ½ an ounce of silver per set of exchanges bringing 15 ounces of silver to the United States), the exchange would be profitable. By 1822 gold coins had disappeared from circulation in the United States.

Though both countries maintained the legal fiction of being on bimetallic standards, France was effectively on a gold standard and the United States was effectively on a silver standard. Using only one of the metals included in the bimetallic definition is known as a *limping standard.* The United States continued to coin gold, but it did not remain in circulation. As a report of the United States Treasury aptly put it, "our coinage of gold was of little benefit, except to purify and prepare bullion for exportation, and for the use of foreign mints." [11]

The problems of the United States were compounded by the fact that even though the United States dollar had been modeled on the Spanish silver dollar, the two coins were not equivalent. On average, Spanish coins were heavier than United States coins. Although most people continued to

---

[11] Woodbury, Levi [Secretary of the Treasury]. "Annual Treasury Report on the State of the Currency after the Devaluations of 1834 and 1837" (1837). Reprinted in Krooss, Herman E., ed. *Documentary History of Banking and Currency in the United States.* vol. 2 (New York: Chelsea House Publishers, 1969): 1050.

accept the coins at face value, some people took advantage of the profitability of melting down Spanish silver coins and presenting the silver for coinage at the United States mint. The result was that Spanish coins were replaced by United States coins, not only in the United States but also throughout the West Indies. By relatively overvaluing silver, the United States found itself producing silver coins for use in other countries.

## Revision of the Bimetallic System—1834

As bimetallism broke down internationally, countries made changes in their mint ratios. The United States Congress reviewed the situation for 15 years before making a decision. It decided to retain bimetallism with a new mint ratio attained by redefining the dollar in terms of gold. Choosing the mint ratio, however, was very difficult. In the world commodity markets, gold and silver exchanged on average at a ratio of 15.7:1, but Mexico, Portugal, Spain, and much of South America and the West Indies had adopted a ratio of 16:1, and Cuba had adopted a ratio of 17:1.

Congress decided that in anticipation of future changes in the market ratio (expected because of the falling price of silver), and in conformity with most other countries, the ratio should be 16:1. This ratio was achieved by redefining the dollar as 23.22 grains of pure gold.[12] Unfortunately, although the United States was then in conformity with many countries, it still had not reckoned with France. By an ordinance of King Louis Philippe, dated February 25, 1835, France adopted a mint ratio of 15.62:1. Also, the anticipated change in the commodity market ratio failed to materialize. In fact, after the influx of gold from the California gold rush, the market ratio fell back close to the old mint ratio of 15:1.

Figure 4.8 shows the situation as of 1835. By Gresham's law, gold flowed into the United States, where it was valued more highly, and silver flowed to France and on to the world commodity markets, where it was valued more highly. The result was that the United States and France were "limping on the other leg." The United States was effectively on a gold standard and France was effectively on a silver standard. Probably some of the same people who had profited by transporting gold to France and silver to the United States now profited by taking it back again.

*Token Coins.* Problems developed in the United States as silver left the country. By 1843 there was hardly a silver coin in circulation. As the smallest gold coin was the dollar, the United States found itself without any small change. This problem was solved in 1853 when the government issued

---

[12]To be absolutely precise, the United States adopted a ratio of 16.002:1 in 1834 by defining the dollar as 23.20 grains of gold and then changed this in 1837 to 15.99:1 by defining the dollar as 23.22 grains of gold.

*Figure 4.8*
**Bimetallic System, 1835: Direction of Metallic Flows**

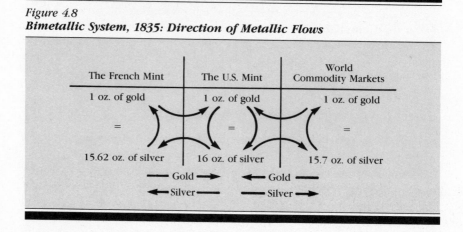

*token* coins that had a face value greater than the market value of the silver contained in the coins. As these coins had their greatest value as United States currency, there was at the time no tendency for them to be melted down and taken to either France or the commodity markets. (*See* "The Great Penny Shortage," page 87.)

## Circulating Nonredeemable Paper with Convertible Currencies

The United States continued on its limping standard until the outbreak of the Civil War, when both the North and the South adopted paper standards as means of financing their war efforts. The way in which the paper standards were adopted, however, differed in a significant way. The Confederacy, having very little ability to tax, issued a paper *fiat*[13] *money,* which was printed at will and put into circulation by paying for personnel and materials to fight the war. The war was very expensive. A great deal of money was printed and the rate of inflation was very rapid. In 1865 Confederate dollar prices were almost 100 times what they had been in 1861. The Union, on the other hand, made a *fiduciary issue*[14] of nonredeemable paper money to circulate *alongside* the old money. The banks still maintained convertibility of the old money in gold, but the United States mint did not buy and sell gold at the official price. The nonredeemable paper money issued by the Union government consisted of United States notes, commonly referred to as *greenbacks.*

---

[13]*Fiat* is the Latin word for "let it be done." The entire money supply is by government decree, and the system will function so long as the public accepts it as money.

[14]*Fiduciary* comes from the Latin *fiducia,* meaning "trust." The government is being trusted not to increase the money supply excessively by issuing "too much" nonredeemable money.

## THE GREAT PENNY SHORTAGE

If you buy a 47-cent item and offer two quarters in payment, you expect 3 pennies in change, but for a while in the early 1970s it was not unusual to be offered 3-cents worth of merchandise instead. This was part of the "great penny shortage" of 1974.

The episode appears to have started in 1973 when, in response to the high cost of minting copper pennies, the Bureau of the Mint requested authority from Congress to begin making aluminum pennies. In expectation of the demise of the copper penny, numismatists apparently rushed to acquire the potentially scarce copper coins (even though over 7 billion were minted in 1973 and almost 9 billion in 1974). The shortage appeared to reach a crisis in April 1974 with the Treasury claim that there were large operators in the penny market. The export and melting of pennies were banned and the maximum penalty of a $10,000 fine and five years in prison imposed. Solutions to the problem abounded from various sources. These ranged from the suggestion that the copper content of the penny (95 percent) be reduced to 70 percent to the suggestion that a new 70 percent copper 2½-cent coin be minted.

Why this shortage of pennies occurred is unclear. It has been suggested that it was the working of Gresham's law, but the market value of the copper in the penny was still far less than 1 cent. It was necessary to melt over 150 pennies to get a pound of copper and, in April 1974, copper was selling for about 70 cents per pound. The coin was far from full-bodied.

During the same period an even greater scarcity of aluminum pennies occurred.[1] To test the feasibility of minting aluminum cents, a test run of 1.5 million was made. Of these, about two dozen were used in lobbying efforts by the Bureau of the Mint on Capitol Hill. About a dozen of them were apparently "mislaid" about the House and the Senate. Even though possession of an experimental coin without proper authorization is illegal, the estimated numismatic value of one was about $35,000.

---

[1]"A Dozen Pennies Vanish, But It's Not a Penny-ante Case," *The Wall Street Journal*, September 19, 1975.
*Sources: The Wall Street Journal* and *The New York Times.*

It might seem that such a system would be doomed to failure because it would be subject to Gresham's law. That is, it would be expected that the "bad" greenbacks would drive out the "good" redeemable money.[15] This was not the case, however, because the two kinds of dollars did not exchange one for one. The price of gold, and the money redeemable in gold, were both free to fluctuate in terms of greenbacks. In 1864, for example, a gold dollar exchanged for over $2 in greenbacks. This kind of activity is known as *agio* phenomenon.

The increase in the money supply increased prices on the Union side, causing the token coins of 1853 to become full-bodied again and to disappear from circulation. Until the mint issued new token coins with a lower silver content, the shortage of small change was overcome by the Treasury printing small denomination paper (called *shinplasters*) and by many private businesses and local governments issuing their own tokens. Even postage stamps were used for making change.

## The Movement to a Gold Standard

The lack of small change during the Civil War was only a minor irritation compared with the more serious problem that faced the United States authorities once the war was over. This was the problem of fulfilling the pledge to return to a redeemable currency. A return to bimetallism at the old mint ratio was out of the question. The relative price of gold to silver in the commodity markets had been greatly changed, so a return to the old system would have become a limping standard all over again.

In an act of 1873 (later to be dubbed the *Crime of '73* by the silver producers), the United States Congress decided that the Treasury would only redeem money in gold, but even this system was to prove difficult. If redeemability were reestablished at the old Mint price (i.e., 23.22 grains of gold to the dollar, or $20.67 per troy ounce of gold), the United States would lose large quantities of gold because prices in other countries (in terms of gold) had not changed. With immediate redeemability at the old price, and with prices in terms of greenback dollars twice what they had been in terms of the pre–Civil War dollar, the most profitable enterprise in the country would have been buying gold at the mint and exporting it to other countries to buy goods for shipment to the United States.

The alternatives were clear. Either the official price of gold could be increased (the gold content of the dollar reduced) and redeemability resumed immediately, or redemption could be postponed until the price level in terms of greenbacks was brought down to prewar levels. Congress decided on the latter method and created the longest deflation the United States has ever recorded. According to contemporaries, those were very

---

[15] *See* "Can 'Good' Money Drive Out 'Bad'"?, page 89.

# CAN "GOOD" MONEY DRIVE OUT "BAD"?

If the common statement of Gresham's law is correct, then "bad" money drives out "good." But this would seem to mean that a money supply can never improve. Once bad money has been introduced, it will always remain current and any better money will be driven out of circulation. Thus, money supplies would seem to be doomed to deteriorate over time and never improve.

This idea stems from a misunderstanding of Gresham's law. One kind of money can "drive out" another only if there is a fixed exchange rate between the two. For example, to use the example Gresham discussed, the debased currency introduced by Henry VIII drove the heavier full-bodied coins from circulation because the coins exchanged one for one. One heavy shilling was exchanged for one light shilling. People thus hoarded the heavy coins or used them in foreign trade while spending the light shillings in the marketplace. Similarly, in the 1960s people hoarded silver coins for their value as silver while they spent the new sandwich coins.

However, if two types of money are free to be exchanged at a market-determined rate, they are both likely to stay in circulation. The higher value of one of the moneys will simply be reflected in lower prices in terms of that unit. In the early seventeenth century in England, both gold and silver circulated with prices expressed in guineas for the gold coins and pounds for the silver coins. So long as people were free to vary the guinea and pound prices as they saw fit, both types of money remained in circulation. As soon as the authorities fixed the guinea-pound rate, the gold coins were driven out of circulation. Also, during the Civil War dollar prices in the North were expressed in gold dollars and greenbacks, and both kinds of money stayed in circulation.

Some economists believe that the best way to reform the United States monetary system is to remove the government monopoly on money production. If people were not restricted in the unit they wished to use, and the monetary authorities were unable to control prices in the current unit, the public could well choose to use a more stable unit. It might well be that a commodity standard could be introduced in this way, and the current paper standard could fall into disuse.[1]

---

[1] See Hayek, F. A. "Choice in Currency: A Way to Stop Inflation," (London: Institute of Economic Affairs, 1976): 9–24. Reprinted in Colander, Donald C., ed. *Solutions to Inflation* (New York: Harcourt Brace Jovanovich, 1979): 93–103.

hard times but overall real output did expand.[16] In late 1878, however, the price level had been decreased far enough, and "Resumption" took place on January 1, 1879.

## SYMMETALLISM AND THE COMPOSITE COMMODITY STANDARD

Although they have never been tried, composite commodity standards have been conceived as a way of having a commodity standard without the problems associated with monometallism and bimetallism. In a composite commodity system, the unit is defined in terms of fixed proportions of various commodities (not necessarily metals).

The symmetallic system is a special case of the composite commodity standard. It is very similar to the bimetallic system, but instead of having coins defined as a specific weight of *either* of two metals, the symmetallic system has coins defined to contain a fixed proportion of *both* the metals. For example, if gold and silver are being used, the unit of money must be defined to contain a given weight of gold *and* a given weight of silver *combined in one coin.* For example, the dollar could be defined as 200 grains of pure silver *plus* 10 grains of gold.

Interconvertibility of all forms of money also would be required. Paper money and bank money would be converted into the symmetallic coins at the fixed rate given by the definition of the unit of money. However, the mint would not exchange gold for silver or silver for gold. Conversion of paper money or bank money would result in the receiving of both metals, and both metals would have to be presented to the mint to be converted into money.

### *The Workings of a Symmetallic System*

A symmetallic system would operate in a manner exactly like the other commodity standards. If prices rose, then gold and silver would have a higher value as commodities than as money. The coins would be melted, and the money supply would be reduced. Similarly, if the price level fell, gold and silver would have a higher valued use as money than as commodities. Gold and silver would be taken to the mint for coinage, the money supply would expand, and the price level would rise.

The advantage of such a system is that it is not sensitive to discoveries of a cheap source of just one of the metals. Under a gold standard, a discovery of cheap gold leads to price increases. With bimetallism, a discovery of *either* cheap gold or cheap silver would ultimately increase prices. Under

---

[16] *See* Friedman, Milton and Schwartz, Anna. *A Monetary History of the United States, 1867–1960* (Princeton University Press, 1963): Chapter 2.

symmetallism, that same discovery of either gold or silver would not lead to an increase in the money supply unless there were a corresponding discovery of the other metal. The chances of a discovery of a cheap source of two metals at the same time is less than the chance of the discovery of one metal. Obviously, the greater the number of metals included in the definition of the unit of money, the lower is the chance that there will be a discovery of a cheap source of all the metals, and the lower is the chance of price rises.

Also, symmetallism does not break down in the manner of bimetallism when countries establish different mint ratios. If two countries establish symmetallism, but the definitions of their respective units give different relative prices for gold and silver, the metals will not flow to the countries where they are valued more highly, because *in both countries, both* of the metals must be presented at the mint in order for money to be coined.

## PAPER STANDARDS

Given the problems associated with commodity standards, it is perhaps not surprising that monometallism and bimetallism have been abandoned in favor of nonredeemable paper standards. With a *paper standard,* the quantity of money available is controlled by the government or another monetary authority *without regard* to its redeemability in a standard commodity or commodities. This break in the direct tie between the quantity of money and some commodity gives governments the ability to influence general economic conditions by altering the supply of money. Under commodity standards, this ability to use monetary policies to influence economic activity is restricted by the availability of the standard commodity.

A relative scarcity of money is important for the functioning of any monetary system. Unless money is sufficiently scarce, people will not believe that the unit of money has value, and it will not be generally accepted as payment for goods, services, and debts. Under a commodity standard, this scarcity is created by the limited availability of the standard commodity. With a paper standard, it is necessary for the government or the monetary authority in some way to restrict the supply of money and to maintain its sufficient scarcity. Otherwise, the paper standard would break down.

There are many mechanisms that could be adopted to restrict the quantity of money available under a paper standard and different mechanisms utilized for altering the quantity of money available. For example, the government simply could print up a limited supply of paper money and put that money into circulation as the government buys goods and services. Declaring that the paper money is legal tender and acceptable as payment for taxes would tend to increase the likelihood that it would be used as money. Alternatively, an independent monetary authority could be established to oversee the creation and distribution of money. This would separate the monetary mechanism from the act of government spending. The

United States has adopted the second type of system, with the Federal Reserve serving as the monetary authority. The exact mechanisms utilized for monetary control under the current paper standard are the subjects of most of the later discussion on central banking.

## SUMMARY

Monetary systems depend on either money's redeemability in given commodities or on control of the quantity of money available by a monetary authority. Those that depend on redeemability are said to be commodity standards and those that are controlled by an authority are said to be paper standards. There are three types of commodity standards: The monometallic standard where the money supply is redeemable in one metal, the bimetallic standard where the money supply is redeemable in either of two metals, and the composite commodity standard where the money supply is redeemable in fixed proportions of a collection of commodities.

All of these commodity standards work in the same free market system. People are free to take the commodity out of the money supply and to sell it in the commodity markets, or to take the commodity out of the commodity markets and to present it to the mint to add to the money supply. The result of this activity is Gresham's law: The commodities will flow to where their values are the highest. The direct consequence is that the money supply will be automatically regulated so that prices tend to be stabilized both domestically and internationally.

## Key Terms

| | |
|---|---|
| monetary standard | Gresham's law |
| commodity standard | gold standard |
| paper standard | gold exchange standard |
| monometallism | Bretton Woods system |
| bimetallism | pegged exchange rate |
| composite commodity standard | fiat money |
| symmetallism | Crime of '73 |
| arbitrage | |

## Questions

1. How will the money supply adjust under a monometallic standard if the general price level starts to rise?

2. If there is an international gold standard, explain what will happen to the money supply in Britain as a result of the discovery of gold in California.

3.  If a gold standard is established, prices will remain stable and the economy will not suffer from either inflation or deflation. Evaluate.

4.  Explain how bimetallic systems have tended to break down into limping systems.

5.  Explain in what sense it is true that monometallism *works* because of Gresham's law, but bimetallism *breaks down* because of Gresham's law.

## Additional Readings

Kroos, Herman E., ed. *Documentary History of Banking and Currency in the United States,* vols. I–IV with Introduction by Paul A. Samuelson. New York: Chelsea House Publishers, 1969.

*This four-volume set contains a comprehensive coverage of the history, laws, regulations, and policies in United States monetary activity. It also contains a review of the economic conditions at the time and the considerations taken in the formulation of those policies.*

Tullock, Gordon. "Competing Monies." *Journal of Money, Credit and Banking* 7 (November 1975): 491–498.

*This article contains a readable discussion of the possible effect of using more than one type of money and the impact of price stability on the use of one or more moneys. The comments by Benjamin Klein, "Competing Monies,"* Journal of Money, Credit and Banking 8 *(November 1976): 513–520 (along with a reply by Gordon Tullock), also are informative.*

# APPENDIX 4A

## *The Quantity of Money under a Gold Standard with Paper and Bank Money*

When a gold standard has been adopted, it is likely that people will choose to use other forms of money than full-bodied gold coins. For example, paper money and token coins may prove easier to transport and more useful in some transactions. The use of these alternative forms of money requires not only that they be less costly for some uses, but also that individuals believe that the other forms of money will be accepted from them as payment for goods, services, and debts. Redeemability of the paper money and token money for gold coins either by the government or through banks not only constrains the amount that can be issued, but also makes it easier for the public to believe that these other forms will retain their value.

People also are likely to choose to use some bank money in the form of bank deposits. The use of checks to draw on these deposits makes them useful for some payments and provides a record of the transaction. As with paper money and token money, the public must again believe that the deposits will be accepted from them as payment. Otherwise, the public would not choose to use the services provided with bank money. To maintain access to the funds deposited and remain in business, banks will stand ready to redeem the deposits for gold coin upon demand. This requires that the banks hold some gold coins to redeem the bank deposits and also to provide a service by redeeming paper money.

The interconvertibility of all forms of money and redeemability in gold causes the amount of gold ($G$) available for monetary use to limit the money supply. The actual quantity of money available, however, is determined by the public's preferences in holding money in various forms.

The money supply ($M$) can be defined as the quantity of gold coins held by the nonbank public ($G_p$) plus the amount of currency (and token coins) held by the nonbank public ($C_p$) plus the amount of bank deposits ($D_p$). Thus,

$$M = G_p + C_p + D_p. \tag{4.1}$$

Gold coin held by banks does not circulate as a medium of exchange and is not counted in the money supply.

Banks will hold some gold coins out of circulation to redeem both paper money (perhaps issued by banks) and bank deposits. If the banks hold for redemption purposes the proportion $r$ of both currency and deposits, then the amount of gold ($G$) available for monetary purposes will be held as

$$G = G_p + rC_p + rD_p, \tag{4.2}$$

where $G_p$ is the amount held by the nonbank public and $rC_p$ plus $rD_p$ is the amount held by banks.

The preferences of the public will determine the proportions of currency to gold coins and deposits to gold coins the public desires to hold. If, on average, the public is willing to hold currency in the proportion $c$ to the amount of gold coins, and if the public is willing to hold the proportion $d$ of deposits to gold coins, then we cay say that

$$c = \frac{C_p}{G_p} \quad \text{and} \quad d = \frac{D_p}{G_p}.$$

Using the ratios $c$ and $d$, the holdings of the amount of gold available for monetary use (from Equation 4.2) can be given as a proportion of gold coins held by the nonbank public

$$G = G_p + r\frac{C_p}{G_p}G_p + r\frac{D_p}{G_p}G_p$$

$$\text{or} \quad G = G_p + rcG_p + rdG_p$$

$$\text{or} \quad G = (1 + rc + rd)G_p. \tag{4.3}$$

Similarly, the money supply (from Equation 4.1) can be expressed in terms of the nonbank public's holdings of gold coins as

$$M = G_p + cG_p + dG_p$$

$$\text{or} \quad M = (1 + c + d)G_p. \tag{4.4}$$

Thus, (combining Equations 4.4 and 4.3) it is possible to express the money supply in terms of the ratios $r$, $c$, and $d$ and the amount of gold available for monetary use as

$$M = \frac{1 + c + d}{1 + rc + rd}G. \tag{4.5}$$

For any given set of ratios $r$, $c$, and $d$, the money supply bears a definite relationship to the amount of gold held for monetary purposes. An increase in the amount of gold available for monetary use will result in an increase in the money supply. For a given amount of gold used for monetary purposes, the money supply could possibly be changed by the public's changing the ratios $d$ and $c$ or, to a limited extent, by the banks' changing the ratio $r$. The banks' ability to control the money supply through changing $r$ is very limited. A change in $r$ will influence the public's desire to hold currency and bank money. Thus if banks attempt to increase the money supply by reducing $r$ and by holding fewer gold coins for redemption purposes, the public may fear that soon the banks may not redeem their money and will reduce both $d$ and $c$.

# CHAPTER FIVE

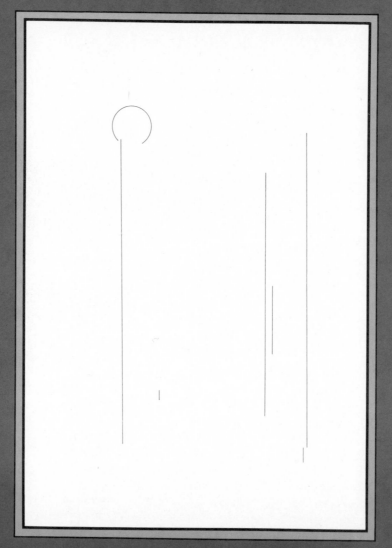

## INTEREST RATES AND
## MARKET ACTIVITY

*Interest rates are market prices that link the past, present, and future. Although nominal interest rates are the most obvious in the economy, real interest rates are more important; they are the prices that are used for the allocation of resources through time.*

T he fundamental problem facing any economy is scarcity. Put simply, there are not enough goods and services available to satisfy all of our wants. Consequently, some method of allocating scarce commodities must be employed. In most economies, markets are one of the main mechanisms used for allocation. Through a series of bids and offers made in the markets, goods and services are allocated between the competing uses to which they may be put.

The decisions that people make are determined by the alternatives that are available; and prices in the markets give the information on which exchanges and substitutions can be made. For example, if oranges are currently selling for 15 cents each and apples are currently selling for 30 cents, one apple may be exchanged for two oranges. This rate of exchange between apples and oranges is the relative price of apples and oranges in terms of each other. As individuals and firms change their bids and offers in the markets, the relative prices are likely to change; so in future periods the rate of exchange between apples and oranges may be different.

As will be remembered from courses in the principles of economics, goods and services are reallocated through markets *from* those who place a low value on their use *to* those who place a higher value on their use. Those who place a lower value on the use of oranges than on apples forgo oranges to acquire apples. Those who place a higher value on the use of oranges than apples forgo apples to acquire oranges. Through the process of exchange, oranges are allocated to those who place a higher value on them, while apples are allocated to those who place a higher value on apples.

## INTEREST RATES AS MARKET PRICES

*Interest rates* perform a central role in the market allocation of goods and services *through time,* by indicating the trade-off between the current and future use of those goods and services. These interest rates appear as prices in markets, and they inform people of the exchanges and substitutions that can be made between periods of time. If individuals or firms decide to forgo the future use of goods and services to have them immediately, the rate of interest reveals the price they must pay. Conversely, those who decide to forgo the current use of goods and services to have them in the future will receive a reward indicated by the interest rate.

Exchanges are often made by using money, and prices are often stated in money terms. As was discussed in Chapter 2, this eases the transfer of information and reduces transactions costs. However, the underlying force for the exchange is not the money being used. It is the desire to forgo the use of one set of goods and services for the use of another set of goods and services.

The forces that drive borrowing and lending activity are the same market forces that drive the exchanges of current goods and services. The decisions are based on the forgone use of one set of goods and services in exchange for the use of another set. The only difference is that the exchange occurs through time.

The substitutions that people make are responses to relative prices or opportunity costs. These are given in units of goods and services.

The opportunity cost for exchanges over time is revealed by an interest rate. This interest rate can be expressed without reference to money. When an interest rate is expressed in physical units of a good, it is a *real rate of interest.* This interest rate expresses the percentage of that good, besides the amount borrowed, to be forgone at some specified future date. Abstracting from money units allows for a concentration on opportunity costs and the motivation for exchange. Also, it simplifies the analysis by avoiding the complication of changes in money's value.

### *Reallocation through Credit Markets*

In order to reveal the reallocation of goods and services that takes place through borrowing and lending in credit markets, we will discuss the exchange of strawberries through time, without immediate reference to the use of money.[1] For example, if the interest rate for strawberries in the credit market is 10 percent, a loan of 100 baskets of strawberries must be repaid after one period with 110 baskets of strawberries. As with any other price, the interest rate serves to indicate the opportunity cost. If the interest rate in the strawberry market is 10 percent per annum, the opportunity cost of the use of 100 baskets of strawberries today is 110 baskets of strawberries one year from now.

If individuals or firms decide to forgo the future use of goods and services in order to have goods and services immediately, the rate of interest is the price they will pay. Conversely, those who decide to forgo the current use of goods and services in order to have goods and services in the future will receive the rate of interest as a reward.

As with markets where currently available goods and services exchange, credit markets reallocate goods and services from lower valued uses to higher valued uses, but the difference is that the reallocation of the use of goods and services is over time. Credit markets, in fact, are created to allow individuals to alter their consumption through time. An individual can lend the use of goods and services today in exchange for the promise of a different level of consumption at some future point in time; or an individual can borrow to increase the number of goods and services used today for the promise of giving up the use of goods and services in the future.

*Alternatives.*   The market process results from individuals comparing the alternatives that are available and then selecting the actions that are expected to make the individuals better off. Suppose, for example, that a consumer receives an income in strawberries.[2] In the absence of a credit market, the individual is faced with only two alternatives: the strawberries can be consumed now or exchanged at current prices for other goods and services. Given the alternatives currently available, the individual may choose to consume some of the strawberries and to exchange the remainder for other goods and services.

The introduction of a credit market expands the alternatives available. The individual now has the ability to exchange some of the currently available strawberries for the promise of a different number of strawberries in the future. In effect, consumers may change their consumption stream by transferring some of the strawberries to a future time. This is not an actual transfer of strawberries into the future. We have assumed that the high

---

[1] The use of an easily spoiled good such as strawberries allows us to ignore the complication of storage by simply assuming that the storage costs of strawberries are prohibitive.

Using strawberries to explain real interest rates dates back to the work of Irving Fisher. *See* Fisher, Irving. *The Theory of Interest.* (New York: Kelley Reprints, 1965): 192.

[2] Most individuals are both consumers and producers, but here we wish to focus attention only on the consumption decision.

storage costs of strawberries preclude this. Only the *use* of currently available strawberries has been transferred. All the existing strawberries are consumed during this period, but the credit market will have changed who consumes them.

If there are credit markets for strawberries, consumers are faced with three alternatives.

1. The strawberries can be consumed.

2. The strawberries can be exchanged for other currently available goods and services.

3. The strawberries can be exchanged for the use of a different number of strawberries at some time in the future.

Actual decisions made by consumers concerning the allocation of their income in strawberries will be determined after a consideration of the relative prices of the goods and services available and the rate of interest in the credit market for strawberries.

*Time Preference.*  Of course, all individuals do not have the same degree of patience with regard to the consumption of their income stream. When people place different values on the current use of goods and services as opposed to their future use, they are said to have different rates of time preference. Because of the different rates of time preference, some individuals will wish to lend strawberries while others will wish to borrow strawberries at any given interest rate. Thus, a credit market is created.

An increase in the market rate of interest increases the reward for lending and increases the opportunity cost of current consumption in terms of future consumption. This induces individuals to increase the quantity of strawberries they supply to the credit market. This is shown as the supply curve (*S*) in Figure 5.1. Changes in any market condition other than this market's rate of interest can shift the supply curve in this market. For example, if income in strawberries increases, there will be an increase in the supply of strawberries to lend with the supply curve shifting to the right. Similarly, an increase in the price of other goods and services most likely will make the lending of strawberries more attractive (as the alternative of exchanging them for other goods and services has become less attractive), and the supply curve of strawberries to lend will shift to the right.

Activity in a credit market, of course, is determined by individuals' desires to borrow as well as to lend. When the interest rate in the credit market for strawberries increases, the opportunity cost of current consumption in terms of future consumption is increased. This will induce individuals who desire to borrow for the purpose of current consumption to reduce the amount they borrow. This decrease in the quantity demanded as the interest rate increases is shown in the demand curve (*D*) in Figure 5.1.

*Figure 5.1*
**The Credit Market for Strawberries**

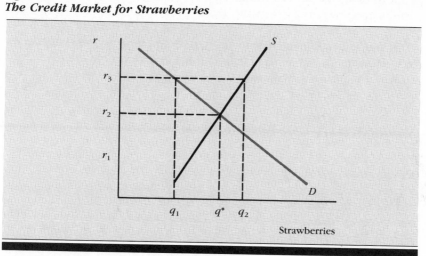

Strawberries also will be borrowed for use in production. If a producer has a process that (say, through planting and cultivation) will yield more strawberries than are required to repay the loan, the producer will desire to borrow strawberries on this credit market. However, as this market's rate of interest increases, fewer of the production processes available will yield a large enough return to warrant the borrowing of strawberries. As this market's rate of interest increases, the desire to borrow strawberries decreases.[3]

The results of the activity in this credit market for strawberries will be determined by an interaction of the desires of the suppliers and the demanders as indicated by the supply and demand curves in Figure 5.1. At an interest rate of $r_3$, the strawberry credit market is out of equilibrium. Both the desires of the borrowers and the desires of the lenders cannot be satisfied simultaneously, as the lenders desire to lend $q_2$ baskets of strawberries and the borrowers desire to borrow only $q_1$ baskets of strawberries. This excess supply of strawberries (equal to $q_2 - q_1$) will put pressure on the market to lower the interest rate. As the interest rate declines, some suppliers will reduce the amount of strawberries they desire to lend and will use them for current consumption instead. At the same time, producers and consumers will respond to the reduced interest rate by increasing the quantity of strawberries they desire to borrow. These adjustments will move the market to equilibrium at an interest rate of $r_2$, where the quantity of strawberries suppliers' desire to lend is equal to the quantity demanders' desire to borrow ($q^*$).

---

[3]This discussion of interest rates and investment is amplified in Part II, Chapter 18.

Similarly, the interest rate $r_1$ shows a disequilibrium that will generate forces to drive the interest rate up. At $r_1$, the borrowers desire a greater quantity of strawberries than the lenders desire to lend. To acquire the quantity of strawberries they desire, some of the borrowers will offer a higher interest rate in an attempt to acquire the short supply. Only when the interest rate is bid up to $r_2$ will both the borrowers and the lenders be capable of realizing their desires.

## INTEREST RATES IN FINANCIAL MARKETS

The credit market for strawberries reallocates the use of currently available strawberries in exchange for the promise to pay strawberries in the future. However, lending and borrowing are usually done in a market for funds. This means that funds are reallocated through time. Funds that could be used to purchase currently available goods and services are exchanged for the promise of funds in the future that can be used to purchase the goods and services later. The difference is that the promise is for funds that have general purchasing power as opposed to being a particular commodity like strawberries.

The supply side of a financial market is made up of a supply of funds made available by surplus-spending units. Surplus-spending units are individuals or corporations who desire to consume a level of goods and services below the level of their current income. By supplying funds to a financial market, they are forgoing the current use of goods and services in exchange for the promise of the use of a different amount of goods and services in the future. They place a lower value on the current use of goods and services than they place on the goods and services that will be made available to them in the future. As interest rates rise, the reward for giving up present consumption rises and the surplus-spending units will be induced to forgo the present use of additional funds and the use of the goods and services those funds could have acquired. This is shown in the supply curves in Figure 5.2.

The demand side of a financial market is made up of a demand for funds by deficit-spending units. Deficit-spending units are individuals or corporations who desire to use a greater number of goods and services in the current period than they can purchase with their current income. The funds demanded may be destined for the purchase of goods and services for current consumption, or they might be destined for the purchase of goods and services for use in the production process, either for the purchase of plant and equipment (planned investment) or for consumer durables like refrigerators or washing machines. As the interest rate increases, the cost of the current use of goods and services in terms of the amount of goods and services forgone in the future will increase, and therefore the desire

*Figure 5.2*
**The Market for Loanable Funds**

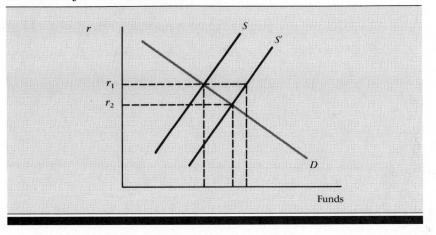

to borrow funds will decrease.[4] This is shown in the demand curve in Figure 5.2.

Lenders and borrowers interact in financial markets to determine the allocation of funds. When, for example, lenders have more funds available (perhaps through an increase in their income), the supply function will shift to the right (shown as the shift from $S$ to $S'$ in Figure 5.2). This shift in the supply function will cause both lenders and borrowers to react. The excess supply of funds at the old interest rate ($r_1$) will cause lenders and borrowers to change their bids and offers until the interest rate is bid down to the new equilibrium interest rate of $r_2$.

The net result of financial market activity is that goods and services that are currently available are reallocated from lower valued uses to higher valued uses; the goods and services that are available in the future are also reallocated from lower valued uses to higher valued uses. The surplus-spending units place a lower value on the use of some currently available goods and services and allocate them through the financial markets to deficit-spending units who place a higher value on the currently available goods and services. Deficit-spending units, on the other hand, place a lower value on the use of some of the goods and services they expect to have in the future and allocate them through the financial markets to the current surplus-spending units who place a higher value on goods and services available in the future.

---

[4]We are assuming that prices are not expected to change.

## Real and Nominal Interest Rates

The borrowing and lending that occurs in financial markets is indicated in units of money, and the interest rates are given in percentages per period of time, usually one year. A loan of $100 at an annual interest rate of 10 percent is an explicit exchange of $100 today for $110 in one year's time. However, there is a problem in the interpretation of the opportunity cost when we are talking about money that is to be received in the future. Although it is clear how many dollars are being exchanged, it is not known how many units of goods and services those dollars are going to buy in the future, as the prices of goods and services may change while the loan is outstanding. To account for the changes in the purchasing power of the dollar, it is necessary for us to make a distinction between nominal and real rates of interest. The interest rates that are observed in financial markets are nominal interest rates, but the borrowers and lenders will assess their opportunity costs in real terms.

A *nominal rate of interest* is expressed in current money units. If $100 is borrowed for one year at a nominal rate of interest of 10 percent, a payment of $110 will be due regardless of any changes in prices over the period. A *real rate of interest* is expressed in ability to purchase goods and services. If $100 is borrowed for one year at a real rate of interest of 10 percent, the repayment due in one year is not necessarily $110 but an amount of money that is *expected* to be able to purchase 10 percent more goods and services than could be purchased with the original $100.

If the price of strawberries is $1 per basket, a loan of $100 is essentially the same as a loan of 100 baskets of strawberries. By lending the $100, the lender is forgoing the ability to acquire 100 baskets of strawberries today. With an interest rate of 10 percent for one period, the payment due after one period is $110. If the price of strawberries remains at $1 per basket, the payment of $110 is equivalent to a payment of 110 baskets of strawberries. Under these conditions, the nominal and actually realized real rates of interest are both 10 percent. The repayment in dollars is 10 percent greater than the original loan in dollars, and the repayment in strawberries is 10 percent more strawberries than the original loan in terms of strawberries.

***Anticipated Changes.***   If, however, the price of strawberries changes over the period of the loan, there will be a divergence between the percentage repayment in dollars and the percentage repayment in strawberries. In this case the nominal and actually realized real interest rates will not be the same. For example, if the price of strawberries rose over the period from $1.00 to $1.05 per basket, the $110.00 repayment would only enable the lender to acquire 104.76 baskets of strawberries ( $110.00/$1.05 = 104.76). Thus, with a nominal rate of interest of 10 percent and a price increase of 5 percent, the actually realized real rate of interest is only 4.76

percent.[5] If the actual change in prices is known, it is possible to calculate the actual percentage that is repaid in goods and services. However, this is not the way the borrowers and the lenders will be making their calculations. The actual price change is not known until the time when the loan is repaid, so it would be impossible for borrowers and lenders to use this information to make their decisions at the time that the loan is being made. Borrowers and lenders can make their decisions only on the price changes that they *anticipate* will take place.

When a price change is expected, borrowers and lenders will alter their behavior to account for the anticipated change. The effect of an anticipated increase in prices will be revealed in an increase in the nominal rate of interest. When the prices of goods and services are expected to rise, lenders expect that additional units of money in the future will be necessary to acquire the same set of goods and services that could be acquired today. Since the expected return in ability to acquire goods and services from the extension of a loan is reduced, because of the expected increase in the price of goods and services, the supply of funds at any nominal rate of interest will decline. This is shown as the shift in the supply of funds from $S$ to $S'$ in Figure 5.3. Borrowers, on the other hand, expect that the dollars used to repay the loan in the future will buy fewer goods and services than they can buy today, so they will react to the anticipated increase in prices by demanding more funds at any given nominal rate of interest. This is shown in Figure 5.3 as the shift in the demand curve from $D$ to $D'$. With a reduction in the supply of funds and an increase in the demand for funds, the nominal rate of interest will rise from $R$ to $R'$ as shown in Figure 5.3. Although the nominal rate of interest definitely will rise, the quantity of funds exchanged may increase, decrease, or remain the same as borrowers and lenders may react differently to the same anticipated changes in prices.

---

[5] The actually realized real rate of interest can be calculated by taking the nominal rate of interest less the actual percentage change in prices and dividing that result by one plus the actual percentage change in prices.

If the nominal rate of interest is $R$, the repayment due after one period for each unit of money borrowed is $(1 + R)$. If the real rate of interest is $r$, the repayment due after one period for each unit of goods and services borrowed is $(1 + r)$. If prices are rising at an annual rate of $P$, the goods and services repaid $(1 + r)$ will have a nominal value of $(1 + r)(1 + \dot{P})$.

Thus,
$$(1 + R) = (1 + r)(1 + \dot{P})$$

or
$$R = r + \dot{P} + r\dot{P}.$$

Similarly,
$$(1 + r) = \frac{(1 + R)}{(1 + \dot{P})}$$

or
$$r = \frac{(R - \dot{P})}{(1 + \dot{P})}.$$

Thus, in our example,
$$r = \frac{0.10 - 0.05}{1 + 0.05} = \frac{0.05}{1.05} = 0.0476.$$

*Figure 5.3*
**The Effect of Rising Prices on Nominal Interest Rates**

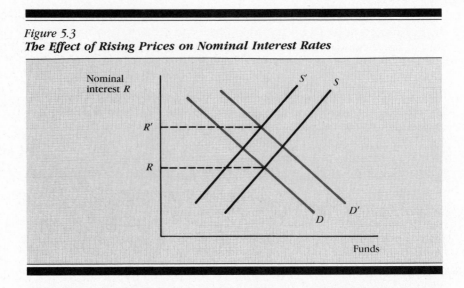

The relationship between the nominal rate of interest $(R)$ and the anticipated real rate of interest $(r)$ is given by the Fisher equation (after Irving Fisher; *see* "Irving Fisher," page 110):

$$R = r + \dot{P} + r\dot{P}, \qquad (5.1)$$

where $\dot{P}$ is the anticipated rate of change in prices. The nominal rate of interest $(R)$ is equal to the real rate of interest $(r)$ plus the expected rate of change in prices $(\dot{P})$ plus the product of the real rate of interest times the expected rate of change in prices $(r\dot{P})$. Since the expected rate of change in prices is difficult to estimate and the cross product term $(r\dot{P})$ usually will be small, the relationship[6] usually is abbreviated to $R = r + \dot{P}$.

If the real rate of interest is 10 percent and prices are expected to rise at a rate of 5 percent per period, the nominal interest rate will be 15.5 percent:

$$R = 0.10 + 0.05 + (0.10)(0.05)$$

$$= 0.155.$$

With an expected increase in prices of 5 percent per year, it is expected that it will take $115.50 in one year to buy what $110.00 will buy today.

The relationship between nominal interest rates and price changes is based on anticipated rates of change in prices not necessarily the actual rate of change in prices. However, the actual rate of change in prices may serve as an estimate of what individuals expected to happen to prices. The relationship between the actual percentage change in the implicit GNP deflator

---

[6]The relationship $R = r + \dot{P}$ holds exactly when the rates are compounded continuously.

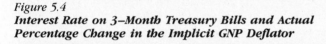

*Figure 5.4*
**Interest Rate on 3–Month Treasury Bills and Actual
Percentage Change in the Implicit GNP Deflator**

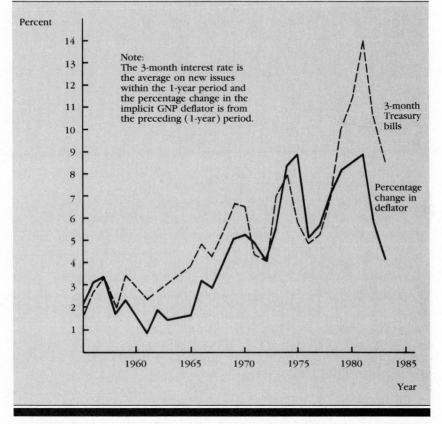

Source: United States Government Printing Office. *The Economic Report of the President to the Congress,* 1979, Tables B-3 and B-65.

(a general price index) and the nominal rate of interest on new issues of 3-month Treasury bills is shown in Figure 5.4.

## PRICE CHANGES AND WEALTH DISTRIBUTION

It is often argued that rising prices benefit monetary debtors at the expense of monetary creditors. With rising prices, monetary debtors are repaying loans with dollars that are worth less than the dollars they borrowed. If prices had not risen, the creditors would be capable of buying more goods and services with the funds they receive in repayment of the loan. However, whether or not the change in the purchasing power of the monetary unit

## IRVING FISHER

*Source: Wide World Photos, Inc.*

Irving Fisher (1867–1947)—economist, mathematician, inventor, and reformer.

It is to Irving Fisher that we owe much of our knowledge about interest rates, particularly about real rates of interest and their relationship to nominal rates. His work on interest rates was concerned with the relationship between impatience (time preference) and the opportunity for investment. He effectively argued that while interest rates may be positive or negative, when a good can be stored at a relatively low cost, then the interest rate in terms of that good (a real interest rate) will never be negative.

Irving Fisher was one of the great "characters" of the economics profession. He started his career as a mathematician at Yale University, but with the opportunities for reform greater in the social sciences, he transferred into Yale's Department of Political Economy in 1895. He is considered a founder of mathe-

actually acts to benefit debtors or creditors depends on whether the change in prices was anticipated correctly by the debtors and creditors.

If the nominal rate of interest is 10 percent, and both debtors and creditors anticipated prices rising by 5 percent per period, the anticipated real rate of interest is 4.76 percent. On a loan of $100.00 at the nominal interest rate of 10 percent, the repayment of $110.00 after one period is expected to be able to purchase what $104.76 could purchase currently. Since both the borrowers and the lenders expected prices to rise by 5 percent, they both were expecting that the dollars used to repay the loan would buy less than the dollars used in the original loan, and they were both expecting a real rate of interest of 4.76 percent. If the prices actually rise by the anticipated 5 percent, the loan repayment is exactly what was

matical economics and with Charles Roos and Ragnar Frisch founded the International Econometrics Society (the publishers of *Econometrica*).

Fisher's work in economics is wide ranging with a primary concentration in the area of monetary economics and price stability. He is probably best known for his statement of the equation of exchange ($MV = Py$), his efforts in making index numbers, and his work on interest rates.

After a bout with tuberculosis, Fisher became a crusader for fresh air and a food faddist. He even had six-inch slits built in around his bed to promote air circulation. With Harold Ley in 1913, he founded the nonprofit Life Extension Institute, which was dedicated to making low-cost periodic health examinations readily available.

He was a continual reformer, always advocating something. His reforms ranged from policies aimed at stabilizing the dollar to the Esperanto movement and the use of acidophilus milk. He was known as a vegetarian and was often seen jogging in his neighborhood. He was also a propagandist for prohibition.

Fisher was an inventor. He made a fortune from his invention of the visible-card index-file system (the round metal file often used in libraries). The company he set up to market this invention was later merged with a competitor and became Remington Rand. The fortune he accumulated during the 1920s was subsequently lost during the Depression.[1]

---

[1]A very readable review of Fisher's life and works is *My Father Irving Fisher* by Irving Norton Fisher (New York: Comet Press, 1956).

expected on both sides, and neither the borrower nor the lender benefits from the change in prices.

If, however, the prices actually had risen by more than was expected, the borrower would have gained at the expense of the lender. If prices actually rise over the period by 10 percent (5 percent more than is anticipated), the $110 repayment would be capable of buying only what $100 could have purchased in the previous period. The actually realized real rate of interest on the loan is then 0.0 percent. The borrower had the use of the funds for one period at a zero charge in terms of goods and services, even though the borrower and the lender both expected a real rate of interest of 4.76 percent. Clearly when prices rise faster than expected, the borrowers gain the use of funds at a lower real rate of interest than is expected.

When prices rise slower than expected, the creditor receives a repayment that will buy more goods and services than is anticipated. In our example, if prices actually rose by 3 percent instead of the 5 percent that was anticipated, the $110.00 repayment on the $100.00 loan would buy what $106.80 would have purchased prior to the price rise ($110.00/1.03 = $106.80). Although both the creditor and the debtor expected a real rate of interest of 4.76 percent, the actually realized real rate of interest was 6.80 percent.

If prices rise at a rate that is *faster* than expected, debtors will be repaying monetary units that buy *less* than expected. The result is an unexpected wealth transfer from creditors to debtors. If prices rise at a *slower* rate than is expected, the debtors will be repaying monetary units that buy *more* than is expected. The result is an unexpected wealth transfer from debtors to creditors.

## PRESENT AND FUTURE VALUES

Interest rates are central to the functioning of markets that allocate the use of goods and services over time. They represent the opportunity cost of the use of goods and services today in terms of goods and services at some future date. Thus, there is a similarity between an interest rate and an ordinary price that shows the opportunity cost of one good in terms of some other good in the same period. However, an interest rate should *not* be thought of as the price of money. The price of money is the number of units of something that must be forgone to acquire a unit of money. If the price of strawberries is $1.50 per basket, the price of money in terms of strawberries is two-thirds of a basket.

The prices of goods and services enable us to translate the value of a quantity of one good into a quantity of another good. If the price of strawberries is $1.00 per basket and the price of apples is $0.50 per pound, then we know that one basket of strawberries is considered to be equivalent in value to two pounds of apples. Similarly, interest rates enable us to translate values in one period into values in another period. A value today ($V_0$) can be converted into the equivalent value one period into the future ($V_1$), using this relationship:

$$V_1 = V_0(1 + R). \tag{5.2}$$

Thus, with an interest rate of 10 percent, a dollar in this period translates into $1.10 in the next period.

The relationship in Equation 5.2 translates values one period into the future. Therefore, we also can state

$$V_2 = V_1(1 + R). \tag{5.3}$$

A value of $1.10 one period from now translates, through an interest rate of 10 percent, into a value of $1.21 two periods from now.

Combining relationships from Equations 5.2 and 5.3, we can translate values in this period to values two periods into the future:

$$V_2 = V_1(1 + R) = V_0(1 + R)(1 + R) = V_0(1 + R)^2. \qquad (5.4)$$

In general, if the interest rate remains the same, we can translate a value in this period into a value $n$ periods into the future by:

$$V_n = V_0(1 + R)^n. \qquad (5.5)$$

## Discounting

Just as the prices of apples and strawberries allow us to convert quantities of strawberries into equivalent quantities of apples *and* quantities of apples into equivalent quantities of strawberries, so the interest rate allows us to translate values now into values in the future *and* values in the future into values now. The process of determining the *present value* of a future value is known as *discounting*. It consists of reversing the procedure used in Equations 5.2 to 5.5.

By solving Equation 5.2 for $V_0$, we have the relationship for the present value of a value one period from now:

$$V_0 = \frac{V_1}{(1 + R)}. \qquad (5.6)$$

Substituting an interest rate of 10 percent in Equation 5.2 shows that a dollar this period translates into $1.10 one period from now. Equation 5.6 shows that the present value of $1.10 one period from now is one dollar today.

In general, with a constant interest rate, the present value of a value to be received $n$ periods from now is given by:

$$V_n = \frac{V_n}{(1 + R)^n}. \qquad (5.7)$$

With a 10 percent rate of interest, a payment of $1.00 five periods from now has a present value of approximately $0.62

$$V_0 = \frac{1.00}{(1 + 0.1)^5} = \frac{1.00}{1.61051} = 0.62.$$

The process of discounting can be used to find the present value of a stream of payments received at different times in the future. For example, suppose that a product generates a stream of benefits over the next five years valued at $100 per year. The present value of that stream of benefits can be found by substituting $100 for $V_1$, $V_2$, $V_3$, $V_4$, and $V_5$

$$V_0 = \frac{V_1}{(1 + R)} + \frac{V_2}{(1 + R)^2} + \frac{V_3}{(1 + R)^3} + \frac{V_4}{(1 + R)^4} + \frac{V_5}{(1 + R)^5}. \qquad (5.8)$$

If the market rate of interest is 10 percent, the present value of the benefit stream of $100 per year for five years is

$$V_0 = \frac{100}{(1 + 0.1)} + \frac{100}{(1 + 0.1)^2} + \frac{100}{(1 + 0.1)^3} + \frac{100}{(1 + 0.1)^4} + \frac{100}{(1 + 0.1)^5}$$

$$= \frac{100}{1.1} + \frac{100}{1.21} + \frac{100}{1.331} + \frac{100}{1.4641} + \frac{100}{1.61051}$$

$$= \$379.08.$$

Alternatively, if the present price of a good is $379.08, and the good yields benefits valued at $100.00 per year for five years, the effective interest rate earned through the purchase of that good is 10 percent. Also, the financial investment of $379.08 at 10 percent will allow $100.00 to be withdrawn each year for five years. In general, the relationship shown in Equation 5.8, which can be extended over any time period, shows how the discounting mechanism links current prices, future benefits, and interest rates.

## INTEREST RATES AND COMMODITY PRICES

Interest rates are not determined in isolation from activity in other markets. Interest rates are determined by market activity, and markets are tied together by the substitutions that can occur. Apples can be substituted for strawberries and short-lived goods can be substituted for longer-lived goods. Prices show the trade-offs that can be made. If any price is changed, different trade-offs will be possible, and the adjustments will spread beyond the market where the original price change took place. This will be reflected throughout the economy by changes in opportunity costs.

Changing the substitutions available in any one market will affect, and be affected by, interest rates and current and future prices. Interest rates are more than a monetary phenomenon. They are influenced by, and influence, commodity prices. The relationships that exist among interest rates, current prices, and future prices flow directly from the discounting process.

Suppose that two different types of shoes exist and that these shoes are identical in all respects except that Type A will last for one year and Type B will last for two years. $S_1$ and $D_1$ in Figure 5.5 show the supply and demand curves for Type A shoes and the market clearing price of $10.

The benefit that can be derived from the purchase of a pair of Type B shoes is identical to the benefits that can be derived from the purchase of one pair of Type A shoes today, along with the purchase of a second pair of Type A shoes one year from now.[7] Assuming that the price of Type A shoes

---

[7]For simplicity, we ignore the additional cost of having to go out one year from now to purchase a second pair of shoes.

*Figure 5.5*
**The Market for Type A Shoes**

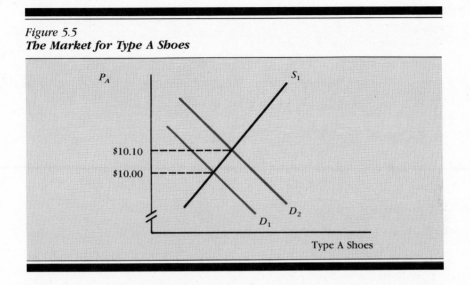

is expected to remain at $10 per pair, the benefit that can be derived from the purchase of Type B shoes is $10 now and $10 one year from now.[8] Since Type A and Type B shoes can be directly substituted, the price that an individual would be willing to pay for a pair of Type B shoes is determined by the present value of the benefits that can be derived from one pair of Type A shoes this year plus one pair of Type A shoes next year. Thus, the price of Type B shoes ($P_B$) is given by

$$P_B = \$10 + \frac{\$10}{(1 + R)}.$$

If the alternatives available in financial markets are indicated by an interest rate of 10 percent, the market for Type B shoes will clear at a price of $19.09.

$$P_B = \$10 + \frac{\$10}{(1 + 0.1)} = \$10 + \$9.09 = \$19.09.$$

This market clearing relationship is shown by the supply and demand curves $S_1$ and $D_1$ in Figure 5.6.

With the short-lived Type A shoes selling for $10.00 and the long-lived Type B shoes selling for $19.09, a customer would perceive no difference between buying one pair of Type B shoes to last the whole two years and buying one pair of Type A shoes each year. A customer buying a pair of Type B shoes would pay $19.09 now, but a customer buying a pair of Type A

---

[8] The $10 benefit from Type A shoes is actually the present value of the use of the shoes over the first year.

*Figure 5.6*
**The Market for Type B Shoes**

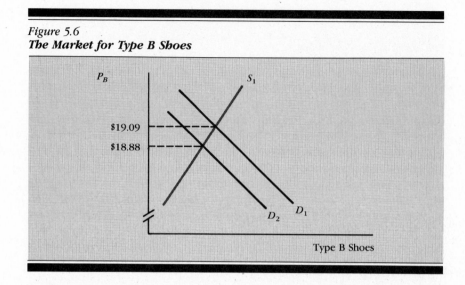

shoes would spend only $10.00 now. The additional $9.09 could then be loaned at 10 percent, and in one year's time it would be worth $10.00, which is the exact amount required for purchasing the second pair of Type A shoes. Alternatively, we might say that the customer spending $19.09 on a pair of Type B shoes has paid $10.00 for being shod the first year and has paid $9.09 for being shod the second year. Since the market price of Type A shoes is expected to remain at $10.00, the purchase of an expected benefit valued at $10.00 in one year's time for $9.09 in the current period shows a 10 percent return on the investment.

A change in conditions in the financial markets can be shown to have an effect on the price of both Type A and Type B shoes. If, for example, the interest rate were to rise to 15 percent, a person buying a pair of Type A shoes at the $10.00 price could lend the $9.09 left over at 15 percent, which would yield $10.45 after one year. This would be 45 cents more than the current price of Type A shoes, which would be an incentive for prospective shoe purchasers to switch from buying Type B shoes to buying Type A shoes. These shifts in demand are shown by the $D_2$ curves in Figures 5.5 and 5.6.

The increase in the demand for Type A shoes will cause the price of Type A shoes to rise, and the decrease in the demand for Type B shoes will cause the price of Type B shoes to fall. The prices will adjust until an individual can purchase a pair of Type A shoes, loan the difference between the new price for Type B shoes and the new price for Type A shoes at the new interest rate of 15 percent, and have exactly the right amount for purchasing the second pair of Type A shoes after one year. For example, if the price of Type A shoes rises to $10.10 (as in Figure 5.5), the price of Type B shoes will fall to $18.88 (as in Figure 5.6). The price differential of $8.78, when loaned for one year at 15 percent, will increase to exactly $10.10 over one year, which is the purchase price of a pair of Type A shoes. At these prices, therefore, both the market for Type A shoes and that for Type B shoes will clear, and there will be no incentive to shift from buying Type B shoes to buying Type A.

Interest rates obviously have an impact on the activity in the markets for short-lived and long-lived assets. Just as the prices of Types A and B shoes react to changes in interest rates, so the prices of all short-lived assets relative to long-lived assets will change with the interest rate. As interest rates rise, it takes less and less today to purchase the same benefit in the future; thus, there will be a shift in demand that will force up the prices of short-lived assets relative to the prices of long-lived assets.[9]

Interest rates should not be thought of as only being of importance in financial markets where they will influence the amounts that people wish to borrow and lend. Instead, it should be realized that rates have a pervasive influence on the types of goods and services that people wish to acquire in commodity markets. The goods and services that are purchased in commodity markets are acquired for the benefits that they will generate over varying periods of time. Cars are purchased for the benefits of transportation over a number of years, pencils are bought as writing instruments that will last some time, and even most food is not bought for immediate consumption. As interest rates change, the desires for the longer-lived of these assets will adjust relative to those that have a shorter life, and the prices will change accordingly. Rising interest rates will cause the prices of shorter-lived assets to rise relative to the prices of longer-lived assets, and falling interest rates will cause the prices of the shorter-lived assets to fall relative to the prices of the longer-lived assets.

## SUMMARY

Credit markets function in the same manner as markets for goods and services. Individuals will determine the alternatives that are available and will desire to undertake those actions they expect will make them better off. As conditions in the market change, the desired behavior of individuals also will change. At higher interest rates, lenders will desire to increase the amount of funds they lend, but borrowers will desire to decrease the amount they borrow. The desires of the borrowers and the lenders will interact in the financial markets to determine the interest rates and the amounts of funds exchanged.

---

[9] It should be noted that the interest rate changes referred to are changes in the real rate of interest. An increase in the nominal rate of interest does not necessarily indicate that it takes less today in terms of goods and services to acquire the same benefit (a good or service) in the future.

Nominal interest rates indicate the trade-off, in money units, of dollars today for dollars in the future. However, anticipated changes in the prices of goods and services over the period of the loan will influence the nominal interest on that loan. Individuals will borrow and lend in anticipation of the amount that will be repaid in terms of goods and services; i.e., the real rate of interest. If prices are expected to rise, lenders will be less willing to lend and borrowers will be more willing to borrow. This will result in a higher nominal rate of interest. The nominal rate of interest will be equal to the real rate of interest plus the anticipated rate of increase in prices plus the product of the real rate of interest and the anticipated rate of increase in prices.

Interest rates also function to translate values through time. By using interest rates, it is possible to determine the future value of a value today. By discounting, it is possible to determine the present value of an amount to be received sometime in the future.

The impact of interest rates is not limited to financial markets and the lending and borrowing of money. Interest rates have an important impact on the demands for long-lived and short-lived assets that will change their relative prices. The impact on the market for goods and services of an increase in the rate of interest will be an increase in the price of short-lived assets relative to the price of those assets that generate benefits over an extended period of time.

## Key Terms

interest rate
real rate of interest
nominal rate of interest
credit market
financial market

loanable funds
anticipated rate of change
  in prices
present value
discounting

## Questions

1.  Explain how individual impatience to spend income affects the rate of interest.

2.  Suppose that corn can be stored indefinitely at zero cost. Why would the interest rate in terms of corn never be negative?

3.  Explain why the naturally given ability of corn to reproduce will tend to make interest rates in terms of corn greater than zero.

4.  Why would observed increases in the general price level tend to increase the nominal rate of interest?

5.  It is observed that nominal rates of interest have increased. Does

this indicate that the cost of borrowing in real terms has also risen? Could it actually be cheaper in real terms to borrow? Explain.

6.  When the real rate of interest rises, what would you expect to happen to the price of consumer durables, such as washing machines, relative to the price of haircuts? Explain.

7.  Since the real rate of interest cannot be observed directly, how would you determine whether the real rate of interest has risen or fallen?

## Additional Readings

Brown, W. W., and G. J. Santoni, "Unreal Estimates of the Real Rate of Interest." *Review.* Federal Reserve Bank of St. Louis (January 1981): 18–26.

*A readable discussion of real interest rates and the problems in their estimation.*

Darby, Michael R. "The Financial and Tax Effects of Monetary Policy on Interest Rates." *Economic Inquiry* XIII (June 1975): 266–276.

*A discussion of the effects of marginal tax rates on the real and nominal rates of interest.*

Fisher, Irving. *The Theory of Interest.* New York: Augustus M. Kelley, 1965 (originally published in 1930)

*A classic book on the determination of interest rates. Chapter 2 (on money interest and real interest), Chapter 4 (on the role of impatience), and Chapter 19 (on the relation of interest to money and prices) are especially relevant to the material in this chapter.*

Shiller, Robert J., and Jeremy J. Siegel. "The Gibson Paradox and Historical Movements in Real Interest Rates." *Journal of Political Economy* (85) 5 (October 1977): 891–907.

*An examination of the correlation between interest rates and prices from 1792 to 1974.*

# CHAPTER SIX

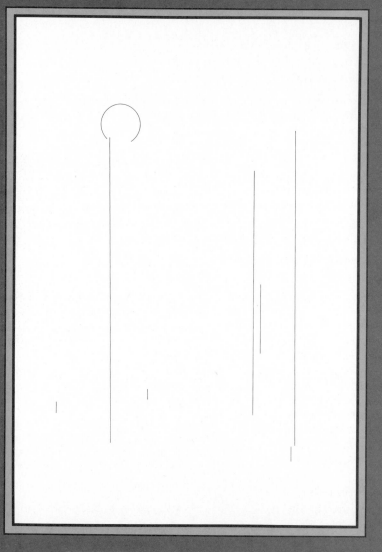

# CREDIT INSTRUMENTS AND
# THEIR MARKETS

*All financial intermediaries are in the business of lending and borrowing, and a great deal of this activity takes place in the markets for the various credit instruments. Credit instruments are issued in primary markets and then traded in secondary markets, where brokers and dealers help to decrease the transactions costs of trading. It is by trading these credit instruments that debt is transferred throughout the economy.*

C hapter 5's discussion centered on the extension of alternatives brought about by the introduction of borrowing and lending. If the benefits from borrowing and lending are to be available extensively in the economy, lending and borrowing must be widespread. Usually, this can be achieved only if borrowing and lending is in the form of money rather than goods, and it is done in such a form that the debts and credits can be transferred easily from one person to another. The total amount of debt (or credit) in the economy will be greatly increased if the debt can be transferred. If you wish to borrow a large amount of money for a long period of time, you probably will have a great deal of trouble finding someone willing to lend that amount for a long time. If, however, the debt is transferrable, it will be much easier to find many people willing to lend the same amount over short periods of time.

## CREDIT INSTRUMENTS

The ability to transfer debt is made possible by the use of *credit instruments.* These are written evidences of the extension of credit. By selling a credit instrument, debt is transferred from one person to another. If, for example, you wish to borrow $1000 for six years, you can do this by issuing a credit instrument that a lender can buy in the market. Ignoring the problem of interest payments for the time being, you could issue the instrument for the $1000 and sell it to someone who wished to lend the money to you. On the instrument, you would promise to pay the money back in six years, but if the owner of the instrument does not wish to lend the money for six years, the instrument could be sold to another lender to recoup the $1000. When the six years are over, you will pay the money to whoever then holds the credit instrument. As the borrower, you will have had the use of the money for the full six years, but the various owners of the instrument will have lent you the money for shorter periods of time. This transferability obviously makes lending and borrowing more attractive and is likely to lead to an increase in the amount of debt in the economy.

## TYPES OF CREDIT INSTRUMENTS

A wide range of specialized credit instruments exists in the United States, each with its own market. None of the markets, however, can be thought of in isolation. Credit instruments are usually so substitutable that a change in any one market will affect many others. Although the details will differ from instrument to instrument, each instrument indicates—

1.  The identity of the debtor (the person or institution borrowing the money and therefore the one responsible for paying it back),

2.  The amount of the debt (specifically, the amount to be paid back at maturity),

3.  The arrangements as to maturity (when the debt is to be repaid), and,

4.  If interest payments are to be made, what those payments are and when they are to be paid.

Credit instruments are broadly classified as being *negotiable* or *nonnegotiable,* but this distinction should not be confused with whether or not they can be *marketed.* Both negotiable and nonnegotiable instruments are marketable and therefore can be used to transfer debt from one person to another. The difference lies in the rights of those who are a party to the transactions when the debt is made and when it is transferred. In the case of negotiable paper, the rights of the parties are covered by special negotiable instruments laws (now embodied in the Uniform Commercial Code). All other credit instruments are said to be nonnegotiable, and the rights of the parties are covered by the general, common, and statute laws of contract.

## *Nonnegotiable*

The effects of these different laws on the rights of transactors can be seen easily in an example. Assume that you buy a stereo from a company called Stereo Inc. and that you pay with a nonnegotiable instrument, promising to pay $2000 at the end of six months. If Stereo Inc. wants the money before the end of the six months, the credit instrument can be sold to, say, Lender A. Because the instrument is nonnegotiable, the transaction is covered by the laws of contract, which means that it must be *assigned* to Lender A (that is, Stereo Inc. must sign over its rights to Lender A). However, under the laws of contract, "the assignee stands in the shoes of the assignor," meaning that Lender A is in the same position as if *he* or *she* had sold you the stereo. If the stereo is not as warranted, you could have refused to pay Stereo Inc. and therefore under the same conditions you also could refuse to pay Lender A. If at the time the payment is due, you claim that Stereo Inc. owes you money that is to be used to offset the debt, you legally can pay Lender A the difference and let Lender A get the remainder from Stereo Inc.

If Lender A assigned the instrument to Lender B before the payment was due, not only does Lender B stand in the shoes of Stereo Inc. but also in those of Lender A. If Lender A stole the instrument, he or she obviously would have no title to the payment, so if the instrument is assigned to Lender B after its theft, Lender B also would have no title to the money.

Negotiable instruments laws are designed to avoid these problems by establishing an *unconditional obligation to pay.* If you bought the stereo and gave Stereo Inc. a negotiable instrument, promising to pay $2000 at the end of six months, your obligation is to pay the full $2000 to Lender B, regardless of whether or not the stereo was as warranted, or even whether Lender A stole the instrument. As no conditions can be attached to the instrument, the person who legally holds the instrument when the payment is due (the holder in due course) has a right to the full amount of the debt.

## *Negotiable*

A negotiable credit instrument is defined in Article 3 of the Uniform Commercial Code as any writing that is—

1.  Signed by the maker or drawer,

2.  An unconditional promise or order to pay a certain amount of money,

3.  Payable on demand or at a fixed or determinable future date, and,

4.  Payable *to order* or *to bearer.*

Negotiable instruments are either promises or orders to pay. If the instrument is a promise, two parties are involved: a maker or payer, and the payee. The maker or payer promises to pay the payee. This kind of instrument is a promissory note, which is defined as

> an unconditional statement in writing made by one person to another and signed by the maker, promising to pay on demand, or at a fixed or determinable future date, a sum certain in money to order or to bearer.

If the instrument is an order to pay, it is called a *bill of exchange* or a draft. There are three parties involved in a draft: the drawer who orders payment, the drawee who is ordered to pay, and the payee to whom payment is to be made. A bill of exchange or draft is defined as

> an unconditional order in writing addressed by one person to another, signed by the person giving it, requiring the person to whom it is addressed to pay on demand, or at a fixed or determinable future date, a sum certain in money to order or to bearer.

A general classification of credit instruments is shown in Figure 6.1. You can see that credit instruments are divided first according to whether or not they are negotiable. The negotiable instruments are divided further into promises or orders. The promissory notes are divided according to who makes the promise. If the party making the promise is part of government, be it federal, state, or local, or a United States government agency, the instruments are referred to as *governments*. The remaining promissory notes are referred to as *private promissory notes*. The promissory notes are classified further according to the length of time to run from issue to maturity.

## United States Treasury Securities

All promissory notes issued by the United States Treasury are referred to as United States Treasury securities, but are divided into three groups. Those securities that are issued for periods of three, six, and nine months and a year are known as *Treasury bills*. The most popular are those for three and six months. *Treasury notes* are issued for periods from one to ten years. *Treasury bonds* are issued for periods from five years on up.

**Treasury Bills.** These short-term promissory notes are secured only by "the full faith and credit of the United States." The minimum par value is $10,000. No interest is stated on the face of the bill, but interest can be earned on the instrument by buying it at less than the face value. They are said to sell "at a discount." Treasury bills are issued in *bearer* form, so the maturity payment (the only payment there is) is paid to the holder.

*Figure 6.1*
**A General Classification of Credit Instruments**

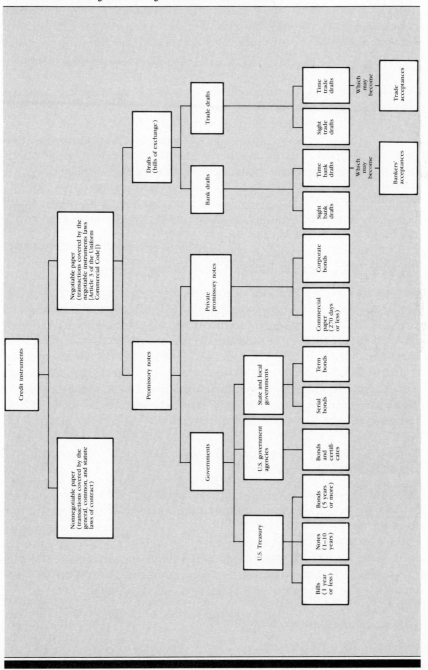

**Treasury Notes.** *Treasury notes* differ from Treasury bills in that they have a coupon rate of interest. This is a contractual rate of interest stated on the face of the note. This contractual interest usually is paid semiannually. Treasury notes are issued in both bearer and *registered* form. If a note is issued in registered form, the name and address of the current owner is registered with the Treasury, and if the note is sold the change of ownership must be recorded by the Treasury. The minimum par value is $1000.

**Treasury Bonds.** Treasury bonds are issued with any maturity but usually are used for long-term borrowing starting at five years. Treasury bonds have a contractual rate of interest stated on the face that usually is payable semi-annually. This contractual rate is limited by law to a maximum of 4¼ per-cent, though from time to time the Treasury has been given permission to borrow certain amounts without regard to this limitation. The par values of Treasury bonds can be as low as $500. Some Treasury bonds are *callable*, meaning that a period is given (usually the last five or ten years of the bond), during which time the Treasury can require the holder to redeem the bond at face value on the date of any interest payment.

## Securities of United States Government Agencies

The securities of the agencies of the federal government take many forms and are supported in many ways by the federal government. Some (for example, bonds that are issued in support of housing loans) are secured by "the full faith and credit of the United States" in the same way as Treasury securities, but others (for example, bonds issued by the Tennessee Valley Authority) are not. Sometimes the agencies issue *participation certificates*. These certificates offer participation in a group of assets (usually a group of mortgages), and the holders of the certificates receive payments of both interest and principal until the entire debt and the interest are paid off.

## Securities of All Branches of State and Local Government

Securities of state and local governments are often called *munis* (short for *municipals*) or *tax-exempts* (because the interest payments are exempt from the federal income tax). The bonds usually are issued in *serial form*, though some issues are of normal *term bonds*. When bonds are issued in serial form, the issue is divided into groups with one group maturing after one year, another after two years, and so on. Municipals usually are issued to an underwriter, who then sells them to the general public.

## Private Promissory Notes

Private promissory notes can be divided into unsecured short-term *commercial paper* and longer-term *bonds* that may or may not be secured.

*Commercial Paper.*   Commercial paper is unsecured, short-term promissory notes issued by banks, corporations, and finance companies. Such securities are issued in denominations of $1000 or more, with maturities up to 270 days. The limit of 270 days exists because of the rules of the Securities and Exchange Commission. If the commercial paper was issued with a maturity date later than 270 days after issue, it would have to be registered; this would add greatly to the expense of making the issue.

*Corporate Bonds.*   Corporate *bonds* come in many different forms, having various arrangements as to the security for the loan. *Mortgage bonds* exist where the debt is secured by a pledge of property. In the event of default on a mortgage bond, a bondholder has a right to the property and may sell it to recoup the loan. *Equipment trust certificates* exist where the debt is secured by specific pieces of equipment that can be sold in the event of a default. *Collateral trust bonds* exist when the debt is secured by other securities that usually are held by a trustee. *Debenture bonds* exist when the debt is unsecured, and when there is a hierarchy of bonds for payment in case of default; those bonds that do not take precedence are called *subordinate debentures.*

## Bills of Exchange or Drafts

Drafts are classified according to the drawee and the length of time before payment is due. When the payment is drawn on a bank, the draft is a *bank draft.* When the payment is drawn on a person or an institution other than a bank, the draft is a *trade draft.* Drafts either are payable on presentation, in which case they are *sight drafts,* or are payable at some determinable future date, in which case they are *time drafts.* A check is a *sight bank draft.*

A draft is only an order to pay; it is not an obligation of the drawee to pay. As such, individuals receiving payment through a draft only have the credit worthiness of the drawer as assurance that payment will be made. For example, if you write a check on your checking account, your bank is not obligated to make payment unless there are sufficient funds in the account. In the case of a time draft, the draft becomes an *acceptance* if the drawee agrees to make the payment (by writing *Accepted* on the draft and signing it ).

*Acceptances.*   Acceptances are extremely important in commerce, both domestically and internationally. They can be used by sellers who wish to receive payment for goods sold before the buyer pays for them. This is very common in international trade because of the time that often elapses between shipment and delivery. Someone selling goods can write a time trade draft on the buyer, ordering the buyer to make payment at a fixed or determinable time. The seller of the goods is the drawer of the draft; the buyer of the goods is the drawee of the draft. Drawers of drafts can make themselves, their banks, or anyone to whom they owe money the payee.

When carriers pick up goods from sellers, they give the seller a receipt for the goods, known as a *bill of lading*. This bill of lading is sent with the draft to a bank in the town where the buyer operates. This *collecting bank* will surrender the bill of lading (which is necessary to be able to take delivery from the carrier) to the buyer if the buyer accepts payment of the draft: if the buyer agrees to pay the draft when it is due by writing *Accepted* on the draft and signing it. At this point the draft has become an *acceptance,* and the payee can sell it on the market for funds. It is sold at a discount (that is, less than the face value) to provide earnings to the purchaser of the acceptance.

This method of financing trade cannot be used easily if the credit of the buyer is not very strong. The acceptance is, in effect, the buyer's promise to pay, but for the acceptance to be salable in the market, there must be reason to expect that the promise will be honored. This problem can be solved, however, by using a time bank draft instead of a time trade draft, so that the bank's credit is used instead of the buyer's. The buyer can arrange for this by getting a *letter of credit* from a bank. The bank that agrees to be the drawee of the draft will send the letter of credit to the seller and charge the buyer an *acceptance fee*. The bank will only do this, of course, if it has received assurance that the buyer will furnish the funds before the draft becomes due. It should be noted that the bank at no time lends money in this transaction to either the buyer or the seller and would only use its own funds if there were a default by the buyer.

Once the seller receives the letter of credit from the bank, the bank can be made the drawee of the draft. When the bank agrees to make the payment, the draft becomes a *bankers' acceptance*. A bankers' acceptance is marketed much easier than a trade draft. Banks that create these acceptances usually do not retain them in their own portfolios; instead they sell them on the secondary market.

Bankers' acceptances that have a short time to run to maturity are often used by depository institutions to increase their liquidity. An institution that is holding this type of bankers' acceptance can sell it to the Federal Reserve to acquire funds. This is one way the Federal Reserve fulfills its role as a reserve on which depository institutions may call when they require funds.

Liberalization of the requirements for eligibility for discounting under the Export-Trading Company Act of 1982 is expected to increase the amount of acceptances that are used to pay for the domestic shipment of goods. However, it usually has been the case that about 90 percent of acceptances are to facilitate international trade.

### Interest Payments

Whenever credit instruments are issued in the market, money is being loaned at interest. The interest payments, however, are made in different ways and seldom are stated explicitly on the credit instrument. Many credit instruments do have a stated interest rate, but his interest rate is seldom the rate being paid on the loan that the instrument represents. Interest is earned in two ways. Either the instrument is sold at a discount, in which case the interest is the difference between the purchase price of the instrument and its maturity value; or installment or coupon payments are made, in which case the interest is a combination of the difference between the purchase price and the maturity value and the payments made to the holder of the instrument before the maturity date.

*Discount Sales.*   Short-term credit instruments, such as bills, commercial paper, and time drafts, are sold at a discount. If a one-year bill with a face value of $10,000 is issued at a price of $9523.81, the holder would earn $476.19 over the year. This rate of return is

$$\frac{476.19}{9523.81} = 0.05, \text{ or 5 percent.}$$

Care must be taken to distinguish between the published rates of discount on credit instruments and the actual rate of return on the loans that the instruments represent. The published rates of discount are for the purpose of indicating the current price of the instrument, not the rate of return on the loan. For example, 90-day commercial paper could be offered at a discount of, say, 16 percent. This does not mean that if you buy the commercial paper at the current price you will earn 16 percent on your money. Instead, it informs you that the price is 96 percent of the face value, i.e., a $10,000 instrument is selling at $9600. The difference between the purchase price and the maturity value is 4 percent on a 90-day instrument when the published rate of discount is 16 percent, because the commercial paper market uses a hypothetical 360-day year for ease in calculations.

$$R_d = \frac{100 - P}{100} \cdot \frac{360}{90},$$

where $R_d$ is the published rate of discount and $P$ is the purchase price, expressed as a percentage of the maturity value.

The actual rate of return on the investment (the *yield to maturity*) must be calculated as a percentage of the purchase price, using a 365-day year

$$R = \frac{100 - P}{P} \cdot \frac{365}{90},$$

where $R$ is the rate of return on the investment. Thus, with a published discount of 16 percent, the rate of return on the investment is

$$\frac{100 - 96}{96} \cdot \frac{365}{90} = 0.16898 \qquad \text{or approximately 16.9 percent.}$$

Though the 360-day year was adopted for the convenience of calculating prices and yields in the 90-day commercial paper market (it was convenient to divide the year into four 90-day periods), it has been adopted universally for the calculation of discount rates on short-term credit instruments regardless of how long they have to run to maturity. In general, therefore, the rate of discount on short-term credit instruments is

$$R_d = \frac{100 - P}{100} \cdot \frac{360}{\text{number of days to maturity}},$$

where $R_d$ is the rate of discount on a per-annum basis and $P$ is the price expressed as a percentage of the maturity value. The rate of return that can be earned by purchasing a credit instrument at the current price and holding it to maturity is

$$R = \frac{100 - P}{P} \cdot \frac{365}{\text{numbers of days to maturity}},$$

where $R$ is the yield to maturity on the loan and $P$ is the price expressed as a percentage of the maturity value.

**_Yield on Coupon Bonds._** The rate of return from a bond can be calculated from the price paid for the bond and the amount received by the holder of the bond, but the calculations are complicated by the fact that not all of the payments are made at the same time. This means that it is necessary to use present value calculations.

The stream of payments to which the holder is entitled can be calculated from the information given on the face of the bond. The face value is paid to the holder at the time of maturity, but the coupon payments are made periodically (usually semiannually, but sometimes annually) throughout the life of the bond. The _coupon rate_ is the percentage of the face value of the bond that is to be paid to the holder annually. It is from the present value of this stream of payments that the yield of the bond can be calculated.[1]

For example, if there is a $10,000 face value bond with a 4 percent coupon (payable annually) that has two years until maturity, the holder is entitled to two annual payments of $400 (4 percent of $10,000) and the maturity payment of $10,000. The present value, $V_o$, of this stream of payments is given by

$$V_o = \frac{\$400}{(1 + R)} + \frac{\$400}{(1 + R)^2} + \frac{\$10,000}{(1 + R)^2}.$$

---

[1] Chapter 5 stated that the present value, $V_o$, of any amount $A_n$ received $n$ periods in the future is equal to

$$\frac{A_n}{(1 + R)^n}$$

As the price in the market is the current evaluation of the present value of the stream of payments, the yield to maturity is that rate of interest that makes the present value of the stream of payments equal to the market price

$$P = \frac{\$400}{(1 + R)} + \frac{\$400}{(1 + R)^2} + \frac{\$10,000}{(1 + R)^2}.$$

If the market price of this bond is currently $9814.06, the yield to maturity is 5 percent, because

$$\frac{\$400}{(1 + 0.05)} + \frac{\$400}{(1 + 0.05)^2} + \frac{\$10,000}{(1 + 0.05)^2}$$

$$= \$380.95 + \$362.81 + \$9070.30$$

$$= \$9814.06.$$

The payments on this bond can be likened to withdrawals from an account that pays 5 percent per annum. If $9814.06 is placed in an account that earns 5 percent per annum, and $400.00 is withdrawn after one year and $400.00 after two years, $10,000.00 will be left in the account after the two years

$$\$9814.06 \times 1.05 = \$10,304.76$$
$$\underline{-400.00}$$
$$\$9904.76 \times 1.05 = \$10,400.00$$
$$\underline{-400.00}$$
$$\$10,000.00.$$

Those who buy this bond at $9814.06 will earn 5 percent on their investment; those who own the bond and sell it at $9814.06 will be giving up a 5 percent return over the next two years.[2]

## THE PRICE OF CREDIT INSTRUMENTS AND THE NOMINAL RATE OF INTEREST

There are two ways of looking at the markets for credit instruments. They can be looked at either as places for the buying and selling of the credit instruments, or as places for the lending and borrowing of funds. Many

---

[2] If, as is common, the coupon payments were made twice a year instead of once a year, the price of the bond would have to be $9811.90 for the yield to be 5 percent.

$$\frac{\$200}{\left(1 + \dfrac{R}{2}\right)} + \frac{\$200}{\left(1 + \dfrac{R}{2}\right)^2} + \frac{\$200}{\left(1 + \dfrac{R}{2}\right)^3} + \frac{\$200}{\left(1 + \dfrac{R}{2}\right)^4} + \frac{\$10,000}{\left(1 + \dfrac{R}{2}\right)^4}$$

$$= \frac{\$200}{(1 + 0.025)} + \frac{\$200}{(1 + 0.025)^2} + \frac{\$200}{(1 + 0.025)^3} + \frac{\$200}{(1 + 0.025)^4} + \frac{\$10,000}{(1 + 0.025)^4}$$

$$= \$195.12 + \$190.36 + \$185.72 + \$181.19 + \$9059.51$$

$$= \$9811.90.$$

different kinds of credit instruments exist, each representing a different kind of loan. Each type of loan—whether between individuals, banks, nonbank financial intermediaries, nonfinancial corporations, or governments—has its own type of credit instrument and financial market. These separate credit markets obviously have individual peculiarities, but they still can be broadly classified as being *primary markets* or *secondary markets.*

## Primary Markets

A *primary market* sale of a credit instrument is a transaction where new credit is being extended. In this market, the initial borrower of funds issues a claim and exchanges it for funds from the initial lender. This is done chiefly by governments and private corporations through an investment banker or an underwriter, or, in the case of the United States Treasury, through the Federal Reserve System acting as the fiscal agent of the government.

## Secondary Markets

A *secondary market* sale of a credit instrument is a transaction where the holder of a credit instrument sells it to a third party. There is no change in the total amount of credit extended, but the ownership of the credit changes. Although the borrower of the funds remains the same, the lenders are changing as the credit instrument is traded. Secondary markets exist wherever owners of credit instruments sell them to others, but many secondary markets are organized by brokers and dealers. If brokers and dealers have organized a secondary market to the extent that any holder of a credit instrument can sell the instrument at any time, the credit instrument is said to be *shiftable.*

***Brokers and Dealers.*** *Brokers* are agents of investors. They earn a commission for the service of bringing together those who wish to sell and those who wish to buy. *Dealers,* on the other hand, buy and sell securities for themselves. They "make the market" by buying for and selling from their own portfolios. Dealers earn an income from the spread between the *bid price,* at which they buy securities, and the *asked price,* at which they sell them.

***Security Prices and Interest Rates.*** Those who trade in the secondary markets for credit instruments either exchange credit instruments for funds or they exchange funds for credit instruments. It is therefore possible to look at this market in terms of the credit instruments being exchanged or the funds being exchanged. The supply of credit instruments to the secondary market and the demand for credit instruments from the secondary market determine the price at which the securities exchange. This is shown in

*Figure 6.2*
**The Market for the Credit Instrument**

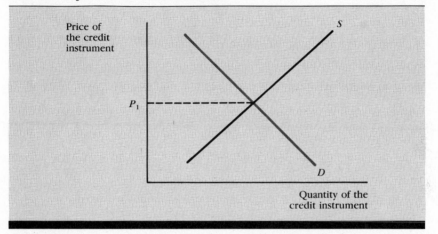

*Figure 6.3*
**The Market for Funds Loaned in this Credit Instrument Market**

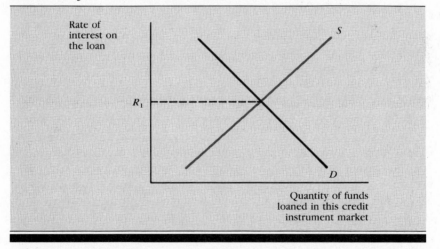

Figure 6.2. However, although no new loans are being made in the secondary market, it is possible to view this market as a supply of funds and a demand for funds. Those who supply funds to this market are purchasing the credit instruments from those who wish to sell them. Those who demand funds in this market are people who already have loaned out money (by buying the credit instruments they are holding) and now demand their money back (by selling the credit instruments). The supply of funds and the demand for funds determine the interest rate at which the funds are loaned, as shown in Figure 6.3.

*Figure 6.4a*
**The Relationship between the Price of the Instrument and the Rate of Interest on the Loan**

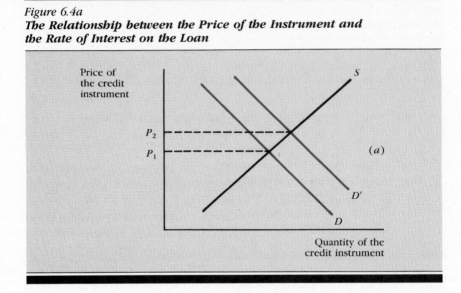

It would be incorrect to think of these two views of the same market as being in any way separate. The supply of the credit instrument shown in Figure 6.2 gives exactly the same information as the demand for funds shown in Figure 6.3; and the demand for the credit instrument shown in Figure 6.2 gives exactly the same information as the supply of funds shown in Figure 6.3.[3] If there is a change in the supply of the credit instrument, there also must be a change in the demand for the funds. If there is a change in the demand for the credit instrument, there also must be a change in the supply of the funds. Suppose, for example, that there is an increase in the demand for a credit instrument that shifts the demand function from $D$ to $D'$ in Figure 6.4a. This will increase the price of the credit instrument from $P_1$ to $P_2$. This price increase also will be reflected in the market for funds, where the rate of interest will be affected. The supply of funds in Figure 6.4b must shift to the right, and the rate of interest will fall from $R_1$ to $R_2$.

Because the two diagrams depict different perspectives of the same adjustment in the same market, one should not think that the price increase *caused* the fall in the interest rate. Rather, one should consider that the increase in the price *is* the decrease in the interest rate.

---

[3] For the supply of funds to increase with a decrease in the price of the credit instrument, the demand for the credit instrument must be price elastic. A 1 percent decrease in the price of the credit instrument will result in more than a 1 percent increase in the quantity demanded, and the funds supplied ($P \times Q$) will increase.

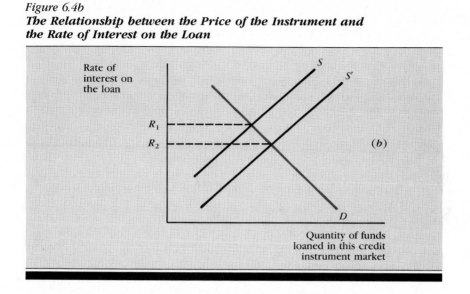

*Figure 6.4b*
**The Relationship between the Price of the Instrument and the Rate of Interest on the Loan**

## Transactions Costs in the Secondary Markets

In making exchanges in markets, buyers and sellers incur costs known as *transactions costs.* Chapter 2 pointed out how money is a device for reducing transactions costs, but even with money in the system there are still significant costs associated with the exchange process. This has had a great effect on the organization of secondary markets for credit instruments. Brokers and dealers have found it possible to make a profit for themselves by reducing the transactions costs of others in the secondary markets.

Investors supply and demand credit instruments on the basis of what they expect to receive in the exchange. For example, the number of bonds that is supplied to the market depends on the price that sellers expect to receive from the sale of the bonds. However, to receive a specific amount of money for a sale of bonds, the bonds will have to be sold at a *higher* price to cover the transactions costs. In Figure 6.5 the quantity of bonds $Q_1$ is sold at the price $P_2$ so that the sellers will receive $P_1$. The difference between the two prices, $P_2 - P_1$, represents the transactions costs incurred in the sale.

Transactions costs also are incurred by the demanders of the bonds. A buyer of bonds must search the market to find a seller, acquire information concerning the alternatives in the market, and make the physical transfer of funds in exchange for the bond. If a purchaser of a bond pays price $P_1$ for a bond, *more* than $P_1$ will be forgone by the purchaser through the use of resources in making the transaction. Figure 6.6 shows the willingness of individuals to buy bonds in the market. With transactions costs, the buyers

*Figure 6.5*
**The Transactions Costs Incurred in Selling Bonds**

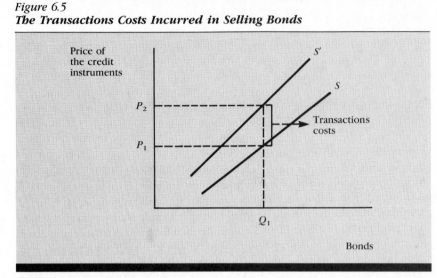

*Figure 6.6*
**The Transactions Costs Incurred in Buying Bonds**

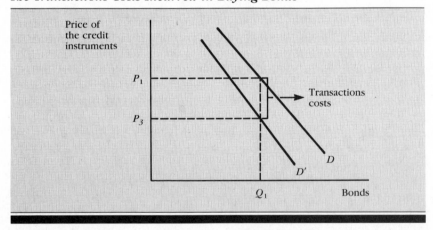

will be willing to acquire a quantity of $Q_1$ bonds only when the price is sufficiently lower than $P_1$ to cover their transactions costs.

When the buyers of the bonds pay price $P_3$, they actually are forgoing the use of resources that are valued at $P_1$. The buyers forgo the value of $P_3$ in the actual purchase, and the additional value, $P_1 - P_3$, is the use of resources in making the transaction.

By putting together the behavior of buyers and sellers, we can determine the impact of transactions costs on the operation of the market. This is shown in Figure 6.7, where the reduction in supply from $S$ to $S'$ is the result of the transactions costs incurred by the sellers, and the reduction in de-

*Figure 6.7*
**The Secondary Market for Bonds with and without Transactions Costs**

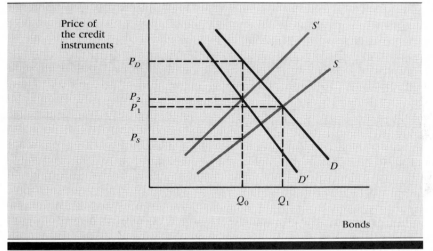

mand from $D$ to $D'$ is the result of the transactions costs that are incurred by the buyers of the bonds.

In a world without transactions costs, the behavior of the market is indicated by supply curve $S$ and demand curve $D$. Under these conditions, a quantity $Q_1$ of bonds will be exchanged at a price of $P_1$. With transactions costs, the quantity exchanged will be reduced to $Q_0$ (determined where $S'$ cuts $D'$). This reduction is the result of the decrease in the quantity that sellers are prepared to bring to the market because of their transactions costs and the decrease in the quantity that buyers are prepared to buy when there are transactions costs. In Figure 6.7 the price that buyers pay to sellers when transactions costs are involved is $P_2$.[4]

Along with a reduction in the quantity of bonds that are exchanged, the impact of the transactions costs is to introduce a "spread" between the price that is received by the seller and the price that is paid by the buyer. Although $P_2$ dollars per unit of bonds sold actually change hands between the buyer and the seller, this $P_2$ does not represent the amount the seller gains from the sale nor the amount the buyer actually forgoes in the purchase. When the transactions costs are included, the value of goods and services forgone by the purchaser is $P_D$, which is equal to the dollar price of

---

[4] In this case the resulting price is higher than the transactions costless price of $P_1$. Whether the actual price is higher or lower than the transactions costless price will depend on shifts in the supply and demand curves because of the transactions costs and the price elasticities of quantity supplied and demanded.

$P_2$ plus the transactions costs forgone by the buyer. Similarly, the price $P_2$ that the seller receives in units of money does not represent the seller's ability to acquire other goods. The seller receives a net payment of $P_s$ dollars, which is equal to the $P_2$ dollars received from the buyer minus the costs incurred by the seller in making the transaction.

The spread that is generated by the transactions costs is the difference between the net proceeds of the seller and the net payment of the buyer. This spread ($P_D - P_S$ in Figure 6.7) is equal to the transactions costs that are incurred by both the buyers and the sellers. Any reduction in the transactions costs will reduce the spread between $P_D$ and $P_S$ and this would benefit buyers or sellers or both.

## Brokers and Dealers in Secondary Markets

As a result of transactions costs in financial markets, brokers and dealers are used in many financial transactions. They are in this position because they economize on the use of resources in making transactions. By having a comparative advantage in the process of making exchanges, brokers and dealers use fewer resources to make an exchange than buyers and sellers would use if they had to make the transactions alone.

If the transactions costs without brokers and dealers are $10 ($P_D - P_S$ in our example is $10), and brokers or dealers can make the same exchange at a cost of $7, brokers or dealers could make the transactions for buyers and sellers, charge them less than what would be the market prices without brokers and dealers, and receive an income from making the transactions. For example, broker could make the exchange and charge the buyer and the seller a total of, say, $9. This would reduce the total amount of transactions costs by $1, allow the buyer of the bond to buy at a net price less than $P_D$, and allow the seller of the bond to receive a net payment of more than $P_S$. In addition, the broker also would gain by charging a total of $9 for a transaction that costs only $7.

We would not necessarily expect in a competitive market that the broker could arbitrarily acquire this $2. Other brokers and dealers would be free to enter the market, so we would expect that competition among brokers and dealers would force down brokerage charges to the amount that covers the cost of making the exchange plus a normal profit.

Brokers and dealers earn their income in different ways: the broker charges a commission on the purchase and sale of the bonds, but the dealer establishes a spread between the prices at which they will buy (the bid prices) and the prices at which they will sell (the asked prices). In order for the dealer to make a profit, of course, the asked price must be above the bid price, but the difference between the two is directly comparable to the commission that is charged by the broker. Market forces also will dictate that the difference between the asked price and the bid price be less than the transactions costs that would be incurred by the buyers and sellers if

*Figure 6.8*
***The Secondary Market for Bonds with or without Brokers and Dealers***

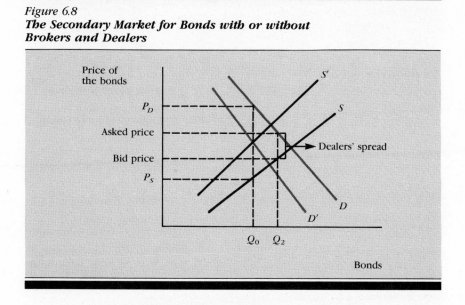

they made the transactions without the aid of brokers and dealers. If this were not the case, buyers and sellers would avoid the brokers and dealers and perform the transactions themselves.

The effect of the activities of brokers and dealers is shown in Figure 6.8. The supply and demand curves with and without transactions costs depicted in the figure are the same as those in Figure 6.7. If there are no brokers or dealers in the market, $Q_0$ dollars worth of bonds will be exchanged. The buyers will pay a price including transactions costs of $P_D$, and the sellers will receive a net price of transactions costs of $P_S$. If there are brokers and dealers in the market, the transactions costs involved are reduced and a greater quantity of bonds are exchanged. The sellers will be better off because the price they receive will be equal to the bid price (rather than $P_S$) and the buyers will be better off because the price they pay will be equal to the asked price rather than $P_D$.[5]

## SUMMARY

Credit instruments facilitate lending and borrowing. Each credit instrument has unique characteristics but all are used in the creation and transference of debt and credit. Credit instruments are issued in primary markets, where

---

[5] This is not strictly accurate in that buyers and sellers will still incur *some* transactions costs. However, with the use of a broker or a dealer, the costs incurred directly by either the buyer or the seller will be reduced to a negligible amount.

The Wizard of Id by Brant Parker and Johnny Hart

*Source:* By permission of Johnny Hart and Field Enterprises Inc.

new credit is created, and are traded in secondary markets, where the credit that already exists is traded. The prices of the credit instruments and the rates of interest on the loans of funds that they represent are market-determined.

Transactions in both primary and secondary markets involve transactions costs. When these transactions costs are high, the level of activity in that market is likely to be small. These transactions costs give rise to brokers and dealers who are able to economize on the resources used in the markets. By having a comparative advantage in bringing together lenders and borrowers, these brokers and dealers reduce the transactions costs and increase the amount of lending and borrowing that takes place in secondary markets.

By facilitating lending and borrowing, credit instruments allow investors to exchange consumption in one period for consumption in another. This characteristic is shared by all credit instruments and therefore tends to make the various credit instruments substitutes for each other.

## Key Terms

| | |
|---|---|
| credit instrument | coupon rate |
| negotiable instrument | primary market |
| nonnegotiable instrument | secondary market |
| bond | brokers |
| Treasury bill | dealers |
| Treasury note | bid price |
| bankers' acceptance | asked price |
| yield to maturity | acceptance |

## Questions

1.  References to *the rate of interest* are common. With the wide variety of credit instruments, and with the different market rates of interest that exist, is it reasonable to talk about only one rate of interest? Why or why not?

2.  "Since brokers operate so as to reduce transactions costs, it is always beneficial to make financial transactions in the credit markets through brokers." Discuss.

3.  Explain why interest rates on credit instruments vary inversely with the prices at which the credit instruments sell.

4.  Why is it incorrect to say that the rise in the price of a credit instrument *causes* the fall in the interest rate?

## *Additional Readings*

Hurley, Evelyn H. "The Commercial Paper Market." *Federal Reserve Bulletin* 63 (June 1977): 523–536.

*A discussion of the technical operations, history, use, and growth in the commercial paper market.*

Maxwell, James A., and J. Richard Aronson. *Financing State and Local Governments.* 3d ed. Washington, D.C.: Brookings, 1977.

*This is the standard reference work for financing state and local government. It is a useful source book for information on state and local debt.*

Purchase and Sales Data Processing Division of the Securities Industry Association. *A Primer on Brokerage Operations.* New York: Institute of Finance, 1973.

*Although this is mainly a how-to book for investors, it explains in simple terms the operation of the securities markets in the United States.*

Zwick, Burton. "The Market for Corporate Bonds." *Quarterly Review* 2. Federal Reserve Bank of New York (Autumn 1977): 27–36.

*A coverage of the corporate bond market, and the issue, sale, and general characteristics of corporate bonds.*

# CHAPTER SEVEN

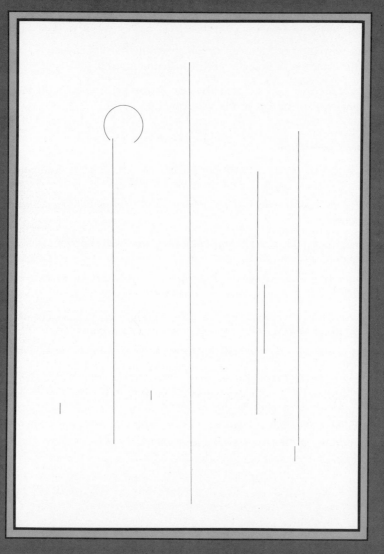

# CREDIT INSTRUMENTS ISSUED BY THE
# UNITED STATES TREASURY

*Financial institutions deal exten-sively in credit instruments that are issued by the U.S. Treasury. These instruments are Treasury bills, Treasury notes, and Treasury bonds. Various theories about the term structure of interest rates have been formulated using the interest rates on the debts represented by these instruments.*

Although United States Treasury securities do not make up a large proportion of a commercial bank's assets (throughout the 1970s and early 1980s they have made up approximately 7 percent), they are prominent among the credit instruments that are *traded* by commercial banks. These are the assets that commercial banks sell off when they wish to acquire funds. As we shall see when we discuss the operations of a commercial bank in Chapter 8, it is very important that the bank's portfolio include highly *liquid* assets that can be sold for cash with a minimum of delay.

*Liquidity* is defined as the ability to sell an asset immediately for cash without making a capital loss. It is an essential ingredient of a commercial bank's portfolio because the bank always must be able to pay cash on demand for any withdrawal from a demand deposit and within thirty days for a withdrawal from a savings account. For a credit instrument to be liquid, it must be able to be sold immediately. Thus, there must be a well-organized secondary market for the instrument. When this is so, the instrument is said to be *shiftable*. However, liquidity is much more than shiftability. In order for the instrument to be sold without making a capital loss, the price at which the instrument can be sold must rise from the time of purchase to the time of sale. If the price of the instrument fluctuates a great deal, losses might be incurred if the asset is sold. If the price fluctuates, the instrument

*Figure 7.1*
**Prices of Hypothetical Credit Instruments from Issue to Maturity**

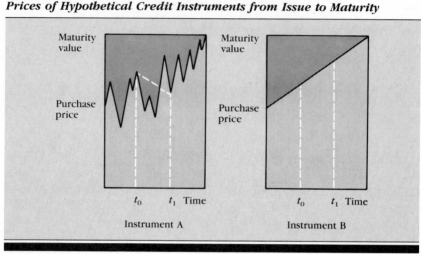

is said to bear interest risk, and it is also less-than-perfectly liquid. If the price of the instrument rises steadily from the time of purchase to the time of maturity, the asset is safe from interest risk and also is liquid.

For example, consider the time path of the two hypothetical credit instruments depicted in Figure 7.1. The prices of both Instrument A and Instrument B rise from the same price of issue to the same maturity value, but because of the fluctuations in the price of Instrument A and the steady rise in price of Instrument B, Instrument A is said to bear interest risk, whereas Instrument B is highly liquid. If Instrument A is bought at $t_0$ and sold at $t_1$, a loss is made on the investment, but if Instrument B is bought at time $t_0$ and sold at $t_1$, a positive rate of return will be received. Indeed, if Instrument B is bought at *any* time between issue and maturity and sold at any later time between issue and maturity, a positive rate of return will be received.

The price of no credit instrument rises as smoothly as that depicted in Figure 7.1 for Instrument B, but the securities of the United States Treasury have been found to have, on average, much less fluctuations than other securities on the market. This relatively low level of interest risk and the almost zero risk of default make United States Treasury securities highly liquid, and an ideal asset for commercial banks to have so that they might be sold to acquire funds at a moment's notice.

The United States Treasury issues credit instruments that are short term (Treasury bills), medium term (Treasury notes), and long term (Treasury bonds). The total gross public debt of the United States Treasury acquired through the issue of securities as of March 31, 1984, was $1,463.7

billion. Of this amount, Treasury bills made up $350.2 billion, Treasury notes made up $604.9 billion, Treasury bonds made up $142.6 billion, and the remainder was in nonmarketable securities. Although not the largest segment, Treasury bills make up a significant proportion, and the secondary market for Treasury bills is most active. The daily average transactions of United States government securities dealers in the secondary market for Treasury bills in, for example, the week ending February 29, 1984, was $25,033 million per day.[1]

Each credit instrument has its own primary market, in which it is initially issued, and each issue of each instrument has its own secondary market, where it is traded after its issue. Because of the extensive use of Treasury bills by the banking industry, the markets for Treasury bills will be used as an example of credit instrument market organization.

## THE PRIMARY MARKET FOR TREASURY BILLS

The primary market for Treasury bills is an auction conducted by the Federal Reserve in its role as the *fiscal agent of the government.* The Treasury announces each offering approximately one week ahead of the auction, on either Monday or Tuesday. The auction is held on Monday unless Monday is a federal holiday, in which case it is held on the previous Friday. An auction for 91-day (13-week) and 182-day (26-week) Treasury bills is held each week, but auctions for other Treasury bills are held less regularly.

Applications are taken for Treasury bills on a competitive or a noncompetitive basis. A *competitive bid* is a bid to buy a specified number of Treasury bills at a specified price. A *noncompetitive bid* is a bid to buy a specified number of Treasury bills at the average price of those sold in the competitive auction. When a competitive bid is made, the bidder is not certain whether the bid will be successful but *is* sure of the price if the bid is successful. When a noncompetitive bid is made, the bidder is certain that the bid will be successful but is not sure of the price at which the purchase will be made. Noncompetitive bids are designed for use by small investors, usually individuals and small companies (including small banks), who typically lack the expertise to make an appropriate competitive bid. There is a limit of $500,000 face value of Treasury bills that can be bought noncompetitively by any one bidder.

The par value of a Treasury bill is the amount that will be paid at maturity. The minimum par value for 91-day and 182-day Treasury bills is now $10,000, though in the past bills with denominations as low as $1000 have been issued. The minimum par value for other Treasury bills is $1000.

---

[1] "Board of Governors, the Federal Reserve System, *Federal Reserve Bulletin* (Washington D.C., April 1984), 28, 30.

No interest is stated on the face of the bill, but interest is earned by the holders. The interest is the difference between the purchase price and the maturity payment.

In the sale of Treasury bills, the Federal Reserve first subtracts the amount of the noncompetitive bids from the total amount to be sold. The remainder is then assigned to the competitive bidders in descending order of their bids. This technique assigns the bills to the highest bidder *at the price bid,* and then to the second bidder *at the price bid,* and so on until the sale is complete. This allows the Treasury to extract the highest payments that bidders are willing to pay. After the bills have been assigned to the competitive bidders, the weighted average of the accepted bids is calculated, and the noncompetitive bids are then accepted at that price.

For the auction held on Monday, January 16, 1984, the following information concerning the 91-day (13-week) Treasury bills was published in the *Wall Street Journal* the following day:

| | |
|---|---|
| Applications | $16,100,450,000 |
| Accepted bids | $6,400,590,000 |
| Accepted noncompetitively | $1,116,645,000 |
| High price (rate) | 97.781 (8.78%) |
| Average price (rate) | 97.771 (8.82%) |
| Low price (rate) | 97.765 (8.84%) |

**SELLING SHORT**

"I know this sounds like heresy, but did you ever stop to think that without federal deficits there might not be Treasury bills?"

This information is shown in Figure 7.2. The amount of the competitive sales was $5,283,945,000 and they were assigned at the prices bid, starting at a price of 97.781 percent of the maturity value and falling to a price of 97.765 percent of the maturity value. The $1,116,645,000 of noncompetitive bids were assigned at the average price of 97.771 percent of the maturity value.

In Figure 7.2, $S_T$ is the total supply of Treasury bills in the auction and $S_C$ is the amount that is sold competitively. The prices are quoted as a percentage of the face value, and for Treasury bills they are always given to three decimal places.

The rates that are published are discount rates based on a 360-day year. These rates are referred to as *Treasury bill rates,* but they should not be confused with the nominal rate of interest earned on the investment (which is also referred to as the *coupon issue yield equivalent*).

The published Treasury bill rate is calculated from this equation:

$$R_{TB} = \frac{100 - P}{100} \cdot \frac{360}{\text{Number of days to maturity}},$$

where $P$ = the price expressed as a percentage of the face value. Although the number 360 is rather cumbersome in a calculation for 91-day and 182-day instruments, it is used to make the calculations comparable to the

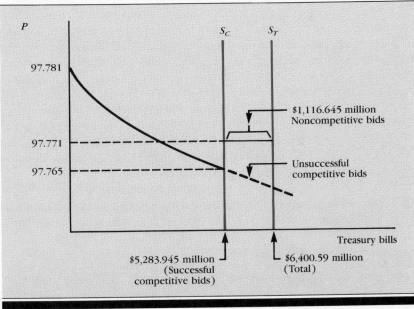

Figure 7.2
**The January 16, 1984, Auction of 91-day Treasury Bills**

published discount rates on commercial paper. Using this calculation on the example above, the Treasury bill rate on the noncompetitive bids is equal to:

$$R_{TB} = \frac{100 - 97.771}{100} \cdot \frac{360}{91} = 0.08818.$$

The nominal rate of interest (*yield*) is determined by calculating the interest payment as a percentage of the purchase price and by using a 365-day year.[2] The yield is calculated from the equation

$$R = \frac{100 - P}{P} \cdot \frac{365}{\text{Number of days to maturity}}.$$

Thus, the yield on the noncompetitive bids in our example is equal to

$$R = \frac{100 - 97.771}{97.771} \cdot \frac{365}{91} = 0.09144.[3]$$

## THE SECONDARY MARKET FOR TREASURY BILLS

The secondary market for Treasury bills operates primarily through a group of United States government security dealers. By standing ready to buy and sell Treasury bills at all times, these dealers ease the purchase and sale of Treasury bills for others by reducing the transactions costs in the market. These dealers, by organizing the secondary market, make Treasury bills shiftable and facilitate their use as short-term, highly liquid assets.

The published information on the secondary markets for Treasury bills consists of the bid and asked Treasury bill rates for currently outstanding bills. These discounts do not represent the yields to maturity of the bills but are instead a means of calculating the prices at which the bills are traded. For example, *The Wall Street Journal* for Tuesday, January 17, 1984, shows Treasury bills that were to mature on April 5, 1984, having (as of January 16, 1984) a bid rate of 8.80 percent and an asked rate of 8.74 percent. These rates mean that the Treasury bills maturing in 80 days could have been sold to a dealer at a bid discount of 1.956 percent ($^{80}/_{360}$ times 8.80 percent), or at a price of 98.044 percent of the maturity value. Also, the same bill could have been bought from a dealer at an asked discount of 1.942 percent ($^{80}/_{360}$ times 8.74), or at a price of 98.058 percent of maturity value.

The nominal interest rate on the loans can be calculated from these asked and bid prices. If a Treasury bill with 80 days left to run to maturity is

---

[2] If the 12-month period beginning on the date of issue includes the "extra day" of a leap year, this number is 366.

[3] As this particular bill was issued in a leap year, the calculation should have been made by using a 366-day year, in which case the answer would have been 9.17 percent.

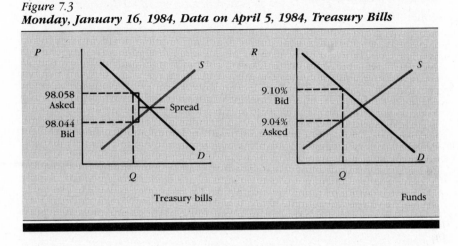

*Figure 7.3*
**Monday, January 16, 1984, Data on April 5, 1984, Treasury Bills**

purchased from a dealer at the asked price of 98.058, the yield to maturity would be:

$$R = \frac{100 - 98.058}{98.058} \cdot \frac{365}{80} = 0.0904 \text{ or } 9.04 \text{ percent.}$$

In general, if a Treasury bill is bought at a price $P_1$ and sold at price $P_2$ after having been held for $n$ days, the rate of return earned on the loan is given by:

$$R = \frac{P_2 - P_1}{P_1} \cdot \frac{365}{n}.$$

If a Treasury bill with 80 days left to maturity is sold to a dealer at a bid price of 98.044, the seller would be *giving up* a yield of:

$$R = \frac{100 - 98.044}{98.044} \cdot \frac{365}{80} = 0.0910 \text{ or } 9.10 \text{ percent.}$$

The rate of return given up by the seller is the same as the yield to maturity of the dealer who buys the bill.

The secondary market activity on January 16, 1984, for the Treasury bills maturing on April 5, 1984, is given in Figure 7.3.

## THE MARKETS FOR TREASURY NOTES AND BONDS

Although all secondary markets are basically the same, some primary markets differ from the primary market for Treasury bills. Treasury notes and bonds, like Treasury bills, are issued through the Federal Reserve, but the markets are not necessarily auctions. Treasury notes and bonds are sold by *auction,* by *exchange,* or by *subscription.* The minimum denomination for

Treasury notes is $1000, and the minimum denomination for Treasury bonds is $500. Treasury notes are offered approximately four times a year, while Treasury bonds are sold irregularly.

When Treasury notes and bonds are sold by auction, either the coupon rate is set prior to the auction so that the notes and bonds will sell close to par (close to their maturity value), or the bids are made in terms of yield to maturity, and the coupon rates are set after the bidding and the price adjusted to give the yield to maturity that was bid. In an exchange, the holders of maturing notes or bonds may exchange their securities for a new issue. Sometimes there is a choice of new issues, so that investors may choose to change the length of time to run to maturity of their debt. If investors do not wish to make the exchange, they may either sell their rights to the new issue to another investor or obtain a cash refund. The amount of the maturing issue that is paid off in cash is known as the *attrition*.

In a subscription the coupon rate is announced at least one week before the subscription takes place. Bidders then purchase them at par. Because bids usually far surpass the amount for sale, all investors are allocated the same proportion of their bid. If total bids are $q_b$ and the total offer is $q_s$, bidders receive $q_s/q_b$ of their bid.

The secondary markets for Treasury notes and bonds are run by United States government securities dealers in exactly the same way as the secondary markets for Treasury bills. The published information is, however, a little more complicated. Not only must the maturity date be published but also the coupon rate of interest. Bid and asked prices are then quoted as a percentage of the maturity value, but the rather odd practice of using the decimal places for 32nds is followed. For example, in *The Wall Street Journal* of Tuesday, January 17, 1984, there is the following information:

|  |  |  |  | bid | asked |
|---|---|---|---|---|---|
| 8⅞ s | 1984 | June | $n$ | 99.23 | 99.27 |

This means that a Treasury note ($n$) maturing in June 1984 and having a coupon rate of 8⅞ percent has a bid price of $99^{23}/_{32}$ and an asked price of $99^{27}/_{32}$. These prices are 99.71875 and 99.84375, respectively.

## CREDIT MARKET INTERACTION

Credit instruments indicate the specific characteristics of the loans that have been extended. To the extent that lenders consider loans with different characteristics as close substitutes, the markets for the credit instruments will be interdependent. The activity in one credit market will affect, and be affected by, the activity in other credit instrument markets.

For example, suppose that there is an increase in the demand for commercial paper. This will increase the price of the commercial paper and

*Figure 7.4*
**Rates on Commercial Paper, Bankers' Acceptances, and
3-Month Treasury Bills (*Monthly Averages of Daily Figures*)**

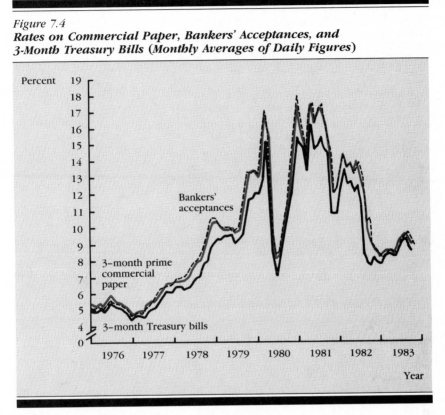

*Source:* Board of Governors. *The Federal Reserve Bulletin,* various issues.

decrease the rate of interest on the loans made in the commercial paper
market. When this happens, it is likely that some lenders in the commercial
paper market will be attracted to the Treasury bill market where interest
rates are now relatively higher. As lenders move from the commercial paper
market to the Treasury bill market, the increase in the demand for Treasury
bills will cause the price of Treasury bills to rise and the rate of interest on
the Treasury bills to fall.

The substitution that occurs between the credit instruments thus links
the credit markets together, and the interest rates are likely to move in the
same direction. The way in which the interest rates on loans in the commercial paper market move with the interest rates on loans in the Treasury bill
market can be seen clearly from Figure 7.4. Although the different characteristics of the different instruments keep the rates separated, the general
phenomenon of the rates moving together can be seen across all credit
markets.

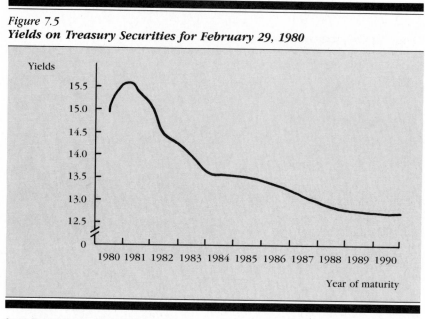

*Figure 7.5*
**Yields on Treasury Securities for February 29, 1980**

Source: *Treasury Bulletin,* March 1980: 79.

Note: The curve is fitted by eye and based only on actively traded issues.

## THE TERM STRUCTURE OF INTEREST RATES

The interaction that occurs in the various credit markets can be used to explain the *term structure of interest rates.* This is the relationship that exists between short-term and long-term interest rates in the markets for credit instruments with similar risks. If we take credit instruments that are alike in all respects except the term that is left to run to maturity, and graph the nominal rates of interest that exist at a particular point in time for the various issues, we have what is known as a *yield curve.* Perhaps the closest we can come to a group of securities that are alike in all respects except maturity is to use the securities that are issued by the United States Treasury. The yield curve for United States Treasury securities as it existed on February 29, 1980, is shown in Figure 7.5.

The yield curve in Figure 7.5 clearly shows that the nominal interest rate on securities that were to mature in one year was higher than the nominal interest rate on three-month and six-month Treasury bills, and that the nominal interest rate on all the maturities after one year declined as the length of time to maturity increased. Although this humped yield curve is not unusual, it is not the only shape that yield curves take. For example, Figure 7.6 shows the yield curve for United States Treasury securities on September 30, 1984. Here the nominal interest rates are higher for longer

*Figure 7.6*
**Yields on Securities for September 30, 1983**

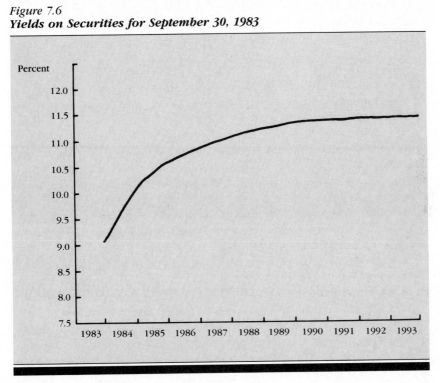

Source: *Treasury Bulletin*, Fall 1983: 31.

Note: The curve is fitted by eye and based only on actively traded issues.

maturities. The differences cannot be caused by different risks, as the United States Treasury securities all share the same risk.

Economists do not agree as to why the yield curve takes on the various shapes that it does. There are several theories of the term structure, but generally these theories hinge on the differences in the substitutability that does or does not exist between the securities with different times to run to maturity.

## The Expectations Theory

The *expectations theory* of the term structure of interest rates explains the shape of the yield curve in terms of the substitutions that investors are likely to make as they expect interest rates in the future to change.

Investors wishing to invest, say, $100 for two years have a choice of either investing for the whole two years or investing for one year and then reinvesting when the first year is over. Obviously, the rate of interest that is *expected* to be available on the reinvestment in one year's time is very important for the decision. For example, if the nominal rate of interest on two-year loans is currently 9 percent, an investment of $100 now will have a return of $118.81 in two-year's time, that is,

$$\$100(1 + 0.09)^2 = \$118.81.$$

If the nominal rate of interest on one-year loans is 8 percent, an investment of $100 now will return $108 in one-year's time,

$$\$100(1 + 0.08) = \$108.$$

If the nominal rate of interest on one-year loans *one year from now* is 10.01 percent, it would be possible to invest $100 now at 8 percent and have $108 in one-year's time that could be reinvested at 10.01 percent for another year. At the end of the two-year period, the investor who chose to invest in two separate investments of one-year's duration would have $118.81: the same as the investor who chose to invest immediately for two years at 9 percent.

If investors expect that the rate of interest for one-year loans one year from now will be 10.01 percent, they will perceive no difference between investing for two years at 9 percent, and investing for one year at 8 percent and the second year at 10.01 percent. So long as the expectation of 10.01 percent for one-year loans in one-year's time persists, there will be no change in the current rates of 8 percent and 9 percent for one- and two-year loans, respectively. These rates are shown in Figure 7.7 by the demand curves ($D_1$) and supply curves ($S_1$).

**Effect of a Change in Expected Interest Rates.**   If there is a change in the expected rates of interest, investors will perceive a difference between investing for one year twice and investing for two years. When investors are no longer indifferent, the supply and demand curves will shift, and the term structure of interest rates will change. Suppose, for example, that investors expect the yield on one-year loans to be 7 percent one year from now (perhaps because of a decline in the expected rate of increase in the general price level during the second year). In this case, the sequential purchase of two one-year loans will yield only $115.56,

$$\$100(1 + 0.08) = \$108$$

$$\$108(1 + 0.07) = \$115.56.$$

This reduction in the return from investing in one-year loans in each of the two years will cause some investors to shift to lending in the market for two-year loans. This change is shown by the supply curves ($S_2$) in Figure 7.7. Similarly, borrowers expect to repay less by sequential borrowing for two one-year periods rather than borrowing for the entire two-year period at one time. Thus, the demand for one-year loans will increase, and the

*Figure 7.7*
**Supplies and Demands for One- and Two-Year Loans**

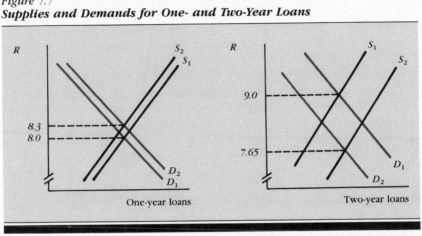

One-year loans

Two-year loans

demand for two-year loans will decrease. These changes are shown by the demand curves ($D_2$) in Figure 7.7.

The result of the change in expectations is a change in the term structure of interest rates. When the expected rate for one-year loans one year from now was 10.01 percent, the rate on one-year loans was 8 percent and the rate on two-year loans was 9 percent. Under these conditions, investors would be indifferent as to whether they invested once for two years or once for one year and then again for a second year, because either way the investment of $100 would yield $118.81. On the other hand, when the expected rate for one-year loans one year from now fell to 7 percent, the current supplies and demand for one- and two-year loans would shift until the rate on one-year loans was 8.3 percent and the rate on two-year loans was 7.65 percent. When the interest rates reached these levels, a two-year investment of $100 would yield $115.88 whether it was invested at 7.65 percent for the entire two years, or whether it was invested for the first year at 8.3 percent and the second year at 7 percent:

$$\$100(1 + 0.0765)^2 = \$115.88$$

$$\$100(1 + 0.083) = \$108.30$$

$$\$108.30(1 + 0.07) = \$115.88.$$

***Effect on Shape of Yield Curves.***  If we look only at the two types of loans that exist in our example, we started with a situation where one-year loans were at 8 percent and two-year loans were at 9 percent (and the expectation that in one-year's time the rate on one-year loans would be 10.01 percent). In this situation the yield curve (at least over one- and two-year maturities) was sloping upward to the right. When the expectations about future rates of interest changed (the rate on one-year loans one year from now fell from 10.01 percent to 7 percent), the yield curve tilted the other way, so that the rate on two-year loans was 7.65 percent and the rate on one-year loans was 8.3 percent. That is, the short-term rate rose above the longer-term rate, and the yield curve sloped downward to the right.

Based on the expectations theory, the yield curve for September 30, 1983, represented a situation like the initial one in our example, whereas the yield curve for February 29, 1980, was like the second situation in our example—when the expectation was that interest rates in the future would be lower than what had previously been thought. The expectations theory tells us that the shape of the yield curve depends on expectations about future interest rates. If the yield curve slopes upward to the right, this is a sign that investors are expecting interest rates to rise in the future. If the yield curve slopes downward to the right, this indicates that investors are expecting interest rates to fall in the future.

The expectations theory tells us that on February 29, 1980, investors were expecting interest rates to fall in the future. This may have been the result of the expectation that the rate of increase in prices was going to decrease. On the other hand, on September 30, 1983, the expectation was that interest rates were going to rise in the future. This may have been the result of the expectation that the rate of increase of prices was going to increase.

It should not be thought that the expectations theory depends on the expectations of price changes. The theory depends on the expectation of changes in future interest rates. Expectations about future changes in prices are one explanation of why interest rates might be expected to change.

## The Liquidity Premium Theory

If the expectations theory is correct, there seems to be no reason to believe that yield curves will slope upward to the right on more occasions than they slope downward to the right. It would seem that on the basis of the expectations theory, a "normal" situation would have a yield curve as a horizontal line, because it would always be equally probable that the yield curve would deviate from the normal by sloping in either direction. Empirically, however, yield curves tend to slope upward to the right on more occasions than they slope downwards. That is, yield curves tend to look like Figure 7.6 on more occasions than like Figure 7.5.

As an explanation of this, the expectations theory has been augmented by what is known as the *liquidity premium theory* of the term structure of interest. This theory maintains that the "normal" yield curve slopes upward to the right (like Figure 7.6) because a liquidity premium must be added to the yields of longer-term maturities. The theory is based on the fact that

although different securities issued by the same borrower share the same
risk of default, they do not share the same interest risk. As we have already
seen, the price of a security varies inversely with its yield. Thus, if interest
rates rise, those holding long-term securities suffer a capital loss on their
investment (the price of the securities fall). For short maturities, there is a
small chance of making a capital loss, and a small chance of making a capital
gain, but as the length to maturity increases, the risk of capital loss (or gain)
also increases. Risk averters, therefore, prefer securities with a shorter maturity. Premiums must be added to the returns on longer-term maturities to
attract the risk-averse buyers.

## The Market Segmentation Theory

Disagreement with the expectations theory of the term structure of interest
comes from those who do not believe that a great deal of substitution can
take place between securities with different maturities. The market segmentation theory is based on the fact that the securities markets are dominated
by large financial institutions that cannot easily make the kind of substitution that the expectations theory requires. In general, the large financial
institutions must match their portfolio of credit instruments to the liabilities
they hold. For example, since commercial banks have primarily short-term
liabilities, the credit instruments they purchase usually are short term; life
insurance companies, on the other hand, have longer-term liabilities and
therefore have longer-term credit instruments in their portfolios.

To the extent that the markets for securities of different maturity are
segmented, the supplies and demands for the different securities would be
capable of generating a yield curve of any shape. For example, if the Treasury increases its issue of long-term bonds, the rate of interest on those
bonds would rise. With other things remaining the same, this would twist
the yield curve so that it sloped upward to the right. On the other hand, if
the Treasury increased its issue of short-term instruments with other things
remaining the same, the short-term interest rates would rise, twisting the
yield curve so that it sloped downward to the right.

The market segmentation theory has important implications for monetary policy in any system where it is thought that interest rates influence
economic activity. If markets are indeed segmented, monetary authorities
can operate in either long-term or short-term credit markets without having
a significant impact on other credit markets. Furthermore, if it is thought
necessary to lower long-term rates, this can be done only by operations in
the long-term markets. Buying and selling in the markets for different securities also could change short-term interest rates relative to long-term interest
rates.

In 1960–1961, an attempt was made to use interest rates in this way.
Short-term interest rates were increased in an attempt to attract short-term
foreign investment into the country, and at the same time long-term interest

rates were decreased in an attempt to increase private domestic investment. In this way, it seemed possible to solve two problems at the same time. By attracting foreign investment, a persistent balance of payments problem could be alleviated, and by increasing private domestic investment, the domestic economy could be stimulated. This attempt to twist interest rates was known as *Operation Twist.* It was to be carried out as part of the Federal Reserve's monetary policy (by buying and selling securities in the secondary markets) and by the Treasury's debt management (by decreasing the issues of long-term bonds and increasing the issues of short-term instruments).

It would seem that Operation Twist would provide an excellent example from which to judge whether in fact markets are segmented. Unfortunately, the evidence is far from clear. Although the Federal Reserve's actions in the markets might be considered to have been in the spirit of the operation, the activities of the Treasury cannot. Throughout the period, the Treasury continued to increase its issues of long-term securities and was able to offset the effects that the Federal Reserve might have had. There has not been any strong evidence to support the market segmentation theory as opposed to the expectations theory, but the true situation may well contain elements of both theories.

## SUMMARY

Many credit instruments are issued by the United States Treasury. Although these securities are issued for the purpose of borrowing funds for the Treasury, the securities, once issued, are an important liquid asset in the financial system. Short-term Treasury securities are, in fact, a prominent part of the portfolio of any financial intermediary that must maintain a high level of liquidity.

The United States Treasury is able to market large amounts of securities, and this amount is greatly enhanced by the existence of well-organized secondary markets. Securities become much more attractive to investors when it is known that the securities do not have to be kept to maturity but can be sold at a moment's notice. A group of United States government security dealers, in fact, has made an active secondary market for Treasury securities. These dealers have greatly reduced the transactions costs that would otherwise have existed.

The degree of interaction between credit markets can be seen clearly in the markets for the United States Treasury securities. Because these securities only differ in their length to maturity, there is a general tendency for their interest rates to rise and fall together. However, interest rates on all Treasury securities do not rise and fall to the same extent. This gives rise to a changing term structure of interest that is depicted in a graph known as a yield curve. Yield curves are of different shapes, and there are various theories as to how these shapes might arise. The expectations theory relates the shapes to expected future interest rates. If investors expect interest rates to rise in the future, the yield curve slopes upward to the right. If investors expect interest rates to fall, the yield curve will slope downward. The market segmentation theory denies that a significant role is played by substitutions between markets for securities with different maturities. Segmented markets would mean that yield curves are predominantly the result of the supplies and demands of the securities of each maturity.

## Key Terms

liquidity                                    exchange
shiftability                                 subscription
fiscal agent of the government    attrition
competitive bid                          term structure of interest rates
noncompetitive bid                    yield curve
Treasury bill rate                       expectations theory
auction                                      market segmentation theory

## Questions

1.  The average price paid at the weekly auction of new 91-day Treasury bills is quoted as 97.000. What would be the published Treasury bill rate for this auction?

2.  A 91-day Treasury bill with 40 days left to run to maturity has an asked price quoted as 99.600 and a bid price quoted as 99.200. If someone buys this Treasury bill and keeps it to maturity, what will be the yield to maturity on the investment?

3.  Currently financial intermediaries issue six-month money market certificates that pay interest equal to the noncompetitive Treasury bill rate in the week of the issue. What is the relationship between the interest earned on the Treasury bill and the interest earned on the money market certificate?

4.  What would you expect to observe in the term structure of interest rates if the rate of inflation was expected to increase in the future? Explain.

## Additional Readings

First Boston Corporation. *Handbook of Securities of the United States Government and Federal Agencies.* Published every second year.

*This handbook gives a complete description of all securities that are issued by the federal government and its agencies.*

Lang, Richard W., and Robert H. Rasche. "Debt-Management Policy and the Own Price Elasticity of Demand for U.S. Government Notes and Bonds." *Review* 59. Federal Reserve Bank of St. Louis (September 1977): 2–7.

*A discussion of the markets for United States Treasury securities and the possible impacts on the term structure of interest rates of debt-management policy.*

Malkiel, Burton G. *The Term Structure of Interest Rates: Theory, Empirical Evidence and Application.* Silver Burdett Company, 1970. Reprinted in Thomas M. Havrilesky, and J. T. Boorman, eds. *Current Issues in Monetary Theory and Policy.* 2d ed. Arlington Heights, Ill.: AHM Publishing Corp., 1980: 395–418.

*A survey of theories advanced to explain the shape of the yield curves.*

Robbins, Sidney. *The Securities Markets: Operations and Issues.* New York: The Free Press, 1966.

*An overview of the United States securities markets, written by the former chief economist for the Special Study of Securities Markets for the Securities and Exchange Commission.*

# CHAPTER EIGHT

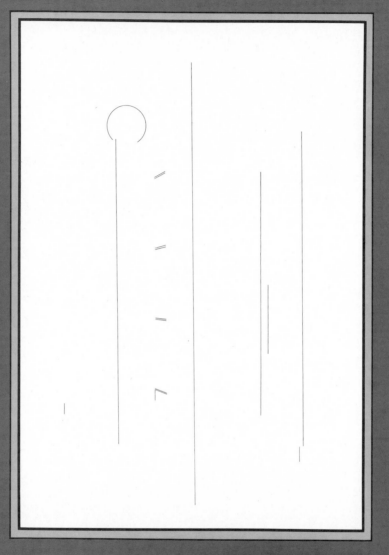

# FINANCIAL INTERMEDIATION AND
# COMMERCIAL BANKING

*Financial intermediaries are important in channeling funds throughout the economy and in the creation of money. Although recent regulatory changes have blurred the boundaries between various financial intermediaries, commercial banks remain the largest and serve as a model for the functioning of other forms of financial intermediaries.*

F inancial intermediation is commonly associated with *commercial banking.* Although many services provided by commercial banks and other financial intermediaries have their origins in the medieval moneylenders and goldsmiths of Europe (indeed, the origin of the word *bank* is thought to be the Old High German word for "moneychanger's table," *Banc*), financial intermediation as we know it is a relatively modern phenomenon. One of the first modern commercial banks was the Bank of Pennsylvania, which was established in 1780 and officially chartered by the Continental Congress as the Bank of North America in 1781. Under the direction of financier Robert Morris, this bank provided significant financial assistance during the American Revolution.

Financial intermediaries are important in the channeling of monetary assets through the economy. By bringing together funds from both small and large lenders with borrowers desiring those funds, financial intermediaries have a significant impact on the velocity of circulation of monetary assets.

Financial intermediaries also have a significant impact on the quantity of money available. As a result of their general business activity, financial intermediaries create transactions deposits, our major medium of exchange, as their liability. Transactions deposits (*demand deposits,* NOW accounts,

ATS accounts, and share draft accounts) constitute over 70 percent of the medium of exchange in the United States (M1). These deposits are transferred by means of checks or checklike instruments. Almost 90 percent of these transactions deposits are housed in commercial banks.[1] The highly liquid nature of these transactions deposit liabilities exerts a strong influence on the financial intermediary's asset portfolio. Highly liquid liabilities gives a distinct bias toward holding highly liquid assets.

## THE ROLE OF FINANCIAL INTERMEDIARIES

A *financial intermediary* is a financial institution that accepts funds from parties who desire to give up their current use, and uses these funds to make loans to (buy securities from) those who wish to acquire the current use of additional funds. The deposits accepted by a financial intermediary are direct claims against the financial intermediary and are not directly related to any of the loans extended by the intermediary. Financial intermediaries induce the deposit of funds either by the payment of interest on the deposit or by offering specific services to the depositor, such as a transferability of the funds by check. The borrowing of funds is induced by the interest rates charged and the low transactions costs of obtaining the funds. Financial intermediaries arise and continue to exist because they are able to offer a higher return net of transactions costs to lenders, and they are able to provide funds at a lower cost net of transactions costs to borrowers.

Financial intermediaries perform a function in financial transactions similar to that of dealers. They act to reduce the transactions costs associated with financial transactions. Unlike the typical dealer, however, financial intermediaries offer deposit liabilities directly against themselves. This significantly reduces the risk to the lender from capital losses resulting from interest rate changes. The diversified portfolio of assets for the financial intermediary also reduces the risk to the lender resulting from loan defaults. In addition, financial intermediaries serve to ease the problem of matching the terms to maturity desired by borrowers and lenders.

As was pointed out in Chapter 6, the matching of the terms to maturity desired by borrowers and lenders is facilitated by the existence of developed secondary markets for credit instruments. A lender is not locked into forgoing the use of the funds until the credit instrument matures, providing that the credit instrument can be resold before its maturity. However, this buying and selling is not costless. To resell the credit instrument, a lender must incur some transactions costs. Since the loan would be tied to a specific credit instrument, the lender is exposed to the *interest risk* of a capital loss or gain should interest rates change during the period that the instru-

---

[1] Board of Governors, the Federal Reserve System, *Federal Reserve Bulletin* (Washington D.C., December 1983),Tables 1.21 and 1.25.

ment is held. Also, with a specific credit instrument, the lender is directly exposed to the *risk of default* in payment by the borrower.

The problems of lending and borrowing in the credit instrument markets are significantly reduced with the use of financial intermediaries. If deposits are made in financial intermediaries instead of the funds being loaned out directly in the credit instrument markets, these deposits can have vastly different conditions attached to them that would not otherwise be available. Some deposits are payable on demand; others have a contracted time period, but the funds may be withdrawn if the depositor pays a penalty. However, whatever conditions are imposed on the deposits, the deposits usually have shorter terms to maturity than the average life of the assets owned by the intermediary.

Financial intermediaries are able to make loans of a longer term than the average term of their liabilities by relying on their ability to predict the behavior of a large set of depositors. Although it is extremely difficult to predict the behavior of one depositor, it is less difficult to predict the behavior of the total deposit liabilities of a financial intermediary. Withdrawal from one account may be offset by deposits in another account, so the total liabilities of the intermediary are more stable than the account of an individual depositor.

By placing their funds into financial intermediaries rather than directly into financial markets, depositors gain in three ways. First, depositors have ease of withdrawal. The funds can be placed in accounts having ready access without substantial penalties. Second, the depositor can be insulated from interest risk by acquiring a deposit with a fixed dollar value (plus interest). This avoids a potential capital loss should interest rates unexpectedly rise. Third, the deposit claims are against the financial intermediary, not one credit instrument. This provides effective diversification and insulation from default risk.

## Financial Intermediation as a Business

Financial intermediation is a business undertaken for profit. If rewards from other activities with the same risk were expected to exceed those from financial intermediation, the forces of the market would induce the owners to engage in those other activities. Though we may think of financial intermediaries only as the industry housing transactions deposits and providing many of the means of exchange, they see themselves differently. They are in the financial intermediation business: accepting deposits, extending loans, and buying securities.

Like other industries, financial intermediaries are multiproduct firms. Apart from providing much of the medium of exchange and acting as an intermediary in financial markets, they provide many related services. Some of these related services provided by commercial banks are listed in Table 8.1.

---

*Table 8.1*
### Some Bank-Related Services Provided by Commercial Banks

| | |
|---|---|
| Credit cards | Payroll accounting services |
| Safe-deposit boxes | Bill collection |
| Wire transfer of funds | Portfolio management of trust accounts |
| Equipment leasing | Access to small bills and coins |
| Traveler's checks | Underwriting and distributing municipal securities |
| Foreign exchange | Financial advice |
| Cash management | Cash concentration |
| Foreign checks | Preauthorized drafts |
| Data processing | Credit investigation |
| Discount brokerage services | |

---

These financial intermediation–related services are provided to contribute to overall profitability. The service may directly generate income through fees charged or provide an incentive to utilize deposit or other services. Traveler's checks may, for example, be provided "free" to depositors with some minimum balance. This provides income in kind rather than an explicit part of the dollar interest payment on deposits.

Deregulation of interest rate ceilings on deposits has moved financial intermediaries away from providing "free" services toward provision on a fee basis. The various services provided by financial intermediaries, along with associated charges, are one form of competition between these financial institutions.

## THE FUNDAMENTAL PROBLEM OF FINANCIAL INTERMEDIATION

*The fundamental problem of financial intermediation* is to arrange the assets and liabilities of the financial intermediary in such a way as to achieve an optimal trade-off between profitability, liquidity, and safety within the legal constraints imposed by regulatory agencies. The concerns over profitability, liquidity, and safety are interrelated in the decisions of the financial intermediary's manager. Actions to increase profitability are likely to increase risk and decrease liquidity, and actions to increase safety and increase liquidity are likely to decrease profitability. An optimal balance must be found between profitability on one hand and liquidity and safety on the other.

*Profitability* relates to the rate of return or the expected rate of return earned for the financial intermediary's owners. It is essential to the continued operation of the financial intermediary. Without sufficient earnings relative to the amount invested by the owners, the owners will move into a more profitable alternative. Profits also can be used to add to equity capital

through retained earnings. The financial concern's equity capital provides a measure of safety by serving as a cushion against failure from loan losses or any other loss.

For a financial intermediary to continue in operation, the depositors must consider its *safety* as a storehouse for their funds. Otherwise, the depositors will take their funds elsewhere. Although the financial intermediary's equity capital helps promote the safety of the firm, the asset portfolio also is important. Financial intermediaries generally carry a high ratio of liabilities to equity capital. Commercial banks, for example, on average have liabilities equal to about 12 times the bank's capital. Thus, financial intermediaries must maintain low risk in their asset portfolios such that the small proportion of capital is expected to be sufficient to cover even unanticipated losses. This low risk in assets to promote safety is not simply a matter of having minimal risk of default on loans, although obviously when an intermediary makes a loan it does so expecting to receive interest payments and the principal at maturity. Financial intermediaries also must face only limited exposure to interest risk. While the capital gains realized in the financial intermediary's portfolio when interest rates fall help to improve profitability, there is risk and threat to safety of a capital loss when interest rates rise. The impact of interest risk on safety binds the concerns over safety and liquidity together.

*Liquidity* is defined as the ability to sell an asset immediately for cash without taking a capital loss. Liquidity adds to the safety of the financial intermediary by limiting interest risk. Also, as long as depositors are able to withdraw their funds readily, depositors will generally consider the financial intermediary a safe storehouse. A liquid portfolio enables the concern to obtain the funds to satisfy depositors' desires for withdrawals.

Liquidity and safety together determine the *solvency* of the financial intermediary. If there is a high probability of insolvency and failure, the intermediary would not be considered safe. Liquidity tends to promote solvency.

Solvency has two distinct aspects: legal solvency and the ability to pay bills on time. Both are concerns of all business firms. Legal solvency occurs when a firm has assets with a value greater than or equal to the value of its liabilities. A financial intermediary is *legally solvent* when it has sufficient assets, given enough time, to pay off the concern's liabilities. However, a firm can be legally solvent and, without sufficient liquidity, be technically insolvent. A firm is *technically insolvent* when it is unable to pay its bills on time. Although a general business firm may be able to continue operating for a short time by putting off some payments, the problem of technical solvency is more acute for a financial intermediary. A financial intermediary that houses transactions types of accounts must have sufficient liquidity to be able to pay cash on demand to depositors who wish to make withdrawals from demand deposits, NOW accounts, ATS accounts, and (for credit unions) share draft accounts. To remain technically solvent, a financial intermediary that houses transactions accounts must arrange its portfolio so that it will always have cash on hand and highly liquid assets that can be sold whenever the cash is depleted.

A financial intermediary can be legally solvent without being technically solvent and technically solvent without being legally solvent. In fact, during the Great Depression of the 1930s, many banks failed because they were technically insolvent even though they remained legally solvent. Also, it should be noted that accounting practice permits financial intermediaries to list their assets at book or par, rather than market, value. Thus, a financial intermediary can be legally solvent with regard to its recorded accounts, yet be insolvent at market values.

## The Role of the Commercial Bank

Commercial banks constitute the largest single group of financial intermediaries, swamping any other group in comparison. In mid-1983, all U.S. domestically chartered commercial banks had total assets over two and one half times those of the next largest group, the savings and loan associations.

Historically, commercial banks were unique as the financial institutions with deposit liabilities that were payable on demand and assets consisting of loans to commercial enterprises. Indeed, these two aspects are often used to define a commercial bank. Recent financial innovations and regulatory changes have removed this distinction.

Following the financial innovation of new interest-bearing transactions deposits in the 1970s, the Depository Institutions Deregulation and Monetary Control Act of 1980 authorized nationwide use of NOW accounts, ATS accounts, and credit union share draft accounts. Housed primarily in commercial banks, these other checkable accounts are also available in the thrift institutions. Other checkable deposits are payable on demand, considered as part of the medium of exchange, and included in the definition of the money supply M1. This regulatory change removed the unique transactions-deposit-housing distinction historically held by commercial banks.

The Garn–St. Germain Depository Institutions Act of 1982 further blurred the distinction between commercial banks and the thrift institutions by authorizing federally chartered savings and loan associations to make commercial and consumer loans. Historical regulatory boundaries between groups of financial intermediaries have been blurred. The distinction between financial intermediaries now rests primarily with the selection of a regulatory and supervisory agency. A *commercial bank* has become, simply, a financial intermediary chartered to operate as a commercial bank.

Regulatory constraints on portfolio selection differ between groups of financial intermediaries. For example, federally chartered *savings and loan associations (S&Ls)* are permitted to invest only up to 55 percent of their assets in commercial loans and the majority of these loans must be secured by commercial real estate (real estate lending being the S&Ls' historical territory). The Garn–St. Germain Act of 1982 also permits the federally chartered S&L to invest up to 30 percent of their assets in consumer loans. Commercial banks face fewer restrictions on asset choice. However, they are subject to many other regulatory constraints. (Regulation of commercial banking is discussed in Chapter 10.)

Besides regulated differences, financial intermediaries differ in their relative expertise and tend to specialize in specific financial markets. This specialization leads to differences in the financial intermediaries' portfolios and to somewhat different solutions to the fundamental problem of financial intermediation.

The commercial bank serves as a model for the analysis of the general activities of the financial intermediaries that operate between lenders and borrowers. An examination of the assets, liabilities, and capital account for a commercial bank gives a general overview of the types of portfolios selected by all financial intermediaries accepting transactions deposits and the uses to which the major forms of assets and liabilities are put. The major differences in portfolio composition of other large groups of financial intermediaries are given in Chapter 11.

## COMMERCIAL BANK ASSETS

The assets of a financial intermediary are determined largely by the nature of its liabilities. The liabilities are, of course, the source of almost all the funds a commercial bank has to purchase assets. The short-term nature of transactions deposits forces the bank into holding a large amount of highly liquid assets. The specific assets selected by a commercial bank are the result of how it chooses to solve the fundamental problem of financial inter-mediation, and it is also the result of many restrictions and regulations imposed on the banking industry. For example, commercial banks in the United States are restricted from holding equity instruments, such as corporate stocks, except as temporary holdings of stock that were posted as collateral for defaulted loans. With the high probability of substantial changes in the value of equity instruments, it is doubtful whether banks would invest significantly in equity in any case. Because the liabilities of banks maintain their nominal dollar value, the banks must choose assets that tend to retain their nominal dollar value also. This is much more likely to be the case with debt instruments than with equity instruments. The assets of banks consist primarily of debt instruments as bank investments or securities or as the debt instruments (generally nonnegotiable) associated with the extension of direct loans.

Within the allowable set of assets, commercial banks acquire a highly diversified portfolio. Each asset generates earnings from different sources in the economy, but each is held with a view to the general level of liquidity and safety of the whole portfolio. Table 8.2 shows the assets selected by the 14,799 domestically chartered commercial banks as of November 1983. This selection does not necessarily indicate the optimal asset portfolio for any one bank. With different local market conditions and different expertise of bank managers, the composition of assets among commercial banks varies widely. However, Table 8.2 does show the relative proportion of the various assets acquired by the banks in business at the time.

### *Cash Items*

Cash items consist of currency and coin (also called vault cash), deposits with Federal Reserve District Banks, deposits at other banks, and cash items (mainly checks) in process of collection. These cash items are the most liquid assets of commercial banks and are important for a bank's technical solvency. Even though these cash items generally do not generate explicit interest earnings, they do provide for a bank's earnings by enabling it to remain in business. A bank can remain in business only so long as it can pay cash on demand for demand deposit withdrawals. Some cash items also are used to satisfy governmentally imposed reserve requirements.

*Currency and Coin.* Currency and coin are held to enable the bank to pay cash on demand and also to provide its customers with access to small

8 FINANCIAL INTERMEDIATION AND COMMERCIAL BANKING

*Table 8.2*
**Assets of all Domestically Chartered Commercial Banks November 1983**

| Assets | Billions of Dollars | Percentage of Total Assets |
|---|---|---|
| **Cash items** | | 179.8 | 9.2 |
| Currency and coin | 22.3 | |
| Reserves with Federal Reserve banks | 17.6 | |
| Balances with depository institutions | 70.9 | |
| Cash items in process of collection | 69.0 | |
| **Total securities** | | 426.8 | 22.0 |
| U.S. Treasury | 180.4 | |
| Other securities | 246.4 | |
| **Loans (excluding interbank)** | | 1,075.5 | 55.3 |
| Commercial and industrial | 372.8 | |
| Other | 702.7 | |
| **Other assets** | | 261.9 | 13.5 |
| **Total assets** | | 1,944.0 | |

*Source:* Board of Governors, the Federal Reserve System, *Federal Reserve Bulletin* (Washington, D.C., December 1983), Table 1.25.

bills and change. Prudent business practice dictates that banks always have some currency and coin available. If a bank's customers and depositors find themselves unable to obtain their desired amounts and the desired composition of currency and coin, they will take their banking business elsewhere. Banks have found by trial and error exactly how much cash is necessary to have on hand. In normal circumstances, this has proved to be a relatively low percentage of demand deposits held. The Federal Reserve allows the vault cash held by commercial banks to be counted in satisfying reserve requirements.

***Reserves with Federal Reserve Banks.*** Reserves with Federal Reserve Banks are the deposits of commercial banks with Federal Reserve District Banks. They are used to facilitate the transfer of funds from one bank to another, and the Federal Reserve uses them in monetary control. The deposits are available for withdrawal in cash for use in satisfying the commercial bank's customers' desires for currency and coin. These deposits also are used for making payments on checks being cleared. When you deposit funds represented by a check, your bank may receive payment on that check through a transfer of deposits held with Federal Reserve District Banks. Reserves with Federal Reserve Banks are also bought and sold on the federal funds market as short-term borrowing and lending.

Commercial banks are subject to governmentally imposed reserve requirements. These requirements stipulate that a determinable amount of specific assets be held as reserves. A bank's *primary reserves* are the bank's holdings of those cash items that can be used to satisfy the reserve requirement. To satisfy reserve requirements, a bank must arrange its asset portfolio such that its holdings of primary reserves are equal to or exceed the amount of required reserves. The Federal Reserve allows a bank's vault cash and reserves held with Federal Reserve Banks to be used in satisfying reserve requirements. By increasing the amount of reserves that must be held by the banks, the Federal Reserve can reduce the amount that commercial banks can lend and, thereby, influence monetary conditions.

Historically, reserves with Federal Reserve District Banks have been required only of banks that are members of the Federal Reserve system, though nonmember banks could choose to hold deposits at the Federal Reserve for direct check clearing with member banks or to acquire direct access to the federal funds market. The Depository Institutions Deregulation and Monetary Control Act of 1980 (The Monetary Control Act) extended the Federal Reserve's reserve requirements to cover all depository institutions (member and nonmember banks plus the thrift institutions). The central housing of funds from various financial institutions facilitates the transfer of funds between a broader range of financial markets.

***Balances at Other Banks.*** Mostly, balances at other banks arise from *correspondent banking* relationships. Usually, small banks will hold deposits at larger banks or at banks in money market centers, such as New York and Chicago, in exchange for certain services. These services include check clearance, securities transactions, access to the federal funds market, and financial advice. Correspondent balances are also held among local banks for check clearance.

The Monetary Control Act has expanded the role of balances at other banks. Institutions that are nonmembers of the Federal Reserve may satisfy their reserve requirements with deposits held on a pass-through basis at approved financial institutions.

***Cash Items in Process of Collection.*** Cash items in process of collection mainly represent the value of the checks that have been presented for deposit into customer accounts but on which the bank has not yet been paid. When a check is deposited in a bank, the amount is listed as a cash item in the process of collection until the funds are transferred into the reserves of the receiving bank, until cash payment is received, or until the funds are transferred into the bank's deposits at another bank.

The cash items in a commercial bank's asset portfolio are necessary to keep the bank operating. Cash must be available for payment on withdrawals, primary reserves must be held so that the bank can satisfy legal reserve requirements, and the other cash items are necessary to provide the services associated with transactions deposits, such as check clearance.

## Security Holdings and Loans

To remain in business, a bank must generate sufficient earnings to prevent the owners from shifting into another business. The bank's securities and loan portfolios provide for these earnings, with the bulk of the income coming from the direct loans extended. A breakdown of security holdings and loans for large commercial banks is given in Table 8.3.

### Federal Funds Sold and Security Resale Agreements.

The federal funds market and the market for security resale and repurchase agreements are closely related in short-term financing for financial intermediaries. Both markets are short term, have relatively low transactions costs, and appear on both the asset side and the liability side of commercial banks' portfolios. As an asset they are a highly liquid, short-term source of interest earnings. As a liability, federal funds bought and repurchase agreements are a valuable source of short-term borrowings.

*Federal funds* are short-term, generally overnight, borrowings and lendings between financial institutions. Although the market is not restricted to these assets, the funds generally traded on the federal funds market are reserves held with Federal Reserve District Banks. The terminology used in this market is *federal funds bought or sold,* even though the banks are in essence borrowing or lending funds. The bought and sold terminology is the result of a 1963 ruling of the Comptroller of the Currency. As purchases and sales rather than borrowing and lending, the legal limitations (15 percent of bank capital) on borrowing and lending from one entity are not violated. Federal funds transactions are usually unsecured, overnight loans made in large units. Although some trading is done in smaller units, the most common unit is $1 million. As an overnight market, the interest rate in this market *(the federal funds rate)* is highly volatile and serves as an indicator of monetary conditions.

*Security resale agreements* are closely related to federal funds sold. A resale agreement is the purchase of a security with a contract to resell the security at a specific date. This gives the commercial bank short-term interest earnings that are tied to temporary ownership of a security, yet avoids the costs of reentering the secondary market for the security. The resale agreements usually are tied to United States government securities and are one reason for commercial bank holdings of these securities.

Table 8.3
**Asset Distribution of Large Commercial Banks (Domestic Assets over $750 Million) October 26, 1983**

| Account | Millions of Dollars | Percentage of Total Assets |
|---|---|---|
| Cash items | | 83,606 | 9.1 |
| Federal Funds sold and security resale agreements | | 41,452 | 4.5 |
|   to commercial banks | 29,380 | | |
|   to nonbank brokers and security dealers | 9,062 | | |
|   to others | 3,010 | | |
| **Securities** | | 139,889 | 15.3 |
| U.S. government | 56,029 | | |
| Other | 83,860 | | |
| **Other loans** | | 512,145 | |
| Commercial and industrial | 215,064 | | 23.5 |
| Real estate | 139,324 | | 15.2 |
|   to individuals for personal expenditures | 81,524 | | 8.9 |
|   to financial institutions | | | |
|     commercial banks in U.S. | 7,491 | | .8 |
|     banks in foreign countries | 8,555 | | .9 |
|     sales finance, personal finance companies | 9,126 | | 1.0 |
|     other financial institutions | 15,220 | | 1.7 |
|   to nonbank brokers and security dealers | 9,384 | | 1.0 |
|   to others for purchasing and carrying securities | 3,225 | | .4 |
|   to finance agricultural production | 7,306 | | .8 |
|   all other | 15,926 | | 1.7 |
| **Other assets** | | 137,931 | 15.1 |
| **Total assets** | | 915,023 | |

Source: Board of Governors, the Federal Reserve System, Federal Reserve Bulletin (Washington D.C., December 1983), Table 1.26.

**Securities.**   Commercial banks hold various types of securities for their interest earnings and for their high degree of liquidity. These securities dominate a bank's secondary reserves. *Secondary reserves* are those highly liquid, short-term assets that can be sold immediately for cash. Secondary reserves are useful for replenishing depleted primary reserves and, by being highly liquid, promote technical solvency for the bank. The assets included in secondary reserves are holdings of United States Treasury securities, state and local securities, federal funds sold and security resale agreements, call loans to brokers and dealers, and the cash item—demand balances at other depository institutions.

The remainder of the security portfolio not included in secondary reserves is the bank's investment portfolio. These financial investments generally are longer-term assets and are held for their interest earnings as well as their marketability. The securities held are similar to the extension of loans by banks. They are indirect loans made on credit markets, usually on negotiable credit instruments.

*United States government securities* held by commercial banks have declined dramatically over the past 20 years. Holdings of these securities have declined from about 24 percent of assets in 1960 to about 13 percent of assets by 1970 to about 6 percent of assets in the 1980s. The shift out of U.S. government securities is due primarily to the development of alternative short-term assets, such as *federal funds*.

Other than the normal considerations of liquidity, profitability, and safety, commercial banks hold government securities as collateral for government deposits. The United States Treasury has a *pledging* requirement that banks hold government securities (plus deposit insurance) equal to the amount of Treasury deposits in the bank. United States government securities are also held for use in *repurchase agreements*.

*Other securities* in commercial bank portfolios include state and political subdivision securities, corporate bonds, and some stock. Almost 70 percent of the other securities are from state and political subdivisions. These securities are held both as secondary reserves and for their tax-exempt interest earnings. The development of secondary markets for municipal securities has made them increasingly liquid, and their use by commercial banks has increased dramatically. State and local securities amounted to only 3.4 percent of commercial bank assets in 1947 but had risen to 10 percent in the late 1970s.

In the United States, commercial banks are severely restricted in their holdings of equity instruments. Member banks of the Federal Reserve System own and hold stock in the Federal Reserve. This stock ownership, however, is divorced from control over the system. In addition, commercial banks are permitted to hold stock in subsidiary corporations engaged in banking-related business, such as Edge Act and Agreement corporations. Holdings of other corporate stock are restricted to the temporary holding of stock received in loan defaults.

*Other loans* are the bank's primary source of income. These are the direct loans extended to the bank's customers. Loans constitute over half of the asset portfolio.

Bank loans generally are associated with nonnegotiable credit instruments and are a relatively illiquid part of the bank's asset structure. Occa-

"I could literally double my income with a 20-foot ladder."

sionally, commercial bank loans are marketed, but when they are, it is generally without the knowledge of the borrower. Interest payments and repayment of the principal will be made to the institution that originally made the loan. In this way, commercial banks can adjust their asset portfolios through the sale or purchase of loans on secondary markets. The specific structure of commercial banks' loan portfolios varies widely and is largely determined by local market conditions. For example, commercial banks in rural areas generally hold a larger proportion of loans to farmers than do urban commercial banks.

*Commercial and industrial loans* traditionally have constituted the largest single group of commercial bank loans. These loans may be short term to finance the production of goods and services or longer term to finance a business firm's capital outlays. Short-term loans are an important source for a business firm's working capital. In addition to receiving the interest income from the commercial loans, the commercial bank also may house the business firm's demand deposits. This gives the bank an additional source of funds that can be used to extend additional loans.

Although banks generally extend short-term loans to match the short-term nature of their liabilities, commercial banks also hold a sizable amount of long-term *real estate* loans extending in term to maturity of upward to 30 years. The growth in longer-term time and savings deposits has in part contributed to the activity in the longer-term markets. A commercial bank may issue more real estate loans than it intends to hold in its portfolio. These loans are then packaged and sold on the secondary market, perhaps to the Federal National Mortgage Association (FNMA). The bank will then earn a fee for processing the loan payments for the term to maturity of the loan.

Consumer loans and other loans to *individuals* also are becoming increasingly important in commercial bank portfolios. In addition to the traditional loans to finance automobiles, mobile homes, and home improvements, there has been an increase in bank credit card loans. On the credit card loans, the commercial bank receives a processing fee in addition to any interest earnings. *Farm loans* generally are seasonal in nature and are issued to finance planting and harvesting. Loans on *security purchases* are restricted by Regulations G, T, and U of the Federal Reserve. These regulations impose margin requirements that allow the bank to finance only 50 percent of the security purchase. Commercial banks also hold a significant amount of loans extended to other *financial institutions,* both domestically and in foreign countries, in their highly diversified loan portfolios.

## COMMERCIAL BANK LIABILITIES

The primary source of funds that enables a commercial bank to earn income by making loans and acquiring other assets is the bank's deposit liabilities. The deposit liabilities of commercial banks are assets of individuals, business firms, and governments, and are held by these parties as assets because the commercial bank offers yields on them in the form of explicit interest payments or in services rendered. The profitability of a commercial bank relates as much to the costs of borrowed funds as it does to the earnings on the bank's asset portfolio. In addition to affecting the bank's profitability, the sources of liabilities affect the liquidity of the bank. Well-developed markets for short-term borrowing, such as the federal funds market, in addition to the bank's highly liquid assets serve as an additional source for cash items.

A commercial bank creates its deposit liabilities when it receives the deposit of an asset, usually in the form of cash or other reserves. Although most of the bank's liabilities are deposits of one kind or another, the holders of these deposits usually do not think of themselves as lending money to the bank. The bank, in fact, is borrowing the funds from the depositors for varying lengths of time. Commercial banks play an active role in attracting deposits, to the extent that a bank can be considered to be managing its liabilities almost to the same extent that it manages its assets. The basic

**Table 8.4**
**Liabilities of all Domestically Chartered Commercial Banks, November 1983**

| Liabilities and Capital Accounts | Billions of Dollars | Percentage of Total Liabilities and Capital |
|---|---|---|
| Deposits | 1,459.2 | |
| Demand deposits | 358.1 | 18.4 |
| Savings deposits | 458.3 | 23.6 |
| Time deposits | 642.8 | 33.1 |
| Borrowings | 219.7 | 11.3 |
| Other liabilities | 112.6 | 5.8 |
| Total liabilities | 1,791.5 | |
| Capital account (Residual assets less liabilities) | 152.5 | 7.8 |
| Total liabilities and capital accounts | 1,944.0 | |

*Source:* Board of Governors, the Federal Reserve System, *Federal Reserve Bulletin* (Washington D.C., December 1983), Table 1.25.

composition of commercial bank liabilities is shown in Table 8.4, which represents the liabilities side of the portfolio whose assets are shown in Table 8.2.

## Demand Deposits

As their name implies, demand deposits are deposits that are payable on demand. These accounts include the other checkable deposits, NOW, ATS, and Super NOW accounts. It is the potential for instant withdrawal from these transactions accounts that causes banks to choose such highly liquid portfolios. The primary holders of these accounts are individuals and business firms, though some are held by governments and their agencies.

The incentive to hold these accounts rests primarily with the services rendered. Banks have been prohibited from paying interest on demand deposits since the Bank Acts of 1933 and 1935. The 1970s innovations in deposit banking created transactions deposits that offer explicit interest payments. NOW and ATS deposits are currently restricted to a maximum interest rate of 5¼ percent. Super NOW accounts are not subject to interest-rate ceilings but require a minimum $1000 balance.

Demand and other checkable deposits are a significant part of the medium of exchange. These deposits provide their owners with the ability to transfer funds by means of checks, a system that has the added advantage of offering protection from theft and a record of the transactions made.

Although this source of funds is not directly managed by banks, changes in the services provided, interest paid (especially on the Super NOW deposits), or charges made for the use of checks do attract or reduce deposits.

In addition to creating demand deposits upon receipt of a deposit, banks generally extend loans by creating a demand deposit for the borrower. Of course, the newly created deposit usually is withdrawn as the borrower uses the funds. Prior to the development of deposits, commercial banks created bank notes as explained in "Bank Notes and Deposits," page 180.

Demand deposits of *individuals and business firms* are held for their convenience in making payments. In addition, business firms often hold demand deposits as *compensating balances* for services they receive, such as payroll services, availability of lines of credit, and cash management. Compensating balances also are a technique used by banks to obtain security on a loan and also to adjust the effective interest rate charged for the loan. On a one-year loan of $10,000 at 15 percent, the repayment due is the $10,000 principal and $1500 interest. If the bank required a compensating balance of $500, the firm would only have the use of $9500. The interest payment of $1500 would represent approximately 15.8 percent on the funds used ($1500/$9500 = 0.158).

In addition to the deposits of state and political subdivisions, other government agencies, other commercial banks, and foreign institutions, commercial banks hold deposits for the United States Treasury. The Treasury holds these deposits in interest-bearing tax and loan note accounts. Government expenditures are not made from these accounts. To make expenditures, the funds are transferred by call to the United States Treasury's deposits in the Federal Reserve District Banks. These deposits arise in commercial banks as the result of the normal payment of taxes and payment for purchases of government securities. The funds then are generally transferred from individual deposits into the Treasury's deposits at the same bank. The authorized banks then have the choice of retaining the deposits in the form of interest-bearing obligations or may remit them directly to the Federal Reserve District Banks. This procedure was adopted to minimize the impact of the Treasury on the availability of funds in local markets and to spread the Treasury's funds throughout the banking system so that no particular private bank serves as "the government's bank." With the transfer of funds between private deposits and the Treasury's deposits in the same bank, the funds remain available to the bank for the extension of loans.

## Savings Deposits

Savings deposits are longer-term deposits of a commercial bank. These deposits include passbook savings accounts and money market deposit accounts. The deposits are less liquid than transactions deposits, and they bear interest.

## BANK NOTES AND DEPOSITS

At the end of 1980, demand deposits accounted for approximately 65 percent of the circulating medium of exchange (M1), or the public held approximately $2.30 in demand deposits in commercial banks for every $1 they held in currency. This widespread use of deposits is, however, a relatively recent phenomenon. In 1853, for example, bank notes in circulation amounted to $146 million, while bank deposits amounted to $145.5 million.[1]

Historically, commercial banks operated by extending loans in the form of bank notes. These bank notes were issued by the banks themselves. Upon presentation to the bank of issue, the notes could be exchanged for *specie* (gold or silver). While deposits were accepted by banks, loans were typically not issued as deposits, and the transfer of funds by check was not common. The use of checks gradually developed in the mid-1800s. The first fully fledged clearinghouse that provided for check clearing, as well as for the clearing of bank notes, was established in New York in 1853.

A significant incentive for the shift from circulating paper to the use of deposits occurred in the 1860s. The National Bank Act of 1864 as amended in 1865 provided for a national cur-

A *passbook savings account* has no stipulated date of maturity. Funds may be deposited into the account at any time, and (subject to the bank's decision on whether or not to require prior notice for a withdrawal) funds may be withdrawn at any time. Small withdrawals from savings accounts are usually paid on demand. These accounts are primarily held by individuals and nonprofit concerns. Firms in business for profit are restricted to holding no more than $150,000 in savings accounts in any one bank.

Commercial banks have actively competed for savings deposits by offering interest payments and services such as "free" safe-deposit boxes or "free" traveler's checks when deposits exceed a certain minimum. The Depository Institutions Deregulation Act of 1980 is phasing out interest rate ceilings. With higher interest-earning accounts available, passbook savings deposits have declined dramatically.

*Money market deposit accounts* were authorized by the Garn–St. Germain Depository Institutions Act. These accounts were devised to

rency. The National Banks (those chartered by the Comptroller of the Currency) were permitted to issue national bank notes that had been printed for them by the Treasury, provided that they also purchased United States government securities. The circulation of bank notes issued by the other banks (the state banks) was halted by the imposition of a 10 percent tax on the amount of state bank notes paid out by any bank.

The intent of the National Bank Act and of the 10 percent tax was to cause banks to apply for federal charters as National Banks. Although the initial effect was to cause banks to shift over to being National Banks, this did not continue. State banks continued in operation and were able to flourish by adjusting to the use of demand deposits rather than note issue. In 1867, currency in circulation amounted to $585 million, and the total amount of deposits amounted to $729 million. By 1877 deposits had grown to $1166 million, and the amount of currency had dropped to $514 million.[2]

---

[1] Redlich, Fritz. *The Molding of American Banking, Part 2, 1840–1910* (New York: Hafner Publishing Co. Inc., 1951): 7.

[2] Friedman, Milton and Schwartz, Anna J. *A Monetary History of the United States, 1867–1960*. NBER study (Princeton University Press, 1963), Table A-1: 704.

allow banks and thrift institutions to compete with the money market mutual funds. Interest paid on these deposits is market-determined. They are not subject to maximum interest rate ceilings unless the average monthly balance falls below $1000 (in which case they are subject to the NOW account ceiling). The rate of interest on these deposits may not be guaranteed for a period longer than one month. Although, as with savings accounts, withdrawals are usually paid on demand, the depository institution must reserve the right to require seven days notice before withdrawals.

Money market deposit accounts have limited transaction account features. The account permits the depositor six preauthorized, telephone, or automatic transfers per month of which three may be by check. Personal withdrawals are unrestricted. The limitations on transactions features makes these accounts closer to savings deposits. Both of these deposits are not considered as part of the means of exchange (M1) but are counted as part of the broader definition of the money supply, M2.

## Time Deposits

*Time deposits* are interest-bearing accounts that have specific dates of maturity ranging upward from seven days. An *open account time deposit* allows the depositor to make additional deposits at any time before maturity, but the time of withdrawal is fixed. Most of these accounts are Holiday Funds, Christmas Clubs, and the like. In a *time certificate of deposit (CD),* the funds are placed in the account at a specific time and are withdrawn at a specific time. These certificates are either negotiable or nonnegotiable. By issuing these certificates, the banks have contracted for the use of the funds for a specific time period.

The 1970s saw the development of a wide range of nonnegotiable time certificates of deposit, including six-month deposits with interest tied to the noncompetitive six-month Treasury Bill rate and 2½ year deposits with interest tied to the rate on Treasury notes. Like savings deposits, time deposits were subject to interest-rate ceilings. The development of this range of certificate accounts was the initial move to allow market adjustment of interest rates on deposits. The Monetary Control Act of 1980 provided for a phase-out of these interest-rate ceilings through 1986. Time deposits issued for more than 31 days to maturity or over 7 days to maturity with $1000 average balance or more currently have no restriction on the maximum interest rate payable. The interest rates paid on these deposits are now determined by market conditions.

Large negotiable certificates of deposit, issued in amounts of $100,000 or more, have become a significant source of deposit funds for banks. The market for these deposits is nationwide and can easily be acquired by altering the interest rate offered. Large negotiable time deposits have been the commercial banks' main access to corporate funds since the early 1960s. These deposits have been free of interest-rate ceilings since the early 1970s.[2]

## Borrowings

Borrowings are important for commercial banks in their portfolio management. These liabilities allow banks access to funds on a national or worldwide market. *Federal funds purchased* and securities sold under *repurchase agreement* are simply the liabilities side of the federal funds and repurchase-resale market. These are short-term funds borrowed by commercial banks, although some banks, especially larger ones, use these markets as a continual source of funds over longer periods of time. Repurchase agreements are sales of securities with contracts to repurchase them at a specific date. Most

---

[2]Interest-rate ceilings on large CDs with maturities of 30 to 89 days were removed in 1970. Those of large CDs with maturities of 90 days or more were removed in 1973. Interest ceilings on time deposits of $1000 or more with maturities of 7 to 31 days were removed in January 1985. Ceilings on all time deposits with initial maturities of more than 31 days were removed in October 1983.

repurchase agreements (RPs) are overnight and almost all mature within two weeks. State and local governments and many business firms have found that RPs are a valuable source of short-term interest income and use them in their cash management programs. If governments or firms are uncertain as to when their cash holdings will be required, they can be invested in RPs and the loan extended indefinitely by rolling over the repurchase agreement. Business firms use cash consolidation services of banks to collect their cash assets in one place for use in repurchase agreements. Commercial banks have found these borrowings a valuable method of maintaining access to business firms' cash funds.

Borrowings on the Eurodollar market are another useful tool in bank portfolio management. *Eurodollars* are United States dollar-denominated deposits in financial institutions outside the United States (*see* "Eurodollars," page 184). Banks have found that they can borrow short-term funds in this market from banks in the Caribbean, as well as from their own branches and subsidiaries overseas. If the borrowing rate in the Eurodollar market falls below comparable rates at which the bank can borrow domestically (for example, the federal funds rate), then banks borrow Eurodollars. Under the Monetary Control Act of 1980, reserve requirements have been imposed on Eurodollar borrowings equal to the rate on nonpersonal time deposits to eliminate any differential incentive to borrow funds overseas.

Banks also borrow funds from the Federal Reserve discount window. This is part of the "lender of last resort" function of the Federal Reserve. These funds are available for short terms to help solve bank cash management problems or for longer terms to supply funds in markets with seasonal loan demands, such as agriculture. The Federal Reserve can control borrowings from the Federal Reserve discount window by restricting the bank's access or can influence borrowing at discount by changing the discount rate. The Monetary Control Act of 1980 extended access to the Federal Reserve discount window to all depository institutions holding reservable deposits.

Among other commercial bank liabilities, *subordinated notes and debentures* are worthy of mention. This item is the result of banks' attempts to circumvent interest-rate ceilings on deposits. Banks borrowed these funds by issuing their own paper in the market, a system the authorities allowed in the early 1960s so long as the paper was subordinated to the claims of depositors. The authorities have restricted the amount of borrowing carried out in this manner by imposing quantity restrictions based on the size of the bank.

## Bank Capital

Bank capital is the residual account that represents the equity claims of the bank's owners. The account consists of the value of stock (at par), a surplus account, and undivided profit. Bank capital provides the initial operating

## EURODOLLARS

Eurodollars are United States dollar-denominated deposits in financial institutions outside the United States (note: not specifically in Europe). The origin of the term *Eurodollar* to describe something we associate with capitalistic high finance is believed to rest with a Soviet-owned Paris bank, the Banque Commerciale pour l'Europe du Nord. In the early 1950s, Soviet-bloc countries shifted their holdings of United States dollars (earned in trade with the United States) from United States banks to the Banque Commerciale pour l'Europe du Nord. This was done to protect them from being either frozen or seized by United States authorities. The transfer of these funds was made by cable, and the term *Eurodollar* was derived from the bank's telex code, *Eurobank*.

The financing of international trade often is made in some generally accepted currency. When the British pound dominated international finance in the 1920s, foreign bank deposits of British pounds were commonly exchanged. While the use of Eurodollars and the development of this market was a result of the cold war's effect on the dollar in international finance, the market was greatly stimulated by regulations imposed on domestic commercial banks in the United States. During the 1960s, interest rates were rising in the United States, and interest-rate ceilings imposed under Regulation Q were effective. As a result, United States residents were induced to find some deposit forms of assets with high rates of return. Since the European banks would accept dollar-denominated deposits and were not subject to interest-rate ceilings, the Eurodollar market attracted funds from the United States.

funds for the bank and enables the bank to acquire its initial fixed assets, bank premises, and equipment. To obtain a charter to operate as a bank, supervisory agencies require a specified minimum of initial capital depending on the size of the community being served by the new bank.

*Bank capital* determines the legal limits on certain bank activities. Banks have been restricted to lending at most an amount equal to 10 percent of their capital and surplus to any one party. The Garn–St. Germain Depository Institutions Act of 1982 has raised this percentage for national

The decline of funds in United States commercial banks caused by this disintermediation induced banks to acquire funds elsewhere. The Eurodollar market was attractive, and United States commercial bank borrowing of Eurodollars reached a peak of about $15 billion in 1969. In late 1969, however, there was a dramatic decline in such borrowing as a result of the imposition of marginal reserve requirements as high as 20 percent on the borrowing of Eurodollars (imposed under Regulation M). These requirements were reduced by stages as the United States authorities tried to induce banks to borrow in the foreign exchange markets, reaching zero in 1978. Reserves were reimposed, however, in October 1979 as part of controls imposed on all managed liabilities of commercial banks. At that time a marginal reserve requirement of 8 percent was imposed.

The Eurodollar market is still predominantly based in Europe, but dollar-denominated deposits also are available in Asia and the Caribbean. The market also has been expanded to include Euromarks, Euro-Swiss Francs, and Euroyen. Because of the interbank nature of the Eurodollar market, and the degree to which funds are transferred from parent to subsidiary banks, the total size of the market is difficult to determine. In 1980 the market was believed to be in excess of $600 billion.

The Eurodollar market is basically short term. Banks tend to think of their Eurodollar borrowings as substitutes for large time deposits. Overnight Eurodollar borrowing, however, is primarily limited to those in Caribbean banks because of the time differences between the United States and Europe. It is because of the high liquidity of these overnight Eurodollar borrowings that overnight Eurodollars issued to United States nonbank residents are included in the definition of money supply 2.

banks to 15 percent plus an additional 10 percent for loans secured by readily marketable collateral.

Regulatory agencies evaluate the condition of a bank, in part, by comparing the asset portfolio and management operations to the size of the bank's capital. Banks and other financial intermediaries function with substantial liabilities relative to the size of their capital. This capital serves as protection for the depositors and demonstrates the financial intermediary's ability to absorb losses. Small loan losses may be written off directly against earnings, although banks may set up special reserves as an asset account (less reserves for loan losses) to spread any losses over an extended period. Loan losses, or other losses in excess of earnings, and special reserves set aside for losses deplete the bank's capital. A bank can absorb losses in excess of earnings and special reserves up to the amount of the bank's capital before becoming legally insolvent.

## SUMMARY

Commercial banks, like other financial intermediaries, function to channel monetary assets through the economy. This is part of the ordinary business process of commercial banking. Commercial banks create deposit liabilities when an asset, such as cash or a deposit held at another institution, is deposited into the bank. Assets acquired by the banks when they create their liabilities are then used to satisfy reserve requirements, maintain sufficient liquidity, and generate a profit for the bank's owners. Liquidity of the bank's portfolio is a primary concern of bank managers, because a substantial portion of the bank's deposit liabilities are demand deposits that are payable on demand and transferred by check.

As a business, a commercial bank's portfolio must generate sufficient earnings for the owners so they will continue in the banking business. The portfolio acquired must be considered sufficiently safe by the owners to protect their equity interest in the bank, and the operation of the bank must be considered as sufficiently safe by depositors to induce them to use the financial intermediary as a storehouse for their assets. In addition, the portfolio must be sufficiently liquid to enable the bank to pay cash on demand to demand depositors. Otherwise, the bank will become technically insolvent.

The process of solving the fundamental problem of financial intermediation and making the optimal trade-offs between profitability, liquidity, and safety is a matter of portfolio management. There are various methods and techniques that can and have been used in commercial bank management, but they all relate to utilizing the available credit markets to satisfy the legal constraints imposed by regulators and to solving the fundamental problem of financial intermediation.

## *Key Terms*

commercial bank
demand deposit
financial intermediary
fundamental problem of
    financial intermediation
profitability
liquidity
safety
solvency

technical solvency
primary reserves
secondary reserves
federal funds
repurchase and resale
    agreements
time deposits
bank capital

## Questions

1. Explain the incentive for borrowers and lenders to use the services of financial intermediaries.

2. What is the relationship between profitability and risk in a financial intermediary's portfolio? Explain.

3. Explain how transactions deposits force a strong consideration of technical solvency on financial intermediaries.

4. How do subordinated notes and debentures serve as protection for financial intermediary depositors? Explain.

5. In the absence of regulators and federal insurance on deposits, why might depositors use only the services of financial intermediaries with high ratios of capital to liabilities? Under what circumstances would you expect depositors to seek out the services of unregulated financial intermediaries or intermediaries with limited capital relative to liabilities? Explain.

## Additional Readings

Garcia, G., Herbert Baer, et al. "The Garn–St. Germain Depository Institutions Act of 1982." *Economic Perspectives.* Federal Reserve Bank of Chicago (March/April 1983): 3–30.

*A summary of this important legislative act and an assessment of its impact on the financial intermediation industry.*

Klein, Benjamin. "The Competitive Supply of Money." *Journal of Money, Credit and Banking* 6 (November 1974): 423–453.

*A discussion of the private issue of money and the role of trust in financial intermediaries.*

Lucus, Charles M., Marcos J. Jones, and Thom B. Thurston. "Federal Funds and Repurchase Agreements." *Quarterly Review* 2. Federal Reserve Bank of New York (Summer 1977): 33–48.

*Coverage of markets for immediately available funds.*

Smith, Wayne J. "Repurchase Agreements and Federal Funds." *Federal Reserve Bulletin* (May 1978): 353–360.

*A Federal Reserve survey of the growth in the use of discretionary sources of funds.*

Thorp, Adrian W. "Eurobanking and World Inflation." *Voice.* Federal Reserve Bank of Dallas (August 1979): 8–23.

*A survey of the Eurocurrency markets and a discussion of the relationship between Eurocurrencies and the medium of exchange.*

# CHAPTER NINE

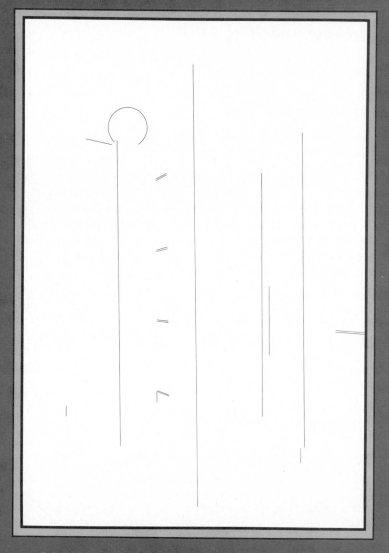

# COMMERCIAL BANK MANAGEMENT

*Financial intermediaries are profit-motivated institutions that facilitate the transfer of funds throughout the economy. Financial intermediary management is a process of providing service and arranging both assets and liabilities to achieve an optimum relationship among liquidity, profitability, and safety. An examination of commercial bank management illustrates the various alternatives and rules of thumb that are used to achieve this optimum.*

The process of financial intermediary management is a matter of portfolio management designed to solve the fundamental problem of financial intermediation. Besides earning a satisfactory rate of return for the owners, the portfolio must also provide for a continuation of those earnings. Thus, the management must ensure continuation of the business and continued access to deposit funds. For the institution to remain in business, the portfolio must also satisfy legal requirements, such as restrictions on asset holdings and reserves. To maintain access to deposit funds, the portfolio must have sufficient liquidity and certain assets to provide the services associated with deposits. Cash must be held for payment of deposit withdrawals. Balances held with other institutions provide for check clearing.

Financial intermediary portfolio management is important in its effect on the flow of credit and on the amount of money available. When a cash asset is accepted for deposit, the financial intermediary creates a deposit liability against itself. The liabilities that are transactions deposits are the majority of the circulating medium of exchange, M1. In managing the portfolio, financial intermediaries extend loans that channel the credit available to various sectors of the economy and influence the credit conditions in various financial markets.

Commercial bank management illustrates the process of financial intermediary portfolio management: the problems, constraints, and solutions encountered in financial intermediaries accepting transactions deposits. The differences between management of commercial banks and the thrift institutions result from regulatory differences and characteristics specific to the markets served. Chapter 11 discusses these differences.

The actual day-to-day management of a commercial bank is an extremely complex and diversified undertaking. After providing for primary reserves sufficient to satisfy reserve requirements and providing for the check-clearing process, bank management decisions turn to the management of the loan and securities portfolio to attempt to provide sufficient liquidity and safety while generating satisfactory earnings for the owners. Commercial bank portfolios and their management vary with local market conditions as well as with changes in national economic conditions. Despite these potential differences, there are generalizations that can provide a general overview of the process of commercial bank management.

## RESERVE REQUIREMENTS

In order to remain in business and provide for a continuation of earnings, financial intermediaries must satisfy specific legal constraints. Commercial banks and thrift institutions are required by regulatory agencies to hold determinable amounts of specific cash items as reserves for their deposits. Vault cash and deposits held at Federal Reserve District Banks are the cash items that can be used to satisfy reserve requirements and are the bank's *primary reserves.* The asset portfolio must be arranged so that the intermediary's holdings of primary reserves are equal to or exceed the amount of its *required reserves.*

The Federal Reserve has authority over reserve requirements for commercial banks, mutual savings banks, savings banks, savings and loan associations, and credit unions, if they are federally insured or eligible for federal insurance. This broad control over reserve requirements is part of the Monetary Control Act of 1980 and is a dramatic departure from the previous system. (*See* "Reserve Requirements Before 1980," page 191.) Reserve requirements are set under *Regulation D* of the Federal Reserve Code.

*Reserve requirements* are one means of monetary control available to the Federal Reserve. By altering the level of reserve requirements, the Federal Reserve can control the amount of each deposit that is available to the bank for lending purposes.

Reserve requirements are imposed on net transactions deposits, nonpersonal time deposits, and Eurocurrency liabilities. *Net transactions deposits* are gross demand deposits, NOW, Super NOW, ATS, and share draft deposits less cash items in the process of collection and transactions balances due from domestic banks. For reserve purposes, money market de-

## RESERVE REQUIREMENTS BEFORE 1980

Financial innovations throughout the 1970s blurred the boundaries between the various financial intermediaries. The development of other checkable deposits altered commercial banks' unique role in housing transactions deposits. The Monetary Control Act of 1980 was a legislative move to adjust for these market changes, broadening the authority of the Federal Reserve. The act altered two major conditions seen as creating difficulties in monetary control: differences in reserve requirement coverage between financial intermediaries and multitiered reserve requirements on demand deposits.

Through 1980 the Federal Reserve had control over the reserve requirements for member banks only. Reserves were required on demand deposits, savings, and time deposits. State banking agencies imposed reserve requirements that constrained the asset portfolios of state-chartered nonmember banks, and the thrift institutions were required to hold a wide range of highly liquid assets.

The reserve requirements imposed by states varied widely. Even when the percentage of demand deposits to be held as reserves was higher than Federal Reserve requirements, the requirements were less restrictive because of the assets the states allowed to be counted as primary reserves. In all states imposing reserve requirements, deposits at approved depository banks were included. Some states also allowed government securities as well as cash items in process of collection to serve as primary reserves.

California had reserve requirements equal to those imposed by the Federal Reserve, but vault cash and deposits at approved depository institutions were included in primary reserves. California's 5 percent reserve requirement on time and

*(continued)*

posit accounts (MMDAs) that permit no more than six preauthorized, automatic, or other transfers (of which no more than three may be checks) per month are considered savings deposits and are subject to the time deposit reserve requirement. *Nonpersonal time deposits,* primarily large certificates of deposit, are time deposits held by depositors other than natural persons.

savings deposits could be met up to 80 percent by holding un-pledged negotiable United States government securities. New York had reserve requirements on net demand deposits 1 per-cent less than those required by the Federal Reserve. Illinois was unique in having no statutory reserve requirements.[1] The rela-tive leniency of state-imposed reserve requirements was one of the reasons for the decline of membership in the Federal Re-serve since World War II.

The broad range of reserve requirements made it difficult to predict the amount of lending that would follow an increase in transactions deposits. The additional lending ability would depend upon whether the financial intermediary accepting the deposit was a bank or a thrift institution and, if it was a bank, whether it was a member or nonmember. The process was fur-ther complicated for banks that were members of the Federal Reserve system. Before the Monetary Control Act, reserve re-quirements on net demand deposits were set in five deposit in-tervals, ranging from a 7 percent requirement for the first $2 million up to 16¼ percent on deposits over $400 million. The amount of additional lending possible from an additional deposit depended upon the size of the deposit-receiving institution. Cur-rently, transactions deposit reserve requirements have only one gradation.

The Monetary Control Act of 1980 was designed to ease monetary control. Currently, no distinction is made between reserve requirements between banks that are members of the Federal Reserve System and those that are not or between com-mercial banks and other depository institutions.

---

[1] For additional discussion, *see:* Gilbert, R. Alton, and Jean M. Lovati, "Bank Reserve Require-ments and Their Enforcement: A Comparison across States," *Review* (Federal Reserve Bank of St. Louis, March 1978): 22–31.

*Eurocurrency liabilities* are the dollar-denominated funds borrowed by domestic institutions offshore (Eurodollar borrowings), primarily from foreign branches or subsidiaries of domestic institutions. In addition, the Federal Reserve (after consultation with Congress and approval of five of the seven members of the Board of Governors of the Federal Reserve) can impose, for a period of 180 days, reserve requirements on any liability of

---

*Table 9.1*
## Reserve Requirements of Depository Institutions

| Type of Deposit | Percentage[1] | |
|---|---|---|
| Net transactions accounts | | |
| $0–$28.9 million | 3 | |
| Over $28.9 million | 12 | |
| Nonpersonal time deposits by original maturity | | |
| Less than 1½ years | 3 | |
| 1½ years or more | 0 | |
| Eurocurrency liabilities | 3 | |

| Legal Limits[2] | Minimum | Maximum |
|---|---|---|
| Transactions deposits (over breakpoint) | 8 | 14 |
| Supplemental requirement | — | 4 |
| Nonpersonal time deposits | 0 | 9 |

---

[1] These reserve requirements result from the Monetary Control Act of 1980 and are being phased in from the previously higher reserve requirements for many member banks and the lower reserve requirements for nonmember depository institutions. The phase-in period for member banks ends October 24, 1985, and for nonmember institutions on September 3, 1987.

[2] For a discussion of changes in reserve requirements, *see:* Cacy, J. A., and Scott Winningham, "Reserve Requirements under the Depository Institutions Deregulation and Monetary Control Act of 1980," *Economic Review* (Federal Reserve Bank of Kansas, September–October 1980): 3–16.

*Source:* Board of Governors, Federal Reserve System, *Federal Reserve Bulletin* (Washington, D.C., January 1984): Table 1.15.

depository institutions. These reserve requirements can be extended for an additional 180 days. The reserve requirements in effect January 1, 1984, are given in Table 9.1.

Reserve requirements on transactions deposits are graduated with a breakpoint that is established to ease reserve position management for smaller depository institutions. Under this graduated system, smaller institutions are able to use a greater percentage of an additional transactions deposit to acquire interest earning loans. The deposit level for the breakpoint in reserve requirements is adjusted each year for the next calendar year by an amount equal to 80 percent of the percentage increase in transactions deposits over the year ending the preceding June 30.

In a move to ease reserve position management and reporting difficulties for very small depository institutions, the Garn–St. Germain Depository Institutions Act of 1982 provided that the first $2 million in reservable liabilities of each depository institution be subject to a zero percent reserve requirement. Like the breakpoint in reserve requirements on transactions deposits, this $2 million exemption is adjusted by an amount equal to 80 percent of the percentage increase in transactions deposits over the year ending the preceding June 30. Beginning January 12, 1984, the exemption was $2.2 million.

In addition to the basic reserve requirements, the Federal Reserve has the authority to impose a supplemental reserve requirement on transactions deposits of up to 4 percent for monetary control purposes only. Any supplemental reserve requirement imposed requires approval of five of the seven members of the Board of Governors and is automatically terminated after 90 days. Primary reserves (the cash items that can be used to satisfy reserve requirements) are generally noninterest-earning assets. However, supplemental reserves, if and when required, are to be held in an earnings participation fund at the Federal Reserve and are to receive interest earnings at a rate not less than the average rate of earnings for the previous quarter on the securities portfolio of the Federal Reserve. This is a first step in the direction of paying interest on reserve deposits.

The new reserve requirements imposed under the Monetary Control Act can be satisfied by financial institutions holding vault cash or deposits at Federal Reserve Banks. In addition, nonmember institutions may *pass* their required reserves to the Federal Reserve *through*—

1.   Another institution holding reserves with the Federal Reserve;

2.   The Federal Home Loan Bank (for savings and loan associations and mutual savings banks) or;

3.   The National Credit Union Administration's Central Liquidity Facility (for credit unions).

Reserve requirements are instituted to restrict the composition of the bank's asset portfolio. With reserve requirements, depository institutions must hold a significant portion of their assets in the highly liquid form of primary reserves. (For a discussion of the required adjustments, *see* "Reserve Position Management," page 195.) Reserve requirements do not, however, provide sufficient funds to satisfy the withdrawal of deposits without some other adjustment in the bank's portfolio.

For example, if a bank with $100 million in net transactions deposits holds exactly the required amount of primary reserves [ $9.399 million = $(0.03 \times \$28.9$ million$) + (0.12 \times \$71.1$ million$)$], a withdrawal of $1 million will reduce the bank's primary reserves by $1 million while required reserves will be reduced by only $0.12 million. If the bank has no excess reserves, it will become deficient by $0.88 million. Some portfolio adjustment will be necessary to acquire these reserves before the reserve averaging period ends. In order to make payments on demand and clear checks without violating reserve requirements, depository institutions must retain access to additional liquidity.

## RESERVE POSITION MANAGEMENT
### (The February 1984 Rules)

One problem faced by depository institutions is managing their primary reserves (currency and deposits at the Federal Reserve) to satisfy the reserve requirements set by the authorities. If reserve requirements were to be met on a daily basis—that is, depository institutions were required to end each day with reserves that are a specific proportion of the deposits held at the end of that day—reserve position management would be extremely difficult. Under such conditions it would be expected that the depository institutions would hold fairly large excess reserves to avoid breaking the law. The Federal Reserve, however, has instituted several mechanisms to ease the reserve management problem. These mechanisms are to be found in Regulation D. The regulation has been amended on many occasions to change the way in which reserves are kept, most recently in February 1984. At that time the Federal Reserve instituted what are known as "contemporaneous reserves."

Depository institutions are not required to satisfy reserve requirements on a daily basis, but as an average over a two-week period. However, the two-week period over which reserves must be kept is not exactly the same as the period over which the calculations are made. Time is divided into two-week computation periods ($C_1$, $C_2$, and so on) and two-week maintenance periods ($M_1$, $M_2$, and so on). The computation periods start on Tuesdays, and the maintenance periods start on the following Thursdays:

| | $C_1$ | | $C_2$ | | $C_3$ | |
|---|---|---|---|---|---|---|

M TW TF(SS)MTWTF(SS)M TW TF(SS)MTWTF(SS)M TW TF(SS)MTWTF(SS)M TW

| | $M_1$ | | $M_2$ | | $M_3$ | |
|---|---|---|---|---|---|---|

*continued*

## THE CLEARING AND COLLECTION OF CHECKS

Deposit liabilities are the primary source of funds for the bank's business of extending loans and purchasing securities. To maintain continued access to deposit funds, the bank provides a return to the depositor through interest payments or through services associated with the deposit. Although recent

The average amount of day-end reserves at the Federal Reserve over the current maintenance period plus the average amount of day-end cash held over the computation period two periods earlier must be the required proportion of the average amount of day-end transactions accounts over the current computation period and the average amount of day-end nonpersonal time deposits of the computation period two periods earlier. For the periods given above, the average deposits at the Fed during $M_3$ plus the average cash holdings over $C_1$ must be the required proportion of the transactions accounts held over $C_3$ and the nonpersonal time deposits held over $C_1$. As the current computation period ends only two days before the current maintenance period, all of the adjustment in reserves must take place in the reserves held at the Federal Reserve over these last two days.

Of course, a depository institution might still end the maintenance period with reserves below the requirement. When this is the case, the deficiency is penalized at an interest charge equal to 2 percent more than the prevailing rate for borrowing from the Federal Reserve ( 2 percent above the current discount rate ). However, depository institutions have the right to be deficient up to 2 percent of required reserves or $25,000 (whichever is the larger) without penalty, provided that the deficiency is made up in the following maintenance period.

Thus an institution with $50 million in required daily averages of reserves could hold an average of $49 million this period provided it held an average of $51 million the next. Also, institutions are allowed to count as reserves this period any excess reserves held the previous period up to 2 percent of required reserves (or $25,000). However, this excess cannot be carried forward for two periods in a row.

financial innovations and the development of new forms of deposit accounts permit explicit interest payments on transactions balances, the primary benefit to the public of the various types of checking accounts is in the services provided. The usefulness of checking accounts to the public does not rest with their safety, but mainly with the ease with which money payments can be made. As an incentive for the public to house transactions balances with a bank, the bank provides easy transfer of deposits, and the assets necessary to facilitate transfers.

Clearly, payment on checks is a simple matter when they are used to withdraw funds from transactions accounts in cash. The bank, holding vault cash for the purpose, makes the payment in cash and reduces the account balance. Also, if payments are to be made between two accounts in the same bank, it is a simple matter for the bank to subtract an amount from one account (the payer's account) and add it to the other (the payee's account). This transaction requires no specific assets, only the ability to maintain accurate records. However, most payments using checks are made between accounts that are not in the same bank. Thus, it is important that there be some system available for transferring funds from one account to another no matter how distant the accounts are.

There are three methods of check clearance in use in the United States today: (1) correspondent arrangements between individual banks, (2) local clearinghouse arrangements, and (3) the national system administered by the Federal Reserve system. There are different circumstances under which these arrangements are used.

## Correspondent Banking

*Correspondent banking* is an arrangement whereby banks hold deposit balances at other banks. The accounts are called *interbank deposits.* Some of these deposits are held as compensating balances for services provided, such as security purchases and sales, foreign transactions, and financial advice. However, the interbank deposits are held primarily for use in check clearing. Commercial banks expect that many of the checks passing through them will be drawn on banks that are close geographically, and they will maintain accounts with each other for clearing these checks.

The method of *check clearance* between correspondent banks is relatively simple and can be seen in Table 9.2. Suppose that Banks A and B are correspondent banks and hold deposits with each other. The payer, banking with Bank B, wishes to make a payment to the payee, banking with Bank A. The payer writes a check instructing Bank B to make a payment of $100 to the payee, and the payee uses the check to make a deposit in Bank A. Bank A will add the amount of the check to its assets as *cash items in the process of collection* (CIIPOC) and add the amount to the payee's account, though the bank may not allow the payee to spend the funds until the check is actually cleared (payment has been made). The account entries are shown with subscripts (1) in Table 9.2. The check is then presented to Bank B for payment. If the payer's account does not contain sufficient funds to pay the check, the check will be returned marked "Insufficient Funds," and the transactions will be canceled. If the payer's account does contain the required amount, Bank B will subtract the amount of the check from the payer's account and also will subtract the amount from the account it has with Bank A. (Alternatively, Bank A's account with Bank B could be increased by the amount of the check.) Bank A will have reduced liabilities

*Table 9.2*
**Check Clearing between Correspondent Banks**

| Bank A | | | | |
|---|---|---|---|---|
| Reserves of A | | | Payee's account | $(+\$100)_{(1)}$ |
| A's account at B | | | | |
| CIIPOC | $(+\$100)_{(1)}$ | $(-\$100)_{(2)}$ | B's account at A | $(-\$100)_{(2)}$ |
| Investments | | | | |
| Loans | | | | |

| Bank B | | | |
|---|---|---|---|
| Reserves of B | | Payer's account | $(-\$100)_{(2)}$ |
| B's account at A | $(-\$100)_{(2)}$ | A's account at B | |
| CIIPOC | | | |
| Investments | | | |
| Loans | | | |

due to Bank B and will reduce CIIPOC by the amount of the payment. These account entries are shown in Table 9.2 with subscripts (2).

   For banks in close proximity, such transactions will take place continuously. The clearing of checks through the addition to or depletion of interbank deposits is undertaken to reduce the amount of cash or other reserves actually transferred between banks. The clearing of checks between two correspondent banks occurs through the exchange of checks drawn on each other. If the amounts of the checks do not exactly offset each other, the net difference is paid through a transfer of interbank deposits. When a bank's deposits in its correspondent banks become too low, the accounts are replenished by an additional deposit. This would transfer reserves between the two banks, increase the receiving bank's ability to extend loans, and reduce its ability to extend loans for the bank incurring a net loss in deposits and making the payment.

## Local Clearinghouses

In many areas the amount of interbank business is so large that transactions costs incurred by banks can be reduced greatly by setting up a local clearinghouse for the exchange of the checks drawn on a group of banks. Clearinghouses originated in London, England, in 1773, but the first American system was the New York Clearing House Association, established in New York City in 1853. This clearinghouse has been the prototype for clearinghouses throughout the United States.

*Table 9.3*
**Local Clearinghouse Arrangements (in Millions of Dollars)**

| Paying Banks / Receiving Banks | Bank A | Bank B | Bank C | Bank D | Totals Received |
|---|---|---|---|---|---|
| Bank A | | 10 | 12 | 8 | 30 |
| Bank B | 7 | | 14 | 16 | 37 |
| Bank C | 10 | 18 | | 5 | 33 |
| Bank D | 13 | 5 | 17 | | 35 |
| Totals paid | 30 | 33 | 43 | 29 | 135 |

A clearinghouse consists of many banks exchanging the checks drawn on one another at a single location. Instead of making individual payments, it is possible to calculate the net payments that have to be made between each bank and then to pay them. For example, Table 9.3 shows the hypothetical payments that are to be made between four banks, Banks A, B, C, and D. The first row shows that Bank A is to receive a total of $30 million, consisting of $10 million from Bank B, $12 million from Bank C, and $8 million from Bank D. The first column shows that Bank A is to pay a total of $30 million consisting of $7 million to Bank B, $10 million to Bank C, and $13 million to Bank D. As the total amount received is equal to the total amount paid, Bank A would neither pay nor receive any net amount at the settlement. The totals for each bank reveal that Bank B is to receive $37 million and pay out $33 million (a net receipt of $4 million), Bank C is to receive $33 million and pay out $43 million (a net payment of $10 million), and Bank D is to receive $35 million and pay out $29 million (a net receipt of $6 million). The net settlement can be made easily between the four banks by Bank C paying $4 million to Bank B and $6 million to Bank D. These two payments will reconcile the balances for a total exchange of $135 million.

Of course, the net payments can be made in the same way as the payments between correspondent banks if the members of the clearinghouse have accounts with each other. In the early days of the New York Clearing House the reconciliation was made in cash. Today, most members of clearinghouses have accounts at Federal Reserve District Banks. The reconciliations can then be made through the Federal Reserve. This is the method used by the New York Clearing House Association. The checks are reconciled on a daily basis.

Through 1980 the Federal Reserve operated the only national check-clearing system. Since check clearing through the Federal Reserve was provided without direct charge to member banks, there was little incentive for

"Thanks to the blessings of automation, you may now insert your credit card in the convenient terminal at your pew, enter the amount of your offering on the keyboard, and our electronic funds transfer system will take it from there."

a competitive system to arise. Following passage of the Monetary Control Act, the Federal Reserve has been required to charge for this service. The result has been a shift away from using the Federal Reserve toward clearinghouse arrangements.

The clearinghouse system seems an obvious place for computerization. The New York Clearing House Association began its computerization in 1970 by setting up CHIPS (the Clearing House Interbank Payments System). Computer terminals in each of the members of the association have established an automated clearinghouse that can eliminate the use of checks from interbank payment transfers. CHIPS is reputed to be the first use of "electronic money." (*See* "Electronic Money," page 201).

### Federal Reserve Check Clearing

Establishing a nationwide check-clearing system was one of the original objectives of the Federal Reserve System. For purposes of check clearing, the United States was divided into 12 districts, each having a Federal Reserve District Bank. As the number of checks to be cleared increased, the

## ELECTRONIC MONEY

Checks, drafts, and other pieces of paper are useful devices for transferring funds. However, processing these records involves the handling of a massive bulk of paper at substantial cost. In 1979 the Federal Reserve processed over 15.9 billion checks at a cost of $279.1 million.[1] The increased cost of check processing and rapidly declining costs of computer services have led to a greater usage of electronic data processing devices for the transfer of financial assets.

Electronic fund transfer is the use of computers or other electronic devices to transfer funds. The Federal Reserve has for years provided member banks with a wire transfer service that enables member banks to shift funds from their reserve accounts to other member banks' reserve accounts and that allows a transfer of marketable government securities throughout the country. During the 1970s banks expanded the use of electronic devices to improve and reduce the costs of providing services to their customers. Automatic teller machines allow customers with special cards and "secret codes" to withdraw cash, deposit funds, shift funds between accounts, and make other banking transactions 24 hours a day.

Receiving deposits and transferring funds to others without the use of paper also is possible. Social Security and other government payments can be deposited automatically. The use of debit cards and point-of-sale terminals allow bank customers to debit their transactions accounts and transfer funds directly into a business concern's account in payment for goods and services. Electronic payment to third parties also can be made through pay-by-phone services.

The use of electronic payments systems speeds up the payments system by avoiding delays in check processing and reduces the handling of paper. However, the use of electronic money does not provide a documentation of the transaction. Requirements for the availability of receipts to record the transfer and the rights of the customers are covered by the Electronic Fund Transfer Act (1978) and Regulation E of the Federal Reserve Code.

---

[1] Board of Governors, the Federal Reserve System, *Annual Report 1979* (Washington, D.C.): 323–324

districts have been divided into smaller regions, each having a regional check-processing center. There is also a system for clearing checks between districts through the Inter-District Settlement Fund in Washington, D.C.

The Monetary Control Act of 1980 requires that the Federal Reserve check-clearing system be available to all depository institutions under the same terms. Before passage of this act, use by nonmember banks was restricted. Nonmember banks were restricted to direct use of the check-clearing process available through one regional check processing center. Any check clearance beyond the territory covered by that one regional center was obtained through correspondent member banks. Since checks require considerable preliminary processing, many smaller depository institutions use correspondent banks for access to the Federal Reserve check-clearing system even though they now have direct access.

The clearing of checks through the Federal Reserve's system in a district goes through four steps. The entries corresponding to each step are indicated by the subscripts in Table 9.4.

1.  Deposit of funds. A check is presented to Bank A for deposit in the payee's account. Bank A lists the amount as "cash items in the process of collection" (CIIPOC) and records the amount in the payee's account.

2.  Presentment for clearing. Bank A sends the check by mail or courier along with many others to the Federal Reserve for clearing. The Federal Reserve Bank records the amount of the check as an asset due from Bank B in the account *Cash in Process of Collection* (CIPC) and as a liability to Bank A in the account *Deferred Availability Cash Items* (DACI).

3.  Payment of reserves to payee's bank. To facilitate the individual bank's reserve position management, the Federal Reserve has eliminated the uncertainty surrounding how soon the reserves will be available to the bank using this check-clearing system. A funds availability schedule based on distance determines when the funds will be added to the depositing bank's reserve at the Federal Reserve Bank. Funds from checks drawn on banks in the local area generally are available overnight. The availability schedule sets shorter times than the actual time it takes for many checks to clear. Regardless of how long it takes for the check to clear, the Federal Reserve will remove the amount of the check from its DACI and give Bank A the use of the funds according to the funds availability schedule. At the same time, Bank A will subtract the amount of the check from its cash items in the process of collection and add the amount to its reserves at the Federal Reserve Bank.

*Table 9.4*
**Federal Reserve Check Clearing**

| Federal Reserve District Bank | | | |
|---|---|---|---|
| **Assets** | | **Liabilities** | |
| Cash in process of collection | $(+\$100)_{(2)}, (-\$100)_{(4)}$ | Deferred availability cash items | $(+\$100)_{(2)}, (-\$100)_{(3)}$ |
| | | Bank A's reserves at the Fed. | $(+\$100)_{(3)}$ |
| | | Bank B's reserves at the Fed. | $(-\$100)_{(4)}$ |

| Bank A | | | |
|---|---|---|---|
| **Assets** | | **Liabilities** | |
| A's reserves at the Fed. | $(+\$100)_{(3)}$ | Payee's deposits | $(+\$100)_{(1)}$ |
| CIIPOC | $(+\$100)_{(1)}, (-\$100)_{(3)}$ | | |

| Bank B | | | |
|---|---|---|---|
| **Assets** | | **Liabilities** | |
| B's reserves at the Fed. | $(-\$100)_{(4)}$ | Payer's deposits | $(-\$100)_{(4)}$ |

4. Presentment by the Federal Reserve for payment. The Federal Reserve presents the check to the payer's bank, Bank B, for payment. The amount of the check is removed from the payer's account, and Bank B's reserves held at the Federal Reserve are reduced. At this time the Federal Reserve will subtract the amount of the check from its CIPC and, also, reduce Bank B's reserves. Thus, the check has cleared. If the payer's account did not have sufficient funds to cover the check, however, the payment would not be made, and the check would be returned marked "Insufficient Funds."

This clearing shifts funds from the payer's account into the payee's account and transfers reserves held at the Federal Reserve from Bank B into the reserves of Bank A.

A more complicated system clears checks between Federal Reserve Districts. Checks cleared between districts may be presented by member banks to the local Federal Reserve office, which then clears the check with the other districts, or banks with relatively large clearings in another district may directly send their checks to the other district for clearing. The direct-send of checks to other districts provides the banks with a more rapid access to the funds. The interdistrict clearing of checks may result in a shift of funds between Federal Reserve District Banks. This transfer of funds is accomplished through shifts in deposits held by Federal Reserve District Banks at the Inter-District Settlement Fund in Washington, D.C. The transfer of funds is not made on a check-by-check basis, but on the net change between districts at the end of each business day.

The Federal Reserve's crediting reserves to one bank before it charges the reserves to another bank causes *both* banks to have the amount of the check counted in their reserves at the same time. The total amount of funds that are included at any given moment in the reserves of receiving banks while still included in the reserves of paying banks is called "the float." The amount of the *Federal Reserve float* is equal to the difference between cash in process of collection (CIPC) and deferred availability of cash items (DACI) on the Federal Reserve's consolidated balance sheet. The check collection fees instituted by the Federal Reserve since passage of the Monetary Control Act include charges that reflect the float's value.

The clearing of checks is an important banking business. Not only is it important as a service that provides an incentive to the public for the use of the bank, but it also results in shifts in reserves between banks. A bank that on net has an increase in deposits is in a position to extend additional loans and to expand its holdings of interest-earning assets. Alternatively, a bank that suffers a net decline in deposits and the loss of reserves must contract its lending activity or look elsewhere for the funds necessary to maintain its loan portfolio.

## THEORIES OF BANKING

When a bank receives a deposit, it gains cash assets, usually in the form of actual cash or in deposits at other institutions such as the Federal Reserve, and it incurs specific liabilities to the depositor. With the receipt of an additional deposit or a gain in deposits through the check-clearing process, the bank must set aside a portion of the assets acquired to satisfy reserve requirements. In addition, some assets will have to be maintained, such as balances at other institutions for check clearing, to provide the services associated with the deposit liability. However, these provisions amount to only a small portion of the assets received from the deposit. Even with a 12 percent reserve requirement on transactions deposits, cash items amount to well under 10 percent of most banks' asset portfolios. Once the cash items are set aside to satisfy reserve requirements and provide for check clearing, the bank management can turn to managing the remainder of its asset portfolio.

Throughout the history of commercial banking various theories about the operation of commercial banks have described how the business of portfolio management should be conducted to generate sufficient earnings while providing for adequate liquidity and safety. In addition, they are useful in predicting the results of banking activity on general economic conditions. In retrospect, the changing nature of the ideas about commercial banking appears to reflect the changing nature of the financial markets available for banking activity. These theories will undoubtedly continue to change as financial innovation continues and financial markets evolve.

## Commercial Loan Theory of Banking

The traditional theory of banking is the *commercial loan theory,* or the *real bills doctrine.* It is from this theory, in fact, that banks became known as commercial. Traditionally, it was thought that a commercial bank could best solve its portfolio problem by investing primarily in self-liquidating commercial paper (real bills). Not only would this solve the bank's portfolio problem, but the quantity of money in the system would fluctuate in a desirable way. Rather oddly, the *quantity* of money was thought to be regulated by the *quality* of bank assets.

A commercial loan was considered self-liquidating if it was issued on goods in the process of production or on goods in transit. When the goods were sold, this would generate the funds necessary to pay the loan. A continuous investment in loans of this type, therefore, would ensure the bank's liquidity. This theory, however, does not have much foundation. No loan is self-liquidating in the sense that repayment is guaranteed. The ability to repay the loan is always dependent on the value of the goods on which the loan was made.

If banks operated in this way, and in the aggregate concentrated primarily on investing in self-liquidating commercial paper, the money supply was thought to fluctuate "according to the needs of trade." As the amount of business increased, it was expected that more self-liquidating commercial loans would be made, banks would create more money, and the money supply would increase. As the amount of business declined, less self-liquidating paper would be issued, banks would make fewer loans, and the money supply would decline.

This argument is flawed. Loans are made on the money value of the goods involved; so during inflation the size of the loans—and hence the money supply—would increase, and during deflation the size of the loans—and hence the money supply—would decrease. Thus, operating according to this theory would cause banks to be a destabilizing influence on the economy, increasing the money supply in inflations and decreasing the money supply during deflations. The banks would function in a way opposite to the mode of operation of the commodity standards. With the development and availability of other financial markets as alternatives to commercial loans, the funds available to the bank could be lent readily in other markets and the mode of operation thought appropriate for commercial banks changed.

## Modern Theories

The abandonment of the real bills doctrine came with the greater develop-ment of liquid security markets in the 1930s. It was then thought proper for banks to hold a portfolio that contained a high proportion of shiftable assets, such as Treasury bills. Using *shiftable assets,* the bank would maintain its liquidity by always having assets that could be sold immediately for cash whenever the amounts of deposits declined. Commercial banks were di-vorced from any notion of operating with the "needs of trade," but instead were concerned with their own liquidity. They maintained their solvency by choosing a particular portfolio of assets. The total amount of money in the system was left to the operation of the central bank.

While operating with a set of shiftable assets does provide a bank with a broader base to satisfy its liquidity requirements than solely relying on commercial paper, it still might not prove adequate. For an asset to remain shiftable, it must be readily salable. Thus, a buyer for the asset must be available. Although an asset may prove shiftable for an individual bank, if there is a general desire to sell the shiftable assets, buyers at acceptable prices may be difficult to find. Also, during periods in which interest rates have risen, banks may be reluctant to sell some of their shiftable assets and realize the capital losses associated with interest rate changes. As a result, banks have expanded their concept of liquidity to rely on their loan portfo-lios as well as their holdings of shiftable assets to provide liquidity.

Loans are extended on the basis of their *anticipated income.* Many loans are amortized and paid off in a series of installments. Thus, a bank's loan portfolio provides for a continual flow of funds which contributes to the bank's liquidity. In addition to this flow of income, the bank's loans may be marketed to provide the bank with additional cash or reserves when desired.

Modern banks have increased the ways in which they manage liquidity and solvency. No longer are they expected to concentrate on the shiftability and liquidity of their assets alone. With the development of markets for short-term borrowing (such as the federal funds market and the market for overnight Eurodollars), banks now use *managed liabilities* along with man-aging their assets.

## BANK ASSET MANAGEMENT

In managing bank assets, some securities are acquired primarily to provide shiftable assets for liquidity purposes and some are held as investments. Security holdings represent loans that are indirectly extended through secu-rity purchases and generate interest income that is generally associated with low risk of default. A commercial bank's primary source of income, how-ever, has traditionally come from the fees and interest it charges on its direct loans. Consumer and commercial loans in their various forms make up the primary lending activity of commercial banks. These loans are part of the personalized depositor-lender relationships of banks and their customers. To continue maintaining access to deposits and extending loans, banks generally will attempt to satisfy any legitimate loan desires of their customers. For many business concerns, a bank's reliability as a source of funds is an important incentive for continuing to use the bank's deposit and other services.

Banks, as with any business concern, are reluctant to turn away any legitimate business and manage their asset portfolios accordingly. If a bank cannot acquire the funds to satisfy a customer's legitimate loan demand at the current market rates of interest, competitors who can are available. The bank may therefore suffer a loss of deposits as well as the loan business. Thus, in a bank's portfolio the liquidity requirements are beyond simply being able to satisfy deposit withdrawals. Anticipated loan demand provides an incentive for banks to manage their assets such that funds will be readily available for the extension of new loans.

Correspondent banking relationships are useful in bank asset management. Not only do large correspondent banks provide check-clearing services and financial advice for smaller banks, but the correspondent relationships permit smaller banks to provide services for their larger customers. Commercial banks are prohibited from extending loans to any one customer in amounts in excess of 15 percent of the bank's capital (raised for national banks by the Garn–St. Germain Depository Institutions Act from the previous 10 percent restriction). This lending restriction prohibits smaller banks from satisfying some of their customers' larger loan demands on their own. However, with a correspondent bank, a smaller bank still may be able to provide customers with sufficiently large sums. If a customer desires a loan in excess of the legal limit for the financial institution and is deemed creditworthy for that loan, the bank can arrange to provide the funds through a loan participation. In a *loan participation* a bank will extend and process the loan and hold as an asset the amount it desires (usually the legal limit). The remainder is lent from correspondent institutions through their participation. Loan participations are useful in helping banks to diversify their asset portfolios.

The selection of an asset portfolio is determined by the bank's solving its fundamental problem: reaching some kind of an optimum among liquidity, profitability, and safety within the allowable set of assets. The actual set of assets selected by a commercial bank is determined largely by local market conditions and the bank manager's expertise. For example, a bank operating in an extremely conservative financial area may be providing services to customers with relatively large savings and low loan demand. With substantial deposits and little local consumer or commercial loan demand, the bank may concentrate its assets in security holdings and serve as a lender to other financial institutions. Alternatively, a bank with large, local loan demands may hold few securities and substantial amounts of consumer loans.

"He wants another 50 bucks . . . pair of nines and a queen."

In addition to being influenced by local market conditions, bank portfolios are adjusted in response to anticipated change in national economic conditions.

## Expected Rate of Return and Risk

In selecting assets a commercial bank's managers are concerned with the *expected rate of return* on the asset and the *risk* involved. Bank management traditionally has been conservative, which means that the portfolio is chosen with an active avoidance of risk. Bank managers are more likely to try to maximize the rate of return for a given level of risk than to choose the rate of return required and then minimize the level of risk. *Risk* includes risk of default and interest risk. Risk of default requires that a bank investigate the creditworthiness of the borrower, whereas interest risk requires that a bank investigate the price fluctuations that are observed in the markets for the credit instruments.

Assets are acquired on the basis of the expected rate of return rather than the current rate of return of the assets. If, for example, interest rates are expected to rise in the near future, investment in credit instruments can lead to capital losses. It is likely, therefore, that a bank manager will elect not to invest funds in credit instruments, but either hold noninterest-bearing primary reserves or invest in some overnight asset like federal funds. If higher interest rates occur, the capital loss will have been avoided, and the manager will be free to invest the funds at the higher rates.

The *expected rate of return* on an asset is the average rate of interest that is expected to be earned. If the portfolio managers expect that half the time interest rates will rise, causing a capital loss and realized earnings of 10 percent, and half the time that interest rates will fall, causing a capital gain and realized earnings of 15 percent, the expected rate of return for that asset would be 12.5 percent ($\frac{1}{2} \times 10\% + \frac{1}{2} \times 15\% = 0.5 \times 0.1 + 0.5 \times 0.15 = 0.125 = 12.5\%$).

When a credit instrument is purchased, the rate of return to maturity is known (provided that the borrower does not default). However, the rate actually earned over the ownership period may be very different. If the instrument is sold prior to maturity, and the interest rate has changed in the market, a capital gain or loss may be realized. For example, if a six-month (182 days) Treasury bill is purchased at 93.100 percent of face value and kept to maturity, the yield would be 14.86 percent:

$$\frac{100 - 93.10}{93.10} \cdot \frac{365}{182} = 0.1486.$$

However, if the Treasury bill is sold after only 90 days at the bid price of 95.500 percent of the face value, the yield over the 90-day holding period is only 10.5 percent:

$$\frac{95.50 - 93.10}{93.10} \cdot \frac{365}{90} = 0.105.$$

The dealer buying the Treasury bill can earn, if the bill is now kept to maturity, 18.7 percent:

$$\frac{100 - 95.50}{95.50} \cdot \frac{365}{92} = 0.187.$$

By selling the bill to the dealer, the original holder has *given up* a return of 18.7 percent for 92 days but has earned 10.5 percent over the past 90 days. The market rate of interest has risen over the period, but the original holder has received a lower yield than the original return to maturity. It is because of such considerations that bank managers base their portfolios on their expectations of future interest rates, rather than current rates.

## Portfolio Diversification

To avoid risk and to stabilize earnings, commercial banks acquire highly diversified asset portfolios. By *portfolio diversification,* bank managers attempt to acquire assets whose rates of return adjust in offsetting ways to changes in market conditions. In this way, the rates of return of the different assets will stabilize the rate of return for the portfolio and decrease the risk associated with the portfolio.

Ideally, a portfolio manager would like to acquire assets whose variability in returns exactly offset each other and completely eliminate the variability in the return for the portfolio. Suppose, for example, that two such assets were available. Asset A has a return of 15 percent half the time and a return of 9 percent the other half. Asset B has equally likely returns of 6 percent and 18 percent. Both assets have an expected rate of return of 12 percent:

$$(0.5 \times 0.15) + (0.5 \times 0.09) = 0.12$$
$$(0.5 \times 0.06) + (0.5 \times 0.18) = 0.12.$$

However, the returns on Asset B are significantly more variable, ranging from 6 percent to 18 percent; therefore Asset B is more risky than Asset A.

If, as assumed, these two assets are subject to movements in returns in opposite directions as a result of the same market conditions, a portfolio of the two can be acquired with significantly less variability than either of the two individually. If Asset A has its high rate of return (15 percent) and B has its low rate of return (6 percent) for the same half of the time, while Asset A has its low rate of return (9 percent) and Asset B has its high rate of return (18 percent) during the other half a portfolio can be acquired with no variability in return. If a portfolio is held that consists of $\frac{2}{3}$ of Asset A and $\frac{1}{3}$ of Asset B (i.e., \$2 of Asset A for every \$1 of Asset B), it will have a return of 12 percent with no variability:

$$(\tfrac{2}{3} \times 15\%) \times (\tfrac{1}{3} \times 6\%) = 12\% \qquad \text{(half of the time)}$$
$$(\tfrac{2}{3} \times 9\%) \times (\tfrac{1}{3} \times 18\%) = 12\% \qquad \text{(half of the time).}$$

Of course, assets that move exactly in the opposite directions under all changes in market conditions are not readily available. Credit instruments generally are substitutes for each other and their yields tend to move in the same direction. However, credit conditions in specific credit markets do not *always* adjust evenly and in the same direction. Conditions in the market for long-term credit instruments may be subject to slightly different market pressures than short-term markets. Conditions for loan demand from different industries may vary. These deviations from the general trend between various financial markets allow some reduction in risk through portfolio diversification. (*See* "Gains from Diversification," page 211.) What is required to reduce risk through portfolio diversification is a degree of independence between credit markets. As long as the returns on different credit instruments do not all move evenly under the same market conditions, a diversified portfolio can generate less variability in the return for the portfolio than is associated with any of the assets individually.

## GAINS FROM DIVERSIFICATION

The process of finding in a portfolio a proper combination of assets to generate lower risk for a given rate of return can get rather technical quickly. In formal financial models, portfolio diversification involves a consideration of standard deviations of, and the covariance between, the anticipated returns from assets under different expected situations.[1] The *standard deviation* of returns is the square root of the average of the squared deviations from the expected return and is used as a measure of variability of returns and risk. The greater the standard deviation, the greater is the variability in the returns, and the greater is the risk associated with the asset. The covariance (or the related measure, the correlation) between returns on different assets is a measure of how the asset returns move "together." So long as the assets have a degree of independence (a correlation of less than $+1$), a combination of the assets in a portfolio can reduce the risk of the portfolio as measured by the standard deviation. The following example demonstrates the point.

*Table 9.5*
**Returns on Assets A and B and a Portfolio**

| Situation | Prob-ability | Return on Asset A | Return on Asset B | Return on Portfolio of 0.76 of A and 0.24 of B |
|---|---|---|---|---|
| a | .25 | 12% | 15% | $0.76 \times 12\% + 0.24 \times 15\% = 12.72\%$ |
| b | .25 | 9% | 9% | $0.76 \times 9\% + 0.24 \times 9\% = 9.0\%$ |
| c | .25 | 8% | 14% | $0.76 \times 8\% + 0.24 \times 14\% = 9.44\%$ |
| d | .25 | 11% | 10% | $0.76 \times 11\% + 0.24 \times 10\% = 10.76\%$ |
| Average return expected | | 10% | 12% | 10.48% |
| Standard deviation of returns | | 1.58 | 2.55 | 1.45 |

*continued*

Suppose that two assets are available and that the portfolio managers expect four, equally likely situations (a–d) that are shown in Table 9.5. The returns for Assets A and B under each of the situations are given in columns 3 and 4, with the expected return on Asset A being 10 percent and on Asset B, 12 percent.

Asset B has a higher expected return than Asset A. However, Asset B also is associated with greater risk. The standard deviation of the returns on Asset A is only 1.58, whereas for Asset B it is 2.55.

While the returns on these two assets under different situations generally move in the same direction (the covariance is 0.75), they do not move together perfectly (note Situations c and d). A portfolio manager can take advantage of the differences in the movement of the returns and acquire a portfolio of the two assets that will have less variability in returns than either of the assets alone.

By including some of Asset B (24 percent of the portfolio) along with Asset A (76 percent of the portfolio), the portfolio manager can gain a higher expected return than is available on Asset A alone with reduced risk. The standard deviation of the returns on the portfolio (shown in column 5) is only 1.45.

---

[1] The standard deviation of the returns on Asset A =

$$\sqrt{\frac{\sum_{i=1}^{n} (R_i^a - R_e^a)^2}{n}} = \sqrt{\frac{(12 - 10)^2 + (9 - 10)^2 + (8 - 10)^2 + (11 - 10)^2}{4}} \cong 1.58,$$

where $R_i^a$ is the return on Asset A under situation $i$, $R_e^a$ is the expected return on Asset A, and $n$ is the number of equally likely situations. The covariance between the returns on Assets A and B is:

$$\text{Cov}(A, B) = \frac{\sum_{i=1}^{n} (R_i^a - R_e^a)(R_i^b - R_e^b)}{n}.$$

Related to the measure of the covariance is the correlation:

$$\text{Corr}(A, B) = \frac{\sum_{i=1}^{n} (R_i^a - R_e^a)(R_i^b - R_e^b)}{\sum_{i=1}^{n} (R_i^a - R_e^a)^2 \sum_{i=1}^{n} (R_i^b - R_e^b)^2} \cong 0.19.$$

THE

SECOND NATIONAL BANK

FORMERLY THE FIRST NATIONAL BANK

## *Practical Portfolio Management*

Acquiring all the available information on probable future conditions and the likely returns under those conditions can be extremely costly. Like any other profit-making business, commercial banks are concerned with the costs of making decisions. Rather than incur all costs associated with all information required to obtain a portfolio with the greatest rate of return for the level of risk the bank is willing to assume, banks have developed general rules on decisions for portfolio management.[1] Banks establishing general rules that more closely approximate the portfolio with the greatest return for a given risk will realize greater profitability at lower risk and will tend to survive in the long run. The use of general rules for selecting portfo-

---

[1] These general "rules of thumb" are akin to the use of mark-up pricing in retail firms as an approximation to pricing at maximum profits where marginal revenue is equal to marginal cost. When market conditions change, the rules are adjusted to compensate.

lios is optimizing behavior such that the commercial bank is economizing on the use of resources in selecting the appropriate assets.

One set of rules used by banks is setting requirements for qualifying for a loan. For example, rather than incur the costs of fully evaluating each individual applying for a new car loan (and charging slightly different rates of interest based on differences in qualifications), a commercial bank typically establishes a set of minimum qualifications and extends loans at the same rate of interest to all who meet the minimum standard. Therefore, some individuals with very sound credit ratings may end up paying the same rate of interest as those with much poorer credit ratings. This procedure reduces costs associated with the acquisition of all necessary information for extending loans on new cars. The practice of having a rule of thumb where loans are made or interest rates are charged, according to the geographic location of the borrower, is known as *red-lining*.[2] When a commercial bank decides that it has extended the appropriate amount of loans on new cars (another rule of thumb), the minimum qualification may be raised, or market forces may change the interest rate that is to be charged.

A prime rate of interest is used by commercial banks as a rule of thumb for determining the interest rates to be charged on different types of consumer and commercial loans. A bank's *prime interest rate* is the rate of interest charged by the bank to its best customers on short-term commercial loans. Rather than adjust the interest rates in each loan category, banks adjust interest rates relative to the prime rate. Customers slightly less creditworthy than prime may be charged the prime rate plus 2 percent, whereas the bank's best long-standing customers may get a differential rate and pay the prime rate less 2 percent.

Commercial banks also use general rules to determine the composition of assets. The basic rule for holdings of primary reserves is set by the reserve requirements of regulatory agencies, but individual banks have learned from experience exactly how much should be held as excess reserves. Rules also are used in selecting the appropriate structure of asset maturities. One common approach is to *ladder maturities* of assets and hold relatively equal amounts of securities, ranging in maturities upward to, say, ten years. When market conditions change, the maturity structure then may be adjusted. For example, if the term structure of interest rates is rising and is expected to remain so, the bank may shift its portfolio to hold slightly more of the longer-term securities. A ladder of maturities in a securities portfolio is a method of providing for a steady stream of interest and repayments of principal that brings funds back to the bank for the purchase of new assets of longer maturity. A more active security management rule is to *barbell* the assets, with the bulk of assets being held in very short-term and very long-term maturities. The barbell maturities rule is more active in that

---

[2] The term *red-lining* comes from the reputed practice of drawing a red line on maps around areas where loans are not to be made or where interest charges are to be higher.

greater adjustments are necessary to maintain the desired composition of assets, and greater adjustments are likely to occur when market conditions change.

One commonly used technique of portfolio management is the *matching* of the maturities of assets and liabilities. The major source of funds for commercial banks is the acquisition of deposit liabilities, but these liabilities have very different characteristics. Demand deposits are short-term (in fact they always have the potential of requiring immediate payment), but negotiable certificates of deposit (negotiable CDs) have longer terms to maturity. When a commercial bank acquires additional funds from the sale of a negotiable CD, the commercial bank may well match this deposit with a loan having the same maturity as the deposit. That way, the repayment of the loan will provide the funds for the deposit when it becomes due. Matching is a simple matter of pragmatism. Matching assets with liabilities means that the assets will be adjusted to the changes in the bank's liabilities.

## BANK LIABILITY MANAGEMENT

Theories on the optimal strategy to solve the fundamental problem of financial intermediation have reflected the changing financial markets that might be used in their profit-maximizing activity. (These changes are an ongoing feature of financial intermediary management. *See* "Financial Futures," page 216.) Following World War II, banks concentrated on managing their asset portfolios. With maximum interest rates payable by the institutions set by government regulation, financial markets afforded little opportunity to influence the financial institutions' supply of funds. During the 1960s, interest rates started to rise and depositors sought the higher rates available in the securities and Eurodollar markets. With the continual flow of funds into financial intermediaries no longer assured, financial institutions moved to active liability management.

*Liability management* is the active adjustment of the financial institution's liabilities to help solve its portfolio problems. Not all liabilities can be actively managed. Transactions deposits and small time deposits have been a

*Source: LA Times*, Feb. 11, 1984

## FINANCIAL FUTURES: A NEW MANAGEMENT TOOL[1]

Volatile interest rates in the 1970s added a new dimension of risk to financial intermediary management. Interest rate increases reduce the market value of securities portfolios and raise the cost of funds. Rapid and unexpected interest rate movements forced management to concentrate on interest risk, taking attention away from their business of bringing borrowers and lenders together.

Historically, interest-rate changes did not present a significant management problem. Helped by interest-rate ceilings on deposits, managers could rely on funds at fixed or relatively constant interest rates. As a result they could concentrate on the business of providing service to both depositors and borrowers. The bank would, for example, make firm commitments today to provide future funds at a stipulated interest rate to finance construction. With rapid interest rate movements, such a commitment often entails more risk than the managers are willing to assume.

Financial, or interest rate, futures were introduced in the 1970s to provide the ability to establish, in advance, an interest rate. *Financial futures* are contracts to buy or sell a standardized credit instrument, at a specific, market-determined price, during a specified month in the future.

Financial futures function as commodity futures have for over a century. The only difference is that financial futures contracts are future delivery of standardized credit instruments instead of pork bellies or soy beans.

In futures market activities, two groups of actors are significant: speculators and hedgers. *Speculators* are individuals who assume risk by buying futures when they expect the price to rise and selling when they expect it to decline. Their income comes from predicting more accurately than others the price changes. *Hedgers* enter the futures market to reduce their exposure to

[1] Financial futures is a continually evolving set of markets. Additional, timely information can be obtained from the Chicago Board of Trade, LaSalle at Jackson, Chicago, IL 60604.

risk. A hedger contracts a future position that will offset a cash market position at that time.

Financial intermediaries are permitted to use financial futures as a hedging tool. With financial futures, the managers can contract to acquire or deliver funds in the future. Suppose, for example, the financial intermediary wishes to commit itself to providing a builder construction loans in six months at a specific interest rate. Providing this service to its customer exposes the institution to substantial risk. Should interest rates unexpectedly rise over that period, any income from this intermediation activity may be lost (or even losses incurred) by the increased cost of funds. The institution can hedge this position with a futures contract to sell ("go short") credit instruments in six months. Should interest rates rise, the increased cost of funds will be offset by the ability to buy the credit instruments contracted to be sold at their reduced market price. Should interest rates fall, the gain in reduced funds costs is offset by the higher-priced credit instruments. However, the financial institution still earns the previously anticipated amount of income on the construction loans.

A wide range of financial futures markets have developed over the past decade. Starting in 1975 with the Chicago Board of Trade's contracts for Government National Mortgage Authority (GNMA) mortgage-backed certificates, the market has expanded to include U.S. Treasury bills, bonds, and notes, and bank certificates of deposit. Each market calls for purchase or delivery of a standardized credit instrument. The futures market used by the financial intermediary in its hedging operations depends upon which credit instrument's price is expected to move with the cash position being offset.

Financial intermediaries' use of financial futures is still in its infancy. With any new market, time and experience must determine how it best fits into management objectives. The larger financial intermediaries are becoming active participants in these markets and smaller institutions are likely to follow. This new tool gives the institutions another way to avoid risk and improves their ability to concentrate on the business of channeling funds from lower to higher valued uses.

highly stable, although decreasingly important, source of funds. These deposits are part of the personal relationship a bank has with its customers. By offering higher interest rates or providing improved services, banks can attract additional deposits. However, this has not proved to be an immediate and sure source of additional liquidity. Without additional sources of funds, a decline in deposit liabilities would force a contraction in the bank's asset portfolio.

In order to compensate for deposit drains and to provide the liquidity to extend additional loans, bank management uses markets for short-term borrowings. *Managed liabilities* are borrowings that can be directly and immediately increased or decreased by the financial institution's management. Additional funds are acquired by borrowing in the federal funds market through the sale of repurchase agreements and large negotiable certificates of deposit, in the Eurodollar market or at discount from the Federal Reserve. These markets are large, nationwide sources of funds. Even small banks can acquire millions of dollars by using money brokers to sell $100,000 negotiable CDs.[3]

The use of managed liabilities depends upon the market-determined interest rate charged for the use of the funds, the ability to use the funds acquired profitably, and the financial institution's desire for additional liquidity. The market for federal funds is very important for managing both short-term assets and liabilities.

## The Federal Funds Market

Federal funds are short-term, usually overnight, borrowings between financial institutions. The federal funds market developed shortly after the Federal Reserve was established. In the 1920s, member banks in New York discovered that although some of them had excess reserves in the Federal Reserve District Bank, others were deficient. An informal method of reallocating the existing reserves among the banks was developed. Banks with excess reserves would lend them overnight to the deficient banks. Funds that were transferred were called *federal funds* because the claims that were exchanged were deposits held at the Federal Reserve District Bank.

The federal funds market expanded rapidly in the 1960s and 1970s. Although the market originally consisted of Federal Reserve System members who lent their excess reserves to fellow members with deficient reserves, it now includes overnight borrowing with other financial institutions. Transactions no longer are limited to the borrowing and lending of claims against the Federal Reserve but include any overnight borrowing from financial institutions where the borrowings would not be subject to

---

[3] The market for $100,000 CDs has become so large, and the relationship between CD depositor and receiving institutions so distant, that in 1984 federal regulators removed complete federal insurance coverage from those deposits acquired through money brokers.

reserve requirements if they were borrowed by members of the Federal Reserve. The market participants now include commercial banks (member and nonmember), federal agencies, mutual savings banks, savings and loan associations, and, to a limited extent, government securities dealers. Although the trading primarily is arranged through several, frequently used brokers, the federal funds market is a national market. However, most business is transacted in New York City.

Although some federal funds transactions are secured with government securities used as collateral, and some transactions are for longer than overnight, the usual federal funds transaction is unsecured and overnight. In a typical overnight transaction of $1 million, the lending (selling) bank makes a wire transfer of funds adding $1 million to the reserves of the borrowing (buying) bank at its Federal Reserve District Bank. On the following day the borrowing bank wire transfers the funds plus interest back into the reserves of the lending bank at its Federal Reserve District Bank.

The interest rate charged in this market is called the *federal funds rate* ($R_{FF}$). If $1 million for one night costs $277.78, the federal funds rate[4] is:

$$\frac{\$1,000,277.78 - \$1,000,000}{\$1,000,000} \cdot \frac{360}{\text{number of days held}}$$

$$= \frac{\$277.78}{\$1,000,000} \cdot \frac{360}{1} = 0.10, \text{ or } 10 \text{ percent.}$$

For many years the federal funds rate was considered to be a key indicator of credit conditions in the economy. The reason for this interpretation rests with the nature of the market in the days when the market was used exclusively by member banks wishing to adjust their reserve positions. In those days, a tightness of credit would mean that more banks would be seeking reserves and fewer banks would have excess reserves. In the market, therefore, the demand for federal funds would increase and the supply would decrease. Thus, the federal funds rate would rise. This interpretation seems less appropriate in the much-expanded market where large banks continually borrow funds, not because they have deficient reserves, but because they can profitably relend the funds they have borrowed, and small banks tend to build up substantial balances at correspondent banks for the express purpose of lending the funds in the federal funds market.

Although the market no longer is tied exclusively to deficient or excess reserves in commercial banks, it still serves as a key indicator of credit conditions. The short-term and volatile nature of the federal funds market causes it to reflect immediately any changes in prevailing credit market conditions. The federal funds market has had a significant effect on bank portfolio management in reducing the amount of excess reserves held. With

---

[4]The federal funds rate is always calculated on a 360-day year.

the federal funds market, banks and other financial institutions have a market immediately available for earning interest overnight on any reserves in excess of required reserves and can readily acquire reserves to make up any deficiency on a short-term basis.

## Inflation and Bank Management

Rapid and upredictable price rises from the mid-1960s through the decade of the 1970s brought about substantial changes in financial markets. Expectations of price level increases drove nominal interest rates up to unprecedented levels. Banks generally extend loans with longer terms to maturity than the average term of their liabilities, the longer-term loans funded by ongoing shorter-term borrowing. During this period, banks found that their cost of funds was rising faster than the earnings on their asset portfolios. Financial intermediaries responded by altering the types of loans extended and the liabilities used to acquire funds.

If inflation is truly unanticipated, little can be done to compensate or to avoid the resulting wealth transfers. Many financial intermediaries suffered significant losses as a result of the unexpectedly high rates of change in prices during the 1970s, failing to record a profit even into the early 1980s.

Adjustments can and have been made when it is anticipated that prices will change, even when the rate of change is highly variable and difficult to predict. Rising uncertainty over future rates of change in prices and nominal interest rates will induce financial intermediaries to avoid long-term, fixed interest-rate commitments. In the early 1980s, financial intermediaries shied away from conventional 30-year, fixed rate mortgages. They often restricted those loans to amounts that could be packaged and resold easily in secondary markets.

Uncertainty also moved the financial institutions toward a partial indexing of the interest rates charged. *Variable* or *adjustable rate loans* let the interest rate charged change automatically with changes in market conditions. The interest rate charged often is tied to a shorter-term interest rate. The indexes used include the prime rate, federal funds rate, rate on 90-day

*Source:* By permission of Johnny Hart and News Group Chicago, Inc.

Treasury bills, and financial institutions' average cost of funds. Beyond automatic adjustments in the interest rate charged, loans are also extended under contract to renegotiate the terms after a specified time period, say four to five years. The adjustability of interest rates on longer-term loans reduces the probability of substantial wealth transfers that result from unpredicted changes in the inflation rate. Also, adjustable rates reduce the necessary costs associated with the immediate inflation-rate prediction for the entire term to maturity of the loan.

## THE INTERACTION OF ASSET AND LIABILITY MANAGEMENT

Modern bank management consists of liability management as much as it consists of asset management. Bank managers make daily adjustments in a particular set of assets (the shiftable assets) and a particular set of liabilities (the managed liabilities) in response to changes in the total amount of deposits. These items are listed in Table 9.6. The day-to-day management of a commercial bank can be seen readily by considering the alternatives available to a bank when it suffers adverse clearings.

*Adverse clearings* are any net decline in deposits realized by a commercial bank at the end of a business day. They result on any day when cash withdrawals and check payments exceed cash deposits and check receipts. The amount of the clearings must be paid from vault cash, deposits at the Federal Reserve, or from interbank deposits. When any bank makes a net payment on its deposits, the amount of the deposits will be reduced by the same amount as the assets. To the extent that this reduces the bank's primary reserves below the requirement, the bank must somehow replenish primary reserves. This can be done either by selling off some of the bank's assets or by additional short-term borrowing.

Which of the methods the bank manager will use to acquire primary reserves will depend on the cost of obtaining the cash items in terms of the

*Table 9.6*
**Markets Used for Obtaining Short-Term Primary Reserves**

| Shiftable Assets | Managed Liabilities |
| --- | --- |
| U.S. government and agency securities | Federal funds |
| State and local securities | Eurodollar borrowings |
| Banker's acceptances | Repurchase agreements |
| Call loans to brokers and dealers | Large negotiable CDs |
| | Discount borrowings from Federal Reserve Banks |

interest forgone, the length of time that the bank expects that it will have to hold the additional primary reserves, and the overall impact the action might have on the commercial bank's portfolio.

The decision over which market or markets to use will depend on the prevailing interest rates in the various markets. If the rates that would be forgone by selling assets (the rate based on the bid price in the secondary markets) are significantly less than the rates that would have to be paid for acquiring cash items (the federal funds rate, the discount rate, the Eurodollar rate, etc.), additional funds will likely be acquired by selling assets. Interest rate differentials will be compared, and with other things remaining the same, banks will choose the least costly way to acquire primary reserves. Bank management requires a continual monitoring of interest rates that would be forgone when selling assets and of interest rates that would be paid when acquiring liabilities.

The length of time the commercial bank's managers expect to require the additional primary reserves is also an important determinant of the market that will be used to obtain funds. If the bank is expecting a deficiency for a very short period, a short-term source like federal funds or repurchase agreements will be used. A longer-term use of funds may induce the use of the market for large negotiable CDs, or the bank will sell United States government or agency securities outright.

The overall impact on the commercial bank's portfolio also is an important consideration in determining which market or markets to use to obtain funds. For example, if market rates of interest have risen over the period that securities have been held, the sale of these securities will result in capital losses to the bank. To avoid this, the bank will not sell such assets but will remain "locked-in" to them. This, of course, will mean that the bank will have to use other markets for obtaining additional primary reserves.

The financial markets that are used are interrelated. The activities of the entire set of financial actors is important. For example, if banks suffering adverse clearings attempt to borrow in the federal funds market, this will drive the federal funds rate up. This will induce some banks to move into other markets. The result will be an increase in the interest rate in that market, too. The result is a general movement of market-determined interest rates in the same direction. To the extent that markets are alternative sources of funds for the banking institutions, the interest rates in those markets will tend to move together.

## SUMMARY

The basic operation of a commercial bank is through adjustments in the bank's portfolio to reach an optimum among liquidity, profitability, and safety within the legal constraints imposed by regulatory agencies. To satisfy legal requirements, banks and other transactions housing institutions are required to hold determinable amounts of primary reserves to satisfy re-serve requirements. In addition, banks hold as cash items some interbank deposits and deposits with Federal Reserve Banks for use in check clearing. Check clearing takes place between correspondent banks, through local clearinghouse arrangements, and, at the national level, through the Federal Reserve. The ability to transfer funds with checks is an important service of banks and serves as a primary incentive for the use of bank demand deposits.

Portfolio management for commercial banks requires adjusting the portfolio to provide for adequate liquidity. Liquidity is required for payment of deposit withdrawals and for available funds to satisfy loan demands of customers. Modern banks provide for liquidity by holding shiftable assets, by arranging the inflow of funds from the anticipated income from loans, and by maintaining access to short-term borrowing through managed liabilities.

The principal source of bank income is the loan portfolio. In managing the loan portfolio, banks have adopted some general rules of thumb for extending loans. These rules include setting amounts to be lent in different loan categories, setting minimum qualification requirements for loans, and adjusting the rates charged on loans relative to the prime rate of interest. These general rules of thumb reduce the costs associated with obtaining an optimally diversified portfolio.

## Key Terms

reserve requirements
correspondent banking
interbank deposits
check clearance
cash items in process of
  collection
deferred availability cash items
Federal Reserve float

commercial loan theory of
  banking
shiftable assets
anticipated income
managed liabilities
expected rate of return
portfolio diversification
adverse clearings

## Questions

1. "In the absence of reserve requirements, commercial banks would not be sufficiently liquid." Evaluate.

2. Explain how reserve requirements constrain bank-lending activity.

3. Explain how the check-clearing process facilitates the flow of funds.

4. Explain how weather affects the size of the Federal Reserve float.

5. Explain how, under the commercial loan theory of banking, the quantity of money would be tied to bank purchases of commercial

paper. How does the availability of other interest-earning assets for commercial banks break this direct tie?

6. Explain why interest-rate ceilings on deposits might serve as an incentive for individuals to forgo the benefits from using financial intermediaries.

7. "Red-lining" is the act of restricting the extension of loans in a selected (red-lined) geographic area. Explain why commercial banks might find this practice useful in selecting the bank's portfolio of assets.

## Additional Readings

Bundy, James M., David B. Humphrey, and Myron L. Kwast. "Check Processing at Federal Reserve Offices." *Federal Reserve Bulletin* (February 1979): 97–103.

*A survey of the use of the Federal Reserve's check-clearing process.*

Brewer, Elijah. "Bank Funds Management Comes of Age." *Economic Perspectives.* Federal Reserve Bank of Chicago (March–April 1980): 3–10.

*A discussion of bank portfolio adjustments in response to volatile interest rates.*

Flanney, Mark J. "How Do Changes in Market Interest Rates Affect Bank Profits?" *Business Review.* Federal Reserve Bank of Philadelphia (September–October 1980): 13–22.

*A survey of the adjustments in a bank's costs and revenues in the face of changes in market conditions.*

Hamilton, Earl G. "An Update on the Automated Clearinghouse." *Federal Reserve Bulletin* (July 1979): 525–31.

*A survey of the growth in automated clearinghouses and their potential commercial use.*

Havrilesky, Thomas M., and John T. Boorman, eds. *Current Perspectives in Banking.* 2d ed. Arlington Heights, Ill.: AHM Publishing Corp., 1980.

*A collection of articles too numerous to list individually. Parts I, II, and IV relate to the material in this chapter.*

Luckett, Dudley G. "Approaches to Bank Liquidity Management." *Economic Review.* Federal Reserve Bank of Kansas (March 1980): 11–27.

*A discussion of the interactions between short-term asset and liability management and the evolving nature of short-term bank management.*

Merris, Randall C. "Business Loans at Large Banks: Policies and Practices." *Economic Perspectives.* Federal Reserve Bank of Chicago (November–December 1979): 15–23.

*A discussion of the changing nature of bank management with respect to the bank's loan portfolio.*

Melton, William C. "The Market for Large Negotiable CDs." *Quarterly Review* 2. Federal Reserve Bank of New York (Winter 1977–1978): 22–34.

*A coverage of the growth and use of large CDs in liability management.*

Schroeder, Frederick J. "Developments in Consumer Electronic Fund Transfers." *Federal Reserve Bulletin* (June 1983): 395–403.

*Review of consumer use and the costs and benefits of regulations on automatic and preauthorized transfers.*

# CHAPTER TEN

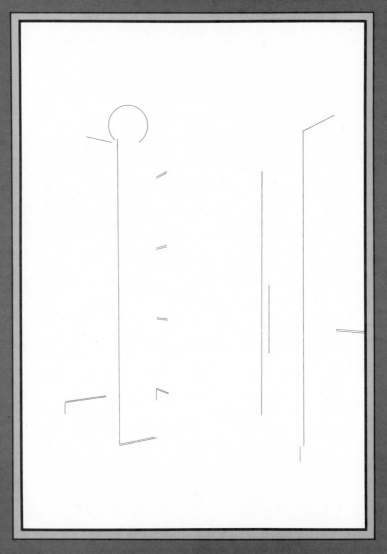

# THE REGULATION OF BANKS AND
# BANKING ACTIVITY

*Commercial banking may well be the most regulated industry in the United States economy. Financial innovation and increased competition from other financial intermediaries have produced sweeping revisions in banking regulations. The major changes come from the Depository Institutions Deregulation and Monetary Control Act of 1980 and the Garn–St. Germain Depository Institutions Act of 1982.*

C ommercial banking may well be the most regulated industry in the United States. Three federal agencies (the Federal Reserve, the Comptroller of the Currency, and the Federal Deposit Insurance Corporation) and at least one agency in each state supervise and regulate the banking industry. This widespread regulation stems from banks serving in the public trust as a storehouse for the savings of a large proportion of the population, and from banking being so all-pervasive in the economy. Through a network of deposits and loans, commercial banks are involved in almost all economic transactions.

The regulation of the banking industry has a direct impact at both the industry level and the level of aggregate economic activity. The regulations discussed in this chapter serve to shape and mold the structure of the banking industry. Regulations constrain entry into, and expansion of, the banking industry and also control exit from the industry. In addition to the micro-impact on the industry structure, the regulation of banks and financial institutions has a direct impact at the macro level through the influence on the flow of credit and the amount of money available.

There are basically two explanations why regulations are imposed. The explanations differ on which groups are perceived to gain from the regulations. Historically, regulations were thought to be imposed to promote the public interest, but more recently it has been theorized that, no matter what the original purpose of the regulatory agency, eventually it is co-opted by the industry and the regulations imposed are those demanded by the private interests of those being regulated.[1]

Regulations are imposed on banking activity to overcome or prevent a perceived deficiency in the market. This deficiency could be some misallocation of resources from the public's standpoint or a perception by members of the industry that the operation of the free market is not in its best interest. It should be realized, however, that some group expects to gain from the regulation; otherwise there would be no incentive for imposing the regulation in the first place. However, the gains for one group may well come at the expense of costs imposed on some other group. It is often difficult to determine exactly who gains and who loses and what they gain or lose. For example, the regulations restricting entry into banking might be thought of as being in the public interest because they generate greater stability in the financial sector, or they might be thought of as protecting the private interests of the existing banks from the competition of new entrants. Whichever might be the case, it is very difficult to determine exactly who might have lost from not being able to enter the industry.

Some regulations are designed to promote a smoother functioning of markets by providing easier access to information. "Truth in lending" (Regulation Z of the Federal Reserve Code) follows this line by requiring uniform information on credit charges. Banking regulations also alter the flow of credit. Legislation constrains the types and extent of lending financial intermediaries may undertake.

Competition is a theme that runs through banking regulation, since it may be reduced if financial institutions are allowed to become too large. Restricting entry and expansion may reduce competition and create market inefficiencies. Alternatively, "excessive competition" may create financial instability.

Regulations are often imposed in response to financial instability. Major banking legislation followed the panic of 1907 and the Great Depression of the 1930s. Regulators' concern with stability stems from the interdependence among various financial institutions. One failed bank would be of little concern as an isolated event. However, if other banks depend on the failed bank (through, perhaps, correspondent balances), they too might be put into jeopardy. Without widespread information as to the cause of the failure, the public might consider that many banks are unsafe. Banking cannot operate without the trust of depositors.

---

[1] See: Stigler, George J., "The Theory of Economic Regulation," *The Bell Journal of Economics and Management Science,* 2 (1, Spring 1971).

## THE REGULATORS

In order to operate a bank it is necessary to obtain a charter. A *charter* is an authorization from a government authority establishing a corporation and defining its rights and privileges. The United States operates under a *dual banking system,* which means that there are two different chartering agencies. *National banks* are chartered by a federal agency, the Comptroller of the Currency, which is an office of the United States Treasury. *State banks* are chartered by a designated agency of the state in which the bank operates. However, there are four kinds of regulating agencies: the state banking agencies, the Comptroller of the Currency, the Federal Reserve, and the Federal Deposit Insurance Corporation.

*State Banking Agencies.*   There are banking departments in each of the 50 states and the United States territories of Guam, Puerto Rico, and the Virgin Islands. The regulations differ from place to place as to the requirements for receiving a charter. Although these agencies have jurisdiction over the majority of the state commercial banks (over 10,000), they have *sole* jurisdiction over only the few noninsured, nonmember banks that numbered 425 in 1982. (*See* Figure 10.1.)

*Comptroller of the Currency.*   Prior to the National Bank Acts of 1863–1864, the United States Congress had chartered only two banks: the first Bank of the United States (1791–1811) and the second Bank of the United States (1816–1836). The National Bank Acts of 1863–1864 established the office of the Comptroller of the Currency as a bank-chartering agency. Any bank receiving a charter from this source is a national bank. The Comptroller has jurisdiction over, directly supervises, and examines all national banks.

*The Federal Reserve.*   Providing effective bank supervision was one reason for establishing the Federal Reserve System in 1913. Membership in the Federal Reserve is mandatory for all national banks. State banks may choose whether or not to join. As Figure 10.1 shows, about 10 percent of state banks have chosen to join. The Federal Reserve Board of Governors has supervisory powers over all *member banks,* but to avoid duplication of effort by the Federal Reserve and Comptroller's Office, the Federal Reserve tends to examine only state member banks.

*The Federal Deposit Insurance Corporation.*   *The Federal Deposit Insurance Corporation* (FDIC) was established by the Banking Act of 1933. It was established principally as an agency for insuring small deposits in commercial banks, but in providing this insurance the FDIC has supervisory

*Figure 10.1*
**Jurisdiction over Commercial Banks, December 31, 1982**

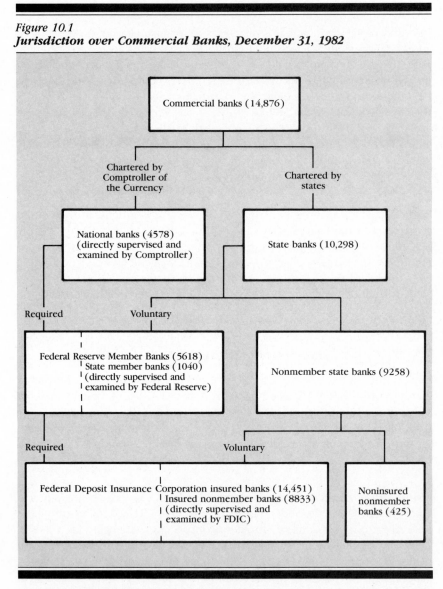

Source: *Charges among Operating Banks and Branches,* FDIC, December 31, 1982, p. 4.

jurisdiction over all insured banks. About 97 percent of commercial banks have FDIC insurance. Such insurance is mandatory for members of the Federal Reserve and for operation in some states. Even without this requirement, most banks choose to be insured. Although the FDIC has this broad jurisdiction, in practice it tends to examine only nonmember insured banks.

## COMPETITIVE REGULATION

Although the law has established overlapping federal banking agencies to supervise the banks, in practice there is a system of competing regulatory authorities. By selecting a status of national bank, state member bank, non-member insured bank, or nonmember noninsured bank, a bank, in fact, can choose whether to be supervised by the Comptroller of the Currency, the Federal Reserve, the FDIC, or only the state banking agencies.

Separating the supervision and examination of commercial banks has the advantage of reducing the costs associated with the examination process for both the banks and the regulators. Supervision costs are reduced when federal agencies avoid duplication of the efforts of other agencies. It is less disruptive for the bank to be examined by only one agency.

The competitive regulatory system is seen as advantageous in the promotion of innovations in the banking system. Any new activity undertaken by a commercial bank usually requires the permission of the supervisory agency. If a national bank had to satisfy all three federal agencies and a state agency before it could experiment with a new technique, the possibilities for innovation would be severely limited.

Competition between agencies tends to temper the severity of the regulations. If one agency becomes stricter than the others, the banks can change their status and shift to a less strict agency. Leniency in regulations can lead to improved banking, but rules being too lenient can lead to a less-stable financial sector.

### Membership in the Federal Reserve System

One result of the competitive nature of bank regulation in the United States has been a steady decline in membership in the Federal Reserve System since World War II. Because banks with state charters are not required to be members, they can leave at any time. National banks can usually change jurisdictions by obtaining a state charter. Membership in the Federal Reserve declined from 49.1 percent of all commercial banks in 1947 to 37 percent of all commercial banks by 1980. (*See* Figure 10.2.) The decline in membership and the percentage of deposits over which the Federal Reserve set reserve requirements were incentives for passage of the Monetary Control Act of 1980.

Historically, one reason for staying with the Federal Reserve System has been the dividend earned on Federal Reserve stock. All members of the Federal Reserve must contribute an amount equal to 3 percent (with an additional 3 percent subject to call) of their paid-in capital and surplus to their Federal Reserve District Bank. The Federal Reserve pays a guaranteed 6 percent on this investment. However attractive this risk-free 6 percent return may have seemed in the 1930s and 1940s, it has not been a sufficient reason for joining the system since the 1960s.

*Figure 10.2*
**Membership Attrition**

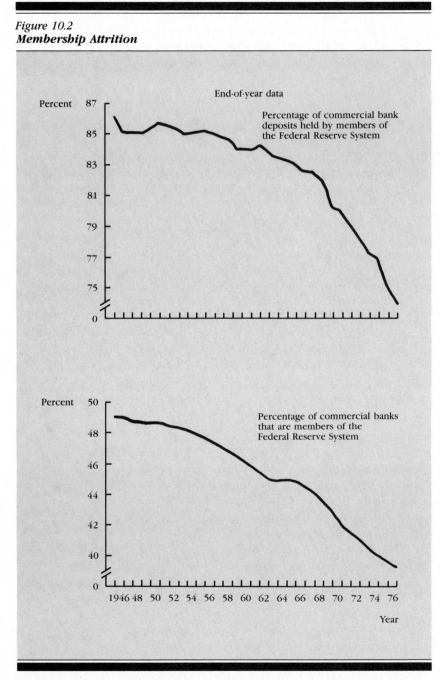

*Source:* Gilbert, R. Alton, "Utilization of Federal Reserve Bank Services by Member Banks: Implications for the Costs and Benefits of Membership," *Review* (Federal Reserve Bank of St. Louis, August 77): 2.

Banks become members because of the costs and benefits that they expect from their association with the Federal Reserve.[2] Through 1980, banks leaving the Federal Reserve System cited the high cost of satisfying reserve requirements. Although most states imposed reserve requirements, they were less stringent than Federal Reserve requirements. Most states allowed a wider range of assets to be counted as reserves. The major benefits of membership came in the form of services provided free to member banks or not provided at all to nonmembers. These services included the following:

*Lending:* The Federal Reserve served as a lender to member banks through the discount window. Nonmembers did not have access to this service.

*Check-collection service:* Nonmember banks had only restricted access to this national check-clearance service. The main cost to a member bank was that of encoding and sorting the checks. Many smaller banks clear their checks through correspondent banks to take advantage of scale economies.

*Currency and coin service:* Free delivery of new currency and removal of defective currency were provided members of the Federal Reserve through armored cars or the mail. Nonmembers received this service at cost.

*Wire transfer facility:* Funds and U.S. government securities may be transferred from one member bank to another through a wire transfer system installed and operated by the Federal Reserve. The system is primarily used in the federal funds market.

*Safekeeping of securities:* The Federal Reserve provided for the safekeeping of securities at no charge to member banks. The securities are commonly held as book entries only. Except in keeping pledged United States government securities, this service was not available to nonmember banks.

The incentives for belonging to the Federal Reserve have changed with passage of the Monetary Control Act of 1980. Reserve requirements imposed by the Federal Reserve have been extended universally to all transactions-deposit-housing financial institutions, as is access to the discount window. The Monetary Control Act also requires the Federal Reserve to charge for its services and to provide them on the same basis to both member and nonmember depository institutions.

---

[2]For an analysis of membership in the Federal Reserve, *see* Gilbert, R. Alton, "Utilization of Federal Reserve Bank Services by Member Banks: Implications for the Cost and Benefits of Membership," *Review* (Federal Reserve Bank of St. Louis August 1977): 2–15.

The Federal Reserve now has control over reserve requirements for all depository institutions. This control has removed any problems caused by limited membership on monetary control. With universal access to Federal Reserve services at the same fees, a bank's membership decision and charter choices now turn on a simple determination of which agency the bank desires to use as its direct supervisor and examiner.

## ENTRY INTO BANKING

One of the cornerstones of competition is the ability to enter the industry. Entry into the activity is induced if profits in the field are greater, adjusted for the risk involved, than the alternatives. *Entry* into the field then increases the supply and causes the price to fall. This drives profits down to the normal rate of return for the amount of risk incurred and eliminates the incentive for further entry. Free entry tends to reduce the costs of services provided by allowing low-cost producers the opportunity to underprice the competition and attract customers away from those with a smaller comparative advantage. Entry into the field of banking, however, is not free because of the necessity of acquiring a charter.

In the early 1800s obtaining a charter to operate a commercial bank was extremely political. Charters were granted directly by state legislatures. Political manipulation and outright corruption were not unknown. The removal of bank chartering from the political process, however, began with the passage of free banking laws in Michigan (1836) and New York (1837). This system spread nationwide and was incorporated in the National Bank Acts of 1863–1864. Under free banking laws, obtaining a charter and entering the banking field required the satisfying of certain rules regarding organization and capital requirements. The dual banking system in the United States arose from the federal and state chartering agencies having different sets of rules with which banks could comply.

Despite the desirable economic effects of free entry into an industry, there have been undesirable effects, particularly in banking. In the short run, there can be large swings in the number of firms in the industry. High profits attract new firms into an industry, and weaker or more poorly managed firms leave. While the exit releases resources for higher valued uses, it can have a disruptive effect in the financial sector of the economy. In the Great Depression of the 1930s, the 25,000 banks that had been in operation in 1929 were reduced by 9000 that suspended operations by 1934. To prevent such a disruption of economic activity, the regulators have attempted to guard against the possibility of instability in the financial markets by restricting entry into banking. Such regulation is not likely to be opposed by the firms already in the industry, as a barrier to entry will give them a certain amount of protection from competition.

*Source:* By permission of Johnny Hart and News Group Chicago, Inc.

Free banking in the United States effectively came to an end with the passage of the Bank Act of 1935. Under this act, national bank charters, membership in the Federal Reserve System, and, most important, approval for an application for insurance of deposits with the FDIC all require a consideration of the following:

1. Financial history and condition of the bank

2. Adequacy of the capital structure

3. Future earning prospects

4. General character of the management

5. *Convenience and needs* of the community served by the bank

Consideration of the "convenience and needs" of the community served by the banks effectively precludes free banking. Unless a new bank can demonstrate that the needs of the community are not being met by the existing banks, that bank cannot become a national, a member, or an insured bank. Few banks are willing to enter banking under these conditions. Meeting the convenience-and-needs requirement can be fairly easy if the population and the personal income of the area is growing.

## Expansion of Banking through Branches

Commercial banks that survive against local competition must have a comparative advantage over those who fail. One way of taking advantage of this kind of expertise is to allow successful banks to expand into other geographic locations. This would allow the public a greater choice of banks and tend to lower the costs of the services offered.

*Branch banking* has been greatly restricted in the United States. Since no state agency can grant permission to operate in another state, state banks are limited to operating in only one state. National banks also are restricted to operating in a single state, because the McFadden Act of 1927 subjects national banks to the branch banking regulations of the state in which they

## INTERSTATE BANKING: THE NEXT PHASE

Historically, banking has been a decentralized, community-oriented business. Banks provided a deposit-accepting service for the local community and concentrated on extending loans to local business and consumers. Over the years, as transportation services improved and the population became increasingly mobile, banks expanded their services to other communities through branching where it was permitted. Branching removed some of the isolation of financial markets, enabled customers to continue banking with the same operation in other communities, and promoted the transfer of funds from communities with lower valued uses to communities willing to pay higher rates of interest.

In the early 1900s, banks began establishing branches across state lines. The McFadden Bank Act of 1927 cut this expansion short by prohibiting it unless specifically authorized by state legislation. Interstate expansion of banking operations continued through multibank holding companies until their activities were severely restricted by the Bank Holding Company Act of 1956.

Banking has become an increasingly complex business. Fluctuating interest rates on deposits and increased competition from nonbank financial intermediaries are changing the mode of bank operations. It is no longer simply a matter of using a stable amount of demand and time deposits acquired at ceiling rates to

operate. Branch banking across state lines thus is precluded.[3] In addition, most states either prohibit or severely limit branch banking *within* the state. Some states have established reciprocal arrangements that would permit banks in either state to branch into the other state. So far such agreements are not widespread (*see* "Interstate Banking: The Next Phase," above.)

The limitations on branch banking range from practices of states that do not allow branching at all (the permitted system is called *unit banking*) to states that allow statewide branching (predominately in the West). In

---

[3]A grandfather clause permitted the operation of existing branches. For example, one national bank in New Jersey has one branch in Pennsylvania. One national bank in California operates three branches in Washington and one branch in Oregon.

finance a series of short-term loans to business. Active liability management and access to funds from national markets are important for even small local banks.

Interstate expansion of banking activities has accelerated in the 1980s. Bank holding companies have aggressively established limited interstate loan and financing operations. This is especially evident in the growing markets in the West and the Sunbelt states. This expansion enables the banking operations to take advantage of differences in local financial market conditions.

Expansion across state lines is likely to increase. Several states have already modified their laws to permit some interstate entry. Three New England states have enacted laws that provide for entry by New England area banks if their home state has a reciprocal agreement.

Regulators are also moving in the direction of interstate banking. The Federal Home Loan Bank Board (regulator of savings and loan associations) allows interstate acquisition to rescue failing institutions. The Garn–St. Germain Depository Institutions Act of 1982 has given bank regulators the authority to permit interstate acquisition of failing institutions.

The future of national banking is still unclear. If we continue in our current direction, we will have a substantial decline in the number of banks, and banks will serve a wider geographic area.

between these extremes, there are states that allow branch banking within the city and county of the head office (Alabama, Indiana, Massachusetts, and New Hampshire); those that allow branching within a hundred-mile radius of the head office (Mississippi); and those that permit only "offices," "agencies," or "stations" (Arkansas, Kansas, Nebraska, Oklahoma, and Wisconsin).[4] (*See* Figure 10.3.)

Unit banking dominates the Midwest. Unit banking is considered desirable by some because it leads to a greater number of individual banks serving the state. With unit banking or limited branching it is considered

---

[4] Munn, Glenn G., *Encyclopedia of Banking and Finance,* revised and enlarged by F. L. Garcia (Boston: Bankers' Publishing Company, 1973): 141–142.

## Figure 10.3
### *State Branch Banking Regulations and Percentage of Commercial Bank Deposits held by Multibank Holding Companies*

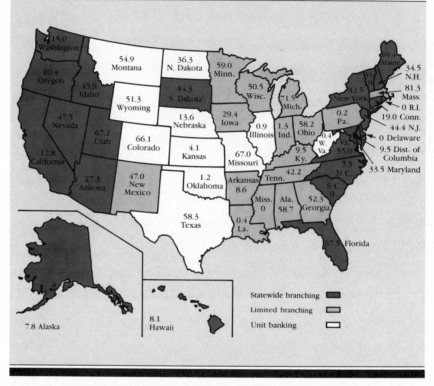

*Source:* Savage, D. T., "Developments in Banking Structure, 1970–81," *Federal Reserve Bulletin,* February 1982, p. 81.

less likely that market power will become concentrated in a few large banks. Also, the concentration of banking in a few large banks that might result from unlimited branching could give those larger banks a greater ability to influence political decisions. In addition, there is a concern that branch banks might siphon funds away from rural areas and take them to the main financial centers. Unit banks also are considered to be more concerned with local conditions.

Not everyone would consider these concerns justified. A unit bank with no competition from the outside could have more market power locally than a large branch bank. Also, it is just as likely that a branch bank would provide a local community with banking services that would not be available from a smaller bank as it is that the branch bank would drain funds away from the area.

*Source:* Drawing by Ed Fisher; © 1984, The *New Yorker* Magazine, Inc.

"I can't sleep. But neither can the city sleep. Nor can justice, health care, round-the-clock banking . . . "

## Bank Holding Companies

One method employed to circumvent the restrictions imposed by branch banking laws is to form bank holding companies. A *bank holding company* is a separate organization that owns or controls a bank or banks. If unrestricted, a multibank holding company could operate multiple banking concerns in states that prohibited branch banking and control banks across state lines. The extent to which multibank holding companies have been able to circumvent branch banking laws can be seen in Figure 10.3. There are several states with unit or limited branching laws in which multibank holding companies account for over 50 percent of commercial bank deposits.

The arguments for restricting multibank holding companies are similar to those for restricting branch banking. Another concern is the potential of bank holding companies for spreading control over other commercial activities. Without restrictions, the bank holding companies pose a threat of competition with nonbanking concerns. Also, allowing bank holding companies into risky alternative activities may pose additional risk to the functioning of the banking system.

The first national legislation recognizing bank holding companies was the Banking Act of 1933. Under this act, the Federal Reserve was given the power to withhold a bank holding company's right to vote its stock in member banks. Bank holding companies had to permit the Federal Reserve to examine their affiliated banks, divest themselves of any securities business, and submit certain reports in order to obtain a permit to vote their stock.

A general restriction of the activities of multibank holding companies did not come until the Bank Holding Company Act of 1956. Corporations owning or controlling 25 percent or more of at least two banks were required to register with, and come under the direct supervision of, the Federal Reserve. Multibank holding companies were required to divest themselves of their nonbanking activities. The acquisition of more than 5 percent of an out-of-state bank was prohibited unless expressly authorized by state law. The activities of multibank holding companies were restricted to "bank-related" activities and required the approval of the Federal Reserve.

*Table 10.1*
**Some Bank-Related Activities Allowed Bank Holding Companies**

| | |
|---|---|
| Mortgage banking | Bookkeeping and data processing services |
| Finance companies | Insurance directly related to credit extension |
| Credit card business | |
| Factoring companies[1] | Underwriting credit life, accident, and health insurance |
| Industrial banking | |
| Servicing loans | Courier service |
| Trust companies | Management consulting service for unaffiliated depository institutions |
| Investment and financial advice | |
| Margin lending | Retail sale of money order, traveler's checks, and U.S. savings bonds |
| Leasing real and personal property (full-payout) | |
| | Investment in export trading companies |
| Equity debt and investment in community welfare projects | |
| Security brokerage | |
| Margin lending | |
| Data basis for financial, economic, and banking data | |

[1] Factoring companies purchase receivables, run a billing and collection agency, and assume the risk from the extension of this credit.

*Source:* Board of Governors, *Federal Reserve Code,* Regulation Y.

(*See* Table 10.1.) The control over multibank holding companies was tightened with an amendment to the Bank Holding Company Act in 1966 that subjected holding company expansion to the convenience-and-needs criterion.

One-bank holding companies were not initially regulated under the Bank Holding Company Act of 1956 and rapidly expanded their activities in the late 1960s. Although one-bank holding companies obviously were not expanding their activities by acquiring additional banks, regulators saw them as an expanding part of the banking industry that was essentially unregulated. In many cases it was easier, and avoided regulations and legal challenges, for a bank to diversify into related areas, such as bookkeeping and data processing, through a holding company than to enter directly into the other business. Also, funds could be raised easily by the holding company's sale of commercial paper. In 1970 the Bank Holding Company Act was amended to bring one-bank holding companies under the same regulations as multibank holding companies. The rapid rise in the number of holding companies can be seen in Table 10.2. The large increase in the number of registered holding companies in 1971 shows the results of registering the one-bank holding companies.

*Table 10.2*
**Bank Holding Companies**

| | All Registered Bank Holding Companies | | | Multibank Holding Companies | | |
|---|---|---|---|---|---|---|
| Year | Number of Companies | Number of Banks | Percentage of Deposits in All CBs | Number of groups[2] | Number of Bank Affiliates | Percentage of Deposits in all CBs[1] |
| 1956 | 53 | 428 | 9.5 | 47 | 428 | 9.5 |
| 1960 | 47 | 426 | 8.0 | 42 | 426 | 8.0 |
| 1965 | 53 | 468 | 8.3 | 48 | 468 | 8.3 |
| 1968 | 80 | 629 | 13.2 | 71 | 629 | 13.2 |
| 1970 | 121 | 895 | 16.2 | 111 | 895 | 16.2 |
| 1971 | 1567 | 2420 | 55.3 | 138 | 1106 | 24.0 |
| 1973 | 1677 | 3097 | 65.4 | 251 | 1815 | 35.0 |
| 1975 | 1821 | 3674 | 67.1 | 289 | 2264 | 37.8 |
| 1977 | 2027 | 3903 | 72.0 | 306 | 2301 | 36.3 |
| 1980 | 3056 | 4954 | 76.7 | 361 | 2426 | 35.4 |

[1] Percentage of deposits in all commercial banks for the states in which bank holding companies operated. In 1956 only 36 states had registered bank holding companies. By 1973 (with the registration of one-bank holding companies starting in 1971), all 50 states and the District of Columbia were included.

[2] Separate banking groups only. This excludes subsidiary banks of bank holding companies that are also registered as bank holding companies.

*Source:* Banking and Monetary Statistics, 1941–1970; Annual Statistical Digests (1971–1977), (1980); (for 1971 figures) Rhoades, S. A., "The Competitive Effect of Interstate Banking," *Federal Reserve Bulletin* (Board of Governors of the Federal Reserve, January 1980).

## International Banking

Expansion of banking and entry into the banking-related field is not restricted to domestic activity. Interstate expansion by foreign banks had become so prevalent that, in the International Banking Act of 1978, reports to Congress were required on the desirability of removing restrictions on interstate banking.

The increase in foreign banking activity has followed the expansion of international trade and improvements in communication and transportation facilities at home and abroad. Just as United States banks have spread overseas, so foreign banks have moved into the United States. The United States has seen two large influxes of foreign banks: one after World War I and the other in the 1970s. By 1979 there were 315 foreign banking institutions operated by 144 foreign banks in the United States, with assets in the United States of over $132 billion.[5]

Foreign banks have operated in the United States under license of the various state agencies. Activities have occurred through agencies, branches, and subsidiary commercial banks. Subsidiary commercial banks operate in the same way as domestic banks; however, although agencies and branches undertake full-scale lending activities, agencies do not have access to funds through the issuing of domestic certificates of deposits. In 1979 foreign banks operated 146 agencies, 122 branches, and 39 subsidiary commercial banks in the United States.

Before the passage of the International Banking Act of 1978, foreign banking operations in the United States had some advantages and disadvantages relative to domestic banks. Through licensing in different states, foreign banks were able to operate as though they had branches across state lines. The McFadden Act prohibited this for all domestic banks. On the other hand, some states restricted foreign banks more than they restricted domestic banks unless there was reciprocal treatment for domestic banks operating in the foreign bank's home country. Foreign banks also were unable to acquire FDIC insurance. This precluded them from accepting deposits in states that require FDIC insurance (such as California).

The International Banking Act of 1978 was passed to provide for uniform national treatment of foreign banks. The act provides for federal licensing and supervision of foreign banks. With a federal license, a foreign bank will be able to branch in states that allow branch banking regardless of reciprocal treatment of United States banks. But foreign banks must select a "home state" for their deposit-accepting operations and keep their deposit-accepting operations restricted to that state. This puts foreign banks on a par with domestic banks. The act also makes FDIC insurance available to foreign banks and requires it for those accepting deposits of less than $100,000.

---

[5] Key, Sidney J. and James M. Bundy. "Implementation of the International Bank Act." *Federal Reserve Bulletin* (October 1979): 785–796.

The International Banking Act also enables the Federal Reserve to impose reserve requirements on deposits of foreign banks whose world-wide operations have assets over $1 billion. Foreign banks also were made subject to all Regulation Q interest-rate ceilings and the nonbanking restrictions of the Bank Holding Company Act (1956 as amended in 1970).

The expansion of United States commercial banks overseas followed the expansion of United States corporations into foreign markets in the late 1960s, but the move was greatly stimulated by credit restrictions imposed in the United States. With restraints imposed on the flow of funds out of the United States to boost the value of the dollar on the foreign exchange, commercial banks expanded into foreign markets to acquire the funds desired by United States businesses operating abroad. Commercial banks also used the foreign markets to raise funds that were not subject to Regulation Q interest-rate ceilings. As interest rate restrictions domestically caused businesses to take their funds out of commercial banks in search of higher returns, the banks tried to recoup the funds they had lost by tapping foreign markets. United States banking abroad expanded from 8 banks operating 131 branches with only $3.5 billion in assets in 1960 to 127 banks operating 731 branches and $219.2 billion in assets by 1976.[6]

If United States banks operating abroad were subject to all United States banking rules, as well as the rules of the country in which they were operating, they would be at a competitive disadvantage relative to the more highly diversified foreign banks. This would be a major problem in countries where the local banks were allowed to provide underwriting services for corporations and hold owners' equity in other businesses. To overcome some of these problems, United States commercial banks have been permitted to establish domestic subsidiary corporations called Edge Act corporations.[7] These subsidiary corporations may hold equity interest in other business firms provided those firms are not primarily engaged in United States production for United States consumption. They also can hold equity interests in foreign financial institutions (located outside the United States). Edge Act corporations are supervised by either the Comptroller of the Currency or the Federal Reserve and are permitted to undertake most of the activities of foreign banking institutions. The Edge Act corporations can accept deposits in the United States, provided those deposits are related to international transactions, and may finance production in the United States provided those goods are intended primarily for export.

The International Banking Act of 1978 has eased the restrictions of the operations of Edge Act corporations. They are now treated in the same way as agencies and branches of foreign banks and are permitted to branch

---

[6]Johnston, Robert, "International Banking, Risk and U.S. Regulatory Policies." *Economic Review* (Federal Reserve Bank of San Francisco, Fall 1977): 36–43.

[7]The Edge Act (1919) added Section 25(A) to the Federal Reserve Act. The section allowed commercial banks to set up subsidiary corporations for the purpose of foreign financial activities.

nationwide. The International Banking Act also has allowed foreign owner-ship of Edge Act corporations. The number of Edge Act corporations grew from 38 in 1964 to 122 in 1977.[8]

The competitive position of banking offices in the United States was further enhanced when permission was granted to establish International Banking Facilities. Starting in December 1981, the Federal Reserve Board permits these facilities to conduct deposit and loan business with foreign residents. This activity is not subject to reserve requirements, deposit inter-est-ceiling rates, or FDIC coverage. During the first nine months, 400 inter-national banking facilities with over $150 billion in assets were established.[9] Of these, 127 were established by United States chartered banks. Although their activities are constrained, several states give these facilities favorable tax treatment.

International banking activity remains a small portion of bank opera-tions. However, increased competition has induced even small banks into the international area. During the growth years of the 1970s, many banks extended sizeable foreign loans. When worldwide recessions hit in the early 1980s, these loans looked exceedingly risky. International banking activity will continue to grow as banking in general moves away from the image of a local institution providing only local services.

## Bank Mergers

A *bank merger* is the combination of two or more banks into one operation. The surviving bank acquires control over the other bank either through an exchange of stock or through a purchase of the bank's assets and an assump-tion of the bank's liabilities.

Bank mergers occur when it is in the private interests of the banks' owners to combine operations. The owners of the surviving bank expect to gain through growth and through employing their management techniques in an additional banking concern. The owners of the merged bank expect to gain from the compensation they receive for the resources forgone. The banking public also may gain through the merger by an improvement in the services provided or through the continuation of an office that otherwise might have closed. However, the banking public might also lose as a result of the reduction in the amount of banking competition.

Direct regulation over mergers by the federal authority supervising the surviving bank was established with the Bank Merger Act of 1960. Prior to 1960 approval of some mergers was required at the federal level, but specific considerations of the factors affecting concentration and competi-tion were absent. The Bank Merger Act requires a consideration of the

---

[8] Pinsky, Neil, "Edge Act and Agreement Corporations: Medium for International Banking," *Economic Perspectives* (Federal Reserve Bank of Chicago September–October 1978): 25–31.

[9] Key, Sydney, "International Banking Facilities," *Federal Reserve Bulletin* 68 (October 1982): 565–577.

convenience and needs of the community served, and the competitive impact of the merger before approval for the merger can be given by the regulatory agency.

The question of antitrust considerations was raised when the attorney general filed against the merger of two banks that had been approved by the Comptroller of the Currency and won on appeal to the Supreme Court (the Philadelphia National Bank case, 1963). The Bank Merger Act was amended in 1966 to include antitrust considerations. The amendment gives the attorney general 30 days after the approval of a bank merger to file against the merger, after which time the merger would become immune from challenge for an antitrust law violation. The amendment specifically allows for mergers when the failure of a bank is imminent and allows for mergers that significantly serve the convenience and needs of the community even though they may be anticompetitive in nature.

## EXIT FROM BANKING

Exit from an industry is as important to the efficient allocation of resources as the ability to enter an industry. With freedom of entry and exit, resources will be induced to flow into those industries in which the public places a higher value on additional services and out of those industries where resources have a lower value. However, the problem with exit from an industry is that it does not come without costs to those involved. Losses are incurred, people are unemployed, and other businesses are disrupted in one way or another.

Exit from the banking industry occurs through a planned liquidation, merger with a stronger firm, or—in the most painful form—through a *bank failure.* A bank failure occurs when the chartering agency places the bank in receivership. A bank suspension is a closing of a bank to the general public by the supervisory agency (other than for general bank holidays). A suspended bank may reopen but usually not in the same form as when it closed. The number of bank closures, 1909–1983, are given in Table 10.3.

Bank failures have a long and dismal history. Outright fraud, dishonesty, and simple mismanagement have been major causes of such failures, though declining general economic conditions also have taken their toll. The first bank failure in the United States (the failure of Farmers Exchange Bank, Glocester, Rhode Island, in 1809) was the result of a rampant overextension of bank notes.[10]

Bank failures impose significant costs on those directly associated with the failed bank. Although *deposit insurance* now has taken care of the de-

---

[10]Sinkey, Joseph F., Jr., *Problem and Failed Institutions in the Commercial Banking Industry,* Contemporary Studies in Economic and Financial Analysis, 4 vols. (Greenwich, Connecticut: JAI Press Inc., 1979): 4:3–5.

### Table 10.3
### Banks Closed Because of Financial Difficulties

| Year or Period | Number of Bank Closures[1] | Commercial Banks Operating at End of Period |
|---|---|---|
| 1909–1919 | 913 | 27,859 |
| 1920–1928 | 5220 | 24,968 |
| 1929 | 659 | 24,026 |
| 1930 | 1350 | 22,172 |
| 1931 | 2293 | 19,375 |
| 1932 | 1453 | 17,802 |
| 1933 | 4000 | 14,440 |
| 1934–1940 | 450 | 14,344 |
| 1941–1978 | 242 | 14,549 |
| 1979 | 10 | 14,533 |
| 1980 | 10 | 15,120 |
| 1981 | 10 | 15,213 |
| 1982 | 42 | 15,329 |
| 1983 | 48 | 15,380 |

[1] Through 1934 this figure gives the number of bank suspensions. Bank suspensions include all banks closed to the public, either temporarily or permanently other than for bank holidays, by the supervising agency or the bank's board of directors because of financial difficulty. Failing banks that have merged with other banks are not counted as suspensions.

Sources: Banking and Monetary Statistics (1943 and 1941–1970); Annual Statistical Digests (1971–1977); Federal Reserve Bulletins (various); Board of Governors of the Federal Reserve System and Annual Report of the FDIC (1983), Table 122.

positors in a failed bank, it should not be forgotten that the losses suffered by depositors in the suspension of 9755 banks between 1929 and 1933 have been estimated at $1.4 billion.[11] One of the most important problems of bank failures comes as a result of the interdependence of the financial system. In the Great Depression, one bank failure led to another as the public generally lost confidence in banks. Between June 1929 and June 1933 deposits in commercial banks declined by $16 billion (28 percent). The means of exchange (demand deposits and currency) declined 27 percent, and loans extended by commercial banks fell 54 percent over the same period.[12]

Even with increased supervision and the stricter entry requirements imposed since the 1930s, bank failures still occur. Aggressive expansion into new areas and adjustments to changing regulations can significantly weaken a bank and lead to its failure. (See "Franklin National Bank," page 247.) Also, bank supervision and examination cannot detect all fraud.

[11] Banking and Monetary Statistics. (U.S. Board of Governors of the Federal Reserve System, 1943), 283.

[12] Ibid. 17–19, 34.

## FRANKLIN NATIONAL BANK[1]

Franklin National Bank is notable in two respects: it was the first bank to issue credit cards, and it was the largest bank failure in United States history. Although these two features are not directly related, the progressive and expansionary nature of Franklin National Bank was the force that eventually led to its failure.

Franklin National Bank was incorporated in 1926 and was a well-established, local bank operating in the Long Island area of New York. From 1934 the bank operated in a market protected from direct competition from the larger New York City banks by New York State's antibranching laws. Franklin's expansion and eventual difficulties stem from the relaxation of these laws. In 1960 New York started to permit limited branching. Franklin was induced by the additional competition to look outside its local area for growth and profits.

In an attempt to grow during the 1960s, Franklin branched into New York City and started expanding its assets by extending relatively unattractive loans at interest rates lower than its competitors'. These loans largely were financed through short-term borrowings. By 1973 federal funds purchased and repurchase agreements amounted to 16 percent of Franklin's liabilities. The 1973–1974 decline in the economy put considerable pressure on the bank. Real output in the United States fell by about 1.4 percent in 1974. The interest rate on federal funds rose from 4 to 5 percent in 1972 to over 13 percent in 1974. The higher cost for short-term funds and the decline in the ability of borrowers to repay the loans made Franklin's economic condition questionable. These problems were recognized relatively early by regulatory agencies. Franklin was listed as a problem bank in 1965 and again in late 1970.

The crisis that directly caused Franklin's failure resulted from its movement into international banking. In the late 1960s and early 1970s many banks moved into the international market to gain direct access to the Eurocurrency markets and the higher profits in the relatively lax regulatory environment of international banking. Franklin followed this movement by establishing branches in the Bahamas in 1969 and in London in 1972. Franklin also undertook considerable speculation in the foreign exchange market by trading on its own account. With a

*continued*

general float in the foreign exchange market only in operation since 1972, general experience with the market was not readily available, and exchange rate movements carried a high level of risk. In the first quarter of 1974 Franklin National Bank lost over $30 million in foreign exchange trading. Much of this trading was unauthorized and hidden. A loss of confidence in Franklin National Bank developed, and it became difficult for the bank to obtain short-term funds. Unsecured federal funds borrowings became unavailable and dropped from $520 million purchased by Franklin National Bank at the beginning of May 1974 to zero by mid-month.

To prevent an immediate closure and a resulting international banking crisis, the Federal Reserve Bank of New York started lending funds at discount to Franklin National Bank in May 1974 and started to oversee an eventual solution to the problem. Federal Reserve lending to Franklin rose from $160 million in May to a high of $1723 million by October. A permanent solution to the Franklin National Bank problem was found on October 8, 1974, when the bank was declared insolvent and acquired by European American Bank and Trust (a chartered bank in New York State owned by an association of European banks). At one time Franklin National Bank was the twentieth largest bank in the United States. At the time of failure the bank had assets of about $3.8 billion.

---

[1] For a complete coverage of the problems of Franklin National, *see*: Spero, Joan Edelman, *The Failure of the Franklin National Bank: Challenge to the International Banking System* (New York: Columbia University Press, 1980). Most data used were taken from the table on pages 72–74.

Deregulation of the banking industry and economic down-turns in the early 1980s have led to a significant increase in bank failures. This moderate upsurge can be seen in Table 10.3. Phasing out of interest-rate ceilings on deposits and increased competition from nonbank financial institutions have placed increased market pressure on bank management. Banking is no longer the staid old business of accepting *core deposits* (demand and savings deposits) at regulated interest rates and extending local commercial loans. Some management has found it difficult to adjust to the new financial environment. Market selection is taking place. Despite the increase in bank failures, the evidence suggests that banking remains an attractive business. The number of commercial banks in operation remains on an increase.

Bank failures remain costly. Even with federal deposit insurance, depositors of amounts in excess of the insurance coverage (currently $100,000) can still lose some of their funds. Smaller depositors may find their funds tied up for extended periods in a failed bank. The interdependence between banks through their correspondent deposits can lead to difficulties for other banks. Any bank failure will cause some loss of confidence in the banking system. In addition to a bank failure's disruption of local business, the public may suffer the loss of previously available banking services.

## Federal Deposit Insurance

Systemwide insurance coverage is provided through the FDIC. Federal deposit insurance now protects small depositors and, by instilling increased confidence in banking in general, has reduced the probability of general bank failures like those that occurred through the 1930s.

The protection offered by the FDIC comes from its supervision and examination of commercial banks, its insurance fund ( $13.77 billion at the end of 1982), its ability to borrow from the federal government, and the methods employed in handling failed banks. FDIC insurance coverage is required for all members of the Federal Reserve System and is available to all nonmember banks that satisfy the FDIC's requirements. An annual assessment of $1/12$ of 1 percent of average total deposits has been levied since 1935 to pay for this coverage.[13]

Insurance protection for bank depositors and other creditors was provided by government bodies as early as 1829 in New York with the passage of the New York Safety Fund Act. This system spread to only a few states and did not survive long. A resurgence of state-provided insurance, however, came in the wake of the bank panic of 1907. Systemwide insurance was not available until establishment of the FDIC in the Banking Act of 1933. Insurance is provided only for small deposits. The initial coverage provided on January 1, 1934, was on deposits up to $2500. This was raised to $5000 on July 1, 1934. Over the years the coverage has expanded and the designation of "small" deposits changed. In 1980 the insurance was raised to cover deposits up to $100,000.

Uniform systemwide insurance coverage provides information at low cost on the safety of deposits in financial institutions. Depositors now primarily rely on the insurance coverage and the regulators' supervision and examination of banks as information on the safety of their deposits. Federal insurance has effectively replaced depositors' evaluations of bank assets and management to discern deposit safety. (See "Market Discipline," page 250.)

---

[13] *Annual Report of the Federal Deposit Insurance Corporation* (1982).

## MARKET DISCIPLINE AND DEPOSIT INSURANCE

Market discipline is a concern about bank safety that arose in the early 1980s. Expansion of federal insurance to $100,000 deposits by the Monetary Control Act of 1980 allowed even large depositors the ability to obtain full coverage. Through money brokers, even large deposits could be split into covered $100,000 units. Large depositors were concerned solely over insurance coverage, not the inherent safety of the banking operation. This attitude was perceived by the FDIC to expose the insurance fund to undue risk and to remove the discipline of the market from deposit placement. About 16 percent of deposits at the 72 commercial banks that failed during 1982 and 1983 came through money brokers.

Historically, banking has been a local business. Deposits were acquired in the local community and used to extend loans to local businesses and the depositors' neighbors. The community retained close working knowledge of the bank's operations. Depositors relied on that knowledge to protect their savings. Financial difficulties (loss of capital, extension of questionable loans, and so forth) would become known to the local community. With this knowledge, the market would discipline the banker by withdrawing the funds necessary to continue in business.

As transportation services improved, financial markets became nationwide. As local banks began working with national markets and having ties to many other banks, depositors' working knowledge of those banks decreased. A bank could run into financial difficulties without local publicity. Bank failures during the 1930s caught many communities by surprise, and trust in even well-run institutions declined.

The establishment of FDIC insurance coverage, restored trust in banking. Small depositors no longer had to evaluate the riskiness of the bank's operations. Federal insurance provided protection for small deposits.

In overseeing banking operations, the insurance program retained some market discipline in addition to its examination and supervision procedures. Large deposits were not covered. Large depositors continued to monitor the banks' operations to protect their assets. Banks that were poorly operated were quickly disciplined by withdrawals of funds. Early on in Franklin

National Bank's trouble, short-term funds became extremely difficult to attract.

With expanded insurance coverage, large depositors no longer find it necessary to expend the resources to evaluate bank portfolios and operations. Like small depositors, they can rely on federal insurance for protection.

The increase in insurance coverage has increased the FDIC's exposure to risk. In 1982 almost 75 percent of deposits in insured banks were covered by FDIC insurance. This was up from 65 percent in the 1970s and 55 percent in the 1950s.[1] A significant element of market-enforced safety of bank operations has been reduced.

Financial institution regulators are concerned with this trend and (in early 1984) have proposed several plans to reinstitute market discipline from larger depositors. These plans include the following:

> *Changing the insurance premium:* If the premium were tied to some measure of risk, the bank would have to be willing to bear the cost of activities that exposed it to more risk.

> *Stronger capital requirements:* Requiring additional capital would expose bank owners to greater losses and induce them to watch the safety of bank operations closely.

> *Altered insurance on large deposits:* Reducing insurance coverage for large deposits would induce those depositors to examine the banks' operations. The market would then impose added considerations to the safety of bank operations.[2]

Changes are only in the planning stages. However, the evidence suggests that over the next few years we will see dramatic changes in the insurance program, a program that brought stability to the banking industry after the turmoil of the 1930s.

---

[1] *Federal Deposit Insurance Corporation Annual Report* (1982): Table 129.

[2] *Economic Report of the President* (Washington, D.C., February 1984).

The knowledge that a bank's deposits are insured has been effective in preventing runs on banks, although the information that a bank is in trouble may still cause a run by those depositors holding large amounts in excess of the insurance coverage. The FDIC is considered important in maintaining the stability of the United States banking system and is credited with the dramatic decline in bank suspensions and failures after 1933. (*See* Table 10.3 on page 246.)

***Bank Examination***   The examination and supervision of banks is another aspect of the New York Safety Fund that has been incorporated into the FDIC. Bank examinations are carried out by the FDIC, the Federal Reserve, the Comptroller of the Currency, and state banking authorities, depending on the kind of charter held by the bank and whether or not it is a member of the Federal Reserve System. Except in the case of nonmember insured banks, which are examined by both the FDIC and state banking authorities, one agency conducts the examination. A report is made available to the other agencies associated with the examined bank.

Bank examinations are important for early detection and correction of problems that might lead to a bank's failure. The bank examiners are not expressly looking for fraud and do not verify the items reported by the bank. Instead, they are looking for unsafe banking practices, such as inadequate capital, insufficient liquidity, insufficient portfolio diversification, and violations of such legislation as federal consumer and investor laws.

The FDIC generally examines banks under its jurisdiction once every 18 months. To correct the deficiencies in banks under its jurisdiction, the FDIC may request changes, issue "cease and desist" orders to stop specific activities, or remove or suspend bank officers; in serious cases where suggested changes are not made the FDIC will terminate insurance. Termination of insurance almost always leads to bank failure.

In the process of examining commercial banks, specific banks are designated as problem banks. A *problem bank* is a bank that the supervisory agency examines more closely and more frequently since its banking practices are giving the bank a high probability of failure. The FDIC examines its problem banks at least once a year. Problem bank lists are not published. Information on individual bank safety acquired by the FDIC is not available to the public.

Although the identification of problem banks makes the surveillance of banks more effective, it cannot identify all bank fraud and mismanagement. Of the 66 insured commercial banks that failed between 1959 and 1973, only 38 had been listed previously as problem banks.[14]

---

[14] Sinkey, *Problem and Failed Institutions,* 45–46.

***Handling Failed Banks.*** When a bank failure is imminent, the chartering agency places the bank into receivership. For insured commercial banks, the FDIC then plays the central role in settling claims against the bank. The two principal methods employed by the FDIC are either to arrange for the assumption of the bank's operations by another bank or to liquidate the bank and pay off the depositors and creditors. In addition, the FDIC can establish a Deposit Insurance National Bank to provide temporary service in the place of the failed bank.

Where possible, the FDIC has arranged for the merger of the failing institution with another bank. The acquiring bank assumes the failing bank's deposit liabilities and may select other liabilities through competitive bidding. Handling the failure through merger protects even uninsured balances at insured banks.

Antibranching banking laws and restrictions on interstate banking have sometimes made finding an eligible bank for a merger difficult. This problem has been removed: the Garn–St. Germain Depository Institutions Act of 1982 gives bank regulators the authority to arrange emergency acquisitions of failing institutions from otherwise restricted geographic areas.

The FDIC is obligated to select the method for handling the closure that will impose the least loss on the insurance fund. Of the 620 bank failures requiring disbursements by the FDIC from 1934 to 1982, 301 were handled by assumption and 319 by deposit payoff.[15]

## Interest-Rate Ceilings on Deposits

Maximum interest rates that may be paid to depositors by commercial banks have been imposed since passage of the Banking Act of 1933. Banks have been prohibited from paying interest on demand deposits, and interest-rate ceilings have been set at various levels for savings and time deposits by the Federal Reserve and the FDIC. Since 1966, thrift institutions similarly have been restricted by their regulators, the Federal Home Loan Bank, the FDIC (for mutual savings banks), and the National Credit Union Association.[16] Although interest-rate ceilings were imposed by various regulatory agencies, they usually were referred to collectively after the Federal Reserve's Regulation Q.

The avowed purpose for imposing *interest-rate ceilings on deposits* was the prevention of interest rate competition between banks to attract funds. It was feared that if banks competed in this way, they would try to earn higher interest rates on their assets by holding riskier portfolios. Interest-rate ceilings also were seen as preserving a viable home mortgage mar-

---

[15] *Annual Report of the FDIC* (1982), Table 124.

[16] A review of interest-rate ceilings is given in "Regulation Q: An Historical Perspective," by S. Winningham and Hagan, D. G., *Economic Review* (Federal Reserve Bank of Kansas, April 1980): 3–17.

ket since funds could be channeled into the thrift institutions by allowing them to pay slightly higher interest rates on deposits than the banks. Competition between banks and between banks and thrift institutions remained, however, in the form of services offered.

As with any market that has a ceiling price imposed, interest-rate ceilings only constrain the market effectively when the market-determined rate would be higher than the ceiling. Between 1935 and 1950 the ceiling rate for time deposits was 2½ percent, and the rates for short-term United States government securities and for commercial paper remained below 2 percent. From the imposition of interest-rate ceilings in 1933 until 1965, ceiling rates basically remained at or above the market-determined rates for similar assets. It is only since 1966 that the ceilings have been effective and have reduced the depository institution's ability to compete for funds.

When imposed constraints restrict individuals or corporations from actions they perceive to be in their best interests, they will seek alternatives that are not subject to the restrictions. Many innovations in banking have resulted from such constraints. NOW accounts were devised specifically to avoid the restriction on paying interest on demand deposits. Bank liability management, the federal funds market, and the use of large certificates of deposit and repurchase agreements expanded as banks sought funds not subject to interest-rate ceilings.

Market rates of interest above the ceiling rates in the late 1960s caused many depositors to remove their funds from the financial institutions and to seek the higher rates on various credit markets. This phenomenon, also responsible for much of the growth in the Eurodollar market, is known as *disintermediation*. Disintermediation led regulators to make some patchwork adjustments in the ceilings. For example, in 1978 permission to link interest rates on six-month certificates to the Treasury bill rate was granted. This innovation and market-related rates on longer-term deposits were not sufficient to stop the growth of other alternatives.

The phenomenal growth of money market mutual funds in the late 1970s is attributable to the effective interest-rate ceilings on other accounts. Money market mutual funds grew from only $3.4 billion in December 1976 to $241 billion in November 1982. These funds offer even small savers access to market-determined interest rates. The mutual funds accept deposits that have properties similar to savings deposits in other financial institutions. Money market funds are not federally insured. The funds' assets are dominated by short-term, highly liquid instruments. Some concentrate on specific money market instruments, such as short-term commercial paper, government securities, or tax-exempt bonds. Money market funds have paid rates of return up to three times the rate paid on deposits subject to Regulation Q.

Although interest-rate ceilings were imposed to create stability in the financial sector, the destabilizing effects of the resulting disintermediation are now apparent. The Depository Institutions Deregulation and Monetary Control Act of 1980 called for a gradual phaseout of all interest-rate ceilings by 1986. The ceiling removal was accelerated by the Garn–St. Germain Depository Institution Act of 1982, which authorized depository institutions to offer an account competitive with money market mutual funds. The new accounts were made available on December 14, 1982, and attracted over $370 billion during the first year.

By 1984 interest-rate ceilings on deposits were almost completely eliminated. Depository institutions could pay market rates on deposits with average balances over $2,500 (providing they reserved the right to require 7 days notice before withdrawal) and on deposits issued with more than 31 days to maturity. The removal of interest-rate ceilings has allowed the depository institutions to compete for and attract funds. However, it has made financial institution management more difficult. With interest-rate ceilings, the decision about how much to pay depositors was already made. Without ceilings, management must continually evaluate its deposit rates to remain competitive and profitable.

## SUMMARY

The banking industry is highly regulated at both local and federal levels. These regulations basically are concerned with attempting to assure that the proper amount of banking and financial activity is provided. The regulations presume that the operations of the free market would provide either too much banking, which would lead to instability, or too little, with a resulting concentration of market power.

To operate a bank, it is necessary to obtain a charter. Commercial banks may obtain charters from either the Comptroller of the Currency (for national banks) or state banking agencies (for state banks). Commercial banks are regulated directly by some combination of state banking departments, the Comptroller of the Currency, the Federal Reserve, and the FDIC.

Entry into banking is restricted. General free banking has been checked since 1933 by subjecting banks to a "needs and convenience" of the community-served consideration to obtain FDIC insurance on deposits. In addition, the entry and expansion of banks into other geographic locations has been limited by both national- and state-imposed restrictions on branch banking. Restrictions on the expansion of banking activity also are imposed on bank holding companies and through restrictions on bank mergers.

Although it can prove costly to both depositors and borrowers, exit from the banking industry is important to the efficient allocation of resources. Liquidations, bank mergers, and bank failures are means of exiting the banking industry. However, although bank failures still occur, entry restrictions, increased supervision and examination, and federally provided deposit insurance through the FDIC have dramatically reduced the probability of general bank failures like those in the early 1930s.

The regulations imposed on commercial banks have served to determine the structure of the banking industry. These regulations also affect general economic conditions by influencing the lending activity of banks and the amount of money that is created.

## Key Terms

| | |
|---|---|
| national banks | bank holding companies |
| state banks | bank failure |
| member banks | deposit insurance |
| FDIC | interest-rate ceilings on |
| entry | deposits |
| branch banks | disintermediation |

## Questions

1. Explain how the "needs and convenience of the community served" influence the structure of the banking industry.

2. "Unless constrained to operate within specific areas and for specific purposes, banks eventually will expand to obtain direct control over most commerce." Evaluate.

3. In whose best interest is it to prevent new entry into banking? Explain.

4. "Bank mergers only should be allowed when a bank is in imminent danger of failing." Evaluate.

5. Canada has not had interest-rate ceilings on deposits. Would you expect to see the development of money market mutual funds in Canada? Why or why not?

6. If the government reduces federal insurance coverage on brokered deposits, which parties will gain and lose? Will this differentially impact large and small depository institutions? If so, how?

## Additional Readings

Brewer, Elijah, et al. "The Depository Institutions Deregulation and Monetary Control Act of 1980." *Economic Perspectives.* Federal Reserve Bank of Chicago (September–October 1980): 3–23.

*A discussion of the historical background of the act, along with a review of its basic provisions.*

Havrilesky, Thomas M., and John T. Boorman. *Current Perspectives in Banking.* 2d ed. Arlington Heights, Ill.: AHM Publishing Corp., 1980.

*A collection of numerous readings on banking; Parts III, IV, and VII–X are related to the material in this chapter.*

Key, Sydney. "International Banking Facilities." *Federal Reserve Bulletin* 68 (October 1982): 565–577.

*A review of the use of a new mechanism for international banking during its first nine months.*

Landy, Laurie. "Financial Innovation in Canada." *Quarterly Review.* Federal Reserve Bank of New York (Autumn 1980): 1–8.

*An overview of financial developments in Canada with some insights into the impacts of interest-rate ceilings on deposits.*

McNeil, Charles R., and Denise M. Rechter. "The Depository Institutions Deregulation and Monetary Control Act of 1980." *Federal Reserve Bulletin* 66 (June 1980): 444–453.

*A description of the details of the 1980 banking and monetary legislation.*

Rhoades, Stephen A. "The Competitive Effects of Interstate Banking." *Federal Reserve Bulletin* 66 (January 1980): 1–8.

*A discussion of the theory and evidence on interstate banking.*

Sinkey, Joseph F., Jr. "Identifying 'Problem' Banks: How Do the Banking Authorities Measure a Bank's Risk Exposure?" *Journal of Money, Credit and Banking* 10 (May 1978): 184–193.

*Contains a brief analysis of the importance of the factors considered in the FDIC's examination of banks in predicting bank failures.*

Smith, W. Stephen. "The History of Potential Competition in Bank Mergers and Acquisitions." *Economic Perspectives.* Federal Reserve Bank of Chicago (July–August 1980): 15–23.

*Contains an overview of the Board of Governors' policies on bank mergers.*

Teeters, N.H., and H. Terrell. "The Role of Banks in the International Financial System." *Federal Reserve Bulletin* 69 (September 1983): 663–671.

*Examination of the expansion of banks' international lending activities and the changing responsibilities of the Federal Reserve.*

# CHAPTER ELEVEN

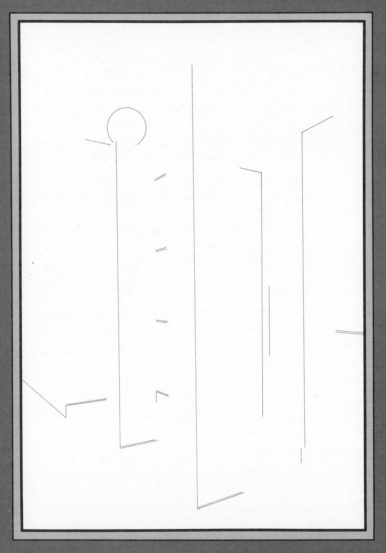

# NONBANK FINANCIAL
# INTERMEDIARIES

*The financial sector of the United
States economy consists of many
nonbank financial intermediaries,
as well as the commercial banks.
Each institution specializes in intermediation between specific lenders and borrowers on the basis of
the institution's comparative advantage. The growth in the size of
nonbank financial intermediaries
since World War II has been a
cause for concern for the monetary
authorities.*

Commercial banks are privately owned financial intermediaries designed to make a profit from acting as middlemen between lenders
and borrowers of funds. The significance of the commercial banks
is primarily that a large part of the money supply is created as a by-product
of their lending activities. However, commercial banks are not the only
financial intermediaries in the economy, and it should not be thought that
the other financial institutions are not important in the money-creating
process.

Numerous *nonbank financial intermediaries* also are important in
both channeling funds and in actually creating the money in the economy.
These nonbank financial intermediaries are either privately owned intermediaries between lenders and borrowers or government creations designed
to supplement private financial arrangements. The importance for the
money-creating process of many of these nonbank financial intermediaries
has been greatly enhanced by the passage of the Monetary Control Act of
1980 and the Garn–St. Germain Act of 1982.

The diversity of nonbank financial intermediaries in the United States
economy is the direct result of specialization undertaken as a result of the
perceived comparative advantage of their owners and managers. Various
intermediaries have gathered considerable expertise in certain financial

markets and therefore have specialized in investing in those particular markets. Many specialize in the mortgage markets, others in consumer lending, others in agricultural lending, and so on. The degree of specialization depends on the size of the particular markets and the amount of government regulation in the markets.

Nonbank financial intermediaries can be classified by their ownership, by the markets in which they operate, by the assets they hold, or by their

---

**Table 11.1**
**A General Classification of Nonbank Financial Intermediaries**

*Thrift institutions*
Credit unions
Mutual savings banks
Savings and loan associations

*Contractual savings associations*
Life insurance companies
Property and casualty insurance companies
Government insurance and social security funds
Government retirement and pension funds
Private pension funds

*Finance companies*
Business and commercial finance companies
  Factors
  Others
Mortgage companies
Personal finance companies
Sales finance companies

*Investment companies*
Closed-end companies
Open-end companies (mutual funds)
  Money market mutual funds
    General purpose and broker/dealer
    Institutional
  Other

*Miscellaneous*
Banks for cooperatives
Federal intermediate credit banks
Federal land banks
Federal home loan banks
Federal home loan mortgage corporation (Freddy Mac)
Federal national mortgage association (Fanny Mae)
Government national mortgage association (Ginny Mae)

liabilities. Perhaps the simplest classification, however, is by their liabilities, as it is through their liabilities that the general public makes contact with them. In this scheme, nonbank financial intermediaries can be divided into four main groups: *thrift institutions* (which together with the commercial banks constitute the depository institutions), *contractual savings institutions* (mainly insurance companies and pension funds), *finance companies* (specialized lenders who borrow from other institutions and sell commercial paper to the public), and *investment companies* (institutions that sell shares in their portfolios).

There are, of course, many other financial institutions that do not fit easily into this classification scheme, but here the only significant ones are government agencies and government-sponsored agencies designed to supplement private activities in various markets. Major nonbank financial intermediaries, classified according to their liabilities, are shown in Table 11.1.

Between 1800 and 1950, the United States saw a proliferation of nonbank financial intermediaries. Only commercial banks and insurance companies operated before 1800; savings and loan associations, and mortgage companies appeared in the nineteenth century; and the first half of the twentieth century brought credit unions, finance companies, investment companies, and pension funds. Since 1950, however, the development of financial institutions has been different. Instead of new institutions being created, the already existing institutions have adapted to the changing demands of the public. With this adaptation has come a tremendous growth in activity. Table 11.2 shows the total assets of selected nonbank financial intermediaries and compares them with the total assets of the commercial banks for the period since 1950.

The 1970s and 1980s have seen a further development in the already existing institutions. The institutions have fought—and won—legal battles to expand their activities. These legal battles led to the passage of the Monetary Control Act of 1980 and the Garn–St. Germain Act of 1982, and this legislation has had a great effect on the development of the various financial institutions, particularly the depository institutions.

Table 11.2 indicates that the dollar value of assets of commercial banks and of nonbank financial intermediaries has grown considerably, but these figures are greatly distorted by the inflation that occurred over the period. To show how the institutions have grown relative to each other, the table lists each institution's assets as a percentage of total assets each year. These percentage figures show that commercial banks declined in relation to other institutions from 56.7 percent in 1950 to 42.6 percent in 1982. Credit unions and savings and loan associations have grown in relation to other institutions over the same period. Mutual savings banks have declined. Excluding the recent phenomenal growth of money market mutual funds, the credit unions, though quite small, have displayed the greatest growth over the period.

*Table 11.2*
*Total Assets of Financial Intermediaries at Year's End*

| | 1950 | | 1955 | | 1960 | | 1965 | | 1970 | | 1975 | | 1980 | | 1982[1] | |
|---|---|---|---|---|---|---|---|---|---|---|---|---|---|---|---|---|
| | Billions | % | Billions | % | Billions | % | Billions | % | Billions | % | Billions | % | Billions | % | Billions | % |
| Commercial banks | $168.9 | (56.7) | $210.7 | (49.2) | $257.6 | (43.1) | $377.3 | (41.0) | $576.2 | (43.0) | $964.9 | (44.9) | $1703.7 | (44.0) | $1972.2 | (42.6) |
| Credit unions | 1.0 | (0.3) | 2.7 | (0.6) | 5.7 | (1.0) | 10.6 | (1.1) | 18.0 | (1.3) | 38.0 | (1.8) | 71.7 | (1.9) | 88.8 | (1.9) |
| Mutual savings banks | 22.4 | (7.5) | 31.3 | (7.3) | 40.6 | (6.8) | 58.2 | (6.3) | 79.0 | (5.9) | 121.1 | (5.6) | 171.6 | (4.4) | 174.2 | (3.8) |
| Savings associations | 16.9 | (5.7) | 37.7 | (8.8) | 71.5 | (12.0) | 129.6 | (14.1) | 176.2 | (13.2) | 338.2 | (15.7) | 630.7 | (16.3) | 706.0 | (15.3) |
| Life insurance companies | 64.0 | (21.5) | 90.4 | (21.1) | 119.6 | (20.0) | 158.9 | (17.2) | 207.3 | (15.5) | 289.3 | (13.5) | 479.2 | (12.4) | 584.3 | (12.6) |
| Private pensions | 7.1 | (2.3) | 18.3 | (4.3) | 38.1 | (6.4) | 73.6 | (8.0) | 110.6 | (8.3) | 146.8 | (6.8) | 286.8 | (7.4) | 336.1 | (7.3) |
| State and local pensions | 4.9 | (1.6) | 10.8 | (2.5) | 19.7 | (3.3) | 34.1 | (3.7) | 60.3 | (4.5) | 104.8 | (4.9) | 198.1 | (5.1) | 253.1 | (5.5) |
| Finance companies | 9.3 | (3.1) | 18.3 | (4.2) | 27.6 | (4.6) | 44.7 | (4.8) | 64.0 | (4.8) | 99.1 | (4.6) | 198.6 | (5.1) | 229.8 | (5.0) |
| Investment companies | 3.3 | (1.1) | 7.8 | (1.8) | 17.0 | (2.8) | 35.2 | (3.8) | 47.6 | (3.6) | 42.2 | (2.0) | 58.4 | (1.5) | 76.8 | (1.7) |
| Money market mutuals | — | — | — | — | — | — | — | — | — | — | 3.7 | (0.0) | 74.4 | (1.9) | 206.6 | (4.5) |
| Total | $297.8 | | $428.0 | | $597.4 | | $922.2 | | $1339.2 | | $2148.1 | | $3873.2 | | $4627.9 | |

[1] Preliminary figures.

Source: *Savings and Loan Source Book '83*: (United States League of Savings Institutions, 1983): Table 50, 36.

# THRIFT INSTITUTIONS

The thrift institutions are the credit unions, the mutual savings banks, and the savings and loan associations. As their collective name implies, a principal source of their funds is the savings of the public. Their portfolios, however, display a difference in their lending patterns. Credit unions specialize in consumer loans (mainly on automobiles and other consumer durables), whereas mutual savings banks and savings and loan associations specialize in mortgages.

Thrift institutions have liabilities that are closest to deposit liabilities of commercial banks. Some of the liabilities held are, in fact, transactions accounts (NOW accounts, demand deposits, and share draft accounts) and are included in the definition of the means of exchange (M1). In accordance with the Monetary Control Act of 1980, thrift institutions must keep reserves for these accounts in vault cash, or in a deposit at a Federal Reserve District Bank, or "passed through" a financial institution that has reserves at a Federal Reserve District Bank. Most of the liabilities of the thrift institutions, however, are *not* transactions accounts.

## Credit Unions

*Credit unions* are nonprofit, cooperative institutions designed to pool the savings of their members and to lend to other members. The aims of the institutions are somewhat contradictory, as they are formed to pay high rates to the savers and to charge low rates to the borrowers. Members of a credit union must have a "common bond," such as being employees of the same firm, members of the same profession, or residents of the same geographical area. Over 90 percent of the credit unions in the United States have an occupational bond.

The Federal Credit Union Act defines a credit union as "a cooperative association organized . . . for the purpose of promoting thrift among its members and creating a source of credit for provident and productive purposes." The moralistic overtones in this definition stem from the religious beginnings of credit unions. Organized credit cooperatives started in Germany in the 1840s and 1850s as a result of suggestions made by the Lutheran writer Victor Huber. There is some evidence that German immigrants started similar societies in New York in the 1860s, but none of these survived. The beginning of credit unions in North America is credited to Alphonse Desjardins, who founded La Caisse Populaire de Levis in Canada in 1900. The idea spread throughout French Canada and eventually to Franco-Americans in New Hampshire. The priest of the Parish of Ste. Marie in Manchester, New Hampshire, invited Alphonse Desjardins to found a credit society, St. Mary's Cooperative Credit Association, which was opened in 1909. The idea soon spread in the United States: first to Massachusetts, then to New York, and eventually to the entire nation. Today a credit union may have a federal charter to operate in any state or may have a state charter from any state except Alaska, Delaware, South Dakota, or Wyoming.

Credit unions accept savings and time deposits, which often are deducted automatically from members' paychecks at their places of employment. The credit unions have been able to take advantage of an interest ceiling on their accounts that is set higher than those allowed commercial banks and savings and loan associations. This advantage has been preserved even after the passage of the Monetary Control Act of 1980. Many credit unions offer share draft privileges to their account holders. These privileges effectively make interest-bearing accounts into checking accounts. A share draft can be used to pay third parties and is almost indistinguishable from a check because each participating credit union maintains balances for draft clearance in a commercial bank (known as the *payable-through* bank). The drafts pass through the ordinary check-clearance mechanism maintained by the commercial banks. Under the Monetary Control Act of 1980, credit unions may set up a check-clearance mechanism through the credit union liquidity facility.

On the asset side, credit unions specialize in consumer loans, mainly for automobiles, consumer durables, vacations, and home improvements and repairs. Competition for consumer loans comes from other depository institutions (commercial banks, mutual savings banks, and savings and loan associations), but the credit unions often have been able to offer the most attractive borrowing rates because of their low overhead. Operating sometimes rent-free on the premises of their employer, with volunteer labor, and under a generally tax-exempt status, credit unions often have a competitive edge over other institutions.

A consolidated statement of condition of all operating federal credit unions is shown in Table 11.3 to give an indication of the assets and liabilities of credit unions. It is clear from this table that credit unions acquire most of their funds from shareholders and mainly lend to their members.

## Mutual Savings Banks

*Mutual savings banks* started in England after a suggestion made in 1697 by Daniel Defoe, the author of *Robinson Crusoe*. The basic idea was taken up in the United States in the early nineteenth century and has spread throughout 17 states. Their number has grown little, however, in recent decades. Their total assets have increased considerably since the 1950s, but they have grown more slowly than the other depository institutions. Therefore, as a percentage of the total assets of the financial institutions, they have declined (*see* Table 11.2).

Mutual savings banks were designed to encourage thrift among the working classes, and they have remained more a philanthropic than a profit-making institution. They are run by self-perpetuating boards of trustees who originally were self-appointed but thereafter were elected. Any earned

*Table 11.3*
**Consolidated Statement of Condition of All Operating Federal Credit Unions December 31, 1981**

| Assets | Millions | % | Liabilities and Equities | Millions | % |
|---|---|---|---|---|---|
| Loans to members | $27,203 | 64.9 | Notes payable | $ 730 | 1.7 |
| Cash | 901 | 2.2 | Accounts payable, etc. | 831 | 2.0 |
| Total investments | | | Savings accounts | 37,789 | 90.2 |
| U.S. obligation | 497 | 1.2 | Regular reserve | 1,218 | 2.9 |
| Federal agency securities | 2,399 | 5.7 | Other reserves | 421 | 1.0 |
| Savings (MSBs, S&Ls) | 4,600 | 11.0 | | | |
| Savings (other CUs, corps, CLF) | 4,118 | 9.8 | | | |
| Common trust investments | 736 | 1.8 | Undivided earnings | 917 | 2.2 |
| Other investments | 267 | 0.6 | | | |
| Other assets | 1,183 | 2.8 | | | |
| | 41,904 | | | 41,906 | |

*Source: 1981 Annual Report of the National Credit Union Administration* (Washington D.C., 1982): Table 1, 36; Table 2, 37; Table 5, 40.

profit in excess of bank operating expenses either is kept in a surplus account or distributed to depositors. Mutual savings banks offer savings accounts, time deposits, and NOW accounts similar to commercial banks. In addition, they hold demand deposits in certain states: Delaware, Indiana, Maryland, New Jersey, New York, Oregon, and those of New England.

There is no federal chartering agency for mutual savings banks. The diverse sets of requirements listed for state charters have given them a rather ambivalent status somewhere between commercial banks and savings and loan associations. In the states where they hold demand deposits, they have been allowed to join the Federal Reserve System, but historically such membership has been minimal. On the other hand, about 18 percent have joined the Federal Home Loan Bank System (the equivalent of the Federal Reserve for savings and loan associations). Despite their excellent safety record even in the days before deposit insurance (for example, very few failed in the Great Depression), all mutual savings banks are now insured. Some 70 percent are insured with the Federal Deposit Insurance Corporation, the remainder with various state insurance funds.

Accepting demand deposits, NOW accounts, savings deposits, and time deposits puts mutual savings banks into direct competition for funds with commercial banks and savings and loan associations. Also, as two thirds of their assets are mortgage investments, they are in direct competition for

*Table 11.4*
**Condensed Statement of Condition of All Mutual Savings Banks**
**December 31, 1981**

| Assets | Millions | % | Liabilities and Reserve Accounts | Millions | % |
|---|---|---|---|---|---|
| Cash | $ 5415 | 3.1 | Savings deposits | $ 49,409 | 28.1 |
| U.S. Treasury and federal agency obligations | 9861 | 5.6 | Time deposits | 103,425 | 58.9 |
| | | | Other deposits | 2079 | 1.2 |
| State and municipal securities | 2274 | 1.3 | Borrowings | 8147 | 4.6 |
| | | | Other liabilities | 2584 | 1.5 |
| Mortgage investments | 113,889 | 64.9 | | | |
| Corporate and other bonds | 20,186 | 11.5 | General reserve accounts | 9969 | 5.7 |
| Corporate stock | 3614 | 2.1 | | | |
| Other loans | 14,740 | 8.4 | | | |
| Other assets | 5632 | 3.2 | | | |
| | 175,611 | | | 175,613 | |

Source: *Annual Report of the President,* National Association of Mutual Savings Banks, New York, 1982: Table 1:5.

lending funds with savings and loan associations (*see* Table 11.4). Competition has been tough, but mutual savings banks have fought back. Many have intensified their competition with savings and loan associations by shifting from the traditional short-term mortgages with large down payments to the longer-term conventional mortgages. In addition, the intense competition with the commercial banks produced NOW accounts. NOW accounts were first introduced in 1970 by the Consumers Savings Bank of Worcester, Massachusetts. After the Massachusetts Supreme Court ruled that the negotiable orders of withdrawal used by Consumers Savings were legal, NOW accounts spread to the mutual savings banks throughout Massachusetts and New Hampshire. Despite initial opposition from the commercial banks and the banking authorities, the practice spread to savings banks, savings and loan associations, and commercial banks throughout the six New England states, New York, New Jersey, and Oregon. Finally, the Monetary Control Act of 1980 authorized NOW accounts for depository institutions nationwide. Obviously, the intense competition between institutions has encouraged banking innovation by the mutuals to maintain their business.

## Savings and Loan Associations

*Savings and loan associations* were designed specifically for operating in the mortgage markets. The original intention was that they would collect the savings of, and make mortgage loans to, the members; but the years have seen a separation of these roles. Today, we can say that savings and loan associations encourage saving by offering interest on various types of savings accounts and that they provide credit for the construction, purchase, repair, and refinancing of residential housing.

Savings and loan associations in the United States were modeled after the British building societies. The first such association in the United States was the Oxford Provident Building Association of Philadelphia, which was founded in 1831. Since that time, savings and loan associations have spread nationwide and, like commercial banks, can be chartered by either federal or state authorities. At the end of 1982, there were 3848 associations, 1730 of which had federal charters (*see* Figure 11.1). The federally chartered savings and loan associations are required to be members of the *Federal Home Loan Bank System* and must be insured by the Federal Savings and Loan Insurance Corporation (FSLIC, which is the FDIC of savings and loan associations). Under the Monetary Control Act of 1980, FSLIC is required to insure deposits up to $100,000. The state-chartered savings and loan associations have a choice. Of the 2118 state-chartered associations at the end of 1982, 1628 chose to be insured by the FSLIC and therefore were required to be members of the Federal Home Loan Banking System. Of the 490 savings and loan associations that chose not to be insured by the FSLIC, 80 chose to join the Federal Home Loan Bank System, even though they were not required to join.

In most states, deposit insurance is optional, but most savings and loan associations choose to have insurance. The number of non-FSLIC-insured associations listed in Figure 11.1, however, is somewhat misleading as to the extent of noninsurance. Most non-FSLIC-insured associations are insured by the various state insurance funds: the Maryland Savings-Share Insurance Corporation, the Co-operative Central Bank of Massachusetts (in Massachusetts savings and loan associations are called *cooperative banks*), the North Carolina Savings Guarantee Corporation, and the Ohio Deposit Guarantee Fund.[1]

As the condensed statement in Table 11.5 illustrates, the business of savings and loan associations consists almost exclusively of channeling funds from savings deposits into mortgage lending. The table reveals that, as of December 1982, over 80 percent of the liabilities of the savings and loan associations consisted of savings deposits, and almost 70 percent of the assets consisted of mortgage loans. The proportion of the assets kept in the form of mortgages has been reduced about 10 percent in recent years, because of efforts to increase liquidity in the portfolios with the advent of checking accounts (actually NOW accounts) into the business of the savings and loan associations. In anticipation of this change, the Monetary Control Act of 1980 authorized the savings and loans to invest up to 20 percent

---

[1] United States League of Savings Associations, *Savings and Loan Fact Book '80* (Chicago, 1980): 50.

*Figure 11.1*
**Savings and Loan Associations by Charter and Membership,
Year End, 1982**

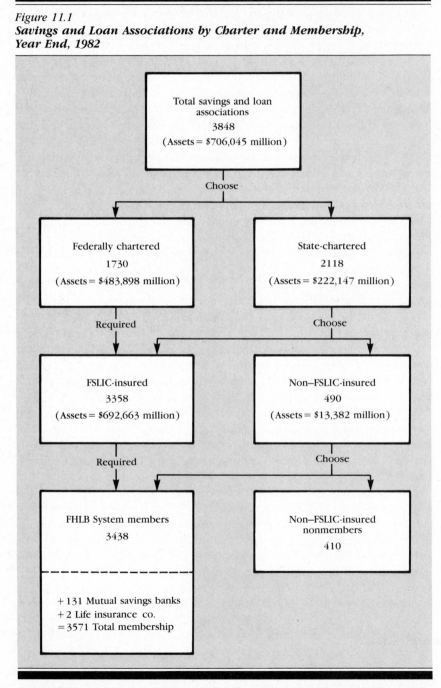

*Source:* United States League of Savings Institutions, *Savings and Loan Source Book '83,* Chicago, 1983, Table 84 (48),
Table 52 (37).

**Table 11.5**
**Condensed Statement of Condition of All Savings and Loan Associations**
**December 31, 1982**

| Assets | Millions | % | Liabilities and Net Worth | Millions | % |
|---|---|---|---|---|---|
| Mortgage loans outstanding | $482,234 | 68.3 | Savings deposits | $566,189 | 80.2 |
| Insured mortgages and mortgage-backed securities | 63,030 | 8.9 | Federal Home Loan Bank Advances | 63,861 | 9.0 |
|  |  |  | Other borrowed money | 34,118 | 4.8 |
| Mobile home loans | 3284 | 0.5 | All other liabilities | 15,720 | 2.2 |
| Home improvement loans | 5534 | 0.8 |  |  |  |
| Loans on savings accounts | 4032 | 0.6 |  |  |  |
| Education loans | 2093 | 0.3 | Net worth | 26,157 | 3.7 |
| Other consumer loans | 5601 | 0.8 |  |  |  |
| Cash and investments eligible for liquidity | 70,179 | 9.9 |  |  |  |
| Other investments | 14,588 | 2.1 |  |  |  |
| Federal Home Loan Bank stock | 5900 | 0.8 |  |  |  |
| Investment in service corporations | 5605 | 0.8 |  |  |  |
| Buildings and equipment | 10,376 | 1.5 |  |  |  |
| Real estate owned | 3600 | 0.5 |  |  |  |
| All other assets | 29,989 | 4.2 |  |  |  |
|  | 706,045 |  |  | 706,045 |  |

*Source: Savings and Loan Source Book '83* (Chicago: United States League of Savings Associations, 1983): Table 64, 41.

of their portfolios in commercial paper, consumer loans, and corporate debt securities.

Savings and loan associations maintain their liquidity with cash reserves, deposits at Federal Home Loan Regional Banks, and deposits at either a Federal Reserve District Bank or a commercial bank that "passes the deposits through" to the District Bank. The Monetary Control Act of 1980 gave savings and loan associations the right to borrow from the Federal Reserve District Banks at the discount window. In addition, members of the Federal Home Loan Bank System may borrow from their Federal Home Loan Regional Bank. Borrowing from the Federal Reserve usually is short-term and at the discount rate, whereas borrowing from the Federal Home Loan Bank is longer-term and at a market rate.

The Federal Home Loan Bank System is open to savings and loan associations, mutual savings banks, and life insurance companies. The system is regulated by the Federal Home Loan Bank Board, a committee whose three

*Figure 11.2*
**Federal Home Loan Bank Districts and Regional Banks**

District 2 also includes Puerto Rico and the Virgin Islands

District 12 also includes Alaska,

Source: *Savings and Loan Fact Book '80,* Chart 45, 97.

members are appointed for four-year terms by the president of the United States. Apart from its regulatory activities, the board also operates the FSLIC and the Federal Home Loan Mortgage Corporation (Freddy Mac), a corporation founded to assist the secondary market for mortgages.

The Federal Home Loan Bank System has divided the country into 12 districts (*see* Figure 11.2), each with its own regional bank. Each regional bank can extend credit to the members in its district for emergencies and for extending mortgage debt in instances where there are insufficient funds deposited in the associations. There have been occasions when the regional banks have behaved counter-cyclically, but generally the regional banks concentrate on facilitating the activities of the members and have therefore been procyclical throughout most of their history.

### DUE-ON-SALE

Savings and loan associations hold a substantial portion of their assets as mortgage loans. Most mortgage loan contracts contain a due-on-sale clause. This clause gives the lender the option to declare the loan due and payable if the property securing the loan is sold. The legality of this clause and its use by savings and loan associations were drawn into question in the late 1970s and early 1980s.

Before the rising nominal interest rates of the 1970s, due-on-sale clauses were used to protect the lender from transfer of a loan to a higher-risk borrower. Since the loan was "due-on-sale," the new buyer would have to apply to the lending institution to have the loan reissued.

With rising interest rates, lenders began using the due-on-sale clause in their portfolio management. Long-term, fixed-interest-rate loans were issued in the expectation that they would be paid off long before the initially established maturity. Mortgages are often repaid before maturity; on average, 30-year mortgages have been paid off in about 12 years.

A low-interest-rate, fixed mortgage loan is a valuable liability to a homeowner during periods of unexpected increases in prices and interest rates. During periods of unexpected increases in interest rates, the average mortgage life also increases. When homeowners can avoid the due-on-sale clause, they can capture the increased value of this liability by passing it on to the new buyer. Homes with assumable financing command higher prices than those without such financing.

*continued*

## CONTRACTUAL SAVINGS INSTITUTIONS

*Contractual savings institutions* are insurance companies and pension funds. They are distinguished from near banks in that they receive funds on a regular, contracted basis. Insurance policies include a contractual payment of premiums. Pension funds receive regular contributions, mainly by paycheck deductions. This steady inflow of funds coupled with a high predictability of payments and claims tends to minimize liquidity problems and to allow the institutions to take advantage of longer-term investments.

Attempts to avoid due-on-sale clauses brought an on-slaught of creative financing in the late 1970s. *Creative financing* in the mortgage market is financing in which the home seller carries some of the paper (lends some of the funds). This financing was used to wrap existing long-term, fixed-interest-rate financing and pass it on to the new buyer. Mortgage payments would be passed through the original buyer. Several states facilitated this type of financing with laws that prohibited the enforcement of due-on-sale clauses.

The inability to enforce due-on-sale clauses placed considerable pressure on mortgage lenders. With higher than expected market rates of interest, the market value of mortgage loans plummeted. Savings and loan associations saw a drastic reduction in the market value of their asset portfolios during a period when their cost of funds was rising. Without enforceable due-on-sale clauses the industry could not recover its funds to relend them at the higher market rates when homes sold.

The initial move around this problem was the shift to adjustable-rate mortgage loans. The interest rates of these mortgages changed with movements in other market rates of interest. The market value of the mortgage contract would remain stable, and the home sellers' advantage in passing the loan to a new home buyer was lost.

The Garn–St. Germain Depository Institutions Act of 1982 brought this matter to a close by providing for a federal override of state restrictions on due-on-sale clauses. This made the clauses enforceable and clarified the gains and losses to lenders and borrowers during periods of changing interest rates.

## Life Insurance Companies

Life insurance companies accumulate funds for investment from premiums paid on the various policies. Term insurance, however, does not usually generate sufficient funds for investment, as the premiums are only high enough to cover administrative costs. Although life insurance companies know very little about the life expectancy of any individual, actuarial tables allow a very accurate prediction of the life expectancy of groups of people. It is this predictability of death, and hence policy payment, that has given life insurance companies a very low liquidity requirement and the ability to invest in long-term markets.

## SO WHO OWNS AMERCIA ANYWAY?

In April 1950, Charles Wilson, president of General Motors, proposed to his workers that a pension fund be set up for them, run by professional asset managers. The idea of a pension fund was not new; there were already some 2000 in operation throughout the United States. What was new was the proposal that the fund be an investment trust, invested mainly in equities bought in the capital market rather than in debt instruments. Moreover, the funds were to be invested in a broad spectrum of American enterprise rather than in General Motors itself. Wilson's fear, that having funds invested in the company would be too tempting for the company not to expropriate the funds if it was ever in financial difficulty, seems to have been borne out by the actions of New York City in 1975. In that year the city used its employees' pension funds to bail out of financial trouble.

Despite initial opposition from the United Auto Workers, the pension fund was established in October 1950, and the idea spread rapidly throughout the country. Today there are approximately 50,000 pension funds covering some 40 million workers. Collectively, they have invested about $600 billion in United States enterprise.

*continued*

The investment portfolio of life insurance companies (*see* Table 11.6) consists primarily of corporate bonds, corporate equities, and mortgages. The acquisition of these assets is rather different from that of most other nonbank financial intermediaries. Bonds are acquired by direct placement; that is, the life insurance companies negotiate directly with the corporations for large blocks of bonds. Mortgages also are obtained in large groups or packages from mortgage companies.[2]

Although life insurance companies have grown absolutely since 1950, they have grown at a slower rate than other nonbank financial intermediaries, so that there has been a relative decline in the share of assets they hold (*see* Table 11.2). This probably has been the result of inflation. As more people have attempted to find a hedge against inflation, they have turned to making direct investments rather than using insurance companies as inter-

---

[2]Mortgage companies originate mortgages (using borrowed funds) and service them, but they do not retain them. The mortgages are resold on secondary markets.

The size of these pension funds has had a significant effect on the stock market. The pension funds, managed mainly by the trust departments of approximately 1300 commercial banks, now dominate stock trading. About 25 percent by dollar value of all publicly traded stocks are owned by the pension funds. They are by far the largest net buyers of new common stock.

The influence of pension funds on the stock market has certainly been great, but their influence on the ownership of capital has been even more profound. The pension funds already own at least one third of the stock in almost all the 1000 largest industrial corporations in the country and in the 50 largest companies in banking, insurance, retail trade, communications, and transportation. The proportion of the United States economy that is owned by employee pension funds is greater than the nationalized proportion of many socialist countries. As the well-known management consultant Peter F. Drucker stated in his book, *The Unseen Revolution,*

> If "socialism" is defined as "ownership of the means of production by the workers" . . . then the United States is the first truly "Socialist" country.[1]

---

[1] Drucker, Peter E., *The Unseen Revolution* (New York: Harper & Row, 1976): 1.

mediaries. As the relative size of life insurance companies has declined, the proportion of their policies that are not term policies has declined.

## Other Insurance Companies

There are many insurance companies besides life insurance companies. They are mainly property and casualty insurance companies. Payments made to such companies are much less predictable than those to life insurance companies. In periods of inflation the size of payments must increase. The result of these problems is that insurance companies, other than those in life insurance, have very different asset portfolios. Because property and casualty insurance companies have higher liquidity requirements than life insurance companies, and because they require a higher return on their investments, they tend to hold a much higher proportion of their portfolios in governments and corporate equities. Investment in state and local securities has been particularly high. (*See* Table 11.7.)

*Table 11.6*
**Condensed Statement of Condition of All Life Insurance Companies
December 31, 1980**

**Assets**                                    **Liabilities**

| | Billions | % | | Billions | % |
|---|---|---|---|---|---|
| Demand deposits and currency | $ 2.8 | 0.6 | Life Insurance reserves | $214.6 | 45.7 |
| | | | Pension fund reserves | 165.6 | 35.3 |
| Corporate equities | 53.0 | 11.3 | Taxes payable | 4.0 | 0.9 |
| U.S. Treasury securities | 5.8 | 1.2 | Miscellaneous | 57.2 | 12.2 |
| Federal agency securities | 11.1 | 2.4 | | | |
| State and local government securities | 6.7 | 1.4 | Capital accounts | 27.7 | 5.9 |
| Corporate and foreign bonds | 178.0 | 37.9 | | | |
| Mortgages | 131.1 | 27.9 | | | |
| Open-market paper | 11.0 | 2.3 | | | |
| Other loans | 41.5 | 8.8 | | | |
| Miscellaneous | 28.1 | 6.0 | | | |
| Total | 469.1 | | | 469.1 | |

Source: *Annual Statistical Digest, 1980* (Washington D.C.: Board of Governors of the Federal Reserve System 1981),
Table 47.B.

*Table 11.7*
**Condensed Statement of Condition of All Other Insurance Companies
December 31, 1980**

**Assets**                                    **Liabilities**

| | Billions | % | | Billions | % |
|---|---|---|---|---|---|
| Demand deposits and currency | $ 2.7 | 1.5 | Taxes payable | $ 1.3 | 0.7 |
| | | | Insurance reserves | 126.0 | 68.1 |
| Corporate equities | 35.1 | 19.0 | | | |
| U.S. Treasury securities | 14.2 | 7.7 | | | |
| Federal agency securities | 7.3 | 3.9 | | | |
| State and local securities | 83.6 | 45.2 | Capital accounts | 57.7 | 31.2 |
| Corporate and foreign bonds | 26.4 | 14.3 | | | |
| Mortgages | 0.7 | 0.4 | | | |
| Trade credit | 15.0 | 8.1 | | | |
| Total | 185.0 | | | 185.0 | |

Source: *Annual Statistical Digest, 1980* (Washington D.C.: Board of Governors of the Federal Reserve System 1981):
Table 47.B.

**Table 11.8**
**Condensed Statement of Condition of Private Pension Funds**
**December 31, 1980**

| Assets | | | Liabilities | | |
|---|---|---|---|---|---|
| | Billions | % | | Billions | % |
| Demand deposits and currency | $ 1.9 | 0.7 | Pension fund reserves | $279.2 | 100.0 |
| Time and savings deposits | 10.3 | 3.7 | | | |
| Corporate equities | 168.2 | 60.2 | | | |
| U.S. Treasury securities | 24.1 | 8.6 | | | |
| Federal agency securities | 6.7 | 2.4 | | | |
| Corporate and foreign bonds | 58.1 | 20.8 | | | |
| Mortgages | 3.7 | 1.3 | | | |
| Miscellaneous | 6.2 | 2.2 | | | |
| Total | 279.2 | | | 279.2 | |

Source: Annual Statistical Digest, 1980 (Washington D.C.: Board of Governors of the Federal Reserve System 1981): Table 47.B.

## Pension Funds

Pension funds include the privately owned corporate pension funds (usually run by a commercial bank's trust department, a life insurance company, or the corporation itself); state and local government employee pension funds, the Social Security System (officially the Old Age, Survivors, Disability, and Health Insurance System); and various federally supervised pension funds (such as the Civil Service Pension Fund). The funds that are either run or supervised by the federal government are invested in special classes of United States Treasury securities.

Pensions usually are at a fixed dollar amount agreed on in advance, so payments made by the funds are accurately predictable. This means that the funds have practically no liquidity problems, giving them greater leeway in the kind of investments they can make. Also, as their low liquidity requirement is coupled with a desire for high returns (for the obvious reason that the higher the return on the investments, the lower the contributions have to be to yield the same pension), pension funds have tended to invest heavily in corporate equities. This has been particularly true of the corporate pension funds. (See Tables 11.8 and 11.9.) The pension funds of state and local government employees have not invested so heavily in equities, mainly because of the many government restrictions placed on the investment of their funds.

Table 11.9
**Condensed Statement of Condition of State and Local Pension Funds**
**December 31, 1980**

| Assets | | | Liabilities | | |
|---|---|---|---|---|---|
| | **Billions** | **%** | | **Billions** | **%** |
| Demand deposits and currency | $  4.6 | 2.2 | Pension fund reserves | $207.9 | 100.0 |
| Corporate equities | 54.3 | 26.1 | | | |
| U.S. Treasury securities | 18.0 | 8.7 | | | |
| Federal agency securities | 18.0 | 8.7 | | | |
| State and local securities | 4.1 | 2.0 | | | |
| Corporate and foreign bonds | 98.0 | 47.1 | | | |
| Mortgages | 10.9 | 5.2 | | | |
| Total | 207.9 | | | 207.9 | |

Source: *Annual Statistical Digest, 1980* (Washington D.C.: Board of Governors of the Federal Reserve System 1981): Table 47.B.

# FINANCE COMPANIES

The term *finance company* is collective, referring to four kinds of institutions: business and commercial finance companies, mortgage companies, personal finance companies, and sales finance companies. These companies are distinguishable from other nonbank financial intermediaries in that their liabilities consist of commercial bank loans and their own issues of short- and long-term paper (*see* Table 11.10). The paper they issue is either *commercial paper* (promissory notes with 270 days or less to run to maturity) or *long-term debentures* (bonds not secured by particular assets). On the asset side of the accounts, the various specialties of the companies can be seen.

## Business and Commercial Finance Companies

Business and commercial finance companies specialize in loans to business, particularly on accounts receivable. In much of this kind of lending the borrower maintains title to the accounts receivable, and the finance company expects the borrower to absorb the loss if accounts are not paid. However, the 1970s saw the development of business companies that purchase the accounts and service them and also suffer the loss if the accounts are not paid. These companies are called *factors,* and the business is known as *factoring.* Although such companies have long existed in the textile industry, it was only in the 1970s that they became important in other busi-

*Table 11.10*
**Condensed Statement of Condition of Finance Companies
December 31, 1980**

| Assets | | | Liabilities | | |
|---|---|---|---|---|---|
| | **Billions** | **%** | | **Billions** | **%** |
| Demand deposits and currency | $ 4.7 | 2.6 | Commercial bank loans | $ 20.7 | 11.4 |
| | | | Open-market paper | 61.2 | 33.7 |
| Mortgages | 13.0 | 7.2 | Corporate and foreign bonds | 64.3 | 35.4 |
| Consumer credit | 91.3 | 50.3 | | | |
| Other loans | 72.3 | 39.9 | Taxes payable | 1.6 | 0.9 |
| | | | Miscellaneous | 21.8 | 12.0 |
| | | | Capital accounts | 11.8 | 6.5 |
| Total | 181.3 | | | 181.4 | |

Source: *Annual Statistical Digest, 1980* (Washington D.C.: Board of Governors of the Federal Reserve System 1980): Table 47.B.

nesses. It is a high-risk business that had traditionally been kept separate from commercial banks, but in the late 1970s some bank holding companies purchased factors to diversify their bank-related business.

## Mortgage Companies

Mortgage companies specialize in financing and servicing mortgages that are then sold to other institutions—particularly to the Federal National Mortgage Association (Fanny Mae). These companies should be distinguished from *mortgage brokers,* who merely bring together borrowers and lenders and earn a brokerage fee for their services. Mortgage companies, on the other hand, originate mortgages by using the funds they have acquired either from bank loans or their own issues of paper.

## Personal Finance Companies

Personal finance companies specialize in small consumer loans. This is a high-cost business, because the administrative costs of investigating and making a loan are about the same regardless of the size of the loan being made. Thus, for small commercial loans, the costs are high and the finance companies charge high rates of interest. In most states, finance companies have been exempt from state *usury laws* (state laws that put ceiling interest rates on lending in an attempt to protect the poor and unwary from high interest costs). The exemption, in fact, has legitimized the small consumer loan business. Where usury laws have been effective, small borrowers have been forced into the hands of illegal "loan sharks," who are, of course, unregulated.

## Sales Finance Companies

Sales finance companies specialize in automobile and other consumer durable lending where repayment is typically on the installment plan. Such companies usually do not lend directly to the public but to large retail stores. Where much buying appears to be financed by the retail stores themselves through credit cards and lines of credit, it is, in fact, financed by sales finance companies who buy sales contracts from the retailers.

## INVESTMENT COMPANIES

*Investment companies* raise money by selling stock and earn income for the stockholders by investing the proceeds in a diversified portfolio of assets. The advantage of such a company to the small saver is that the portfolio can be much more diversified than a small portfolio. The investment company offers the advantages of a large portfolio, with both the safety that can come from diversification and the expertise of highly qualified investment managers.

There are many kinds of investment companies, each specializing in a different kind of portfolio. Some portfolios are only stocks, some are only bonds, and others are mixed. However, investment companies can be classified broadly according to the way in which the shares in the company are sold. There are *closed-end companies* that do not offer to redeem their shares and do not sell new shares regularly, and *open-end companies* that redeem their shares on demand and regularly sell new shares to the public.

## Closed-end Investment Companies

Closed-end investment companies do not sell shares directly to the public. Fixed amounts of shares are sold through investment banks and thereafter the shares are traded on stock exchanges. The shares are not, however, sold back to the company. This kind of company was in existence before the stock market crash of 1929, but few new companies have been formed in recent years.

## Open-end Investment Companies

Open-end investment companies sell shares to the public on a continuous basis and stand ready to redeem shares held by the public. These companies are also called *mutual funds*. They can expand the size of their portfolios whenever the new shares sold exceed the redemption of shares by shareholders. The portfolios, of course, will contract when redemptions exceed sales, but contractions do not necessarily mean that funds are becoming less profitable. The performance of a fund is more a function of the management of the fund than of the size of the portfolio.

One particular type—the *money market mutual fund*—has risen spectacularly since the mid-1970s. The total value of these funds was negligible before 1976, but they started to climb in 1978. In that year, the total value reached only $10 billion, but after that the volume increased rapidly, reaching almost $80 billion in 1980, $150 billion in 1981, and $190 billion in 1982. Since then, there has been some decline, but they still constitute a major factor in the market for loanable funds.

The funds have been invested in a variety of fixed income securities: short-term government securities, short-term corporate securities, commercial bank certificates of deposit, and other short-term debt instruments. These funds became popular when short-term interest rates rose above the interest ceilings imposed on savings and time deposits. The attraction of such funds has been greatly enhanced by the introduction of a liquidity factor. By holding an account in a commercial bank (known as the *transfer agent*), the money market mutual funds have allowed shareholders to cash their shares at any time in any amount and to write checks to third parties in amounts above some minimum (usually $500). Despite this transaction-balance characteristic, the turnover rate of funds is about the same as that for ordinary savings accounts (approximately three times per year), and for this reason the money market mutual fund shares are included in money supply 2 (M2) rather than the means of exchange, money supply 1 (M1).

Money market mutual funds were so successful in attracting funds that the depository institutions complained bitterly that these funds had a competitive edge over them. The congressional response (included in the Garn–St. Germain Act of 1982) was to authorize MMDAs that could be placed in depository institutions. These accounts are federally insured and pay unregulated interest rates.

## MISCELLANEOUS NONBANK FINANCIAL INSTITUTIONS

There are many government agencies and government-sponsored agencies that raise funds by selling their own paper and use these funds to supplement activities in various financial markets, particularly in agricultural and housing finance.

### *Banks for Cooperatives*

There are 12 banks for cooperatives, each serving its own district. These banks do not deal directly with the farmers, but indirectly through cooperatives that are set up by the farmers for marketing products and purchasing supplies.

## Federal Intermediate Credit Banks

There are 12 federal intermediate credit banks, each serving its own district. As with the banks for cooperatives, they do not deal directly with farmers but make short- and intermediate-term loans through farmers' cooperatives for the purpose of buying feed, seed, and fertilizer.

## Federal Land Banks

There are 12 federal land banks, each serving its own district. They were established to provide agricultural mortgage and other long-term credit to farmers through cooperatives owned by the farmers.

## Federal Home Loan Banks

The Federal Home Loan Bank System was established to provide a central credit facility to supplement the resources of its members (mainly savings and loan associations). *See* "Savings and Loan Associations," page 266.

## Federal Home Loan Mortgage Corporation (Freddy Mac)

Officially known as the *Mortgage Corporation,* but popularly known as *Freddy Mac,* the Federal Home Loan Mortgage Corporation was established in 1970 to strengthen existing secondary markets in residential mortgages insured by the Federal Housing Administration or guaranteed by the Veterans' Administration. It buys from, and sells to, commercial banks, savings and loan associations, and mutual savings banks, allowing these institutions to sell off low-yield mortgages and to reinvest the proceeds in higher-yield mortgages.

## Federal National Mortgage Association (Fanny Mae)

The Federal National Mortgage Association, popularly known as *Fanny Mae* (after its initials, *FNMA*), was created by the federal government to provide assistance in the residential mortgage market. By offering to buy mortgages on residential property held by other institutions, and by being ready to sell mortgages from its portfolio when the demand for mortgages is on the increase, Fanny Mae increases liquidity in the mortgage markets when the normal participants in the market are not active. Fanny Mae became a private corporation in 1968 and has since grown to be one of the largest corporations (by dollar value of assets) in the country.

## Government National Mortgage Association (Ginny Mae)

The Government National Mortgage Association, popularly known as *Ginny Mae*, was created by the federal government in September 1968 when Fanny Mae became a private corporation. Ginny Mae was designed to take over some of the duties of Fanny Mae. Ginny Mae is officially "a corporate instrumentality of the United States within the Department of Housing and Urban Development." It operates in the secondary mortgage markets under the supervision of the secretary of HUD.

## SUMMARY

There are many financial institutions in the economy other than the commercial banks that act as intermediaries between lenders and borrowers. All are important in the flow of funds through the economy and in the allocation of resources. These nonbank financial intermediaries were formed to exploit the comparative advantage gained from expertise developed in certain financial markets. Many nonbank financial intermediaries (particularly the thrift institutions) have come to resemble commercial banks over the years in many of their operations. In response to this development, the monetary authorities decided to change institutional arrangements so that now they are able to control the lending of many nonbank financial institutions in exactly the same way as they control the lending of the commercial banks.

## Key Terms

nonbank financial
 intermediaries
depository institutions
credit unions
mutual savings banks
savings and loan associations

Federal Home Loan Bank
 System
contractual savings institutions
finance companies
investment companies
money market mutual funds

## Questions

1. How do near banks differ from commercial banks? How are they the same?

2. How do thrift institutions differ from contractual savings institutions?

3. In what way is the Federal Home Loan Bank System like the Federal Reserve System? How do they differ?

**4.** What effects have Fanny Mae, Ginny Mae, and Freddy Mac had on mortgage markets?

## Additional Readings

A great deal of information on the operations of the thrift institutions appears in the annual publication of the United States League of Savings Associations (Chicago). This publication, formerly called the *Savings and Loan Fact Book,* has now been replaced by a similar publication called the *Savings and Loan Source Book.* Other information is published in the *Annual Report,* published annually by the National Credit Union Administration (Washington, D.C.), and in the *National Fact Book of Mutual Savings Banking,* published annually by the National Association of Mutual Savings Banking (New York).

# CHAPTER TWELVE

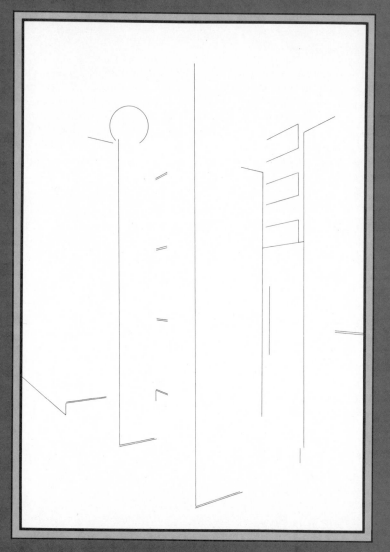

# THE MONEY SUPPLY AND THE
# MULTIPLE EXPANSION OF DEPOSITS

*Without intending it, managers of depository institutions create money. Whatever definition of the money supply is adopted, the quantity of that money is related to the monetary base by a multiplier consisting of several crucial ratios, most of which are not under the direct control of the authorities.*

An important aspect of the relationships among the various financial institutions in the system is that they are able to create money as a by-product of their lending and investing activities. No matter what definition of the money supply is being used, most money is created by private financial institutions rather than monetary authorities. The transfer of funds into a financial institution does not of itself change the total supply of funds in the system. However, because financial institutions hold fractional reserves (that is, the reserves held are only a fraction of the total amount of the deposits), a part of each deposit is loaned out. When loans are extended out of new deposits received by the banking system, additional money is created.

If all banks are holding reserves of 20 percent, then for every $100 placed in a demand deposit one bank can make a loan of $80. The amount loaned out may be in the form of direct loans to the bank's customers or in the form of investments, which are indirect loans made by purchasing credit instruments. These loans, whichever form they take, are the means whereby the banks are able to create money. Borrowers spend the money they borrow; those who receive this money in payment cannot distinguish between this borrowed money and any other. The loaned money is part of the money supply, even though the deposit from which the loan was made is still intact. Until the loan is paid back, the money supply has been increased.

This is only the first step, however, in a rather lengthy procedure. A person who receives money in payment from a bank borrower is likely to place these funds in another bank account, and the lending process will be repeated. The bank receiving the funds will keep fractional reserves and loan out the remainder. The funds will be spent again, deposited in another account, and so on. The *multiple expansion of deposits* is illustrated in Figure 12.1.

If all money loaned out by a bank is spent and then deposited in another bank, and if all banks keep the same proportion of their deposits in reserves, it is possible to calculate exactly how much money is created by the banking system from any deposit placed in a bank. For example, continuing the example used in Figure 12.1, all banks are assumed to be holding 20 percent of their deposits in the form of reserves. As each loan made is subsequently deposited in another bank account, each deposit is exactly 80 percent of the previous deposit. Thus, starting with a deposit of $1000 in

*Figure 12.1*
***The Multiple Expansion of Bank Deposits:* Assuming That All Loans Are Spent and Then Deposited into Another Bank**

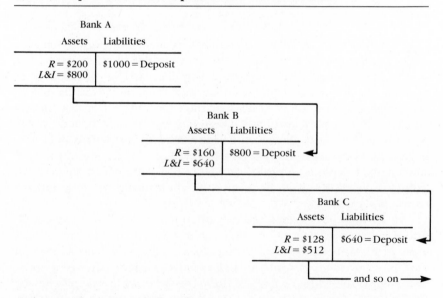

$R$ = reserves. $L\&I$ = loans and investments made by the bank.

Bank A, the loans and deposits made will follow the sequence illustrated in Figure 12.2.

The series of loans and deposits derived in this way ends when the amount that may be loaned out reaches zero. This occurs when the total amount of the initial deposit is being held in reserves by the banks involved. In this example, the initial deposit was $1000; therefore, the series ends when the total amount of the reserves is $1000. As the reserves in our

Figure 12.2
**The Multiple Expansion of Deposits by the Banking System**

| Bank(s) | Deposits | Reserves | Loans and Investments |
|---|---|---|---|
| Bank A | $1000.00 | $200.00 | $800.00 |
| Bank B | 800.00 | 160.00 | 640.00 |
| Bank C | 640.00 | 128.00 | 512.00 |
| Bank D | 512.00 | 102.40 | 409.60 |
| Bank E | 409.60 | 81.92 | 327.68 |
| Bank F | 327.68 | 65.54 | 262.14 |
| Bank G | 262.14 | 52.43 | 209.72 |
| Bank H | 209.72 | 41.94 | 167.77 |
| Bank I | 167.77 | 33.55 | 134.22 |
| Bank J | 134.22 | 26.84 | 107.37 |
| Bank K | 107.37 | 21.47 | 85.90 |
| All others | 429.50 | 85.91 | 343.60 |
| | $5000.00 | $1000.00 | $4000.00 |

example are equal to 20 percent of the deposits, the total amount of the deposits ($D$) is equal to the initial deposit divided by 0.20,

$$D = \frac{\text{Reserves}}{0.20} = \frac{\text{Initial deposit}}{0.20} = \frac{\$1000.00}{0.20} = \$5000.00,$$

or, in general,

$$D = \frac{R}{r},$$

where $r$ = the reserve ratio held by the banks (whether required or not), and $R$ = the total amount of reserves held.

This simple calculation does not tell the whole story of how money is created by the banking system, but it does convey the basic concept. The problem is complicated by, first, that we have so far assumed that all loans made are returned to a bank account when they are spent, and, second, that we have assumed that banks only keep reserves for demand deposits. Neither assumption is true. It is possible to relax each to gain a clearer idea of exactly how much money is created by the system.

## NONBANK FINANCIAL INTERMEDIARIES IN THE MULTIPLE EXPANSION PROCESS

There has been considerable controversy regarding the position that non-bank financial intermediaries hold in the money creation process, but their position is clear once the *definition* of the money supply specifies what is and what is not included. If we are discussing money supply 1, for example, we know exactly what is included in the definition: currency held by the nonbank public, plus traveler's checks issued by nonbank companies, plus transactions accounts issued by all depository institutions. To illustrate the effect of the nonbank financial institutions, let us begin by looking at the first step in the expansion of deposits, assuming that only commercial banks and demand deposits are involved. If $1000 is deposited in Bank A, and Bank A keeps 20 percent reserves, $800 is loaned out. If this $800 is then deposited in Bank B, $800 that must be included in money supply 1 has been created. This is shown in Figure 12.3a. In calculating money supply 1, the $1000 in Bank A's demand deposits and the $800 in Bank B's demand deposits are included. The two banks are contributing $1800 to money supply 1.

If a nonbank financial institution is involved in the lending process, and we allow accounts other than demand deposits, then the situation becomes a little more complicated. If the $800 loaned by Bank A is deposited in a passbook savings account in a savings and loan association (as shown in Figure 12.3b), and the savings and loan association keeps 20 percent reserves, the savings and loan lends out $640. If this $640 is then deposited in a demand deposit in Bank B, the amount of money supply 1 that has so far

*Figure 12.3a*
**Multiple Expansion Only in Commercial Banks**

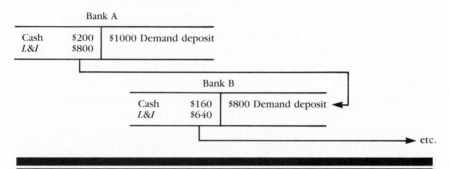

**a. In Commercial Banks Only**

*Figure 12.3b*
**Multiple Expansion in Commercial Banks and Nonbank Financial Intermediaries**

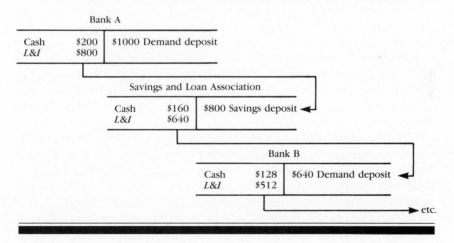

**b. In Both Commercial Banks and Nonbank Financial Intermediaries**

been created is exactly the same as in the case when the savings and loan association was not involved in the process. In calculating money supply 1, the amounts included are the $1000 demand deposit in Bank A, the $640 demand deposit in Bank B, and the $160 cash held as reserves in the savings and loan association. The two banks and the savings and loan association together are contributing $1800 as before.

It should not be thought, however, that the two situations are exactly alike. If the savings and loan association keeps the $160 in reserves in cash, the effect on the multiple expansion of deposits will be a reduction in the total amount of money created. As Figure 12.3 shows, Bank B lends $640 when there is no nonbank financial intermediary involved, but lends only $512 when the savings and loan association intervenes in the lending process. Any reduction in the amount loaned out by Bank B, of course, will reduce the amount of the multiple expansion of deposits that are subsequently involved. However, it is rather artificial to assume that the savings and loan association keeps its reserves in cash. Savings and loan associations keep very low cash reserves. It is much more likely that the savings and loan association's reserves will be placed in a demand deposit in a commercial bank. In *that* case, the amount of money supply 1 created will be exactly the same as if the savings and loan association had not been included in the process. This process is shown in Figure 12.4. The $160 reserve deposit of the savings and loan association is a demand deposit at Bank Z. Bank Z keeps 20 percent reserves and therefore lends $128. Bank B and Z then jointly loan out $640, and the process continues as before.

If the $800 deposited in the savings and loan association had been a NOW account (or a share draft account, had the institution been a credit union), then that deposit would have been included in money supply 1. Using the same procedures as before, money supply 1 would include the $1000 deposited in Bank A, the $640 deposited in Bank B, the $800 in the NOW account, and the $160 deposited in Bank Z. This is a total of $2600. In this example, clearly the savings and loan association is as much a part of the multiple expansion process as were the commercial banks. There is some double counting involved here, as the $160 deposited in Bank Z is the reserve held for the $800 in the NOW account, but the Federal Reserve has allowed this because the amounts are, as yet, minimal. If transactions accounts in nonbank financial intermediaries grow significantly, an adjustment will have to be made.

If the $800 in the savings and loan association had *not* been a NOW account (but a passbook savings account or a time deposit), it would have been counted in money supply 2 rather than money supply 1. Money supply 2 includes all savings accounts (and all small time deposits) in all financial institutions whether they are transactions accounts or not. Using the definition of money supply 2, therefore, makes the savings and loan association in our example a part of the money creation process just the same as it is when creating a NOW account as part of money supply 1.

However, there is a difference in the way that the money supply is counted. If a nonbank financial intermediary keeps reserves on deposit in a commercial bank for deposits that are included in money supply 2 but not included in money supply 1, the double counting mentioned above is avoided. Savings and loan associations are not required to keep reserves for savings accounts, but they are for nonpersonal time deposits. The reserves held in commercial bank demand deposits for these nonpersonal time deposits is subtracted out as part of the M2 consolidation component.

*Figure 12.4*
**Multiple Expansion of Deposits when Reserves of a Nonbank**
**Financial Intermediary Are on Deposit in a Commercial Bank**
**12a-gd Ratio of Currency to Demand Deposits**

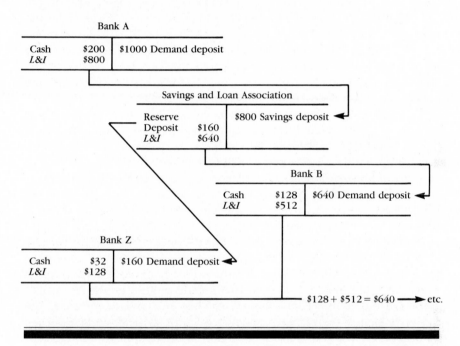

In general, it can be said that, insofar as the accounts held in the nonbank financial intermediaries are part of the money supply definition, the nonbank financial intermediaries are as much a part of the money creation process as the commercial banks. When the accounts in the nonbank financial intermediaries are not part of the money supply definition, then the effect on money supply creation of the nonbank financial intermediaries depends on the form in which they hold their reserves. If they hold cash reserves, these reserves will reduce the total amount of money created by the other institutions.

## The Monetary Base

The amount of money created by the banking system depends on the amount of reserves held by the financial intermediaries that hold the transactions accounts (demand deposits, NOW accounts, ATS accounts, and share draft accounts). These institutions are called *depository institutions.*

The larger the amount of reserves $(R)$ held, the larger the amount of deposits $(D)$ created:

$$D = \frac{R}{r},$$

where $r =$ the reserve ratio actually held by the depository institutions.

The total amount of funds *available* to be used as reserves by the financial institutions (the monetary base) is decided by the monetary authorities, but the proportion of the base actually held as reserves is decided to a great extent by the public. Thus, the amount of money created by the depository institutions is partly determined by the portfolio decisions of the public. If the public decides to hold part of its wealth in the form of currency, this currency becomes unavailable for the depository institutions to use as reserves on which they could create money. If, on the other hand, the public chooses to transfer funds into the depository institutions, these funds become part of the reserves on which money is created.

The *monetary base* $(B)$ is the amount of funds available to be used as reserves for deposits in the depository institutions. It is also equal to the total amount of currency that would be in circulation if everyone withdrew the money from their deposits in currency. This is not equal to the amount of currency that exists in the system but the amount that *could* be converted into currency by making withdrawals from deposits. The difference lies in the fact that the depository institutions do not hold all their reserves in currency but also hold deposits with Federal Reserve District Banks. These deposits in the Federal Reserve can be withdrawn in currency. The monetary base is, therefore, the amount of currency held by the nonbank public *plus* the reserves of the depository institutions either in vault cash or as deposits at the Federal Reserve District Banks.

$$B = C_p + R,$$

where $B =$ the monetary base, $C_p =$ the currency held by the nonbank public, and $R =$ the reserves held by the depository institutions in vault cash or deposits at the Federal Reserve. Amounts of the monetary base and its two components are shown in Table 12.1.

The reserves of the depository institutions, whether they are held as vault cash or as deposits at the Federal Reserve, are held for three reasons. They are held as required reserves for transactions accounts, as excess reserves, and as required reserves for nonpersonal time deposits. Nonpersonal time deposits (the only deposits for which reserves are required apart from transactions accounts) are defined as time deposits that are transferable or are held by a depositor other than a natural person.[1] The reserve require-

---

[1] *See:* Cacy, J. A., and Scott Winningham, "Reserve Requirements Under the Depository Institutions Deregulation and Monetary Control Act of 1980," *Economic Review* (Federal Reserve Bank of Kansas City, September–October 1980): 4.

**Table 12.1**
***The Monetary Base***

| | Monetary Base (B) Billions | Reserves (R) Billions | Currency Held by the Nonbank Public ($C_p$) Billions |
|---|---|---|---|
| **1982** | | | |
| Jan. | $169.1 | $45.8 | $123.3 |
| Feb. | 166.8 | 43.8 | 123.0 |
| Mar. | 165.4 | 41.6 | 123.8 |
| Apr. | 167.6 | 42.0 | 125.6 |
| May | 169.2 | 42.0 | 127.2 |
| June | 170.4 | 42.1 | 128.3 |
| July | 172.3 | 42.5 | 129.8 |
| Aug. | 172.8 | 42.8 | 130.0 |
| Sept. | 172.3 | 42.1 | 130.2 |
| Oct. | 173.8 | 42.6 | 131.2 |
| Nov. | 176.0 | 43.3 | 132.7 |
| Dec. | 179.3 | 44.1 | 135.2 |
| **1983** | | | |
| Jan. | 177.9 | 44.7 | 133.2 |
| Feb. | 176.0 | 42.3 | 133.7 |
| Mar. | 175.9 | 40.5 | 135.4 |
| Apr. | 178.4 | 41.0 | 137.4 |
| May | 179.8 | 40.9 | 138.9 |
| June | 181.6 | 41.3 | 140.3 |
| July | 183.7 | 41.7 | 142.0 |
| Aug. | 183.8 | 41.7 | 142.1 |
| Sept. | 183.5 | 40.9 | 142.6 |
| Oct. | 184.7 | 40.8 | 143.9 |
| Nov. | 187.2 | 41.1 | 146.1 |
| Dec. | 190.6 | 41.9 | 148.7 |

*Source:* Board of Governors, Federal Reserve System, *Federal Reserve Bulletin* (Washington, D.C.: Board of Governors): Tables A13, A14, A15, various issues.

ment currently applies only to those nonpersonal time deposits with an initial maturity of less than one and a half years. Also, this reserve requirement has currently been applied to any Eurodollar borrowing by the depository institutions. This was done to avoid giving an incentive to the depository institutions to borrow from overseas, rather than domestic, markets.

Dividing the reserves of the depository institutions into three components, we have

$$R = r_D D_T + e D_T + r_T T_{NP},$$

where $R$ = the total amount of reserves held by the depository institutions; $D_T$ = the total amount of transactions deposits held in the depository institutions; $T_{NP}$ = the total amount of nonpersonal time deposits held in the depository institutions; $r_D$ = the required reserve ratio for transactions accounts; $e$ = the excess reserve ratio of depository institutions expressed as a proportion of the transactions accounts; and $r_T$ = the required reserve ratio for nonpersonal time deposits. Using this definition of the total amount of reserves held by the depository institutions allows us to define the monetary base as

$$B = C_P + r_D D_T + e D_T + r_T T_{NP}.$$

These four components of the monetary base allow us to see how the portfolio decisions of the public and of the depository institutions contribute to monetary expansion. The required reserves for nonpersonal time deposits ($r_T T_{NP}$), of course, are used to support nonpersonal time deposits. This means that any dollar included in this amount is supporting part of any money supply that is defined to include the nonpersonal time deposits (for example, M2), but is not supporting any part of a money supply that does not include these deposits (M1).

If the public decides to change the way in which it holds its wealth, it can change the amount of the money supply by causing funds to be shifted from one part of the monetary base to another. If, for example, the public decides to increase the proportion of its wealth that it holds in the form of currency, this will increase $C_P$ and decrease some other part of the monetary base. If the funds transferred to $C_P$ come from the required reserves being held for transactions accounts, the transactions accounts will have to be reduced by more than $C_P$ increased. This would reduce the total amount of money supply 1. On the other hand, if the funds transferred to $C_P$ come from the excess reserves held by the depository institutions, $C_P$ will increase without the amount of the transactions accounts being reduced, therefore increasing the amount of money supply 1.

## TRANSACTIONS ACCOUNTS

Transactions accounts consist of all checking-type accounts in the system. A large proportion of these accounts are demand deposits in commercial banks, which are noninterest-bearing checking accounts. There also are some demand deposits in savings and loan associations and mutual savings banks.

Apart from the ordinary demand deposits, however, there are several other kinds of checking accounts in both commercial banks and nonbank financial intermediaries. Commercial banks hold some checking accounts that are interest bearing. These are the NOW and the ATS accounts. NOW accounts are simply demand deposits that bear interest, whereas ATS accounts are savings accounts that bear interest and have an automatic transfer service that moves funds from the savings account to the checking account whenever a check is presented for payment. The checking accounts that exist in nonbank financial institutions include interest-bearing NOW accounts, noninterest-bearing NOW accounts (NINOW accounts), and share draft accounts in credit unions.

Traveler's checks issued by nonbank companies have posed a problem for the Federal Reserve in defining the money supply. All traveler's checks are used as currency and clearly should be counted as money, but it has not been easy to count them. When traveler's checks are issued by a commercial bank, there is no problem. The funds to be used when the checks are cashed are placed in a special demand deposit at the bank, and this is counted as part of transactions accounts. However, because nonbank companies do not keep the funds to pay off their traveler's checks in demand deposits at commercial banks or transactions accounts at any depository institution, these funds are not part of transactions accounts or of the money supplies unless they are specifically added. Until June 1981, these nonbank-issued traveler's checks were omitted, but improved data collection has made it possible to include them. Traveler's checks are now included in all money supply definitions. For simplicity, we will include traveler's checks issued by nonbank companies as part of transactions accounts ($D_T$).

To see how the total amount of transactions accounts in the system can be calculated and to see how that amount relates to the monetary base, we must know the portfolio choices made by members of the nonbank public. Each member of the public makes a decision regarding the holding of wealth in the form of currency, transactions accounts, and other deposits. First, the *ratio of currency in the hands of the nonbank public to transactions accounts* ($c$) is defined as the amount of currency held by the non-bank public divided by the total amount of transactions balances in the depository institutions:

$$c = \frac{C_P}{D_T}.$$

In addition, members of the public also make a portfolio choice regarding the holding of nonpersonal time deposits. We define the *ratio of nonpersonal time deposits to transactions accounts* ($t$) as being equal to the total amount of nonpersonal time deposits divided by the total amount of transactions accounts:

$$t = \frac{T_{NP}}{D_T}.$$

These two ratios then allow us to define both the currency held by the nonbank public and the total of nonpersonal time deposits in terms of the total amount of transactions accounts in the system:

$$C_P = cD_T$$

and $$T_{NP} = tD_T.$$

As both currency in the hands of the nonbank public and the total of nonpersonal time deposits appear in our definition of the monetary base, we now can redefine the monetary base in terms of the transactions accounts.

$$\text{If} \quad B = C_P + r_D D_T + e D_T + r_T T_{NP}$$

$$\text{then} \quad B = c D_T + r_D D_T + e D_T + r_T t D_T.$$

Rearranging this equation to define $D_T$ in terms of the monetary base gives us

$$B = (c + r_D + e + r_T t) D_T.$$

$$\text{Therefore,} \quad D_T = \frac{1}{c + r_D + e + r_T t} B.$$

This equation shows that there are six determinants of the total amount of transactions accounts in the depository institutions: the monetary base ($B$) and five ratios. Of these six determinants, three are determined by the monetary authorities ($B$, $r_D$, and $r_T$), two are determined by the general public ($c$ and $t$), and one is determined by the commercial banks ($e$).

*If it could be assumed that the five ratios remained constant,* the monetary authorities would know exactly what the effect of changing the monetary base would be on the amount of transactions deposits. If the monetary base is increased by an amount $\Delta B$, the total amount of the transactions deposits will increase by an amount equal to $\Delta D_T$, where

$$\Delta D_T = \frac{1}{c + r_D + e + r_T t} \Delta B.$$

If the monetary base is decreased by an amount $\Delta B$, the total amount of transactions deposits will decrease by the amount $\Delta D_T$.

If the ratios $c$, $e$, and $t$ remain constant, and the monetary base ($B$) is unchanged, the monetary authorities would be able to change the total amount of transactions deposits by changing the reserve requirements on transactions accounts and on the nonpersonal time deposits. If $r_D$ or $r_T$ is increased with other factors remaining the same, the total amount of $D_T$ decreases. Similarly, if banks increase their excess reserve ratio ($e$) with other things remaining the same, the total amount of $D_T$ decreases.

Unfortunately for the ease with which monetary policy might be carried out, the ratios that represent private portfolio decisions ($c$ and $t$, which are the results of decisions made by individuals and nonbank companies, and $e$, which is the result of decisions made by the depository institutions) cannot be relied on to remain constant while the monetary authorities change the monetary base or the reserve requirements on the various kinds of accounts. Any increases in $c$, $t$, or $e$, with other factors remaining the same, will result in decreases in the total amount of transactions deposits; and any decreases in $c$, $t$, or $e$, with other remaining the same, will result in increases in the total amount of transactions deposits. Any instability in the ratios will be reflected in instability in the amount of transactions deposits, and therefore will increase the difficulty of any monetary policy designed to change the total amount of deposits in the system.

The ratio

$$\frac{1}{c + r_D + e + r_T t}$$

is known as a *money multiplier*. This particular multiplier—the money multiplier for transactions deposits—is the number by which the monetary base must be multiplied to find the total amount of transactions deposits in the system. It should not be thought of as a constant, as it will vary with any changes in any of the five ratios included in it. It is true that $r_D$ and $r_T$ are set by the authorities, but the other three ratios are the results of portfolio decisions and may vary considerably over time.

## Money Supply 1

Money supply 1 (considered to be the Federal Reserve's best estimate of the means of exchange) is defined as being equal to the total amount of transactions deposits in the system plus the currency held by the nonbank public:

$$M1 = D_T + C_P.$$

If the two components of this money supply definition are expressed in terms of the total amount of transactions deposits in the system, it is a simple matter to find another money multiplier, one that relates M1 to the amount of the monetary base $(B)$. $C_p$ has already been defined as being equal to $cD_T$; therefore, we can say that

$$M1 = D_T + cD_T$$

$$\text{or} \quad M1 = (1 + c)D_T.$$

However, as

$$D_T = \frac{1}{c + r_D + e + r_T t} B,$$

$$M1 = \frac{1 + c}{c + r_D + e + r_T t} B$$

$$\text{and} \quad \Delta M1 = \frac{1 + c}{c + r_D + e + r_T t} \Delta B.$$

The amount

$$\frac{1 + c}{c + r_D + e + r_T t}$$

is the money multiplier for money supply 1. It is the number by which the monetary base must be multiplied to give money supply 1. The multiplier contains the same five ratios as the multiplier for transactions accounts; therefore, money supply 1 has the same six determinants as the total amount of transactions accounts in the system: the ratio of currency held by the nonbank public to transactions accounts, the ratio of nonpersonal time deposits to transactions accounts, the excess reserve ratio of depository institutions, the required reserve ratio for transactions accounts, the required reserve ratio for nonpersonal time deposits, and the monetary base.

The monetary authorities have the same three ways of influencing money supply 1 as they have of influencing the amount of transactions deposits. In fact, they cannot change transactions deposits without changing money supply 1. The authorities can change the size of the money multiplier by changing the required reserve ratio for transactions deposits and the required reserve ratio for nonpersonal time deposits. Any increase in the required reserve ratios, with other things remaining the same, causes the money multiplier to decline. Any decrease in the required reserve ratio, with other things remaining the same, causes the money multiplier to increase. Any increase in the monetary base, with the money multiplier remaining the same, will cause money supply 1 to increase. Any decrease in the monetary base, with the money multiplier remaining the same, will cause money supply 1 to decrease.

The public also has some influence over the amount of money supply 1. As with the other money multipliers, the money multiplier for money supply 1 may be changed whenever the nonbank public changes the ratio of currency to transactions deposits; whenever the nonbank public changes the ratio of nonpersonal time deposits to transactions deposits; or whenever the depository institutions change their excess reserve ratio. All three ratios are the results of portfolio choices made by either the nonbank public or the depository institutions. All three are likely to be influenced by interest rates. Any increase in the rate of interest paid on transactions accounts could influence members of the public to decrease the ratio of currency to transactions accounts. Any decrease in this ratio will be reflected in an increase in the money multiplier for money supply 1. Similarly, any increase in the interest rates paid on nonpersonal time deposits relative to other rates may cause the ratio of nonpersonal time deposits to transactions deposits to increase; and any increase in this ratio, with other things remaining the same, is reflected in a decrease in the money multiplier for money supply 1. In addition, as excess reserve holdings entail forgone interest costs, a general rise in interest rates will give depository institutions an incentive to reduce their excess reserve ratio. Any decrease in the excess reserve ratio, with other things remaining the same, is reflected in an increase in the multiplier for money supply 1.

## Money Supply 2

Money supply 2 defines money as much broader than the means of ex-change. Apart from the means of exchange (money supply 1), money supply 2 includes a selected list of short-term financial assets (SSTA) that can be converted easily into cash with little or no loss in nominal value. These SSTAs include all savings accounts in the depository institutions (other than those already included in money supply 1), all small (less than $100,000) time deposits in the depository institutions, all overnight repurchases in commercial banks, all overnight Eurodollars issued to United States residents by United States banks abroad (mainly in the Caribbean and London), all money market deposit accounts, and all general purpose and broker-dealer money market mutual funds. Although including these financial assets greatly increases the size of the definition of money beyond the means of exchange, it is a simple matter to make the change from the definition of money supply 1 to money supply 2.

Because the decision to hold these SSTAs is again a portfolio decision made by members of the public, we can define $d$ as the *ratio between the selected short-term assets to transactions accounts in the depository institutions.* Thus,

$$d = \frac{SSTA}{D_T}$$

or   $SSTA = dD_T$.

By substituting this expression in the definition of money supply 2, we have

$$M2 = M1 + SSTA$$

or   $M2 = M1 + dD_T$
or   $M2 = D_T + C_P + dD_T$
or   $M2 = D_T + cD_T + dD_T$
or   $M2 = (1 + c + d)D_T$.

but   $D_T = \dfrac{1}{c + r_D + e + r_T t} B.$

Therefore   $M2 = \dfrac{1 + c + d}{c + r_D + e + r_T t} B$

and   $\Delta M2 = \dfrac{1 + c + d}{c + r_D + e + r_T t} \Delta B.$

Again we see that the money supply is determined by the authorities when they decide on the monetary base ($B$) and the reserve requirements for transactions accounts ($r_D$) and nonpersonal time deposits ($r_T$); by the

*Table 12.2*
**Monetary Aggregates and Components**

| 1983 | Jan. | Feb. | Mar. | Apr. | May | June | July | Aug. | Sept. | Oct. | Nov. | Dec. |
|---|---|---|---|---|---|---|---|---|---|---|---|---|
| $D_T$ | 352.6 | 342.8 | 349.5 | 362.7 | 356.4 | 363.1 | 367.6 | 364.3 | 366.6 | 370.8 | 373.1 | 382.1 |
| $TC_{NBC}$ | 3.9 | 4.1 | 4.3 | 4.4 | 4.5 | 4.9 | 5.2 | 5.1 | 5.0 | 4.8 | 4.6 | 4.6 |
| $C_P$ | 133.2 | 133.7 | 135.4 | 137.4 | 138.9 | 140.3 | 142.0 | 142.1 | 142.6 | 143.9 | 146.1 | 148.7 |
| M1 | 489.7 | 480.6 | 489.2 | 504.5 | 499.8 | 508.3 | 514.8 | 511.5 | 514.2 | 519.5 | 523.8 | 535.4 |
| M1 | 489.7 | 480.6 | 489.2 | 504.5 | 499.8 | 500.3 | 514.8 | 511.5 | 514.2 | 519.5 | 523.8 | 535.4 |
| ORP + Eu $ | 47.3 | 49.1 | 48.6 | 50.6 | 55.1 | 55.9 | 52.7 | 52.0 | 53.0 | 56.7 | 55.3 | 56.1 |
| SD | 332.1 | 321.0 | 319.5 | 324.3 | 324.6 | 326.3 | 326.6 | 321.5 | 318.2 | 318.0 | 313.8 | 310.1 |
| STD | 798.6 | 758.5 | 737.7 | 728.6 | 722.7 | 723.9 | 734.3 | 746.0 | 754.8 | 769.3 | 781.3 | 786.7 |
| MMMF | 166.7 | 159.6 | 154.0 | 140.1 | 135.0 | 132.9 | 138.8 | 139.1 | 137.6 | 137.8 | 138.7 | 138.0 |
| MMDA | 180.7 | 277.7 | 320.5 | 341.2 | 356.8 | 367.3 | 368.4 | 366.3 | 366.9 | 367.4 | 369.1 | 372.4 |
| − M2CC | −3.2 | −4.0 | −3.5 | −0.2 | −0.1 | −0.6 | −7.8 | −7.2 | −7.6 | −7.7 | −7.6 | −7.3 |
| M2 | 2011.9 | 2042.5 | 2066.0 | 2089.1 | 2093.9 | 2114.0 | 2127.8 | 2129.2 | 2137.1 | 2161.0 | 2174.4 | 2191.4 |

*Legend:* $D_T$ = transactions accounts, $TC_{NBC}$ = traveler's checks issued by nonbank companies, $C_P$ = currency in the hands of the nonbank public, M1 = money supply 1, ORP = overnight repurchases in commercial banks, Eu $ = Eurodollars issued to U.S. residents other than financial institutions, SD = savings deposits, STD = small (<$100,000) time deposits, MMMF = general purpose and broker-dealer money market mutual funds, MMDA = money market deposit accounts, M2CC = M2 consolidation component, M2 = money supply 2.

*Source:* Board of Governors, Federal Reserve System, *Federal Reserve Bulletin,* (Washington D.C.): Tables A13, A14, A15, various issues.

Table 12.3
**Movement in Portfolio Ratios (Nonseasonally Adjusted Data)**

| Date | c | d | Date | c | d |
|------|------|------|------|------|------|
| 1982 | | | 1983 | | |
| Jan. | 0.3781 | 4.2993 | Jan. | 0.3778 | 4.1375 |
| Feb. | 0.3969 | 4.5544 | Feb. | 0.3900 | 4.5680 |
| Mar. | 0.3968 | 4.5753 | Mar. | 0.3874 | 4.5216 |
| Apr. | 0.3857 | 4.4149 | Apr. | 0.3788 | 4.3797 |
| May | 0.4055 | 4.6216 | May | 0.3897 | 4.4731 |
| June | 0.4040 | 4.6026 | June | 0.3863 | 4.4239 |
| July | 0.4068 | 4.6302 | July | 0.3862 | 4.4091 |
| Aug. | 0.4074 | 4.6738 | Aug. | 0.3901 | 4.4603 |
| Sept. | 0.3998 | 4.5969 | Sept. | 0.3890 | 4.4476 |
| Oct. | 0.3923 | 4.5117 | Oct. | 0.3881 | 4.4477 |
| Nov. | 0.3885 | 4.4364 | Nov. | 0.3916 | 4.4444 |
| Dec. | 0.3844 | 4.1965 | Dec. | 0.3892 | 4.3530 |

*Source:* Board of Governors, Federal Reserve System, *Federal Reserve Bulletin,* (Washington D.C.): Tables A13, A14, A15, various issues.

depository institutions when they choose their excess reserve ratio ($e$); and by the public when they make their portfolio choices ($c$, $d$, and $t$).

The monthly data for M1 and M2 and their components for 1983 are shown in Table 12.2. Apart from showing how M1 and M2 changed over this period, the information in the table allows us to see how the ratios $c$ and $d$ from our multipliers have changed over the same period. Table 12.3 shows the ratios $c$ and $d$ for the period January 1982 through December 1983.

## MONEY MULTIPLIERS AND THE MARKET

Looking at the money multipliers, it would be easy to conclude that there was a simple mechanical connection between the monetary base ($B$) and the money supply, and that the connection is not affected by market forces. This would not be the case, however. Market forces affect some of the ratios in the multipliers. Obviously, the market does not affect those ratios that are set by the authorities ($r_D$, $r_T$), but the ratio of currency to deposits ($c$), the ratio of nonpersonal time deposits to transactions accounts ($t$), the excess reserve ratio ($e$), and the ratio of "selected short-term assets" ($SSTA$) to transactions accounts ($d$) are all influenced by the market to some extent.

If all of the ratios expressing portfolio choices of the public ($c$, $d$, $e$, $t$) were to remain constant, it would be clear to the monetary authorities exactly how much of a change in the monetary base would be required to achieve any desired change in the money supply. However, the monetary authorities are faced with a more difficult problem. There can be significant

## THE CHANGING MONEY SUPPLY DEFINITIONS[1]

| | Pre–1980 $M_1$ | 1980–1982 M1A | 1980–1982 M1B | Post–1982 M1 | Pre–1980 $M_2$ | 1980–1982 M2 | Post–1982 M2 |
|---|---|---|---|---|---|---|---|
| Currency of the nonbank public | X | X | X | X | X | X | X |
| **At commercial banks** | | | | | | | |
| Demand deposits exclusive of those due to foreign commercial banks and official institutions | X | X | X | X | X | X | X |
| Demand deposits due to foreign commercial banks and official institutions | X | | | | X | | |
| NOW accounts | | | X | X | | X | X |
| Super NOW accounts | | | X | | | | X |
| ATS accounts | | | X | X | | X | X |
| Overnight repurchases | | | | | | X | X |
| Savings deposits | | | | | X | X | X |
| Small time deposits (<$100,000) | | | | | X | X | X |
| Money market deposit accounts | | | | | | | X |
| **At thrift institutions** | | | | | | | |
| Demand deposits | | | X | X | | X | X |
| NOW accounts | | | X | X | | X | X |

changes in the ratios that will be reflected in changes in the money multipliers. For example, a significant "run" on the depository institutions (that is, the conversion of deposits to cash by members of the public) could cause a drastic change in the money multipliers and in the money supply. Before the days of deposit insurance, periodic bank panics did have this effect. As people lost confidence in the banks as a safe repository for funds, the ratio of currency to deposits ($c$) would rise, causing a decrease in the money multipliers and the money supply. Volatility in the ratio of currency to deposits also could cause instability in the other ratios. When banks fear panics and runs on banks (as in the 1930s), it is not uncommon for them to increase their holdings of excess reserves. If ratio $e$ rises, the amount of money that

| | Pre–1980 $M_1$ | 1980–1982 M1A | 1980–1982 M1B | Post–1982 M1 | Pre–1980 $M_2$ | 1980–1982 M2 | Post–1982 M2 |
|---|---|---|---|---|---|---|---|
| **At thrift institutions (continued)** | | | | | | | |
| Super Now accounts | | | | X | | | X |
| Credit union share draft balances | | | X | X | | X | X |
| Savings deposits | | | | | | X | X |
| Small time deposits (<$100,000) | | | | | | X | X |
| Money market deposit accounts | | | | | | | X |
| **Other** | | | | | | | |
| Traveler's checks issued by nonbank companies | X | X | X | | | X | X |
| Overnight Eurodollars issued to United States residents | | | | | | X | X |
| General purpose and broker-dealer money market mutual funds | | | | | | X | X |
| M2 consolidation component | | | | | | X | X |

---

[1] The money supply definitions used in this book are those adopted in the Monetary Control Act of 1980 as adapted by the Garn–St. Germain Act of 1982. The changes in the money supply definitions have meant that published statistics are not strictly comparable. This chart compares the definitions.

---

*Source:* Hafer, R. W., "The New Monetary Aggregates," *Federal Reserve Bank of St. Louis Review* (February 1980); Garn–St. Germain Act of 1982.

can be created from any particular monetary base declines.

The ratio of currency to deposits ($c$) is decided by the general public when they decide whether to hold their money in the form of currency or transactions accounts. However, the public's decision will be affected by market forces. Some transactions accounts bear interest directly, so obviously any change in this rate will influence how members of the public decide to hold their money. In addition, the decision will be affected by the (market-determined) costs involved in changing from one form of money to another and also by whether certain transactions can (or must) be made in a particular form (for instance, coin-operated machines can only accept coins, some retailers will only accept cash).

Source: Drawing by Ross; © 1983, The New Yorker Magazine, Inc.

The ratio of nonpersonal time deposits to transactions accounts ($t$) is also determined by the public. This time, the decision is greatly influenced by that part of the general public that holds nonpersonal time deposits (businesses). Where a business decides to hold its wealth over even short periods of time is greatly influenced by the market: rates of return on nonpersonal time deposits; transactions accounts; many alternative assets (overnight repurchases, overnight Eurodollars, term repurchases, term Eurodollars, Treasury bills, Treasury notes); and the transactions costs involved in changing from one kind of asset to another.

The excess reserve ratio ($e$) is a decision made by the commercial banks, but this decision too is influenced by the market. When a commercial bank decides to hold excess reserves, it is deciding to forgo the interest that could otherwise be earned on the funds. Thus, the decision to hold such reserves will be influenced by the rates of return on all the alternative assets that the bank could have held, as well as the many liquidity considerations that led to the holding of excess reserves. The liquidity considerations are influenced by the bank's portfolio holdings and the public's decision as to whether to put money into their accounts or take money out of their accounts; this decision also results from the public reaction to market forces (those market forces that influenced $c$ and $t$).

The ratio of SSTA to transactions accounts ($d$) is also market-determined. Remembering the definition of this ratio:

$$\frac{ORP + OEu\$ + SA + STD + MMDA + MMMF}{D_T}$$

## THE DEMAND FOR CURRENCY AND
## THE UNDERGROUND ECONOMY

Financial innovations over the past 30 years have consistently increased the possibility that substitutes for currency will be used by the general public. For example, the rise in the use of check guarantee cards has increased the acceptability of demand deposits. Also, the widespread availability of credit cards has made it easy for individuals to draw on anticipated future earnings to make current purchases. It is surprising, therefore, to discover that there has been a dramatic increase in the use of cash relative to demand deposits since the early 1960s. The rise in the ratio of currency relative to demand deposits can be seen in the figure below. By 1979 the average currency holdings for a family of five had been estimated at $2500.

The rise in currency holdings has led many to suspect that there has been a marked growth in illegal transactions in what is known as "the underground economy." As rising prices and rising nominal incomes have shifted individuals into higher and higher marginal tax brackets, the government has taken a greater proportion of individual real income. This has provided an incentive for many people to arrange to receive income payments that are difficult to trace. For example, lower prices might be charged to those who pay in cash and offer the recipient a chance to avoid taxes. (It is an interesting sidelight on the underground economy that a tax reduction could induce more activity to be brought out of the underground economy, where it can be taxed, thus increasing total tax revenues.)

Apart from lost tax revenues, heavier tax burdens on those not involved in illegal activities, increased use of resources to hide transactions, and increased use of resources to detect illegal activities, any increase in the size of the underground economy could pose a problem in monetary control. As the underground economy grows, so does the demand for currency. As the de-

*continued*

it will be clear that its value will be influenced by any market forces that would influence the public's holdings of any of the included items. Thus the *relative* rates of return on overnight repurchases, overnight Eurodollars, savings accounts, small time deposits, money market deposit accounts, money market mutual funds, and transactions accounts will all have an ef-

mand for currency grows, there will be significant changes in the money multipliers. If it proves difficult to predict the changes in currency demand, the Federal Reserve will find it much more difficult to control the money supply by changing the monetary base.

*Source:* The information for this insert was largely extracted from: Bowsher, Norman N., "The Demand for Currency: Is the Underground Economy Undermining Monetary Policy!" *Review* 62 (Federal Reserve Bank of St. Louis, January 1980): 11–17, figure, 12.

fect on the value of *d*. It is also possible, of course, that the rates of return on other assets (not included in this definition) relative to the rates of return on the assets included in the definition could also have an effect on *d*.

The actual stability of the money multipliers for M1 and M2 can be judged from the numbers shown in Table 12.4.

*Table 12.4*
**Money Multipliers**

| 1982 | Money Multiplier for M1 (M1/$B$) | Money Multiplier for M2 (M2/$B$) |
|---|---|---|
| Jan. | 2.6813 | 10.9332 |
| Feb. | 2.6201 | 11.0456 |
| Mar. | 2.6602 | 11.2545 |
| Apr. | 2.7172 | 11.2584 |
| May | 2.6306 | 11.1637 |
| June | 2.6438 | 11.1872 |
| July | 2.6355 | 11.1735 |
| Aug. | 2.6273 | 11.2234 |
| Sept. | 2.6727 | 11.3250 |
| Oct. | 2.6716 | 11.3470 |
| Nov. | 2.7188 | 11.2909 |
| Dec. | 2.7384 | 10.9565 |
| 1983 | | |
| Jan. | 2.7527 | 11.3451 |
| Feb. | 2.7313 | 11.6051 |
| Mar. | 2.7811 | 11.7453 |
| Apr. | 2.8274 | 11.7085 |
| May | 2.7798 | 11.6457 |
| June | 2.7990 | 11.6410 |
| July | 2.8019 | 11.5830 |
| Aug. | 2.7835 | 11.5843 |
| Sept. | 2.8016 | 11.6463 |
| Oct. | 2.8127 | 11.7766 |
| Nov. | 2.7981 | 11.6154 |
| Dec. | 2.8085 | 11.4974 |

*Source*: Board of Governors, Federal Reserve System, *Federal Reserve Bulletin* (Washington D.C.): Tables A13, A14, A15, various issues.

## THE GURLEY-SHAW HYPOTHESIS

The stability (or the lack of it) in one of our ratios has been used to shed light on an important controversy in money and banking. This controversy, known as the *Gurley-Shaw hypothesis,* concerns the place that nonbank financial intermediaries hold in the economy. In particular, the controversy concerns the ability of the various institutions to create money and the place of nonbank financial intermediaries in the allocation of funds throughout the economy.

The controversy was sparked by two economists from Stanford, John G. Gurley and Edward S. Shaw, who claimed that it was necessary to treat nonbank financial intermediaries in exactly the same way as commercial banks if the amount of lending in the economy were to be controlled.[2] The issue is not simply that broad definitions of the money supply such as M2 have risen substantially over M1, but whether it is possible to control the amount of the broad definitions simply by controlling the monetary base and the activities of the commercial banks. It is partly in response to this controversy that the Monetary Control Act of 1980 has extended Federal Reserve control to the transactions accounts created by the thrift institutions.

The problem can be seen in perhaps its simplest form by considering the money multipliers we have been using in this chapter. M1 is defined as

$$\frac{1 + c}{c + r_D + e + r_T t} B,$$

and M2 is defined as

$$\frac{1 + c + d}{c + r_D + e + r_T t} B.$$

Clearly, the difference between them lies in the ratio $d$, which is the ratio of the selected short-term assets held in nonbank financial intermediaries to the amount of transactions accounts held in the depository institutions ($D_T$). If, therefore, the authorities are able to control M1 but cannot control M2 at the same time, ratio $d$ accounts for the difference. If authorities reduce the monetary base ($B$), which leads to a reduction of M1 but an increase in M2, $d$ must have risen.

Gurley and Shaw feared that monetary control was impossible so long as reserve requirements were imposed only on commercial banks (as was the case until the passage of the Monetary Control Act of 1980). Their hypothesis was that when the authorities imposed tight money, borrowers who were being turned down for loans by the commercial banks would go to nonbank financial intermediaries. As their lending was not controlled by the authorities, they would be able to expand their loans. Thus, the total amount of lending could rise in the face of tight money. In terms of the monetary aggregates that we have been using, M2 could rise during periods when the authorities were causing M1 to be reduced.

**Table 12.5**
**Ratio d Since 1961**

| Year end | 1961 | 1962 | 1963 | 1964 | 1965 | 1966 | 1967 | 1968 | 1969 | 1970 | 1971 |
|---|---|---|---|---|---|---|---|---|---|---|---|
| Ratio $d$ | 1.56 | 1.72 | 1.88 | 2.01 | 2.14 | 2.21 | 2.32 | 2.37 | 2.38 | 2.40 | 2.59 |

| Year end | 1972 | 1973 | 1974 | 1975 | 1976 | 1977 | 1978 | 1979 | 1980 | 1981 | 1982 |
|---|---|---|---|---|---|---|---|---|---|---|---|
| Ratio $d$ | 2.79 | 2.90 | 2.99 | 3.24 | 3.62 | 3.88 | 3.94 | 4.02 | 4.20 | 4.28 | 4.48 |

[2] Gurley, John G., and Edward S. Shaw, *Money in a Theory of Finance* (Washington, D.C.: The Brookings Institution, 1960).

*Figure 12.5*
**Rates of Growth of the Ratio d since 1961**

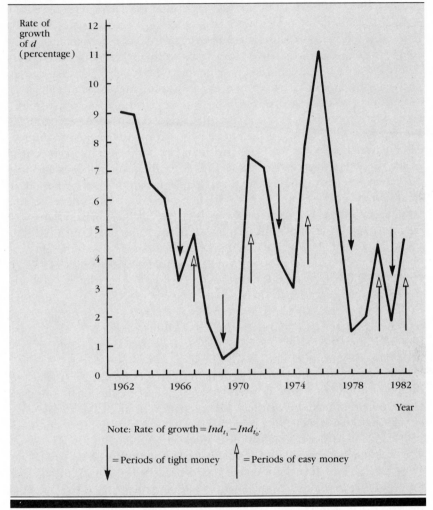

Note: Rate of growth $= Ind_{t_1} - Ind_{t_0}$.

↓ = Periods of tight money    ↑ = Periods of easy money

*Source: Annual U.S. Economic Data* (Federal Reserve Bank of St. Louis, May 1980, May 1981, May 1982, May 1983).

If we look at the monetary aggregates, the hypothesis is reduced to an empirical question. How does ratio *d* behave in periods of tight money? The answer is not immediately obvious because the ratio has risen continually throughout the 1960s, the 1970s, and into the 1980s (*see* Table 12.5). The *rate* at which ratio *d* has increased, however, shows a very strong relationship to monetary conditions. Since the beginning of the 1960s, the rate of increase of ratio *d* has risen only in periods of easy money and fallen during periods of tight money. This is shown in Figure 12.5.

Figure 12.5 clearly shows ratio *d* responding to monetary policy. The rate of increase of *d* fell in the "credit crunch" of 1966, rose in the easy money of 1967, fell during the tight money that led up to the "minirecession" of 1970–1971, rose during the expansion that started at the end of 1971, fell again during the contraction that led up to the recession of 1974, rose in the following expansion, fell again as the rate of growth of the money supply was restricted in 1978, rose again with the monetary expansion before 1980, and then alternately fell and rose with the decrease and increase in the rate of change of the money supply in 1981 and 1982.

The cause of these changes in the rate of growth of the ratio of short-term assets in nonbank financial intermediaries to transactions accounts in the depository institutions is the phenomenon known as *disintermediation*. Although this phenomenon helps the monetary authorities to keep control of the monetary aggregates, it is a serious problem for nonbank financial intermediaries, particularly savings and loan associations. During periods of tight money, interest rates tend to rise in money markets. In order to take advantage of these rates, the public will disintermediate; that is, they will take their funds out of the financial intermediaries and invest them directly in the markets. By buying the credit instruments issued by governments and corporations, the public is taking funds away from nonbank financial intermediaries and banks and is lending them directly to governments and corporations that traditionally keep their funds in deposits in commercial banks. The net result is that short-term financial assets in nonbank financial intermediaries tend to fall relative to transactions accounts in the depository institutions. Thus, in periods of tight money there is an automatic tendency for there to be a downward pressure on the ratio *d*.

Disintermediation in periods of tight money has had a great effect on the flow of funds to certain intermediaries and therefore on the flow of funds to certain financial markets. The reduction in funds flowing through savings and loan associations, for example, has a large effect on the mortgage markets. As disintermediation takes place, the flow of funds to mortgage markets is curtailed and residential construction is likely to decline. This can trigger a recession, but to try to prevent it (as both the Federal Reserve and the Federal Home Loan Bank Boards have tried to do) could jeopardize the effectiveness of monetary policy.

Much of the Depository Institutions Deregulation and Monetary Control Act of 1980 appears to be a response to many of the points made by Gurley and Shaw. By establishing reserve requirements for all transactions accounts, the act moves toward an equitable treatment of all depository institutions, and regulation of lending by banks and near banks alike. At the same time, by opening the Federal Reserve discount window to all depository institutions as a lender of last resort, the act tends to reduce the effects of disintermediation and could reduce the ability of the authorities to carry out monetary policy. Also, the elimination of interest-rate ceilings that the act called for and the creation of money market deposit accounts in the depository institutions are likely to reduce the incentive of depositors toward disintermediation.

## SUMMARY

An important aspect of commercial banking that can be seen by considering the entire banking system is the way in which the depository institutions are able to create money as a by-product of their lending activities. No matter what definition of the money supply is used, most of the money supply is created through the lending activities of banking institutions. Monetary authorities place in circulation a monetary base that consists of currency and deposits at the Federal Reserve Banks. Depository institutions create money based on this amount. Money creation depends on the fact that funds loaned by depository institutions are returned to other depository institutions in the form of other deposits.

Using information concerning the portfolio decisions of members of the public and the depository institutions, it is possible to devise money multipliers that relate the money supply to the monetary base. The various ratios that appear in these money multipliers inform the authorities how the determinants of the money supply are changing and therefore what actions they have to take to compensate for these changes. Apart from the monetary base, the determinants of money supply 1 and money supply 2 are included in the following ratios: the ratio of currency to transactions accounts held by the nonbank public, the ratio of selected short-term assets to transactions accounts held by the nonbank public, the ratio of nonpersonal time deposits to transactions accounts held by the nonbank public, the excess reserve ratio of depository institutions, the reserve requirements on transactions accounts, and the reserve requirements on nonpersonal time deposits.

### Key Terms

multiple expansion of deposits
monetary base
excess reserve ratio of the
  depository institutions ($e$)
ratio of currency in the hands
  of the nonbank public to
  transactions accounts ($c$)
ratio of nonpersonal time
  deposits to transactions
  accounts ($t$)

money multipliers
ratio of selected short-term
  assets (SSTA) to transactions
  accounts ($t$)
Gurley-Shaw hypothesis
disintermediation

## Questions

1. On the average depository institutions hold $5 in excess reserves for every $100 of transactions accounts they hold. In addition, the authorities require that they hold 15 percent of transactions accounts and 5 percent of nonpersonal time deposits in reserves. The monetary base is $140 billion. If the general public, on the average, holds $10 in transactions accounts and $10 in nonpersonal time deposits for every $1 it holds in currency, what is the amount of money supply 1 in the system?

2. Using the information in question 1, what would happen to money supply 1 if reserve requirements on transactions accounts were increased to 20 percent?

3. Choose any one-month period and calculate the annual rate of change in the M1 multiplier (from the information in Table 12.4). If the Federal Reserve had held the rate of change of the monetary base constant over the one-month period, how much would the rate of change of M1 have changed? What does your answer tell you about the ease or difficulty of maintaining a steady growth rate of the money supply?

4. What is the Gurley-Shaw hypothesis?

5. To what extent does the existence of disintermediation disprove the Gurley-Shaw hypothesis?

6. Is the existence of Super NOW accounts and money market deposit accounts in the depository institutions likely to affect disintermediation? Does this mean that Gurley and Shaw are more likely or less likely to be proved correct?

## Additional Readings

Burger, Albert E. *The Money Supply Process.* Belmont, Calif.: Wadsworth, 1971.

*A comprehensive coverage of the factors affecting money multipliers.*

Balbach, Anatol, and David H. Resler. "Eurodollars and the U.S. Money Supply." *Review* 62. Federal Reserve Bank of St. Louis (June–July 1980): 2–12.

*A discussion of the impact of Eurodollars on commercial bank portfolio management with a concentration on the possible effects on money multipliers.*

Gurley, John G., and Edward S. Shaw. *Money in a Theory of Finance.* Washington, D.C.: The Brookings Institution, 1960.

*This is the classic presentation of the Gurley-Shaw hypothesis. This book is the first attempt to give a theory explaining the relationship between commercial banks and the nonbank financial intermediaries.*

*For more information on the growth and measurement of the underground economy and the changing nature of currency holdings by the public see:*

Feige, Edgar L. "How Big Is the Irregular Economy?" *Challenge* (November–December 1979): 5–13.

Gutmann, Peter M. "Statistical Illusions, Mistaken Policies." *Challenge* (November–December 1979): 14–17.

Laurent, Robert D. "Currency and the Subterranean Economy." *Economic Perspectives.* Federal Reserve Bank of Chicago (March–April 1979): 3–6.

*"The Underground Economy." U.S. News and World Report,* October 22, 1979, 49–52.

# CHAPTER THIRTEEN

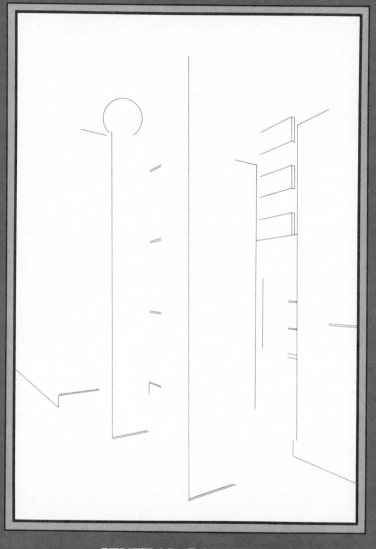

## CENTRAL BANKING

*The Federal Reserve System was es-
tablished in 1913 as a lender of
last resort for the commercial
banking system, but it has since
evolved into a much more active
central bank, concerned mainly
with the monetary control of the
economy. Although there are several instruments of monetary control, most monetary management
is carried out through open market
operations, a procedure run under
the direction of the Federal Open
Market Committee.*

A consideration of the money multipliers allows us to see how it might be possible for some central authority to control the amount of money in the system. Each money supply is equal to the monetary base multiplied by the appropriate money multiplier. Therefore, the money supply might be changed by changing either the multiplier or the amount of the base. Under a commodity standard, the monetary base is established automatically by the system. Authorities can influence the money supply only by changing the multiplier. Under a paper standard, authorities can affect the base, the multiplier, or both.

The authority that usually has assumed this role is the central bank. However, *central banks* have not traditionally limited themselves to this particular activity. Most financially developed nations have established central banks that perform several important functions. They act as lenders of last resort for commercial banks suffering liquidity problems; act as fiscal agents of government; establish banking rules and monitor compliance with them; and manage, in one way or another, the money supply and credit conditions.

## CENTRAL BANKING IN THE UNITED STATES BEFORE 1913

Although central banks have existed for over three hundred years (the Bank of Sweden was founded in 1656 and is reputed to be the first), the United States did not establish one until 1913. Even then a great deal of opposition to the notion of a central bank had to be overcome. Commercial banking in the United States historically has been decentralized, and many traditional functions of central banks have been performed by other agencies or not at all. Much of the supervision of commercial banks has rested with state banking agencies, and any centralized banking supervision was done by the Treasury. The federal government either has used private banks as its fiscal agent or it has done without.

The first *Bank of the United States* (chartered by the federal government from 1791 to 1811), and the second *Bank of the United States* (chartered by the federal government from 1816 to 1836) did provide some of the services traditionally performed by central banks, but they were principally private commercial banks. The control they exercised over commercial banks was limited to forcing a constraint on private bank-note issue (the principal means of creating money open to the commercial banks at that time) by systematically presenting notes for payment in specie.

The Banking Act of 1863 brought about some federal government supervision of banks, but this supervision was restricted to those banks that chose to have a national charter. Admittedly, it was initially intended that *all* banks apply for these national charters, but that is not how it worked out, and today most commercial banks are not national banks. The national banks were (and are) chartered by the federal government to operate within a particular state, and they were (and are) supervised by the Comptroller of the Currency, an office of the United States Treasury. In the Banking Act of 1863, reserve requirements were set for notes issued by the national banks and for the deposits in national banks; capital requirements were set; and provision was made for frequent bank examination. However, the emphasis of the legislation was on the safety of the national banks and the safety of the currency they issued. The national banking system offered no monetary control over either the money supply or interest rates.

The desirability of some centralized control in the monetary sector became an issue after the various financial panics that occurred in the late nineteenth century. After the serious economic disruption that accompanied the panic of 1907, the United States Congress became actively involved in the issue. The result was the passage of the *Federal Reserve Act* on December 23, 1913. This act established the Federal Reserve as the central bank for the United States.

The Federal Reserve Act provided for the following:

1.  A centralized holding of commercial bank reserves

2.  An *elastic currency* (a currency whose quantity was varied on demand through the lending of reserves to banks)

3.  A more effective supervision of commercial banks

4.  A fiscal agent for the government

5.  A national check-clearing mechanism

The Federal Reserve Act of 1913 did not provide for monetary control in the sense that we know it today: control of interest rates and the money supply. However, more and more monetary powers have been given to the Federal Reserve over the years. Historically, the Federal Reserve took on the full powers of a central bank only after the passage of the Banking Act of 1935.

## THE STRUCTURE OF THE FEDERAL RESERVE

The Federal Reserve System is a curious mixture of centralization and decentralization. This has resulted from the attempt that was made to satisfy diverse views held by members of Congress and by the banking community in the period from 1907 to 1913. The commercial banking system was decentralized, the only centralization coming from the supervision of the national banks by the office of the Comptroller of the Currency. Adding a central bank to a banking system that already was in place was no easy task. Inevitably, some would not approve of the way it was done. The Federal Reserve System that was established resulted from a series of compromises between what were often conflicting opinions.

### Membership

Some wanted membership in the Federal Reserve System to be mandatory; others wanted it voluntary. The result was that membership was mandated for national banks and was voluntary for state banks. Most state banks, in fact, have chosen not to join the system. (*See* Chapter 10.)

### Ownership

The *Federal Reserve district banks* are owned by the member banks in each district. Each member bank subscribes an amount equal to 3 percent of the member's paid-in capital plus surplus. An additional 3 percent is subject to call by the Federal Reserve Bank. The Federal Reserve, however, is not run as a profit-making business. Owners receive a stipulated 6 percent annual dividend on their stock in the district bank.

Paying the owners of the Federal Reserve a stipulated amount has caused a problem with the substantial earnings Federal Reserve banks have from their holdings of government securities and from their other lending. At one time the Federal Reserve's earnings were used to establish the FDIC, at other times the earnings have been retained by the Federal Reserve, and at others they have been turned over to the Treasury. Currently, the Federal Reserve voluntarily turns over whatever it earns above its expenses to the United States Treasury as "an interest payment on Federal Reserve Notes." In the early 1980s the payment to the Treasury has averaged approximately $10 billion per annum.[1]

## Control

Control of the Federal Reserve is divorced from ownership. Although the power in the Federal Reserve System initially rested with district banks, it has come to rest more and more with the Board of Governors. The seven members of the *Federal Reserve Board of Governors* are appointed by the president of the United States (with the advice and consent of the Senate) for 14-year terms. The terms are staggered in such a way that one new appointment must be made every two years. The chairman of the Board of Governors (who also serves as chairman of the Federal Open Market Committee) is appointed by the president of the United States for a four-year term that is renewable.

The Board of Governors supervises the operations of the Federal Reserve System, issues regulations on banking activity, directs the supervision and examination of member banks, and oversees the economic research and publications of the Federal Reserve staff. The main power of monetary management held by the Board of Governors is exercised through their service as a majority on the Federal Open Market Committee. They also set reserve requirements on various kinds of deposits held by the depository institutions.

In addition to their powers at the federal level, the Board of Governors also have a hand in the appointment of the directors of each of the Federal Reserve District Banks. Each district bank has a nine-member board of directors. Three of the members are appointed by the Board of Governors. A board of directors consists of three Class A directors, who are elected by the member banks to serve banking interests; three Class B directors, who are elected by the member banks to serve business interests; and three Class C directors, who are appointed by the Board of Governors to represent the general public. For purposes of the Class A and Class B elections, member banks in each district are divided according to the size of their asset portfolios. One Class A and one Class B director is elected by the small, medium, and large banks, respectively. The chairman and the deputy chairman of the board of directors are always chosen from Class C directors.

---

[1] See the *Annual Reports* of the Board of Governors for each year.

*Figure 13.1*
**The Federal Reserve System (Boundaries of Federal Reserve Districts and Their Branch Territories)**

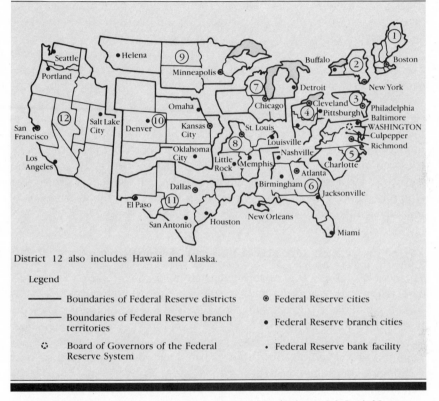

District 12 also includes Hawaii and Alaska.

Legend

——————  Boundaries of Federal Reserve districts  ◉  Federal Reserve cities

——————  Boundaries of Federal Reserve branch territories  •  Federal Reserve branch cities

✿  Board of Governors of the Federal Reserve System  •  Federal Reserve bank facility

*Source:* Board of Governors, Federal Reserve System, *Federal Reserve Bulletin* (Washington, D.C.: Board of Governors, September, 1984): A 76.

    The Federal Reserve System has been divided into 12 districts, each having a district bank (*see* Figure 13.1). The supervision and examination of member banks, as well as the day-to-day operation of the system, are carried out through the district banks and their branches. The nine-member board of directors oversees the operations of each district bank and appoints the president and vice president of each district bank.

    The division of the country into 12 districts was designed to decentralize power within the system. The main power over banking that initially was given to the Federal Reserve was the establishment of district banks as *lenders of last resort* for member banks in each district. The service was to be provided by each district bank through its discount window. At the discount window a member bank would be able to borrow at the discount rate. The original idea was that with each district's board of directors determining its own discount rate, there could be a decentralized monetary policy. It was expected that the district bank would be able to use the discount policy to serve its own community. Discount rates can be different in each district, but in general they are not. The local autonomy in discount rate determination, however, is not complete as the Board of Governors do in fact have veto powers over the rate that is set.

As the Federal Reserve has developed, it has acquired more power over monetary affairs in the economy; and as it has done this, the power has become more and more centralized. This has been the case particularly since the Banking Act of 1935. Reserve requirements on deposits have been set centrally by the Board of Governors since that time, but today most of the power rests with the Federal Open Market Committee (FOMC). Although this committee includes the presidents of five of the district banks, the Board of Governors represents a permanent majority on the committee, and it can, therefore, be the deciding influence on monetary affairs. The structure of the Federal Reserve System as it relates to the instruments of monetary policy is shown in Figure 13.2.

## INDEPENDENCE OF THE FEDERAL RESERVE

The Federal Reserve was established as an independent agency of the federal government. It was designed to separate control of the banking system from the political whims of both the executive and the legislative branches of government. The overlapping 14-year terms are part of this design, making it impossible (without deaths or resignations) for any president to appoint a majority on the Board in less than eight years. The prohibition on reappointment for two terms also reduces the incentive for any Board member to serve the specific interests of the executive branch.

The Federal Reserve also is insulated from congressional pressure by having an independent budget. The interest earned on the Federal Reserve's large holdings of United States Treasury securities is more than enough to cover the expenses incurred in operating the system. Because of this self-sufficiency, the Federal Reserve is not subject to outside supervision. Audits are conducted only internally.

However, the independence of the Federal Reserve may be more apparent than real. The Federal Reserve was created by an act of Congress, so Congress by additional acts or amendments to the original act, could alter the form, structure, or even the existence of the system. These possibilities may serve to induce the Federal Reserve to respond to the wishes of Congress. Also, the Full Employment and Balanced Growth Act of 1978 requires that the Federal Reserve report on its monetary activities and intended policies for the coming year to Congress on an annual basis. These reports could portend a closer relationship between the Federal Reserve and the legislature.

Figure 13.2
**Structure of the Federal Reserve System**

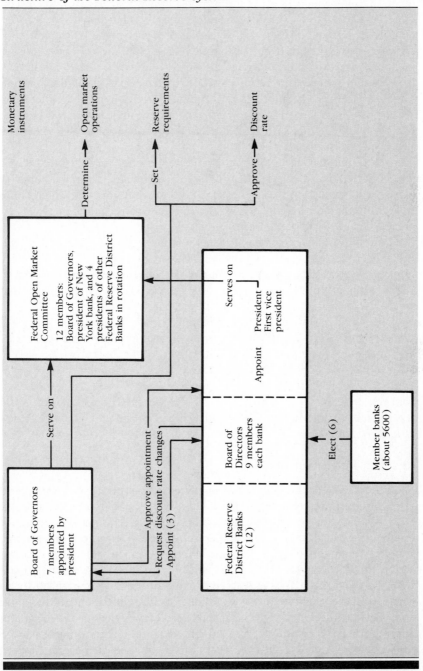

## MONETARY MANAGEMENT

The Federal Reserve System has three instruments of monetary management through which it generally affects monetary aggregates and credit conditions. The three include changing reserve requirements on various kinds of deposits in the depository institutions, changing the discount rates charged by the district banks, and undertaking open market operations. In addition, the Federal Reserve has the powers of *moral suasion,* whereby bankers are exhorted in various ways to behave in a particular manner. Moral suasion usually is attempted through speeches made by Federal Reserve personnel. For that reason, it often is included under the heading of "jaw-boning." Less charitably, it has been known also as the Federal Reserve's "open mouth policy."

Moral suasion has not been particularly successful in the United States, probably because it is extremely difficult to persuade a large number of banks to do something that is inimical to their profit motive. In such countries as the United Kingdom, where there are few banks, moral suasion has a greater chance for success. Perhaps the only instance of obvious success of this kind of policy in the United States was the Voluntary Credit Restraint Program, which was instituted during the Korean conflict. During that period the Federal Reserve asked commercial banks to direct their loans to certain segments of the economy by supplying lists of the types of loans that were encouraged and those that were discouraged.

Although moral suasion is considered a rather weak means of affecting monetary conditions (with the exception of what might be possible in periods of national emergency), many still believe that much can be said in favor of the kind of public relations attempted. When monetary policies are implemented, Federal Reserve personnel are able to explain the policies to bankers, and this may have an effect on policy effectiveness. Whether or not it really is effective, the amount of it carried out would seem to indicate that at least Federal Reserve personnel *think* it works.

### Reserve Requirements

The Federal Reserve was not originally delegated authority over the setting of reserve requirements on deposits in any of the depository institutions. When the Federal Reserve was established reserve requirements were not thought of as instruments of monetary control, but as crucial to ensuring safety and soundness in banking. As such, the reserve requirements for the national banks were set by Congress and the reserve requirements for the state banks were set by the state banking authorities. Some authority to change reserve requirements within limits to influence the expansion and contraction of credit was given to the Board of Governors in the Banking Act of 1935. However, the act only gave the Federal Reserve power over the reserve requirements of those banks that chose to join the Federal Reserve System (a distinct minority of the banks). Not until the Monetary Control

Act of 1980 did the Federal Reserve have control over the reserve requirements of all depository institutions whether or not they are members of the Federal Reserve System. However, the Board of Governors' powers are still limited to changing reserve requirements between limits that are set by Congress.

Everything else held constant, an increase in reserve requirements on transactions accounts or on nonpersonal time deposits reduces the money multiplier and results in a reduction in the supply of money. With higher reserve requirements, banks are able to lend only a smaller proportion of funds that are deposited with them, and the multiple expansion of deposits is reduced.

The exact impact of a change in reserve requirements on the supply of money is unclear because of the possible effects on the other factors in the money multiplier. This problem can be seen from the Federal Reserve's first attempt to use variable reserve requirements as a policy instrument in the 1930s. In June of 1936 the member banks (at that time the only depository institutions that had reserve requirements set by the Federal Reserve) were holding considerable excess reserves. Reserves in excess of the amount required were almost 27 percent of demand deposits and amounted to 5.4 percent of total deposits. The Federal Reserve apparently mistook this desire of member banks for highly liquid assets as a potential for an expansion of loans. The Federal Reserve saw it as a limit to their control of credit and so attempted to absorb the existing excess reserves by increasing reserve requirements. As this failed to decrease the excess reserves held, the Federal Reserve again increased the requirements. The changes in reserve requirements seemed to have no effect on the excess reserves held, and the reserve requirements were increased sequentially until they reached the maximum allowed under the law, which was double the original level (*see* Table 13.1).

If changes in the reserve requirements actually had been met by the banks decreasing their excess reserves dollar for dollar, the impact on the money supply would have been zero. However, although they were somewhat reduced, member banks continued to hold significant amounts of excess reserves. By December of 1937 excess reserves in member banks had been reduced to only 12 percent of demand deposits, or 2.2 percent of total deposits. The increase in reserve requirements resulted in an increased holding of total reserves by members, from 13.4 percent of total deposits in June 1936 to 14.6 percent of deposits in December 1937.[2] More important for a period of economic decline, the supply of money was reduced. Even though the monetary base was increased from June 1936 to December 1937 by $1.954 billion, the supply of currency in the hands of the public

---

[2]Board of Governors of the Federal Reserve, *Banking and Monetary Statistics,* (Washington, D.C., 1943): 19, 82, 396.

*Table 13.1*
**Required Reserve Ratios Imposed by the Federal Reserve**

| Effective Date | June 21, 1917 | August 16, 1936 | March 1, 1937 | May 1, 1937 |
|---|---|---|---|---|
| **Designation of Deposit and Bank**[1] | | | | |
| On net demand deposits in | | | | |
| Central reserve city | 13 | 19½ | 22¾ | 26 |
| Reserve city | 10 | 15 | 17½ | 20 |
| Country | 7 | 10½ | 12¼ | 14 |
| On time deposits | 3 | 4½ | 5¼ | 6 |

[1] The central reserve city designation was for banks located in Chicago and New York City. Reserve city and country designations were made by the Federal Reserve on the basis of the population of the town in which a bank was located. The central reserve city designation has since been abolished. Since 1972 the reserve city and country designations have been made on the basis of bank size.

*Source:* Board of Governors of the Federal Reserve, *Banking and Monetary Statistics* (1943): 400.

plus the total amount of demand deposits in commercial banks declined by $541 million.[3]

The ability to control the money supply through reserve requirement changes depends on the responses of the depository institutions and the general public. Whether or not the depository institutions will decide to absorb reserve requirement changes in excess reserves will depend on the costs imposed on them. If reserve requirements are changed continually in attempts to alter monetary conditions, the adjustment costs imposed on the depository institutions could become significant. If the costs of adjusting the reserves are greater than the income forgone on excess reserves, it would be expected that the depository institutions would hold greater amounts of excess reserves to cover the adjustments in the required reserves.

Throughout the 1970s, major overall changes in reserve requirements were infrequent. Changes made were designed to alter the direction of the flow of credit rather than to change the total amount of credit available. Reserve requirements have been imposed on funds from specific credit markets to control selectively the expansion of certain types of credit such as Eurodollars, commercial-bank-managed liabilities other than deposits, and money market mutual funds.

The most significant change in reserve requirement legislation in recent years was that brought about by the Monetary Control Act of 1980, but

[3] Friedman, Milton, and Anna J. Schwartz, *A Monetary History of the United States, 1867–1960,* NBER Study (Princeton: Princeton University Press, 1963): 714–715, 804.

## EVEN THE FEDERAL RESERVE HAS TROUBLE CALCULATING RESERVES

In July 1980 the Federal Reserve noticed a large increase in excess reserves in the system. At the same time, the interest rate in the federal funds market was rising. The question was, Why would banks hold higher and higher levels of excess reserves and yet pay more and more to borrow from each other? By the end of the first week in August, excess reserves had reached a 20-year high of $1 billion. Officials at the Federal Reserve thought the whole affair "quite mysterious."

By the end of August the officials were more embarrassed than mystified and had to admit that they had calculated required reserves incorrectly. Having underestimated required reserves by some $300 million, they had overestimated the excess reserves held by the same amount.

The problem started when the Federal Reserve removed a 2 percent reserve requirement that had been placed on CDs. To find the new level of required reserves, the Federal Reserve officials simply found 2 percent of the total amount of CDs held and subtracted this amount from the previous total of required reserves. However, the officials had forgotten one of their own rules (although the member banks had not): that any member bank's reserves for CDs must not fall below 3 percent. Thus no bank could reduce its reserves by the full 2 percent if that reduction would leave them with less than an average of 3 percent for all CDs held.

For approximately three weeks, the Federal Reserve System had been operating on the mistaken belief that excess reserves were $300 million more than they actually were.

*Source: The Wall Street Journal,* August 26, 1980: 35.

it is expected that this is a once-and-for-all change. Under this act, the Federal Reserve imposes its reserve requirements on all depository institutions. Specific reserve requirements were set at that time for transactions accounts and certain nonpersonal time deposits (*see* Chapter 9). The Board of Governors retains the right to change the reserve requirements, but it seems unlikely that the Federal Reserve will be using this as an active part of monetary policy. Since the Monetary Control Act of 1980, the only change has been one of deciding which deposits are eligible for reserve requirements and which are not. This issue was addressed in the Garn–St. Germain Act of 1982.

## *The Discount Rate*

One of the original purposes for establishing the Federal Reserve was to provide an elastic currency to fluctuate with public demand without causing tight money in the system. In the early 1900s it was felt that the amount of credit available should expand or contract in keeping with the "needs of trade." However, prior to the establishment of the Federal Reserve System, the quantity of funds was determined by the availability of specie plus the national bank note issue (that was secured by United States Treasury securities deposited with the Comptroller of the Currency). There was no mechanism available to change the amount of credit or the money supply in response to economic conditions.

The Federal Reserve's lending of funds through the discount window provided for an elastic currency by making additional reserves available. Originally, the Federal Reserve issued loans as discounts to member banks through the purchase of high-grade, self-liquidating commercial paper from the member banks. Such an extension of loans increased Federal Reserve credit and expanded the monetary base. In periods when the economy was expanding, the "need" for additional credit would be evidenced by additional borrowing from the banks and the issue of more commercial paper. Banks, finding themselves unable to satisfy this demand for loans at the current interest rate, could sell acceptable commercial paper to the Federal Reserve banks and receive additional reserves in exchange. Thus, the supply of credit would expand in response to the "need" indicated by the economy. This mechanism is simply an outgrowth of the old commercial loan theory of banking, or the real bills doctrine (*see* Chapter 9). Unfortunately, the mechanism had the drawback of expanding credit when the economy expanded and reducing the credit available during recessions and depressions.

The discount process provides for both an elasticity of the supply of monetary base and an increased liquidity in commercial bank portfolios. The Federal Reserve's availability as a buyer of last resort for paper that is eligible for discount increases the marketability and liquidity of that paper. Originally, the type of paper eligible for discounting was very limited. However, the eligibility (set out in Regulation A of the Federal Reserve Code) has been expanded over the years, and—perhaps most important—the Federal Reserve has been authorized to extend loans directly to the depository institutions as *advances*. In a discount of eligible paper, a depository institution sells the securities to the Federal Reserve District Bank. In an advance, a loan is secured by eligible paper, but no exchange of ownership of the securities takes place. Most of the borrowing by the depository institutions from the Federal Reserve is in the form of advances secured by United States Treasury securities. Before 1933 advances often were secured by commercial paper, but this rarely occurs today.[4]

***Access to the Discount Privilege.***   Before 1980, only member banks of the Federal Reserve System had access to the discount mechanism, but the Monetary Control Act of 1980 extended the privilege to all depository institutions. Discounts and advances extended by the Federal Reserve historically have fallen into three categories. The principal type of discounts are *adjustment discounts,* issued for short terms to ease problems of reserve position management temporarily. *Seasonal discounts* are available for longer terms (up to 90 days) to smaller banks that have a seasonal pattern of loans (primarily from agricultural lending). These longer-term loans, however, must be arranged in advance. Lending to nonmember institutions was considered to be *emergency credit,* but since the passage of the Monetary Control Act of 1980, normal discount lending has been made to any depository institution whether they are members of the Federal Reserve or not. Thus the third category is now subsumed under the first two.

In the case of ordinary adjustment discounts, a depository institution will ask the Federal Reserve District Bank for an overnight loan whenever it finds that it has a reserve problem. This will almost certainly be granted, to the extent that it might be considered that discounting takes place at the discretion of the depository institution rather than by the choice of the Federal Reserve. However, the automatic borrowing ends after the first overnight loan. From then on the Federal Reserve will scrutinize the request very closely and may very well refuse to continue the loan any further. The Federal Reserve always has maintained that the use of the discount mechanism by a depository institution is a privilege, *not* a right.

For those institutions eligible for this service, borrowing from the Federal Reserve at the discount window is an additional source of funds similar to borrowing from the federal funds market or the Eurodollar market. As such, the cost to the depository institution of borrowing at the discount rate, relative to the other rates of interest at which the institution could borrow, is a significant determinant of the use of this service. Even though borrowing from the Federal Reserve to profit by lending the funds out at a higher rate of interest is not considered appropriate, the borrowing still is quite sensitive to changes in interest rates. The financial intermediaries tend to find themselves short of reserves more frequently and resort to borrowing at the discount window more often, when short-term interest rates rise in relation to the discount rate. The response of borrowing by the

---

[4] Federal Reserve Board of Governors *Banking and Monetary Statistics, 1941–1970,* (Washington, D.C., 1976): 514.

*Figure 13.3*
**Member Bank Borrowings, Federal Funds–**
**Discount Rate Differential**

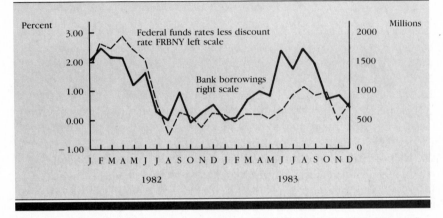

*Source:* Board of Governors, Federal Reserve System, *Federal Reserve Bulletin* (Washington, D.C.: Board of Governors), Tables 1.11, 1.35, 1.14 various issues.

depository institutions to the difference between the federal funds rate and the discount rate charged by the Federal Reserve District Bank of New York for 1982–1983 is shown in Figure 13.3.

***Effect on the Monetary Base.***  On the aggregate level there is a significant difference between borrowing from the Federal Reserve System at the discount rate and borrowing from the federal funds market. When funds are borrowed from the discount window, the monetary base is increased. This is because the funds borrowed are newly created reserves. This is not the case with borrowing federal funds or using other managed liabilities. These other sources simply serve to reallocate the existing set of assets that may serve as reserves. The effect of borrowing from the Federal Reserve on the assets and liabilities of both the Federal Reserve and the borrowing depository institution can be seen in Table 13.2.

In Table 13.2 a depository institution has borrowed $100 from the Federal Reserve District Bank. To borrow the funds, the depository institution would have presented the district bank with its own promise to repay the funds. The depository institution would then list this amount as a liability under borrowings, and the Federal Reserve would list the amount under assets as an advance. The $100 of reserves then would be listed as a liability of the Federal Reserve District Bank and as an asset of the depository institution. The transaction leaves the accounts of both institutions balanced, but the reserves of the system (and hence the monetary base) would have been increased by $100. The $100 then could be used by the depository institu-

*Table 13.2*
**Effect of Borrowing from the Federal Reserve**

| Federal Reserve | | Depository Institution | |
|---|---|---|---|
| **Assets** | **Liabilities** | **Assets** | **Liabilities** |
| Advance   +100 | Reserves of depository institution   +100 | Reserves   +100 | Borrowings from the Federal Reserve   +100 |

tions for the multiple expansion of deposits. The increase in the monetary base, and the increase in the money supply, then would persist until the loan matured, and the depository institution repaid the funds to the Federal Reserve.

***Use as a Monetary Instrument.***   The Federal Reserve discount rate can be used as an instrument of monetary policy because changing the rate *in relation to other interest rates* can change the incentive of the depository institutions to borrow from the Federal Reserve District Banks. When the Federal Reserve raises the discount rate relative to other short-term rates, the depository institutions are given the incentive to look elsewhere for funds. As the depository institutions reduce their borrowing from the Federal Reserve and pay back their previous borrowing, the monetary base is reduced. When the Federal Reserve lowers the discount rate below other short-term rates, the depository institutions are induced to borrow from the Federal Reserve in cases where they would otherwise have looked elsewhere. As the borrowing is increased, the monetary base is increased.

Up until about 1970 the discount rate was changed relatively infrequently. Between January 1, 1960, and January 1, 1970, the discount rate at the New York Federal Reserve was changed only 13 times. As a result, any change in the discount rate was considered significant as an indicator of a change in monetary policy. A lowered discount rate was thought to indicate an easier money policy. An increased rate was thought to indicate a tighter policy. However, apart from the fact that the true indicator of policy is the discount rate *relative* to other rates, it does not necessarily follow that a change in the rate indicates a change in policy. Between January 1, 1970, and January 1, 1980, the discount rate at the Federal Reserve in New York was changed 36 times.[5] This did not indicate that the rate was being used

---

[5] Board of Governors, *Federal Reserve Bulletin,* for March 1976 (A6) and for March 1980 (A8).

more as an instrument of monetary policy. What was happening was that short-term interest rates were changing much more frequently; and it was necessary for the Federal Reserve to change the discount rate more frequently simply to keep pace with the changes in the other rates. The 1970s made it clear that many discount rate changes are *defensive;* that is, they are changed as other interest rates change so as not to cause an undesirable monetary policy accidently, rather than to try to impose a policy. The same discount rate can mean easy or tight money, depending on what the other short-term interest rates are. Only *defensive discount rate changes* in response to other rate changes can prevent this.

Figure 13.4, which shows the discount rate charged by the New York Federal Reserve District Bank, the federal funds rate, and the three-month Treasury bill rate for more than fifty years, reveals that changes in the discount rate often followed, rather than preceded, changes in the other rates. Clearly, the more volatile the short-term rates of interest, the more active a merely defensive discount policy would have to be.

As an instrument that changes the quantity of the monetary base, the discount rate no longer is considered to be particularly significant, but it does continue to play a role in monetary policy. First, it *can* have a significant effect on short-term interest rates. If the discount rate is lowered below other short-term rates, and the Federal Reserve District banks do in fact lend funds to the depository institutions that ask for loans, other short-term rates of interest will fall. If the discount rate is raised above other short-term interest rates, the other short-term interest rates will rise. Second, changing the discount rate is considered by some to have a *demonstration effect.* When the rate is raised, it demonstrates to the people in the economy that the Federal Reserve wishes to pursue a tight monetary policy. When the rate is lowered, it demonstrates to the people in the economy that the Federal Reserve wishes to pursue an easy money policy.

Whether or not there really is a demonstration effect is a controversial issue. Obviously, the Federal Reserve could use the discount rate to make announcements about the future path that monetary policy is going to take, but that could be done without changing the rate. Moreover, changing the rate to demonstrate what policy is going to be followed would mean that defensive changes in the rate would be impossible. Making a defensive change in the rate can only demonstrate that the Federal Reserve does not wish to change monetary policy, or at least it wishes to pursue a policy that allows the short-term interest rates to fluctuate in the way that they are already doing.

There also is the added problem that, even if the discount rate was used for demonstration purposes, it could have the opposite effect from what was intended. Suppose that the Federal Reserve wishes to follow a tight money policy, and "demonstrates" this fact to the public by increasing the discount rate. In the minds of the public, this increase in the discount rate could well herald higher interest rates generally. If the public expects

Figure 13.4
**Short-Term Interest Rates, 1930–1983 (Discount Rate,
Effective Date of Change; All Others, Quarterly Averages)**

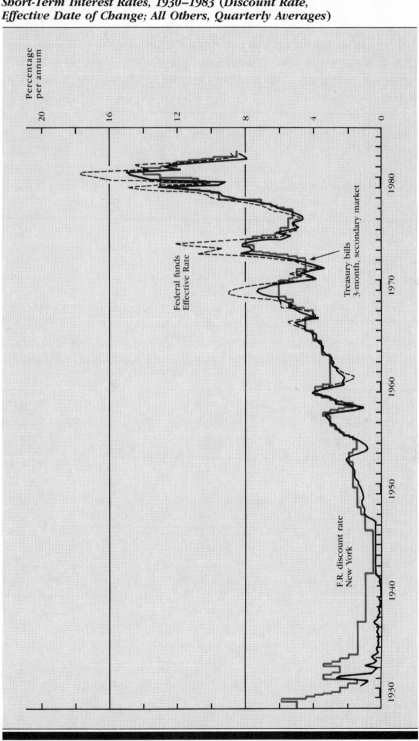

interest rates to rise in the future, it is likely that it will attempt to borrow funds before the rates rise. The increased demand for loanable funds will push up interest rates, and as this increases the opportunity costs of the depository institutions (in the form of interest forgone), it is possible that the depository institutions might increase, rather than decrease, their lending. In such a case as this, the demonstration effect would be perverse, and the effects of discount policy would be unpredictable.

## Open Market Operations

*Open market operations* are the most important and most frequently used instrument of monetary control. Open market operations consist of purchases and sales of United States Treasury and federal government agency securities. These purchases and sales are carried out by the systems' open market managers (one for each of domestic and foreign operations) at the direction of the Federal Open Market Committee. The written and verbal instructions given to the managers by the committee are known as Federal Open Market Committee directives. Open market operations are based on the very simple facts that an open market purchase of securities by the Federal Reserve increases the monetary base, and an open market sale of securities by the Federal Reserve decreases the monetary base.

Open market operations generally are carried out on a day-to-day basis by the account managers through changes in the System Open Market Account, which is in the New York Federal Reserve District Bank. Account managers are vice presidents of the New York Federal Reserve. Daily purchases or sales of securities are made through a few, special United States government securities dealers who are in New York City. Each dealer keeps an account in Manufacturers' Hanover Trust, a private commercial bank in the city.

Once the managers have decided on the appropriate actions to satisfy the FOMC directive, the open market purchase or sale is made through bids solicited from security dealers. If the managers wish to make an open market purchase, they will buy securities from the dealers who will acquire them from the public. In practice, the securities take rather a circuitous route, being sold by the public to the dealers, then by the dealers to Manufacturers' Hanover Trust, and then by Manufacturers' Hanover Trust to the New York Federal Reserve. However, the way in which a security purchase increases the reserves of the monetary base can be seen by looking at a simplified set of accounts like those in Table 13.3

***An Open Market Purchase.*** Table 13.3 omits accounts of dealers and Manufacturers' Hanover Trust. It shows the transaction as though a member of the public dealt directly with the Federal Reserve. The accounts shown are those of the New York Federal Reserve District Bank, of the commercial

*Table 13.3*
**Open Market Purchase of Securities**

**Federal Reserve**

| Assets | | Liabilities | |
|---|---|---|---|
| Securities | + $100 | Reserve of commercial bank | +100 |

**Commerical Bank**

| Assets | | Liabilities | |
|---|---|---|---|
| Reserve of commercial bank | + $100 | Deposit of a member of the public | + $100 |

**Member of Public**

| Assets | | Liabilities | |
|---|---|---|---|
| Deposit of a member of the public | + $100 | | 0 |
| Securities | − $100 | | 0 |

bank where a member of the public has an account, and of the member of the public who sells the securities to the Federal Reserve. In the example, the Federal Reserve buys $100 worth of securities from a member of the public. The securities are subtracted from the assets of the member of the public and added to the assets of the Federal Reserve Bank. The Federal Reserve then pays for the securities by writing a check for $100 that the member of the public deposits in a commercial bank. As the check clears through the banking system, the $100 will be added to the deposit of the member of the public and also to the reserves of the commercial bank (both as an asset of the bank and as a liability of the Federal Reserve). When the deposit of the member of the public and the reserves of the commercial bank both have been increased by the value of the security purchase ($100 in this case), the commercial bank will have excess reserves. As the commercial bank decreases its excess reserve ratio, there will be a multiple expansion of deposits, and the money supply will be increased.

This kind of transaction increases the money supply because the Federal Reserve creates reserves. When the Federal Reserve's check clears through the system, reserves are added to those of the depository institutions without any funds being removed from any other account. Once the reserves have been increased, the depository institutions generally can be relied on to increase the money supply.

*An Open Market Sale.*   The way in which sales of securities by the Federal Reserve decrease the reserves in the monetary base can be seen by looking at the simplified set of accounts in Table 13.4. As in the case of the purchase of securities, these accounts are simplified so as to omit the transactions with the dealers and Manufacturers' Hanover Trust. Again, the accounts shown are those of the New York Federal Reserve District Bank, of the commercial bank where a member of the public has an account, and of a member of the public who buys the securities that the Federal Reserve is selling.

In this example, the Federal Reserve sells $100 worth of securities on the open market, and these are purchased by a member of the public. It should be emphasized that the Federal Reserve is selling in the open market securities that it already purchased. This is a secondary market transaction that is quite separate from the Federal Reserve's selling of securities for the Treasury when it is operating as the fiscal agent of the government. When the Federal Reserve operates as the fiscal agent of the government, it is borrowing money on behalf of the government. It is borrowing funds that are already in existence. When the Federal Reserve sells securities from its portfolio in the secondary market, it is doing this to decrease the amount of reserves in the system.

In our example, the $100 of securities are subtracted from the assets of the Federal Reserve and they become an asset of a member of the public. The reason that this transaction leads to a reduction in the monetary base is the result of the way in which payment for the securities is made. The member of the public purchasing the securities that are being sold by the Federal Reserve will write a check on an account in a depository institution (in this case, a commercial bank). The check then will clear through the banking system. The $100 will be subtracted from the deposit of the member of the public, and it will also be subtracted from the reserves of the commercial bank (both as an asset of the bank and as a liability of the Federal Reserve). Significantly, the $100 reduction in Federal Reserve liabilities is offset by the $100 reduction in the securities held as assets. The $100 subtracted from the reserves of the commercial bank are not added to any other account. The result is that there is a decrease in reserves of the full $100.

The commercial bank has suffered a loss in deposits of $100 and also a loss in reserves of $100. Assuming that the bank was not holding more reserves before this event than it wanted to hold, the bank now will find

**Table 13.4**
***Open Market Sale of Securities***

**Federal Reserve**

| Assets | | Liabilities | |
|---|---|---|---|
| Securities | − $100 | Reserves of commercial bank | − $100 |

**Commercial Bank**

| Assets | | Liabilities | |
|---|---|---|---|
| Reserve of commercial bank | − $100 | Deposit of member of public | − $100 |

**Member of Public**

| Assets | | Liabilities | |
|---|---|---|---|
| Deposit of member of public | − $100 | | 0 |
| Securities | + $100 | | 0 |

itself with deficient reserves. In order to rectify this situation, there will have to be a multiple contraction of deposits among the depository institutions. This, of course, will lead to a reduction in the money supply. An amount of reserves (included in the monetary base) has been destroyed in this process equal to the amount of the sale of securities by the Federal Reserve.

## The Federal Open Market Committee (FOMC)

When the Federal Reserve was established in 1913, discount policy was considered to be the primary mechanism for changing monetary conditions. The use of open market operations and its evolution to the primary instrument of monetary control followed the increase in the size of the marketable public debt and the resulting development of the secondary market for United States Treasury securities. In 1916 the marketable public issue of United States government debt totaled only $972 million. By December

1919 the marketable United States government debt had risen to $25,595 million.[6] Although some limited open market operations were carried out in the 1920s by individual Federal Reserve District Banks, the formal systemwide use of open market operations as an instrument of monetary control started only when the Banking Act of 1933 created the Federal Open Market Committee.

Meetings of the Federal Open Market Committee usually are conducted every three weeks, and a directive is issued to the system's open market account managers. The twelve voting members of the committee are the seven members of the Board of Governors, the president of the Federal Reserve Bank of New York (in whose district the operations take place), and the presidents of four other Federal Reserve banks chosen in rotation. The seven presidents of the other Federal Reserve banks not currently serving as members of the committee usually are in attendance, too, but they cannot vote. The directives of the Federal Open Market Committee are not immediately made known to the public. Eventually they are published, but there is a delay to prevent speculative use of the information.

Putting the directives of the FOMC into effect is not a straightforward operation. The directives do not simply state "add to our security holdings," or even "add to the amount of Federal Reserve credit." Rather, the directives contain broad statements about desirable economic conditions and ranges of growth rates for specific monetary aggregates and ranges for specific interest rates. Even though open market operations directly affect the monetary base, the directives do not specify even a range of growth rate for the monetary base. It is left to the system's open market account managers to determine the daily open market adjustments that are necessary to satisfy the directives. It should not be thought, however, that the managers have complete freedom to interpret FOMC directives. If members of the FOMC feel that the managers are not conducting monetary policy in the way in which they intended, they can (and will) modify the directive before the next formal meeting of the committee.

***FOMC Directives.***   The tenor of open market directives and the concerns of the FOMC have changed over the years. Historically, the directives have concentrated on the rather ill-defined notion of "credit conditions," which somehow are indicated by interest rates, bank reserves, and bank loans. Open market operations, in fact, often have been carried out exclusively in response to prevailing interest rates.

Although the Federal Reserve System only directly sets the discount rate, the purchase and sale of securities as part of open market operations will at least affect short-term interest rates in the short run. A large purchase

[6]Board of Governors of the Federal Reserve, *Banking and Monetary Statistics* (Washington, D.C., 1943): 509.

"This just in, folks! In an effort to stimulate consumer confidence, all future announcements of the federal reserve board will be unintelligible!"

of United States Treasury securities by the Federal Reserve can be made only if the public (through the government security dealers) can be induced to forgo the securities. The incentive to sell a large volume of securities to the Federal Reserve would come as a result of an increase in the price offered (the dealer's asked price), with the simultaneous reduction in the yield on the securities. This decline in the nominal interest rate on some particular kind of security then would induce a decline in the rates of interest on other substitute financial obligations.

Directing open market operations to have a specific effect on the money supply is only a recent development. Target ranges for different definitions of the money supply have been included in open market directives only since 1970. Since that time, target ranges have been given for the federal funds rate and various definitions of the money supply. However, the range for the federal funds rate has been fairly narrow and the range for growth rates in money supplies relatively wide. This would mean that monetary policy was very much influenced by the federal funds rate and influenced less by the rates of change of the money supply.

A significant change in open market directives occurred in October 1979, indicating a stronger concern for the growth in the money supply relative to a concern for interest rates. At the FOMC meeting of September 18, 1979, a range of ½ of 1 percent (from 11¼ percent to 11¾ percent) was specified for the federal funds rate. The range of growth rates for the old $M_1$ (present M1 plus demand deposits of foreign commercial banks and official institutions minus all interest-bearing checking accounts) was set at 5 percent (from 3 to 8 percent). At the following meeting, on October 6,

1979, the range for the federal funds rate was broadened to 4 percent (from 11½ percent to 15½ percent), and the range for the growth rate of old $M_1$ was narrowed to 3 percent (from 4½ percent to 7½ percent).

The narrowing of the range on monetary aggregate growth rates and the widening of the range on the federal funds rate signify that the FOMC has changed the emphasis of its policy. Rather than emphasizing interest rates, the committee is emphasizing the money supply. It should be remembered, however, that this is only a change of emphasis, not a change in targets. The significant difficulty faced by the account managers of reconciling conflicts between the targets still remains. For example, the directive on interest rates still can conflict with the target on money supply 1. It may be that it is impossible to stay within the range for the federal funds rate and at the same time carry out open market operations that cause money supply 1 to grow at a rate that is within the specified range. At the same time, staying within the range for federal funds would cause the rate of growth of money supply 1 to be outside its range. The FOMC has not given the account managers any guidance on how to reconcile this kind of conflict.

## SUMMARY

Most financially developed countries have established an institution known as a *central bank*. Central banks have functions very different from those of commercial banks. They usually do not deal directly with the public but instead act as a "bankers' bank," holding reserve deposits for commercial banks. Central banks traditionally have had certain roles to play in an economy. These often have had to do with maintaining the safety of the private banking industry in one way or another. However, in this century the emphasis has shifted to include monetary management, whereby the central banks intervene in the economy to affect the money supply and credit conditions measured in various ways.

The United States established the Federal Reserve as its central bank in 1913. Initially it was a "lender of last resort" for the member banks, but currently it is much more than that. It still is a lender of last resort, but it is a lender of last resort for all depository institutions. In common with other modern central banks, the Federal Reserve has three instruments of monetary management. These are (1) changing reserve requirements on various kinds of deposit in depository institutions, (2) changing the discount rate at which depository institutions might borrow reserves, and (3) undertaking open market operations, whereby the Federal Open Market Committee is able to change the monetary base.

The most important instrument of monetary policy is the use of open market operations. In open market operations, the purchase of securities in the open market by the Federal Reserve increases the reserves of the private depository institutions. The sale of securities in the open market from the

Federal Reserve's portfolio decreases the reserves of the private depository institutions. Although the other instruments have some effect on the economy, they do not compare with open market operations for having a direct effect on the money supply. Open market operations are the easiest policy to use, they can be used on a day-to-day basis, and they have a more definite effect than other instruments.

## Key Terms

central bank
First Bank of the United States
Second Bank of the United
   States
Federal Reserve Act
Federal Reserve District Bank
Federal Reserve Board of
   Governors

FOMC
lender of last resort
moral suasion
changing reserve requirements
defensive discount rate changes
demonstration effect
open market operations

## Questions

1.  "The Federal Reserve is an independent agency of the United States government." Evaluate.

2.  "An increase in reserve requirements for deposits held by the depository institutions will reduce the supply of money." Evaluate.

3.  "An increase in the discount rate means that the Federal Reserve is tightening monetary policy." Evaluate.

4.  Some economists have advocated the discontinuation of discount policy as part of monetary policy. Why would you expect this to be the case?

5.  "An open market purchase by the Federal Reserve will increase the money supply." Evaluate.

6.  Could open market operations be carried out by buying and selling furniture? Explain.

## Additional Readings

Board of Governors of the Federal Reserve. *The Federal Reserve System—Purposes and Functions.* Washington, D.C., 1974.

*A comprehensive coverage of the organization, role, and function of the Federal Reserve System.*

Brewer, Elijah. "Some Insights on Member Bank Borrowing." *Economic Perspectives.* Federal Reserve Bank of Chicago (November–December 1978): 16–21.

*A discussion of the Federal Reserve discount mechanism and the incentive for banks to borrow from the Federal Reserve.*

Eastburn, David P. *The Federal Reserve on Record: Readings on Current Issues from Statements by Federal Reserve Officials.* Federal Reserve Bank of Philadelphia, 1965.

*A collection of statements made by Federal Reserve officials over the first 50 years of operation that describe the problem-solving nature of Federal Reserve actions.*

Kane, Edward J. "Good Intentions and Unintended Evil." *Journal of Money, Credit and Banking* 9 (1) (February 1977): 55–69.

*A paper presented as a public lecture on "The Case Against Selective Credit Controls."*

Minsky, Hyman P. "The Federal Reserve: Between a Rock and a Hard Place." *Challenge.* (May–June 1980): 30–36.

*A view of the conflict between the Federal Reserve's monetary control function and its function as a lender of last resort.*

# CHAPTER FOURTEEN

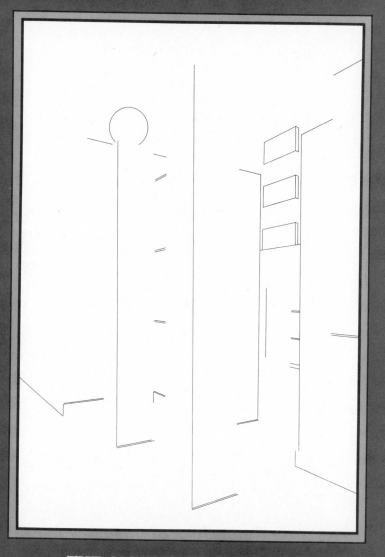

# THE MONETARY BASE AND
# MONETARY CONTROL

*The Federal Reserve's open market operations have a predictable effect on the monetary base, and hence on the money supply. However, there are many factors affecting the monetary base that are not under the control of the system's open market managers. Open market operations must be used to offset any adverse changes in these outside factors as well as to accomplish an active monetary policy. Most of the factors affecting the monetary base can be seen in the Federal Reserve's balance sheet.*

The Federal Reserve's monetary control rests with its ability to influence the quantity of money and general monetary conditions (including interest rates). This generally is accomplished by changing the amount of the monetary base through open market operations or through the discount mechanism. However, this is not as simple as it might seem from the ease with which open market operations can be accomplished, because there are many factors affecting the monetary base that are not controlled directly by the Federal Reserve. Such factors include the monetary activities of the United States Treasury, the float that is generated as a by-product of the check-clearance mechanism of the depository institutions, and the official interventions in the foreign exchange markets.

Even if the Federal Reserve had complete control over the monetary base, it would not have complete control over the money supply. All money multipliers are influenced by portfolio decisions of the public and the depository institutions; and the Federal Reserve does not have direct control over any of these. The Federal Reserve's ability to exercise monetary control, therefore, depends on its ability to offset all other factors beyond its control. Open market operations have a precise effect on the monetary base *with all other factors remaining the same;* but having to predict the changes in other factors and then having to offset them makes open market operations very difficult to use. A great many open market operations are defensive operations that offset changes in the money multipliers or in the factors that affect the monetary base.

## MONETARY CONTROL

As the Federal Reserve has developed into the monetary authority in the United States, it has come to rely more and more on the actions taken by the Federal Open Market Committee. Although some control obviously can take place through the other instruments of monetary control—through moral suasion and reserve requirements changes by the Board of Governors and through discount rate changes made by district banks—the most accurate form of control comes through changes in the monetary base that are brought about through open market operations authorized by the FOMC.

As we have seen in previous chapters, relationships have been developed between the *monetary base* ($B$) and the various definitions of the money supply (M1 and M2). For example, the relationship between the monetary base and money supply 1 is

$$M1 = \frac{1 + c}{c + r_D + e + r_T t} B.$$

Clearly, if account managers are able to predict accurately the changes in ratios $c$, $e$, and $t$, changes in $B$ could come about through open market operations to offset these changes. Any increase in $c$, $e$, or $t$, with all else remaining the same, would decrease the amount of money supply 1. Therefore, if these increases are predicted, $B$ can be increased in such a way as to keep M1 at the desired level. It now must be a part of the work of account managers to predict changes in the ratios, so that defensive open market operations can be carried out to offset them. Offsetting ratio changes in the money multipliers is, in itself, no easy task. As we saw in Chapter 12, some of the ratios have changed considerably over time.

More important, the Federal Reserve does not have complete control over the base. The monetary base consists of the balances of depository institutions held with Federal Reserve District Banks (either directly or through pass-through accounts) plus currency in circulation (outside the Federal Reserve and the United States Treasury). Well over 90 percent of the monetary base is liabilities of the Federal Reserve, either in the deposits of the depository institutions or in Federal Reserve notes outstanding. These Federal Reserve liabilities are affected by the size of all other assets and liabilities of the Federal Reserve. On a day-to-day basis, adjustments in the Federal Reserve's portfolio in items that it does not control directly can alter the monetary base. For example, the check-clearing process may slow and the float rise or funds may be withdrawn from the deposits other than those of the depository institutions held with the Federal Reserve banks. The monetary activity of the United States Treasury also can affect the monetary base. The circulating coin, an obligation of the United States Treasury, also is part of the monetary base.

While many factors not controlled directly by the Federal Reserve can affect the monetary base, and some portfolio decisions made by the public can alter the money multiplier and change the quantity of money available, the Federal Reserve has sufficient power to offset the effects of changes in these variables. The Federal Reserve's ability to exercise control over the money supply depends on its ability to *predict* the changes in uncontrolled factors. After effects of these factors' changes on the money supply have been predicted, appropriate changes in open market operations can be undertaken to offset the undesired effects. Clearly, with lags in data collection and the difficulty in determining hour-to-hour and day-to-day adjustments in portfolios of the financial sector, the Federal Reserve's ability to predict changes and to control the money supply is greater over a longer period of time than it is on a day-to-day basis.

The primary instrument utilized by the Federal Reserve for monetary control is open market operations. Through the purchase or sale of United States government securities by the Federal Reserve, the amount of reserves potentially available to the depository institutions is altered, and this change in the monetary base will affect the supply of money. Open market operations can be classified broadly as being either dynamic or defensive in nature.

*Dynamic open market operations* are the purchase or sale by the Federal Reserve of United States government securities that are designed to alter the general level of economic activity. These operations are undertaken to affect the rate of inflation, the level of employment, or some other normative goal of monetary policy. Such open market operations generally are undertaken through the outright purchase or sale of securities.

*Defensive open market operations* are designed to stabilize monetary conditions by offsetting factors deemed to be temporary or seasonal in nature. For example, additional open market purchases may be undertaken to offset the increased desires by the public to hold currency in, say, December. The defensive activity generally is undertaken through repurchase agreements to indicate the temporary nature of the open market operation. When the Federal Reserve purchases securities under a repurchase agreement, additional reserves and monetary base are supplied for a few days. In addition, the reserves and the monetary base may be lowered temporarily by the open market desk's sale of securities through a matched sale/purchase agreement. The vast bulk of open market activity is in the form of repurchase agreements or matched sale/purchase agreements. For 1983 the temporary open market operations in repurchase or matched sale/purchase agreements were valued at $685 billion, compared to only $26 billion in outright purchases or sales of government securities.[1]

---

[1] Board of Governors, Federal Reserve System, *Federal Reserve Bulletin* Washington, D.C. (Board of Governors, (March 1984): A9.

## THE FEDERAL RESERVE BALANCE SHEET

The Federal Reserve exerts its principal control over the monetary base through the management of its portfolio of assets and liabilities. Since the monetary base primarily consists of two of the Federal Reserve's liabilities: Federal Reserve notes outstanding, and the balances of depository institutions held with Federal Reserve District Banks, the composition of the consolidated balance sheet for the 12 Federal Reserve District Banks is important in determining monetary conditions. One important aspect of balance sheets is that they balance. Total assets equal total liabilities plus the capital accounts. Unless directly offset elsewhere, every item on the Federal Reserve balance sheet will have an effect on the amount of Federal Reserve notes outstanding or the balances of depository institutions held with Federal Reserve banks and will alter the monetary base. The composition of the consolidated balance sheet of the Federal Reserve Banks is given in Table 14.1.

*Federal Reserve notes* are the amount of paper currency issued and circulated by the Federal Reserve. This amount includes the notes held in the vaults of depository institutions, holdings of the nonbank public, and

*Table 14.1*
**Consolidated Balance Sheet, Federal Reserve Banks December 28, 1983 (Millions of Dollars)**

| Assets | | | Liabilities and Capital | | |
|---|---:|---:|---|---:|---:|
| Gold certificate account | | $ 11,123 | Federal Reserve notes | | $157,702 |
| SDR certificate account | | 4,618 | Deposits | | 27,270 |
| Coin | | 409 | Depository institutions | 22,813 | |
| Loans | | 1,311 | U.S. Treasury general | 3,636 | |
| Acceptances (under repurchase agreement) | | 0 | account | | |
| Federal agency obligations | | 8,645 | Foreign-official accounts | 263 | |
| U.S. government securities | | 152,570 | Other | 558 | |
| | | | Deferred availability cash items (DACI) | | 8,822 |
| Bought outright | 152,570 | | Other liabilities | | 2,266 |
| Held under repurchase agreement | 0 | | Total liabilities | | 196,060 |
| Cash items in process of collection (CIPC) | | 11,877 | Capital accounts | | 3,230 |
| Other assets (includes bank premises and foreign currencies) | | 8,737 | | | |
| Total assets | | 199,290 | Total liabilities and capital | | 199,290 |

*Source:* Federal Reserve Bulletin, Board of Governors, Washington, D.C. (January 1984): Table 1.18.

some cash holdings of the United States Treasury. Federal Reserve notes held by Federal Reserve banks are not currently circulating and are not counted in this obligation of the Federal Reserve.

*Deposits of depository institutions* are assets of the depository institutions held at Federal Reserve District Banks. Along with vault cash, these deposits are used to satisfy legal reserve requirements. Through 1980, only member banks were required to satisfy reserve requirements with deposits held with Federal Reserve banks; prior to December 1959, only deposits with Federal Reserve banks could be used to satisfy member bank reserve requirements (vault cash did not satisfy reserve requirements).

Depository institutions also find these deposits useful for making transfers between institutions and for lending on the federal funds market. As part of the Federal Reserve's pricing for use of its services, depository institutions with zero or small required reserve balances are required to hold *clearing balances.* Unlike other deposits with the Federal Reserve, clearing balances earn credits at the average federal funds rate for the week to offset charges for Federal Reserve services. In addition, the Federal Reserve charges deficiency fees.

Federal Reserve notes and deposits of depository institutions are exchangeable directly by the depository institutions. The composition of these two liabilities depends on the desires of the depository institutions and the nonbank public for paper currency. When the public desires more paper currency, deposits are withdrawn from depository institutions in the form of currency. The depository institutions then will replace their inventory of currency (vault cash) by withdrawing balances held with Federal Reserve banks. When the public desires less currency, the currency is deposited in depository institutions. This transaction is recorded in the accounts shown in Table 14.2 with the subscripts $(a)$ for the amount of $10. Those depository institutions acquiring more currency than desired may exchange it for a more readily transferable asset by depositing the Federal

*Table 14.2*
**An Exchange of Federal Reserve Notes for Reserve Deposits**

| Depository Institution | | Federal Reserve | |
|---|---|---|---|
| Assets | Liabilities | Assets | Liabilities |
| Vault Cash   $+\$10_{(a)}$  $-\$10_{(b)}$<br>Balances with Federal Reserve   $+\$10_{(b)}$ | Deposits   $+\$10_{(a)}$ | | Federal Reserve notes outstanding   $-\$10_{(b)}$<br>Reserve balances   $+\$10_{(b)}$ |

Reserve notes with their Federal Reserve District Bank in exchange for reserve balances as shown in Table 14.2 with subscripts (*b*). The amount of Federal Reserve notes outstanding goes down, and reserve balances increase by an identical amount.

However, shifts between Federal Reserve notes outstanding and balances held with Federal Reserve Banks do not alter the monetary base. Only the composition of the items in the monetary base is changed. What alters the level of the monetary base are the changes in the other assets and liabilities of the Federal Reserve. Although most of the monetary base is a liability of the Federal Reserve, the monetary base cannot be determined by considering only the assets and liabilities of the Federal Reserve. The monetary activities of the United States Treasury also must be considered.

## THE MONETARY BASE

The monetary base is the set of assets that puts the ultimate constraint on monetary growth through the multiple expansion mechanism. It is the set of assets available to the public which, if held by depository institutions, could be used to satisfy the Federal Reserve's legal requirement for reserves. The monetary base consists of balances of depository institutions held in Federal Reserve Banks and currency in circulation (outside the Federal Reserve and the United States Treasury).

Currency in circulation includes the obligations of the Federal Reserve in Federal Reserve notes and the obligations of the United States Treasury. The predominant form of the Treasury's issue is coin. The Treasury coin issue was $14,073 million or about 9.5 percent of the total currency and coin circulating outside the Treasury and Federal Reserve Banks at the end of September 1983.[2] The circulating currency consists of the currency held by the nondepository institution public plus the vault cash held by depository institutions.[3]

---

[2] *Treasury Bulletin,* Department of the Treasury, (Washington, D.C., Fall 1983): 86.

[3] At least two different measures of the monetary base are available. The Board of Governors of the Federal Reserve has published monetary base data since March 16, 1979. This statistic is an outgrowth of the factors affecting reserve funds of depository institutions (Table 11.1, *Federal Reserve Bulletin*). The Federal Reserve Bank of St. Louis has published monetary base data since 1968. The figures differ in some minor technical aspects. The principal difference is in the treatment of vault cash. Since vault cash held by depository institutions two periods ago are currently included in the institutions' reserves, they also are included in the Board of Governors' monetary base statistic. This statistic is calculated by adding up the reserve balances at Federal Reserve Banks in the current period plus the vault cash held two periods earlier used to satisfy reserve requirements at all depository institutions plus currency outside the United States Treasury, the Federal Reserve Banks, and the vaults of depository institutions plus the surplus vault cash at depository institutions. The St. Louis Federal Reserve Bank's monetary base statistic is calculated from balance sheet items and includes the vault cash of depository institutions during the current period. The Federal Reserve Bank of St. Louis also adjusts the monetary base statistic for changes in reserve requirements. For a discussion of the statistics, *see:* Burger, Albert E., "Alternative Measures of the Monetary Base," *Review* (Federal Reserve Bank of St. Louis, June 1979), 3–8.

---

*Table 14.3*
**Factors Influencing the Monetary Base**
**December 28, 1983 (Millions of Dollars)**

| Factors Influencing the Monetary Base | | | Composition of the Monetary Base | | |
|---|---|---|---|---|---|
| Federal Reserve credit | | $174,318 | Balances of depository institutions with Federal Reserve Banks | | $ 22,774 |
| U.S. government securities | 152,570 | | | | |
| Federal agency securities | 8,645 | | Currency in circulation | | 170,616 |
| Acceptances | 0 | | Currency held by the nondepository institution public | 149,254 | |
| Loans | 1,311 | | | | |
| Float (CIPC − DACI) | 3,055 | | | | |
| Other Federal Reserve assets | 8,737 | | Vault cash of depository institutions (est.)[1] | 21,362 | |
| Gold stock | | 11,123 | | | |
| SDR certificate account | | 4,618 | | | |
| Treasury currency outstanding | | 13,786 | | | |
| *Less* | | | | | |
| Treasury cash holdings | | 462 | | | |
| Deposits, other than reserves with Federal Reserve Banks | | 4,497 | | | |
| U.S. Treasury general account | 3,636 | | | | |
| Foreign official | 263 | | | | |
| Other | 598 | | | | |
| Other Federal Reserve liabilities and capital | | 5,496 | | | |
| Monetary base | | 193,390 | Monetary base | | 193,390 |

[1] Vault cash held 2 weeks earlier to satisfy reserve requirements plus surplus vault cash.

*Source: Federal Reserve Bulletin,* Board of Governors, Washington, D.C. (January 1984): Tables 1.18, 1.11.

***The Accounting Framework.***  The monetary base can be calculated directly from the assets in the "composition of the monetary base." Alternatively, it can be computed from the assets and liabilities of the Federal Reserve and Treasury. A computation from the balance sheet indicates the "factors influencing the monetary base." These are given in Table 14.3.[4]

---

[4] The factors influencing the monetary base given in Table 14.3 are an adaptation of the "sources" and "uses" of reserve bank credit used by the Federal Reserve. The "factors influencing the monetary base" are the "sources": the assets supplying monetary base *less* the factors absorbing monetary base.

The assets of the public that the monetary base comprises are primarily liabilities of the Federal Reserve Banks. Federal Reserve notes outstanding and balances of depository institutions with Federal Reserve Banks make up over 92 percent of the monetary base. Since the composition of the monetary base is part of the liabilities of the Federal Reserve, we can investigate the Federal Reserve's influence on the monetary base by examining its assets and other liabilities. The factors influencing the monetary base primarily consist of Federal Reserve's assets less its liabilities not in the composition of the monetary base. Some adjustments are then made to account for the monetary activity of the Treasury. For example, the gold stock (against which gold certificates are issued) replaces the Federal Reserve asset of gold certificates, and the Treasury's currency and coin issue less its holdings of cash are included.

## Federal Reserve Credit

When the Federal Reserve acquires an asset (other than coin), monetary base is created. Most activity that supplies and influences the monetary base is recorded as *Federal Reserve credit* and results from open market operations. When the Federal Reserve buys an asset, payment is made that either increases the amount of Federal Reserve notes outstanding or increases the balances of depository institutions. For example, when the open market desk purchases United States government securities from a dealer (either outright or through a repurchase agreement), the Federal Reserve immediately credits the balances of the dealer's bank. As Federal Reserve credit (United States government securities held by Federal Reserve Banks) increases, so does the monetary base.

*United States Government Security Holdings.*   This asset is the principal factor influencing the monetary base and is the primary asset used in open market operations. As can be seen from Tables 14.1 and 14.2, the Federal Reserve held over $152 billion in United States government securities in December 1983.

*Federal Agency Securities.*   As part of open market operations, the Federal Reserve also acquires some obligations of federal agencies. The credit extended through this source, however, is relatively small. Federal agency obligations generally are acquired as part of the Federal Reserve's support of these financial markets.

*Acceptances.*   Bankers' acceptances were acquired by the Federal Reserve as part of its development of the market for real bills. Through 1955 these were acquired at an established rate, and the extension of this Federal Reserve credit was at the initiative of the commercial banks rather than that of the Federal Reserve.

Acceptances were acquired as part of open market operations. The market has expanded to a scale that no longer requires continuing support. The use of repurchase agreements on bankers' acceptances in open market operations was abandoned in July 1984.

*Loans.*  Loans are principally extended to authorized financial institutions through the discount window. Most loans are advances issued to financial institutions on their own promise to repay secured by acceptable securities, such as issues of the United States government. In addition, commercial paper can be rediscounted by depository institutions. Most loans are short term and supply reserves in cases of temporary deficiencies.

*Other Assets.*  Other assets include the value placed on bank premises, holdings of foreign currencies, and balances of foreign currency held at other foreign central banks. Foreign currency holdings are valued at market rates and are used to supply domestic banks with foreign exchange and to intervene in foreign exchange markets. When the Federal Reserve acquires these assets, the payments for them create monetary base, and they are included in the amount of Federal Reserve credit outstanding.

## The Float

The *Federal Reserve float* is the amount of credit given to depository institutions by the Federal Reserve as a result of the check-clearing mechanism. This factor influencing the monetary base is the Federal Reserve's asset of cash items in the process of collection (CIPC) less the liability of deferred availability cash items (DACI). These balance sheet items are grouped together because they both result from the check-clearing process. (See Chapter 9.)

The float was created by the Federal Reserve and results from its payment on checks it is clearing (reducing DACI) before it receives payment (reducing CIPC). The Federal Reserve effectively gave up control over the float by establishing the funds availability schedule for check clearing.

The float has resulted in an extremely volatile amount of Federal Reserve credit. Movement in the float is shown in Figure 14.1. It should be noted that Figure 14.1 actually masks much of the daily movement in the float because the figures plotted are weekly *averages* of daily figures.

Volatility in the float limits the Federal Reserve's ability to control the monetary base on a short-term basis. The float is subject to seasonal variation and to changes in weather conditions that slow down transportation and the collection of checks.

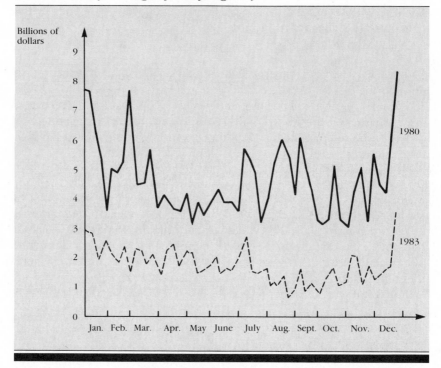

Figure 14.1
**Federal Reserve Float, 1980 and 1983**
**(Plotted: Weekly Average of Daily Figures)**

*Source:* Board of Governors, Federal Reserve System, *Federal Reserve Bulletin,* (Washington, D.C.: Board of Governors, February 1980–February 1981 and February 1983–February 1984): Table 1.11.

The monetary control problems related to the float changed dramatically after the Monetary Control Act of 1980 passed. In order to improve on monetary control the Federal Reserve has been charged with reducing the float. They have succeeded by accelerating the check-clearing process. As can be seen in Figure 14.1, during 1983 the float was reduced both in size and volatility.[5]

Through 1980 the float was effectively an interest-free, short-term loan to depository institutions using the Federal Reserve's check-clearing mechanism. It was also seen as a loss of income to the United States Treasury. To maintain a given level of monetary base (or of depository institutions' reserves), the Federal Reserve would hold fewer United States government securities to offset the amount of Federal Reserve credit extended

---

[5] From 1980 to 1983 the average of the weekly average figures declined from $4.7 billion to $1.8 billion and the standard deviation was reduced to $0.58 billion from $1.26 billion.

through the float. The Treasury ultimately would receive the interest paid on those securities, if held by the Federal Reserve, because the Federal Reserve returns its earning in excess of expenses to the Treasury. The Federal Reserve now charges for its services and includes in check-clearing charges an amount to compensate for the float. This fee has served as an incentive to use check-clearing services outside of the Federal Reserve and further reduce the float.

## Circulating Currency

The monetary base is composed of balances of depository institutions with Federal Reserve Banks and currency in circulation. The circulating currency consists of Federal Reserve notes and obligations of the United States Treasury. The Treasury's activities related to its issue of currency and coin influence the monetary base.

***Treasury Currency Outstanding.***  Treasury currency outstanding is the total amount of currency and coin issued by the Treasury. While primarily coin, some United States notes and silver certificates remain outstanding and are included in this figure. This represents all the Treasury's issue of paper currency and coin, including that held in Federal Reserve Banks, the vaults of depository institutions, and in the vaults of the Treasury.

***Treasury Cash Holdings.***  Treasury holdings of its own cash issue or Federal Reserve notes reduce the monetary base. Treasury cash also includes the amount of free gold held by the Treasury. *Free gold* is the nonmonetized segment of the gold stock and is the difference between the gold stock and the amount of gold certificates. The Treasury could issue gold certificates against its free gold and add the amounts to its deposits with the Federal Reserve. Thus, effectively, free gold is cash. The amount of the Treasury's cash holdings is a factor that influences the monetary base that is not directly controlled by the Federal Reserve. However, the balances are small and the impact on the monetary base minimal.

Some of the United States Treasury's issue of coin is held as an asset of Federal Reserve Banks in their vaults. This asset of the Federal Reserve is not listed as a factor that influences the monetary base. Treasury issue of coin supplies monetary base. The Federal Reserve's holdings of part of this issue simply result from the desires of the public for different forms of funds.

The Federal Reserve circulates the Treasury's issue of coin in response to the public's demand. When the public demands more coins, depository institutions find themselves short of coins and replenish their stocks by requesting coins from the Federal Reserve. The Federal Reserve ships the requested coins and the Federal Reserve's asset of coin declines. This effect is offset by a reduction in the balances of depository institutions held with

Federal Reserve Banks. The composition of the monetary base is altered, with fewer balances of depository institutions and more currency in circulation. With the amount of monetary base available unaltered, the only possible effect on the money supply would be through a change in the money multiplier. The public's demand for additional coin might reflect a change in its desired ratio of currency holdings to transactions deposits.

The Federal Reserve acquires its coin holdings from deposits made by depository institutions and from the Treasury. The Treasury deposits coin into the *Treasury general account* at the Federal Reserve. When the Treasury makes expenditures out of the general account, the monetary base increases.

Since the Federal Reserve does not control the issue of currency and coin by the Treasury, this factor reduces the Federal Reserve's control over the monetary base. However, the issue of coin is a response to the public's demands for different denominations. Changes in this issue are usually relatively small. The effect on the monetary base can be predicted and, if desired, offset by Federal Reserve open market operations.

## Gold and Special Drawing Rights

***The Gold Stock.***   Under a monometallic gold standard, the amount of gold available for monetary use serves as the monetary base for the multiple expansion of deposits (and bank note issue).[6] Although the United States abandoned gold coin circulation in the early 1930s, the tradition of a monetary base in gold has kept the gold stock listed as a factor influencing the monetary base (and reserves of depository institutions). Although the *gold stock* currently remains almost constant, increases in the United States gold stock during the 1930s, resulting from an inflow of gold from abroad, added considerably to the monetary base. This factor influenced the Federal Reserve's decision to forestall additional monetary expansion in the late 1930s. The gold stock rose from $7.4 billion in early 1934 (valued at the official price of $35 per troy ounce) to over $22 billion in 1941.[7]

With a commodity gold standard, the monetary base is not determined by the entire gold stock, only that portion available for monetary use. Likewise, under the paper standard controlled by the Federal Reserve, the gold stock that influences the monetary base is the amount of monetized gold. Gold is monetized when the Treasury issues gold certificates and deposits them in the Treasury accounts at the Federal Reserve. The amount of monetized gold, therefore, appears as an asset of the Federal Reserve in the *gold certificate account.* The value of gold certificates and the gold stock is not determined by the free market price of gold. Since 1973, gold has been valued officially at $42.22 per troy ounce.

---

[6] *See* Chapter 4.

[7] Board of Governors, Federal Reserve, *Banking and Monetary Statistics* (1943): 537–538.

For many years the Federal Reserve was required to hold gold certificates as reserves against its note issue, but this is no longer the case (*see* "Gold," page 356.) Currently, gold certificates are used only for internal bookkeeping by the Federal Reserve and the Treasury. For example, check clearances made through the Interdistrict Settlement Fund are accomplished by a transfer of gold certificates between district banks.

**The Special Drawing Rights Certificate Account.**   Special drawing rights certificates affect the monetary base in a manner similar to that of monetized gold. Just as gold certificates are issued against gold, so special drawing rights certificates are issued against special drawing rights (SDRs), and both kinds of certificates are deposited into Treasury accounts at the Federal Reserve. *SDRs* are claims issued by the International Monetary Fund (IMF) to increase international liquidity and provide additional international reserves. Although originally considered to be "paper gold," SDRs are not connected to gold in any way and are now valued in terms of a composite bundle of currencies. SDRs allocated to the United States are placed in the Exchange Stabilization Fund.

Either a gold sale or the sale of SDRs will reduce the monetary base through a retirement of certificates issued. Both the gold stock and the *SDR certificate account* are extremely stable. Since the decline in the official use of gold, these accounts have had little impact on changes in the monetary base.

## Factors Reducing the Monetary Base

In addition to the Treasury's activity represented by Treasury cash holdings, several other factors listed in Table 14.3 reduce the monetary base. All of them are liabilities or capital accounts of Federal Reserve Banks. Deposits in Federal Reserve Banks, other than the balances of depository institutions, reduce the monetary base. These deposits are not controlled by the Federal Reserve and limit its ability to control the monetary base on a short-term basis. However, apart from the Treasury's general account, these other deposits are relatively small and tend to remain fairly stable.

*Foreign-official accounts* are deposits of other central banks with Federal Reserve Banks. These generally are small and are used by foreign central banks for international payments and for some activity in foreign exchange markets. The Federal Reserve also houses *other deposits* from other international organizations and government-sponsored agencies.

The Federal Reserve's *capital account* reduces the monetary base by offsetting some Federal Reserve credit. The capital account represents stock held by member bank owners of the Federal Reserve and a generally equal amount of accumulated surplus. During the year, earnings in excess of expenses are accumulated in this account until payment is made to the Treasury.

## GOLD

Gold is a soft metal that has desirable properties for functioning as a commodity money. It is durable, portable, easily divisible, and can be readily coined to be standardized and recognizable. Also, gold's natural scarcity instills people with a faith in its continuing value that is required for the use of something as money. It is this natural scarcity and the constraint that it places on the quantity of money that leads to the nostalgic yearning for a return to the "good old days" of a gold standard.

A shift from the use of only a commodity as money to the use of paper warehouse receipts that may be more easily transported requires the leap of faith that the paper will continue to remain relatively scarce and, hence, retain value. Initially, the faith in the scarcity of the paper is maintained through the redeemability of the paper bank notes for the commodity money. When the Federal Reserve was established, a tie between the circulating paper issued by the Federal Reserve and gold was built into the system. The Federal Reserve Banks were required to hold as reserves either gold or lawful money (lawful money held as reserves was basically silver dollars, silver certificates, and United States notes) equal in amount to at least 35 percent of its deposits and 40 percent of the Federal Reserve's note issue.

One difficulty seen in the tie between the natural forces in the gold market and the quantity of money is the lack of direct government control over monetary conditions. Adjustments may be made simply to offset actions in the gold market. For example, to forestall the growth of credit in the early 1930s that resulted from the inflow of gold, the Federal Reserve increased the discount rate. In October 1931 the discount rate at the Federal Reserve Bank of New York was raised from 1.5 to 2.5 percent. The ability of the government to have more direct control over monetary conditions is an incentive to break the tie between gold and money and establish a paper standard.

It was the banking and monetary problems of the 1930s that led to the break between gold and the money supply. As a result of the national emergency in banking, presidential orders prohibited the private holding of gold or its sale in the United

States, except under license, in 1933. The Gold Reserve Act of 1934 gave ownership of the Federal Reserve's gold to the United States Treasury, and the official price of gold was changed for the first time in a century from $20.67 to $35 per troy ounce.

The illusion of a tie between gold and the Federal Reserve's liabilities was still maintained, although the relationship was stretched. Gold certificates were issued by the Treasury against the gold stock held by the Federal Reserve. However, these new gold certificates were not like the old, previously circulating gold certificates that were essentially warehouse receipts for gold coin. The new gold certificates became simply a means of internal bookkeeping. A semblance of a tie between gold and Federal Reserve liabilities was maintained through the requirement that the Federal Reserve Banks hold gold certificates as reserves in an amount equal to at least 35 percent of its deposits and 40 percent of its notes.

Gold continued to be used to settle international payments and to maintain the fixed exchange rate for the dollar in the foreign exchange markets into the 1960s. Whenever the outflow of gold and the resulting reduction in gold certificates, or the expansion of the Federal Reserve's liabilities, appeared to place a constraint on monetary expansion, the relationship between the Federal Reserve's liabilities and its holdings of gold certificates was changed. In 1945 the reserve requirements for holdings of gold certificates against both the Federal Reserve's deposit liabilities and its note issue was reduced to 25 percent. The gold certificate holding requirement against the Federal Reserve's deposit liabilities was completely dropped in 1965, and the gold certificate requirement against Federal Reserve notes was eliminated in 1968.

It is perhaps ironic that the final severing of the bookkeeping tie between gold and Federal Reserve liabilities set the stage for the ability of United States citizens to exchange money for gold. Although there is not official convertibility with the government at the official price of $42.22 per troy ounce, citizens of the United States have been able to convert their money into gold on the free market at a market-determined price since the mid-1970s.

Of all the factors affecting the monetary base, the movements in the float and the Treasury general account are the most difficult to predict, and they have inhibited the Federal Reserve's ability to control the monetary base on a short-term basis.

## Treasury Cash Management

The day-to-day impact of the Treasury's activities on the monetary base occurs through its management of its cash position. Although the Treasury's actual holdings of currency and coin (listed in the account entry *Treasury cash holdings*) are small and have little impact on the monetary base, the Treasury's working balance in the general account held with the Federal Reserve Banks does have a significant impact on the monetary base and the Federal Reserve's ability to control the monetary base.

One purpose for establishing the Federal Reserve was to provide a fiscal agent for the government. As part of this service, Federal Reserve Banks serve as storehouses for the Treasury's working balances held in the Treasury's general account. Expenditures that are made by the Treasury are drawn almost always on these deposits held in Federal Reserve Banks. Additions to the Treasury's general account reduce the monetary base. Fluctuations in the Treasury general account frequently lead to defensive open market operations by the Federal Reserve. These offset the resulting impact on the reserves available to depository institutions and on the monetary base.

The Treasury continually receives payments from the collection of taxes and the sale of its securities and continually makes payments for goods and services purchased by the government. To minimize the monetary impact of the day-to-day financing of government expenditures, the Treasury uses a two-tiered system for holding its deposit balances. The funds used directly for expenditure are housed in the general account with the Federal Reserve Banks. The bulk of the Treasury's temporary cash holdings are stored in tax and loan accounts held at private depository institutions.

Financial institutions become depositories for the Treasury's tax and loan accounts through application to the Federal Reserve. Government securities are pledged as collateral for these deposits. Depository institutions may select the manner in which they participate in the Treasury's tax and loan program. Those depositories that wish to retain the funds place the Treasury's deposits received in interest-bearing tax and loan note accounts. Alternatively, the depositories may remit the funds directly to the Federal Reserve.

The use of *tax and loan accounts* is designed to minimize the impact on the reserves of individual depository institutions when the Treasury receives payment. In most cases when a customer of a depository institution makes tax payments or pays for the purchase of government securities, the funds are transferred from the customer's account to the Treasury's tax and

*Table 14.4*
**The Use of Tax and Loan Accounts**

| Federal Reserve Banks | | |
|---|---|---|
| **Assets** | **Liabilities** | |
| | Reserve balances of depository institutions | $\begin{cases} -\$100_{(b)} \\ +\$100_{(c)} \end{cases}$ |
| | Treasury-general account | $\begin{cases} +\$100_{(b)} \\ -\$100_{(c)} \end{cases}$ |

| Depository Institutions | | |
|---|---|---|
| **Assets** | | **Liabilities** |
| Reserve balances with Federal Reserve Banks | $\begin{matrix} -\$100_{(b)} \\ +\$100_{(c)} \end{matrix}$ | Deposits—customers' $\quad\begin{cases} -\$100_{(a)} \\ +\$100_{(c)} \end{cases}$ |
| | | Tax and loan deposits $\quad\begin{cases} +\$100_{(a)} \\ -\$100_{(b)} \end{cases}$ |

loan account in the same institution. This transaction is shown in Table 14.4 with subscripts ($a$). The depository institution retains the use of its reserves, and the monetary base remains unchanged. In addition, the geographic distribution of the monetary base is retained.

As the Treasury's general account becomes depleted through expenditures made by the Treasury, the general account is replenished by calling some of the funds from the tax and loan accounts. This increases the general account, reduces the reserve balances of the depository institution, and results in a temporary reduction in the monetary base. These transactions are recorded in Table 14.4 with subscripts ($b$). For the purpose of calling in funds from the tax and loan accounts, the depository institutions are divided into three groups (A, B, and C) that are based on size. The deposits in the smallest banks (group A banks) are generally called once a week, the group B tax and loan deposits are subject to call after three days, and the largest depository institutions may have special calls placed on their tax and loan deposits daily.[8]

As the Treasury makes expenditures out of the general account, the funds are restored as part of the monetary base. Assuming that they become reserve balances of depository institutions through customer deposits, the transaction is shown in Table 14.4 with subscripts ($c$). The net effect of this set of transactions to finance government expenditure is to leave the mone-

---

[8]Brewer, Elijah, "Treasury to Invest Surplus Tax and Loan Balances," *Economic Perspectives* (Federal Reserve Bank of Chicago, November–December 1977): 14–20.

tary base at its original level. The monetary base was temporarily reduced as the funds were transferred into the general account, and then was restored to its original level through the expenditure.

The impact of the Treasury's cash management on the monetary base and the ability of the Federal Reserve to control the monetary base in the short run depend on the stability of the Treasury general account. By maintaining a fairly constant level of deposits in the general account, the adjustments in the Treasury's cash flow will occur in the tax and loan accounts, and the monetary base will be stabilized. A relatively constant level was maintained in the general account until 1974. At that time the Treasury started to hold the bulk of its deposit assets in the general account to reduce the subsidy that was being given to private depository institutions. The Treasury's tax and loan deposits were noninterest-bearing accounts. The Treasury reduced the level of the tax and loan deposits to a level considered sufficient to compensate the depository institutions for their services provided in the collection and handling of government obligations. In addition, the Treasury receives implicit interest on its general account balances. As more funds are held in the general account, the Federal Reserve generally will acquire more United States government securities and extend additional Federal Reserve credit to offset the impact of the general account on the reserve balances of depository institutions and the monetary base. The Treasury will effectively receive the interest earned on these additional securities held by the Federal Reserve when the Federal Reserve returns its earnings in excess of expenses for the year to the Treasury.

The transfer of the bulk of the Treasury's working cash balances to the general account transferred the volatility in the Treasury's cash flow to the monetary base, and called for additional defensive open market operations by the Federal Reserve to stabilize reserves and the monetary base. The movement in the Treasury general account for 1976 is shown in Figure 14.2.

After October 28, 1977, the Treasury was allowed to earn interest on its tax and loan deposits. This interest-earning ability has served as an incentive for the Treasury to reduce its general account balances and has reduced substantially the volatility in the general account as shown in Figure 14.2 for 1979.

## FINANCING GOVERNMENT EXPENDITURE

Government expenditure can have a significant impact on monetary conditions through changes in interest rates and adjustments in the flow of credit. The monetary impact of government expenditure in the United States, however, is not through a direct change in the monetary base. Neither government expenditure nor the government's collection of taxes serves as a source of monetary base. To finance government expenditures, taxes are

*Figure 14.2*
**Movement in Treasury General Account**

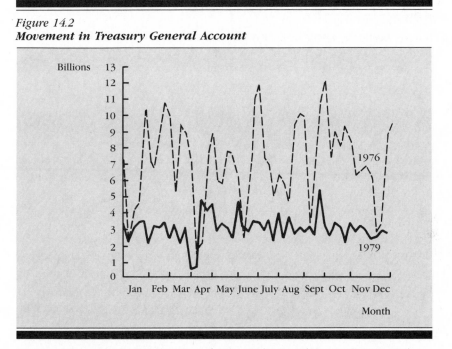

*Source:* Various *Federal Reserve Bulletins* (February 1976–January 1977): A10, A12 (February 1979–January 1980): Table 1.18. Wednesday figures plotted.

collected and additional United States Treasury securities are issued to finance any expenditures in excess of tax receipts through borrowing. For these additional securities to alter the monetary base, they must be added to the Federal Reserve's asset portfolio. This would occur only through an active decision by the Federal Reserve to undertake a policy of expanding Federal Reserve credit and the monetary base. When government expenditure is financed through tax collection or through the issue of Treasury securities, except for some minimal transitory effects, the monetary base remains unchanged unless the Federal Reserve is induced to alter its open market policy.

***Financing Government Expenditure by Tax Collection.***  The bulk of government expenditure is financed through the collection of taxes. When taxes are collected, the funds are transferred into the Treasury's interest-earning tax and loan note balances held in depository institutions. This leaves the reserves with the individual depository institution, leaves the monetary base unchanged, and does not force a change in the amount of lending activity of the depository institutions. As the government spends the proceeds of the tax collections, the funds are transferred on call into the general account held with the Federal Reserve Banks, and the funds are put back into circulation through government expenditures. The monetary base will be reduced temporarily, but only for the period that the funds are held in the general account.

***Financing Government Expenditure by Issuing New Debt.*** When government expenditures exceed tax receipts, the budget deficit is financed through additional borrowing. The gross public debt of the United States Treasury in December 1983 was $1,410.7 billion, or about 41 percent of annual nominal GNP for the United States. Of this debt, $1,050.9 billion was in marketable United States Treasury securities (bills, notes, and bonds). The remainder was in nonmarketable securities, primarily savings bonds and notes and accounts held for the United States government agencies and trust funds.[9]

As the fiscal agent for the government, the Federal Reserve serves as the agent in the sale of newly issued government securities. The proceeds from the sale of securities are placed into tax and loan accounts or into the general account. The shift of funds into the general account will temporarily reduce the monetary base. However, when placed into the tax and loan accounts or spent out of the general account, the funds will be returned to their use in the monetary base. The net impact of this debt financing is to leave the monetary base unchanged.

The financing of government expenditure through borrowing would increase the monetary base only if the issue of new securities was bought by the Federal Reserve. In that case, the Federal Reserve's holdings of government securities would have increased. However, this type of debt financing, which directly increases the monetary base, has only limited use. The purchase of securities by the Federal Reserve directly from the Treasury is subject to statutory limit, and is used primarily as a temporary measure to provide the Treasury with additional funds to finance tax refunds.

***Financing Government Expenditure Through New Currency Issue.*** To a limited extent, government expenditure could be financed by an additional issue of currency and coin by the Treasury. This would increase the amount of Treasury currency outstanding, a factor supplying monetary base, and would increase the monetary base. However, although some foreign countries have resorted to printing additional currency to finance their government expenditures, this technique is not generally used in the United States. The amount of currency and coin issued and in circulation is determined by the public's demand for these specific types of money, and most of the currency in circulation is the obligation of the

---

[9]*Federal Reserve Bulletin* (February 1984): A30.

Federal Reserve rather than the Treasury. The Federal Reserve could off-set, if desired, any impact of the Treasury's use of newly issued coin to finance government expenditure on the monetary base through open market operations.

## Effect of Government Finance on the Money Supply

Although the methods used to finance government expenditure do not alter the monetary base directly, the financing of government expenditure may still influence the supply of money. Changes in the portfolios of depository institutions and the nonbank public may occur systematically and, through changes in the money multiplier relationship, the money supply may change. The Treasury's tax and loan accounts, for example, are not included in the definitions of the money supply (M1 or M2). Thus, a shift in funds from a member of the public's demand deposits into a tax and loan account (either by the payment of taxes or the purchase of a government security) would immediately reduce M1 by an identical amount. However, since the depository institution retains the reserves, it is not forced to alter the amount of loans it has extended. Indeed, since the Treasury's tax and loan note balances are nonreservable, funds will be released from the depository institutions' required reserves, and additional loans may be extended. Unless the funds become housed permanently in tax and loan accounts, however, these impacts on the money supply will be only temporary.

The purchase by a depository institution of a United States Treasury security used to finance government expenditure also could alter the money supply. If the security was purchased out of excess reserves held by a depository institution, the money supply (with an unchanged monetary base) would immediately rise by the amount of securities purchased. However, the same increase would occur even without the additional sale of government securities if the depository institution had simply extended loans to the public out of its excess reserve holdings. For this to have any lasting effect on the money supply, there must be a change in the money multiplier, as the depository institutions decide that it is optimal to hold fewer excess reserves. This might occur as a result of the higher interest rates brought on by the additional borrowing by the government. However, considering that depository institutions currently hold few, if any, excess reserves, it seems highly unlikely that any substantial adjustment will occur.

**Response by the Federal Reserve.** The most significant impact on the money supply of the financing of government expenditure is the possible response by the Federal Reserve. As the Treasury enters the financial markets to undertake additional borrowing, interest rates are likely to rise. The additional competition for the available funds and the additional availability of new securities in substantial amounts will drive down the price of credit instruments and drive up market rates of interest. To forestall a general increase in interest rates, the Federal Reserve may supply additional Federal Reserve credit through increased open market operations. This response by the Federal Reserve, if made, will increase the monetary base and, through the multiple expansion process, will result in increases in the money supply. This change in the monetary base, however, is the result of an active decision by the Federal Reserve concerning the appropriate monetary policy to follow, and does not necessarily result from increases in government expenditure.

## FOREIGN EXCHANGE MARKET INTERVENTION

Under a commodity standard, the international flow of the commodity money will automatically alter the domestic monetary base and change the money supply. Under the gold standard used into the 1930s, gold flows dramatically limited the monetary authorities' ability to exercise control over domestic monetary conditions. The limitations placed on domestic monetary control were an incentive for the change to the current paper standard and to flexible exchange rates between currencies.

Since 1973, foreign exchange markets have made widespread use of floating exchange rates. The general level of the dollar is left to the market forces that determine the supply and demand for foreign currencies. However, exchange rates are not determined without official government interference.

Economic policymakers are concerned over fluctuations and unstable movements in foreign exchange rates. Both the Federal Reserve and the United States Treasury, through its Exchange Stabilization Fund, occasionally intervene in foreign exchange markets in attempts to prevent "speculative" movements in the value of the dollar relative to other foreign currencies. The Federal Reserve Bank of New York is the agent for these operations, which are directed by the systems open market account manager for foreign operations. The Federal Open Market Committee issues occasional directives to guide these operations.

Government intervention in foreign exchange markets has made the floating exchange rate system a "dirty" float. Governments intervene in the free market operations for foreign exchange to stabilize temporarily the adjustments in the currency's value. In terms of the market for dollars, government purchase of dollars with foreign exchange (when the foreign exchange value of the dollar is falling "too rapidly") or of foreign exchange with dollars (when the dollar's value is rising "too rapidly") stabilizes the exchange rate.

Foreign exchange market interventions can be either sterilized or unsterilized. A *sterilized intervention* leaves unchanged the monetary accounts of both countries and eliminates direct changes in the money supplies of both countries. *Unsterilized operations* have a greater impact on the exchange rate. Suppose that it is determined that the dollar's value is falling too rapidly and an unsterilized operation is undertaken. The government will purchase dollars with foreign exchange. This increases the demand for dollars on the foreign exchange market and drives up or reduces the decline in the dollar's value. In addition, the dollars purchased are removed from the system, thus reducing the monetary base and the domestic money supply. According to the naive quantity theory of money, domestic prices decline and further increase the foreign exchange demand for dollars to buy the now cheaper United States goods.

Unsterilized foreign exchange operations have a direct impact on the domestic money supply and limit the monetary authorities' ability to control domestic monetary conditions. The interventions mechanisms are designed to sterilize the foreign exchange operations and to improve domestic monetary control.

Foreign exchange market interventions can alter the United States monetary base by changing balances on the Federal Reserve's balance sheet. The accounts that could be affected are foreign-official deposits with the Federal Reserve and the Federal Reserve's "other assets," which include its deposits in foreign central banks and its holdings of foreign currency. Since they are noninterest-earning accounts for the holder, these accounts generally contain only minimal balances. Foreign central banks, for example, generally keep their dollar-denominated assets in the form of interest-earning United States government securities. With minimal balances maintained in central banks, one must acquire the funds for foreign exchange market interventions elsewhere.

In order to avoid holding substantial amounts of foreign exchange for use in interventions and to enable sterilized operations, the Federal Reserve maintains a swap network with foreign official institutions. The *swap network* is a system of reciprocal currency arrangements that permit short-term borrowing of foreign currencies in exchange for deposits in central banks. In 1983 the Federal Reserve maintained over $30 billion of these reciprocal currency arrangements.[10]

Reciprocal currency arrangements ease the sterilization of foreign exchange market interventions. To drive up the dollar's value the Federal Reserve borrows funds from a foreign central bank, which receives a deposit with the Federal Reserve as the Federal Reserve receives foreign exchange. The foreign exchange is used to buy dollars on the foreign exchange market. The amount removed from the monetary base is replaced as the foreign central bank reduces its deposits with the Federal Reserve to acquire interest-earning United States government securities.

---

[10] Cross, S.Y., "Foreign Exchange Operations: Interim Report," *Federal Reserve Bulletin* (December 1983): 893.

Foreign exchange market interventions by the United States Treasury are similar to those of the Federal Reserve. The difference is that the operations occur through the Exchange Stabilization Fund, which was established in 1934. The swap network provides funds for the operations, using SDRs to obtain funds from foreign central banks or from special deposits with the Federal Reserve for the stabilization fund. Any impact on the monetary base will be small and can be sterilized by the Federal Reserve through additional open market operations.

The mechanisms used for foreign exchange market interventions have little impact on the domestic monetary base and do little to inhibit the Federal Reserve's ability to control it. However, although foreign exchange market operations do not alter the monetary base directly, they may have significant effects on economic conditions through changes in exchange rates and relative prices of domestic and foreign goods. Although they do not severely limit the Federal Reserve's monetary control, changes in foreign exchange markets may cause the monetary authority to alter its domestic monetary policy.

## SUMMARY

The Federal Reserve is the central bank and the monetary authority for the United States. The quantity of money available and the flow of credit are influenced and controlled by the Federal Reserve. The most significant of the Federal Reserve's instruments for monetary control is the ability to engage in open market operations that alter the amount of Federal Reserve credit outstanding and change the monetary base. Open market operations may be either defensive or dynamic in nature. Dynamic open market operations are undertaken in an attempt to alter domestic economic conditions. The vast majority of open market operations are defensive in nature and are designed to offset the monetary impacts of factors that are beyond the Federal Reserve's direct control.

The Federal Reserve float and the cash management activity of the United States Treasury are the factors that most severely limit the Federal Reserve's ability to control the monetary base on a short-term basis. The float is the result of the Federal Reserve's check-clearing process; it is extremely volatile and difficult to predict. The Treasury's deposits in the general account with the Federal Reserve is a factor that absorbs monetary base. While this account has been very volatile, with the advent of interest-earning tax and loan note accounts, the general account balance has stabilized significantly and has given the Federal Reserve additional short-term control over the monetary base.

With the ability to control the monetary base, the Federal Reserve now is faced with the problem of determining the appropriate monetary policy to follow. This is the subject matter for the second part of this book.

## Key Terms

monetary base
dynamic open market
   operations
defensive open market
   operations
Federal Reserve credit
Treasury general account

gold stock
gold certificate account
SDR certificate account
tax and loan accounts
foreign exchange market
  intervention

## Questions

1. "Although the Federal Reserve cannot control the supply of money, it does have control over the monetary base." Evaluate.

2. "The Federal Reserve's ability to control the monetary base is only limited by its ability to predict the float." Evaluate.

3. "Increases in the government's budget deficit will increase the monetary base and increase the supply of money." Evaluate.

4. What factors that influence the monetary base are not directly controlled by the Federal Reserve? How do these factors limit the Federal Reserve's monetary control?

5. "Federal Reserve credit extended results in interest income for the United States Treasury." Evaluate.

6. "Activity in the foreign exchange market dictates changes in domestic monetary policy." Evaluate.

## Additional Readings

Balbach, Anatol B. "The Mechanics of Intervention in Exchange Markets." *Review* 60. Federal Reserve Bank of St. Louis (February 1978): 2–7.

*A detailed "T-account" analysis of interventions in the foreign exchange market and their possible impacts on the monetary base.*

Brewer, Elijah. "Treasury to Invest Surplus Tax and Loan Balances." *Economic Perspectives.* Federal Reserve Bank of Chicago (November–December 1977): 14–20.

*A discussion of the effect of allowing the Treasury to earn interest on tax and loan balances.*

Burger, Albert E. "Alternative Measures of the Monetary Base." *Review* 61. Federal Reserve Bank of St. Louis (February 1978): 2–7.

*A comparison of the Board of Governors and the Federal Reserve Bank of St. Louis's measures of the monetary base.*

Gilbert, R. Alton. "Revision of the St. Louis Federal Reserve's Adjusted Monetary Base." *Review* 62. Federal Reserve Bank of St. Louis (December 1980): 3–10.

*A description of the process used to calculate the reserve adjustment magnitude in computation of the adjusted monetary base.*

Henderson, D., and S. Sampson. "Intervention in Foreign Exchange Markets." *Federal Reserve Bulletin* (November 1983): 830–836.

*A brief summary of ten Federal Reserve staff studies, which discusses the experience and major intervention activities of the Federal Reserve over the past decade.*

Lang, Richard W. "TTL Note Accounts and the Money Supply Process." *Review* 61. Federal Reserve Bank of St. Louis (October 1979): 3–14.

*A review of the effects of the change in Treasury cash management procedures on bank reserves and money multipliers.*

Kubarych, Roger M. "Monetary Effects of Federal Reserve Swaps." *Quarterly Review* 2. Federal Reserve Bank of New York (Winter 1977–1978): 19–21.

*Provides additional insights into the effects of the Federal Reserve's use of swaps.*

Tatom, John A. "Issues in Measuring An Adjusted Monetary Base." *Review* 62. Federal Reserve Bank of St. Louis (December 1980): 11–29.

*An overview of the issues involved in measuring a monetary base that accounts for all of the Federal Reserve actions that affect the supply of money.*

# II

## MONETARY THEORY
## AND POLICY

# CHAPTER FIFTEEN

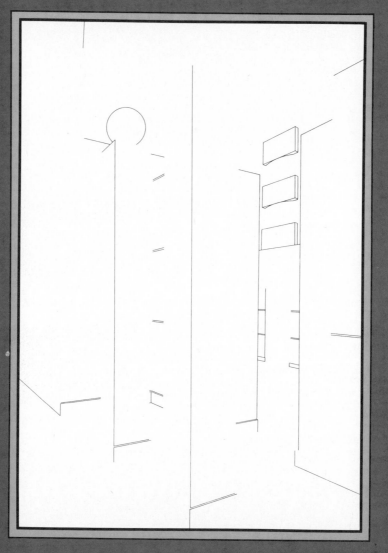

# INTRODUCTION TO MONETARY
# THEORY AND POLICY

*To understand how monetary policy is possible, it is necessary to understand the functioning of the economy. Unfortunately, that process is so complex that it is necessary to use models that simplify the economy. Those models—mainly the neoclassical and Keynesian models—do not agree in all details, but they are similar enough that the empirical evidence is not sufficient to reject either of them.*

The Federal Reserve has evolved into the monetary authority for the United States. As an agency of the federal government, the Federal Reserve shares in the responsibilities set forth in the Full Employment and Balanced Growth Act of 1978 (Humphrey-Hawkins Act) to undertake policies designed "to promote full employment, production, and real income . . . and reasonable price stability." Along with its regulatory and supervisory powers over banking, the Federal Reserve is, therefore, responsible for undertaking monetary policies designed to achieve ultimate targets or goals in terms of GNP growth, unemployment levels, and price levels.

Part I explained how the monetary authority is able to exert control over the monetary base and influence the money supply and interest rates, but determining the appropriate monetary policy to pursue remains a problem because money supply and interest changes are not by any means the ultimate goals of the policies being carried out. The design of a monetary policy depends on policymakers' interpretations of available information about the effects of instruments under their control on the ultimate targets. We have seen how the monetary base (and hence the money supply) and interest rates can be influenced by the authorities, but we must also know how the money supply and interest rates affect the levels of output, employment, and prices. In order to proceed, we must consider the way the aggregate economy is perceived to function. Unfortunately, this is not an easy task. No one knows exactly how the economy functions. Instead of a detailed description of its actual functioning, we have an incomplete model of the economy that necessarily does not account for some of the relationships that actually exist in the economy. In addition, economists do not agree about what is the best model of the economy for a monetary or any other kind of policy.

Although experience has demonstrated that changing the money supply and interest rates has a profound effect on economic activity, much more must be known about economic relationships before we can determine exactly what the results of monetary policy on the economy are. It is known, for example, that the effects of monetary policies are only felt after considerable time lags. The actual conduct of day-to-day operations of monetary policy depends therefore on how policymakers interpret the relationships between currently observable changes in policy tools and the ultimate targets that such policies are designed to affect, including the origins of lags and the ramifications of policy changes throughout the economy. Both the design and the conduct of monetary policy depend on how policymakers perceive the economy functioning.

Monetary policy is not conducted in isolation. Through its expenditure and taxation policies, government (federal, state, and local) also can have a significant effect on output, employment, and prices. Monetary policy must, therefore, be based on a model of the economy that takes into consideration not only monetary changes, but also the economic activity of the government and any adjustment that might occur in the markets that transmit policy changes to output, employment, and prices.

In order for us to consider the *normative* problem of whether a particular monetary policy might be advisable, it is necessary to investigate the *positive* economic analysis of how the economy functions. The expected results of both monetary and other government policies depend on an analysis of models of how the economy functions. From these models economists derive their predictions of the long-term results of policy measures.

## ECONOMIC MODELS

By constructing economic models, it is possible to deduce the implications of various policy changes for such economic variables as levels of employment, output, and prices, and rate of economic growth. Economic models are highly simplified, reducing the economy to a set of relationships that describes how economic variables interact. By reducing the complex world to a few simple relationships, we can concentrate on only those actions and interactions that are important in predicting the outcome of policy changes.

Though economic models often have been criticized on the grounds that the degree of abstraction involved makes them unrealistic, the opposite is in fact the case. It is the simplification of the complicated economy that makes the models useful. Only by completely abstracting from some relationships and downplaying others is it possible to single out what is really important.

## Microeconomic Models

Perhaps the easiest way to demonstrate the usefulness of such simplification is to look at the most common type of economic model: the supply and demand model commonly used in microeconomics. Typically, a small market is selected, and the effect on price and quantity of a change in, say, technology is analyzed. If it is found that the technological change lowers costs of production, producers will be willing to supply more of the good in question at any given price. This increase in supply will result in an excess supply at the original market-clearing price, so the price will be bid down. Thus, the implication of the improvement in technology is a decrease in price and an increase in the quantity exchanged.

A large number of other things may result from this change, but they are not considered to be crucial to the solution of the particular problem. For example, the decrease in the price of this good will make it relatively cheap when compared with other goods. This, in turn, will shift the demands for other goods and alter their prices. Relative prices again will have changed, and further adjustments will take place in the original market. Although such repercussions are known to exist, they are deliberately ignored in the model. A relatively small market will have a minimal impact on other markets, but the fact remains that the market has been simplified so that only the bare essentials are considered.

## Macroeconomic Models

The same type of selective myopia used in microeconomic models is employed in the construction of the *macroeconomic model*. However, since large markets are being considered, the interactions among markets cannot be ignored. In fact, the way one large market affects another may be the most important factor in the model. Choices still have to be made, however, as it must be decided which variables adjust to clear each market and which variables have the greatest impact on other markets. Not surprisingly, opinions differ as to which variables are important, and many different models have been constructed. There are perhaps more models or versions of models of the aggregate economy than there are economists. Since macroeconomic models are designed to describe the same economy, they must by nature have many similar aspects. They differ, however, in their interpretation of what is important in the specific markets analyzed.

Many people do not understand why economists disagree about which model best describes the economy and conclude that since the economists themselves do not agree, then none of the models can be of much use in describing what is going on. This, however, is an erroneous conclusion. Different models can exist side by side because empirical evidence is not strong enough to distinguish between the models. Obviously, if empirical data show that the economy does not operate as the model suggests, then that model should be rejected. In fact, such theories *have* been rejected. The models that we retain are those that have *not been proved wrong* by empirical testing. If, say, the implications of policy changes that are derived from different models are consistent with the empirical evidence available in the economy, then we have no way of rejecting the models. This does not mean that the models have been proved correct; it merely means that they cannot be rejected on the basis of the evidence.

In our discussions of the effectiveness of monetary policy, we are concerned with two basic types of macroeconomic model: the *neoclassical model* (derived from an updating of the theories held by classical economists) and the *Keynesian model* (derived from the thinking of the eminent British economist John Maynard Keynes and his followers). Both types are formulated to answer basic macroeconomic questions about the determination of employment, aggregate output, prices, and economic growth, but they differ in their selection of the adjustment processes deemed present in the money market (the supply of and demand for money), labor market, and product market.

Neoclassical and Keynesian models are not completely different. Indeed, many of the details of the models are exactly the same, but the ways in which markets are thought to interact with each other are different. Neoclassical economists assume that the amount of employment is determined in the labor market. Supplies of and demands for labor are adjusted through changes in the real amount of payments made to employees. If wages and prices are flexible, the neoclassical economists believe that an unemployment situation is automatically corrected by adjustments in the labor market. With an excess supply of labor, the unemployed actively bid against each other for jobs by lowering the wage at which they are prepared to work.

Competitive market forces within the labor market, therefore, ensure full employment. If wages and prices are not flexible, there is no automatic tendency to full employment, although monetary policy can be used to achieve the same result. When the money in circulation is increased, spending increases, and prices are likely to be bid up. If prices rise in relation to money wages, the real wage can be forced down and the level of employment increased. Not all neoclassical economists agree that this kind of policy is possible, however. Many believe that when prices rise, money wages will eventually rise at the same rate, with the result that the real wage, and hence employment, will not be affected.

Crucial to neoclassical monetary theory is the belief that adjustments in the money market are made primarily through changes in the general level of prices. If prices can be changed in relation to money wages, the real wage and the level of employment can be changed. With both the capital stock and the level of technology given, the determination of employment also fixes the level of output produced, and the product market then allocates these goods and services to other demanders. If prices cannot be changed in relation to money wages, then the monetary authorities must take great care not to introduce instability into the economy by causing what is essentially unnecessary inflation or deflation.

In the depression of the 1930s, one of Britain's most famous monetary economists, John Maynard Keynes, became dissatisfied with this approach to macroeconomic problems (*see* "John Maynard Keynes (1883–1946)," page 377). Believing that the failure of authorities to cope with the depression was a direct result of the use of the economic theory constructed by the classical economists,[1] he set out to revolutionize economic thinking. He presented his case to his fellow economists in a path-breaking book, entitled *The General Theory of Employment, Interest and Money.*[2]

In this book, Keynes reversed what he perceived to be the basic cause-and-effect relationship of macroeconomics. He characterized classical thought by the now famous phrase, "supply creates its own demand," believing that classical theory showed no concern for the aggregate demand for output, only concern for the output that would be produced by the market-determined levels of labor and capital employed.[3] This classical (and neoclassical) view is characterized in Figure 15.1, where the relationship between employment and aggregate output is such that the level of output can be determined only once the level of employment is known. This interpretation differed from Keynes's analysis of the way producers of output (and employers of labor) actually would operate. Keynes based his analysis on the entrepreneurial decision to produce an output. The key to Keynes's theory rests with the notion that entrepreneurs will produce output only if they expect a demand for that output. Given the demand, producers will decide to hire workers so as to maximize profit while producing the output that is demanded. This can be seen in Figure 15.2, where the Keynesian relationship between employment and aggregate output shows that the level of employment is determined once the level of output is known.

When an economy shows instability in the level of output and employment, it results from instability in the level of aggregate demand, according

---

[1] The neoclassical system presented here is an updated version of the classical system referred to by Keynes.

[2] Keynes, John Maynard, *The General Theory of Employment, Interest and Money,* (London: Macmillan, 1936).

[3] Keynes identified this phrase with "the law of markets" of the classical French economist Jean Baptiste Say, although apparently neither Say nor any of his pre-Keynesian followers used it to express their arguments.

*Figure 15.1*
**The Classical and Neoclassical View (The Output Is Produced Because the Labor Is Employed)**

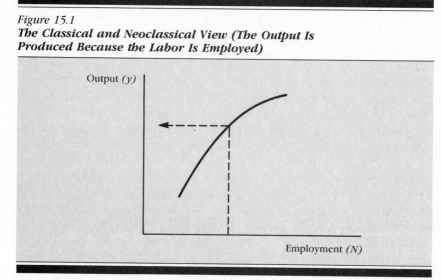

*Figure 15.2*
**The Keynesian View (Labor Is Employed Because the Output Is Demanded)**

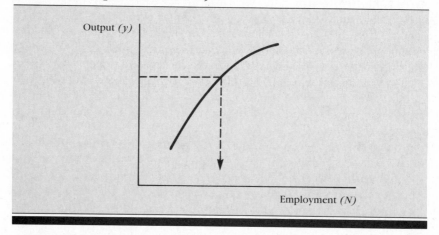

to the Keynesian view. Also, if economic policy is to be effective in reducing unemployment, it must be aimed at increasing aggregate demand. To reduce unemployment, neoclassical economic policy is aimed at the pricing of inputs in the factor markets; Keynesian economic policy is aimed at the level of aggregate demand.

If classical and neoclassical economic thought is characterized by the phrase "supply creates its own demand," Keynes's thought might be typified by "demand calls forth its own supply." If the economy is depressed—that is, it is producing less than the fully employed economy can produce—the

## JOHN MAYNARD KEYNES (1883–1946)

*Source: Bettman Archive*

John Maynard Keynes, after whom *Keynesian economics* is named, was the son of another eminent British economist, John Neville Keynes. He had an upper-class upbringing, attending both Eton and Cambridge University. After initially studying mathematics and philosophy, he was persuaded by Britain's leading economist, Alfred Marshall, to take up the study of economics. On graduation he entered the India Office as a civil servant, remaining there for three years before returning to Cambridge as a Fellow of King's College—a post he held until his death.

As a Fellow of King's College, Keynes was at the center of academic life, but he also was involved with literature, the arts, and public life at the national and international levels. He was a member of the famous literary and artistic elite known as the Bloomsbury set, numbering Lytton Strachey and Leonard and Virginia Woolf among his closest friends. He married Russian ballerina Lydia Lopokova. He financed and built the Cambridge Arts Theatre.

Keynes entered public affairs as a member of the Royal Commission on Indian Finance and Currency in 1913. His work on this commission so impressed members of the Treasury that at the outbreak of war in 1914 Keynes was called to the Treasury. Suspect in the minds of many because he had registered as a conscientious objector, he nonetheless climbed to prominence in the civil service. At the end of the war, he was the principal representative of the British Treasury at the peace conference in Versailles. Horrified by the severity of the reparations to be visited on the Germans, he resigned his post and wrote *The Economic Consequences of the Peace.* Loved by the Germans and vilified by the French, Keynes had achieved worldwide acclaim. Thereafter, his views were sought on every economic issue both at home and abroad.

*continued*

At the academic level, Keynes's studies focused mainly on money. His first book was about the monetary problems of India. This was followed in 1923 by *The Tract on Monetary Reform.* Although the economics in the book was fairly orthodox, it stunned many of Keynes's old Treasury colleagues by declaring the gold standard a "barbarous relic." After six more years of intensive work, Keynes then published the two-volume *Treatise on Money.* This book presented new ideas on inflation and deflation and clearly stated the problems of national autonomy in the international economy. However, by the time Keynes had finished writing the *Treatise,* his ideas on macroeconomics had changed so much that he decided a revolution in economic thinking was necessary. To this end he wrote his most famous work, *The General Theory of Employment, Interest and Money.* Macroeconomics has never been the same. Even those who disagree with Keynes's conclusions use much of his framework as the basis for their analysis.

As the editors of *The Collected Writings of John Maynard Keynes* have stated:

> No other writer in this century has done more than [John] Maynard Keynes to change the ways in which economics is taught and written. No other economist has done more to change the ways in which nations conduct their economic and financial affairs.[1]

---

[1] *The Collected Writings of John Maynard Keynes* (New York: St. Martins Press, 1971).

Keynesian explanation is that demand for output is inadequate. Full employment can be restored only by an increase in aggregate demand. As demand is increased, producers will respond by increasing their output; as a consequence of this increase, they will hire more workers and unemployment will be reduced.

Wage and price flexibility, which is so prominent in neoclassical economics, holds no such place in the Keynesian system. Even if workers actively bid against each other for jobs by lowering the wage at which they are prepared to work, full employment is not assured. Wage and price flexibility only reduces unemployment if the wage and price adjustments stimulate aggregate demand, and many Keynesians, including Keynes, have been skeptical of this outcome. Keynes stated in *The General Theory* that if lowering wages would increase aggregate demand, then so would an expansionary monetary policy, and the latter would always be preferable to lowering money wages.

In the Keynesian view, production and output are demand-oriented, so the size and composition of aggregate demand are important for what goods and services will be produced. Crucial to Keynesian monetary theory is the belief that investment demand may be manipulated by changing interest rates that are determined in the money market. Changes in the money supply therefore will lead to changes in interest rates and changes in aggregate demand, and these changes will lead to changes in output and employment. Contrary to neoclassical theory, the labor market may be completely dominated by the product and money markets.

Many people are surprised when they first read Keynes's *General Theory* to find that the book does not contain what they consider to be the Keynesian policy prescriptions that are taught in macroeconomics courses. The truth of the matter is that policy prescriptions can only be inferred from what Keynes wrote in this book. This does not mean that what are usually called *Keynesian policies* have nothing to do with what Keynes might have prescribed. The policy measures were developed by Keynes's disciples, particularly Joan Robinson and Abba P. Lerner, but Keynes's own position was well known, because he was a vocal advocate of such policies in the economic debates that took place in the United Kingdom in the 1920s and 1930s. Many Keynesian policies can be found in pamphlets that Keynes wrote in support of Lloyd George and his Liberal Party's unsuccessful political campaign of 1929.

*The General Theory* introduces the idea of an active government fiscal policy; Keynes states that government expenditure on even a useless project could be useful in increasing employment when there is idle capacity in the economy. The kind of fiscal policy included in Keynesian macroeconomics books today was developed in the United States mainly in the fiscal policy seminars conducted at Harvard by Professor Alvin Hansen. Keynes's views on monetary policy were not stated strongly in *The General Theory*. He was somewhat skeptical of the success of what he called "merely monetary policy," but he was not opposed to its use. Keynes advocated the use of low interest rates as a stimulus to the economy and suggested that open market operations should be carried out in long-term rather than short-term instruments, so that the impact of the policy might be felt more quickly in the long-term markets.

## MONETARISM AND MONETARY THEORY

Modern policy discussions often are couched not in terms of neoclassical theory versus Keynesian theory, but in terms of *monetarism* versus *Keynesianism* (or, somewhat less charitably, *fiscalism*). However, it would be a mistake to identify monetarism solely with the policy implications of *neo-*

## KARL BRUNNER, A PIONEER OF MONETARISM

Karl Brunner was born in Zurich, Switzerland, in 1916 and attended the University of Zurich. His interest in economic problems convinced him to switch from the study of history to the
study of economics, but he found that the economics that was
being taught was rather unsatisfying. It consisted of a description
of Swiss economic institutions and a history of thought that
barely reached the twentieth century. However, while visiting
the London School of Economics in 1937–1938 he was introduced to modern economic theory and became interested in
Anglo-American economic literature.

After receiving his doctorate from the University of Zurich
in 1943, he joined the economics department of the Swiss National Bank. Much of his free time, however, was spent discussing economic theory in an artists' café in old Zurich. In 1946 he
became a lecturer at the Handels-Hochschule in St. Gallen, but
this position failed to provide the intellectual stimulus he
craved. In 1949, his situation changed significantly when he received a three-year Rockefeller Fellowship to visit the Cowles
Commission at the University of Chicago. As the commission
was housed with the Economics Department, he was in constant
contact with perhaps one of the greatest collections of eco-

*classical theory* and opposition to monetarism with the policy implications
of *Keynesian theory.* The use of *Keynesianism* to mean *nonmonetarism* is
somewhat unfortunate, as, many monetarist conclusions, in fact, can be derived from Keynesian theory.[4] It is not unusual to find economists who
claim to be monetarists explaining their policies entirely in terms of the
Keynesian model. The word *fiscalist,* however, is no better, as it tends to
identify opposition to monetarism with a belief that only fiscal policy is
effective and monetary policy is completely ineffective. This could lead to
the quite erroneous notion that monetarism means merely that monetary
policy can have *some* effect on the economy.

The term *monetarism* was originated by Karl Brunner in 1968.[5] (*see*
"Karl Brunner, A Pioneer of Monetarism," above). It often is narrowly de-

---

[4] *See:* Stein, Jerome L., "A Keynesian Can Be a Monetarist," in *Monetarism,* J. L. Stein, ed. (Amsterdam:
North Holland, 1976).

[5] Brunner, Karl, "The Role of Money and Monetary Policy," *Review* 50 (Federal Reserve Bank of St.
Louis, July 1968): 8–24.

nomic theorists who had ever worked under one roof. His first publication from Chicago—on the relationship between real and nominal variables—is still considered a classic.

In 1951 he joined the faculty of the University of California, Los Angeles, where he made a great impact on the students by using formal logic and mathematics in the classroom and by his emphasis on empirical verification. Also, in his own research, he arrived at the set of hypotheses that would later be termed *monetarism.*

In 1966 he moved to The Ohio State University, where he occupied the chair of Money and Banking for five years. While at Ohio State he continued his teaching and research and also founded the *Journal of Money, Credit, and Banking.* During this period, Brunner made the first of several visits to the University of Konstanz, where he established the famous Konstanz seminars in Monetary Theory and Policy, and he also re-established contacts in Switzerland that eventually led to a position at the University of Bern.

In 1971 Brunner joined the faculty of the Graduate School of Management at the University of Rochester. There he established another journal, *The Journal of Monetary Economics,* and helped found a new series of conferences: The Carnegie-Rochester Public Policy Conferences.

fined as the view that changes in the money supply are the predominant factor in explaining changes in money income, but it has come to mean a great deal more.[6] For example, Brunner has defined monetarism as the acceptance of four propositions:

1.  The money supply is the predominant influence on aggregate money income.

2.  When the money supply is increased, the excess money balances placed in the hands of the public are disposed of through increased expenditure on goods and services as well as on credit instruments.

3.  The private sector of the economy is inherently stable.

---

[6]Mayer, Thomas, *The Structure of Monetarism* (New York: W. W. Norton and Co., 1978): 1.

*Source:* Reprinted by permission: Tribune Company Syndicate, Inc.

". . . First I was a Keynesian . . . next I was a monetarist . . . then I was a supply-sider . . . now I'm a bum . . ."

4.    The allocative details of aggregate demand between sectors are irrelevant for explaining short-run changes in money income.

Several other propositions have been added to this list by non-monetarists. These propositions are not accepted by all those who call themselves monetarists, but they are sufficiently common to be considered monetarist propositions. James Tobin (a leading nonmonetarist) lists these additional propositions:[7]

1.    The quantity of money should be the *target of monetary policy.*

2.    A fixed rule of monetary growth should replace discretionary monetary policy.

3.    There is no short-run trade-off between unemployment and inflation.

One of the most hotly debated issues in monetary theory is whether monetarism is "better" or "worse" than Keynesianism for purposes of mone-

---

[7]*Ibid,* p. 3, where Mayer attributes these propositions to Tobin's discussion in *The New Economics One Decade Older* (Princeton, N.J.: Princeton University Press, 1974).

tary policy. Unfortunately, distinctions between the two often are quite blurred. In addition the debate has been greatly complicated by the tendency of popularizers of various monetary policies to use the terms *monetarist* and *Keynesian* as pejoratives with which to label the opposition.[8] Part II of this book attempts to avoid this kind of name calling by classifying the theory in terms of neoclassical and Keynesian models. However, it will be pointed out that neoclassical theory *does* lead to monetarist policy implications, and Keynesian theory *can* lead to policy implications that may or may not be monetarist.

## Key Terms

**Macroeconomic model**  **Keynesian theory**
**Neoclassical policy**  **Monetarism**
**Keynesian policy**  **Targets of monetary policy**
**Neoclassical theory**

## Questions

1. How can the abstractions included in an economic model explain a real-world economy that is so much more complicated?

2. What is the difference in the cause-and-effect relationship between employment and output in the economy as viewed by the neoclassical and Keynesian economists?

3. What is monetarism, and how does it differ from neoclassical theory?

## Additional Readings

Brunner, Karl. "The Role of Money and Monetary Policy." *Review* 50. Federal Reserve Bank of St. Louis (July 1968).

Keynes, John Maynard. *The General Theory of Employment Interest and Money.* (London: Macmillan, 1936).

Mayer, Thomas. *The Structure of Monetarism.* New York: W. W. Norton & Co., 1978. *A collection of writings that represents the general form of monetarist thinking.*

Stein, Jerome L., ed. *Monetarism* (Amsterdam: North Holland, 1976).

---

[8]Johnson, Harry G., "Comment on Mayer on Monetarism," in Thomas Mayer, *ibid,* 126.

# CHAPTER SIXTEEN

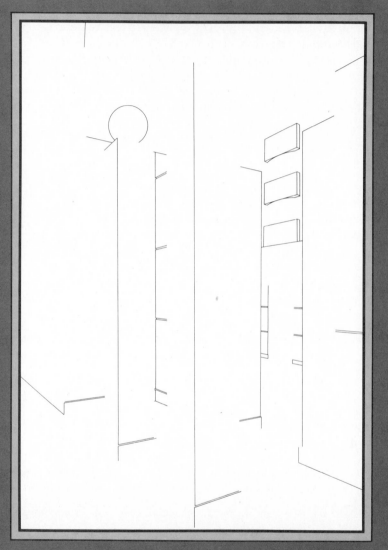

# THE MONEY MARKET IN THE
# NEOCLASSICAL SYSTEM

*The neoclassical system defines the effect of money in terms of the various quantity theories of money. These theories, from the "naive" theory to the modern quantity theory, all show that the money supply has its effect on the economy through impact on the general price level. Any effect on real variables results from the way price level changes impinge on the input markets.*

Money enters the neoclassical system as the primary determinant of the general price level. Thus, the impact of monetary policy on the economy can be found only through a consideration of how changes in the money supply and changes in credit conditions affect the general price level, and how these price changes affect the level of economic activity. This chapter will focus on the ways in which money supply changes can affect the general level of prices. Subsequent chapters will focus on the ways in which the price changes can affect the level of employment and output in the economy.

## THE EQUATION OF EXCHANGE

As was pointed out in Chapter 3, the effects of money supply changes on the economy can be summarized by using Irving Fisher's *equation of exchange,*

$$MV = Py,$$

where $M$ = the quantity of money in circulation (by whatever definition), $V$ = the velocity of circulation (the number of times that the money supply would have to be spent in a given period to purchase the real amount of output produced in that period), $P$ = the general price level (a price index that expresses the average price level), and $y$ = the real amount of output produced in the given time period. However, it always must be remembered that the equation itself is a truism, merely equating two definitions of the aggregate level of expenditure in the economy over some time period. The left-hand side of the equation expresses expenditure in terms of the money that is spent; the right-hand side expresses expenditure in terms of the value of the goods and services that are produced. Using real gross national product as the measure of the level of output, $P \cdot y$ represents the market value of the gross national product at current market prices. As the velocity of circulation is the number of times that the money supply would have to be spent to purchase the market value of the gross national product, $V$ is defined as $(P \cdot y)/M$. Thus

$$M \cdot \frac{P \cdot y}{M} = P \cdot y,$$

which is obviously true. Theories can be derived from the equation only when assumptions are made about the behavior of some of the variables in the equation. Given these assumptions, the equation could be used to indicate the implications of changes in the money supply.

## THE CAMBRIDGE EQUATION

An alternative version of Fisher's equation of exchange has proved to be much more useful for monetary analysis. This is known as the *Cambridge equation,* as it was first used at Cambridge University in England.[1] In the Cambridge equation, the demand for money ($M^d$) is expressed as a proportion of the money value of gross national product,

$$M^d = kPy,$$

where $M^d$ = the demand for money (in nominal terms), $P$ = the price level, $y$ = the level of real output, and $k$ (sometimes referred to as *Cambridge k*) = the proportion of the money value of the gross national product that people in the economy wish to *hold* in the form of money.

Although there is little difference in these equations algebraically, they do differ in concept. The Cambridge version allows us to view the holding of money as a market phenomenon and allows us to talk about the *money market.*[2] Equilibrium exists in the money market when the demand for

---

[1] Various versions of the equation were used by Alfred Marshall, Arthur Cecil Pigou, Dennis Robertson, and John Maynard Keynes, the chief monetary economists at Cambridge before 1930.

[2] We refer here to the money market, where there is a supply of money and a demand for money. Care should be taken to avoid confusing this concept with the common practice of referring to the markets for short-term securities as "the money market."

money is equal to the supply of money (M), that is, when

$$M^d = M.$$

Thus, in equilibrium, we have

$$M = kPy,$$

where $M$ = the money supply and $(kPy)$ = the demand for money.

## The Demand for Money

The *demand for money* is the desire, given the current market circumstances, for people to *hold* money as a store of value before spending it on goods and services. When people receive their income, they have a choice of holding all the money until it is spent or investing the money where it can earn interest and "disinvesting" it as it is required to make expenditures on goods and services. The problem faced by the individual is then one of deciding how much wealth to keep invested and how much cash should be held for the purposes of making the purchases. Whenever cash is held, interest is forgone, but whenever cash has to be disinvested, transactions costs are incurred. The problem then becomes one of minimizing these costs. Individuals will decide on their money balances (and hence the number of times they will disinvest) by minimizing the costs.

For example, if a person is to spend $5000 at a constant rate over a given period, and it costs $10 to disinvest money while the interest rate is 10 percent, then the cheapest way to carry out the transactions is to make five disinvestments of $1000.[3] That way, the person will hold $500 on average throughout the period (*see* Figure 16.1). Other things remaining the same, if the interest rate increases to 40 percent, the cheapest system would be to disinvest $500 ten times throughout the period and thus hold an average of $250.

Assuming that expenditure is positively related to money income, the Cambridge economists were able to conclude that the individual's demand for money was positively related to money income, and aggregating for the whole economy, they expressed the aggregate demand as $kPy$. The Cambridge equation, however, opens up the way for the inclusion of variables other than money income. *Cambridge k* is not assumed to be constant, but to be subject to several market forces. The explanation we have just given of

---

[3] If the total expenditure to be made is $T$, the rate of interest is $R$, and the cost of a disinvestment is $b$, then the amount of the withdrawal is given by $C$, where

$$C = \sqrt{\frac{2bT}{R}}.$$

This result is found by minimizing the costs $(bT/C + RC/2)$ with respect to $C$. Those unfamiliar with calculus can verify the result by trial and error. *See* Baumol, W., "The Transactions Demand for Cash: An Inventory Theoretic Approach," *Quarterly Journal of Economics* 66 (1953): 545–556.

*Figure 16.1*
**A Changed Expenditure Pattern**

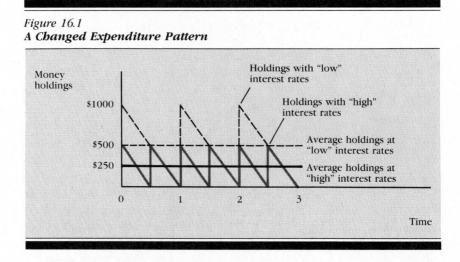

the transactions demand, for example, implies that $k$ is a function of the rate of interest and the cost of disinvesting funds. Because of the algebraic equivalence of the Cambridge equation and Fisher's equation of exchange, we can state that anything that is found to influence $k$ must also affect the velocity of circulation. In effect, anything that increases $k$ decreases $V$, and anything that decreases $k$ increases $V$.

## THE NAIVE QUANTITY THEORY OF MONEY

Any assumption about the behavior of variables in the equation of exchange (or equivalently in the Cambridge equation) will yield a quantity theory of money. If the velocity of circulation is assumed constant (which also means that the Cambridge $k$ has been assumed constant) and the real level of output is assumed constant, we have the *naive quantity theory of money.* The only implication for monetary policy that comes from this theory is that an increase in the supply of money will lead to a proportionate increase in the average price level. That is, if the money supply is increased by 10 percent, the average level of prices will increase 10 percent.

$$M\overline{V} = P\overline{y} \quad \text{and} \quad M = \overline{k}P\overline{y}.$$

Although observations of the relationship between changes in the supply of money and changes in the general price level do not correspond exactly to this implication, sustained rises in the general price level have not been observed without increases in the money supply, and sustained increases in the money supply have not been observed without increases in prices. This was a major conclusion reached by Milton Friedman (*see* p. 398) and Anna J. Schwartz in *A Monetary History of the United States,*

*Figure 16.2*
**Money Stock and Money Income**

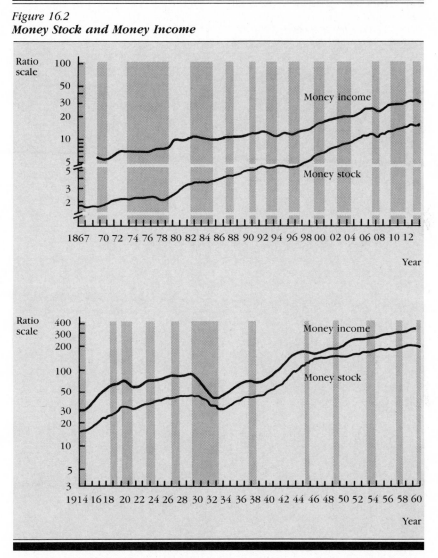

*Source:* Friedman, Milton, and Anna J. Schwartz, *A Monetary History of the United States, 1867–1960* (Princeton, N.J.: Princeton University Press, 1963): 678. (Money stock is currency plus deposits in banks.)

*1867–1967* (Princeton, N.J.: Princeton University Press, 1963). Although a simple statistical relationship says nothing about causality, the relationship between the money supply (defined here as currency plus deposits at commercial banks) and nominal income ($P \cdot y$) is shown in Figure 16.2. The relationship between price changes and money supply changes for recent years is shown in Figure 16.3. This figure shows the basis for the belief that

*Figure 16.3*
**Rate of Change in Prices (Implicit GNP Deflator)
and the Rate of Change in M2**

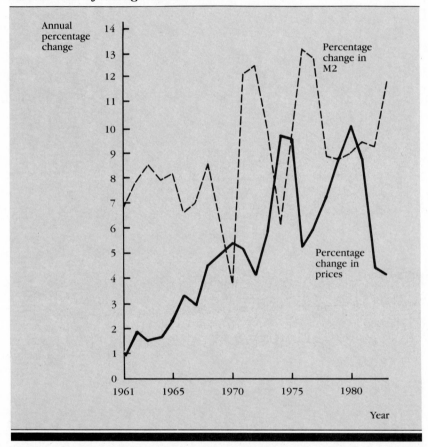

*Source:* Federal Reserve Bank of St. Louis, *Monetary Trends; Annual U.S. Economic Trends,* various issues.

measured price changes lag behind changes in the money supply by two to three years.

Although it certainly would be naive to assume that prices will always change in exactly the same direction and proportion as the money supply, it should not be thought that the assumptions underlying the theory are naive. Calling the theory *naive* is somewhat unfortunate, as those economists who devised the theory certainly were not being naive. They were in no way deluded into thinking that there was always and everywhere a direct relationship between the money supply and the price level. Much of the theorizing that accompanied this equation related to a search for the conditions under which it would be the case that money was "neutral": that changing the money supply only affected prices and did not affect the real variables, $V$ and $y$. The naive theory will hold true under any circumstances where the velocity of circulation and the level of real output do not change as a result of money supply changes. Thus any model that generates these conclusions must contain assumptions about economic behavior that would ensure that $V$ (or $k$) and $y$ remain constant.

As will be explained in Chapter 17, the level of real output in the neoclassical system is determined by the level of capital and labor employed and the level of technology. In the short run, therefore, when capital and technology can be assumed constant, the level of output depends on the level of employment of labor. However, as the level of employment depends on the real wage in the labor market, a constant level of employment requires a constant level of real wages. If there is any change that would cause a change in real wages, there must be some mechanism whereby the real wages must be restored. If the average price level rises relative to money wages, this would cause a fall in the real wage and an increase in employment and output. If the real wage, employment, and output are to remain the same, it is necessary that money wages change to keep pace with the price changes. Once the level of employment of labor is set by the labor market, however, the level of real output in the equation of exchange and the Cambridge equation is constant.

The stability of the *velocity of circulation* (or of Cambridge $k$) depends to a great extent on the definition of the money supply that is being used in the equation. Both $M$ and $V$ (or $k$) incorporate the activities of the financial institutions in the money market. The particular activities of any financial intermediary can be included in either $M$ or $V$ (or $k$) by using a different definition of the money supply. The broader the definition of money, the more activities of financial intermediaries are included in $M$ rather than $V$ (or $k$).

As financial institutions have evolved over the past several decades, the definitions of the money supply have been broadened. In general, neoclassical economists have included these changes in the money supply used in their models and have used a broad definition of the money supply such as M2. As the activities of more of the financial institutions are included in $M$, it is the relatively stable payments activities of the nonfinancial institution public that determines $V$. Over an extended period of time, the velocity of circulation of M2 has remained relatively constant (it has shown a constant trend), while the velocity of circulation of M1 has shown a marked upward trend. This can be seen in Figure 16.4.

Assuming that both the velocity of circulation and the level of real output are constant, the naive quantity theory shows how prices will vary in direct proportion to the money supply. Given that the Federal Reserve has control over the quantity of money in the system through open market operations and reserve requirements changes, the Federal Reserve controls the price level if the naive quantity theory holds.

*Figure 16.4*
**Income Velocity of Money**

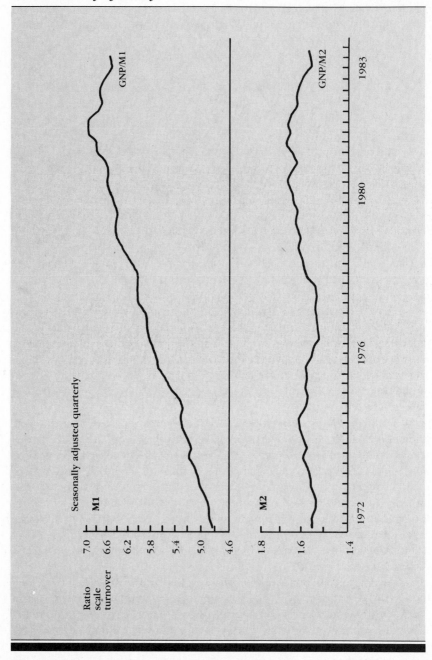

*Source:* Board of Governors, Federal Reserve System, *Federal Reserve Chart Book* (1983): 5.

*Figure 16.5*
**Determination of the Aggregate Price Level According
to the Naive Quantity Theory of Money**

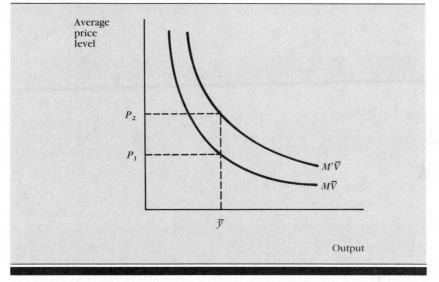

The determination of the price level under the conditions of the naive quantity theory is shown diagrammatically in Figure 16.5. Once the Federal Reserve has set the money supply, a constant velocity of circulation means also that the Federal Reserve has set the level of expenditure in the economy. This level of expenditure is shown on the graph as a rectangular hyperbola. A fixed level of expenditure does not specify either $P$ or $y$; only the product of the two, $Py$, must remain constant. If this constant product is drawn on a graph with prices and real output on each of the axes, the line traced out is a rectangular hyperbola. If the level of output is fixed by activities in the labor market, the price level is fixed by the positioning of the rectangular hyperbola. If the Federal Reserve moves the rectangular hyperbola from $M\bar{V}$ to $M'\bar{V}$ by increasing the money supply from $M$ to $M'$, the general price level will rise from $P_1$ to $P_2$.

The same result, but with a more market-oriented explanation, can be achieved using the Cambridge equation. If the level of output, $y$, and the Cambridge $k$ are both constant, only the general price level remains as a direct means of adjustment in the money market. Changes in the supply of money put direct pressure on nominal prices to adjust, and these changes will alter the demand for money until the demand for money is equal to the amount of money available. If there is an increase in the money supply with other things remaining the same, individuals will discover that they have more money than they wish to hold. This excess supply of money will be removed as individuals attempt to exchange the additional nominal money balances for goods and services. However, since the amount of goods and services available is determined by conditions in the labor market, the response will be an increase in the average price of those goods and services. As the general price level of goods and services rises, the demand for nominal money balances will rise, and this will continue until the nominal demand for money is equal to the nominal money supply. In terms of the Cambridge equation,

$$M = \overline{k}P\overline{y}.$$

Using the Cambridge equation, the adjustment mechanism in the money market can be seen to be no different from the adjustment mechanism in the market for any other good. If there is an increase in the supply of beef, for example, with all other things remaining the same, the price of beef is bid down. Similarly, if there is an increase in the supply of money, the *price of money* is bid down.

Care should be taken to understand the relationship between the price of money and the general price level. The price of money is the inverse of the general price level (the price of money is $1/P$). Whereas the general price level is an index showing the number of units of money required to purchase an average commodity bundle, the price of money is the number of average commodity bundles required to purchase a unit of money. For example, if the index of the general price level is two, then two units of money are required to buy one average commodity bundle. In this case, half an average commodity bundle would be required to purchase one unit of money, so the price of money is $\frac{1}{2}$. An increase in the general price level is, therefore, a decrease in the price of money. Or, put simply, an increase in the general price level is a reduction in *the purchasing power of money.* The supply of and demand for nominal money balances is shown in Figure 16.6.

## THE MODERN QUANTITY THEORY OF MONEY

The market-oriented concept of the Cambridge equation has allowed a closer study of the forces of supply and demand in the money market than is possible from a study of Fisher's equation of exchange. Among the neoclassical economists, advocates of the *modern quantity theory of money* have used the Cambridge equation as a starting point for their work. However, as will be apparent in later sections of this book, the Keynesian economists also used this same equation as a starting point for their monetary theory.

Quantity theorists have long realized that many economic factors affect the velocity of circulation. Even though it is true to say that the velocity of M2 has remained relatively constant over long periods of time, it is equally obvious that there have been significant changes in the short run.

*Figure 16.6*
**The Price of Money, Determined by Supply and Demand**

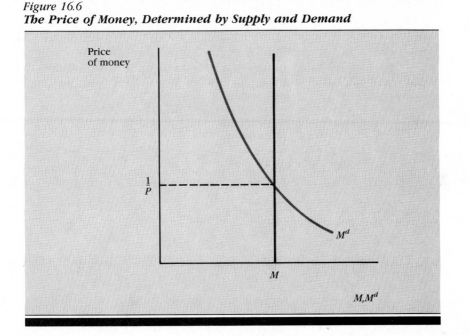

These movements in the velocity of circulation are apparent from the annual rates of change shown in Figure 16.7. The quantity theorists have studied the demand for money (Cambridge $k$), but the factors they have discovered as influencing $k$ also can be stated as the factors affecting $V$.

## The Asset Demand for Money and the Modern Quantity Theory

Modern quantity theorists view the demand for money as part of the demand for wealth.[4] The *asset demand for money* is formulated as a portfolio choice decision between holdings of *real* money balances and holdings of all other assets that can be included in wealth. *Real money balances* are nominal money balances divided by the price level ($M/P$). They are used in this formulation of the demand for money because the decisions are assumed to be made in real terms.

In a simplified form, the various types of wealth holdings can be classified as money, bonds, equities, physical goods, and human capital. *Money* is defined as the asset that has fixed nominal value and that is accepted as a

---

[4] *See:* Friedman, Milton, "The Quantity Theory of Money—A Restatement," in *Studies in the Quantity Theory of Money,* Milton Friedman, ed. (Chicago: University of Chicago Press, 1956): 3–21.

*Figure 16.7*
**Annual Rates of Change in Income Velocities**

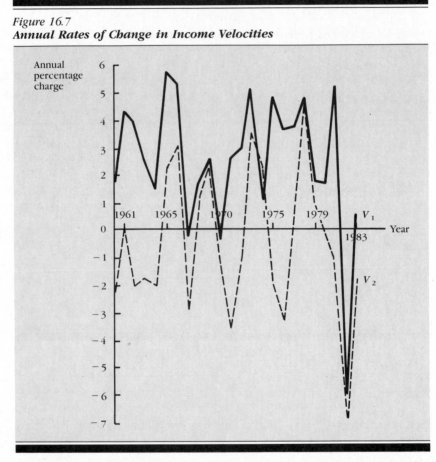

*Source:* Simpson, Thomas D., "The Redefined Monetary Aggregates," *Federal Reserve Bulletin,* February 1980 (for 1961–1979); Calculated from data in Federal Reserve Bank of St. Louis, *Monetary Trends,* February 1984 (for 1980–1983).

means of payment. *Bonds* are interpreted as claims to streams of payment that are fixed in nominal terms. *Equities* are interpreted as claims to shares in the returns to enterprises. *Physical goods* are the physical assets owned by individuals, including owner-occupied houses, automobiles and other consumer durables, land, antiques, and the like. *Human capital* is the result of investment in human beings through education and job training. Of the four nonmoney forms of wealth, human capital is the least liquid. In a modern, nonslave society, the market for human capital is extremely limited.[5]

The incentive to hold real money balances will depend on the *expected* rate of return for money holdings relative to the *expected* rates of

[5]*Ibid,* 5–8.

return to other types of wealth. An individual's total wealth serves as a constraint on the holdings of money balances. The demand for real money balances in the modern quantity theory can be expressed as

$$\left(\frac{M}{\dot{P}}\right)^d = f(r_b, r_e, \dot{P}, h, y),$$

where $r_b$ is the expected rate of return on bonds, $r_e$ is the expected rate of return on equities,[6] $\dot{P}$ is the expected rate of change of prices, $h$ is the ratio of human to nonhuman wealth, and $y$ is expected real income.

## The Expected Rates of Return on Wealth Forms

Because the demand for money depends on relative expected rates of return, it is necessary to understand what the expected rates of return on the various wealth forms are.

**Money.**  The expected rate of return on money results from both explicit interest payments made on some forms of money and from the services provided by money as a medium of exchange. For real balances this return comes from buying real goods and services. When there is an increase in the amount of real goods and services available, as represented by $y$, real money balances will become more useful. Thus an increase in real money balances will increase the demand for real money balances. This can be viewed as a *transactions demand for money.*

An increase in the expected rate of change in the general price level will reduce an individual's desire to hold money. If money is being held and the general price level rises, the purchasing power of those money balances will have declined and money will have yielded a lower rate of return. When average prices are expected to rise, individuals will adjust their portfolios of assets and reduce their holdings of money by shifting into other forms of wealth. An increase in the expected rate of change in the general price level ($\dot{P}$) will reduce the demand for real money balances.

**Bonds.**  Credit instruments compete with money as a form of holding wealth. Bonds, collectively, are the debt instruments not included in the definition of money that is being used. The expected rate of return on bonds comes from the interest payments received and includes any expected capital gains or losses resulting from interest rate changes. Any increase in the expected rate of return on bonds relative to the expected rate of return on

---

[6]The expected rates of return on both bonds and equities are in real terms. However, since the expected rate of change in prices also is included in the formulation, nominal rates of return can be used. The nominal rates can be converted into real rates by adjusting for the expected rate of change in prices.

# MILTON FRIEDMAN

Milton Friedman is a leading proponent of the importance of the money supply for economic activity. Relying on both economic theory and statistical evidence, Friedman has found that changes in the supply of money are the best predictor in the economy of the level of economic activity. From this he has deduced that control of the money supply is crucial for maintaining economic stability. However, because the instruments of monetary policy are so blunt, and the abilities of the policymakers to discern when policy changes are necessary are so questionable, he does not consider that short-run changes in the money supply should be used to "fine-tune" the economy. Instead, the money supply (whatever definition is used) should be changed continually at a constant rate to avoid economic disruptions being caused by the monetary authorities.

Milton Friedman was born of immigrant parents in Brooklyn, New York, in 1912. He received his Ph.D. from Columbia University in 1946. In 1948 he joined the faculty of the University of Chicago and remained there until his retirement in 1977. Since that time Friedman has been a senior research fellow at the Hoover Institution at Stanford University.[1]

At the University of Chicago, Friedman reformulated the old quantity theory of money, tested it, and produced what is considered to be the modern quantity theory of money. Working with Anna J. Schwartz, Friedman produced *A Monetary History of the United States, 1867–1960* (Princeton: Princeton University Press, 1963) in which the blame for the depth of the depression of the 1930s was attributed to the policies of the Federal Reserve.

Probably no other economist in modern times has contributed so much to the discussion of monetary economics. At a time when economists and policymakers had relegated monetary policy to a minor role, Friedman marshaled his forces in the Money and Banking Workshop at the University of Chicago and launched a counteroffensive that led to a neoclassical resurgence in macroeconomic theory and to a restoration of money to a position of preeminence for economic policymaking both at home and abroad.

Friedman's work, however, has not been restricted to monetary economics. For example, he has made important contributions to consumption theory, to the use of permanent income in statistical applications, to unemployment theory, and to the discussions of the inherent stability of a free market economy. In 1976 Friedman was awarded the Nobel Memorial Prize in economics.

Apart from his work in economic theory, Friedman has become a popular and controversial economist through his continuous advocacy of a classical liberal position in public policy discussions. He has argued consistently against government interference in the workings of the free market economy not only in numerous articles and books, but also through a column in *Newsweek* magazine, testimony before congressional committees, television appearances, and the popular best-seller, *Free to Choose* (co-authored with his wife, Rose Friedman, and based on their television series of the same name).

---

[1]An overview of the life and works of leading economists, including Milton Friedman, is contained in *The Academic Scribblers* by William Breit and Roger L. Ransom (Hinsdale, Ill: Dryden Press, 1982).

money would induce a shift out of money holdings and into bonds. Similarly, any increase in the expected rate of return on money relative to the expected rate of return on bonds would induce a shift out of bond holdings and into money.

**Equities.** Equity instruments represent ownership and pro-rata, residual claims to the earnings of an enterprise (any sole proprietorship, partnership, or corporation). The expected rate of return on equities comes from stock dividends and any expected appreciation or depreciation in the value of the enterprise. Any increase in the expected rate of return on equities relative to the expected rate of return on money would induce a shift out of money holdings and into equities.

Both $r_b$ and $r_e$ are included in the formulation of the demand for real money balances to capture any differential impact that might result from changes in the *term structure of interest rates.* The expected rate of return on bonds represents relatively short-term credit instruments, and the expected rate of return on equities captures the longer terms to maturity. To the extent that short- and long-term credit instruments are considered to be close substitutes, their expected rates of return will move in the same direction. As a simplification, the real rate of interest can be substituted for both $r_b$ and $r_e$. A higher rate of interest from assets other than money (a higher $r$) will reduce the demand for real money balances.

**Physical Goods.** The rate of return on physical goods includes not only the return in terms of the utility received by the owner, but the rate at which the value of the goods is changing. Thus, rising prices add to the rate of return of the goods, and falling prices subtract from the rate of return of the goods. As the general level of prices ($P$) is used to measure the value of all goods and services at a point in time, the expected rate of change in prices ($\dot{P}$) can be used to measure the expected rate of return of the physical goods held. Increases in the expected rate of return on goods with other things remaining the same will induce individuals to shift out of money and into goods; that is, the demand for money will fall. Decreases in the expected rate of return on goods with other things remaining the same will induce individuals to shift out of goods and into money; the demand for money will rise. Thus, the demand for money is an inverse function of the expected rate of inflation. As the expected rate of inflation increases, the demand for money falls; as the expected rate of inflation decreases, the demand for money rises.

**The Wealth Constraint.** An individual can acquire additional money holdings by reducing the holdings of some other form of wealth. Thus, an individual's total wealth serves as a constraint on money holdings. However, all nonmoney wealth does not consist of types of wealth that can be substituted easily for money. Markets are readily available where bonds, equities, and physical goods can be exchanged for money balances, but individuals hold some of their wealth in human form, which is relatively illiquid.

Human capital is the result of investment in the human being by way of education, training, or some other form of self-improvement. Developed markets for the sale of such things that are embodied in the human being are not readily available. Certainly, over time, human capital can be used to generate an income stream through the sale of human capital *services* (that is, labor services), but the outright sale of human capital is slavery, and this is prohibited.

In formulating a constraint on the ability to acquire money holdings, the amount of assets held in liquid form (nonhuman form) is very important. As more of an individual's wealth is held in nonliquid, human form, the ability to shift wealth holdings into money is reduced. Thus, the wealth constraint not only is set by the total amount of wealth, but also must include the ratio of human to nonhuman wealth ($h$). If the ratio of human to nonhuman wealth is high, the individual has fewer assets that can be exchanged for money. For that reason, a higher proportion of nonhuman wealth will be held in the form of money. As $h$ rises (other things remaining the same), the demand for money increases.

## THE MODERN QUANTITY THEORY AND CAMBRIDGE $k$

The factors that affect the demand for money in the modern quantity theory can be stated in terms of their impact on Cambridge $k$. If expected real income is represented by the current real income, and we assume that a change in $y$ does not directly affect the other variables in the demand for money relationship, the formulation of the demand for real money balances in the modern quantity theory can be written as

$$\left(\frac{M}{P}\right)^d = g(r, \dot{P}, h) \cdot y,$$

where the real rate of interest ($r$) has replaced the expected rates of return on bonds and equities.

If we also assume that the general price level ($P$) does not directly affect the other variables in the demand for real money balances relationship, both sides of this equation can be multiplied by the price level. This yields a formulation for the demand for nominal money balances ($M^d$).

$$M^d = g(r, \dot{P}, h) \cdot Py$$

It is only necessary to recall that

$$M^d = kPy,$$

to see that

$$k = g(r, \dot{P}, h).$$

As a comparison of the equation of exchange with the Cambridge equation reveals that $k = 1/V$, then

$$M \cdot V(r, \dot{P}, h) = P \cdot y.$$

## Adjustments within the Money Market

The modern quantity theory of money draws attention to the factors that affect the demand for money. Although the theory encompasses all effects that money market conditions have on the economy, greater emphasis is given to the demand for money. The rationale for this approach is that the supply side of the money market had been analyzed much more in the past. The apparent bias of the modern quantity theory to the demand side really redresses the imbalance that had existed before.

If we are to know what effects the monetary authority can have when the money supply is changed, it is necessary to know which factors in the demand for money function are responsive to monetary changes. Simply because the real rate of interest and the ratio of human to nonhuman wealth are factors that affect the demand for money does not mean that either of these variables can be affected by the monetary authority. As will be explained in detail in Chapter 18, the real rate of interest in a neoclassical system is determined by activity in the product market through the interaction of saving and investment. The interest rate effect on the demand for money, therefore, serves as a link between the activities in the product market and the activities in the money market. In addition, the ratio of human to nonhuman wealth ($h$) is not a monetary phenomenon. However, it is still the case that the monetary authority can have an effect on the velocity of circulation and the demand for money through its effect on the expected rate of change of prices.

*Expectations.*  Expectations of changes in the general price level have a significant effect on the money market. When prices are expected to rise at a faster rate, the demand for money will decline and the velocity of circulation will increase. This means that the way in which individuals determine their expectations about future price changes is very important and can have an effect on the impact of monetary policy on the economy.

A relatively simple method of determining expected rates of change in prices is to base the expectations on recent observations of price changes. If prices have recently been rising at a relatively slow rate, it may be reasonable to assume that they will continue to rise at about the same rate. As the rate of change in prices is observed to increase, expectations on price changes will be revised upward.

If price change expectations are simply determined by directly observing price changes, a change in the money supply will not affect the velocity of circulation until *after* the prices actually change. Since it would take some time before the population revised its expectations of price changes, the monetary authority could "fool" the population in the short run and change prices at a rate that was different from what was expected. This could give the monetary authority the ability to induce a short-run change in real variables like unemployment and output. As will be explained in Chapter 17, an unexpected change in prices can affect the real wage, and a decrease in real wages (other factors remaining the same) causes employment and aggregate output to rise.

*Rational Expectations.* A recent development in economics that is relevant here is the theory of *rational expectations.*[7] In this theory, the formulation of expectations is based on all the available, relevant information rather than a simple statistical observation of the recent past. Through observations of the effects of changes on the economy in the past, the public is assumed to be able to formulate some kind of model of how the economy functions. The model, for example, can incorporate a relationship between price changes and monetary policy. If the public has become convinced that increases in the money supply ultimately increase the price level, this information will be incorporated into the determination of expected changes in the price level.

If expected rates of change in prices are arrived at by rational expectations that incorporate a direct relationship between money supply changes and price changes, the short-run impact in the money market of a change in the money supply will be a more rapid adjustment of prices. If the money supply is increased, and it is believed that it will be increased at the same rate in the future, expectations of price rises will be revised immediately and the demand for money will decrease. If the demand for money decreases as the money supply rises, this can mean only that the velocity of circulation rises as the money supply rises. With an increase in both $M$ and $V$, the price level change from a given increase in the money supply will be greater.

## Equilibrium in the Money Market

The equilibrium position in the money market occurs when the demand for money has adjusted to equal the level of money supplied. With a transactions demand for money based on nominal income, and the other factors

---

[7] Rational expectations were first introduced into economics by John F. Muth in 1961, but the subject did not get wide attention until the 1970s. For a general survey, *see:* Kantor, Brian, "Rational Expectations and Economic Thought," *Journal of Economic Literature,* 17 (4, 1979): 1422—1441. For a nonmathematical overview, *see:* McCallum, Bennett T., "The Significance of Rational Expectations Theory," *Challenge* (January–February 1980): 37–43.

*Figure 16.8*
**Determination of the Aggregate Price Level According to the Modern
Quantity Theory of Money, When Output Is Assumed to Be Constant**

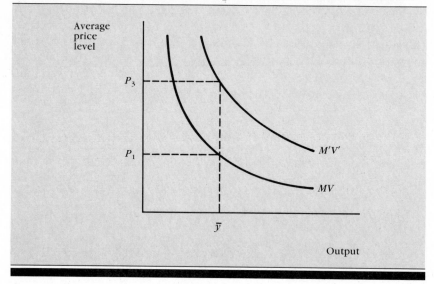

affecting the asset demand for money included in the velocity of circulation,
the equilibrium still can be discussed in terms of the equation of exchange,
$MV = Py$, but we must revise the diagram we used in Figure 16.5, which
showed the equilibrium positions with a constant velocity of circulation.
With a variable velocity of circulation, the change in the equilibrium price
level brought about by an increase in the money supply from $M$ to $M'$ is
shown in Figure 16.8.

An increase in the money supply from $M$ to $M'$ will shift the equilibrium curve to the right as before, but the expected increases in prices will
cause the velocity of circulation to rise from $V$ to $V'$. Thus, assuming the
level of output remains constant (as determined by activities in the labor
market), the increase in the money supply from $M$ to $M'$ will cause prices to
rise from $P_1$ to $P_3$, which is larger than the increase from $P_1$ to $P_2$ shown in
Figure 16.5. In terms of the equation of exchange, we have

$$M\uparrow \cdot V\uparrow = P\uparrow \cdot \bar{y}.$$

## SUMMARY

Activity in the money market consists of the interaction between the supply
of money and the factors that determine the demand for money. Given
enough time, the Federal Reserve can control the supply of money through
open market operations, discount rate policy, and changes in the reserve

requirements on deposits. However, changes in the money supply put pressure on the average price level to change, causing an adjustment to be made in the quantity of money demanded.

The demand for money is the desire to hold money balances. The principal motive for holding money comes from its usefulness in making transactions. The amount of money demanded for transactions purposes is directly related to the level of nominal income (or, what amounts to the same thing, the market value of real output). However, as money also serves as an alternative form of holding wealth, the asset demand for money is related to the real rate of interest, the expected rate of change of prices, and the proportion of human to nonhuman wealth. Increases in the real rate of interest, increases in the expected rate of increase of prices, and decreases in the ratio of human to nonhuman wealth will lead to decreases in the demand for money and increases in the velocity of circulation.

The way in which expectations of price changes are formed also can have a direct impact on the demand for money. If the public have rational expectations, price level changes will be anticipated before they actually occur. This allows the public to adjust their activities to the price changes, and the monetary authorities then could be severely limited in the effects that they might have on the real variables in the economy.

## Key Terms

equation of exchange  
demand for money  
Cambridge *k*  
naive quantity theory of money  
velocity of circulation  
modern quantity theory of money  

transactions demand for money  
asset demand for money  
human capital  
rational expectations  

## Questions

1. "The equation of exchange tells us that an increase in the money supply will increase the general price level." Evaluate.

2. "All that is necessary to change the velocity of circulation is a change in the definition of money." Evaluate.

3. How would an individual's expenditure pattern be altered if prices were expected to rise at a faster rate than they are currently rising? What effect would this have on the demand for money?

4. Why does it make sense to talk about an "excess supply of money" when we all know that everyone wants more money?

5. Explain what happens to the general price level if the money supply is decreased.

## Additional Readings

Baumol, W. "The Transactions Demand for Cash: An Inventory Theoretic Approach." *Quarterly Journal of Economics* 66 (November 1952): 545–556.

*A seminal article formalizing the theory of the transactions demand for money incorporating the impact of forgone interest income as a cost of holding an inventory of money.*

Carlson, Keith M. "The Lag from Money to Prices." *Review* 62. Federal Reserve Bank of St. Louis (October 1980): 3–10.

*A statistical analysis of the changing relationship between monetary growth and price level changes.*

Feige, Edgar L., and Douglas K. Pierce. "The Substitutability of Money and Near-Monies: A Survey of the Time Series Evidence." *Journal of Economic Literature* 15 (June 1977): 439–469.

*A survey of studies on money demand with a concentration on the degree of substitutability between narrow money and liabilities of nonbank financial intermediaries.*

Friedman, Milton, and Anna J. Schwartz. *A Monetary History of the United States 1867–1960. Princeton, N.J.: Princeton University Press, 1963.*

*A comprehensive tour of monetary policy in the United States concentrating on the effects of changes in the supply of money.*

Tobin, James. "Liquidity Preference as Behavior towards Risk." *Review of Economics and Statistics* 25 (February 1958): 58–86.

*A classic in the presentation of risk and the demand for money as part of a general portfolio problem.*

Yeager, Leland B. "Essential Properties of the Medium of Exchange." *Kyklos.* 21 (1968): 45–68.

*A discussion of the properties that distinguish the medium of exchange from other assets; of interest in determining an appropriate definition of money.*

# CHAPTER SEVENTEEN

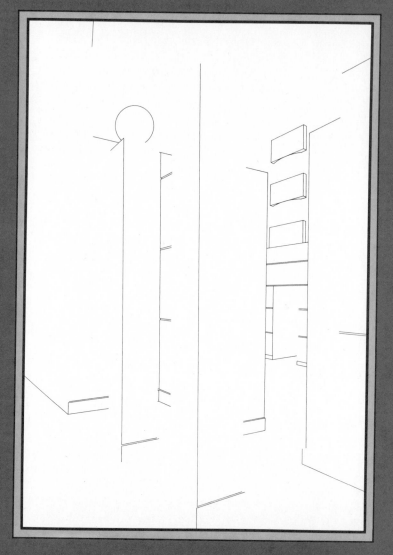

# THE SUPPLY SIDE

*High levels of unemployment ac-
companied by rapidly rising prices
have focused attention on the markets for factors of production. By
inducing price level changes and
corresponding changes in real
wages, the monetary authority may
be able to affect the level of employment and hence the level of
aggregate output. In addition, output may be affected by increases in
the amount of capital employed
and by improvements in technology. Because the effects appear in
the supply of output, this theory is
known as* supply-side economics.

I n the neoclassical system, the determinants of output and employment
are in the markets for the factors of production: the markets for labor,
capital, and technology. As these markets are commonly referred to as
the *supply side* of the economy, the neoclassical system is said to be *supply-
oriented.* As shown in chapters 20 through 22, the Keynesian system is
based on the assumption that output and employment are determined more
by the level of aggregate demand for output, and is therefore *demand-
oriented.* Keynesian economists do not ignore the supply side, but their
emphasis is always on demand.[1] To a neoclassical economist, however, aggregate demand *allocates* the goods and services produced, but it does not
determine the aggregate quantity of output. This fact is the origin of the
neoclassical notion that "supply creates its own demand."

---

[1] *See,* for example, the presidential address to the American Economic Association of the 1980 Nobel
Laureate, Lawrence Klein, "The Supply Side," *American Economic Review*  68 (1, March 1978): 1–7.

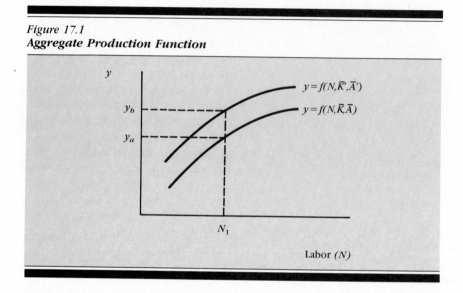

*Figure 17.1*
**Aggregate Production Function**

## THE SUPPLY OF OUTPUT

In the neoclassical system, the aggregate supply of real output depends on the quantities of labor and capital employed and the state of technology.[2] An increase in the utilization of labor ($N$) or capital ($K$), or an improvement in technology ($A$) will result in increases in the supply of real output. The *aggregate production function* is usually written as

$$y = f(N, K, A). \tag{17.1}$$

This relationship for given levels of capital ($\overline{K}$) and technology ($\overline{A}$) is shown in Figure 17.1.

If there is an increase in the capital stock or an improvement in technology, the entire production function will shift upward, as shown in Figure 17.1. Not only would this result in the availability of more newly produced goods and services, but also it could result in a general decrease in prices. If the money supply ($M$) and the velocity of circulation ($V$) remained unchanged, the increased output would be available at a lower price level:

$$MV = P \downarrow y \uparrow.$$

In addition, with more (or perhaps improved) capital and technology with which to work, labor's productivity is likely to increase, and wage rates and employment also could increase.

The *short run* is defined as being a period that is too short to change the capital stock, so a policy aimed at shifting the production function could

---

[2]The effects of aggregate demand in the neoclassical system are described in Chapter 18.

be only a long-run policy. In the short run, the availability of the capital stock and the level of technology remain fairly constant. Both capital and technology are very firm-specific and cannot be shifted readily from one use to another. It is possible for the capital stock to be underutilized, but apart from this variation, the only short-run variable remaining is the level of employment of labor.

When unemployment of labor exists, additional labor is available in the very short run, and the amount of labor utilized in production easily could be changed. In addition, some segment of the population not currently in the labor force could be induced to join the labor force. As of June 1983, only 64.7 percent of the noninstitutional population of the United States 16 years of age or over was currently in the labor force.[3] Thus a short-run policy to change the level of output must have its effect in the factor market for labor, and the design of any short-run policy depends on how the *labor market* is perceived to function.

## THE LABOR MARKET

Employment decisions are made by the individual employer and the individual employee. Each firm decides whether or not it is profitable to increase or decrease the amount of labor that it employs. Each potential employee compares the additional benefits from employment with the additional costs that are incurred.

### A Firm's Labor Demand

A firm's employment decisions are based on the firm's ability to produce an output that can be sold in the market. The output that is produced, however, is determined by the firm's utilization of the factors of production, capital, and labor and of the technology employed. In the short run, we can assume that the level of capital is given and the technology remains the same. Thus, the *production function* for output of the $i^{\text{th}}$ firm may be written as a function of its employment of labor ($N^i$), conditional on its capital stock ($\overline{K}^i$) and its level of technology ($\overline{A}^i$) as

$$y^i = f^i(N^i, \overline{K}^i, \overline{A}^i). \tag{17.2}$$

The form of this production function is given in Figure 17.2. When $N_1^i$ units of labor are employed, the firm will produce $y_1^i$ units of final output. An increase in the employment of labor to $N_2^i$ units will increase the level of final output to $y_2^i$. The production function is assumed to be *well behaved,* in the sense that it starts at zero, initially increases at an increasing rate, and

---

[3] Board of Governors, Federal Reserve System, *Federal Reserve Bulletin* (Washington D.C., Board of Governors, September 1983): A.46.

*Figure 17.2*
**Production Function for a Firm**

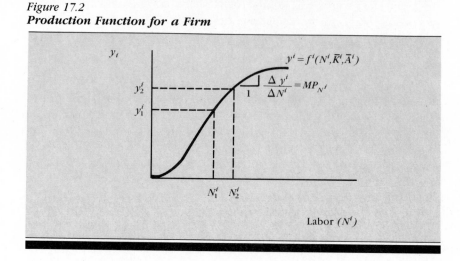

eventually increases at a decreasing rate. This is the *law of diminishing marginal productivity of labor.*

The *marginal product of labor ($MP_N$)* is the additional output that results from the employment of an additional unit of labor holding the inputs of the other factors of production constant. The law of diminishing marginal productivity of labor simply states that, after some point, the additional output produced from an additional unit of labor decreases. The function relating the marginal product of labor to the level of employment is shown in Figure 17.3.

A *firm's demand for labor* indicates the desire of that firm to employ labor. The demand is, however, a derived demand, because the demand for labor derives from the fact that the labor produces output of goods and services. The labor is demanded only if the goods are demanded. As with any economic decision, the decision to hire labor is based on a comparison of the additional benefits expected to be received from the labor with the additional costs of hiring the labor. A firm will wish to hire labor only if the expected additional benefit exceeds the expected additional costs.

The marginal product of a unit of labor is a measure *in real terms* of the additional benefits that a firm receives from hiring that particular unit of labor. On the other hand, the cost to the firm of employing the additional unit of labor is the wage that prevails in the labor market. The payment in money units is the *nominal wage (W)*. In order to compare this cost with the real marginal benefit, it is necessary to reduce the nominal wage to a *real wage.*

The additional cost to the firm of a unit of labor in real terms is given by the amount of output forgone by the firm to acquire that unit of labor.

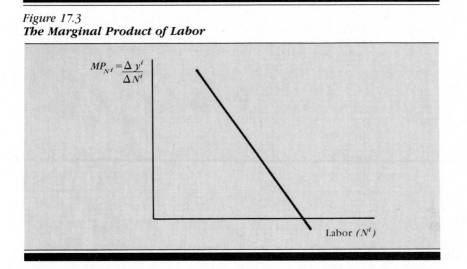

*Figure 17.3*
*The Marginal Product of Labor*

Since the firm knows the price of its output ($P^i$), the firm easily can calculate the real wage that is being paid by that firm ($w^i$). This real wage from the point of view of the firm is given by the nominal wage divided by the price of the firm's output:

$$w^i = \frac{W}{P^i} \qquad (17.3)$$

If the nominal wage is $10 per hour, and the price of the firm's output is $2 per unit, the additional cost to the firm for that unit of labor is five units of output.

Individual firms in the economy are small relative to the size of the market. As such, they do not have control over either the prevailing nominal wage rate or the market price of their output. Firms are thus considered to be *price takers*. With both $W$ and $P^i$ given, the real wage (which is the marginal cost of a unit of labor to the firm) also is given. The firm's decision to employ labor is made by comparing this marginal cost in real terms to the firm's marginal benefit as represented by the marginal product of labor. This can be seen from Table 17.1.

In Table 17.1, the first two columns represent the production function, as they show the output of the firm varying with the level of employment. The third column shows the marginal product of labor, which is the additional output for the employment of the additional units of labor. With the price of the output ($P^i$) determined by the market at $2 (column 4), the value of the marginal product ($VMP^i$) can be calculated. These values are shown in column 5. The money wage ($W$) is established in the labor market at $10 (column 6), and so the real wage from the point of view of the firm,

Table 17.1
A Firm's Employment Decision

| $N^i$ | $y^i$ | $MP^i$ | $P^i$ | $VMP^i$ | $W$ | $\dfrac{W}{P^i}$ | $\dfrac{W}{MP^i}$ |
|---|---|---|---|---|---|---|---|
| — | — | — | — | — | — | — | — |
| — | — | — | — | — | — | — | — |
| 12 | 300 | — | — | — | — | — | — |
| 13 | 310 | 10 | 2 | 20 | 10 | 5 | 1 |
| 14 | 319 | 9 | 2 | 18 | 10 | 5 | $1\frac{1}{9}$ |
| 15 | 327 | 8 | 2 | 16 | 10 | 5 | $1\frac{1}{4}$ |
| 16 | 334 | 7 | 2 | 14 | 10 | 5 | $1\frac{3}{7}$ |
| 17 | 340 | 6 | 2 | 12 | 10 | 5 | $1\frac{2}{3}$ |
| 18 | 345 | 5 | 2 | 10 | 10 | 5 | 2 |
| 19 | 349 | 4 | 2 | 8 | 10 | 5 | $2\frac{1}{2}$ |
| 20 | 352 | 3 | 2 | 6 | 10 | 5 | $3\frac{1}{3}$ |
| 21 | 354 | 2 | 2 | 4 | 10 | 5 | 5 |
| — | — | — | — | — | — | — | — |
| — | — | — | — | — | — | — | — |

$N^i$—number of units of labor employed

$y^i$—level of output produced

$MP^i$—marginal product of labor in real terms

$P^i$—price in dollars per unit of output

$VMP^i$—value of the marginal product to the firm (in dollars)

$W$—nominal wage rate

$\dfrac{W}{P^i}$—real wage, from the firm's point of view

$\dfrac{W}{MP^i}$—marginal wage cost per unit of output

$w^i = W/P^i = 5$, is shown in column 7.[4] The marginal labor cost per unit of output is shown in column 8. This is calculated by dividing the nominal money wage by the marginal product of labor.

The firm will hire workers up to the point where the marginal product of labor is equal to the real wage. At levels of employment less than this, workers will add more to output in real terms than they will cost in real terms. To employ more workers would cost more per unit of labor in real terms than would be added to output in real terms. In our example, when

---

[4]It is necessary to distinguish between the real wage from the point of view of the firm and the real wage from the point of view of the employee. The firm will divide the nominal wage ($W$) by the price of the firm's output ($P^i$) to find the real cost *to the firm*. The employee interested in his or her real wage will divide the nominal wage by the level of prices for the goods purchased with those wages.

*Figure 17.4*
**A Firm's Employment of Labor**

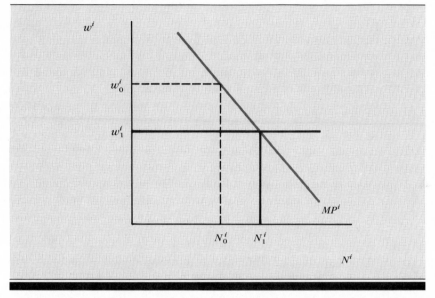

18 workers are hired, the marginal product of labor equals the real wage from the point of view of the firm which equals five. At the same level of employment, it can be seen that the value of the marginal product is equal to the nominal wage, and the price of the output is equal to the marginal labor cost. These are simply alternative ways of stating the same thing: employing 18 workers is the profit-maximizing level of employment.

The firm's demand for labor curve is the marginal product of labor curve with real wages (from the point of view of the firm) on the vertical axis. The demand for labor represents the firm's desire to employ a flow of labor services per period of time (hours per year) and is shown in Figure 17.4. At a real wage of $w_1^i$, it is optimal for the firm to employ $N_1^i$ units of labor. If the firm employed only $N_0^i$ units of labor, the marginal product would be greater than the real wage, and therefore the firm could gain by employing more workers. Similarly, if the firm employed more than $N_1^i$, the cost of the additional workers would be greater than the additions to the firm's output. On the other hand, an increase in the real wage to $w_0^i$ would induce the firm to reduce its workforce to $N_0^i$.

***Increasing Employment within a Firm.***   A firm can be induced to increase its employment of labor either through an increase in labor's pro-ductivity or through a reduction in the cost of labor through a reduction in the real wage paid by the firm. An increase in labor's productivity is reflected through a shift in the marginal product curve of labor. Such a shift would require a shift in the production function. This can happen through a change in the quantity of capital employed, a change in labor skills brought about by labor-training programs, or through changes in technology. Any change that shifts the firm's production function so that the marginal product of labor increases will increase the demand for labor by the firm. As labor becomes more productive, there are additional benefits to the firm from the employment of additional units of labor.

A decrease in the real wage faced by the firm also will induce an increase in the quantity of labor demanded by the firm. Such a reduction in the real wage can be the result of either a reduction in the nominal wage prevailing in the labor market or an increase in the price of the firm's output. If, for example, there is an increase in the demand for a firm's output, the price of the firm's output is likely to be driven up. As a result, the value of the marginal product of labor will rise. The amount paid to a unit of labor in terms of units of output will decline, and the firm will increase its employment.[5] If a nominal wage is $10 per hour, and the price of the firm's output rises from $2 per unit to $5 per unit, the real wage paid in terms of the firm's output will have declined from five to only two units per hour.

The increase in employment within a specific firm, industry, or geographic area that results from an increase in demand for output is a type of response that can be observed in the labor markets. However, this is the impact in a specific segment of the labor market. Even though the labor market is the sum of its parts, an observation of an impact on one segment of the market is not necessarily an indication of the impact on the aggregate market. An increase in demand in one segment of the market could be accompanied by a decrease in demand in another segment.

## The Aggregate Demand for Labor

The *aggregate demand for labor* is determined by adding together the demands for labor of the individual firms. Each firm has a demand for labor that indicates the firm's desire to employ labor at different real wage rates. As the real wage declines, the benefits to the firm from employing the next additional unit of labor will exceed the additional costs in real terms and the firm will desire to employ more labor. The position of each firm's labor demand curve depends on the marginal product of labor that in turn is

---

[5] In addition to this movement along the marginal product of labor curve, there may be a shift in the curve itself. A shift will depend on the firm's success in bidding capital away from other firms. The size of the impact, therefore, will depend on the adaptability of the capital stock. If plant and equipment are highly product specific, for example, there is little possibility for an industry to increase its capital input in the short run.

influenced by the capital stock utilized and the firm's technology. In the short run the utilization of capital and technology can be assumed as given.

At any point in time the aggregate demand for labor is the sum of all demands of individual firms at each real wage rate. This, of course, does not mean that the increase in demand for labor by one industry leads to an increase in the demand for labor in the aggregate. There can be changes in labor demand at the level of the firm or industry that are offset by other changes in the aggregate.

Adding up the demands of individual firms immediately presents a problem because labor is evaluated in terms of the real wage *as perceived by that firm*—which means that the real wage is equal to the nominal wage divided by the price of the particular firm's output. In the aggregate, it is necessary to make an adjustment so that the real wages faced by each firm in each industry is the same. Just as we use the average of all nominal wages as the nominal wage rate, we use a price index to measure the average level of prices. This real wage is

$$w = \frac{W}{P},\tag{17.4}$$

where $W$ is the average nominal wage rate in the labor market and $P$ is an index for the general level of prices. For any set of nominal wages and prices, it is possible to determine the level of demand for labor for each firm and to calculate the average real wage. By adding the amounts of labor demanded at the different average real wages, it is possible to derive the aggregate demand for labor.

Suppose that the economy consists of two firms, $a$ and $b$, whose labor demand curves are shown in Figure 17.5. Assume, further, that Firm $a$ sells its output at \$2 per unit and Firm $b$ sells its output at \$4 per unit and that the two sell identical amounts of output. The average price per unit of output is then \$3 per unit. If now the nominal wage rate is at \$10 per hour, Firm $a$ will employ $N_1^a$ units of labor and Firm $b$ will employ $N_1^b$ units of labor. For the real wage in average units of output of 3.33 (i.e., \$10/\$3), the aggregate amount of labor demanded is $N_1 = N_1^a + N_1^b$. A decline in the nominal wage to \$6 per hour will induce both firms to desire to increase their labor input. With a new real wage of 2 (\$6/\$3), the quantity of labor demanded in the aggregate will have risen to $N_2$ units, where $N_2 = N_2^a + N_2^b$. From a determination of the levels of employment desired by firms at the different real wage rates, the aggregate demand for labor curve shown in Figure 17.5 can be derived.[6]

---

[6]There are some aggregation problems present in the derivation of the aggregate demand for labor. For example, two different sets of prices may yield the same price index yet induce firms in the aggregate to desire different amounts of labor. If the firms are sufficiently similar, these differences will be minimal. Also, after the decline in the nominal wage to \$6 from \$10 per hour, the average price of output would not necessarily remain at \$3. With more employment, there would be additional output, and the price level may decline.

*Figure 17.5*
***Derivation of the Aggregate Demand for Labor***

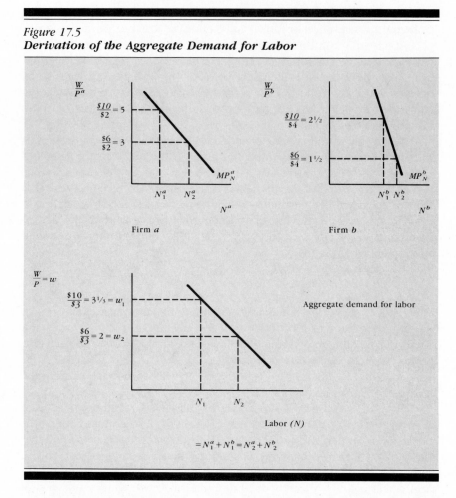

Firm *a*

Firm *b*

Aggregate demand for labor

Labor *(N)*

***Increasing Aggregate Employment.*** The aggregate demand for labor curve shows the amount that all firms taken together are willing to employ at different real wage rates. It is a derived demand: derived from the marginal products of labor in various employments. Any shift in the aggregate function is the net change of the shifts in the various firms' marginal product curves.

The aggregate demand for labor curve is shown in Figure 17.5. It shows the limits of aggregate employment for each real wage rate. Firms demand $N_1$ units of labor when the real wage is $w_1$ and demand $N_2$ units of labor when the real wage is $w_2$. Firms, however, can be induced to increase the aggregate quantity of labor they demand in two ways. First, if the aggregate demand for labor curve shifts to the right through changes in marginal productivities, firms will demand more labor at each real wage rate. Second, if the real wage falls, the aggregate quantity of labor demanded will increase through movements along the demand curve.

Shifts in the aggregate demand for labor curve occur through changes in the marginal productivity of labor. This can be the result of increases in the capital stock, improvements in technology, or improvements in the quality of labor through, say, personnel training programs. When there is an increase in the capital stock, the same amount of labor can produce a greater output. When there is an improvement in technology or an improvement in the quality of labor, the same amount of labor working with the same amount of capital can produce a greater amount of output. However, these changes are not generally short-term adjustments that can be used for short-run policies for increasing employment. Changes in the capital stock, technology, and the quality of labor all take considerable time.

Short-run changes in the level of employment are more likely to come from changes in the real wage rate. As the real wage consists of two components—the average nominal wage and the average price level—changes in the real wage, and hence the level of employment, can be the result of changes in either of the components. An increase in the level of employment can come from a decrease in the nominal wage for a given average price level or from an increase in the average price level for a given nominal wage.

An increase in the demand for one specific good or service will not result necessarily in an increase in the aggregate level of employment. Whether or not employment will rise in the aggregate depends on the impact on the average price level. Employment will rise in the expanding industry as a result of the increase in the price of the output. From the point of view of the expanding industry, there will be a decrease in the real wage of labor *in units of the output of that industry*. However, unless the average price level has risen, there will be offsetting reductions in employment in other industries.

The average price level is not determined simply by the demand for specific goods and services but also by the aggregate level of output, the money supply, and the velocity of circulation. In terms of the equation of exchange

$$P = \frac{MV}{y}.$$

If the money supply and the velocity of circulation do not change, the level of expenditure must remain the same. If, in addition, the level of aggregate output does not change, the price level cannot change. If the output of one industry increases, but this increase is offset by decreases in other industries, any price increase must be offset by a price decrease. If aggregate output increases, while the level of expenditure remains the same, then the average price level must fall.

## The Aggregate Supply of Labor

The *aggregate supply of labor* is the result of individual comparisons of the additional benefits received from employment to the additional costs that are incurred. The decision to supply additional labor is similar to the decisions individuals make in purchasing one good over another. The benefits expected to be received from a good are compared to the benefits forgone by not acquiring the alternative good. Individuals then allocate their budgets over the goods available so as to maximize the expected total benefits from their expenditures. In supplying labor services, individuals compare the benefits expected from the goods that can be acquired from the wage payments to the benefits that could be received from the additional consumption of leisure. Individuals then allocate the time they have available between supplying labor and consuming leisure so as to maximize the expected benefits from the allocation of their time.

The additional benefit from employment is the increased ability to acquire goods and services. The increase in purchasing power from employment is given by the real, rather than the nominal, wage. By dividing the nominal wage received by a price index representing the general price level, the amount of compensation for supplying labor services is measured in terms of real goods and services.

The additional cost to the individual of supplying another unit of labor is primarily the value placed on the forgone good, leisure. As more and more leisure is forgone, it is likely that an individual will place a higher value on the next additional unit of leisure to be forgone. Thus, to induce individuals to forgo additional leisure and, thereby, increase the quantity of labor supplied, the reward offered for additional forgone leisure must increase.

Increases in the real wage will increase the quantity of labor that individuals desire to supply.[7] The aggregate supply of labor is simply the sum of the quantities of labor that individuals desire to supply at each real wage rate. In the neoclassical system, the aggregate supply of labor is shown as a function of the real wage. As shown in Figure 17.6, if the real wage increases from $w_1$ to $w_2$, the quantity of labor supplied in the aggregate will increase from $N_1$ to $N_2$. As the real wage increases, the increase in quantity of labor supplied comes from those already in the labor force offering to supply additional units of labor and from those new entrants to the labor market who are attracted by the higher real wage rate.

### A Keynesian Critique.

A major distinction between neoclassical and Keynesian models of the economy comes in the assumptions concerning the operation of the labor market in the short run. In particular, the models differ in the assumption that the supply of labor depends on the real wage in

---

[7]Although it is true that some individuals may find that as their real wage increases, the increase in their income induces them to consume more leisure and therefore supply less labor, this does not appear to be the case for the economy as a whole.

*Figure 17.6*
**The Aggregate Supply of Labor**

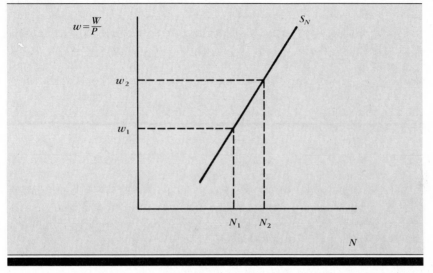

the short run. While it may be reasonable to assume that firms base their demand for labor decisions on the real wage, this may not be appropriate for the decisions of the individuals who supply labor services.

For a firm to know the real wage that it is paying for its labor, all that the firm requires is knowledge of the nominal wage it is paying and the price of its output. However, the real wage from the point of view of the employee depends on the nominal wage rate as well as the prices of the goods and services being purchased. With purchases of a large number of different goods, considerable information is required to determine the magnitude of the effect of price changes on the real wage. Although some information is available from published general price indexes (such as the CPI), this may not reflect accurately the impact of the price changes on the individual employee.

In the short run, the decisions to supply labor will be based on the available information and may be determined on the basis of the nominal wage and nominal wage rate changes rather than the real wage. Where this is the case, workers are said to suffer from *money illusion*. In the long run, employees will become aware of the effect of price changes on their real wage. However, in the short run limited changes in the price level and the resulting changes in the real wage may not induce a change in the quantity of labor supplied. At any given real wage, with different price levels, different quantities of labor may be supplied (corresponding to the different nominal wages), and the aggregate supply of labor will not be a well-defined function of the real wage in the short run.

# EQUILIBRIUM IN THE LABOR MARKET

In the neoclassical system, the level of employment is determined through the interaction of the aggregate supply and demand for labor. The aggregate supply and demand curves show the desired behavior in response to the real wage of both sides of the labor market: the employers and the employees. Through an interaction of these desires, the market conditions in the labor market can adjust until both sides realize their desired behavior and have no further incentives to change. This equilibrium condition occurs when the quantity of labor demanded at the prevailing real wage rate is equal to the quantity of labor supplied at the real wage rate. The aggregate labor market is depicted in Figure 17.7.

Suppose that (in Figure 17.7) the current real wage is $W_1/P_1$, which is above the market-clearing real wage. Employers will desire to employ less labor than is supplied; this excess supply is, of course, unemployment. If some of the unemployed start to offer their labor services at a lower nominal wage than $W_1$ in an attempt to get work, the real wage will be bid down. As the real wage falls, the offers of employment increase and the number of employees offering to work decreases. When the real wage reaches $W^*/P_1$, the desires of both the employers (the demanders) and the employees (the suppliers) are satisfied, and there is full employment.

> Full employment is defined as that state of affairs in the labor mar-
> ket that exists when the number of people who want to work at
> the going real wage rate is equal to the number who are offered jobs.

Similarly, when the real wage is $W_2/P_1$ (which is below the market-clearing real wage), the employers will have the incentive to bid up the real wage to attract more employees into the market. At the real wage $W_2/P_1$, only $N_1$ units of labor offer to work, but from the point of view of the employers the marginal product of the $N_1^{\text{th}}$ unit of labor exceeds its marginal cost in real terms. This will induce employers to offer higher nominal wages in order to eliminate the excess demand. As the real wage is bid up, the excess demand will be removed by both an increase in the number of employees offering to work and a decrease in the quantity demanded by the employers. Eventually the real wage will reach the market-clearing real wage of $W^*/P_1$ with $N^*$ units of labor employed.

# UNEMPLOYMENT IN A NEOCLASSICAL SYSTEM

*Unemployment* exists when those actively seeking employment at the *current market wage* are unable to obtain it. In the long run, pressures in the labor market will eliminate this unemployment. When there is an excess supply of labor, sooner or later some of the unemployed will offer to work for a lower nominal wage or will accept offers for employment at lower nominal wages. This will lower the real wage, increase the quantity of labor

*Figure 17.7*
**The Aggregate Labor Market**

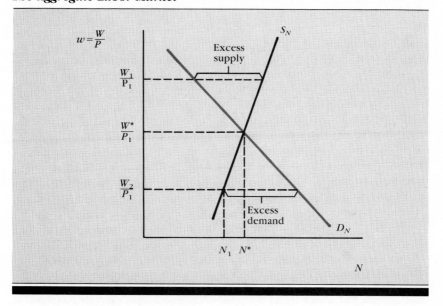

demanded, and reduce the quantity of labor supplied. The real wage will fall until full employment is reached.

However, this is a long-run phenomenon. The downward adjustments in the real wage may not occur as rapidly as economic policymakers desire. In the short run the nominal wage may be rigid in a downward direction. This means that unemployment can exist and indeed persist for extended periods of time in the absence of economic policy changes.

A downward rigid nominal wage will generate a perfectly elastic (flat) segment in the supply of labor at the current market real wage. In the short run workers are unwilling to supply their labor services for a lower nominal wage. Since the price level is determined in the money market, the result is that the real wage does not adjust to the market-clearing price. This unemployment situation is shown in Figure 17.8, where the current market real wage is $W_1/P_1$. In the short run, while the nominal wage is downward rigid at $W_1$, $N_1$ units of labor are employed, and $N_2 - N_1$ units of labor are unemployed.[8]

---

[8]Unemployment, as measured by the United States Bureau of Labor Statistics, is the percentage of the labor force that is not currently employed and is actively seeking employment. It is a stock measure, whereas the measure in this model is a flow. These measures may differ because of continual shifts into or out of the labor market and movements between jobs. The overlaps between durations of unemployment for individuals may alter the stock measure (at a point in time) for the same flow of unemployed hours per period.

*Figure 17.8*
**Unemployment in the Neoclassical System**

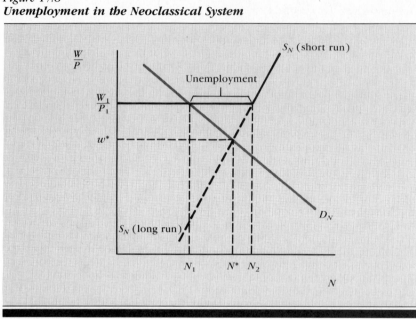

Given time, adjustments in the labor market will lower the real wage to the market-clearing rate, $w^*$, and the level of employment will reach $N^*$. Employment will rise by the amount $N^* - N_1$, but the number of units of labor offering to work will decline by the amount $N_2 - N^*$. The $N_2 - N^*$ will drop out of the labor force, having found higher valued uses of their time. This result, however, can be achieved only if the nominal wage is allowed to fall.

A large number of institutional factors contribute to the lack of downward mobility in the nominal wage. One of the most frequently cited is the existence of minimum wage legislation. With minimum wage laws, firms legally cannot hire workers at a nominal wage below the legislated minimum even if there are workers who are willing to accept the work (*see* "Experience Puerto Rico," p. 425). Labor contracts also contribute to the rigidity of nominal wages. In the absence of a new labor contract, the nominal wage is specified by the old contract, so as long as workers refuse a contract with lower money wages a *rigid nominal wage* exists. Unemployment compensation and other benefit programs also may contribute to the downward rigidity of nominal wages by reducing the incentive to accept a lower wage offer. Unemployment compensation, for example, is related to the old wage, not necessarily to the new market-clearing wage.

## EXPERIENCE PUERTO RICO

Minimum wage laws make up one institutional factor that prohibits the downward mobility of the nominal wage to reduce unemployment. In the United States, federal minimum wages, imposed since passage of the Fair Labor Standards Act of 1938, generally have been kept at about one half the average wage rate in manufacturing. As such, minimum wages probably have had only limited impact in the United States.

In Puerto Rico, however, the legal minimum wage historically has been kept close to the average hourly wage rate. In 1955, for example, in 76 export industries, 44.7 percent of all employees were earning the minimum wage, and 68.5 percent were within five cents of the legal minimum.[1] Moreover, minimum wage rates were set by industry committees for each industry and were adjusted upward frequently, often annually, raising average wages. The high unemployment rate in Puerto Rico, ranging between 13.0 and 16.2 percent in the 1950s, has been attributed in part to the minimum wage rates imposed. An estimated unemployment of 29,000 workers in only manufacturing industries in the mid-1950s resulted from wage increases. This was almost one third of total unemployment in Puerto Rico in 1955.[2]

In the United States the impact of minimum wage laws is primarily in entry-level positions and temporary jobs for individuals who have not yet acquired sufficiently high marginal products. This impact is apparent in teenage unemployment. In 1954 the "real" minimum wage, based on the CPI, in 1967 dollars was only $0.94. By 1978 the minimum wage gradually had been increased in nominal terms from the 1950 level of $0.75 to $2.65. In 1967 dollars this was an increase in the real minimum wage to $1.37. In 1954 the unemployment rate of 16–19-year-olds was only 2.57 times the rate of unemployment for males over 20 years of age. By 1978, with the increase in the real minimum wage, teenage unemployment had risen to over 4.6 times the rate for males over 20.[3]

---

[1] Reynolds, Lloyd G., and Peter Gregory, *Wages, Productivity, and Industrialization in Puerto Rico* (Homewood, Ill.: Richard D. Irwin, Inc., 1965): 54–55.
[2] *Ibid*, 38, 305.
[3] *Economic Report of the President* (Washington, D.C., 1979).

## *Search Behavior*

If the problem of labor market adjustments were only the result of institutional factors, the institutions simply could be altered, and the nominal wage then would adjust as required. However, the persistence of unemployment and the downward rigidity in the nominal wage also is the result of individuals pursuing their own best interests as they search the labor markets for employment opportunities.

When an individual enters the labor market in an attempt to obtain employment, information concerning employment opportunities is obtained through a search of the labor market. Such information is valuable and costly to obtain. It is not necessarily in the best interest of an unemployed person to accept the first job offer. Additional search will yield additional information concerning employment alternatives and may yield a higher wage offer or better working conditions. Individuals will continue to search the labor market as long as the expected additional benefit from anticipated higher wage offers exceeds the costs (primarily from forgone current income) incurred from not accepting a previous offer.

Unemployment is in large part the result of change. Changes in the relative demands for products will cause reductions in the employment in some firms and start a search for employment opportunities in other firms or industries. However, transferring from one job to another is not always easy. The labor services offered by many are to some extent job-specific, and considerable search is necessary to find similar work. Also, the extent of the unemployment is not known immediately by either employers or employees. The loss of a job in one firm only indicates that the demand for one specific type of labor service in one specific firm has declined. This may be related directly to the management of the one firm, or it may be industry-wide. It may be only a temporary decline in the demand for one type of labor service, or it may be a more permanent decline in the aggregate demand for labor. The widespread use of temporary lay-offs (as opposed to outright terminations) is a mechanism whereby firms, having little or no knowledge of the extent of unemployment, maintain contact with an inventory of workers.

A search of the labor market eventually will reveal the extent and nature of unemployment. Until an individual has sufficient information about the changed labor conditions, accepting employment at a lower nominal wage is highly unlikely. If the change that caused the unemployment proves to be related to one firm, or is only temporary in nature, a search probably will yield a job offer at the old nominal wage. If the decline in the demand for a particular labor service proves to be more permanent, new bargains will be struck at lower nominal wages. Only when a search has been made will the wage rate start to decline. There are various employment agencies and government employment services that act to increase the flow of information concerning labor market conditions, but even with

"Look, kid, there's almost never an opening for Master of the Revels."

this kind of assistance it takes time for the information to filter through the market and for the nominal wage to decline to eliminate unemployment. Search behavior does not prohibit the real wage from declining. However, it does make the real wage less flexible downward in the short run.

Because of the amount of searching that is going on in the labor market, the measured rate of unemployment will not fall to zero even if the real wage reaches the "full employment" market-clearing level. At any moment, some workers will be between jobs and searching for better alternatives elsewhere. Those engaged in this activity are the *frictionally unemployed*. Those who search the market, but find that the labor services they offer are no longer demanded because of significant changes in the goods and services demanded, are the *structurally unemployed*. With a very low value placed on their skills by the market, drastic reductions in their real wage or a manpower retraining program would be required to eliminate this kind of unemployment.

## The Natural Rate of Unemployment

The *natural rate of unemployment* is the rate of unemployment that would exist if the rate of inflation were anticipated correctly and individuals adjusted their nominal wage rates to compensate for the anticipated price changes.[9] This is the proportion of the labor force that would be unemployed at the level of full employment that can be sustained by the economy. Through adjustments in wages and prices, the economy tends to adjust to the natural rate of unemployment over time. The number of jobs available equals the amount of unemployment, but movements into and out of jobs, lack of information, search duration, and the problems of matching potential employees to the job skills desired by employers result in some measured unemployment. Estimates of the natural rate of unemployment vary widely but usually have been between 3 and 7 percent.

At the natural rate of unemployment, nominal wages and prices are adjusting at the same rate and the real wage rate remains constant. Altering the level of unemployment from this natural rate is only a short-run phenomenon and depends on movements in the real wage away from the real wage associated with the natural rate of unemployment.

When the monetary authority increases the money supply at a rate greater than the rate of growth of real output, it is to be expected that the average price level will rise. This will have a profound effect on wage bargaining. If average prices rise relative to the nominal wage, the real wage will fall. Although this will increase the quantity of labor demanded, it also will have an acute effect on the standard of living of those already employed. As real wages are eroded, wage bargainers will attempt to change nominal wages to keep pace with changing prices. Whether or not monetary policy can be used to generate movements in the real wage will depend on how individuals formulate their expectations of price level changes and on the ability of individuals to alter their nominal wages to compensate for anticipated price changes.

## EXPECTATIONS: RATIONAL OR ADAPTIVE

Individuals have a strong incentive to predict future economic events accurately. This is especially clear in relation to predicting the future level of prices. An accurate prediction of future price changes would enable the individual to contract for payments that would compensate for any erosion in purchasing power. The expectations of price level changes are important in determining the level of the nominal rate of interest, investment decisions, and the formulation of wage contracts.

How individuals formulate their expectations is important in the design of economic policy. If, for example, a monetary policy is designed to increase employment by increasing the price level and lowering the real wage, the viability of that policy will depend on whether or not individuals

---

[9] The concept of a natural rate of unemployment is from: Friedman, Milton, "The Role of Monetary Policy," *American Economic Review* 58 (March 1968): 1–7.

anticipate the price level increase and can adjust their nominal wage rate to compensate for the expected price level increase.

A relatively simple method of formulating expectations of changes in the price level (or any other variable) is to base the expectation on recent past movements in that variable *(adaptive expectations)*. If prices have remained constant in the past and are now observed to be rising, individuals will adjust their expectations and, perhaps, anticipate that prices will be rising in the future (although probably not as fast as this most recent one-time occurrence). A crucial implication of this method of formulating expectations is that the variable must change *before* individuals will begin to anticipate further changes, and a reduction in the expectations of, say, the rate of increase in the price level would not occur until *after* prices were observed to be rising at a slower rate than previously expected.

As was pointed out in Chapter 16, the theory of *rational expectations* states that individuals formulate their expectations on *all* available and relevant information rather than solely on observed changes in one variable.[10] Under rational expectations, it is assumed that the model of how the economy functions used by individuals to formulate their expectations includes the effects of monetary and fiscal policy. In a sense, rational expectations extend adaptive expectations by including more information. Clearly, the information included in the formulation of expectations depends on the costs of obtaining the information relative to the additional benefits received from the use of that information. When prices remain relatively stable, the formulation of price expectations is not extremely important. However, when prices start to change dramatically, inaccurate expectations or the inability to adjust to expected price level changes can result in significant transfers of wealth. Thus, individuals have an incentive when prices change substantially to seek additional information with which to formulate their expectations.

As a result of observing past changes in, say, prices and the relationships between changes in monetary and fiscal policy to those observed changes, individuals will formulate a view of how macroeconomic policy changes affect future conditions. These models may be relatively simple or very complex. However, policy changes are taken into consideration. Those who more accurately predict the impact of those changes will predict more accurately the changes in prices and can benefit, relative to the rest of the economy, from those predictions. With substantial benefits to be realized, the predictions will tend to become increasingly accurate. The possibility of outside shocks and the nonavailability of some information make it highly unlikely that expectations will be formulated as though people had perfect foresight.

---

[10] *See:* McCallum, Bennett T., "The Significance of Rational Expectations Theory," *Challenge* (January–February 1980): 37–43.

The implication of rational expectations is that expectations will be reformulated sooner than under adaptive expectations based on observations of actual changes in the variable alone. For example, the rate of increase in prices would not necessarily have to decrease before individuals anticipated that prices would be rising at a slower rate. All that would be necessary for the reformulation of expectations is the realization of a change in monetary or fiscal policy that would lead to a reduction in the rate of increase in prices.

Rational formulation of expectations would reduce dramatically the monetary authority's ability to reduce the real wage through policies designed to increase the price level. The change in policy would lead to an immediate change in expectations and individuals would attempt to alter their nominal wages to compensate for the anticipated price rise. The monetary authority's ability to reduce the real wage would then depend on possible inaccuracies in the formulated expectations (which would equally likely be too high as too low) and on the inability of some employees under longer-term contracts to adjust their nominal wages.

## AGGREGATE OUTPUT IN THE NEOCLASSICAL SYSTEM

If we bring together the labor market and the aggregate production function, it is possible to see what the possibilities are for changing output and employment in the short-run through policies aimed at the labor market. Figure 17.9 shows that once the level of employment is known, the level of output is determined. If the nominal wage is downward rigid at $W_1$, and the current real wage is $W_1/P_1$, then the amount of labor employed is $N_1$, and the level of aggregate output is $y_1$. If the monetary authorities are able to increase prices, say to $P_2$, then as the real wage falls to $W_1/P_2$, the level of employment will rise to $N_2$ and the level of output to $y_2$.

Traditionally, neoclassical monetary policy has been discussed in terms of raising average prices relative to the nominal wage. However, with the development of theories that allow money wage bargains to keep pace with average price changes (as in the rational expectations theory), there has been a growing skepticism about such a policy. If, in fact, wage bargains can be made so that real wages do not change, alternative methods of changing the level of employment must be sought. In what has been termed *supply-side economics*, emphasis has been placed on policies to change employment through changes in the capital stock and in the level of technology. The results of such policies are shown in Figure 17.10.

If the real wage remains at $w_1$, either through money wages and prices remaining constant or through money wages and prices both rising at the same rate, increases in employment can be achieved only through shifts to the right in the aggregate demand for labor function. If incentives are given

*Figure 17.9*
**Changing Employment and Output through Price Changes**

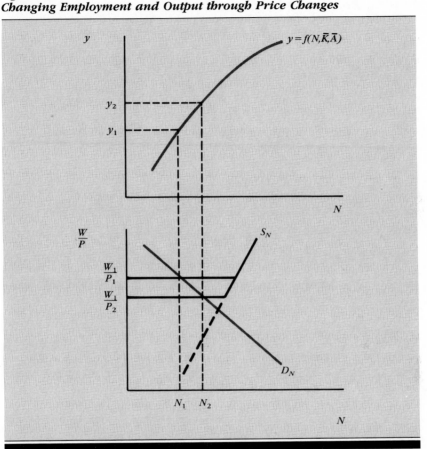

to firms to accumulate more capital or to improve technology, the aggregate production relationship might be moved up. As this happens, the demand for labor by individual firms will increase, and the aggregate demand for labor curve will shift from $D_N$ to $D_N{'}$. Thus, without the real wage being affected, employment will rise from $N_1$ and $N_2$, and output will rise from $y_1$ to $y_2$.

Fiscal policies might also be used to stimulate the supply side and to affect economic growth in real output per capita. Fiscal policy is the use of government expenditure or taxation to affect economic activity. In affecting the supply side through the factor markets, fiscal policy has an advantage in that it can be applied to specific markets. Fiscal policy could be utilized, for example, to stimulate investment demand. By a program of investment tax

*Figure 17.10*
**Changing Employment and Output through Technological and Capital Changes**

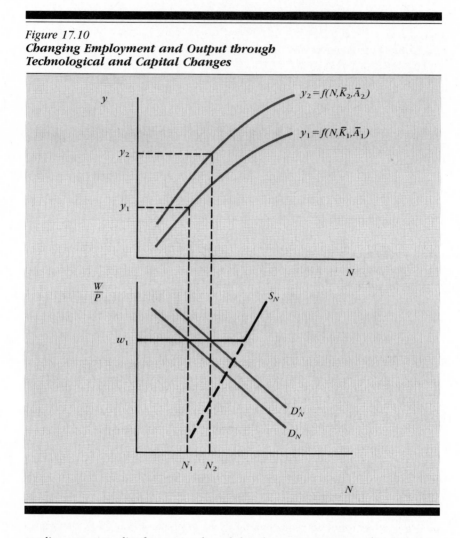

credits or tax credits for research and development programs (both reducing taxes for business firms and undertaking additional investment expenditures), additions to the capital stock or improved technology could be stimulated.

In addition, policies could be designed to improve the quality of the labor force and directly increase labor's productivity. For example, fiscal policy could be used to subsidize job training programs in the private sector. By the government paying part of a worker's wage in a training program, firms could be induced to undertake increased investment in worker training. The training of workers in those skills desired by the private sector would increase labor's productivity and result in increases in wage rates or employment without putting pressure on the general level of prices.

Monetary policy, in general, is not as amenable to affecting specific markets as is fiscal policy. Open market operations, for example, while initially affecting the availability of reserves in New York, have an impact that is rapidly spread through the federal funds market to all financial markets across the country. It is possible, however, through the use of *selective credit controls,* for the monetary authority to channel funds into specific sectors of the economy and therefore stimulate activity on the supply-side markets. For example, by imposing constraints on lending for consumer purchases—such as requiring reserves to be held against each additional dollar lent on credit cards, as occurred in early 1980—the monetary authority could curtail the flow of funds into consumer purchases and, thereby, release funds that could be used for additional business investment expenditures.

Monetary policy can have a general impact on long-term supply-side conditions through the ability of the monetary authority to influence interest rates. By increasing the availability of credit and, perhaps, reducing its cost, the monetary authority could induce increased investment expenditure in plant and equipment.

Perhaps monetary policy's most substantial impact on long-term supply-side conditions comes from its stabilization activities. Investment decisions, which augment the capital stock and technology, depend on firms' expectations of future events. If the monetary sector is subject to substantial short-run changes, this will likely result in increased uncertainty over the future benefits of an investment plan. If, for example, monetary policy results in price level increases that vary and are difficult to predict, it will become increasingly difficult to determine what nominal rate of interest will compensate for actual price changes. In addition, it will be difficult to predict the prices that will be charged for the goods produced by the investment project and the benefits to the firm of the project. By following a monetary policy designed to stabilize prices and the expectations of price changes, the improved ability to predict future events will likely lead to increased investment, additions to the capital stock, and increased economic growth.

## SUMMARY

The operations of the labor market are central to the workings of the neoclassical system. In this system, the decisions to employ labor services or to supply labor services are determined by the purchasing power of the nominal wage payment; that is, labor demand and labor supply are functions of real wages. While adjustments in either the capital stock or the level of technology can make labor more productive and therefore induce firms to increase their labor input, in the short run such increases can only be brought about by changes in the real wage.

Unemployment above the natural rate of unemployment exists when the real wage is above the long-run, market-clearing real wage. If nominal wages are downward flexible, the nominal wage would fall and the reduction in real wage would reduce the level of unemployment. However, in the short run, nominal wages are extremely "sticky" in the downward direction primarily as the result of the market search behavior. Workers are likely to spend considerable time searching the job market before they are fully aware that the demand for their specific labor services has declined and that they should accept employment at a lower nominal wage. If nominal wages are rigid in the downward direction, real wages can be reduced only by the application of some economic policy by the authorities.

Effective policy prescriptions aimed at the reduction of unemployment in a neoclassical system must be guided toward making some adjustment in the labor market. In the short run, this implies undertaking an activity that will reduce the real wage rate. However, in a world where money wages appear to be quite sensitive to price changes, this might prove difficult. Rational expectations on the part of wage bargaining might even make such policies impossible. In the longer run, supply-side economics suggests that policies aimed at increasing capital or improving technology might be successful.

## Key Terms

supply-side economics
aggregate production function
labor market
marginal product of labor
demand for labor
nominal wage

real wage
aggregate demand for labor
supply of labor
unemployment
rigid nominal wage
rational expectations

## Questions

1. In what way would a change in the capital stock in the neoclassical system affect the aggregate demand for labor and the aggregate level of output?

2. Can unemployment exist in the neoclassical system in the long run?

3. Explain how a change in the average price level will affect a neoclassical system that has some unemployment.

4. If a neoclassical system is at full employment, what is likely to be the result of an increase in the general price level?

**5.** Is full employment the "natural equilibrium position" for the labor market in a neoclassical system?

**6.** Would rational expectations of wage bargainers make monetary policy impossible?

## *Additional Readings*

Brown, Weir M. "Employment vs. Unemployment Data as Macro-policy Guides." *Journal of Post Keynesian Economics* 1 (Summer 1979): 70–82.

*A discussion of employment and unemployment data as measures of economic activity.*

Gramley, Lyle E. "The Role of Supply-Side Economics in Fighting Inflation." *Challenge* (January–February 1981): 14–18.

*A discussion by a member of the Board of Governors of the Federal Reserve on the usefulness and limitations of supply-side tax policies in long-term policies to cool inflation.*

McElhatten, Rose. "Should Discouraged Workers Be Counted in the Labor Force? A Job-Search Approach." *Economic Review.* Federal Reserve Bank of San Francisco (Winter 1980): 7–24.

*A study of the impact of unemployment benefits and real wage rates on the labor market.*

*The Federal Reserve Bank of Minneapolis has become known for its work on rational expectations. Among the articles of general interest are the following:*

Sargent, Thomas J. "Rational Expectations and the Reconstruction of Macroeconomics." *Quarterly Review.* Federal Reserve Bank of Minneapolis (Summer 1980): 15–19.

Willes, Mark H. "The Future of Monetary Policy: The Rational Expectations Perspective." *Quarterly Review.* Federal Reserve Bank of Minneapolis (Summer 1980): 1–7.

# CHAPTER EIGHTEEN

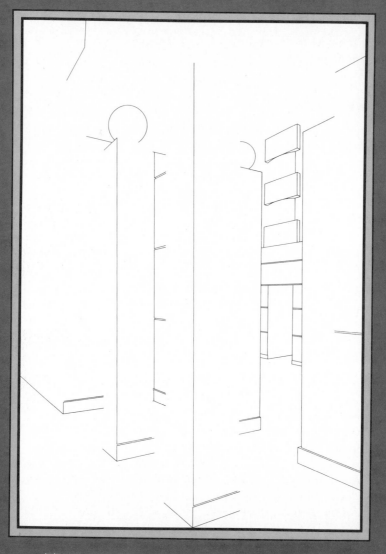

# THE PRODUCT MARKET IN THE
# NEOCLASSICAL SYSTEM

*Although the level of aggregate output is mainly determined on the supply side in the neoclassical system, the demand side of the product market is also important for the allocation of that output between consumer goods and producer goods. An important factor is the natural rate of interest, which is determined by real saving and real investment. Factors affecting real saving and real investment affect greatly the allocation of aggregate output in the economy.*

In the neoclassical view, the aggregate quantity of real goods and services exchanged in the product market is determined by the inputs of capital and labor, not by the level of the aggregate demand for the output. Although the nominal value of the aggregate demand for output can be changed, the demand for output in real terms always adjusts to the amount of real output supplied. It is for this reason that economic policies in a neoclassical system are always aimed at making adjustments on the *supply side* of the product market. Aggregate output can be changed only by inducing individual firms to change their employment through changes in the real cost of labor and capital.

Even though changes in aggregate demand cannot be used to change the aggregate level of output, the demand for output is still important because it can induce important changes in the *composition* of aggregate output. If the demand for specific goods and services is not forthcoming, the prices of those goods and services will fall. As production becomes less profitable, the output of these specific goods and services will be reduced. However, the demand in real terms for any good can only be expanded if the demand in real terms for some other good is reduced.

Some of the most significant changes in the product market occur as a result of changes in the real rate of interest. This rate of interest reflects the relative values of short-lived to long-lived goods and services. As these relative values change, the composition of output will change. In particular, the real rate of interest is important in determining the aggregate level of investment in capital equipment. This investment is important in generating growth in per capita output, and for the continuing ability to produce additional output in the future.

## PRODUCT MARKET EQUILIBRIUM

As with any market, equilibrium in the *product market* occurs when there is no incentive for the buyers or the sellers of goods and services to alter their behavior, given current market conditions. This occurs when the aggregate demand for real output is equal to the amount of real output supplied. In a neoclassical system, although the composition of aggregate demand and aggregate supply may change, it is the aggregate demand that adjusts to the amount of aggregate supply.

In any economy, real aggregate demand ($d = D/P$, where $D =$ the money value of aggregate demand and $P =$ the average price level) for domestically produced output consists of four components: aggregate real consumption ($c = C/P$, where $C =$ the money value of the consumer goods); aggregate real investment ($i = I/P$, where $I =$ the money value of the investment goods); aggregate real government expenditure ($g = G/P$, where $G =$ the money value of government expenditure); and aggregate real *net* exports ($e_x - i_m = (E_x/P - I_m/P)$, where $E_x =$ the money value of the goods exported by this country and $I_m =$ the money value of the goods imported by this country). Aggregate real demand is simply the sum of the four components:

$$d = c + i + g + (e_x - i_m).$$

The aggregate supply of real output ($y = Y/P$, where $Y =$ the nominal value of all final goods and services produced) is determined in the neoclassical system by the inputs of labor and capital. However, since the supplying of this output generates the incomes of all those involved in the production process, aggregate output in real terms is equal to aggregate income in real terms. Thus, the supply of real output can be divided into the three separate uses to which individuals put their real income: real consumption, real taxes ($t = T/P$, where $T =$ the money value of the amount paid in taxes), and real saving ($s = S/P$, where $S =$ the money value of the amount saved).

When individuals have received their real disposable income (the amount of their real income after their real taxes have been paid), they decide whether or not to spend it on real consumption. Whatever part of their real disposable income is not used for consumption is called *real saving.* Real saving is simply forgone current real consumption. In terms of our symbols

$$y - t = c + s$$

or
$$y = c + s + t.$$

The level of supply ($y$) does not change unless the inputs of labor and capital change, but changes in the composition of real income (the proportions of $c$, $s$, and $t$) can occur.

Equilibrium in the product market occurs when the aggregate demand for real output has adjusted to equal aggregate real output. In terms of the components of aggregate demand and aggregate supply, this equilibrium is given by

$$c + i + g + (e_x - i_m) = c + s + t.$$

Since the amount of real consumption appears on both sides of the equation, equilibrium can be expressed as

$$i + g + (e_x - i_m) = s + t.$$

The product market is in equilibrium when the aggregate demand for output for *other than current consumption* equals the amount of real goods and services supplied for *other than current consumption.*

If there was no government and no foreign sector, equilibrium in the product market simply would be where the desired amount of investment is equal to the desired amount of saving, that is,

$$i = s.$$

If the product market is in disequilibrium and (in the absence of government and foreign sectors) desired saving is not equal to desired investment, the amount of saving or the amount of investment, or both, would have to change. In the neoclassical system, this adjustment is made through changes in the real rate of interest.

## Saving

*Saving* is a flow. It must be distinguished from the stock known as savings. Although saving represents the part of the flow of disposable income that is not used for current consumption,

$$s = (y - t) - c,$$

savings are an accumulation of what has been saved. Saving is the act of forgoing current consumption.

For every dollar's worth of real income generated during a period of time, there exists a dollar's worth of goods and services. Thus, the act of saving (the nonuse of the goods in current consumption) supplies the goods or services for purposes other than current consumption. Without saving (and taxation), goods and services for investment, government expenditure, or net exports would not be available.

The supply of goods and services for purposes other than current consumption resulting from saving occurs regardless of the form used by individuals to store the amount saved. The income from producing some good or service usually is received in the form of a monetary payment, but the amount of this income that is saved may be deposited in a savings account, used to buy a bond, or even stuffed in a mattress or an old shoe box. The decision as to how to store this extra wealth is part of the portfolio choice decisions made by the individual in determining the composition of wealth holdings. However, regardless of the form used to store this wealth, the goods produced still exist; and, since they are not being demanded for current consumption purposes, they are being made available as a supply for other purposes. From the point of view of the saver, the choice of different forms of wealth holding simply serves to facilitate the functioning of the financial markets in reallocating current purchasing power and hence reallocating the existing supply of goods and services.

Saving is undertaken to postpone the consumption of goods and services. Those individuals who save are transferring some of their ability to consume from the present into the future. At the same time, they are transferring current goods and services to others who wish to consume immediately. There are two basic economic factors that affect real saving decisions: the level of real income and the real rate of interest.

As an individual's real income and current consumption increase, the marginal benefit from the current consumption of goods and services relative to the marginal benefit from the future consumption of goods and services probably declines. Thus, at a given real rate of interest, real saving most likely will increase with increases in real income. In general, with an increase in real income, a portion of that income is consumed and a portion saved. The *marginal propensity to consume (mpc)* is the change in current consumption per unit change in real income (real disposable income when there are taxes). If a portion of each increment of real income is saved, the marginal propensity to consume lies between zero and one. With a marginal propensity to consume of 0.9, a one-dollar increase in real disposable income will increase real consumption by 90 cents and real saving by 10 cents. The marginal propensity to save is equal to one minus the marginal propensity to consume ($mps = 1 - mpc$).

Even though real income directly affects the amount of real saving, this is not an important factor in the neoclassical system. In the neoclassical system, the rate of real output, and hence real income, is determined by adjustments made in the labor market. Thus, unless there are changes in the labor market, the level of real income will not change in the short run.

Neoclassical theorists consider the real rate of interest to be a much more important variable. The real rate of interest affects real saving by

*Figure 18.1*
**The Real Saving Curve**

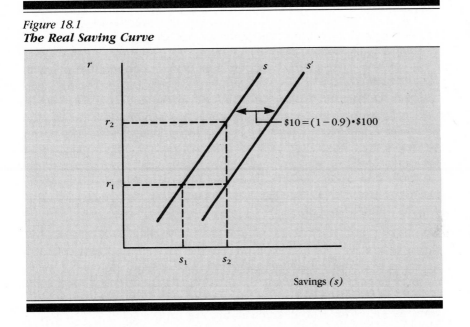

changing the reward in terms of goods and services in the future for forgone current consumption. Thus, an increase in the real rate of interest will induce individuals to forgo more current consumption. This increase in the quantity of real saving is shown on the $s$ curve in Figure 18.1. An increase in the real rate of interest from $r_1$ to $r_2$ will move the economy along the saving curve from real saving of $s_1$ to real saving of $s_2$.

A change in the level of real income would show up as a shift in the saving curve in Figure 18.1. If the marginal propensity to consume is 0.9, an increase in real income of $100 will shift the saving curve to the right by $10. If, at the same time, the real rate of interest remained at $r_1$, real saving would increase by $10 to a position on $s'$. Either the increase in the real rate of interest from $r_1$ to $r_2$ while income remained the same, or the increase in real income of $100 while the real rate of interest remained the same, would increase the real amount of saving by $10. However, in the neoclassical system, only the real rate of interest is an adjustment factor in the aggregate product market.

## Investment

*Investment* also is a flow. It is the flow of additions to the existing capital stock. Real investment ($i$) is the amount of *currently produced* goods and services that is set aside for use in producing goods and services in the future. It comes either in the form of new plant and equipment or in the form of additions to inventory. Care should be taken to distinguish this real investment from financial investments. Even though many people refer to their purchases of common stock in a corporation or even their purchases of credit instruments as investment, this kind of activity does not add to the existing real capital stock.

The way in which the flow of real investment per period varies with the real rate of interest can be determined only in a market setting. It is necessary to consider both the demand and supply sides of the market for real capital goods.[1] In the market for capital goods, moreover, the decision to increase the capital stock at the level of the individual firm is not necessarily an investment from the point of view of the economy. An increase of the capital stock of one firm may simply be a reallocation of the existing stock of plant, equipment, and inventory. Only when the decisions of the individual firm increase the aggregate capital stock can we consider that real investment takes place.

***Rates of Return.***   The *demand for capital goods* is determined by the decisions of the owners and managers of business firms, who will demand capital goods only if they expect the *real* rate of return to the capital goods to exceed the *real* rate of return to the alternatively available financial assets with the same risk. The decision to acquire capital goods is based on a comparison between the internal real rate of return to capital goods and the market real rate of interest. The market real rate of interest is the real rate of return on the alternative financial assets. The *internal real rate of return* to capital goods is the real rate of interest that makes the present value of the net real revenues from the capital goods equal to the current price of the capital goods.

As market real rates of interest rise, some owners and managers of business firms will find the alternative returns in financial markets relatively more attractive, and the demand for capital goods will decline. When the market real rate of interest declines, the real rate of return on capital goods becomes relatively more attractive, and the demand for capital goods will increase.

The internal real rates of return to capital goods depend on the *net* real revenues from the capital goods and on the current price of capital goods. To determine the expected net revenues from a capital good, it is necessary to subtract from the gross expected revenues the amounts that are expected to be paid to the other factors involved in the production. For example, if a machine is purchased, workers no doubt will be required to run the machine, and therefore the net revenues from selling the product can be found only by subtracting the amounts that are expected to be paid

---

[1] For a full explanation of this method of deriving the investment function, *see:* Witte, James G., "The Microfoundations of the Social Investment Function," *The Journal of Political Economy* (1963): 441–456.

to the workers for operating the machine:

| The net revenue, | The gross revenue | The expected |
|---|---|---|
| $V_t$, expected in | = expected in that | − payments to |
| any period $t$ | period | other factors. |

Once these expected nominal revenues ($V_t$) have been predicted, it is then necessary to take the future expected price changes into account to determine the expected net real revenue ($v_t = V_t/P_t$). Each expected net nominal revenue must be divided by the expected level of prices in that period to give the expected net real revenue:

$$v_1 = \frac{V_1}{P_1}, \; v_2 = \frac{V_2}{P_2}, \ldots, v_n = \frac{V_n}{P_n}.$$

Since the internal real rate of return to a capital good depends on the expected net real revenues from the capital good and on the current price of capital, the demand for capital goods will depend on these factors as well as the market real rate of interest. When there is an increase in the expected net real revenues from capital goods, the real rate of interest that makes them equal to the current price of capital goods will be greater. Thus, an increase in the expected net real revenues from capital goods (a condition we shall refer to as *improved expectations*) will increase the internal real rate of return to capital, and the demand for capital goods will increase.

***Effect on Present Value.*** Similarly, if the current price of capital goods increases, the real rate of interest that makes the present value of the expected net real revenues from the capital goods equal to the new higher price of capital goods is a lower real rate of interest. The reduction in the internal real rate of return to capital goods will act to decrease the quantity of capital goods demanded.

If the expected net real benefits from capital goods increase, the present value of the net real revenues stream will increase. These improved expectations will act to increase the demand for capital goods. Similarly, when the market real rates of interest increase, the present value of the expected net real revenues from capital goods will decline.[2] Thus, an increase in the market real rates of interest will reduce the demand for capital goods.

---

[2] The present values obtained by discounting the expected *real* net revenues by the *real* rate of interest are the same as the present values obtained by discounting the expected *nominal* net revenues by the *nominal* rate of interest:

$$\begin{aligned}
\text{P.V.} &= \frac{V_1/P_1}{(1+r)} + \frac{V_2/P_2}{(1+r)^2} + \frac{V_3/P_3}{(1+r)^3} + \cdots + \frac{V_n/P_n}{(1+r)^n} \\
&= \frac{V_1/(1+\dot{P})}{(1+r)} + \frac{V_2/(1+\dot{P})^2}{(1+r)^2} + \frac{V_3/(1+\dot{P})^3}{(1+r)^3} + \cdots + \frac{V_n/(1+\dot{P})^n}{(1+r)^n} \\
&= \frac{V_1}{(1+\dot{P})(1+r)} + \frac{V_2}{(1+\dot{P})^2(1+r)^2} + \frac{V_3}{(1+\dot{P})^3(1+r)^3} + \cdots + \frac{V_n}{(1+\dot{P})^n(1+r)^n} \\
&= \frac{V_1}{(1+R)} + \frac{V_2}{(1+R)^2} + \frac{V_3}{(1+R)^3} + \cdots + \frac{V_n}{(1+R)^n}.
\end{aligned}$$

*Figure 18.2*
**The Demand for Capital Goods**

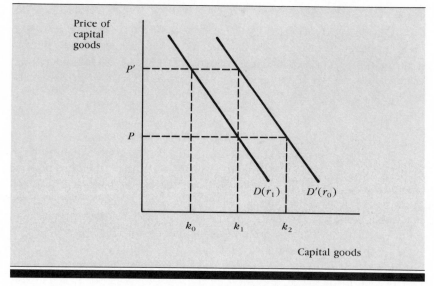

An increase in the current price of capital goods will increase the cost of acquiring the expected net real benefit stream, and the quantity of capital goods demanded will decline.[3] The relationships among the price of capital goods, the market rates of interest, and the demand for capital goods are represented in Figure 18.2.

When the price of capital goods increases from $P$ to $P'$, with a real interest rate of $r_1$, the quantity of capital goods demanded decreases from $k_1$ to $k_0$. A decrease in the market real rate of interest from $r_1$ to $r_0$ will increase the demand for capital goods. This is seen as a shift in the demand for capital goods curve from $D$ to $D'$. If the price of capital goods remains at $P$, the quantity of capital goods demanded will rise from $k_1$ to $k_2$ as a result of the reduction in interest rates.

***Changes in Capital Stock.***   At any time, the capital stock in the economy is fixed. If we assume no change in the quantity of this capital, the shifts in demand for capital goods will lead only to changes in the price of capital goods. If the capital stock remains at $k_1$, the increase in demand for capital

---

[3] It should be noted that our discussion of the demand for capital goods parallels the discussion of the relationship between interest rates and long- and short-lived assets in Chapter 5. Capital goods are long-lived assets. As market rates of interest fall, the benefits from the long-lived assets become relatively more attractive, and the demand for long-lived assets will increase relative to short-lived assets.

*Figure 18.3*
**Supply of Capital Goods per Period**

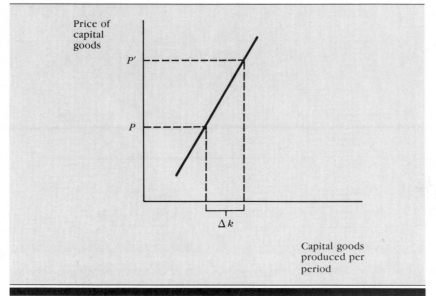

goods caused by the decrease in the market real rate of interest from $r_1$ to $r_0$ simply will cause the price of capital goods to rise to $P'$ from $P$. As a result, the existing capital stock will be reallocated throughout the economy.

However, we cannot assume that the capital stock remains fixed. During even a fairly short period of time, an increase in the selling price of capital goods will induce a response in the *supply of capital goods* produced per period. As the price of capital goods starts to rise, there will be an induced increase in the quantity of capital goods produced during the current period. The short-run supply curve for capital goods (a flow) is represented in Figure 18.3.

A decrease in market real rates of interest will act to increase the demand for capital goods. As the demand for capital goods increases, the price of capital goods will rise. If the price of capital goods increases from $P$ to $P'$, the quantity of capital goods produced this period will increase by an amount equal to $\Delta k$. The quantity of capital goods produced represents the net additions per period that are made to the capital stock.

From the amount that the demand for capital goods increases in response to a decrease in the market real rate of interest, and the short-run supply function of the capital-goods-producing industry, it is possible to derive the investment response to interest rate changes. This is shown in Figure 18.4. If the market real rate of interest falls from $r_1$ to $r_0$, investment demand per period will increase by the amount shown by $i = \Delta k$.

*Figure 18.4*
**The Investment Function**

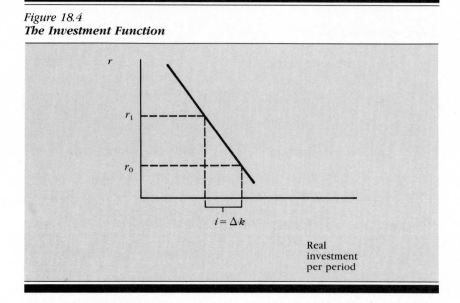

$$i = \Delta k$$

Real
investment
per period

## The Natural Rate of Interest

The *natural rate of interest* is the underlying real rate of interest that equili-brates the product market. This market real rate of interest is determined by the preferences for current, as opposed to future, consumption as repre-sented in the aggregate demand for other than current consumption pur-poses relative to the aggregate supply of current output for other than cur-rent consumption purposes. In the absence of government expenditure ($g$), taxes ($t$), and the foreign sector ($e_x - i_m$), the natural rate of interest is the market real rate of interest that equates real investment demand with real saving.

Both real saving and real investment demand are influenced by the real rate of interest. As was shown above, a higher real interest rate will increase the amount of saving per period and decrease the amount of invest-ment demand per period. These responses are shown in Figure 18.5.

Suppose that the labor market has adjusted to the natural rate of un-employment. At this level of employment, wages and prices will continue to adjust at the same rate and maintain the same real wage with the same level of employment and a corresponding constant level of real output. We will assume that this "full employment" level of output ($y_f$) is $1000.

If the current market real rate of interest is $r_1$ in Figure 18.5, real saving will exceed real investment demand, and aggregate supply will be greater than aggregate demand as shown in Table 18.1. The excess of real saving over real investment demand becomes an *unintended inventory*

*Figure 18.5*
**The Product Market**

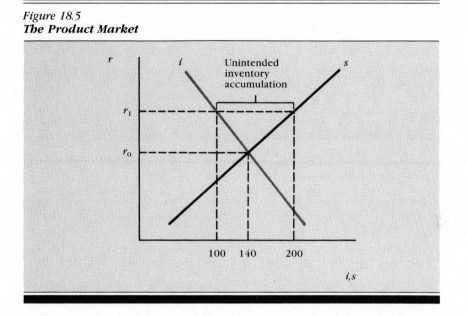

*accumulation.* This is an undesired addition to the existing capital stock that will act to bid down the internal real rate of return to capital and the market real rate of interest. As the real interest rate declines, the flow of investment demanded will increase and the flow of saving will decrease. This will continue, with movements *along* the curves in Figure 18.5, until the product market is in equilibrium at the natural rate of interest $r_0$. As Table 18.1 shows, the deficiency in aggregate demand is removed by an increase in both investment and consumption and a decrease in the flow of saving.

Similarly, if the real interest rate is below the natural rate of interest, investment demand exceeds real saving, and real aggregate demand exceeds real aggregate supply. The excess aggregate supply results in an *unintended inventory decrease,* which is an unintended reduction in the existing capital stock. To replenish inventories, the market real rate of interest is bid up to induce an increase in forgone current consumption until real saving and real investment demand are equal and the market real rate of interest is equal to the natural rate.

The real rate of interest serves as the adjustment variable in the neoclassical product market. Through market forces, set off by unintended inventory accumulations and decreases, the real rate of interest changes until the market is cleared. Such changes induce adjustments in real aggregate demand until it is equal to the level of real aggregate supply that is determined by the operation of the labor market.

*Table 18.1*
**Demand Adjustments in Product Market**

| Before Adjustment (at $r_1$) | | After Adjustment (at $r_0$) | |
|---|---|---|---|
| **Real Demand** | **Real Supply** | **Real Demand** | **Real Supply** |
| $c = 800$ | $c = 800$ | $c = 860$ | $c = 860$ |
| $i = 100$ | $s = 200$ | $i = 140$ | $s = 140$ |
| $d = c + i = 900$ | $y_f = c + s = 1000$ | $d = c + i = 1000$ | $y_f = c + s = 1000$ |

## Changes in Real Income

It must be remembered that not only does the product market affect other parts of the economy, but that it can be affected by other segments of the economy. For example, changes in the labor market will affect the product market. Changes in the level of employment change the level of output, but as this also changes the level of real income, there will be a change in the natural rate of interest as the saving function shifts. If, say, there is an increase in real income of $100, and the marginal propensity to consume is 0.9, the real saving function will shift to the right by $10, as shown in Figure 18.6.

The increase in real aggregate supply causes real saving to exceed real investment demand, and aggregate supply to exceed aggregate demand by $10 at the natural rate of interest of $r_0$. The difference between the increase in aggregate supply of $100 and the resulting excess aggregate supply of $10 is the $90 that real consumption demand is induced to increase as a result of the increase in real income. The excess aggregate supply and the unintended inventory accumulation put pressure on the market real rate of interest, so that a new equilibrium will be reached at the natural rate of $r'$. The fall in the real rate of interest generates real aggregate demand to meet the increased real aggregate supply by decreasing the flow of saving and increasing the demand for real investment.

## FISCAL POLICY

An important aspect of government expenditure and taxation policy is the attempt that is made to stabilize the economy by changing the aggregate amount of government expenditure and taxation. This is known as *fiscal policy*. At the national level, such policy is the joint responsibility of the executive and legislative branches of the government, guided by the Employment Act of 1946 as amended by the Full Employment and Balanced Growth Act of 1978.

Regardless of any notion government might have concerning its ability to stabilize the economy, the neoclassical economists believe that the aggre-

*Figure 18.6*
**The Effect of an Increase in Real Income**

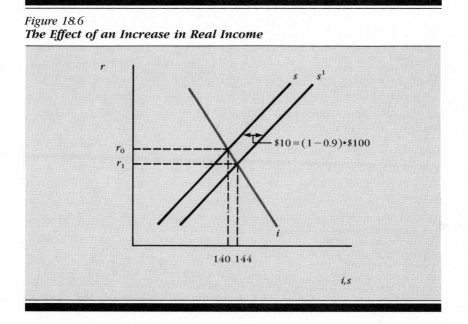

gate effects of fiscal policy are quite limited. This is *not* to say that they believe that government expenditure and taxation will have little effect on the economy, but they believe that the aggregate amounts of government expenditure and taxation can have little effect on the levels of employment and output. In a neoclassical system, fiscal policy has its initial impact on the market real rate of interest, and through such changes it mainly alters the composition of real output.

Although state and local government expenditure and taxation policies usually are not undertaken with a view to changing the aggregate level of economic activity, these policies also must be considered since state and local fiscal policies may augment or offset federal fiscal policy. At the state and local level, government expenditure and taxation appear to be closely related to interest rates and the level of real income. At lower real rates of interest, this expenditure tends to increase similar to private investment demand since the real cost of borrowing to finance the expenditure is lower. Also, taxes are closely related to income and tend to rise as income increases.

To the extent that government expenditure and taxation (at any level) respond to real interest rate and real income changes, they can be considered part of investment and saving in the private sector. However, our concern here is with government expenditure and taxation that is deliberately undertaken to change economic activity rather than those automatic changes that simply respond to the current level of activity.

Fiscal policy *must not* be confused with monetary policy. Monetary policy is undertaken by the Federal Reserve System (the monetary authority) through open market operations, the discount mechanism, and variable reserve requirements. Government expenditure and taxation do not affect money multipliers, nor do they serve as sources or uses of the monetary base. If in the process of financing government expenditure the money supply is changed, this is a monetary act quite separate from the fiscal change and is the result of an active decision on the part of the monetary authority.

***Government Expenditure.***  Real *government expenditure* is a demand for real goods and services. Like private investment, it is a demand for output that is not part of current private consumption. If we ignore taxes and the foreign sector for the time being, it can be said that equilibrium in the product market occurs when

$$i + g = s.$$

That is, real saving serves as the supply of goods and services for use in real private investment and for real government expenditure.

Suppose that the product market is initially in an equilibrium position without government expenditure at the natural rate of interest $r_0$ as shown in Figure 18.7. Aggregate real supply, determined through the labor market,

*Figure 18.7*
***The Product Market with Government Expenditure***

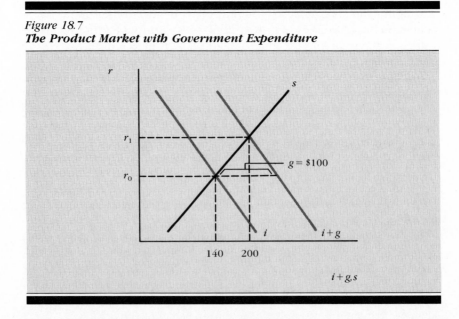

is $1000, and saving equals investment at $140. A real government expenditure of $100 will shift the demand for purposes other than current private consumption to the right and generate an excess demand for real output of $100, as shown in Figure 18.7 and accompanying Table 18.2. This will result in an unintended inventory decrease that will induce a rise in the market real rate of interest to $r_1$.

The increase in the market real rate of interest will induce an increase in the amount of real saving with a corresponding decline in current private consumption. Also, the increase in the real interest rate will induce a decline in the quantity of real investment demanded. The government acquires the $100 of desired goods and services by reducing the amount of goods and services used by the private sector for investment and consumption purposes. This reduction in the private use of goods and services will be divided between reductions in consumption and investment depending on the relative responsiveness of real investment demand and real saving to the market real rate of interest. The example shown in Table 18.2 has $40 of the reduction coming from private investment and $60 from private consumption.

The shift in the use of goods and services from the private to the government sector is a form of *crowding out.* In the absence of changes in the labor market, which would affect the level of aggregate employment and output, no additional output will be forthcoming as a result of the government expenditure. The only change will be a shift in employment from producing goods and services for the private sector to producing for the government sector. While some transitory changes may occur as the economy adjusts the composition of output to satisfy the government demand, without a change in the real wage, additional real output will not be forthcoming in the short run. Whether or not there is a change in the level of aggregate employment and output, or a complete crowding out of the private sector, will depend on the interactions that occur between the money, labor, and product markets.

*Table 18.2*
**Adjustments with Government Expenditure**

| Before Adjustment (at $r_0$) | | After Adjustment (at $r_1$) | |
|---|---|---|---|
| **Real Demand** | **Real Supply** | **Real Demand** | **Real Supply** |
| $c = 860$ | $c = 860$ | $c = 800$ | $c = 800$ |
| $i = 140$ | $s = 140$ | $i = 100$ | $s = 200$ |
| $g = 100$ | | $g = 100$ | |
| $c + i + g = 1100$ | $c + s = 1000$ | $c + i + g = 1000$ | $c + s = 1000$ |

*Figure 18.8*
**The Effect of Taxation on the Product Market**

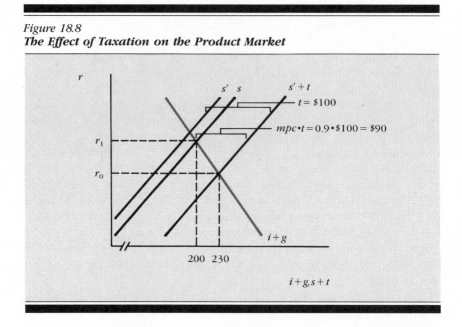

**Taxation.**     Taxes are one means of financing government expenditure. They directly affect the product market by extracting purchasing power away from the private sector. The imposition of taxes reduces disposable income and therefore affects current consumption and current saving in the private sector.[4] By reducing current private consumption, taxation acts to increase the supply of goods and services for purposes other than current consumption, and therefore induces a decline in the market real rate of interest. In the absence of a foreign sector, equilibrium in the product market occurs when the real rate of interest has adjusted so that

$$i + g = s + t.$$

Suppose, for example, that a real tax of $100 is imposed and the marginal propensity to consume out of disposable income is 0.9. Of the $100 in real income that is taxed away, current real consumption is reduced by $90 and real saving is reduced by $10. This decline in real saving is shown by the shift in the saving curve from $s$ to $s'$ in Figure 18.8. As the real amount of the tax also is included as part of the real supply of goods and services for other than current real consumption, the net change in the function is a shift from $s$ to $s' + t$. Accompanying Table 18.3 shows the resulting changes in the composition of output.

---

[4]As government transfer payments (such as welfare and social security payments) are not demands for goods and services, but supplements to private disposable income, they are included as "negative taxes" as far as their impact on the product market is concerned.

### Table 18.3
### Adjustments with Taxation

| Before Adjustment (at $r_1$) | | After Adjustment (at $r_0$) | |
|---|---|---|---|
| **Real Demand** | **Real Supply** | **Real Demand** | **Real Supply** |
| $c = 710$ | $c = 710$ | $c = 770$ | $c = 770$ |
| $i = 100$ | $s = 190$ | $i = 130$ | $s = 130$ |
| $g = 100$ | $t = 100$ | $g = 100$ | $t = 100$ |
| $c + i + g = 910$ | $c + s + t = 1000$ | $c + i + g = 1000$ | $c + s + t = 1000$ |

Taxes increase the supply of goods and services for purposes other than current consumption simply by reducing the amount of current consumption. This results in an excess supply of aggregate output and an unintended accumulation of inventory at the current real rate of interest. Pressure is thus put on the market real rate of interest to decline from $r_1$ to the new natural rate of interest, $r_0$, as shown in Figure 18.8. As the real rate of interest falls, the amount of real saving is reduced and the amount of investment demand is increased. While the actual amounts of the changes in the composition of output will depend on the relative responses of real saving and real investment to changes in the real rate of interest, and on the marginal propensity to consume, the direction of the changes is evident from Table 18.3. Again, without some impact on the real wage in the labor market, taxes will not affect the aggregate level of real output, only the composition of that output.

### A Balanced Budget.
Government expenditure and taxation are not tied together directly. In general, the decisions to spend and to tax are made at different times for different reasons. The federal government can spend without taxing and can impose taxes without increasing spending. Expenditures without taxes are financed by borrowing, and taxes without spending are used to retire some of the existing national debt.

If the federal government decides to finance additional government expenditure with an additional increase in taxes, there will still be an impact in the neoclassical product market. Identical increases in government expenditure and taxation still affect the market real rate of interest because government expenditure affects demand in a different way than the same amount of taxation affects the supply of goods and services for purposes other than current consumption. Government expenditure directly affects the level of aggregate demand, but taxation only indirectly affects the level of the supply of goods and services for purposes other than current consumption through changes in disposable income.

If real government expenditure and real taxation are both increased by $100, the $i + g$ function shifts to the right by the full $100, but the $s + t$

*Table 18.4*
**Impact of Identical Government Expenditures and Taxation**

| Before (at Lower $r$) | | After (at Higher $r$) | |
|---|---|---|---|
| Real Demand | Real Supply | Real Demand | Real Supply |
| $c = 860$ | $c = 860$ | $c = 770$ | $c = 770$ |
| $i = 140$ | $s = 140$ | $i = 130$ | $s = 130$ |
| $g = 0$ | $t = 0$ | $g = 100$ | $t = 100$ |
| $c + i + g = 1000$ | $c + s + t = 1000$ | $c + i + g = 1000$ | $c + s + t = 1000$ |

function only shifts to the right by $100 *minus* the marginal propensity to save multiplied by the $100. Thus, there is a *net* increase in the demand for goods and services for purposes other than current consumption, and the market real rate of interest must rise.

The results of an identical increase in government expenditure and taxes can be seen by comparing the position without a government sector, as shown in Table 18.1, with the final result of both a $100 increase in real government expenditure ($g$) and real taxes ($t$) as shown in Table 18.3. The results are reproduced in Table 18.4.

## THE FOREIGN SECTOR

The foreign sector influences the product market in the neoclassical system through changes in the aggregate demand for *domestic* output for purposes other than current, private consumption of domestic output. The *net* effect of the foreign sector on aggregate demand for current output is the amount of net exports ($e_x - i_m$). An increase in *net real exports* is an increase in aggregate real demand for other than current consumption out of domestic output. This shifts the $i + g + (e_x - i_m)$ curve to the right. The resulting unintended decrease of inventory will induce a rise in the market real rate of interest and a change in the composition of domestic output.

Real exports and imports are influenced by a wide variety of economic factors. For example, changes in the general price level, the rate of exchange in foreign exchange markets, and the market real rate of interest all can cause a change in net exports. To the extent that these effects are significant, monetary and fiscal policies must take them into consideration. Exports and imports do have a substantial effect on the foreign exchange rate of the dollar, and domestic economic policy (particularly monetary policy) has become increasingly concerned with conditions in the foreign exchange market. However, the concern with the foreign sector's impact on aggregate demand and the composition of real output remains relatively small. It is only the level of net exports that affects the level of aggregate demand. This is not surprising, as the foreign sector of the United States is relatively small. General imports for the United States for 1982 was approximately 10.7 percent of nominal output, and the value of *net* exports was $17.4 billion, a little over ½ of 1 percent of nominal output.[5]

## INDIRECT EFFECTS OF FISCAL POLICY ON AGGREGATE OUTPUT

Although the direct effect of fiscal policy in a neoclassical system, at least in the short run, is on the composition of output rather than on the aggregate level of output, there are *indirect* ways in which fiscal policy can affect the level of output. Whenever fiscal policy has an effect on the level of employment of labor or capital, it has an effect on the level of real output. For example, fiscal policy can have an indirect effect on the labor market through its effect on the money market. Because fiscal policy has a great effect on the real rate of interest, it can have an effect on the demand for money (or the velocity of circulation), and this will affect prices. If prices change relative to money wages, there is a change in real wages, employment, and output.

When unemployment above the natural rate of unemployment exists because of rigidities in the nominal wage, expansionary fiscal policy from either an increase in real government expenditure or a reduction in real taxes can cause an increase in employment and output in the short run. An increase in government expenditure increases aggregate demand for goods and services for purposes other than current consumption. The resulting unintended inventory decrease will induce a rise in the market real rate of interest. The higher real rate of interest causes the demand for money as an asset to decline. With a constant money supply, there will be an excess supply of money, and as individuals attempt to remove the excess supply, the velocity of circulation will rise, and the general price level will rise. If the nominal wage remains the same in the face of price increases, the real wage falls, employment rises, and the level of real output increases. These events can be expressed as

$$g\uparrow \;\rightarrow r\uparrow \rightarrow V\uparrow \;\rightarrow P\uparrow \rightarrow \frac{W}{P}\downarrow \;\rightarrow N\uparrow \rightarrow y\uparrow$$

| Product market | Money market | Labor market |

Although the events resulting from the change in government expenditure have been shown as happening sequentially, it should be noted that the adjustments actually take place simultaneously. As a disequilibrium ap-

---

[5] Board of Governors, the Federal Reserve System, *Federal Reserve Bulletin* (Washington, D.C., September 1983).

*Figure 18.9*
***Fiscal Policy and Market Interaction:***
***A Change in Government Expenditure***

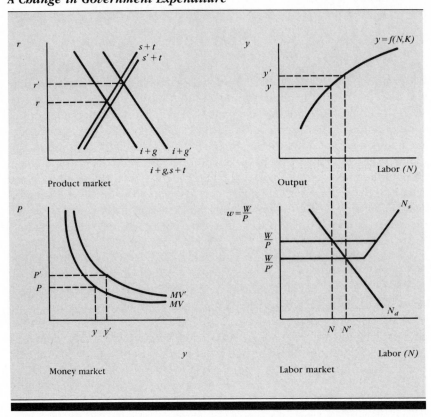

Product market

Output

Money market

Labor market

pears in one market, it will be immediately reflected in one or more other markets. Adjustments toward equilibrium in all markets will take place simultaneously. Some partially offsetting adjustments also will occur between the markets. For example, as real income increases, real saving increases, and this partially offsets some of the initial rise in the market real rate of interest. Also, the increase in output will reduce somewhat the increase in the general price level.

The results of an increase in government expenditure in the markets for labor, money, and output are shown in Figure 18.9. Before the change in government expenditure, the economy is in equilibrium with output equal to $y$, employment equal to $N$, the real rate of interest at $r$, and the price level at $P$. After the fiscal policy, a new equilibrium is reached with output equal to $y'$, employment equal to $N'$, the real rate of interest at $r'$, and the price level at $P'$.

In a neoclassical system, fiscal policy is relegated to a distinctly secondary role relative to monetary policy for influencing economic activity. Although fiscal policy does have an effect on the real market rate of interest, and hence on the composition of output, the link with the level of aggregate output and the level of employment is extremely tenuous. In the short run, only *if* there is unemployment, and *if* the velocity of circulation is significantly affected by the market real rate of interest, and *if* the changes in prices are not offset by changes in nominal wages, can fiscal policy have an impact on the aggregate level of employment. If the neoclassical labor market tends to adjust to the natural rate of unemployment, there can be no significant effect on output in the short run caused by fiscal policy.

## SUMMARY

Activity in the product market is determined by the aggregate supply and aggregate demand for real goods and services. In a neoclassical system, the level of aggregate demand adjusts to the quantity of aggregate supply that has been determined by the level of employment of labor and capital. Within the product market, adjustments in aggregate demand and the composition of aggregate demand are made through changes in the market real rate of interest. Whenever there is a change in the demand for goods and services for purposes other than current consumption, there will be an unintended accumulation or decrease of inventory. This will cause the market rate of interest to adjust. The market real rate of interest that is determined by society's preferences for current, as opposed to future, consumption is called the *natural rate of interest.*

Fiscal policy is the use of government expenditure and taxation to influence economic activity. It has its impact through the product market. In the neoclassical system, an increase in government expenditure generates an excess demand for goods and services for purposes other than current consumption. This will induce a rise in the market real rate of interest. The resulting decrease in both private real investment and private current consumption is known as *crowding out.*

Although the direct effect of fiscal policy in the neoclassical system is on the composition of aggregate output, and not on the level of aggregate output, there are some indirect ways in which fiscal policy can affect aggregate output. In the short run, this can happen through the effects that fiscal policy has on the money and labor markets. Increases in government expenditure can increase the real rate of interest and therefore have an effect on prices through changes in the velocity of circulation. If prices change relative to the nominal wage, there will be an increase in employment and aggregate output. In the long run, fiscal policy also can have an effect through changes in the capital stock. Government expenditure can divert goods and services into capital accumulation, and this can bring about economic growth in both employment and output.

## Key Terms

| | |
|---|---|
| product market | unintended inventory decrease |
| saving | fiscal policy |
| investment | government expenditure |
| marginal propensity to consume | crowding out |
| internal rate of return | taxation |
| natural rate of interest | net exports |
| unintended inventory accumulation | |

## Questions

1. An increase in real income will increase real saving, and an increase in the market real rate of interest will increase the quantity of real saving. Explain.

2. An increase in the expected *net* real benefits from capital goods will increase the internal real rate of return to capital goods, increase the price of capital goods, increase investment demand, and increase the market real rate of interest. Explain.

3. Explain the impact of a decrease in taxes on the composition of output between private investment and private consumption uses.

4. "For fiscal policy to be 'neutral' and to have no impact on the market real rate of interest, an increase in government expenditure must be matched by an even greater increase in taxes." Evaluate.

5. With a downward rigid nominal wage, a decrease in government expenditure will increase unemployment. Explain.

## Additional Readings

Mayer, Thomas. *Permanent Income, Wealth and Consumption.* Berkeley, Calif.: University of California Press, 1972.

*An evaluation of theories of consumption and related empirical evidence.*

Wicksell, Knut. *Interest and Prices (Geldzins und Guterpreise).* Reprints of Economic Classics. New York: Augustus M. Kelley, Bookseller, 1965. Published in German in 1898 and published in English in 1936.

*This book introduced the concept of the natural rate of interest and explained its connection to the nominal rate.*

Witte, James G. "The Microfoundations of the Social Investment Function." *Journal of Political Economy* (1963): 441–456.

*This is a market-oriented approach to the development of the aggregate investment function. It specifically takes into account the supply of and demand for capital goods.*

# CHAPTER NINETEEN

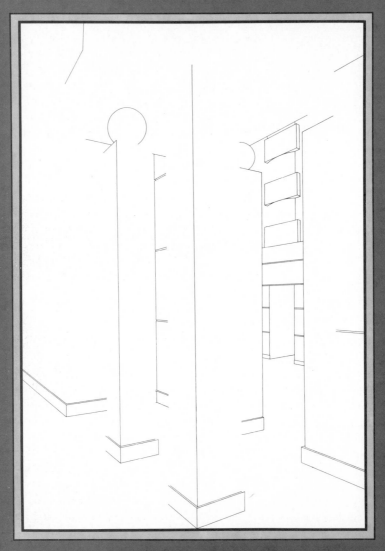

# MONETARY POLICY IN THE
# NEOCLASSICAL SYSTEM

*The monetary authority attempts to influence general economic activity by changing the money supply. In both the long run and the short run, neoclassical economists consider that monetary policy has its effect through price changes. Therefore, in the neoclassical system, the supply of money is the most important determinant of nominal income, and monetary aggregates are considered to be the appropriate targets of monetary policy. However, the difficulties created through changing inflationary expectations have led some economists to advocate a fixed rule of monetary expansion.*

As part of the Full Employment and Balanced Growth Act of 1978 (the Humphrey-Hawkins Act), the monetary authorities, along with other policy-making bodies, are mandated to follow a policy of high levels of employment and "reasonable" price stability. To carry out such a policy, some knowledge of how the economy functions is necessary. One model the authorities can use is the neoclassical model. In this system, monetary policy is carried on primarily by changing the money supply.

It is important to realize that in the neoclassical system the supply of money is considered to be the most important determinant of *nominal* output and *nominal* income, rather than *real* output and *real* income. *Monetary policy* has its impact through the effects that money supply changes have on the general price level. While some impact may be felt in real variables through changes in the real wage and the real rate of interest, the monetary impact is generally limited to changes in nominal variables. Only if the monetary policy is able to change the real wage can the level of employment and the level of output be changed, and only if the real rate of interest is changed can the composition of real output be changed.

Although neoclassical economics always has emphasized the importance of the money supply for nominal output, it is only recently that there has been an increase in the concern for the supply of money as a policy tool.

This is the result of the work of the *monetarists*.[1] Although some monetarists reached their conclusions through the use of theories other than the neoclassical, most of them are, in fact, neoclassical economists. By using models similar to the one explained in the preceding chapters, they have reached the conclusion that *money matters* as the singularly most important driving force behind the level of nominal income. Although it certainly cannot be said that "all monetarists are alike," they share common conclusions concerning the importance of money for nominal variables, the relative unimportance of fiscal policy for changing the level of aggregate output, and the destabilizing influence of much discretionary monetary policy.

## MONETARY POLICY IN AN ECONOMY WHERE WAGE FLEXIBILITY ASSURES FULL EMPLOYMENT

If wages are flexible in the labor market in the neoclassical system, the nominal wage will adjust to price changes in such a way that the real wage will remain stable at the level that generates full employment. This constant level of employment, together with the output relationship, will determine the aggregate level of real output and real income. With a constant level of output and an unchanged set of preferences between current as opposed to future consumption, the flow of saving will be determined. The real rate of interest then will be determined where saving is equal to investment, and the composition of output between consumer and producer goods will be determined. In this kind of situation, monetary policy can have no lasting impact on *real* economic conditions. However, it can have an effect on nominal variables since it will change prices.

If open market operations are carried out to increase the money supply, the public will find themselves holding fewer debt instruments and more money balances than they desire. As some of these excess money balances will be spent on goods and services in an economy where there are no extra goods and services to be had (the economy is already at full employment), the general price level will rise. With a higher price level and an unchanged level of output, nominal income ($Py$) has increased, and there will be a direct relationship between the increase in the money stock and the increase in prices. Although it is possible that there be some transitory effects on the level of real output when the money supply is increased, eventually the original, full-employment output is restored.

### Real Effects of Monetary Policy

As the money supply is increased and prices start to rise, the initial impact on the real wage may be a reduction. However, in a fully employed economy this will generate an excess demand for labor in the labor market and

---

[1] *See* Chapter 15.

*Figure 19.1*
**Money Supply Changes in a Fully Employed Economy**

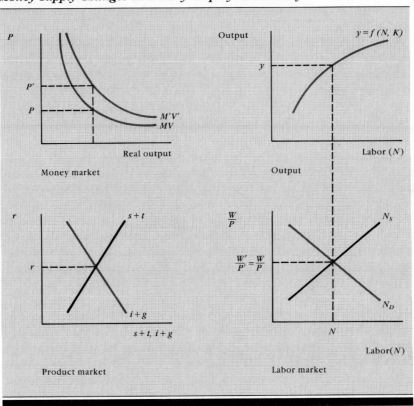

will cause the money wage level to rise until the full employment real wage is restored. As a result, there will be no change in employment or real output. Furthermore, if there is no effect on real saving and real investment, the market real rate of interest also will be unaffected. This is shown in Figure 19.1, where prices rise to $P'$ without any change in real variables. The money wage rises to $W'$, so the real wage, the level of employment, and the level of real output all remain unchanged.

Obviously, where full employment is assured by wage and price flexibility, monetary policy has the impact that would be predicted from the naive quantity theory of money. If the money supply increases by 10 percent, the general price level will increase by 10 percent. However, if *expected price level changes* are taken into account, the impact of monetary policy on the price level may be even greater than that predicted by the naive quantity theory. If expectations of price changes are revised upward as a result of the increase in the money supply, individuals will economize on their money holdings to avoid the expected loss of purchasing power. This is a decrease in the demand for money balances, which will be evidenced in an increase in the velocity of circulation. With the money supply and the velocity of circulation both increasing, prices will rise by a larger proportion than the money supply.

An increase in the expected rate of increase in prices also will have an effect on the nominal rate of interest ($R$). Even though the real rate of interest remains the same (because real saving and real investment have not changed), a greater expected rate of change in prices will cause the nominal rate of interest to rise as people adjust their borrowing and lending to compensate for the expected loss in the purchasing power of future money payments.

It is to be expected that expansionary monetary policy in a fully employed economy will have some temporary effects on the level of real economic activity. When the money supply is changed, the additional money is not uniformly distributed across all sectors of the economy. Thus, the expenditure of the excess supply of money is likely to have different impacts on the markets for different products in the economy. What the exact changes will be depends on how the money is distributed and how this money disturbs the asset portfolios of those receiving the money. The result is that even though the general price level may rise by, say, 10 percent, prices in some sectors of the economy may rise by a greater percentage and prices in others may rise by less. Price changes usually are not uniform. This changes the relative prices of goods and services, and so production will respond to these changes. Even though the economy eventually returns to the same aggregate level of output, there may be some expansions in certain sectors before other sectors contract. For a time at least, aggregate output will have increased.

Temporary adjustments in output and employment are most likely to occur when individuals are not aware of the impact of price changes on their real wages. As prices rise, the initial response is a reduction in the real wage. Firms will respond to this reduction in the real cost of labor by offering a higher nominal wage to attract workers. In the short run, some workers perceive this nominal wage increase as an actual increase in real wages. Therefore, the quantity of labor supplied will increase until the workers become aware of the reduced purchasing power of their nominal wage payments.

A temporary change in the market real rate of interest also may occur as a result of monetary policy. After the nominal money supply has been increased, but before the price level has risen, there is an increase in real money balances held. This will induce a wealth portfolio shift out of real money balances and into goods, bonds, and equities. The prices of these alternative assets will be driven up temporarily, and there will be a temporary decline in the market real rate of interest. However, without a lasting change in the preference for current as opposed to future consumption, as indicated in the product market by the real saving and real investment functions, the market real rate of interest will return to the original natural rate of interest.

## *Inflation in a Fully Employed Neoclassical System*

*Inflation* is defined as a continuous increase in the general price level. Obviously, in a fully employed economy, it occurs whenever the money supply is continuously increased at a rate greater than the rate of growth in real output. Thus, inflation may well be *caused* by monetary policy in this system. Although the obvious solution to a problem caused by the policy is to stop the policy, things are not quite that simple.

Growth in the labor force through population growth, and increases in labor's productivity through improved technology and increases in the capital stock serve to generate a fairly continual increase in real output over time. With this increase in real output and no change in the money supply, the price level will fall. Unless money wages fall along with the price decreases, real wages will rise and there will be unemployment. As money wages do not adjust easily to such price decreases, the alternative is to increase the money supply so as to maintain the same price level as before. Thus, in a growing economy, a continuous increase in the money supply is necessary in order to maintain the price level. The problem is knowing exactly at what rate to increase the money supply. If the money supply increases at exactly the same rate as real output, prices will remain constant. However, if the money supply increases too slowly there is likely to be unemployment, and if the money supply increases too quickly there will be inflation.

## MONETARY POLICY IN AN ECONOMY WITH UNEMPLOYMENT

The interesting policy issues of the neoclassical system are not related to a fully employed economy, but to an economy in which there is unemployment greater than the natural rate. The question is whether there are short-run policy measures that can be taken to alleviate the unemployment. In the long run, pressures within the labor market can cause the nominal wage to be bid down and with it the real wage. This effect reduces the level of unemployment. However, as these effects may take considerable time, the question of whether it is possible in the short run to have the same effect by increasing the money supply so that prices rise relative to money wages arises.

The increase in the money supply certainly will create an excess supply of money, and the result will be that the general price level will rise. If prices rise relative to the nominal wage, the real wage will fall, and firms will be induced to increase their labor input; that is, they will hire more workers. Thus, employment will rise, output will rise, and the level of unemployment will fall. The increase in output then will have further effects through the product market. As real saving is a function of real income, real saving will increase. The resulting excess supply of aggregate output, and the unintended inventory accumulation from the excess of real saving over real investment, will cause the market real rate of interest to be bid down.

The monetary expansion may well have effects on the velocity of circulation, but the direction of the change is somewhat ambiguous as two opposing effects are likely to be exerted. The rise in the supply of money may cause an increase in the expected rate of change of prices. If this is the case, velocity will likely be increased. However, if there also is a reduction in the market real rate of interest, there will be an increase in the demand for money balances having the opposite effect on the velocity of circulation. Whether the velocity of circulation ultimately rises or falls depends on to what extent there is a change in expectations, and the effect that this has on velocity relative to the effect of the interest rate change.

The effects of a monetary expansion—where it is assumed that the real wage is in fact reduced—is shown in Figure 19.2. (The diagram is intentionally ambiguous as to whether $V'$ is greater or less than $V$.)

## Expectations

Expectations of price level changes, and the response of nominal wages to these expectations, play crucial roles in monetary policy's ability to affect the level of employment in the neoclassical system. If the labor force actively seeks to maintain the purchasing power of nominal wages (as they usually do), the monetary authority's ability to change real wages will be undermined, and the monetary policy will have little impact on the level of employment and real output.

Even during the depths of the depression in the 1930s, the vast majority of the labor force was employed. Thus, in almost any situation where the monetary authorities increase the money supply and drive up prices, this is seen by the majority as a simple reduction in real wages. Workers, therefore, will strive to maintain their real wages and will attempt to bid up money wages along with the price level. If nominal wages in fact increase at about the same rate as prices, employment remains relatively unchanged, and the purchasing power of nominal wages remains relatively constant.

Nominal wage adjustments to maintain real wages have become partially institutionalized with the increased use of COLA clauses in wage contracts. Even though these adjustments occur after the price rises have been revealed, and even though the wage adjustment may be only a portion of the price change, this continual movement in the nominal wage in response to price level changes reduces the monetary authority's ability to reduce the real wage. Also, since the CPI used in many nominal wage adjustments only contains a small set of commodities, its use may actually overstate the

Figure 19.2
***Monetary Policy and Market Interaction:
An Increase in the Money Supply***

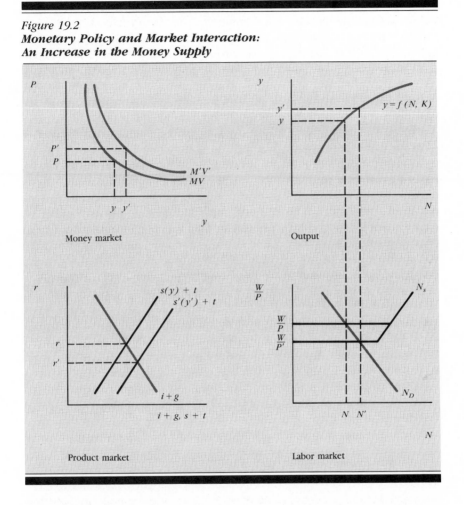

Money market

Output

Product market

Labor market

actual impact of price level changes on the purchasing power of particular nominal wages. The adjustment may maintain, or even increase, the real wage rate.

Even when there are no COLA clauses in the wage contracts, the expectations of price level changes will enter into nominal wage determination. When workers expect prices to rise in the near future, wage contracts will be negotiated to adjust the nominal wage to compensate for the expected price level changes. When this is the case, the only way that the monetary authorities are able to decrease the real wage is to increase the general level of prices at a rate greater than the expected rate. The workers are then "fooled" by the unexpected monetary policy. There is a short-run decrease in real wages, bringing with it a short-run increase in employment and output.

Neoclassical economists, however, believe that the ability to fool the workers by increasing prices at a faster rate than is expected is doomed to failure. With *rational expectations,* workers will incorporate the expected impact of money supply changes into their expectations of price level changes. Although the monetary authorities may be able to have a short-run effect on employment and output at some particular time, they are not likely to be able to repeat their success. Workers quickly will become aware of the impact of monetary policy on their real wages, and nominal wages therefore will be adjusted to compensate for the attempted reduction in worker purchasing power.

The attempt by monetary authorities to decrease unemployment by reducing real wages can have the opposite effect from that intended. This is because workers, having observed the behavior of the monetary authorities, may extend the search time they are prepared to undergo while looking for employment at a particular wage. Rather than accept a lower nominal wage offer, unemployed workers will be aware that sooner, rather than later, they will get a nominal wage offer at the old nominal wage. Since in the past the monetary authority has acted to raise the general price level and to reduce the real wage, downward mobility in the nominal wage may be reduced.

When the monetary authority has pursued an expansionary policy for an extended period of time, it will to some extent become locked into maintaining that policy. From observations of past policy, wage contracts will have been made that incorporate the expected price level changes from an expansionary monetary policy. Thus, unless those expected price level increases are actually realized, the market real wage will increase as nominal wages rise relative to actual increases in the general price level. The real wage increase will increase unemployment, and this will persist until expectations and nominal wage contracts are revised in keeping with the new, less-expansionary monetary policy.

When workers make adjustments in nominal wages that are consistent with general price level changes, substantial unemployment *and* rising prices can exist, and indeed persist, side by side. The monetary authority's attempt to reduce unemployment by driving up prices is offset consistently by rises in nominal wages designed to maintain the existing real wage. The reduction of the unemployment may then be beyond the control of the monetary authority. If the monetary authorities should try to revise their policy, the nominal wages may continue to rise, causing the real wage and the unemployment to increase. Any reduction in unemployment then will have to wait until pressures in the labor market serve to reduce the market real wage.

## MONETARY TARGETS

Policymakers have certain normative goals that they wish to achieve concerning unemployment, inflation, growth, and the balance of payments. However, these goals are not controlled directly by the monetary authori-

## THE VOICE FROM ST. LOUIS

Historically, the Federal Reserve never has been overly concerned with the quantity of money available, either as a monetary target or as an indicator of monetary conditions. It was not until 1945, 33 years after they started operations, that the Federal Reserve started to collect a monthly series of money supply data, and money stock statistics based on average daily figures were not published until the 1960s. It was as recent as 1970 that the Federal Open Market Committee started to include the money supply as a target variable for monetary policy, and only in 1979 did the money supply target receive as much prominence as the interest rate targets.[1]

In the early days of the Federal Reserve, the money supply was still linked to a commodity standard, so the monetary authorities rightly concerned themselves only with the credit extended by banks. However, the concern with "credit conditions" (usually interpreted as a concern with interest rates) persisted long after the demise of the gold standard. Before 1970 the only monetary aggregates discussed by the Federal Reserve were free reserves (member bank excess reserves minus member bank borrowing from the Federal Reserve) and, since the mid-1960s, bank credit (total bank loans and investments minus interbank loans). The Board of Governors and the FOMC consistently used some short-term interest rate as the key indicator of monetary and credit conditions. The prominence that is now given to the money supply in monetary policy decisions largely is attributable to the persistent advocacy of a monetarist position by the economists at the St. Louis Federal Reserve Bank.

Each of the 12 Federal Reserve Banks and the Board of Governors have staff economists engaged in monetary research.

*continued*

ties, are observable only with a considerable time lag, and have many other influences besides monetary policy affecting them. For this reason, the monetary authorities set certain *monetary targets,* which are observable economic variables, that can be used to guide monetary policies. Targets are different from goals, in that goals are the ultimately desired results of policy whereas targets are used only to determine the adjustments that are necessary to reach the goals.

Late in the 1960s economists at St. Louis achieved some fame as the voice of monetarism in the system. Through publication of monetary data and articles in the *Review* (Federal Reserve Bank of St. Louis), explaining the monetarist conclusions that can be drawn from the data, the St. Louis economists have attracted significant attention in the system, in Congress, and among the public. Widespread notice of their position was achieved with the publication of the results of the "St. Louis equation" of Leonall Andersen and Jerry Jordan.[2] Using statistical techniques, Andersen and Jordan found that a $1 million increase in the money supply led to an increase in nominal GNP, of $1.5 million within one quarter, and an increase of over $5.8 million within a year. On the other hand, fiscal policy was found to have little impact. A $1 million increase in government expenditure increases nominal GNP by $0.36 million after one quarter, and this increase then decreases to $0.07 million within a year.

Despite the fact that the techniques used in the original study have been called into question, the St. Louis Federal Reserve has remained the chief exponent of monetarism within the system, and the FOMC has at least been made aware of the importance of monetary aggregates. Whether or not this relatively small Federal Reserve Bank (number 11 out of 12 in total assets) will have a significant impact on monetary policy still remains to be seen.

[1] Wallich, Henry C., "The Role of Operating Guides in U.S. Monetary Policy: A Historical Review," *Federal Reserve Bulletin* (September 1979): 679–691.
[2] Andersen, Leonall C., and Jerry L. Jordan, "Monetary and Fiscal Actions: A Test of Their Relative Importance in Economic Stabilization," *Review* 50(10), Federal Reserve Bank of St. Louis (October 1968): 11–23.

A monetary target variable must be causally related to the desired goal, have a fairly predictable relationship to the goal, be controllable by the monetary authorities, and be directly observable in a short period of time. With a predictable relationship between the target variable and the goal, appropriate adjustments in monetary policy necessary for achieving the goal can be made. For example, if the authorities decide that they wish to reduce the rate of increase in the general price level, and the authorities have selected the money supply as the target variable, an observed increase in the rate of growth of the money supply would signal that the authorities should initiate a reduction in open market purchases or an increase in open market sales to reduce the growth in the monetary base which will reduce the rate of growth in the money supply.

The causal relationship between the money supply and the price level is clearly derivable from neoclassical theory. In the neoclassical system, a reduction in the rate of growth of the money supply leads directly to a reduction in the rate of increase in prices. Even though any change in the rate of increase in the general price level may not be directly observable immediately, the adjustment in the rate of growth in the supply of money will cause adjustments in the various markets in the economy toward a realization of the goal of slower price level increases. (*See* "The Voice from St. Louis," p. 469–470.)

Neoclassical economists believe that some *money supply target* should be used to conduct monetary policy. There is some debate among neoclassical and monetarist economists over which definition of the money supply to use, but in general a broad definition is preferred. The money supply definition is usually chosen on the basis of the predictability of the relationship between the money supply and nominal income, and therefore there is a tendency to choose M2 over M1. However, regardless of any differences of opinion the neoclassical economists might have, the consensus is that *any* definition of the money supply is a preferable target over the use of interest rates. Monetarists in particular believe that the causal link between the money supply and economic conditions is both more direct and more predictable than the relationship between interest rates and economic conditions.

## Interest Rate Targets

The Federal Reserve System historically has used various interest rates as monetary targets. Even with the shift toward monetarism that has had the authorities include money supply definitions in Federal Open Market Committee directives since 1970 (and expand their use since late 1979), interest rates, as they reflect credit conditions, have had a primary place in the determination of short-term monetary policy. In general, even when the FOMC has chosen a rate of growth for the money supply, they have estimated the range for an interest rate that is consistent with that growth in the money supply, and then targeted on the interest rate. The interest rate that has most commonly been used is the short-term overnight federal funds rate.

The appeal of *interest rate targets* is that the rates are readily observable. The Federal Reserve's Open Market account managers can obtain hourly information on movements in the federal funds rate and the interest rates on United States government securities. Thus, with what has come to be called "a feel for the market," the open market managers have been able to make almost instantaneous adjustments in the money supply through open market operations to accommodate changing market conditions.

Using an interest rate target, daily open market operations are easily decided. When the targeted interest rate rises toward the top of the specified range, it is taken to imply that credit is less available than is desired (money is said to be tight), and additional Federal Reserve credit is supplied through open market purchases. When the targeted interest rate falls toward the bottom of the specified range, it is taken to imply that credit is more available than is desired (money is said to be easy), and Federal Reserve credit is reduced through open market sales.

The adjustments that seem so easy using an interest rate target seem to be much more difficult when the money supply itself is used as the monetary target. Hourly, or even daily, information on the existing money supply is difficult to obtain. Also, the broader the definition of money supply that is being used, the more difficult it is to obtain the relevant information. For example, using the current definition of M1, the credit union share draft balance component may not be available until monthly reports are submitted. Short-term adjustments in the portfolio decisions of financial intermediaries and the nonbank public can have significant effects on the money multiplier and hence on the money supply, but this information will be available to the authorities with a considerable lag, and will be of little use in determining day-to-day open market operations. With interest rate targets, on the other hand, the information is readily apparent, and adjustments can be made the same day.

Interest rate targets, however, do have significant problems of their own. The main difficulty is that only *nominal* interest rates are directly observable. As these nominal rates are made up of the real rate and the expected rate of change of prices, the Federal Reserve must always be aware of why the nominal rate is changing: whether it is a result of a change in the real rate or whether it is a result of a change in price expectations. Depending on which it is, the Federal Reserve's reaction varies greatly.

## MONETARY POLICY AND NOMINAL INTEREST RATES

The *nominal rate of interest (R)* is composed of the real rate of interest $(r)$ and the expected rate of change in the general price level $(\dot{P})$. The precise relationship is

$$R = r + \dot{P} + r \cdot \dot{P}.$$

As individuals adjust their desires to borrow or lend monetary units to compensate for expected changes in the purchasing power of the monetary units used to repay loans, the nominal rate of interest will change relative to the real rate of interest. Increases in the expected rate of change of prices will lead to increases in the nominal rate of interest relative to the real rate.

According to neoclassical theory, it is possible for monetary policy to have a lasting effect on the market real rate of interest, but this only happens through the changes that can be brought about in employment and output. If an increase in the money supply actually succeeds in reducing the real wage (by increasing prices relative to nominal wages), there will be an increase in employment and output. If saving is a function of real income, the increase in real income will cause an increase in real saving and a decrease in the real rate of interest. However, if there are rational expectations in the labor market to the extent that nominal wages are always adjusted to price level changes, monetary policy will be unable to change the level of employment, and at the same time it will be unable to change the real rate of interest. In this situation, monetary policy will have an effect only on the nominal rate of interest through the changes in the expected rate of change of prices ($\dot{P}$).

In the short run, an unanticipated increase in the money supply can have a temporary effect on the real rate of interest. As the money supply is increased, wealth holders will find themselves holding excess money balances. As they attempt to shift their wealth out of money and into bonds, equities, and goods, the prices of these other assets will be bid up. In the process the market real rate of interest will decline, but unless these short-term changes actually change real saving and real investment, the market real rate of interest will return to the old natural rate.

The excess money balances spent on goods and services, of course, will drive up the general price level, and if this causes the expected rate of price increase to increase, the nominal rate of interest will rise. The net result is that the nominal rate of interest will follow a pattern similar to that shown in Figure 19.3. At first the nominal rate will fall because the real rate has been reduced

$$R \downarrow \; = r \downarrow \; + \dot{P} + r \downarrow \cdot \dot{P},$$

but after the real rate has returned to the natural rate, the nominal rate will rise because of the increases in the rate of expected price changes:

$$R \uparrow \; = r + \dot{P} \uparrow \; + r \cdot \dot{P} \uparrow.$$

It has been estimated that the initial decline in the nominal rate of interest lasts for approximately six months.[2]

If rational expectations of price level changes are built into the public's response to monetary policy, the period of decline in the nominal rate of interest will be reduced. As a result of observing the ultimate impact on the price level of an increase in the rate of growth of the money supply,

---

[2] Friedman, Milton, "Factors Affecting the Level of Interest Rates," in *Proceedings of the 1968 Conference on Savings and Residential Financing* (Chicago, 1969): 11–27. Reprinted in *Current Issues in Monetary Theory and Policy,* edited by T. M. Havrilesky and J. T. Boorman (Arlington Heights, Ill.: AHM Publishing Corporation, 1980): 378–394.

*Figure 19.3*
**The Time Path for Nominal Interest Rate Changes**

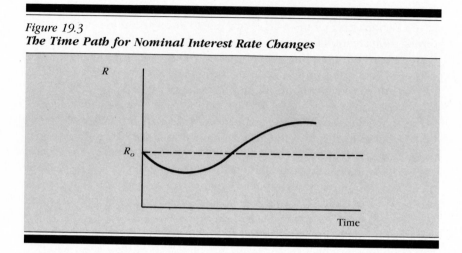

expected price level changes will be formulated directly from observations of changes in the money supply. The simple observation of an increase in Federal Reserve open market purchases will result in an upward adjustment in the expected rate of change of prices, and the nominal rate of interest will rise. Thus, monetary expansions can cause nominal rates of interest to rise rather than fall. To reduce interest rates when they are rising because of an increasing expected rate of change in prices, the Federal Reserve must decrease the rate of increase in the money supply, or even decrease the money supply.

## THE INTEREST RATE TARGET AND FISCAL POLICY

As the government changes its levels of expenditure and taxation, the market real rate of interest will be changed. However, if the market real rate of interest is used as a monetary target, monetary policy necessarily will accommodate the fiscal policy. New money will be injected into the system to finance the new government expenditure. Worse, if the nominal interest rate is used as the monetary target, fiscal policy may instigate an accommodating monetary policy that is inflationary. (*See* "Monetary Policy: 1942 to the Present," p. 476–477.)

Figure 19.4 shows the effects of an increase in government expenditure when the monetary authority successfully maintains the market real interest rate. The level of government expenditure is increased in real terms so that the $i + g$ function in the product market shifts to $i + g'$. This action alone would increase the real rate of interest, but if the monetary authorities can successfully prevent it from rising, they do this by increasing the money supply. If prices rise relative to the nominal wage, real wages will fall and the level of employment and real output will increase. If saving is then a

*Figure 19.4*
**Effect of Government Expenditure Increase When the
Monetary Authority Follows an Interest Rate Target**

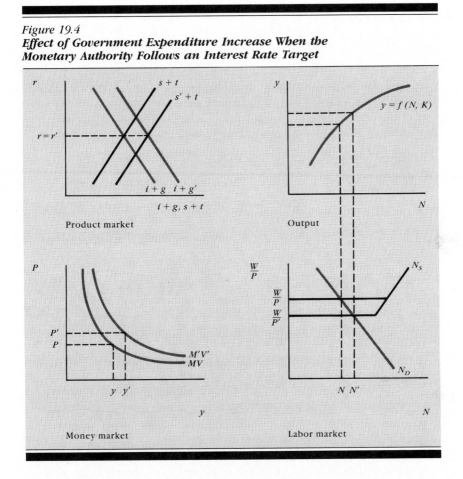

positive function of real income, the saving function will shift to the right also. The monetary authorities then will continue this policy until the $s + t$ function has shifted to $s' + t$ and the real rate of interest is restored. As a result of pursuing the interest rate target, the monetary authorities have effectively decided to follow a policy of providing the funds that the government wishes to spend.

In a neoclassical system with unemployment, the use of an interest rate target by the monetary authorities can serve to reduce or even eliminate the crowding-out effect of government expenditure. Crowding out occurs as a result of rises in the market real rate of interest. If government expenditure is increased, the market real rate of interest will rise, which will cause decreases in private real investment and real consumption. In this way the government can acquire additional goods that would have gone to the private sector. However, if at the same time as the government expenditure is being increased the monetary authorities are able to decrease real

## MONETARY POLICY: 1942 TO THE ACCORD

In April 1942, shortly after the United States entered World War II on the side of the Allies, the Federal Reserve reached an agreement with the Treasury to accommodate government expenditure as an aid to financing the war effort. The Federal Reserve agreed to maintain a yield of ⅜ of 1 percent on three-month Treasury bills and a yield of 2½ percent on longer-term bonds. This reduced the Treasury's direct interest cost of borrowing, but it involved the Federal Reserve in a program of buying and selling Treasury securities at fixed prices.

As the federal government ran substantial deficits during World War II (e.g., $54.9 billion in 1943, $47.0 billion in 1944), the Federal Reserve acquired large quantities of United States government securities. The Federal Reserve's holdings of United States government securities increased from $2.25 billion in December 1941 to $24.26 billion by December 1945. This policy simply amounted to the Federal Reserve creating the money with which to purchase the securities. The money supply (currency plus demand deposits) rose from $48.5 billion in December 1941 to $102.3 billion by December 1945.[1]

The dramatic rise in the money supply and the substantial decline in the availability of consumer goods placed considerable pressure on prices. However, the pressure was suppressed by wage and price controls, rationing, and regulation of credit. When controls were relaxed at the cessation of hostilities, the pressure on prices became evident. From 1945 to 1951 the CPI

wages by driving up prices relative to the nominal wage, it is possible to hold the market real rate of interest constant. When this is the case, private investment remains the same, and the government acquires the goods and services out of the increase in production.

## THE FOREIGN SECTOR

Since flexible exchange rates were reinstituted in foreign exchange markets in the mid-1970s, the Federal Reserve has become increasingly concerned with the exchange rate of the United States dollar and with the United States balance of international payments. Since August 1979 the Federal Reserve System has had a special Manager for Foreign Operations of the System's

rose at an average annual rate of 6.6 percent.[2] Despite the rising prices, only a gradual adjustment in interest rates was allowed. The Treasury did not wish to impose costs on those who had invested in the securities, and so did not wish to have the price on the securities fall (which, of course, would have happened if the interest rates had been allowed to rise). By the end of 1950, the three-month Treasury bill rate had risen only to 1.367 percent.[3]

After a political battle in which the Treasury insisted that the Federal Reserve must continue its policy of pegging interest rates and the Federal Reserve tried to reassert its independence from the government, an agreement was reached in 1951 known as "the Accord." Under this agreement, the Federal Reserve was allowed to follow its own policy in accordance with prevailing monetary and credit conditions. Accommodation of Treasury policy was relegated to avoiding monetary policy changes during periods of Treasury financing (about four times a year). This was known as keeping "an even keel," and was the only assistance afforded the Treasury by the Federal Reserve. The Accord of 1951 thus restored independence to the Federal Reserve as the monetary authority and removed Treasury dominance that had lasted a decade.

---

[1] *Banking and Monetary Statistics, 1941–1970* (Board of Governors, 1976): 5, 17, 468–469, 526–529.
[2] *Economic Report of the President, 1979,* 195, 239.
[3] *Banking and Monetary Statistics, 1941–1970,* 693.

Open Market Account to carry out the Federal Open Market Committee's authorized foreign currency operations. These occasional directives authorize the purchase or sale of foreign currency and also direct the maintenance of reciprocal currency arrangements with foreign central banks.

In the short run, orderly foreign exchange market conditions can be maintained by the Federal Reserve and the Treasury through the use of borrowings in the swap network (*see* Chapter 14). However, these borrowings are only for temporary adjustments in the supply and demand for dollars in the foreign exchange market, and are used to forestall undesirable changes in the foreign exchange rate of the United States dollar. Monetary policy can be used to influence the basic conditions that determine the supply of and demand for United States dollars in the foreign exchange markets, and therefore it can be used to have a permanent effect on the exchange rate.

## Foreign Exchange Market

In the current flexible exchange rate system, market-induced changes in the exchange rate ensure the equality between supplies of and demands for the currencies. Thus, foreign exchange market adjustments will generate a balance of international payments between the supply of dollars coming from United States residents wishing to buy overseas and the demand for dollars from foreign residents wishing to buy in the United States.[3]

The *exchange rate (e)* is the price of the dollar in units of a foreign currency. With respect to the British pound (£), an exchange rate of ½ means that half a pound sterling is required to buy one United States dollar or, equivalently, it takes two dollars to buy one pound sterling. An increase in the exchange rate from ½ to 1 means that the value of the dollar in terms of the British pound has increased, and one dollar can be exchanged for one pound sterling (*see* Chapter 3). By altering the basic conditions that determine the demand and supply of dollars relative to the pound sterling, monetary authorities in the United States and in the United Kingdom can influence the exchange rate for the dollar relative to the pound.

The demand for dollars in the foreign exchange market is determined by residents of foreign countries who wish to buy goods and services and financial assets from the United States. At a higher exchange rate (*e*), it takes more pounds sterling to buy a dollar, and the cost of United States goods in terms of pounds is higher. Thus, at a higher exchange rate the quantity of dollars demanded by residents of the United Kingdom to buy United States goods and services is less. This is shown by the downward sloping demand curve (*d*) in Figure 19.5. Similarly, the supply of dollars in the foreign exchange market is determined by United States residents who wish to buy goods and services and financial assets from foreign countries. At a higher exchange rate, the dollar price of foreign goods and services is lower and the quantity of dollars supplied to the foreign exchange market is greater. This is shown by the upward sloping supply curve (*s*) in Figure 19.5.

## Factors Affecting the Exchange Rate

The basic economic conditions (other than the exchange rate) that influence the demand for and supply of dollars in the foreign exchange market are the general price level in the United States relative to the United Kingdom, the market real rate of interest in the United States relative to the United Kingdom, and the levels of real income in the United States and in

---

[3] A balance of payments should not be confused with a simple balance of trade. Trade is balanced when the value of goods and services exported from the United States equals the value of the imports coming into the United States. International payments include this trade flow as well as the flow of funds for securities purchases, transfer payments, and other currency flows. Thus, if imports exceed exports, a payments balance (in a flexible exchange rate system) still will be struck with an additional demand for dollars from foreign residents buying securities issued in the United States.

*Figure 19.5*
**Effect of a Price Level Increase in the United States on the**
**Foreign Exchange Rate for the United States Dollar**

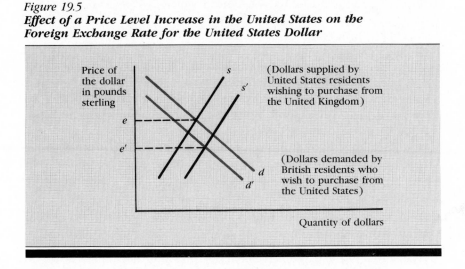

the United Kingdom. Any changes in price levels, interest rates, and income levels relative to conditions in the other country will affect the supply and demand conditions in the foreign exchange market.

If the general price level in the United States rises relative to the level of prices in the United Kingdom, at the existing exchange rate, goods and services in the United States will be relatively more expensive compared with those in the United Kingdom. This would cause an increase in the demand for goods and services from the United Kingdom on the part of United States residents. This would increase the supply of dollars in the foreign exchange market as shown by the shift from *s* to *s'* in Figure 19.5. There also will be a decrease in the demand for dollars in the foreign exchange market as the residents of the United Kingdom find United States goods and services relatively more expensive. This is shown in Figure 19.5 by the decrease in demand from *d* to *d'*. The resulting excess supply of dollars at the old exchange rate, *e*, will induce a decline in the exchange rate to *e'*.

If the market real rate of interest in the United States rises relative to the rate in the United Kingdom, financial assets in the United States will be generating a relatively higher rate of return.[4] This would induce an increase in the demand for dollars in the foreign exchange market as residents of the United Kingdom buy more financial assets in the United States. There also

---

[4] In computing the desirability of these financial shifts, wealth holders in Britain are likely to consider the nominal interest rate in the United States, adjusted for any anticipated changes in the exchange rate, and the anticipated rate of change in prices in Britain. This would yield the anticipated real rate in pounds to compare with the domestic alternatives.

would be a decline in the supply of dollars on the foreign exchange market as financial assets in the United Kingdom became relatively less attractive to United States residents. Thus, an increase in the real rate of interest in the United States relative to the United Kingdom would induce an increase in the foreign exchange rate for the United States dollar.

An increase in real income in the United States also will increase the supply of dollars on the foreign exchange market. With a higher level of real income, real consumption demand will rise and with it there will be an increased demand for imports. This will tend to drive down the exchange rate for the dollar. Similarly, an increase in the level of real income in the United Kingdom will increase the demand for United States exports to the United Kingdom. This will increase the demand for dollars on the foreign exchange market and induce a rise in the exchange rate for the dollar relative to the British pound.

## Use of Monetary Policy

A relatively more expansionary monetary policy in the United States, as compared with the United Kingdom, will tend to reduce the value of the dollar relative to the pound sterling. The desire to pursue a monetary policy that attempts to increase employment and real output may be at odds with attempting to maintain a relatively high foreign exchange rate. By expanding the money supply in an attempt to reduce unemployment, the monetary authority, in the neoclassical system, will be directly generating an increase in the general price level. If this policy is successful in increasing employment by lowering the real wage, there also will be an increase in real income. The higher price level generates both an increase in the supply of dollars and a decrease in the demand for dollars on the foreign exchange market. The increase in real income will increase the demand for imports and further increase the supply of dollars on the foreign exchange market. Also, any decline in the market real rate of interest brought about by increased real saving will increase the supply of dollars and decrease the demand for dollars on the foreign exchange market as individuals attempt to acquire the relatively higher real rate of return on financial assets in the United Kingdom. Unless the expansionary monetary policy in the United States is equally offset by an expansionary policy in the United Kingdom, the increase in the supply of dollars and the decrease in the demand for dollars on the foreign exchange market will reduce the exchange rate for the dollar.

Monetary policy alone is not sufficient for carrying out an economic policy aimed at both reducing unemployment and maintaining the existing exchange rate. Some other policy, say fiscal policy, also would be required. In the neoclassical system, monetary policy could be used in an attempt to increase employment by reducing the real wage. The resulting downward pressure on the exchange rate for the dollar could be offset by expansionary fiscal policy, which would drive up the market real rate of interest. If this combination of policies is successful in increasing the market real rate of interest sufficiently, the attracted foreign financial investment in securities issued in the United States would offset the downward pressure on the foreign exchange rate for the dollar and act to maintain the value of the dollar relative to foreign currencies. Of course, this combination policy has its drawbacks. On average, prices in the United States will be rising at a faster rate, and the increase in the market rate of interest may reduce per capita growth in real output through an induced decrease in real investment demand.

## RULES VERSUS AUTHORITIES

Although we have seen how it might be possible to carry out a short-run monetary policy designed to change the level of real output and employment, it should not be thought that all neoclassical economists are of the opinion that such a *discretionary monetary policy* should be attempted.[5] Many neoclassical economists, particularly those who consider themselves monetarists, believe that more can be achieved in the economy with a longer-run approach to the problem. Rather than being concerned with a short-run change in output or employment, these economists believe that monetary policy should be conducted in such a way as to create long-run stability in monetary conditions.

Using the simple neoclassical system that we have used so far, these economists advocate a system whereby the attempt to change prices relative to the money wage is not made, but instead monetary policy is aimed at creating long-run price stability. The discretionary change in the money supply that is intended to change prices relative to the money wage fails because of the changes made in the money wage rate as wage bargains take the price change into account. In fact, it can be argued that the attempt to change prices relative to the money wage causes instability in the labor market as workers attempt to maintain their real wage. The problem is that changes in real wages are brought about by *unanticipated* changes in prices, and wage-bargainers maintain their real wage by second-guessing the monetary authority's price changes.

Many neoclassical economists believe that the best way to avoid this instability is to have a *monetary rule* of fixed money supply changes. Instead of changing the money supply on a discretionary basis every time the level of output or employment deviates from some accepted level, the money supply is increased at a constant rate at all times, regardless of any short-run changes in output and employment. This policy is based on an

---

[5]*Discretionary* monetary policy occurs when the monetary authority deliberately changes the money supply or interest rates in an attempt to cause a short-run change in the level of real output and employment.

attempt to maintain stable prices in an economy where the level of output is growing.

If it is possible to maintain prices at some particular level, there no longer is a need for wage-bargainers to try to second-guess the monetary authority. The anticipated price level will be the current price level. As wage-bargainers adjust to the current price level, the labor market will settle at the natural rate of unemployment. However, many neoclassical economists expect more from price stability than stability of the unemployment rate. They argue that the certainty stable prices afford is conducive to growth in real aggregate output. In a stable price and wage environment, entrepreneurs can plan ahead with much certainty. This, it is argued, will lead to increased investment, increased capital stock, and an increased level of output for any given level of employment. In terms of the production function, the curve will shift upward.

If price stability, in fact, does lead to economic growth in aggregate output, a consideration of the equation of exchange reveals that a monetary policy other than keeping a constant money supply is necessary. If real output ($y$) is rising, a constant money supply ($\overline{M}$) and a constant velocity of circulation ($\overline{V}$) implies that the general price level ($P$) must be falling:

$$\overline{MV} = P\downarrow \cdot y\uparrow.$$

To maintain a constant price level when real output is growing, it is necessary that the money supply also grow.

Using the neoclassical diagrams we have employed so far, it is possible to see how the money supply must be increased if there is in fact economic growth. In Figure 19.6 growth in real output is shown by shifting the production relationship upward. The level of real output for any given level of employment is increasing. If, therefore, the level of employment remained at $\overline{n}$, the level of output would grow from $y_1$ to $y_2$. If the money supply were not changed, and the velocity of circulation remained at $\overline{V}$, the price level would fall from $P_1$ to $P_2$. However, if the money supply is increased at the same rate as output is growing, the price level will remain at $P_1$.

If a stable real wage is achieved by the monetary authority's managing the money supply so that there is a constant price level, there is likely to be economic growth in output and an increase in the level of employment. However, the money supply would have to be increased at the same rate as real output was growing to maintain constant prices. Therefore, the monetary rule usually advocated is that the money supply be increased at the same rate as the rate of growth of real output. Neoclassical supporters of the monetary rule, however, have always emphasized that the stable growth rate in the money supply is more important than the actual rate at which the money supply is increased. As it is usually considered that an economy is better able to cope with slowly rising rather than slowly falling prices, the tendency would be to have the money supply increase at a rate slightly above, rather than slightly below, the rate of growth of real output.

*Figure 19.6*
**The Fixed Monetary Rule**

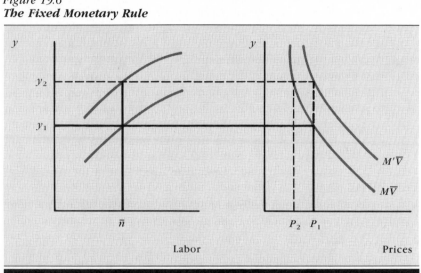

*Note:* As real output grows from $y_1$ to $y_2$, the money supply is increased from $M$ to $M'$ so that prices remain at $P_1$.

## SUMMARY

In the neoclassical system, the supply of money is the most important driving force behind the determination of nominal income. Monetary policy therefore is given the primary role in any attempt to change the general price level or the rate of change of the general price level. Because monetary policy has a direct effect on general prices, it is possible to use it in attempts to change the level of employment and output through changes in the real wage. If the general price level can be changed relative to the nominal wage rate, the real wage will change and the monetary policy will affect employment and real output.

It is by no means certain that monetary policy actually will change the real wage. If there is unemployment above the natural rate of unemployment, an expansionary monetary policy might be successful in lowering the real wage. However, with rational expectations, the level of unemployment will remain at the natural rate and expansionary monetary policy will result only in increases in prices. When the monetary policy *is* successful, real wages will fall, employment will rise, and real output will rise. In the product market, real income will increase, which will cause real saving to increase and the market real rate of interest to decline.

The ability of monetary policy to reduce unemployment in a neoclassical system depends on the monetary authority's ability to reduce the real wage through raising prices relative to the nominal wage. As the employed become increasingly aware of the impact of monetary policy on their real wage (either through simple observation or rational expectations), the nominal wage will tend to be adjusted to compensate for any loss in purchasing power. When this happens, the real wage remains relatively constant, and the impact of monetary policy on unemployment is greatly reduced if not eliminated.

In the neoclassical system, the appropriate choice of a target for monetary policy is some definition of the money supply. This follows from the fact that monetary policy has its effect through price changes and that the money supply has a direct effect on prices and the expected rate of change of prices. The Federal Reserve quite consistently has used interest rate targets for monetary policy, but neoclassical monetary theory would consider this a mistaken approach. Since only nominal rates of interest are observable, the effect of expected price level changes on these nominal rates of interest may give rise to misleading signals as to the appropriate monetary policy.

## Key Terms

monetary policy

expected price level changes

inflation

monetary targets

money supply target

interest rate targets

nominal rate of interest

exchange rate

foreign exchange market

discretionary monetary policy

monetary rule

## Questions

1.  In the neoclassical system, will an increase in the money supply increase nominal income?

2.  Under what conditions will an open market purchase by the Federal Reserve reduce unemployment and increase real output in the neoclassical system?

3.  Evaluate the monetarist notion that it makes no difference which definition of the money supply is used so long as the monetary authority uses a consistent money supply target.

4.  If the Federal Reserve uses an interest rate target, will an increase in government expenditure generate an increase in the money supply?

5.  Will a decrease in the Federal Reserve's discount rate induce a decline in the value of the dollar in relation to foreign currencies?

## Additional Readings

Andersen, Leonall, and Keith Carlson. "A Monetarist Model for Economic Stabilization." *Review* 52. Federal Reserve Bank of St. Louis (April 1970): 7–25.

*This article develops the St. Louis model designed to analyze stabilization policies with a focus on the impact of monetary expansion.*

Andersen, Leonall, and Jerry Jordan. "Monetary and Fiscal Actions: A Test of Their Relative Importance in Economic Stabilization." *Review* 50. Federal Reserve Bank of St. Louis, 11–23.

*This article contains the initial results of the St. Louis equation and is usually designated as the root of the Federal Reserve Bank of St. Louis's monetarist position.*

Andersen, Leonall, and Denis S. Karnosky. "Some Considerations in the Use of Monetary Aggregates for the Implementation of Monetary Policy." *Review* 59. Federal Reserve Bank of St. Louis (September 1977): 2–7.

*An argument that the monetary base rather than broader definitions of the money supply should be considered for use as the appropriate monetary aggregate in the implementation of monetary policy.*

Federal Reserve Bank of Boston. *Controlling Monetary Aggregates* (1969).

*The proceedings of a conference on monetary control with several articles and discussions by leading monetary economists on the appropriate use of monetary aggregates.*

Friedman, Benjamin M. "Even the St. Louis Model Now Believes in Fiscal Policy." *Journal of Money, Credit and Banking* 9 (May 1977): 365–367.

*A presentation of the results of reestimating the St. Louis equation. These results draw into question the strong monetarist results of the initial estimates of the equation.*

Pierce, James L., and Thomas D. Thompson. "Some Issues in Controlling the Stock of Money." *Controlling Monetary Aggregates II, The Implementation.* Federal Reserve Bank of Boston (1972): 115–136.

*A discussion with simulations of the problems involved in controlling monetary aggregates.*

Poole, William. *Money and the Economy: A Monetarist View.* Reading, Mass.: Addison-Wesley, 1978.

*A survey of monetary economics concentrating on the first-order monetary effects on important economic variables.*

Tavlas, George S. "Some Initial Formulations of the Monetary Growth-rate Rule." *History of Political Economy* 9 (Winter 1977): 535–547.

*This article traces the monetary rule back to the writings of Jeremy Bentham and Henry Thornton in the early 1800s.*

# CHAPTER TWENTY

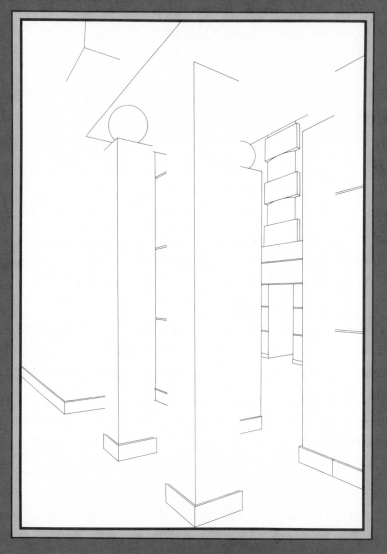

# THE PRODUCT MARKET IN THE
# KEYNESIAN SYSTEM

*In Keynesian theory, the level of aggregate demand for goods and services greatly influences the level of output and employment. This means that to be effective in the Keynesian system, monetary policy must affect aggregate demand. According to Keynesian theory, monetary policy has its chief effect through interest rates and their effect on real investment. The effect on aggregate output of changes in interest rates is shown in the is curve.*

T he Great Depression of the 1930s caused substantial changes in macroeconomic thought. With the unemployment rate rising to over 20 percent, the classical approach to macroeconomic problems was questioned.[1] John Maynard Keynes, in *The General Theory of Employment, Interest and Money*, set out to revolutionize economic thought. The theories presented by Keynes as adopted into the Keynesian system have dominated macroeconomic thought and policy since the 1940s.

Because Keynes believed that the expected demand for output was the crucial determinant of entrepreneurs' decisions to produce goods and services and to hire labor, the level and composition of aggregate demand is central to the Keynesian system. When Keynes constructed his model of the economy, he used money values throughout: the money value of the demand for goods and services ($D$), the money value of consumer expenditures on goods and services ($C$), the money value of business expenditures on new plant and equipment ($I$), the money value of government expenditures on goods and services ($G$), and so on, but the traditional development

---

[1] The neoclassical system presented in Chapters 16–19 is an updated version of the classical approach.

*Figure 20.1*
**Keynesian Aggregate Demand Curve**

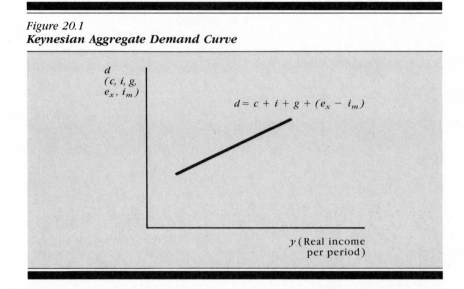

of Keynesian macroeconomics followed by Keynes's disciples deviates considerably from what is written in the *General Theory.*[2] In particular, the model is developed by using the real terms that are obtained by dividing the nominal money values by the price level.[3] In this way, an increase in the general price level will not increase aggregate demand directly, though the real variables may well be affected by changes in the price level or the anticipated rate of change in prices, a point that will be important in our discussion of inflation.

Real *aggregate demand* ($d = D/P$) for domestically produced output consists of four components: aggregate real consumption ($c = C/P$); aggregate real investment ($i = I/P$); aggregate real government expenditure ($g = G/P$); and aggregate real net exports $[(e_x - i_m) = (E_x/P - I_m/P)]$. Aggregate real demand is the sum of these four components:

$$d = c + i + g + (e_x - i_m). \qquad (20.1)$$

It has been empirically verified that real aggregate demand increases with real income. This relationship is shown in Figure 20.1, where the vertical

---

[2] *See:* Leijonhufvud, Axel, *On Keynesian Economics and the Economics of Keynes* (Oxford: The University Press, 1968).

[3] Dividing nominal variables by the price level to obtain real amounts does not apply, of course, to nominal and real rates. If prices are expected to remain constant, the real rate of interest ($r$) is equal to the nominal rate ($R$). However, in periods of expected price changes:

$$r = \frac{R - \dot{P}}{1 + \dot{P}},$$

where $\dot{P}$ is the expected rate of change in prices. (*See* Chapter 5.)

*Figure 20.2*
**Equilibrium in the Product Market**

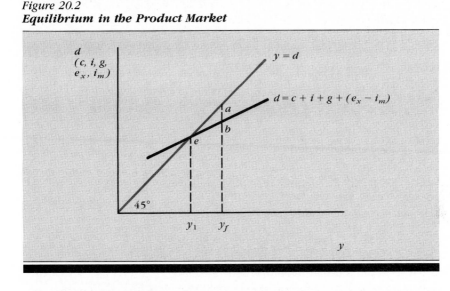

axis measures demand in real terms and the horizontal axis measures real output and real income per period.

The aggregate supply of goods and services plays a secondary role in the Keynesian system. Producers of output are assumed to respond to the level of aggregate demand per period and simply produce the level of output demanded. This assumption about the supply side of the product market is a key notion in Keynesian thought. This passive response of aggregate supply to aggregate demand makes the Keynesian system demand-oriented.

The response of producers to aggregate demand is given by the relationship:

$$y = d. \tag{20.2}$$

That is, the amount of real output produced (and real income) is equal to the amount of aggregate demand per period. This relationship is represented by the 45° line in Figure 20.2.

## PRODUCT MARKET EQUILIBRIUM

Equilibrium in the product market occurs when the level of real output supplied per period is equal to the level of aggregate demand for that level of real income. When this position is reached, the *desires* of both suppliers and demanders are satisfied under current market conditions. For the given level of aggregate demand per period, the product market equilibrium is represented in Figure 20.2 by point $e$, with the level of real output being produced at $y_1$.

In the Keynesian system, equilibrium in the product market is generated by producers adjusting the level of output in response to the realization that aggregate demand differs from current output. For example, suppose that the economy represented in Figure 20.2 initially is producing the level of output that corresponds to full employment of the labor force. This level of output is indicated by $y_f$ in Figure 20.2. This level of output will not persist because aggregate demand is insufficient to sustain a continued supply of $y_f$ units of real goods and services.

The pressure on producers to adjust their levels of output is realized through *undesired* flows of goods into investment. Investment includes not only the real value of purchases of new plant and equipment, but also any changes in the level of inventory. When the supply of goods and services is in excess of the amount that is demanded (desired) for consumption, for net exports, by the government, and for investment (including desired inventory accumulation), the excess supply is added to investment as an *unintended inventory accumulation.* Similarly, if producers supply fewer goods and services than are demanded, the excess demand for goods and services will be realized as an unintended inventory decrease. It is these unintended inventory increases or decreases that induce producers to adjust the amount of goods and services that they supply per period.

At the output and income level $y_f$ (Figure 20.2), the level of aggregate demand is represented by point *b*. This is the amount of goods and services desired at the income level of $y_f$. The amount of goods and services available in that period is represented by point *a*. The difference between *a* and *b* is the amount of surplus production (the excess supply of output) that flows into investment as an unintended inventory accumulation. Although this unintended inventory accumulation could be reduced by a reduction in prices or (as in the neoclassical system) with a reduction in interest rates, the response of producers will be to reduce the level of output per period in the Keynesian system. As output is reduced, the amount that is unintentionally added to inventory will decline, and the economy will move toward the equilibrium point, *e*.

Similarly, if the level of output is less than the equilibrium level of output $y_1$, the aggregate demand for output will exceed the amount of available goods and services. Producers will observe this excess demand as an *unintended inventory decrease* and will respond by increasing their output to replenish the depleted inventories. The response of producers in reducing output when inventories are unintentionally increasing and increasing output when inventories are unintentionally decreasing will move the level of output per period to the equilibrium point *e* in Figure 20.2.

Equilibrium in the product market occurs when the desires of both producers and demanders of output simultaneously are satisfied. This point, *e* in Figure 20.2, is referred to as "the point of effective demand." It is the equilibrium level of real output per period. In the Keynesian system, with aggregate demand as represented in Figure 20.2, the number of people employed will be equal to the number that can produce the level of output $y_1$ per period.

The difference between the Keynesian and neoclassical approaches is apparent from this diagram. To the Keynesian economist, the labor market will adjust to that level of employment that will produce the level of output $y_1$. The neoclassical economist, on the other hand, believes that the aggregate demand schedule will adjust to the level of output produced by the number of workers employed. If there is perfect flexibility in the labor market, the neoclassical economists believe that the *point of effective demand* will move to the full employment level of output. To the Keynesian economist, the economy is not self-correcting in the short-run. If full-employment is to be reached, the aggregate demand function will have to shift until it crosses the 45° line at point *a*.

## COMPONENTS OF AGGREGATE DEMAND

Aggregate demand can be divided into four components: consumption demand, government demand, net exports, and investment demand. Each of these components is affected by economic conditions, but the most important effects are considered to be the effect that income has on consumption, and the effect that interest rates have on investment.

### *Consumption Demand and the Multiplier*

The flow of consumption expenditure is by far the largest of the four components of aggregate demand. It consists of the real amount (the money value divided by the price level) of the purchases per period of all private households in the economy. Although the volume of this real flow per period obviously will be subject to many different influences, it is thought to be primarily a function of the real flow of aggregate income per period

$$c = c(y). \qquad (20.3)$$

Keynes considered it to be "a fundamental psychological law" of human behavior that aggregate real consumption would increase as aggregate real income increased, but that the increase in real consumption would be less than the increase in real income.[4] This notion (now empirically verified) is shown in Figure 20.3. The change in consumption demand ($\Delta c$) per unit change in real aggregate income ($\Delta y$) is called the *marginal propensity to consume.* The fundamental psychological law states that the marginal propensity to consume ($\beta$) is positive and less than 1. If real aggregate income increases by \$1, real consumption demand will increase by less than \$1.

---

[4] *See: The General Theory,* 96.

*Figure 20.3*
**The Consumption Function**

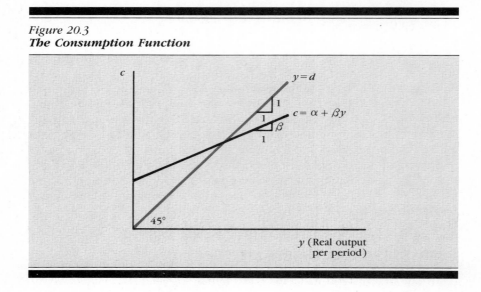

This simple representation of aggregate real consumption demand can be expressed as the algebraic function

$$c = \alpha + \beta y, \qquad (20.4)$$

where $\alpha$ is the intercept term in Figure 20.3 and $\beta$ is the marginal propensity to consume.

This functional relationship for consumption demand can be substituted into our definition of aggregate demand (Equation 20.1) to yield

$$d = \alpha + \beta y + i + g + (e_x - i_m). \qquad (20.5)$$

By using the 45° line relationship ($y = d$) in Equation 20.2, we have

$$y = \alpha + \beta y + i + g + (e_x - i_m). \qquad (20.6)$$

When Equation 20.6 is solved for real aggregate income, we have an expression for equilibrium real output in terms of the marginal propensity to consume and the components of aggregate demand:

$$y - \beta y = \alpha + i + g + (e_x - i_m)$$

$$y = \frac{\alpha + i + g + (e_x - i_m)}{1 - \beta} \qquad (20.7)$$

From the expression for equilibrium output (Equation 20.7), it is easily shown how the level of aggregate output reacts to any change in the components of aggregate demand. For example, if the real investment component is changed by an amount equal to $\Delta i$ per period, the output per period will change by an amount equal to $\Delta y$, where

$$y + \Delta y = \frac{\alpha + i + \Delta i + g + (e_x - i_m)}{1 - \beta}$$

$$y + \Delta y = \frac{\alpha + i + g + (e_x - i_m)}{1 - \beta} + \frac{\Delta i}{1 - \beta}$$

$$\Delta y = \frac{1}{1 - \beta}\Delta i. \tag{20.8}$$

The quantity $(1/1 - \beta)$, by which we multiply $\Delta i$ to find $\Delta y$, is called the *investment multiplier.* Because the marginal propensity to consume is positive and less than 1, the investment multiplier is greater than 1.[5] An increase in real investment demand of \$1 will cause an increase in real aggregate output of more than \$1.

The multiplier process is not simply the mechanical relationship indicated in the mathematical expressions above. It is the result of the behavior of producers and demanders in the product market. In the Keynesian product market, producers expand output in response to increases in real aggregate demand. As output is increased in response to an increase in investment demand, income will increase and bring forth *induced consumption demand.* As producers respond to satisfy the increase in investment demand and the induced consumption demand, real aggregate output will increase by more than the initial increase in investment demand. This *multiplier effect* can be seen in Figure 20.4.

## Government Expenditure and Net Exports

When government (either federal, state, or local) increases its expenditures, or when exporters sell more goods and services abroad, or when the private sector shifts from purchasing foreign goods to purchasing domestically produced goods (a reduction in imports), aggregate output will expand through the multiplier relationship in a manner that is similar to the expansion when investment demand increases.

It should not be thought that the quantities in the aggregate demand function denoted by $g$ and by $(e_x - i_m)$ are free of outside influence. Although the federal government has a great deal of leeway in deciding the level of government expenditure on goods and services, it is still limited by

---

[5] Those familiar with calculus will notice immediately from the expression for equilibrium output that

$$\frac{dy}{di} = \frac{1}{1 - \beta} > 1.$$

*Figure 20.4*
**The Multiplier Effect**

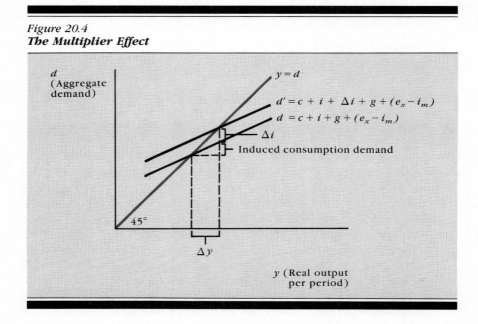

the taxes it is able to levy and by its ability to finance deficit spending. Perhaps more important, state and local governments are limited by the revenues they are able to collect, and these usually are an increasing function of aggregate income. This will mean that the government expenditure component almost certainly is an increasing function of income and that there will be some induced government expenditure in the multiplier process as well as induced consumption demand.

Aggregate levels of exports and imports per period will be influenced greatly by relative prices and relative interest rates among countries and also by many trade and financial restrictions placed on international trade. In general, for any given exchange rate between two currencies, any increase in the price level in one country relative to the price level in the other will cause a decrease in the first country's exports and an increase in its imports. Similarly, if relative prices among countries remain the same, but exchange rates are changed, exports and imports of the affected countries are likely to change.

For purposes of this simple exposition of the Keynesian product market, we will assume that these influences on government expenditure and international trade are absent. However, as we shall find when we discuss Keynesian stabilization policies, these are not matters to be ignored. Monetary policy has become increasingly concerned with accommodating government expenditure and with inducing changes in international trade patterns.

## Investment Demand and Interest Rates

Undoubtedly, one of the most important features of aggregate demand in Keynesian monetary theory is the relationship that exists between that demand and the real rate of interest. Monetary policy is thought to operate primarily through the real rate of interest. Any component of aggregate demand could be a function of the real rate of interest, but traditionally the interest rate has been considered to be of primary importance in the investment decision. Keynesian monetary policy is possible to the extent that aggregate demand is a decreasing function of the real rate of interest.

Real investment is the addition per period to the capital stock. The flow of real investment demand per period is derived from the desires of producers to acquire capital goods and the ability of the capital-goods-producing sector to alter its output. Thus, to determine the relationship between investment demand and the real rate of interest, it is necessary to consider both demand and supply in the market for capital goods.[6]

The *demand for capital goods* is determined as part of portfolio decisions made by members of the economy over their desired forms of wealth holding. Other than holding wealth in the form of money balances, the basic forms of wealth holdings are such financial assets as credit instruments or such capital goods as plant, equipment, housing, consumer durables, or the accumulation of goods as inventory. The determination of the desire to hold different amounts of these various wealth forms depends on the expected real rate of return on each asset. The market real rate of interest serves as a measure of the real rate of return available on the alternatives to capital goods, such as financial assets. The expected real rate of return on capital goods is the internal real rate of return. The *internal real rate of return* is the real rate of interest that makes the present value of the expected net real benefits (future revenues or services from, say, housing less costs) from capital goods equal to the current price of capital goods. When expected net real benefits from capital goods increase, the expected real rate of return on capital goods will increase. If the current price of capital goods increases, it will take a lower real rate of interest to equate the present value of the net benefits stream to the current price of capital goods, and the real rate of return on the capital goods will decline.

Capital goods are acquired because the expected stream of net future benefits exceeds the net benefits from holding alternative forms of wealth. The differences between these net benefit streams are indicated by the relative real rates of return to the alternative assets. When market real rates of interest increase, financial assets will generate a relatively higher real rate of return, and the demand for capital goods will decline. Similarly, when the expected net real benefits stream from capital goods increases, capital

---

[6]For a more detailed discussion of the relationship between the real interest rate and investment demand, *see* Chapter 18.

goods will have an expected higher internal real rate of return and the demand for capital goods will increase. These changes in the demand for capital goods will affect the price of capital goods. For example, an increase in the market real rate of interest will decrease the demand for capital goods and the current price of capital goods.

If the supply of capital goods was completely fixed, no investment would take place. Change in the demand for capital goods would result only in a change in the price of capital goods and a reallocation of the existing capital stock. However, even in a fairly short period of time the capital-goods-producing sector of the economy does supply a flow of newly produced capital goods. These goods are part of current real output and are real aggregate investment.

When the real rate of interest declines, capital goods become attractive relative to alternative forms of wealth. Thus, a decline in the real rate of interest will increase the demand for capital goods and drive up the price of capital goods. With an increase in the price of capital goods relative to other goods and services available in the economy, the capital-goods-producing sector of the economy will respond by increasing output. This additional production of capital goods is the additional investment for the economy. The increase in real investment demand as a result of a decrease in the real rate of interest is shown in Figure 20.5. If, in fact, it is possible for the monetary authorities to lower the real rate of interest from $r_1$ to $r_2$, as shown in Figure 20.5, real investment demand per period will increase from $i_1$ to $i_2$.

*Figure 20.5*
**The Investment Function**

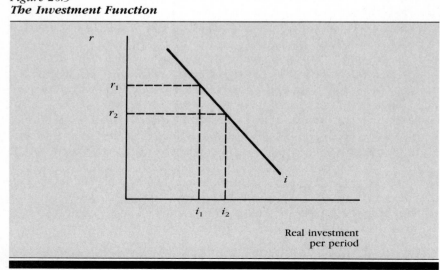

## INTEREST-INDUCED CHANGES IN AGGREGATE DEMAND AND THE *is* CURVE

Clearly, the investment function is of great importance to Keynesian theory. If investment demand is a function of the real rate of interest, as we have shown in the previous section, the mechanism whereby the authorities might change aggregate demand is readily apparent. If the authorities can change the real rate of interest, aggregate demand per period will change. If the level of employment is considered too low, it can be remedied when the authorities decrease the real rate of interest. A decrease in the real rate of interest will induce an increase in investment per period and hence an increase in the level of aggregate demand per period. Producers will then respond to the increase in demand by increasing their output, which in turn will require that they increase their level of employment.

A decrease in the real rate of interest from $r_1$ to $r_2$ will increase investment demand from $i_1(r_1)$ to $i_2(r_2)$. This is shown in Figure 20.6 as an increase in aggregate demand from $d_1$ to $d_2$. This increase in aggregate demand causes the equilibrium level of output per period in the product market to increase from the real amount $y_1$ to the real amount $y_2$.

The relationship between the real rates of interest and the corresponding equilibrium levels of real output per period in the product market

*Figure 20.6*
**The Effect of a Change in the Real Rate**
**of Interest on Equilibrium Output**

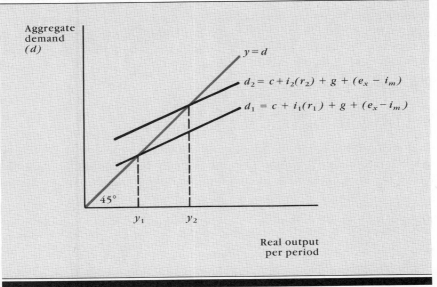

*Figure 20.7*
***The* is *Curve***

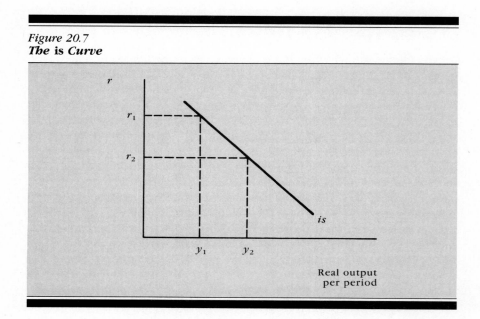

is called the *is curve*.[7] For the real interest rate $r_1$, the equilibrium level of real output per period is $y_1$. When the real rate of interest is reduced to $r_2$, real investment demand increases and the equilibrium level of real output per period increases to $y_2$. These equilibrium relationships are shown on the *is* curve in Figure 20.7.

At lower real rates of interest, aggregate demand is increased through increases in investment demand and the equilibrium level of output per period will be higher. Since the *is* curve shows all possible equilibrium positions in the product market, it shows the authorities exactly what real rate of interest is required to achieve any desired level of output and employment.

## STABILITY IN THE PRODUCT MARKET

In deriving the *is* curve, we have assumed that producer expectations have not changed. In other words, we have assumed that investors have not had cause to revise their estimations of the real net revenues expected from

---

[7]The *is* curve was derived first by Sir John Hicks in "Mr. Keynes and the Classics: A Suggested Interpretation," *Econometrica* (1937): 147–159. It gets its name from the equality between the flow of real investment ($i$) and the flow of real saving ($s$) in a simple model with no government and no foreign trade. Since product market equilibrium occurs when $y = d = c + i$, and since income can either be consumed or saved ($y = c + s$), we have

$$i = s.$$

*Figure 20.8*
**A Shift in the is Curve**

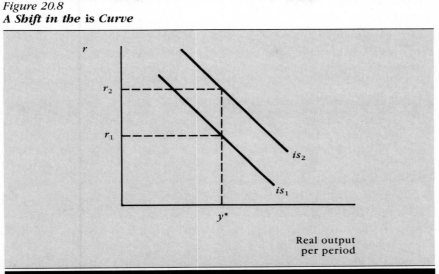

capital goods. When Keynes wrote *The General Theory,* he took great care to show that the investment function was dependent on investor expectations of net revenues. To predict the net real revenue from capital goods, investors must predict not only what can be sold in the market for the product (a flow that depends on the expectations of many factors involved with the production and marketing of the product produced as well as relative product prices), but also how much will be spent on other factors of production involved in producing the product and on changes in the general price level. Since these net real revenues are predicted for some time in the future, there obviously is a great deal of uncertainty involved. As investor expectations change, the demand for capital goods will change.

If investors have improved expectations, the demand for capital goods will increase, causing an increase in investment demand for any real rate of interest. The result is a shift in the aggregate demand function and in the *is* curve. The *is* function will shift out from $is_1$ to $is_2$, as shown in Figure 20.8. With this shift, the real rate of interest required to keep the level of real output at $y^*$ will change from $r_1$ to $r_2$. As expectations about the future change, it will be necessary for the monetary authorities to change the real rate of interest continually to maintain the desired level of output per period. Even if we assume that it is a simple task for the monetary authorities to change the real rate of interest (which is by no means clear), it is not necessarily advisable to change the rate continually. Continually changing the rate of interest seems likely to increase, rather than decrease, the amount of instability in the economy.

Because of the changes in investor estimates of the net real revenues (caused by what Keynes chose to call their "animal spirits"), Keynes believed that the investment schedule was very unstable. This led him to be very skeptical of the degree to which monetary policy alone could be effective.[8] Keynes therefore advocated a combination of monetary policy and "fiscal policy." The fiscal policy would consist of manipulating the level of government expenditure ($g$) per period to offset the swings in private investment. Then, when this activity had stabilized the investment schedule, the monetary authorities could try to regulate the quantity of investment per period by changing the real rate of interest.

## SUMMARY

The Keynesian product market is demand-dominated. Producers of output are assumed to alter output in response to changes in aggregate demand. An unintended inventory accumulation signals to producers that the supply of real goods and services exceeds demand, and producers will respond by reducing output and employment. Similarly, unintended inventory decreases signal to producers that demand for real goods and services exceeds their supply. Producers will respond by increasing the output of real goods and services per period. These adjustments in aggregate output per period continue until aggregate supply has adjusted to the point of effective demand.

If authorities are able to change the level of any of the components of aggregate demand, there will be an increase in equilibrium output that is greater than the original increase in demand. The reason for this is that consumption is an increasing function of income. As output is increased in response to an increase in demand incomes will increase, causing an induced increase in consumption (the *multiplier effect*). The size of the multiplier depends on the marginal propensity to consume.

Monetary policy is possible in the Keynesian system because of the relationship that exists between investment demand and real interest rates. If the monetary authorities can reduce the real interest rate, investment demand will increase. The resulting increase in aggregate demand will induce producers of output to increase the supply of goods and services and the level of employment. However, the investment demand function is believed to be highly unstable because of uncertainties involved in predicting the net real revenue stream from capital goods. It is this instability in investment demand that led Keynes to advocate the use of fiscal policy as a supplement to monetary policy in stabilizing the economy.

---

[8] *The General Theory,* 164.

## Key Terms

aggregate demand
unintended inventory
    accumulation
unintended inventory decrease
point of effective demand
marginal propensity to
    consume

investment multiplier
the multiplier effect
induced consumption demand
the *is* curve
stabilization policy

## Questions

1.  "An unintended inventory accumulation implies that the supply of output is greater than demand and employment will decline." Evaluate.

2.  "In the simple Keynesian system with a marginal propensity to consume of 0.75, a $1 increase in government expenditure will increase aggregate demand and will shift the *is* curve to the right by $4." Evaluate.

3.  "The greater the marginal propensity to consume, the greater will be the increase in output resulting from an increase in investment demand." Evaluate.

4.  "The greater the marginal propensity to consume, the greater will be the increase in output resulting from a decrease in the real rate of interest, and the flatter will be the *is* curve." Evaluate.

5.  Explain why the *is* curve might be unstable and how government expenditure possibly could be used to stabilize aggregate demand.

## Additional Readings

Hicks, John R. "Mr. Keynes and the Classics: A Suggested Interpretation." *Econometrica* 5 (April 1937): 147–159.

*The classic article in which the* is-lm *framework for the analysis of Keynes's theory was introduced.*

Keynes, John Maynard. *The General Theory of Employment, Interest and Money.* New York: Harcourt Brace and Company, 1936.

*Perhaps the classic book in macroeconomics. Difficult to read and harder to interpret, this book is the basis for the systems that evolved into Keynesian economics.*

Patinkin, Don. *Money, Interest, and Prices,* 2d ed. New York: Harper & Row, 1965.

*An advanced-level general equilibrium approach to monetary theory with an integration of microeconomic value theory into macroeconomics.*

Samuelson, Paul A. "The Simple Mathematics of Income Determination." (1948). Reprinted in Johnson, Walter L., and David R. Kamerschen. *Macroeconomics Selected Readings.* Boston: Houghton Mifflin Company, 1970: 39–49.

*A mathematical exposition of a Keynesian model.*

Smith, W. L. "A Graphical Exposition of the Complete Keynesian System," in *Readings in Money, National Income, and Stabilization Policy,* edited by W. L. Smith and R. L. Teigen. Homewood, Ill.: Richard D. Irwin, 1974: 61–67.

*A graphical exposition of the workings of different forms of the Keynesian model.*

# CHAPTER TWENTY-ONE

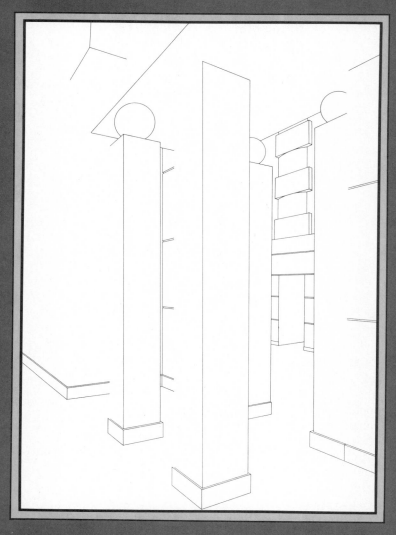

# THE MONEY MARKET IN THE
# KEYNESIAN SYSTEM

*The demand for money for transac-*
*tions purposes is an increasing*
*function of income, and the asset*
*demand for money is a decreasing*
*function of the rate of interest.*
*Therefore, at higher levels of in-*
*come, a higher rate of interest is*
*required to equilibrate supply and*
*demand in the money market. This*
*equilibrium is represented by the*
*lm curve. Interactions between the*
*product market (the is curve) and*
*the money market (the lm curve)*
*determine equilibrium in the*
*Keynesian system, and policies de-*
*signed to change output and em-*
*ployment must affect either the is*
*or the lm curve.*

The money market enters the Keynesian system in the determination of the market real rate of interest. As in the neoclassical system, monetary policy operates through changes in the money supply, but the emphasis here is very different. Because the Keynesian system is demand-oriented, changes in levels of output, income, and employment only occur through activities that change the level of aggregate demand per period. When the money supply is changed, conditions in the money market change (there are changes in "credit conditions"). If these changes affect the market real rate of interest, the change in the money supply can have the effect of changing real investment—and hence employment and output.

As is the case in the neoclassical system, equilibrium in the money market occurs when factors that affect the demand for money adjust until the demand for money is equal to the supply of money. However, there is a significant difference between the Keynesian and neoclassical systems in both the importance of the money market and the adjustment factors in the market. In the neoclassical system, the quantity of money available and money market conditions directly affect the general price level and the anticipated rate of change in prices. In the Keynesian system, while these price level factors are important in their influence on the demand for money and conditions in the money market, they are not the primary adjustment factor in the money market.

The basic apparatus of the Keynesian system was developed as an outgrowth of the experiences of the Great Depression of the 1930s, so it is not surprising that the model has emphasized the problem of unemployment. However, in the post–World War II period, the problems of inflation have been much more intense, and this has meant that the basic Keynesian system has had to be adjusted to take price changes into consideration. In order to bring the Keynesian system up to date, therefore, it is necessary to include the price level, and expected rate of change of prices.

## THE DEMAND FOR REAL MONEY BALANCES

The factors affecting the demand for *real money balances* are remarkably similar in the Keynesian and neoclassical systems (*see* Chapter 16).[1] However, there is a difference of emphasis. The usual Keynesian function is expressed in much simpler terms than the neoclassical function. The demand for real money balances is expressed as a function of market interest rates and the level of real income per period:

$$\left(\frac{M}{P}\right)^d = \ell(R, y).$$

The level of real income per period is included to show that there will be an increase in the demand for real money balances associated with higher levels of real income, and the market interest rate is included to show that the demand for real money balances will be sensitive to changes in the rates of return available on alternative assets.

In order to show the place of price expectations in this demand function, however, it is possible to make use of Fisher's equation ($R = r + \dot{P} + r\dot{P}$), and state the demand function as:

$$\left(\frac{M}{P}\right)^d = \ell(r, y, \dot{P}).$$

The market real rate of interest captures the effect of the real rate of return that is available on alternative assets, but price expectations can now be considered separately. If the prices of goods and services are expected to increase in the future (if $\dot{P}$ is positive), then—other factors remaining the

---

[1] Important work on the demand for money function has been carried out by the leading proponents of both the Keynesian and neoclassical approaches to macroeconomics. Though their overall view of the economy may be different, it is clear that their studies of this particular component have been remarkably similar. *See,* for example: Friedman, Milton, "The Quantity Theory of Money—A Restatement" in *Studies in the Quantity Theory of Money,* ed. Milton Friedman (Chicago: University of Chicago Press, 1956): 3–21; and Tobin, James, "Liquidity Preference as Behavior Towards Risk." *Review of Economics and Statistics* 25 (February 1958): 58–86.

same—individuals are likely to shift their wealth out of money and into goods: the demand for real money balances will fall. When prices are not expected to change, there is no difference between the nominal and real rates of interest (if $\dot{P} = 0$, then the demand function $\ell(r, y)$ is equivalent to the demand function expressed as $\ell(R, y)$). We will first discuss money market equilibrium on the assumption that prices are not expected to change, and add in price expectations later.

In discussing the demand for money function, it is common today to distinguish between (1) the transactions demand for money and (2) the asset demand for money, though originally Keynes had made a distinction between (1) the transactions demand, (2) the precautionary demand, and (3) the speculative demand. Keynes, however, had collapsed his three demands into two by showing that each was a function of only income or the interest rate (Keynes did not consider price expectations explicitly in the function).

## The Transactions Demand for Money

Because money is the generally accepted means of exchange, one of the principal benefits from holding money balances is in having these balances available for acquiring goods and services. Real money balances represent immediate command over, and the ability to purchase, real goods and services. When individuals receive their income, they will decide to spend some proportion of that income on real goods and services before the next part of their income is received. Having made that decision, a part of the income will be kept to purchase those goods and services. The higher the level of income, the higher the level of expenditure, and therefore the higher the demand for real money balances. Thus, the *transactions demand* for money is directly related to real income (*see* Figure 21.1). As the amount of real goods and services produced per period increases, the increase in real income will induce individuals to hold additional real money balances for use in purchasing the additional real goods and services.

## The Asset Demand for Real Money Balances

People hold real money balances as part of their wealth holdings. The *asset demand for real money balances* depends on the rate of return for holding real money balances relative to the alternative rates of return that are available on other assets. In real terms, the rate of return to the alternative forms of wealth holdings, which represent future command over goods and services such as bonds and other credit instruments, is given by the market real rate of interest. An increase in the market real rate of interest will make bonds attractive, relative to real money balances, and the quantity of real money balances demanded will decline. At lower real interest rates, the opportunity cost of holding the highly liquid real money balances will be

*Figure 21.1*
**The Transactions Demand for Real Money Balances**

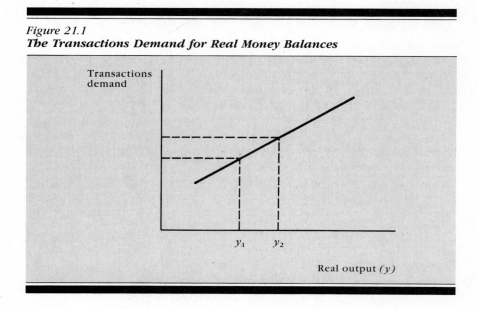

lower and the quantity of real money balances demanded will increase. This relationship is indicated in the demand for real money balances curve in Figure 21.2, where prices are not expected to change.

**The Speculative Demand for Money Balances.** When Keynes developed his analysis of interest rates and the money market, he was principally concerned with the form in which individuals held their command over future goods. This is basically a choice between longer-term bonds or shorter-term, highly liquid assets. Money was considered a form of immediate, highly liquid command over future goods and services, and the interest rate was viewed as the price being paid for holding highly liquid assets.[2] The price was the cost incurred in terms of forgone interest income. The demand for real money balances was part of people's preferences for liquidity in short-term assets as opposed to longer-term, less liquid assets, such as bonds. Historically, this *liquidity preference* has evolved to a consideration of the demand for real money balances rather than a demand for a wider set of liquid assets.

In Keynes's view, one of the more significant determinants of liquidity preference resulted from the uncertainty that exists in future interest rates. The possibility that interest rates on longer-term credit instruments might change generates the possibility that individuals might profit by correctly

---

[2] *The General Theory*, 166–167.

Figure 21.2
**The Supply of and Demand for Real Money Balances**

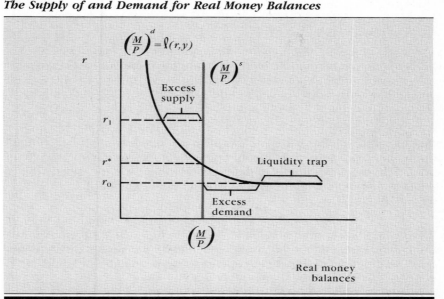

anticipating the interest rate movements. These gains can be realized by shifting individual holdings between shorter-term liquid assets and longer-term bonds.

If individuals feel that the current rate of interest is "too low," relative to what is considered to be "normal," this is the same thing as individuals expecting that interest rates will rise in the near future. If interest rates in the future in fact do rise as expected, the price of bonds will decline, and those holding bonds will suffer a capital loss. Thus, when interest rates are considered to be "too low," there will be a speculative demand for real money balances to avoid the expected capital loss from holding less liquid, long-term bonds.

Alternatively, if some individuals consider the current interest rate "too high," relative to what is considered to be "normal," they are expecting interest rates to fall. These individuals then will speculate and attempt to realize capital gains by holding greater amounts of their wealth in longer-term bonds as opposed to holding money. If interest rates actually fall as these individuals expect, the price of bonds will rise, and these individuals will realize capital gains from their increased holdings of bonds.

The speculative demand for real money balances is a demand for money in anticipation of future interest rate changes. The speculative motive for holding money (like the asset demand for money) makes the demand for real money balances a decreasing function of the real rate of interest as shown in Figure 21.2. Different individuals have different opinions as to what will happen to interest rates because they have different opinions about what is "normal." At higher rates of interest it is likely that a larger segment of the economy will consider the current rate of interest "too high" and will expect interest rates to fall in the future. Thus, there is likely to be a greater demand for bonds and a smaller quantity of real money balances demanded as individuals speculate in anticipation of realizing capital gains. Also, when the current market real rate of interest is low, it is likely that more individuals will perceive the current interest rate "too low" and that future interest rates are likely to be higher. This will generate a greater quantity of real money balances demanded as individuals speculate by holding money (and other short-term, highly liquid assets) in an attempt to avoid suffering a capital loss in the event that interest rates actually rise as they expect. Thus, the quantity of real balances demanded will increase when the market real rate of interest is lower.

One outgrowth of the idea of a speculative demand for money is the concept of the Keynesian liquidity trap. A *liquidity trap* would occur if the demand for liquid assets were sufficiently strong that the economy could absorb either increases or decreases in the amount of liquid assets available *without* a change in market rates of interest. This would occur if the demand for real money balances (or other short-term, highly liquid assets) were perfectly elastic (flat in the diagram) with respect to the interest rate.

The liquidity trap no longer is considered to be the essential part of the Keynesian system that it was once thought to be, but as a limiting case it is still of some theoretical interest. Empirically, the existence of a liquidity trap never has been proved, but it was thought in the early days of the development of the Keynesian system that a highly elastic demand for money could occur at low interest rates. This was thought to be possible because of the way in which the speculative demand for money depends on expectations of future changes in interest rates. It was thought that there would be an effective lower limit below which individuals would not expect interest rates to fall. Since goods can be held for use in the future, and goods can be used to produce additional goods and services in the future, generally it is not expected that real interest rates will become negative. Also, it does not seem reasonable to expect that funds would be lent at an interest rate less than the amount necessary to cover the transactions costs involved in extending and collecting the loan. If interest rates actually fell to such a lower limit, the only expected changes in interest rates would be increases. Under that situation, whatever amount of liquidity was supplied to the economy would be absorbed at the current rate of interest. A liquidity trap segment of the real money balance demand curve is included in Figure 21.2.

## EQUILIBRIUM IN THE MONEY MARKET

Equilibrium in the money market occurs when the demand for real money balances is equal to the supply of real money balances. The supply of money in real terms is given by the nominal money supply divided by the general price level $(M/P)^s$. The supply of real balances will increase with increases in the nominal money supply or with decreases in the general price level. Since the general price level in the Keynesian system is determined by activities within the various sectors of the economy, the monetary authorities do not have direct control over the supply of real money balances. However, the supply of real balances can be affected directly by changes in the nominal supply of money. The nominal supply of money $(M)$ is determined (as shown in Part I) by the decisions of the Federal Reserve, the depository institutions, and the monetary portfolio decisions of the non-bank public (holdings of currency and coin, demand deposits, and time deposits). As we have seen, changes in the nominal supply of money occur through changes in the money multiplier or in the monetary base. Through open market operations, the discount mechanism, and control over variable reserve requirements, the money multiplier, and the monetary base can be broadly influenced by the Federal Reserve and, over time, the monetary authority can determine the nominal supply of money. Assuming, in the short run, that prices remain constant, control over the nominal supply of money will determine the supply of real balances. Equilibrium in the money market will occur when factors in the money market adjust the quantity of real balances demanded to the quantity that is being supplied.

If real income, the general price level, and price expectations remain the same, then adjustments in the money market occur through changes in the market real rate of interest. If the market real rate of interest is $r_1$ in Figure 21.2 (which is above the market-clearing real interest rate) there will be an excess supply of real balances. Individuals will attempt to dispose of these excess holdings of highly liquid assets by lending the funds to others and by buying credit instruments. This will bid up the price of credit instruments and drive down the market real rate of interest. As the real rate of interest declines, the quantity of real balances demanded will increase, and the money market will move to the equilibrium real rate of interest indicated by $r^*$ in Figure 21.2.

Similarly, if the market real rate of interest is at $r_0$, which is below the market-clearing real interest rate, there will be an excess demand for real money balances. To acquire the additional real balances desired, individuals will increase their borrowings or sell off some of their holdings of credit instruments. The price of credit instruments will decline, and the market real rate of interest will increase to the equilibrium real interest rate $r^*$ as shown in Figure 21.2.

In the Keynesian money market, the real interest rate adjusts to equate the demand for real balances with the quantity supplied. The adjustment in the market real rate of interest occurs as individuals attempt to either borrow or lend to remove an excess demand or excess supply of real money balances. The money market adjustments that occur in the Keynesian system are adjustments in the allocation of credit.

## The Demand for Real Money Balances and the lm Curve

The demand for real money balances is found simply by adding together the transactions demand for money and the asset demand for money. As the transactions demand for real money balances is an increasing function of real income, the total demand for real money balances can be shown as a function of the real rate of interest that shifts to the right as real income is increased. This is shown in Figure 21.3a. As real income increases from $y_1$ to $y_2$, the demand for real money balances shifts from

$$\left(\frac{M}{P}\right)^d (y_1) \qquad \text{to} \qquad \left(\frac{M}{P}\right)^d (y_2),$$

and so on as income increases in real terms through $y_3$ and $y_4$.

*Figure 21.3a*
***The Money Market (Assuming That Prices
Are not Expected to Change)***

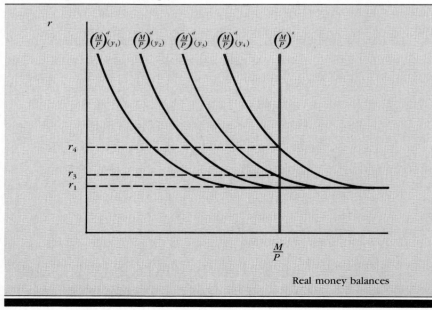

Real money balances

Suppose that the economy is initially in an equilibrium position with real income at $y_3$ and the real interest rate at $r_3$. This equilibrium position for the money market is shown in Figure 21.3a. If conditions in the product market change, the level of real income being generated will change and equilibrium in the money market will be disturbed. For example, if real aggregate demand increases, real output from the product market will rise and the additional real income will increase the demand for real money balances. If this product market adjustment increases real income to $y_4$, the demand for real balances curve will shift to the right to

$$\left(\frac{M}{P}\right)^d (y_4)$$

as shown in Figure 21.3a. The increased transactions demand for real money balances will generate an excess demand for real money balances at the old equilibrium rate of $r_3$. This excess demand for real money balances will induce adjustments in the money market. The market real rate of interest will rise as individuals sell off some of their holdings of bonds and attempt to borrow the additional real money balances desired. The market real rate of interest will rise until the money market reaches the new equilibrium position at the real interest rate $r_4$. Different equilibrium positions in the money market for various levels of real income per period are shown in Figure 21.3a.

The relationship between levels of real income (or output) per period and the corresponding equilibrium real interest rate in the money market is called the *lm curve*.[3] For the real income level $y_3$, equilibrium between the demand for real money balances and the quantity of real balances supplied occurs at real interest rate $r_3$. When real income increases to $y_4$, equilibrium in the money market occurs at real interest rate $r_4$. The equilibrium positions in the money market for a given supply of real money balances (that is, both a given price level and a given nominal money supply) and a constant anticipated rate of change in prices is shown as the *lm* curve in Figure 21.3b. The upward sloping nature of the *lm* curve is the result of the shifts in the demand for real money balances function as the level of real output increases. At higher real income levels the demand for real money balances is greater. Thus, a higher real rate of interest is necessary to reduce the quantity of real balances demanded for asset purposes to bring about equality between supply and demand in the money market.

The *liquidity trap* segment of the liquidity preference curve (demand for real money balances curve), shown in Figure 21.2, also shows up in the *lm* curve. If in fact there is a minimum expected level of real interest rates

---

[3] The *lm* curve (along with the *is* curve) was first derived by J. R. Hicks in "Mr. Keynes and the Classics: A Suggested Interpretation," *Econometrica* (1937): 147–159. Hicks originally called the curve the *LL* curve, but it is now called the *lm* curve from the equality between the demand for real money balances (*l* standing for liquidity) and the supply of real money balances (*m*).

*Figure 21.3b*
**Derivation of the lm *Curve***

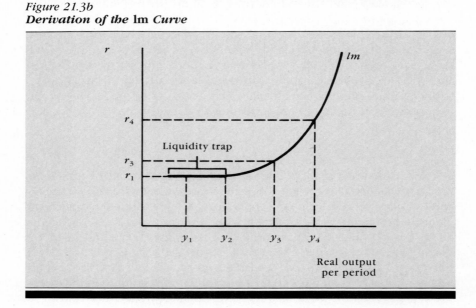

where the asset demand for real money balances is perfectly elastic with respect to the market real rate of interest, the *lm* curve also will be perfectly elastic in this region. For example, in Figure 21.3b an increase in real income per period from $y_1$ to $y_2$ increases the demand for real money balances (the liquidity preference function) in Figure 21.3a shifts from

$$\left(\frac{M}{P}\right)^d (y_1) \qquad \text{to} \qquad \left(\frac{M}{P}\right)^d (y_2),$$

but this is not sufficient to induce a rise in the market real rate of interest. The same quantity of real balances demanded at the real income level of $y_2$ and the real interest rate of $r_1$ would have been demanded at lower levels of real income per period.

## EXPECTED PRICE CHANGES AND THE *lm* CURVE

So far we have assumed that prices are not expected to change. This makes the discussion easier, but it cannot be assumed that this is true in the economy. It is likely that people expect that the price level will change, and this will have an effect on the demand for real money balances. As prices rise, money balances lose their value, so it is to be expected that if prices are expected to rise in the future, people will attempt to move out of money balances and to hold goods. This means that the demand for real money balances will decrease as prices are expected to increase. The effect will be that the *lm* curve will shift to the right.

Changes in the general price level in the Keynesian system affect the money market directly by changing the supply of real money balances. If money demand remains unchanged, an increase in the nominal money supply with a constant price level shifts the *lm* curve to the right. Also, price level increases with a constant nominal money supply shift the *lm* curve to the left. In the same way, if the real money supply remains unchanged, changes in the demand for money will shift the *lm* curve. If price expectations cause a decrease in the demand for real money balances, then (other factors remaining the same) the *lm* curve shifts to the right. If the nominal money supply is increased, we cannot know what the result will be until we know the effect that the change will have on prices and on price expectations. If prices rise at the same rate as the nominal money supply, there will be no change in the real money supply; however, if the expected rate of change in prices has changed, there will still be an effect on the *lm* curve.

## EQUILIBRIUM IN THE KEYNESIAN SYSTEM

Equilibrium in the Keynesian system occurs when both the money market and the product market are simultaneously in equilibrium. These two large markets interact, and the adjustments that occur in either of the markets will induce adjustments in the other market. For example, if product market conditions change, and this alters the level of real output per period, the demand for real money balances will change, inducing adjustments in the market real rate of interest. Similarly, if conditions in the money market change, causing an adjustment in the market real rate of interest, the level of investment demand will change. This change in the level of aggregate demand then will induce a change in the level of real output in the product market. The interaction between these two markets can be analyzed with the use of the *is* and *lm* curves. The *is* curve (derived in Chapter 20) represents the relationship between the real interest rate and the level of real output per period, which generates equilibrium in the product market. The *lm* curve represents the relationship between the level of real output and the real interest rate, which generates equilibrium in the money market. These curves, for given levels of government expenditure, taxation, net exports, prices, and anticipated rates of change in prices, are shown in Figure 21.4. Any changes in the conditions that are assumed given for these two curves would be shown as shifts in either the *is* or the *lm* curve.

Suppose that the economy were initially at a real interest rate of $r_2$ and a level of real output per period of $y_2$ (position $a$ in Figure 21.4). At $a$, both the product market and the money market are out of equilibrium. For the real interest rate of $r_2$ there is not sufficient aggregate demand for real output to sustain the real income level of $y_2$. Equilibrium in the product

*Figure 21.4*
**Market Interaction: The is and lm Curves**

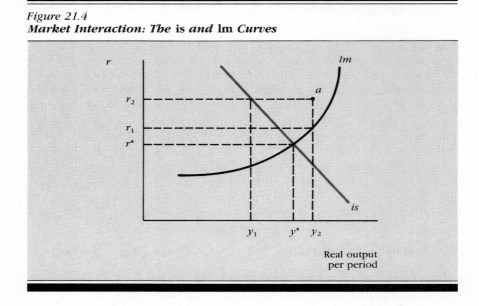

market for a real interest rate of $r_2$ would occur at the level of real output $y_1$. At point $a$ there is a deficiency of aggregate demand. The unintended inventory accumulation will induce producers to cut back on their production. As a result real income and employment will decline.

Similarly, at the real income level of $y_2$, the real interest rate of $r_2$ is too high for equilibrium in the money market. At point $a$ there is an excess supply of real money balances. *Credit conditions* will change as individuals attempt to remove these excess holdings of real money balances by acquiring additional bonds, and the market real rate of interest will decline.

Both markets will continue to adjust until simultaneous equilibrium is reached. This equilibrium position for both the product and the money markets is given by the intersection of the *is* and the *lm* curves at the real income level $y^*$ with the real interest rate $r^*$.

### Shifts in the lm Curve

If the *real* money supply is changed with no change in the demand for money, the resulting disturbance in the money market will also have effects in the product market. In Figure 21.5 the real money supply is increased from

$$\left(\frac{M}{P}\right)^s_1 \quad \text{to} \quad \left(\frac{M}{P}\right)^s_2.$$

Figure 21.5a shows the effects of this change in the money market. As the real money supply increases, the equilibrium real rate of interest for any

*Figure 21.5a*
**An Increase in Real Money Balances Supplied**

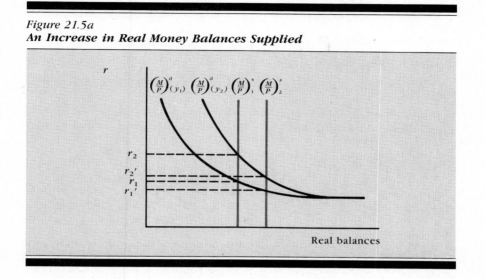

given level of real income decreases. If the level of output is at $y_1$, the demand for real money balances is represented by the curve

$$\left(\frac{M}{P}\right)^d (y_1).$$

Thus, the increase in real money balances causes the equilibrium real rate of interest to fall from $r_1$ to $r_1'$. If the level of output is at $y_2$, the demand for real money balances is represented by the curve

$$\left(\frac{M}{P}\right)^d (y_2),$$

and the increase in real money balances causes the equilibrium real rate of interest to fall from $r_2$ to $r_2'$. This same information is shown in Figure 21.5b as a rightward shift in the *lm* curve from $lm_1$ to $lm_2$.

The effect that the change in the money market will have on the economy is shown in Figure 21.5c, where the shift in the *lm* curve is superimposed on the *is* curve. When the real money supply is at $(M^s/P_1)$ (in Figure 21.5a), the *lm* curve is at $lm_1$ in Figure 21.5b and Figure 21.5c. Given the conditions in the product market (represented by the *is* curve), the economy then will be in equilibrium at point *a* (in Figure 21.5c), where output is $y_a$ and the rate of interest is $r_a$. If the money supply is increased from

$$\left(\frac{M}{P}\right)^s_1 \quad \text{to} \quad \left(\frac{M}{P}\right)^s_2$$

(in Figure 21.5a), the *lm* curve will shift to $lm_2$ in Figure 21.5b and Figure 21.5c. If the rate of interest remained at $r_a$ when the *lm* curve moved to

*Figure 21.5b*
**The Resulting Shift in the lm Curve**

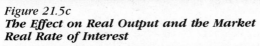

*Figure 21.5c*
**The Effect on Real Output and the Market
Real Rate of Interest**

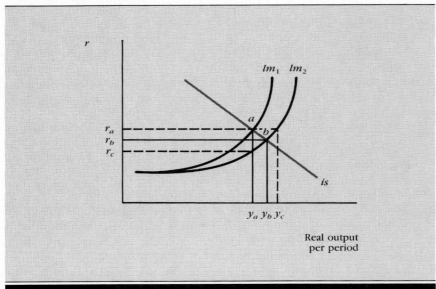

### JAMES TOBIN

James Tobin was born in Champaign, Illinois, in 1918. He attended Harvard University, where he received his Ph.D. in 1947. He has spent all of his academic career at Yale University, where he is currently the Sterling Professor of Economics. From January 1961 to July 1962, Tobin was a member of President Kennedy's Council of Economic Advisers. Wholly trained in the Keynesian period, he has been a leading exponent of Keynesian economics and a leading opponent of monetarism.

Tobin has researched many areas of macroeconomics, and many of the building blocks used today are the result of his work. His earliest work was on money wages and their role in Keynesian macroeconomic theory. In 1955 his attempts to identify the modifications in Keynes's model that would be necessary

*continued*

$lm_2$, the money market could not be in equilibrium unless real output increased to $y_c$. On the other hand, if the level of real output remained at $y_a$, the money market could not be in equilibrium unless the real rate of interest fell to $r_c$.

The disequilibrium is resolved by the actions of individuals in the money market. At interest rate $r_a$, there is an excess supply of real money balances as soon as the real money supply is increased. Those individuals who find that their portfolios have excess money balances then will attempt to reduce their money holdings by spending the money in the markets for credit instruments. This increase in the demand for credit instruments will cause the market prices of the credit instruments to rise and the rates of interest to fall. As interest rates fall, the economy will move along the *is* curve. A new equilibrium will be reached at point $b$, where the level of real output is $y_b$ and the real interest rate is $r_b$.

to generate neoclassical results contributed greatly to the establishment among North American economists of what came to be called the *neoclassical synthesis* and is now used in most textbooks.

Tobin's writings on monetary economics, for which he received the Nobel Memorial Prize, have shown that money holdings can be treated as part of the more general problem of portfolio choice in the face of risk. Believing that the medium of exchange differs only in degree from other assets that are held and not used in exchange, Tobin became an early advocate of the Gurley-Shaw hypothesis. His research into the linkage between the real and monetary sectors of the economy led to important conclusions concerning the effectiveness of open market operations.

Tobin's fame in recent years has stemmed from the fact that, in the face of the monetarist onslaught, he stalwartly has defended the Keynesian position. Emphasizing the monetary aspects of the Keynesian system, he accuses the monetarists of overstating their case: jumping from the discovery that "money matters" to the erroneous notion that money is *all* that matters. He also accuses the monetarists of defining away many of the macroeconomic problems of today by considering that economies are at "full employment" whenever unemployment is sufficiently high to bring about price stability.

## INFLATION IN THE KEYNESIAN SYSTEM

If expansionary monetary or fiscal policy is carried out when the economy is already at full employment, there will be an effect on the general price level. Assume, as is the case in Figure 21.6a, that the *is* and *lm* curves cross at full employment ($y^*$). If monetary policy is then used so that the *lm* curve shifts to the right to $lm_2$, as in Figure 21.6b, it is clear that equilibrium in the markets for goods and services and for money is possible only at a level of output beyond the amount that the fully employed economy can produce. An excess aggregate demand for output beyond the level required to create full employment may result in a temporary increase in output beyond the full-employment level. However, this additional output requires inducing more individuals into the labor force, the employment of some less-productive employees (from the structurally unemployed), and an increased utilization of the capital stock. Production costs will increase in

Figure 21.6a
**Full Employment Equilibrium**

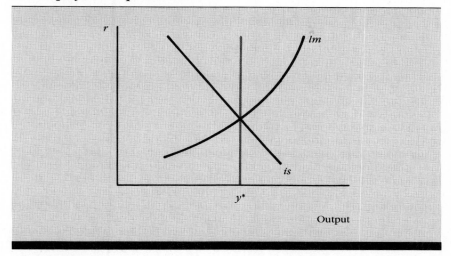

Figure 21.6b
**Monetary Expansion Causing Prices to Rise**

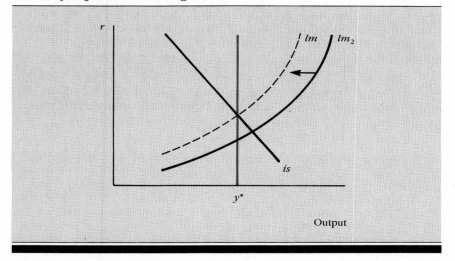

response to the excess in aggregate demand, and the general price level must increase. As long as the excess demand persists, prices will continue to rise and to reduce the real money supply. This will continue until the decline in the real money supply has shifted the *lm* curve back into equilibrium at the full-employment level and the excess demand pressure on prices is released.

*Figure 21.6c*
**Fiscal Expansion Causing Prices to Rise**

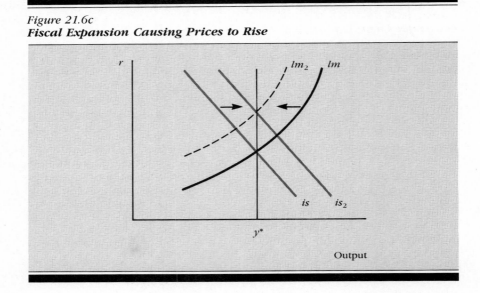

Alternatively, if the economy is in equilibrium at full employment but fiscal policy is then used to shift the *is* curve to the right to *is*₂, as in Figure 21.6c, the result on the general price level will be almost the same. If the *is* curve is at $is_2$, there would be an excess demand for goods and services because the fully employed economy cannot sustain production beyond $y^*$. The excess aggregate demand causes the general price level to rise, and the *lm* curve then shifts to the left as real balances are reduced. Equilibrium is restored and the excess demand pressure on prices to rise is released when the *is* and *lm* curves cross at full employment.

The Keynesian system is demand-oriented, and shifts in aggregate demand, whether they are caused by monetary or fiscal policy, can create excess demand and cause the general price level to rise. If these rises in the general price level are sustained, there is inflation. Because this inflation is caused by changes in aggregate demand, it is called *demand-pull inflation*.


## THE PHILLIPS CURVE

The Keynesian explanation of demand-pull inflation is not entirely satisfactory for explaining the inflation that we see in the economy. In Keynesian terms inflation is caused when aggregate demand exceeds full employment output, an explanation that seems to indicate that inflation is associated with the attainment of full employment. This clearly does not agree with the facts. Much of the post–World War II period in the United States has been characterized by the simultaneous existence of unemployment and infla-

*Figure 21.7*
*A Phillips Curve*

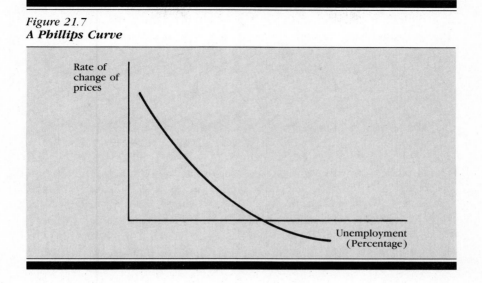

tion. For this reason, the causes of inflation have been sought in phenomena other than excess aggregate demand for output.

The relationship between unemployment and inflation has usually been represented in what is known as a *Phillips curve*.[4] Along a Phillips curve, higher rates of change in prices are associated with lower levels of unemployment, as shown in Figure 21.7. Such a trade-off between employment and inflation is not difficult to explain. It can be viewed, for example, as the result of changes in real wages. Increases in aggregate demand will induce producers to expand output, but an increase in demand for raw materials could cause a general rise in prices. If the prices rise in relation to nominal wages, the real wage will decline and firms will be induced to expand employment. In addition, individuals who are searching for employment will receive employment offers sooner, and this effect also will contribute to the decline in the rate of unemployment. Thus the amount of unemployment could decline as prices were rising, and the real wage was falling. Expansionary policies could, therefore, be accompanied by higher employment but also by a faster increase in prices.

The trade-off between the level of unemployment and the rate of change in prices can be attributed to a lag in nominal wage rate changes behind changes in the general price level. There are two general factors that contribute to this lag: the existing wage contracts and lags in obtaining

[4] The Phillips curve is named after A. W. Phillips, who found a statistical relationship between the level of unemployment and the rate of change of money wages. *See:* Phillips, A. W., "The Relationship Between Unemployment and the Rate of Change of Money Wage Rates in the United Kingdom, 1861–1957," *Economica* 25 (November 1958): 283–299.

information. Many labor contracts extend for two to three years in time, and it is difficult to alter the nominal wage from that contracted for during that period. Even when it is known that the real wage has declined, it may be too costly to find a method of adjusting the nominal wage to compensate. Certainly, the employee with the reduced real wage could quit and seek employment elsewhere that was not subject to the contract. However, without extremely large changes in prices, the gains from a new position would be unlikely to compensate for the costs incurred when unemployed. Workers also may suffer from *money illusion* and base their employment decisions on the nominal rather than the real wage. Basing decisions on the nominal rather than the real wage is probably due to a lack of information on the actual change in prices and their effect on the individual employee's real wage. In the short run, decisions may be based on the information that is available, which is the nominal wage rate. With some lags in the adjustment of nominal wages to changes in the general level of prices, increases in the rate of change in prices will likely be associated with lower levels of unemployment.

## SUMMARY

In the Keynesian system, aggregate demand for real output is the primary determinant of output, income, and employment. The money market is important in the Keynesian system through its effect on aggregate demand, an effect that is transmitted mainly through changes in the market real rate of interest. When conditions in the money market change, the adjustment that occurs is in credit conditions as indicated by real interest rates. A decline in the market real rate of interest will generate an increase in investment demand and this, by increasing aggregate demand, will cause an expansion of output and employment.

Equilibrium in the money market occurs when the demand for real money balances is equal to the quantity that is being supplied. While the monetary authority generally can control the nominal supply of money, the supply of real money balances is not controlled directly because it cannot control the general price level. The most important element that determines the demand for real money balances is the market real rate of interest. At higher real interest rates, the quantity of real money balances demanded declines as real money holdings become relatively less attractive in asset portfolios and as some individuals speculate on future decreases in interest rates by holding bonds rather than money. In the Keynesian system, the money market adjusts through changes in the market real rate of interest as individuals change their portfolios by buying or selling bonds until the demand for real money balances has adjusted to equal the quantity that is supplied.

The demand for real money balances is the sum of the transactions demand for money and the asset demand for money. Although both of these demands will be affected by changes in price expectations, the transactions demand is considered to be primarily a positive function of real income, and the asset demand a negative function of the real rate of interest. Thus, equilibrium can exist in the money market at different levels of income and interest. The higher the real rate of interest (the lower the asset demand for money), the higher must be the level of income (the higher the transactions demand for money) in order for equilibrium to exist in the money market. These equilibrium positions are shown on the *lm* curve, and the *lm* curve will shift when there are changes in real money supply and/or real money demand.

The demand for real money balances is the sum of the transactions demand for money and the asset demand for money. As the transactions demand is principally a positive function of real income, and the asset demand is principally a decreasing function of the real rate of interest, equilibrium can exist in the money market at different levels of income and interest rates. The higher the real rate of interest (which decreases the asset demand for money), the higher must be the level of income (which increases the transactions demand for money) in order for equilibrium to exist in the money market. These equilibrium positions are shown on the *lm* curve.

Equilibrium in the Keynesian system occurs when the product and money markets are both simultaneously in equilibrium. This occurs at the real interest rate and level of real income where the *is* and *lm* curves intersect. If the economy is not at that position, the disequilibrium in the product market will generate changes in the level of output, and the disequilibrium in the money market will cause changes in the market real rate of interest until both markets are adjusted to that equilibrium position.

The Keynesian system allows for inflation as the result of excess aggregate demand for output, but the simultaneous existence of unemployment and inflation has led to the introduction of Phillips curve analysis. This curve is basically a trade-off between unemployment and inflation. The usefulness of this apparent trade-off has, however, been questioned. It appears that in the long run it would be difficult, if not impossible, to buy a reduction in unemployment with a simple increase in the rate of inflation.

## Key Terms

real money balances
transactions demand for money
asset demand for real money
 balances
liquidity preference

speculative demand for money
liquidity trap
*lm* curve
credit conditions
Phillips curve

## Questions

1.  In what sense can it be said that the demand for money in the Keynesian system is similar to the demand for any set of highly liquid assets?

2.  What effects will an increase in the general price level have on the demand for real money balances?

3.  An increase in the supply of real money balances will cause a decline in the market real rate of interest and an increase in real output and employment. Explain.

4.  How do price expectations affect the *lm* curve?

## Additional Readings

Bronfenbrenner, M., and T. Mayer. "Liquidity Functions in the American Economy." *Econometrica* 28 (October 1960): 810–834.

*An early attempt to find empirical evidence for Keynesian money demand functions.*

Laidler, David E. W. *The Demand for Money: Theories and Evidence.* 2d ed. New York: Dun-Donnelly, 1977.

*An examination of the state of knowledge concerning the demand for money with a survey of empirical evidence.*

Tobin, James. "The Interest Elasticity of Transactions Demand for Cash." *Review of Economics and Statistics* 38 (August 1956): 241–247.

*One of the seminal articles on the transactions demand for money.*

Whalen, E. L. "A Rationalization of the Precautionary Demand for Cash." *Quarterly Journal of Economics* (May 1966): 314–324.

*An analysis of the factors determining optimal precautionary cash balances as an inventory problem in the face of uncertainty over receipts and disbursements.*

# CHAPTER TWENTY-TWO

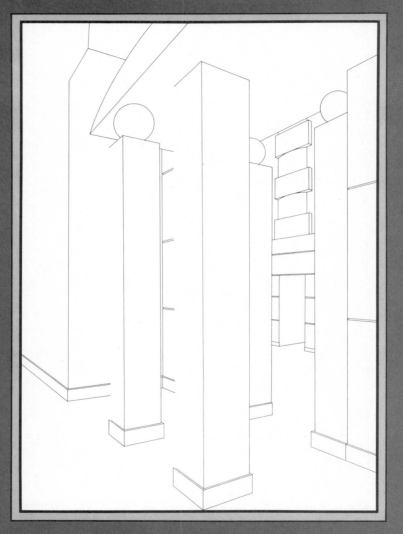

# MONETARY AND FISCAL POLICIES IN
# THE KEYNESIAN SYSTEM

*The effects of monetary policy and fiscal policy on aggregate real output in the Keynesian system can be seen easily from a consideration of is-lm curves. Government expenditure and taxation have their main effects through shifting the is curve; monetary policy has its main effects through shifting the lm curve. Problems arise in the Keynesian system in predicting to what extent nominal changes will affect real variables.*

Keynesian economists consider that the economy may well move toward full employment in the long run, but Keynes made his views plain concerning the advisability of waiting for that position to be reached. In one of his more famous quotes, he said:

> this *long run* is a misleading guide to current affairs. *In the long run* we are all dead. Economists set themselves too easy, too useless a task if in tempestuous seasons they can only tell us that when the storm is long past the ocean is flat again.[1]

Even if it can be assumed that the system will return to full employment eventually, the Keynesian system has an important role for short-run monetary and fiscal policies. By adopting policies that change aggregate demand in the short run, the economy can be moved toward full employment in that short run. Also, since instability in aggregate investment demand and in conditions in the money market may generate economic disruptions, monetary and fiscal policies may provide a useful stabilization to quell the tempestuous seas in the short run rather than waiting for the long run adjustments finally to bring about the calm of full-employment equilibrium.

---

[1] Keynes, John Maynard, *A Tract on Monetary Reform* (London: Macmillan, 1923), reprinted in *The Collected Writings of John Maynard Keynes,* vol. IV (London: Macmillan/St. Martin's Press, 1971): 65.

## FISCAL POLICY

*Fiscal policy* is the use of government expenditure and taxation policy to improve or stabilize general economic conditions. In the Full Employment and Balanced Growth Act of 1978 (which is itself an amendment of the Employment Act of 1946), the normative goals of fiscal policy are set at reducing unemployment, stabilizing the general price level, stimulating growth, and stabilizing the foreign exchange rate for the United States dollar (*see* Chapter 3). National fiscal policy is determined jointly by the legislative and executive branches of government in accordance with these goals.

In general, Keynesian economists believe that fiscal policy can be extremely effective in stabilizing the economy because it has a direct impact on the level of aggregate demand. Government expenditure is an integral part of aggregate demand, and therefore it will play an important role in determining both the amount of output that is supplied and the number of workers employed. Thus, fiscal policy has its impact on the economy through the product market and can be analyzed through its effects on the *is* curve.

### Government Expenditure

An increase in government expenditure has a stimulative effect on the economy. When government expenditure in real terms ($g$) is increased, aggregate demand for output is increased directly. Producers perceive the increase in aggregate demand through an unintended inventory decrease and

*Source:* Drawing by Lorenz, © 1981, The New Yorker Magazine, Inc.

"With your permission, gentlemen, I'd like to offer a kind word on behalf of John Maynard Keynes."

respond to it by expanding output and employment. This initial expansion of output sets into operation an additional sequence of induced consumption demands known as the *multiplier effect*. The additional output that directly results from the increase in government expenditure will increase real income. As real income increases, consumers are induced to increase their consumption expenditures. Individuals will increase the consumption expenditures by their own marginal propensity to consume, multiplied by the increase in their own real income. But for the whole economy we can say that aggregate consumption will increase by the marginal propensity to consume ($\beta$) multiplied by the increase in aggregate output. This induced consumption demand then will further stimulate aggregate demand, resulting in further increases in real income and output. The effect of an increase in real government expenditure in the product market is shown in Figure 22.1 as the shift from $is_1$ to $is_2$. The rightward shift in the *is* curve is equal to $[1/(1 - \beta)]$ multiplied by the increase in government expenditure.

## Crowding Out

The impact of this expansionary fiscal policy on the economy ultimately depends on the interaction between the product market (as represented by the *is* curve) and the money market (as represented by the *lm* curve). If the market real rate of interest remained constant, the full multiplier effect

**Figure 22.1**
**Fiscal Policy: Effect of an Increase in Government Expenditure**

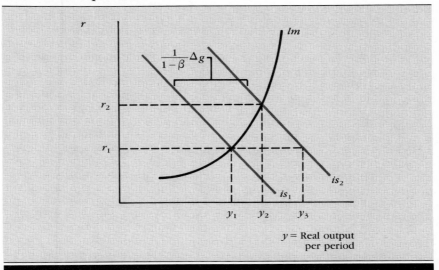

$y$ = Real output per period

would be felt, and real output and real income would increase from $y_1$ to $y_3$, as shown in Figure 22.1. However, to some extent the increase in output and income is offset by the changing conditions in the money market. As real income starts to increase, the transactions demand for real money balances also will increase, and a disequilibrium excess demand for real money balances will appear in the money market. As wealth holders adjust their portfolios to acquire the additional real money balances, the selling of some of their holdings of bonds will drive up the market real rate of interest. Since private real investment is influenced by the market real rate of interest, the increase in the real interest rate will reduce the quantity of real investment demand, which will offset some of the expansionary impact of the increase in government expenditure.

The reduction in private real investment that occurs as a result of the higher market real interest rate is viewed as a *partial crowding-out* of the increased government expenditure. Even though there is more output of real goods and services, and both the government sector and the consumption sector of the economy acquire more goods and services, additions to the capital stock may well be reduced as the private investors are being pushed out of the market by the higher rates being offered on financial assets (such as bonds). Thus, apart from the stimulative impact of the government expenditure on output and employment, there will be a reduction in the stimulus to future economic growth in the private sector brought about by the higher interest rates. Unless the additional government expenditure is being used to make additions to the existing capital stock, the reduction in private investment will reduce the ability of the economy to expand output in the future.

The degree to which private real investment is crowded out by increases in government expenditure depends on the elasticities of the *is* and *lm* curves. The steeper the *lm* curve, the greater is the rise in the interest rate for any given increase in government expenditure; that is, the more interest inelastic the demand for real money balances, the larger the increase in the interest rate for any given shift in the *is* curve. In addition, the more interest elastic the *is* curve (the more interest elastic the private investment function), the greater the reduction in private investment brought about by any given change in the interest rate. Thus, the amount of crowding-out increases as the *lm* curve becomes more interest inelastic and the *is* curve becomes more interest elastic. Conversely, the amount of crowding-out decreases as the *lm* curve becomes more interest elastic and the *is* curve becomes more interest inelastic.

## Taxation Policy

The aggregate level of taxation also affects the economy through changes in the level of aggregate demand. However, unlike government expenditure, taxes only affect aggregate demand indirectly: by changing consumers' disposable incomes. An increase in real taxes ($t$) will reduce aggregate real disposable income dollar for dollar, but since all income is not used for consumption purposes, it will initially reduce real aggregate demand by less than the amount of the increase in taxes. The proportion of aggregate income spent on consumption goods is indicated by the marginal propensity to consume ($\beta$). Thus, an increase in real taxes initially will reduce aggregate demand through a reduction in consumption demand by the marginal propensity to consume multiplied by the increase in the amount of real taxes. Whatever the initial reduction in aggregate demand, the ultimate reduction in output (for any given real interest rate) will be $[1/(1 - \beta)]$ multiplied by the initial decline in aggregate demand. Since, in the case of taxes, the initial decline in real aggregate demand is given by the amount $-\beta \, \Delta t$, the total effect of the tax increase when coupled with the multiplier effect is

$$\Delta y = \frac{1}{1 - \beta} (-\beta \, \Delta t).$$

This is shown in Figure 22.2 as the shift in the *is* curve to the left from $is_1$ to $is_2$.

As is the case with changes in government expenditure, the effect on the economy of a change in real taxes depends on the interaction between the product and money markets. When real output and income start to

*Figure 22.2*
**Fiscal Policy: Effect of an Increase in Taxes**

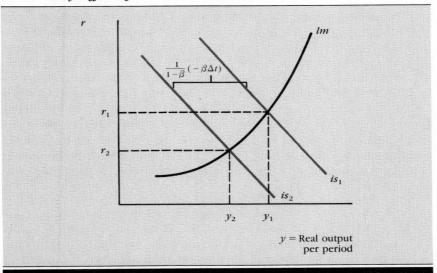

$y$ = Real output per period

decline as a result of a decrease in aggregate demand brought about by an increase in taxes, the demand for real money balances for transactions purposes also will start to decline. This will cause an excess supply of real money balances in the money market. As wealth holders attempt to remove this excess supply of money balances by buying bonds, the market real rate of interest will fall. At lower real rates of interest, the quantity of real investment will increase, and some of the contractionary effect of the increase in real taxes will be offset by this increase in real aggregate demand. As the amount of real taxes is increased, the product and money markets will adjust to a new, short-run equilibrium position at a lower level of real output per period and a lower real rate of interest. This is shown in Figure 22.2 as the movement from the initial equilibrium position at $y_1$ and $r_1$ to the new equilibrium position at $y_2$ and $r_2$.

An interesting aspect of the relationship between government expenditure and taxation is their differential impacts on aggregate demand. Increases in government expenditure directly increase aggregate demand dollar for dollar. However, increases in taxes affect disposable income dollar for dollar, and aggregate demand by less than a dollar per dollar of taxes. Thus, because of the stronger impact of the government expenditure, a policy of financing government expenditure with taxes still will have a stimulative effect on the level of aggregate demand. The impact will be less than for a government expenditure financed by additional borrowing, but it will still be positive.

## MONETARY POLICY

As has been emphasized throughout this book, *monetary policy* must be responsive to the goals established in the Full Employment and Balanced Growth Act of 1978 (and before that, to those established in the Employment Act of 1946). This means that when the Federal Reserve carries out its monetary policy, it must attempt to reduce the level of unemployment, stabilize the general price level, and stimulate economic growth.

However, in the Keynesian system the transmission mechanism differs somewhat from that of the neoclassical system. The effects of monetary policy are transmitted to the economy through the credit markets and changes in market real rates of interest. By changing real rates of interest, the authorities are able to influence the level of aggregate demand through the effects that these interest rates have on aggregate investment.

Equilibrium in the money market occurs when conditions in the money market have adjusted to equate the demand for real money balances to the amount that is being supplied. The Federal Reserve, therefore, influences money market conditions through changes in the supply of real money balances. However, real money balances are the nominal money supply divided by the general price level $(M/P)^s$, so even if the Federal Reserve had complete control over the nominal money supply, it would not necessarily have direct control over the supply of real money balances. The general level of prices is not controlled directly by the monetary authority. If we consider a time period that is so short that the general price level does not have time to adjust, changes in the nominal money supply will be changes in the real money supply. When this is the case, changes in the nominal supply will affect conditions in the money market directly.

In the Keynesian system, the effects of monetary policy are analyzed through the impact of monetary changes on the *lm* curve, but the *lm* curve reflects only changes in the demand for and supply of *real* money balances. The Federal Reserve—through open market operations, discount policy, and reserve requirement changes—can generate changes in the nominal money supply, but the effect of these nominal changes depends on how the nominal money supply changes in relation to the general price level.

*If the general price level remains constant,* the effects of monetary policy easily can be seen from a consideration of the *is-lm* curve diagram. If the Federal Reserve System increases the nominal money supply, the result will be an increase in the real money supply. At the current level of real output and income, an increase in the supply of real money balances will create an excess supply of money in real terms. In an attempt to reduce these excess holdings of money by purchasing bonds or other financial obligations, wealth holders will force down the market real rate of interest. This is shown in Figure 22.3 by the shift in the *lm* curve from *lm₁* to *lm₂*.

*Figure 22.3*
***The Effects of Monetary Expansion***

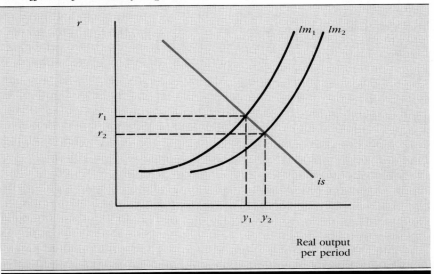

Real output
per period

Similarly, a decrease in the supply of real money balances at the current level of real output and income will create an excess demand for money. Attempting to satisfy this demand for money by selling bonds or other financial obligations will force up the market real rate of interest. This would be shown as a shift in the *lm* curve to the left. Monetary actions that increase the supply of real money balances shift the *lm* curve to the right. Monetary actions that decrease the supply of real money balances shift the *lm* curve to the left.

*If the general price level does not remain constant* when the nominal money supply is changed, the outcome is not so clear-cut. The effect that monetary policy has on general economic conditions depends on the effect it has on the *lm* curve. Whether or not the *lm* curve shifts depends on the changes in the supply of and demand for real money balances. The real money supply increases only if the price level rises at a slower rate than the nominal money supply. In addition, there will be a reduction in the demand for real money balances if the price increase causes a change in the expected rate of change in prices. The *lm* curve will shift to the right whenever the nominal money supply rises in relation to the price level for any given money demand, or whenever there is a reduction in the demand for real money balances for a given real money supply.

The effects of an expansionary monetary policy depend on the interactions between the product and money markets. As the increase in money balances forces down the market real rate of interest, there are repercussions in the product market. Since the quantity of investment demand depends on the market real rate of interest, any decline in that interest rate generates an increase in the quantity of investment demand, which is an increase in aggregate demand for output. The increase in aggregate demand will reveal itself to producers as an unintended decrease in their inventories, and the producers will respond by increasing output and employment. Thus, an increase in the real money supply leads to a new equilibrium position with a higher level of output and a lower real market rate of interest.

## EFFECTIVENESS OF MONETARY AND FISCAL POLICIES

In the Keynesian system, monetary and fiscal policies are effective in changing the level of employment and output only if they can change the level of real aggregate demand. However, from the *is-lm* curve framework, it is obvious that this effectiveness depends on both the elasticities[2] of the curves and on the ability of policymakers to shift them. The more elastic the *is* curve, the greater is the change in output that results from a given change in the interest rate.

---

[2] *See:* Mayer, Thomas, *The Structure of Monetarism* (New York: W. W. Norton and Co., 1978): 1.

## Interest Inelastic Aggregate Demand

The shape of the *is* curve, of course, is greatly influenced by the shape of the real investment function. The more elastic the investment function, the more elastic the *is* curve; the more inelastic the investment function, the more inelastic the *is* curve. In the short run, it is likely that investment demand will be relatively inelastic with respect to the market real rate of interest. When interest rates change, many investment projects already underway are extremely costly to terminate. Also, considerable time often is required to reevaluate decisions to change the size of existing plant and equipment. In the short run, therefore, changes in the market real rate of interest may have little impact on the quantity of real investment demand, and consequently the *is* curve will be interest inelastic.

A highly inelastic *is* curve with respect to the interest rate will mean that fiscal policy will be relatively effective, whereas a monetary policy that is designed to influence the market real rate of interest will be relatively ineffective in changing real output and employment. Even if the monetary authority was effective in reducing the market real rate of interest by expanding the supply of highly liquid assets, little additional investment demand would be forthcoming, and there would be little or no change in output and employment. The effects of a perfectly interest inelastic *is* curve are shown in Figure 22.4. Figure 22.4a shows the effect of an increase in the real money supply when the *is* curve is interest inelastic and does not shift

*Figure 22.4a*
**Monetary Policy: Effect of an Increase in the Supply of**
**Money with a Perfectly Inelastic Demand**

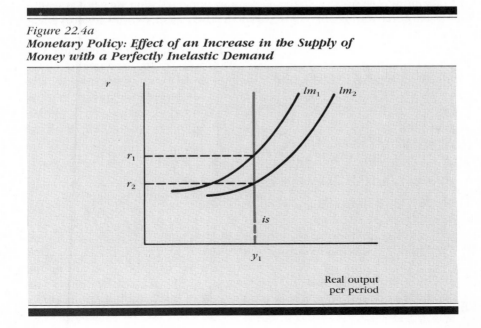

*Figure 22.4b*
***Fiscal Policy: Effect of an Increase in Government
Expenditure with a Perfectly Inelastic Demand***

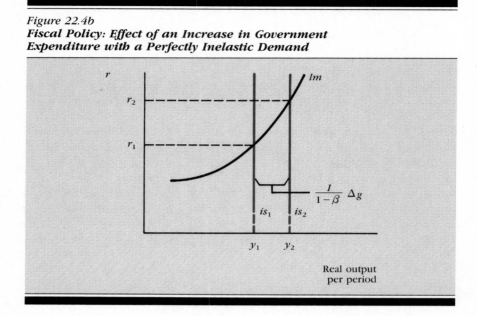

as a result of the increase in the real money supply. The shift in the *lm* curve
from $lm_1$ to $lm_2$ decreases the rate of interest from $r_1$ to $r_2$, but the level of
real output remains at $y_1$. If the monetary policy shifts the *is* curve, as well as
the *lm* curve, the change in output will be the result of the amount of the
shift in the *is* curve.

Figure 22.4b shows the effect of fiscal policy when the *is* curve is
interest inelastic. If the *is* curve shifts from $is_1$ to $is_2$ because of the change
in real government expenditure $\Delta g$, the level of real output increases from
$y_1$ to $y_2$. This is an expansion in output by the full multiplier effect of
$[1/(1 - \beta)]\Delta g$. The interest rate can be seen to rise from $r_1$ to $r_2$, but because the *is* curve is perfectly interest inelastic, this has no effect on the
change in output.

## Interest Elastic Aggregate Demand

Similarly, if real investment demand is highly elastic with respect to the
market real rate of interest, monetary policy aimed at changing the interest
rate can become much more effective in changing the level of output, and
fiscal policy can become much less effective. This is shown in Figure 22.5.
Figure 22.5a shows the effect of increasing the real money supply. As the
real money supply increases, the *lm* curve shifts from $lm_1$ to $lm_2$. This shift
reduces the market rate of interest only a very small amount, from $r_1$ to $r_2$.
However, because of the elasticity of investment demand, this has a large

*Figure 22.5a*
**Monetary Policy: Effect of an Increase in the Supply of**
**Money with an Interest Elastic Investment Demand**

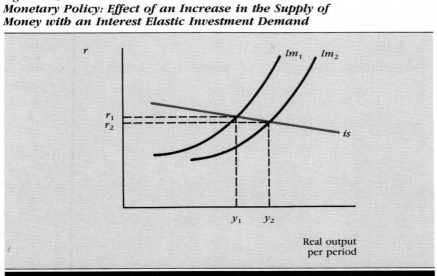

effect on output, increasing it from $y_1$ to $y_2$. Figure 22.5b shows the effects of fiscal policy: if government expenditure is increased by $\Delta g$, the *is* curve will shift to the right by the amount $[1/(1 - \beta)]\Delta g$, from $is_1$ to $is_2$. This rightward shift of the *is* curve moves the economy up the *lm* curve, raising the market rate of interest from $r_1$ to $r_2$. The increase in real output can be seen to be rather small ($y_1$ to $y_2$) and certainly smaller than the amount $[1/(1 - \beta)]\Delta g$. This is the phenomenon known as *crowding-out.* The fiscal policy has shifted the *is* curve to the right, but the increase in the market interest rate causes a reduction in investment to offset the increase in the government expenditure. When the investment function is elastic, it is likely that even a small increase in the interest rate will be sufficient to decrease the amount of private investment by an amount that almost offsets the government expenditure completely.

## Liquidity Trap

The responsiveness of the demand for real money balances to changes in the market real rate of interest (that is, the interest elasticity of the *lm* curve) is also important for determining the effectiveness of monetary and fiscal policies. Although modern Keynesian economists have modified their position somewhat, Keynesians traditionally have claimed that it would be possible for the demand for real money balances to become perfectly elastic with respect to the interest rate because the speculative demand for money

*Figure 22.5b*
**Fiscal Policy: Effect of an Increase in Government
Expenditure with an Interest Elastic Investment Demand**

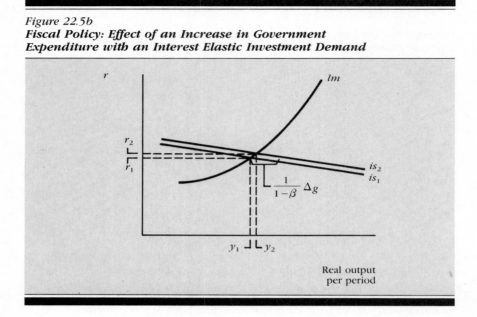

balances could become infinite at low interest rates. This condition, known as the *liquidity trap,* results in a portion of the *lm* curve being perfectly horizontal.

In the liquidity trap, expansionary monetary policy is ineffective in changing the level of output and employment unless it shifts the *is* curve. In the absence of *is* curve changes, changes in the *lm* curve cannot affect the market real rate of interest. Any additional units of money supplied to the system will be absorbed into wealth holders' portfolios at the current rate of interest. Thus, because the rate of interest doesn't fall as the quantity of money is increased, there is no effect on the quantity of real investment. If there is no increase in aggregate demand, there is no increase in output or employment. This is shown by the rightward shift in the *lm* curve from $lm_1$ to $lm_2$ in Figure 22.6a. Clearly, without a shift in the *is* curve, the level of output must remain at $y_1$ so long as the economy remains in the liquidity trap.

Fiscal policy is extremely effective in changing output and employment in liquidity trap situations. Increases in government expenditure directly increase aggregate demand and, therefore, real output. Within the liquidity trap region, this expansion will not cause a rise in the market real rate of interest and there will not be an offsetting reduction in the quantity of real investment demand. Within the liquidity trap region, therefore, the multiplier will have its full effect of $[1/(1 - \beta)]\Delta g$ on the level of real output. This is shown in Figure 22.6b.

*Figure 22.6a*
**Monetary Policy: Effect of an Increase in the
Supply of Money with a Liquidity Trap**

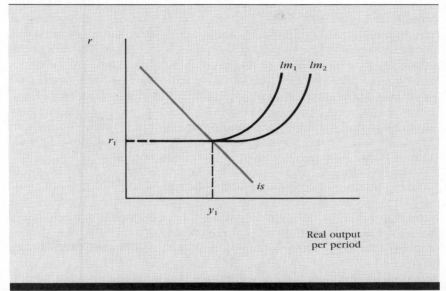

*Figure 22.6b*
**Fiscal Policy: Effect of an Increase in Government
Expenditure with a Liquidity Trap**

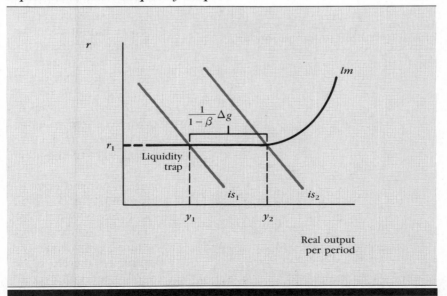

## *The Classical Region*

If the demand for real money balances becomes highly inelastic with respect to the market real rate of interest, fiscal policy becomes relatively
ineffective in changing the level of output, and monetary policy becomes
very effective. This condition is likely to occur at relatively high market real
rates of interest. At high market real rates of interest, the quantity of real
money balances held for speculative purposes is very small, and most of the
money supply is being held for transactions purposes. Thus, small changes
in the market real rate of interest will have little effect on the total demand
for real money balances. A perfectly inelastic demand for real money balances with respect to the market real rate of interest results in a vertical *lm*
curve. Because of the similarity between the results of the Keynesian system
with a vertical *lm* curve and the classical (or neoclassical) results, the vertical part of the *lm* curve is known as the *classical region.*

   In the classical region, monetary policy is effective in generating
short-run increases in real output and employment. By increasing the supply of real money balances, the funds are provided to finance the increased
transactions at higher levels of output. The increased supply of funds causes
the market real rate of interest to fall and induces an increase in the quantity
of investment demand. The additional real aggregate demand then induces
producers to expand both output and employment. The effect of monetary
policy in the presence of a vertical *lm* curve is shown in Figure 22.7a.

*Figure 22.7a*
***Monetary Policy: Effect of an Increase in the Supply
of Money (in the Classical Region)***

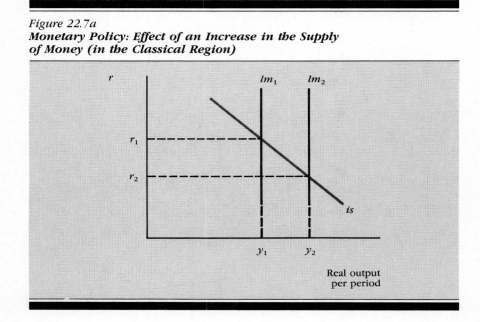

Expansionary fiscal policy, however, is not effective in increasing real output and employment in the classical region, because of the lack of funds to finance the transactions at a higher level of output. Any increase in government spending may start to generate an increase in real output, but this increases the transactions demand for real money balances and forces the market real rate of interest to rise. This results in a reduction in the quantity of investment demand, and the interest rate will continue to rise until real aggregate demand has declined to its original level. In the classical region there is *total crowding-out,* and expansionary fiscal policy results only in a higher market real rate of interest with no increase in real output. This is shown in Figure 22.7b.

The amount of crowding-out in the Keynesian system easily can be seen to be related to the elasticities of the *is* and *lm* curves. The amount of crowding-out is greater the more inelastic the *lm* curve and the more elastic the *is* curve. The amount of crowding-out is smaller the more elastic the *lm* curve and the more inelastic the *is* curve. Obviously, those economists who believe that the *lm* curve is inelastic and the *is* curve is elastic also would tend to believe that fiscal policy is ineffective and monetary policy is effective. Also, those economists who believe that the *lm* curve is more elastic and the *is* curve is more inelastic would tend to believe that fiscal policy is more effective and monetary policy is less effective.

**Figure 22.7b**
***Fiscal Policy: Effect of an Increase in Government Expenditure (in the Classical Region)***

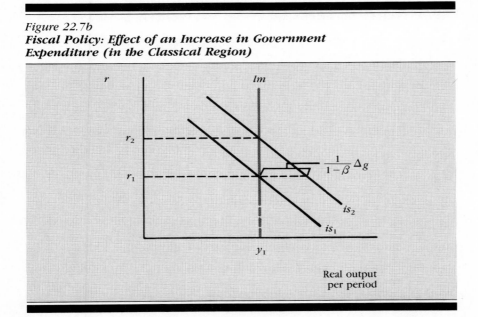

Real output
per period

## MONETARISM AND THE *is-lm* CURVE ELASTICITIES

The issue of crowding-out and the crucial elasticities of the *is* and *lm* curves raises the further issue of the usefulness of *is-lm* curves for explaining monetarism. Originally, monetarism was derived from the neoclassical system. An increase in the money supply affected the prices of goods and services, and through various supply-side effects (mainly in the labor market), this led to changes in the levels of employment and output. However, if the *lm* curve is in fact inelastic, this appears to be a sufficient condition for reaching monetarist conclusions using the Keynesian *is-lm* curves.

If the *lm* curve becomes vertical, or even close to vertical, the money supply clearly becomes the predominant influence on aggregate output and employment. If the *lm* curve is vertical, there is complete crowding-out and the allocative details of aggregate demand are irrelevant. Even though the government expenditure component of aggregate demand has increased, for example, the crowding-out will ensure that the amount of private investment will decrease to offset the change. In addition, if the money supply is increased, the *lm* curve will move to the right, and the output of goods and services will increase. Provided these conclusions are linked to a belief in the inherent stability of the private sector of the economy, the description fits almost exactly the four propositions of monetarism listed by Karl Brunner. (*See* Chapter 15).

## REAL BALANCE EFFECTS IN THE *is* CURVE

So far we have assumed that changes in the supply of real money balances affect only the *lm* curve and not the *is* curve. This means that we have *assumed* that monetary policy can affect the level of output in the economy only through changes in the interest rate. If the money supply is increased in such a model, the rate of interest falls, and the economy moves down the *is* curve to a higher level of output and employment (Figure 22.8). As the *lm* curve moves from $lm_1$ to $lm_2$, output increases from $y_1$ to $y_2$. However, if the monetary policy has a direct effect on the *is* curve, shifting it to the right, output will increase to $y_3$. This is known as the *real balance effect* or the *Pigou effect.*[3]

---

[3] The effect is usually named for Arthur Cecil Pigou, professor of economics at Cambridge University, England, teacher of John Maynard Keynes. Pigou described the effect in Chapter 7 of *Employment and Equilibrium* (London, 1941), but it is incorrect to ascribe the discovery to Pigou, as the effect was well known before Pigou's book was written. The effect is mentioned by Gottfried Haberler in *Prosperity and Depression* (Geneva, 1937) and by Tibor Scitovsky in "Capital Accumulation, Employment and Price Rigidity," *Review of Economic Studies* 8 (1940–1941).

*Figure 22.8*
***Monetary Policy When the* is *Curve Is Also
Affected by Real Money Balances***

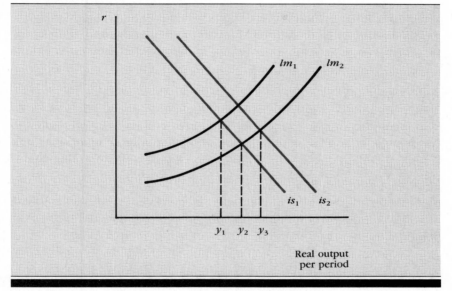

Many economists believe that the real money supply, in fact, will affect the *is* curve directly.[4] If the real money supply is increased, this will create an excess supply of real money balances in wealth holders' portfolios. The attempts by wealth holders to remove this excess supply will entail the purchasing of real goods and services as well as credit instruments. The goods and services demanded may be consumption goods or investment goods, but either way, the *is* curve will shift to the right.

The inclusion of a real balance effect in the demand for aggregate output strengthens the monetarist-type conclusions that can be derived from the *is-lm* curve analysis. Even if the *lm* function were perfectly elastic (which most economists now concede would be an unlikely event), monetary policy still would be effective in changing the level of real output and employment. If the real money supply is increased, the *is* curve moves to the right, and even though the market real rate of interest does not change, the level of output increases.

---

[4] This real balance effect relies on an increase in real money balances' increasing household wealth and inducing an increase in consumption demand. However, it should be noted that an increase in the money supply does not necessarily increase wealth for the economy. The asset holdings of money are offset by liabilities on the balance sheets of financial institutions.

## STABILIZATION POLICY

Fundamental to the Keynesian system is the belief that the level of aggregate demand is somewhat unstable. The economy cannot be relied on to return to full employment in the short run. Relatively minor changes in economic conditions (or even in the perception of economic conditions) are likely to generate substantial changes in the level of aggregate demand. Unless some kind of economic policy is implemented to offset these changes, the adverse conditions are likely to persist.

One source of instability has been the investment demand function. This instability is the result of the highly subjective nature of the decision to invest. The decision to undertake an investment depends on the *expected* real rate of return to capital goods. This expected real rate depends on the expected net receipts from the sale of the goods produced in the future and on the anticipated rate of change in prices. Thus, the expected rate of return to capital goods depends on the perceptions of the investor concerning the economic conditions in the future, and for that reason the level of aggregate real investment may be highly unstable. If investment demand is unstable, real aggregate demand will fluctuate, the *is* curve will fluctuate, and output and employment will fluctuate.

Another possible source of instability is the demand for real money balances. Any instability in the demand for money will be reflected in an instability of the *lm* curve. The cause of the instability here, too, is likely to be expectations. The demand for real money balances depends on, among other things, expectations about future interest rates and about future prices. If people's expectations about the future change, the demand for real money balances is likely to change. This will cause fluctuations in the *lm* curve and will result in fluctuations in output and employment.

Using monetary and fiscal policy in an attempt to offset these fluctuations in economic conditions (whether they are caused by fluctuations in investment demand or fluctuations in the demand for money or any other source) is called *stabilization policy.* However, the cause of the fluctuation is very important for the decision as to what kind of stabilization policy to follow. Translating the instability into movements of the *is* and *lm* curves helps to show how different policies will have an effect.

### Stabilization with Fiscal Policy

In the Keynesian view of the economy, fiscal policy has a key role in policy. The use of fiscal policy to stabilize aggregate demand, to some extent, has been built into the institutional structure of the economy to respond automatically to changes in economic conditions. These "built-in stabilizers" automatically help to maintain the existing level of aggregate demand. If, for example, investment demand declines, real aggregate output will decline by a greater amount because of the multiplier effect. The built-in stabilizers act to reduce the multiplier effect by reducing the decline in disposable income. When such stabilizers are effective, the system operates as though the marginal propensity to consume were less. Typical built-in stabilizers are the progressive income tax system, unemployment compensation programs, and general welfare programs: all of which reduce the multiplier effect by giving some kind of compensation to cover a portion of the lost income when aggregate demand falls.

However, the built-in stabilizers only serve to reduce the impact on economic conditions of any change in the level of aggregate demand. They do not prevent the initial change in demand. Since government expenditure directly affects aggregate demand, it can be used in the Keynesian system to stabilize economic activity directly by offsetting other changes in aggregate demand. A judicious use of government expenditure and taxation policy can maintain the level of $c + i + g + (e_x - i_m)$ at a fairly constant level and therefore avoid fluctuations in output and employment by avoiding fluctuations in aggregate demand.

### *Stabilization with Monetary Policy*

It is also possible for monetary policy to be used to offset fluctuations in aggregate demand. If aggregate demand declines, an expansionary monetary policy can increase aggregate demand again either by lowering the market real rate of interest or through real balance effects. However, deciding to use monetary policy to offset the fluctuations in aggregate demand involves a further decision. That is the decision as to what should be used as the monetary target. Because of the lags in the effect of monetary policy on real output and employment, it is necessary to have some intermediate targets like interest rates or the money supply for the authorities to use in the stabilization policy.

If the instability is in the *is* curve (regardless of which component of aggregate demand is the cause of the fluctuation), it is clear from the *is-lm* curve diagram that a policy aimed at a money aggregate such as the monetary base, or M1 or M2, is preferable to an interest rate policy. The *is-lm* curve diagram can be used to choose between intermediate targets.[5] In Figure 22.9, the instability is assumed to be represented by movements in the *is* curve between $is_1$ and $is_2$. If the monetary authorities react to this instability by keeping the money supply constant, so that the *lm* curve does not move, the interest rate will fluctuate between $r_1$ and $r_2$ and the level of output will fluctuate between $y_1$ and $y_2$. If, on the other hand, the monetary policy were aimed at keeping the interest rate constant at $r_1$, the monetary policy would result in the level of output fluctuating between $y_1$ and $y_3$, which is a greater fluctuation than would result if the authorities had kept the money supply constant.

---

[5] *See:* LeRoy, Stephen F., and David E. Lindsey, "Determining the Monetary Instrument: A Diagrammatic Exposition," *American Economic Review* 68 (December 1978): 929–934.

*Figure 22.9*
**Monetary Policy Targets in the Face of Instability in the is Curve**

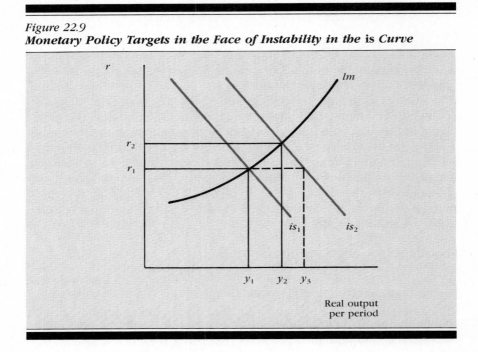

***Instability in the Money Market.***   If the source of the instability is in the demand for money function, the intermediate policy target would likely be different. Figure 22.10 shows the fluctuations in the *lm* curve. If the *lm* curve fluctuates between $lm_1$ and $lm_2$, the level of output will fluctuate between $y_1$ and $y_2$. If the monetary policy were aimed at keeping the money supply constant, output would continue to fluctuate between $y_1$ and $y_2$; but if the monetary policy were aimed at keeping the interest rate at $r_3$, output would be stabilized at $y_3$.

***Selecting a Target.***   Of course, we cannot assume that the instability can be identified easily as being in the *is* curve or the *lm* curve. It may be that both curves are unstable. However, the target used for monetary policy will be different depending on whether the *is* curve or the *lm* curve is thought to be the more unstable of the two. If the *is* curve fluctuates more than the *lm* curve, a money supply target will cause a smaller instability in output than an interest rate target. If the *lm* curve fluctuates more than the *is* curve, an *interest rate target* will cause a smaller instability in output than a *money supply target.*

This kind of analysis shows how important it is to locate the source of instability in the economy. Those who believe that the greatest instability comes from the demand for money function will advocate a monetary pol-

*Figure 22.10*
**Monetary Policy Targets in the Face of Instability in the lm *Curve***

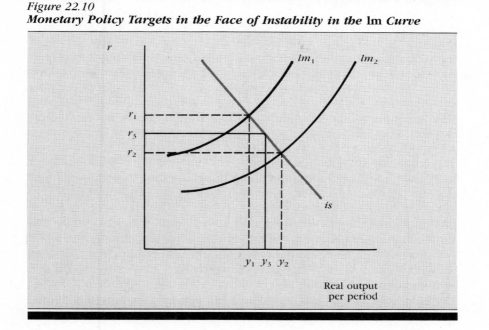

icy aimed at a stable interest rate. Those who believe that the greatest instability comes from the investment function will advocate a monetary policy aimed at a stable money supply. It is these economists who have adopted a monetary policy that is closest to monetarism. Even though they may not believe the neoclassical theory is the best explanation of how the economy functions, they still will conclude that a stable money supply (in a growing economy a growing money supply rather than a constant money supply) is preferable to a stable interest rate. This even may lead people to conclude that a monetary rule is preferable to discretionary monetary policy. When that is the case, these economists will be almost indistinguishable from neoclassical economists in their policy prescriptions.

Interestingly, Keynes himself believed that the instability was in the investment function. His conclusion was that a monetary policy aimed at the interest rate was not likely to be successful. This was, in fact, a large part of the reason for Keynes's advocacy of fiscal policy over monetary policy. In *The General Theory,* Keynes stated:

> it seems likely that the fluctuations . . . will be too great to be offset by any practicable changes in the rate of interest.[6]

---

[6]Keynes, John Maynard, *The General Theory of Employment, Interest and Money* (London: Macmillan, 1936): 164.

## *The Stability of a Phillips Curve*

If the trade-off between the rate of change in the general price level and the rate of unemployment actually exists *and* is highly stable or predictable, policy decisions of both monetary and fiscal authorities will be greatly affected. Clear alternatives would be available: increase government expenditure or increase the money supply and reduce unemployment *but* cause a higher increase in the rate of change in prices; or, alternatively, undertake a contractionary policy to reduce the rate of increase in the general price level *but* suffer additional unemployment. Furthermore, the decisions could be spelled out in specific numerical trade-offs of, say, either an 8.0 percent rate of increase in prices with a 3.8 percent rate of unemployment or a 5.0 percent rate of change in prices with a 5.2 percent rate of unemployment.

Such a simple trade-off between price changes and unemployment does not appear to exist. Relatively high levels of unemployment have been associated with high rates of change in prices, and low levels of unemployment have existed with relatively low rates of change in prices. Annual data for the relationship between the rate of change in the CPI (urban) and the overall rate of unemployment for the United States economy since 1970 are shown in Figure 22.11. Although curves have been drawn through the data showing a shift in the Phillips curve from *a* in the early 1970s to *b* in the late 1970s and early 1980s, the same data might be used to suggest that a trade-off between unemployment and the rate of change in prices does not exist.

The apparent lack of a stable trade-off between unemployment and inflation has led to the belief that, if the Phillips curve exists, then it is subject to changes brought about by expectations. Suppose that the economy is initially in equilibrium with a low rate of change in prices (2 percent per year) and unemployment at the natural rate, assumed to be 6 percent. This is shown by position *a* in Figure 22.12. One difficulty in making policy decisions is that the natural rate of unemployment is not known. Policymakers may perceive, for example, that the natural rate of unemployment and full employment exists at, say, a 5 percent unemployment level. This is shown by the dashed line in Figure 22.12. The economy is initially on the Phillips curve, labeled $PC_1$. Policymakers may decide to speed up the adjustment to their perceived level of full employment with some expansionary policy. The expansionary policy is designed to move the economy to position *b* in Figure 22.12, with a 1 percent reduction in the level of unemployment with only a ½ percent increase in the rate of change in prices. By using an expansionary monetary or fiscal policy to increase aggregate demand, prices will begin rising at a faster rate. If this price rise is at a faster rate than nominal wage increases, the real wage rate will fall and unemployment will decline toward 5 percent.

However, anticipations of price changes will affect wage bargains and also may affect the rate of change in prices associated with a given level of unemployment. As the employed become aware that prices are rising at 2-½ percent instead of the previously slower rate of only 2 percent per year

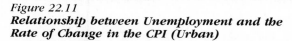

Figure 22.11
**Relationship between Unemployment and the
Rate of Change in the CPI (Urban)**

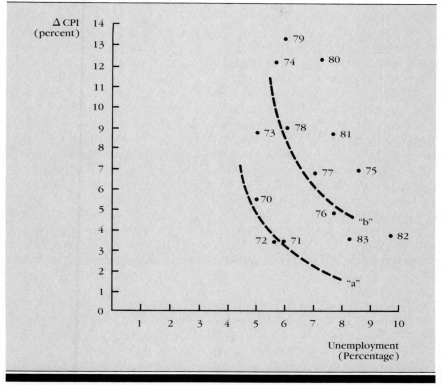

Source: Board of Governors, Federal Reserve System, *Federal Reserve Bulletin* (Washington, D.C.): Tables A47, A51, various issues.

(as indicated by position *b* in Figure 22.12), wage bargains will be struck to achieve a higher rate of change in the nominal wage to compensate for the decline in purchasing power. These higher wage costs then will cause firms to hire less labor, and unemployment may in fact return to the previous level. Instead of an adjustment from position *a* to position *b* in Figure 22.12, and remaining on the Phillips curve $PC_1$, adjustments in expectations and changes in the nominal wage to compensate for price level changes may shift the Phillips curve type of trade-off to a new higher position indicated by $PC_2$. The result of this shift is a movement toward position *c* with only a short-term reduction in the level of unemployment. To sustain a higher level of unemployment than the natural rate, even faster rates of change in prices then would be required as indicated by a movement toward position *d* in Figure 22.12. A continuing attempt to utilize monetary or fiscal policy

*Figure 22.12*
**Anticipations and a Shifting Phillips Curve**

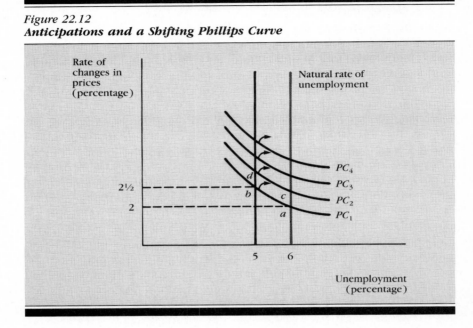

to reduce unemployment below the natural rate could, over time, shift the Phillips curve type of trade-off from $PC_1$ to, say, $PC_4$ with the difference between the two curves being the result of changes in anticipations of price level changes and compensating changes in nominal wages.

In the short run it might be possible to reduce the rate of unemployment without a substantially faster rise in prices. However, as people become aware of price rises and change their behavior in anticipation of a faster change ahead, any short-run trade-off is likely to change. The speed of this shift in the Phillips curve type of trade-off will depend on how individuals formulate their expectations of price level changes and on how rapidly nominal wages can be adjusted to compensate. Since determining any shift in the trade-off depends on changes in expectations that are difficult to predict, determining the exact position of any short-term Phillips curve for use in policy decision making will be difficult.

The gains in employment when the economy is close to full employment usually come from the labor force being "fooled" with a faster than expected rate of change in prices and a decline in the real wage. When price level increases are anticipated, workers will attempt to adjust nominal wages in advance of the actual price increase so that little or no change in the real wage will occur. If expectations are formulated by an adaptive approach based on recent observed changes in prices, it may be possible to increase prices faster than expected, and, thereby, reduce the real wage and unemployment. With this form of *adaptive expectations,* prices actually would have to increase at a faster than expected rate before expectations would be revised upward.

The formulation of anticipations based on *rational expectations* has significant implications on the ability to "buy" reductions in unemployment with a faster than expected rate of increase in the general price level. Rational expectations incorporate the past observed impacts of economic policy in the formulation of expectations of future events. As workers become increasingly aware of the fact that increases in aggregate demand, for example, are brought on by a faster rate of increase in the money supply or, perhaps, increases in government expenditure are associated with price rises, which erode their purchasing power, economic policy changes will be taken into consideration in the formulation of expectations. Any extended use of monetary or fiscal policy to increase aggregate demand could lead to this awareness by the public, and the policy would become less useful in changing unemployment. With any change in policy, employees would anticipate an impact on the general price level and adjust their expectations of the rate of change in prices accordingly. Thus, it will become increasingly difficult (if not impossible) to gain a reduction in the market real wage with a faster than expected rate of change in prices. Real wage reductions then would rely on the inability of workers to alter wage contracts and adjust their nominal wages to compensate for the anticipated price changes.

The practice of *indexation,* an automatic adjustment of nominal wages to actual price increases, makes it increasingly difficult to obtain even short-run reductions in the real wage. When there is an automatic adjustment in money wages through indexation, little or no reduction in the real wage can take place. Even if workers are fooled by a faster than expected increase in prices, nominal wages will adjust automatically to at least partially compensate and unemployment might not decrease even if prices are rising at very high rates.


## SUMMARY

In the Keynesian system, both monetary and fiscal policy have an impact on employment and output by changing the level of aggregate demand. Increases in government expenditure and decreases in taxation are both expansionary fiscal policies. Government expenditure has the stronger impact per dollar because it directly changes aggregate demand in the product market, whereas taxation only has an indirect impact on the level of aggregate demand through changes in disposable income and the effect of those changes on consumption. Monetary policy has its impact on the economy through its effect on aggregate demand. This can be through the changing of interest rates (which will primarily affect investment) or through the real balance effects on the demand for goods and services (which will shift the *is* curve).

The effect of both monetary and fiscal policies on aggregate economic activity depends on the interaction between the product and money markets. For example, the impact that fiscal policy has on the product market may be partially, or even totally, offset by changes in the money market. An increase in government expenditure will have a direct impact on aggregate demand, but it also will have an indirect effect on the economy through its impact on interest rates. As government expenditure is increased, interest rates will be increased and private investment will be decreased. The expansionary impact of the government expenditure is offset by the crowding-out of the private investment.

The extent to which monetary and fiscal policies are effective in changing output and employment, to a great extent, depends on the responsiveness of investment demand to the market real rate of interest, and on the responsiveness of the demand for real money balances to interest rate changes. When investment demand is highly elastic, with respect to the market real rate of interest, monetary policy will be relatively effective in changing output and fiscal policy will be relatively ineffective. When investment demand is highly inelastic, with respect to the market real rate of interest, monetary policy will be relatively ineffective and fiscal policy will be relatively effective in changing output.

Similarly, when the demand for real money balances is highly elastic with respect to the market real rate of interest, monetary policy will be relatively ineffective and fiscal policy will be relatively effective in changing output and employment. When the demand for real money balances is highly inelastic with respect to the market real rate of interest, monetary policy will be relatively effective and fiscal policy will be relatively ineffective in changing output and employment.

The correct monetary policy to use to stabilize the economy depends on the source of the instability. If the investment function is unstable, a monetary policy aimed at a stable money aggregate would be more successful in minimizing fluctuations in output and employment than an interest rate policy. However, if the demand for money function is the source of the instability, a monetary policy aimed at a stable interest rate would be more successful in minimizing fluctuations in output and employment than a policy aimed at a stable money aggregate.

## Key Terms

| | |
|---|---|
| fiscal policy | Pigou effect |
| partial crowding-out | stabilization policy |
| monetary policy | interest rate target |
| liquidity trap | money supply target |
| classical region | elastic and inelastic *lm* curves |
| total crowding-out | elastic and inelastic *is* curves |

## Questions

1.   What will be the effect of an increase in government expenditure in the Keynesian system when substantial amounts of unemployment exist?

2.   If substantial amounts of unemployment exist in a Keynesian system, what will be the effects of an expansionary monetary policy on real and nominal interest rates?

3.   Assuming that the monetary authorities follow an interest rate target, what impact will an expansionary fiscal policy have on the supply of money? Explain.

4.   Should the monetary authorities always follow an interest rate policy if the demand for money function is unstable?

5.   Is there a role in the economy for monetary policy if all instability is attributable to an unstable investment function?

6.   "A Phillips curve does not have to remain in the same position to be useful in the design of monetary policy. What is necessary is predictability." Evaluate.

## Additional Readings

Lerner, Abba P. "Functional Finance and the Federal Debt." *Social Research* 10 (February 1943): 38–51.

*An early discussion of the functions performed in the economy by government spending, taxing, borrowing, and lending in light of the new fiscal theory put forth by J. M. Keynes.*

Lucas, Robert E. Jr., and Thomas J. Sargent. "After Keynesian Macroeconomics." *Quarterly Review* 3 Federal Reserve Bank of Minneapolis (Spring 1979): 1–15.

*A discussion of the problems with Keynesian models, especially in terms of the role of expectations.*

Modigliani, Franco. "The Monetarist Controversy; or Should We Forsake Stabilization Policy?" *American Economic Review* 67 (March 1977): 1–19.

*An analysis of instability generated by demand and supply shocks with a comparison of Keynesian and monetarist approaches to stabilization policy.*

Tobin, James. "How Dead is Keynes." *Economic Inquiry* 15 (October 1977): 459–468.

*An article containing a good defense of Keynesian systems, especially in situations of rising prices, rational expectations, and unemployment.*

# CHAPTER TWENTY-THREE

# THE CONDUCT OF MONETARY POLICY

*The Federal Reserve formulates monetary policy according to its best interpretation of economic theory and its best estimates of economic conditions. Nevertheless, determining the appropriate course of action in any given situation has not been easy. Various proxy targets have been used over the years, but the choice between interest rates and money aggregates still remains at the center of the Federal Reserve's ideological conflict.*

Decisions to undertake particular monetary policies are made by committees in the Federal Reserve. Most crucial decisions are made by the twelve voting members of the FOMC: the seven members of the Board of Governors, and five presidents of district banks of the Federal Reserve System. The Board of Governors always constitutes a majority of the committee. The governors also have additional powers affecting monetary policy: they set certain reserve requirements (between limits set by Congress), and their advice and consent must be sought for discount rate changes made by district banks. However, under the present Federal Reserve procedures, the crucial decisions of monetary policy are made through a consensus of the opinions of the twelve voting members of the FOMC.

As a group of individuals serving in a committee framework, the FOMC is not wedded to any specific economic theory, nor are the policies derived from any particular economic theory. Chapters 15 through 22 of this text have presented the neoclassical and Keynesian theories of how the economy functions, but these are only two general views of how various markets in the economy interact and how they are linked together. There is no reason to believe that the members of the FOMC follow any particular version of either of these general views. However, it can be safely assumed that the views expressed at FOMC meetings will cover a broad spectrum of ideas. Input can be given by the FOMC members themselves, the staff economists who serve the Board of Governors, the nonvoting presidents of the other Federal Reserve District Banks who attend the meetings, and the staff economists who serve the presidents of the district banks. The consensus that is eventually reached, however, does not necessarily comply with the policy implications of any of the theories we have described.

Fortunately, there is at least basic agreement among neoclassical and Keynesian theorists concerning the monetary policies required for reaching intermediate and long-term results. When the economy has high levels of employment and high rates of increase in the general price level, both views of the economy call for a contractionary monetary policy that ultimately will bring about some reduction in the rate of monetary expansion. Similarly, when there are substantial unemployment and relatively stable prices, both views of the economy suggest that an expansionary monetary policy might serve to alleviate the problem. Also, both views of the working of the economy recognize the problems generated by inflationary expectations, which most likely would make it difficult for an expansionary monetary policy to reduce unemployment.

Conflicts do arise, however, when it comes to determining the discretionary use of monetary policy and the short-run guides for implementing expansionary or contractionary policies. Unfortunately, the actual practice of discretionary monetary policy forces the FOMC to stress a series of short-term guides for the day-to-day conduct of open market operations.

In its approximately 10 meetings per year, the FOMC gives directives to the system's open market account manager for domestic operations. The directives serve as guides for the day-to-day open market operations. Although the FOMC may change the directives between meetings, when economic conditions warrant it, the FOMC directives set out specific rules and guides for the conduct of monetary policy until the next general meeting. The short-term nature of the directives make it almost inevitable that monetary policy be carried out as a series of short-term adjustments without a longer-term monetary policy ever being considered.

It was only with a congressional resolution in 1975, and the passage of the Full Employment and Balanced Growth Act of 1978, that the FOMC was specifically required to set out some goals for monetary policy that extend beyond the next general meeting. The Full Employment and Balanced Growth Act requires a semiannual report to Congress specifying the target ranges for the growth in monetary aggregates (such as M1 and M2) over the coming year. While these ranges may be modified, or may be set so wide as to present no real constraint on short-term policy, they do require some consideration of a longer-term objective. Nevertheless, it is still true to say that monetary policy is concentrated in the day-to-day operations set out in the FOMC directives.

## THE BASIC CONFLICT: RULES VERSUS AUTHORITIES

One basic conflict in the conduct of monetary policy is evident in the debate over establishing set rules for monetary growth as opposed to allowing the monetary authorities to pursue discretionary policies. Discretionary economic policy is the use of monetary or fiscal policy instruments on a short-term basis to stabilize economic activity. A problem with discretionary policy, and with the design of short-term monetary policy, is the timing of the policy change. There are substantial lags between an actual change in economic conditions that warrants a policy change and the impact of that policy change. These lags have led to a conflict between the use of discretionary monetary policy and the use of fixed rules for the conduct of monetary policy. The lags apparent in the conduct of discretionary monetary policy are those of recognition, implementation, and impact.

The *recognition lag* is the time it takes to discern that economic conditions have changed sufficiently to warrant a policy change. The ultimate targets and areas of concern for economic policy are generally related to real GNP, unemployment, and stability in domestic and foreign exchange prices. However, ultimate targets are observed with substantial lags. For example, it may take several months or quarters to have clear evidence that aggregate real output is changing at a different rate. Changes in economic conditions are not always evident when they occur, and it takes time to discern their extent.

The *implementation lag* is the time it takes, once a change in economic conditions is recognized, to alter economic policy. Monetary policy does have an advantage over fiscal policy in the speed of possible policy adjustments. Although Congress may take several quarters, or even years, to alter tax rates or the level of government spending, the FOMC has general meetings at which monetary policy can be changed every four to six weeks. In addition, FOMC open market directives can be, and have been, altered between general meetings.

The *impact lag* is the time it takes for a policy change to alter economic conditions. Whether monetary policy transmits its impact on output and prices through interest rate or price level changes, the markets take time to adjust and respond to any changes in the direction of policy. With increased attention being paid to economic policy and movement toward rational expectations, the impact lag is likely being reduced.

When there are lags before changes are made and produce effects, discretionary economic policies can result in policy changes that exacerbate current economic problems. Since economic conditions may change, the policy adopted may destabilize rather than stabilize the economy. Instead of offsetting cyclical tendencies in the economy, additional expansionary pressure may result when the economy is already in an expansionary phase.

The possibility that discretionary monetary policy actually could destabilize economic conditions has led some economists (primarily monetarists) to call for general rules for the conduct of monetary policy. A rule for the conduct of monetary policy would eliminate the possibility of short-term discretionary policy changes that could contribute to destabilizing economic conditions. In addition, a set rule is perceived to promote confidence and longer-term planning by eliminating the uncertainty of the short-run changes. Inherent in the argument for a monetary rule is the belief in the basic stability of the private sector. In general, the monetary rules advocated consist of constant growth rates for the various definitions of the money supply.

The argument for rules as opposed to discretion, however, is not clear-cut. Even if mistakes in monetary policy have been made in the past (and the evidence of general destabilizing activities is ambiguous), constantly improving forecasting techniques, and adjusting policy decisions in the light of past experience, should bring about an improvement in the conduct of discretionary policy. The ultimate goals of economic policy are fairly diverse, and a fixed rule would not permit the Federal Reserve to adjust policy to changes in conditions unanticipated when the rule was adopted. In addition, it is not clear what an appropriate monetary rule would be. A rule for a specific rate of growth of M1, for example, could have significantly different effects from a rule set in terms of M2. At present, the correct rate of growth for any rule is unclear, but it should be remembered that many monetarists claim that *having* the rule is what is important, not the actual rate of change of the money supply.

The debate about monetary rules and discretionary monetary policy has produced no clear victor, but policymakers appear to have more confidence in their own abilities to pursue discretionary policy than they have in any general rule of monetary growth. However, the requirement that the FOMC establish longer-term (annual) targets for the rates of growth of various monetary aggregates mandated in 1975 is something of a compromise on the issue. Short-term discretionary policy is still allowed and is undertaken, but that short-term discretionary policy is partially constrained by the longer-term considerations.

## CONFLICT: MONETARY AGGREGATES OR INTEREST RATES

Apart from the debate over rules vs. authorities, there is a conflict in the choice of specific guides for the day-to-day conduct of discretionary monetary policy. The Federal Reserve does not have direct control over the ultimate targets set in terms of GNP, unemployment, and prices. However, it can influence economic activity through open market operations and its other monetary instruments. Monetary policy can be guided in the short run by attempting either to alter monetary aggregates, such as various definitions of the money supply, or to control "money market conditions" (usually interpreted to mean a set of interest rates).

Holding everything else constant, it would make little difference whether an interest rate or a money supply was used as a guide to expansionary or contractionary monetary policy. A larger money supply (other things equal) would result in lower interest rates. Undertaking open market operations in which Treasury securities are purchased will result in increases in the prices of those credit instruments, decreases in the rates of interest of those credit instruments, and an expansion in the money supply. However, everything else does not remain constant. Inflationary expectations may change, and the feedbacks between the markets could result in significantly different effects being achieved when different targets are used as a guide to short-run discretionary policy. The different views of how the various markets interact and adjust in the face of uncertainty have led to a difference in the design of short-run stabilization policy and those policies used to reach the longer-term goals.

## Neoclassical View

The neoclassical view of the operation of the economy implies that the supply of money is the crucial guide for short-run monetary policy and for monetary stabilization policy. Interest rates are not considered to be an appropriate guide because of the impact of inflationary expectations and the possible confusion between real and nominal interest rates. More important, interest rates are not considered to be the linkage between monetary actions and general economic activity. While monetary actions may change both nominal and real interest rates, real rates of interest are viewed as being the result of time preference decisions and generally are not altered significantly. For the neoclassical economist, the supply of money is the most important driving force behind the determination of nominal income, is central to the determination of the general price level, and strongly influences employment decisions in the short run.

The appropriate monetary stabilization policy in the neoclassical view is the maintenance of a stable rate of growth in the supply of money. Fluctuations in the supply of money brought about by a policy designed to maintain constant interest rates are considered more likely to disrupt economic activity and employment than to stabilize them. According to the neoclassical view, a fluctuating rate of growth in the supply of money is likely to cause prices to change at different rates. This will generate considerable uncertainty about price changes, difficulty in formulating nominal wage contracts, and fluctuations in business firm employment decisions.

## Keynesian View

In the Keynesian view of the economy, aggregate demand is the driving force behind economic activity, and interest rates are the link between monetary actions and aggregate demand. An expansionary monetary policy calls for a reduction in interest rates to stimulate investment demand, and a contractionary monetary policy calls for an increase in interest rates to curtail investment demand. By keying on the appropriate level of interest rates, monetary policy can be used to adjust the level of real aggregate demand. However, using interest rates as a day-to-day guide for monetary policy also changes the money supply. Either interest rates or the money supply could be used as a guide to policy changes. In the short run, for example, higher interest rates can be brought about by increased open market sales. This will bid down the price of United States Treasury securities and increase the interest rates in the market. At the same time, these increased open market sales will bring about a reduction in Federal Reserve credit, a reduced monetary base, and a reduction in the supply of money. So long as monetary actions serve to change the underlying *real* interest rates, and do not generate misleading signals from nominal interest rates influenced by inflationary expectations, the supply of money generally will adjust in the opposite direction to the interest rates and, alternatively, interest rates will adjust in the opposite direction to changes in the supply of money. Given the difficulty of interpreting nominal interest rate changes and the impact of inflationary expectations, longer-term monetary policy adjustments generally are guided by considerations of monetary aggregates.

In the short run, however, for monetary stabilization purposes, a conflict still exists in the Keynesian view between the use of interest rates or monetary aggregates as the guide for day-to-day conduct of monetary policy. Whether interest rates or monetary aggregates are the appropriate short run guide depends on the stability of the money market relative to the stability of the product market.[1] When there is greater instability in the money market (as reflected by movements in the *lm* curve), an interest rate guide will result in greater economic stability. When there is greater instability in the product market (as reflected by movements in the *is* curve), a monetary aggregate will guide the economy toward greater stability.

## Market Instability

Instability in the money market results from fluctuations in the demand or the supply of money or both. Even if the Federal Reserve had complete control over the monetary base, adjustments in the portfolio decisions of financial institutions and the public could change the money multiplier and probably would result in unpredictable changes in the money supply. Coupling the short-run fluctuations in the money supply with a possible instability in the money demand would result almost certainly in fluctuations in interest rates. A monetary policy aimed at controlling the monetary base (and through it the various definitions of the money supply) would not eliminate this interest rate instability. Fluctuations in interest rates would

---

[1] *See* Chapter 22.

likely cause uncertainty in investment decisions and fluctuations in aggregate demand and would change economic conditions. If the instability is in the money market and the *lm* curve, a short-run monetary stabilization policy guided by interest rates would make compensating adjustments in the monetary base. This would tend to stabilize interest rates and economic conditions.

If, however, the instability in output and economic conditions is the result of fluctuations in aggregate demand in the product market and the *is* curve, a monetary aggregate guide to short-run stabilization policy would result in increased economic stability. For example, an unanticipated decrease in investment demand would result in a reduction in aggregate demand and generate a decline in output. By maintaining a constant money supply, interest rates would decline in the short run and offset some of that reduction in aggregate demand with an increase in the quantity of investment demand. Under an interest rate guide, the supply of money would be reduced to offset the reduction in interest rates, and the decline in aggregate demand actually would increase.

The conflict between the choice of an appropriate short-run guide for monetary stabilization policy has led to the not-too-surprising result that both interest rates and monetary aggregates are employed as short-run guides for the conduct of monetary policy. However, even though monetary aggregates are given increased consideration in longer-term policies (especially during inflationary periods), and both interest rates and monetary aggregates are given consideration in the short run, there is an apparent bias in favor of a consideration of short-run adjustments based on interest rates. Unlike the money supply or the monetary base, interest rates (at least nominal interest rates) can be observed directly in the very short run. Also, the link between interest rates and investment decisions and costs is known to the business sector. This consideration seems to have had a significant effect on the way the FOMC thinks of short-run monetary policy. Henry Wallich, a member of the Board of Governors (who apparently favors longer-term control over monetary aggregates), stated in a May 1980 speech:

> To the market, the money supply is a statistical abstraction. . . . Interest rates are the reality which governs quotations, contracts, profits and losses. . . . There is no direct effect running from the money supply to the economy. The effect runs via interest rates.[2]

Even though it is a mere "statistical abstraction" that serves as the underlying cause of changes in certain variables, it obviously is relatively easy for the FOMC to respond to something that can be observed easily. In addition, the FOMC can concentrate on market conditions where businesses operate rather than making adjustments in the money supply that may go unnoticed by the business sector.

---

[2] Davenport, John A., "A Testing Time for Monetarism," *Fortune,* October 6, 1980, 44.

## THE ROLE OF TARGETS AND INDICATORS

The conduct of monetary policy relies on the use of certain target and indicator variables as guides for the monetary adjustments that are to be made. The basic goal of economic policy has been to improve the level of economic well-being. This is an extremely vague notion, and for the purpose of guiding economic policy certain quantifiable ultimate targets are used. The general targets to be considered are set forth in acts of Congress. The ultimate goals for monetary policy are generally set in terms of unemployment rates, output, and price levels. However, it is impractical to attempt to conduct policy in the short run based on observations of the ultimate target variables. The lags in observation are sufficiently long that economic conditions could change and current monetary policy would be inappropriate. Thus, in the short run, the conduct of monetary policy is based on other readily observable target and indicator variables.

### *Targets*

A *target variable* is used as a specific guide for the conduct of monetary policy. The day-to-day conduct of open market operations is designed to adjust the selected target variable toward its desired level. Reasonable monetary target variables are variables that can be directly controlled or at least strongly influenced by actions of the Federal Reserve, can be readily observable in the short run so that adjustments can be made, and are causally linked in a discernable manner to the desired longer-term goals. With a causal link to the desired goals, adjustments in the level that is selected for the target can be used to influence general economic conditions over time.

Target variables can be grouped as either operating or intermediate targets. An *operating target* is used for the actual day-to-day conduct of monetary policy through open market operations. Specific interest rates, various measures of bank reserves, and the monetary base are possible operating targets. An *intermediate target* is a target variable used as a guide for adjustments and corrections in the day-to-day operations of monetary pol-

icy. Operating targets are selected to make the day-to-day adjustments in monetary policy to realize the desired levels for the intermediate targets over a short-term period of time. For example, an interest rate may be used as the operating target with an intermediate target set in terms of the money supply. On a day-to-day basis open market operations will be keyed on the selected interest rate with the policy designed to adjust the money supply to the desired intermediate target level or rate of growth over the following two to three months.

## Indicators

An *indicator* is a variable that reflects the effect of the use of monetary policy instruments on economic activity and the relationship between that activity and ultimate policy goals. Such an indicator would serve as a gauge of the "ease" or "tightness" of monetary policy relative to general economic activity. While variables that serve as intermediate or operating targets often are employed as monetary indicators, a separation of these functions might be advantageous.

Suppose, for example, that an expansionary monetary policy is deemed desirable and that the Federal Reserve targets for and achieves an increase in the supply of money. Whether such a policy proves expansionary relative to general economic activity will depend on any changes in economic conditions that are outside the Federal Reserve's control. If there has been an unanticipated increase in the demand for money, the targeted increase in the supply of money actually may have resulted in a decline in the availability of money *relative* to the amount demanded. Under such conditions, the use of an interest rate indicator might reveal that monetary policy has actually tightened relative to economic conditions rather than eased.

While interest rates and monetary aggregates are generally recognized as monetary indicators, neither of them taken alone is generally unambiguous. Observed interest rates, for example, can convey different and conflicting information about changes in economic conditions. High nominal interest rates could indicate that credit is tight and investment demand is likely to fall or could be the result of an increase in the expected rate of change in prices. Even if expectations of price level changes remain constant, interest rate changes may not clearly indicate the direction of changes in output and employment. If interest rates rise because of an increase in the demand for money (shifting the *lm* curve to the left), output will decline. Alternatively, if the interest rate rise is because of an increase in aggregate demand (shifting the *is* curve to the right), output and employment will increase. Changes in monetary aggregates have similar problems as indicators in the short run. The money supply (especially M2) is observable only with a lag and the data may be subject to revisions over several months. Also, changes in the money supply in the short run may reflect the changing monetary portfolio decisions of the public and the money multipliers without a discernible change in general economic activity. Generally, some combination of indicators is used to give clearer evidence of the adjustments that are occurring in the various markets.

Also, once a variable has been selected as a monetary target variable, it *may* no longer serve as a reliable indicator of the impact of monetary policy.[3] For example, *free reserves,* which equal nonborrowed reserves minus required reserves (when negative, this variable is called *net borrowed reserves*), have been used as a monetary target by the FOMC. Free reserves measure the potential additional loans that could be extended without additional borrowing from the Federal Reserve by the banking system. Free reserves may indicate the future expansion or contraction of loans by banks. By increasing free reserves (or reducing net borrowed reserves) the FOMC, through open market operations, can supply additional reserves to the banking system, which might start an expansion of loans. However, when free reserves actually are used as a target variable and are kept at a constant level by open market operations, free reserves no longer will adjust to market conditions, so they can no longer serve to indicate the direction of policy changes to be made. Some other indicator of economic conditions then is required to inform the authorities when the free reserve target should be changed.

The current conduct of monetary policy is the result of an evolution in the use of monetary targets and indicators since World War II. The current set of intermediate targets, operating targets, and specific side constraints on other variables perhaps can be best understood in the context of a historical overview of monetary policy. The adjustments in monetary targets over the past three decades occurred in light of the problems discerned in previously used targets and indicators and changes in prevailing economic conditions brought on, in part, by the conduct of monetary policy.

## MONETARY POLICY FOLLOWING WORLD WAR II

During the 1940s the Federal Reserve helped to finance the war effort by maintaining a market for United States Treasury securities. With a pegged minimum price and the corresponding maximum interest rate on the securities, open market operations simply responded to prevailing market conditions providing a ready buyer for existing United States Treasury securities. Monetary policy was not changed or even determined on the basis of prevailing economic conditions. The ongoing purchase of United States Treasury securities by the Federal Reserve was generating inflationary pressure in the late 1940s. This is evident in the rate of change in prices shown in

---

[3]The target variable, however, will still serve as an indicator to the public of the direction of policy changes being taken by the monetary authority.

*Figure 23.1*
**Annual Rates of Change in Prices**

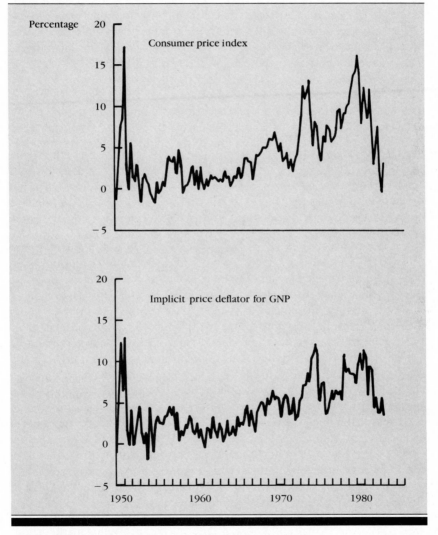

*Source:* Board of Governors, Federal Reserve System, *Historical Chart Book* (1983): 37.

Figure 23.1. The expansionary pressure being placed on the economy by monetary actions (or inactions) moved the Federal Reserve to decide that it was time to resume an active monetary policy. When *the Accord* between the Federal Reserve and the Treasury was reached in March 1951, the Federal Reserve embarked on its first active monetary policy since the Great Depression.

## Monetary Targets After the Accord

During the second World War, and the period immediately thereafter, the interest rates on United States Treasury securities had been pegged, and the financial markets had adjusted to that situation. Any rapid departure from a system of pegged interest rates would have dramatically upset the operations of financial markets. This gave the Federal Reserve the incentive to guide monetary policy on the basis of interest rate targets.

After the Accord, the FOMC keyed short-run monetary policy on select short-run interest rates and free or net-borrowed reserves. The combination of an interest rate target and a free reserve target allowed the FOMC to have an indirect effect on aggregate demand through the interest rate and a direct effect on the availability of funds for additional loans through free reserves. The short-term interest rate generally used for monetary policy was the rate in the very active market for 90-day Treasury bills.

## MONETARY POLICY IN THE 1950s: DOMESTIC

The Federal Reserve started its first active policy in the period after the Federal Reserve–Treasury Accord with a note of extreme caution. Conditions at the time called for a tight money policy as prices were rising quite rapidly (the CPI rose 7.6 percent from 1950 to 1951; *see* Figure 23.1). However, shifting to a policy that would cause interest rates to rise would have been extremely disruptive. One of the difficulties stems from an internal conflict that is built into the Federal Reserve. While the Federal Reserve is in charge of monetary policy, it also is a supervisor of banks and is greatly concerned with the safety and viability of banks. A shift to higher interest rates (called for in a tight money policy) would have adversely affected the commercial banks that had been most helpful during the pegging period. The banks had helped the pegging policy by holding substantial amounts of their assets in United States Treasury securities. Higher interest rates, particularly on longer-term bonds, would impose substantial losses on these banks. Thus, in undertaking the required monetary policy, the Federal Reserve chose to move very slowly so as to maintain an orderly adjustment of the financial markets away from the previous pegging.

One part of the policy of maintaining this orderly adjustment was the "bills only" policy that was adopted after the Accord. This policy simply restricted open market operations to the purchase and sale of Treasury bills. With only minor exceptions, this policy continued until the 1960s. The market for longer-term Treasury securities was simply considered to be of inadequate depth for use in open market operations. In such a thin market (as it was at the time), even small open market purchases and sales were likely to cause substantial changes in the prices of the long-term instruments. Thus, in order to avoid being at fault for any capital losses the banks might have suffered from interest rate changes in the longer-term markets, the Federal Reserve restricted open market operations to the more robust market for Treasury bills, where open market purchases and sales would have smaller effects on prices and interest rates.

Monetary policy during the 1950s can be considered to have been one of general restraint. From 1949 through 1959, the money supply (then defined as currency plus demand deposits) grew at an annual average rate of only 2.46 percent. A broader definition of the money supply, which was defined to include time deposits, grew at an annual average rate of 3.47 percent over the same period. As might be expected from such a restrained rate of increase in the money supply, prices rose very slowly during the 1950s. From 1951 through 1959, the CPI rose at an annual rate that averaged less than 1.5 percent.

During the 1950s monetary policy was guided by interest rates. From 1951 through 1953 unemployment had remained around 3 percent and the rate on prime commercial paper (four–six months) had risen from an average of 1.45 percent in 1950 to an average of 2.52 percent in 1953. However, when the unemployment rate rose to 5.5 percent in 1954, the monetary authorities responded by easing monetary conditions. The rate on prime commercial paper dropped to an average of 1.58 percent as the money supply (currency plus demand deposits) increased over 1954 at a rate of 3.05 percent.

Following the recovery, unemployment remained at a little over 4 percent from 1955 through 1957. Then, in 1958, unemployment rose to an average annual rate of 6.8 percent. This rise in unemployment followed an extremely contractionary monetary policy during 1957. The supply of money (currency plus demand deposits) declined during 1957 at an annual rate of 1 percent, and the interest rate on prime commercial paper rose to an average rate of 3.81 percent. In the following recovery, unemployment declined to about 5 percent, and the Federal Reserve felt that it could attack the inflationary pressures that were building by tightening monetary conditions. In 1959 the interest rate on prime commercial paper averaged 3.97 percent. At the end of the decade, interest rates were comparatively high, unemployment was rising, and a new problem appeared with the balance of payments.

## MONETARY POLICY POST–WORLD WAR II: INTERNATIONAL PAYMENTS

Following World War II, Western countries established a quasi-gold standard for international transactions. This was the Bretton Woods system. Under this system, one currency's value was set as a fixed amount of gold, and the other currencies had their values defined in terms of the first currency. The value of the dollar was already set at $35 per troy ounce. With the dollar being the primary currency used for international payments, the other currencies in the system had their values set in terms of the United States dollar.

## THE BALANCE OF INTERNATIONAL PAYMENTS ACCOUNTS

The concept of a balance of international payments deficit is relatively straightforward. A balance of payments deficit is the amount of excess supply of a currency (payments in excess of receipts) on the foreign exchange markets. The amount of any deficit or surplus is a measure of the pressure being placed on the foreign exchange value of the currency to decline or increase. However, arriving at a well-defined measure of a deficit (excess supply) or surplus (excess demand) is relatively difficult. As is the case with all goods, the amount purchased will exactly equal the amount sold. This is shown in the United States Balance of International Payments Account for the second quarter 1980 in Table 23.1. The total balance of payments account will always balance. Measures of the pressure being placed on the foreign exchange value of the dollar are arrived at by considering only a portion of the total payments account.

A measure of the pressure on the exchange rate is arrived at by attempting to separate those balance of payments account items that represent the desired actions in the supply and demand for the currency from those that represent accommodating transactions. An *accommodating transaction* is the purchase or sale of the currency designed to maintain the exchange rate at the current level or to maintain stable conditions in the foreign exchange market. The transactions considered to be accommodating are placed "below the line" in determining a bal-

This international payments system was designed to maintain stable exchange rates and yet allow each country to follow its own domestic policy relatively unconstrained by international payments considerations at least in the short run. The Bretton Woods system differed from a gold standard or a gold exchange standard in that no automatic mechanism existed to adjust the foreign exchange market so as to achieve a balance in international payments. When a country suffered from a balance of payments deficit (*see* "The Balance of International Payments Accounts," above), the excess supply of the country's currency was bought up by the country using its official reserve assets.[4] The loss of official reserve assets, however, would

---

[4] Official reserve assets include gold, convertible currencies, the country's gold (tranche) position in the International Monetary Fund, and, since the early 1970s, SDRs.

ance of payments deficit or surplus. When the amount of payments ( − ) exceeds the amount of receipts ( + ) in the items included "above the line," it is a balance of payments deficit by that measure.

A commonly used measure of a balance of payments deficit or surplus is arrived at by considering changes in official assets to be accommodating transactions. Changes in domestic official reserve assets and in foreign official assets are placed below the line. Transactions recorded above the line are those considered to be undertaken by the private sector in response to basic foreign exchange market conditions.

However, it is not clear that all transactions other than official settlements should be included as being in response to underlying foreign exchange market conditions. For example, the purchase and sale of securities can be the result of adjustments in monetary policy designed to affect foreign exchange market conditions on a short-term basis.

With some difficulty in determining whether or not financial capital flows (recorded in the capital account) are being altered by short-term policies aimed at the foreign exchange market, the current account may give a better measure of the underlying market pressures. Also, since international trade is the primary motivation for continuing use of the foreign exchange market, some economists consider the balance of merchandise trade to be a good long-term measure of likely adjustments in the foreign exchange value of a currency.

*continued*

not cause an automatic adjustment in the country's domestic conditions so that further excess supplies of the currency would be eliminated. In the short run, a country could run a balance of payments deficit as long as it had sufficient reserves to buy up the excess supply of its currency in the foreign exchange markets. Sooner or later, some adjustment in the exchange rate or in the country's basic economic conditions would have to be made if a prolonged balance of payments problem was to be eliminated.

The United States incurred substantial balance of payments deficits throughout the 1950s. These deficits generally were not considered to be undesirable, or even a problem, at the time. Sufficient official reserves existed to cover the deficits and to accommodate the excess supply of the United States dollar at the existing exchange rate for a considerable period of time. The deficits actually were considered to be beneficial because the

Table 23.1
**U.S. Balance of International Payments Account Quarter III,
1983 [Quarterly Data, Seasonally Adjusted Net Figures
(Receipts Less Payments), Millions of Dollars]**

| Current account | | Net Receipts (+) or Payments (−) |
|---|---|---|
| Merchandise trade balance (exports − imports) | | −18,169 |
| Services | | 8,254 |
|    Military transactions | −21 | |
|    Investment income | 6,928 | |
|    Other services | 1,347 | |
| Balance of goods and services | | −9,915 |
| Transfers | | −2,061 |
|    Remittances/pensions and other | −656 | |
|    U.S. government grants | −1,405 | |
| Balance of current account | | −11,976 |
| **Capital account (change in assets)** | | |
| U.S. government assets | | −1,188 |
|   (other than official reserves) | | |
| U.S. private assets abroad (increase, −) | | −5,770 |
|    Reported claims | −498 | |
|    Purchases of foreign securities, net | −1,122 | |
|    Direct investment abroad | −4,150 | |
| Foreign private investment in U.S. (increase, +) | | 21,722 |
|    U.S. reported liabilities | 16,344 | |
|    Purchases of U.S. securities | 2,970 | |
|    Direct investment in U.S., net | 2,408 | |
| Statistical discrepancy | | −82 |
|   (of which −1,355 is for seasonal adjustment) | | |
| Balance excluding changes in official assets | | 2,706 |
| Changes in foreign official assets (increase, +) | | −3,235 |
| Changes in U.S. official reserve position (increase, −) | | 529 |
| Overall balance | | 0 |

Source: Federal Reserve Bulletin (February 1984): A52.

shifting of official reserve assets to other countries helped to supply international liquidity and to finance the postwar recovery of international trade. However, by the end of the decade the decline in official reserves came to be treated more seriously. The $24,299 million of official reserves held by the United States in 1951 had declined to $19,359 million by 1960. As can

*Figure 23.2*
**U.S. Reserve Assets (Amount Outstanding, End of Month)**

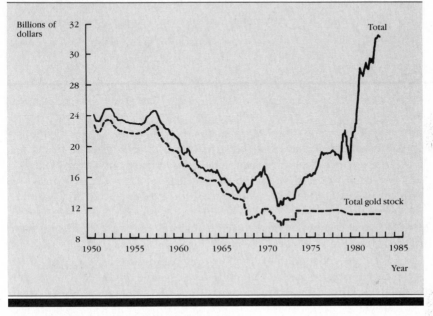

Source: Board of Governors, *Historical Chart Book* (1983): 106.

be seen in Figure 23.2, the amount of United States reverse assets started a substantial and prolonged decline in the late 1950s.

## International Payments in the 1960s

As the economy entered the decade of the 1960s, unemployment was on the rise (by 1961 unemployment had reached 6.7 percent), and the continuing *balance of payments* deficit became a matter of concern. However, there is a serious conflict in the policies necessary to correct these problems. The balance of payments deficit could have been eliminated by lowering the foreign exchange value of the dollar. If the dollar bought less foreign currency, foreign goods would be more expensive to United States residents, and the supply of dollars to the foreign exchange market would decline. Unfortunately, the Bretton Woods agreement did not contain a provision for devaluation of the dollar.

The United States was forced into the position of eliminating the balance of payments deficits by changing domestic policies. Higher interest rates and lower prices would attract foreign financial investment and make United States' goods attractive to foreign residents. The resulting demand for U.S. dollars on the foreign exchange markets would reduce or even eliminate the balance of payments deficit (*see* Chapter 3). However, during the same period, unemployment and economic stagnation in the United States called for monetary stimulus. The tight monetary policy called for to solve the international payments problems would aggravate domestic problems.

## Operation Twist

Federal Reserve policymakers were very much aware of this conflict, but eventually they were able to devise at least a temporary solution. This solution came to be known as *Operation Twist*. As its name implies, Operation Twist was an attempt to twist the structure of interest rates so that short-term interest rates would rise and long-term interest rates would fall. This was based on the notion that short-term capital flows are responsive to short-term interest rates, and that domestic investment is responsive to long-term interest rates. To achieve this result, the authorities launched a campaign whereby long-term credit instruments in the market were *swapped* for short-term credit instruments. By purchasing long-term bonds, and selling an equal amount of short-term Treasury bills, the Federal Reserve could increase short-term interest rates and decrease long-term rates without affecting the money supply.

Monetary policy at the time was concerned primarily with interest rates. Operation Twist followed that policy and can be considered a Keynesian policy in the sense that interest rates were considered to be of primary consequence. However, Operation Twist also depends on some rather questionable premises. The policy presumes a market segmentation theory of the term structure of interest rates so that short-term interest rates can be systematically altered relative to long-term interest rates. In addition, there is some evidence that international capital flows are affected as much by long-term interest rates as they are by short-term interest rates, which would mean that the policy was doomed from the start. The evidence shows that Operation Twist was not an overwhelming success. Regardless of whether a twisted term structure can have the desired effect, the simple truth is that the interest rates were little affected by the operation. Table 23.2 shows the way in which short-term and long-term interest rates compared during the operation.

The lack of a dramatic change in the term structure of interest rates was probably more the result of what the United States Treasury was doing rather than what the Federal Reserve was doing. To keep the rates twisted, a great deal of cooperation was required of the Treasury. New government debt would have to have been overwhelmingly short term, but the Treasury resorted more and more to long-term borrowing and succeeded in frustrating the Federal Reserve's efforts.

*Table 23.2*
**Yields on Treasury Securities During Operation Twist**

| Date | 3-month Treasury Bills | 3–5 Year Treasury Securities |
|---|---|---|
| June 1960 | 2.46 | 4.06 |
| June 1961 | 2.33 | 3.70 |
| June 1962 | 2.73 | 3.51 |
| June 1963 | 2.99 | 3.67 |
| June 1964 | 3.48 | 4.03 |

Source: *Banking and Monetary Statistics 1941–1970,* 695.

Operation Twist was only one of the stop-gap measures that authorities tried as temporary solutions to the balance of payments problem. Among the measures attempted were the fiscal policy measure of an interest equalization tax imposed in 1964 (retroactive to 1963) and a system of voluntary credit controls in 1965 that became mandatory in 1968. These measures were imposed to forestall the flow of financial capital out of the United States. All measures were to help reduce the balance of payments deficit, but in spite of these efforts the stock of United States official reserve assets declined throughout the 1960s to $14,487 million in 1970.

## Breakdown of Bretton Woods

The stop-gap measures of the 1960s did not solve the international payments problems, and the decade of the 1970s started with a complete breakdown of the Bretton Woods exchange rate system. The United States in 1971 officially closed the gold window and suspended convertibility of the dollar into reserve assets. An attempt to salvage a Bretton Woods type of fixed exchange rate system was made in December 1971 with the Smithsonian Agreement. This agreement made it possible to devalue the dollar by changing the official price of gold. The price of gold was officially raised to $38 per troy ounce, which effectively devalued the dollar by 7.89 percent. However, this did not prove sufficient to solve the United States' international payments problems. A further devaluation occurred in February 1973, when the price of gold was officially raised to $42.20 per troy ounce.

In spite of the two devaluations of the dollar, the measures to maintain a fixed exchange rate system like the Bretton Woods system failed. Continuing pressure on the exchange rates to change eventually caused the abandonment of fixed exchange rates and the establishment of floating exchange rates where market pressures change the relative values of currencies on a daily basis. The exchange rate system, adopted in mid-1973, is a *managed float* with official intervention in the exchange markets to maintain orderly adjustments. The managed float system has given the international payments mechanism a calm unknown throughout the recurring crisis period of the 1960s. This calm, however, did not come without some costs being imposed on some people who had to learn the ways of the new system (*see* for example, the Franklin National Bank case in Chapter 10).

### Effect on Monetary Targets

During the period of fixed exchange rates under the Bretton Woods system, maintaining the established exchange rate for the dollar occupied a considerable amount of the Federal Reserve's time and effort. This was especially apparent during Operation Twist in the early 1960s. The shift to a floating exchange rate system allows additional freedom in the conduct of monetary policy. Automatic adjustments in response to market forces eliminate prolonged pressure on the exchange rate. Exchange rate considerations no longer dictate changes in monetary policy.

However, the floating system adopted is a managed float. The very notion of management of the exchange rate requires that the monetary authority make decisions to intervene in the market. This intervention is undertaken to maintain orderly adjustments in exchange rates.

The shift to a floating exchange rate system has reduced the concern over international payments in the conduct of monetary policy. The monetary authority is no longer concerned with having to maintain a fixed foreign exchange rate for the United States dollar. United States monetary policy generally is conducted on the basis of domestic concerns. International payments considerations enter into the actual operation of monetary policy as a side constraint of avoiding unsettled conditions in foreign exchange markets. As a side constraint, domestic monetary policy and other monetary targets are forsaken only when sufficient instability is apparent in the foreign exchange markets that could not be dealt with under established arrangements. With growth in international financial markets and increasing international exposure of domestic banks, international payments concerns are again returning to importance in the conduct of monetary policy.

## MONETARY POLICY IN THE 1960s: DOMESTIC

Unemployment was a major economic concern at the start of the 1960s. The relatively high unemployment rate can be seen in Figure 23.3. The high unemployment rate caused the Federal Reserve to implement a relatively restrained monetary expansion. Over the decade, M2 rose at an average annual rate of about 6.8 percent and M1 rose at an annual rate of 3.8 percent. As measured by the rate of growth in M1, the first half of the 1960s showed considerable restraint on the part of the authorities who were generally following interest rate targets. The annual rates of growth in M1 and

*Figure 23.3*
**Unemployment Rate (Seasonally Adjusted, Quarterly)**

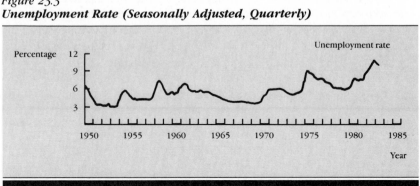

*Source:* Board of Governors, *Historical Chart Book* (1983): 20.

M2 are given in Figure 23.4. M1 increased at an average annual rate of only 2.7 percent for the first half of the decade. Prices remained relatively stable (*see* Figure 23.1), and the GNP deflator rose at an annual average rate of only 1.4 percent through 1965. Operation Twist may not have solved the balance of payments problem, but a combination of restrained monetary expansion and a fiscal policy tax cut in 1964 left the economy in 1965 with only 4.5 percent unemployment (and falling) and prices rising at less than 2 percent per annum.

By 1966 Operation Twist no longer was appropriate. The balance of payments problem remained, but the domestic problems had changed. The economy went into boom conditions, fueled to a great extent by government expenditures related to the escalation of the war in Vietnam. Domestic and international problems both called for monetary restraint and higher interest rates. By 1969 the rate of unemployment was down to 3.5 percent, but this improvement in the employment situation was accompanied by increases in the rate of increase of prices. In the second half of the decade the Federal Reserve showed considerable ambivalence in its policies. The rates of increase in the money supply fluctuated from year to year. In 1966 the Federal Reserve undertook a contractionary policy to try to stem the rising inflation. The rate of growth of M2 dropped from 8.0 percent for 1965 to 4.9 percent for 1966. The rate of growth of M1 dropped from 4.4 percent in 1965 to 2.7 percent in 1966. Funds for bank loans became exceptionally tight. The federal funds rate rose to an average rate of 5.11 percent for 1966. The period was the famous "credit crunch" of 1966. It caused considerable disruption in commercial and near-banking circles. As interest rates rose, disintermediation took place. Some financial institutions (particularly the savings and loan associations) found themselves in considerable trouble.

The Federal Reserve appears to have feared that the contraction had been overdone and proceeded to expand the money supply in 1967 and

*Figure 23.4*
**Annual Rates of Change in Monetary Aggregates, 1960–1983**

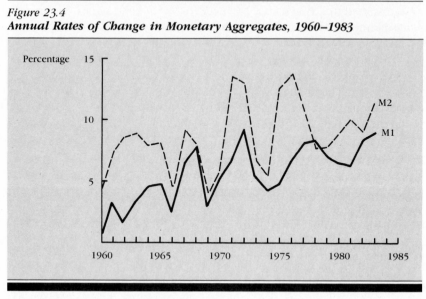

Source: *Economic Report of the President,* 1984, 291.

1968. M2 rose at 9.3 percent and 8.0 percent, and M1 rose at 6.33 percent and 7.47 percent, respectively, for 1967 and 1968. The result of this policy was that unemployment declined, but inflation increased rapidly. Once again, the Federal Reserve reversed the monetary policy and in 1969 virtually repeated the policies of 1966, with the same result. The end of the decade saw high levels of unemployment *and* high rates of increase in prices.

## Changes in Monetary Targets

Changes in market conditions and the results of past monetary policy will bring about changes in monetary targets. The 1960s saw some adjustments in the day-to-day conduct of monetary policy. The interbank market for the borrowing and lending of reserves was expanding rapidly. Following the development of the federal funds market, the FOMC shifted in the mid-1960s from using the 90-day Treasury bill rate to the more volatile overnight rate in the federal funds market as an operating target.

During the 1950s and early 1960s prices had remained relatively constant. General price rises and inflationary expectations apparently were not having a dramatic effect on nominal rates of interest. Interest rates and the rate of growth in the money supply generally were moving in opposite directions so that monetary restraint guided by higher interest rates generally brought about reductions in the rate of monetary expansion. However, rising prices in the late 1960s caused the use of interest rate targets to be questioned.

By the mid-1960s the monetarists had attracted some attention. The FOMC shifted to giving some consideration to monetary aggregates as well as to money market conditions. Interest rates and free reserves still served as the primary day-to-day guides and targets for monetary policy, but a *proviso clause* was added to FOMC directives during and after 1966 to consider bank credit and the money supply.[5] Although the Open Market Directives issued in the 1960s did not generally contain specific target ranges, they did serve to give a general feel for the concerns of the FOMC and to indicate the basic direction taken in short-term monetary policy. For example, the Directive issued at the meeting of November 22, 1966, which contained a proviso clause, included these statements:

> While there has been some slowing in the pace of advance in broad price measures, upward pressure still persists. . . . Bank credit and money have shown no expansion in recent months. Long-term interest rates have risen somewhat. . . . The balance of payments remains a serious problem. . . . [T]he Federal Open Market Committee's policy is to maintain money and credit conditions conducive to noninflationary expansion.

> To implement this policy, System open market operations until the next meeting of the Committee shall be conducted with a view to attaining somewhat easier conditions in the money market, unless bank credit appears to be resuming a rapid rate of expansion.[6]

By the late 1960s it became apparent that the observed nominal interest rates no longer were effectively serving as indicators of the tightness or ease of monetary policy. Rising prices and inflationary expectations had created a significant spread between real and nominal interest rates. This spread, coupled with uncertainty over the future rate of change in prices and pressure from monetarist economists, led the FOMC to an increased concern over monetary aggregates in the short-term conduct of monetary policy. The FOMC embarked on the decade of the 1970s with the money supply and bank credit listed as primary targets and money market conditions as represented by interest rates as secondary targets.

## MONETARY POLICY IN THE 1970s: DOMESTIC

The United States entered the decade of the 1970s in the aftermath of the credit squeeze of 1969. The rate of unemployment rose steadily throughout 1970. The Federal Reserve was back to an expansionary monetary policy. The rate of inflation was picking up again. Conditions did not improve in

---

[5] Bank credit is total loans plus investments less interbank loans.

[6] Board of Governors, Federal Reserve System, *Annual Report* (1966): 195.

1971. By August the administration decided on drastic measures. On August 15, 1971, President Nixon imposed wage and price controls. Phase I was to be a 90-day period of fixed wages and prices. This was to be followed by a period of unspecified duration in which the controls would be more flexible. At the same time, as the freeze was to hold down inflation, fiscal policy was to be used to increase the level of employment. A tax cut was proposed that would shift the *is* curve to the right. Domestic monetary policy was given no specific part to play in these policies, but it is clear that the Federal Reserve followed a rather expansionary policy. In 1971, M1 rose at 6.6 percent and M2 rose at 13.5 percent. In 1972, M1 rose at 9.2 percent and M2 rose at 13.0 percent (*see* Figure 23.4).

Not surprisingly, given the rate of increase in the money supply, the removal of the controls brought on a further round of inflation. In 1973 the CPI rose 8.8 percent. The Federal Reserve responded to this with a tighter monetary policy. M1 and M2 were increased at 5.5 percent and 6.9 percent, respectively. However, this did not have an immediate and obvious effect on prices. Another two months of wage and price controls were introduced in the middle of 1973. The result of the monetary restraint and the second price freeze was a recession that lasted through 1975. Unemployment rose to 8.9 percent. In the recovery from the recession, unemployment did not improve rapidly. The average levels of unemployment in 1977 and 1978 were 7 percent and 6 percent, respectively.

By 1978 policymakers in the United States faced very serious problems. Unemployment was still high. The rate of inflation continued to accelerate. In 1978 the CPI rose at an annual average rate of 9 percent. The end of the year saw the famous "double-digit" inflation. The conditions seemed to defy simple Keynesian analysis. The unemployment called for easy money and low interest rates, but the inflation called for tight money and high interest rates, a contradictory situation not helped by the fact that the easy money policy that had been followed had driven nominal interest rates to unprecedented heights. In the second half of the 1970s, the problems of unemployment and inflation were exacerbated by the drastic changes in oil prices and oil availability from the Middle East. The steep rise in the price of oil imports had an impact on consumer prices. Also, expensive energy caused a downturn in industrial production. The expansionary monetary policy followed by the Federal Reserve may have helped industry to overcome the external shock of the increased oil prices, but the effect on prices continued to be inflationary. Over the second half of the decade, M1 and M2 increased at annual average rates of 6.75 percent and 10.42 percent, respectively. The rate of inflation hovered around 8 and 9 percent.

## Consistency of Monetary Targets

Short-term monetary targets throughout the 1970s were specified for several definitions of the money supply as well as for the federal funds rate of interest.[7] One difficulty with this multitude of short-term targets is that, with the limited tools available to the Federal Reserve, it may not be possible to achieve all the desired target levels set. For all targets to be reached, the targets must be selected so as to be consistent. Whenever the selected targets prove to be inconsistent, one or more of the targets must be forsaken in order to realize the desired levels for the other targets. With a large set of targets used to guide monetary policy, some target variables will come to dominate the actual conduct of short-term monetary policy.

The problem of consistent selection of target ranges is readily apparent in selecting a target range for the federal funds rate. Selecting a range for the federal funds rate that is consistent with a desired rate of growth in various monetary aggregates requires a prediction of likely changes in the demand for money. Instability in the demand for money in the short run and unpredicted changes in money demand would make a consistent selection extremely difficult over short-term periods of time.

In selecting target ranges, monetary aggregates have been listed as primary targets because they were generally used during the 1970s to determine the basic direction of short-term monetary policy. Once the FOMC has determined the basic direction of monetary policy through the use of forecasts, an interest rate operating target range is selected that is estimated to be consistent with the desired rates of growth in monetary aggregates. Given a consistent selection of targets, and assuming that monetary conditions do not change during the inter-meeting period from their predicted paths, either target could be used to guide open market operations with similar results. However, basic monetary conditions do change. It usually is necessary to concentrate on one specific target for the day-to-day operations of open market policy and to fail to realize some of the other targets specified. Even with a set of monetary aggregates selected as primary targets, interest rates dominated the short-term conduct of monetary policy during the 1970s. The ease with which interest rates (at least nominal interest rates) can be observed, and the perceived link between interest rates and economic activity, appear central to the day-to-day operations of monetary policy.

The dominant role of interest rates in the short-term conduct of monetary policy is apparent in monetary operations during 1978, shown in Figure 23.5. During the period the FOMC directives specified a broad range (4 to 5 percent) for the targeted rates of growth in monetary aggregates and a narrow range (usually ½ of a percent) for the weekly average federal funds rate. As can be seen in Figure 23.5, monetary policy was conducted successfully in achieving a weekly average federal funds rate in the limited target

---

[7]During a brief period (1972–1975) reserves against private deposits (RPDs) also were used as a target. RPDs net out of reserves the volatile effect of changes in reserves held against Treasury tax and loan deposits. The shifting composition of private deposits made RPDs extremely volatile. The target was soon dropped from specific consideration.

*Figure 23.5*
**FOMC Ranges for Short-Run Monetary Growth and
for the Federal Funds Rate, 1978**

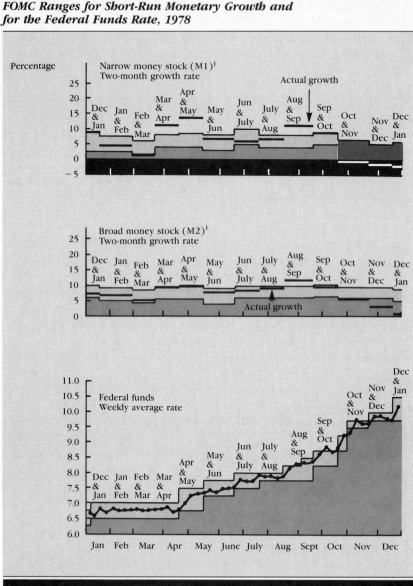

*Note:* Shaded bands in the upper two charts are the FOMC's specified ranges for money supply growth over the two-month periods indicated. No lower bound was established for Ml at the October and November meetings. In the bottom chart, the shaded bands are the specified ranges for federal funds rate variation. Actual growth rates in the upper two charts are based on data available at the time of the second FOMC meeting after the end of each period.

[1]Seasonally adjusted annual rates

*Source:* "Monetary Policy and Open Market Operations," *Quarterly Review* 4 (1) (Federal Reserve Bank of New York, Spring 1979): 60.

range. However, the relative stability in interest rates came at the cost of substantial variability in the growth rates for money supplies M1 and M2. Even with the broad ranges for monetary aggregates, there were substantial misses for the target ranges. The variability in monetary growth rates evident in Figure 23.5 occurred throughout the 1970s as the Federal Reserve concentrated on interest rates for the short-term conduct of monetary policy.

## A SHIFT TOWARD MONETARISM

Over the 1970s, money supply M2 had been increased at an annual average rate of 9.58 percent. This was accompanied by an annual average rate of increase in real output of 2.99 percent and an increase in prices (the GNP implicit deflator) at an annual average rate of 6.68 percent. However, even with major adjustments in monetary policy throughout the 1970s, high unemployment and persistent inflation continued to plague the economy. Indeed, the concentration on interest rates in the short run and the accompanying volatility in monetary aggregates may have contributed to the uncertainty over inflation rates and the continuation of the problems.

The first shift in the conduct of monetary policy in the 1970s came as Congress moved, with a resolution in 1975 and the Full Employment and Balanced Growth Act of 1978, to force a consideration of a longer-term monetary policy. Perhaps more important, the pervasive influence of inflation and inflationary expectations along with the uncertainties and distortions in markets moved the Federal Reserve to attempt to gain stronger control over monetary expansion. Additional power was given to the Federal Reserve in the Depository Institutions Deregulation and Monetary Control Act of 1980.

The high and volatile rates of price changes in the late 1970s left nominal interest rates suspect as a means of attempting to control the rates of growth in monetary aggregates. To maintain control over credit and monetary expansion, on October 6, 1979, the Federal Reserve shifted its emphasis to controlling in the short run the provision of bank reserves, and through reserves to control other monetary aggregates, as an operating target. Interest rates still retained their importance, but the concern over day-to-day or even weekly changes in the federal funds rate was lessened.

To emphasize monetary aggregates the target range for the federal funds rate was broadened. The typical target range expanded from ½ percent spread of pre-1979 to a spread of 4 percent or more. Interest rates, in essence, became a side constraint in the conduct of short-run monetary policy. Interest rate movements would force an adjustment in operations only when substantial changes occurred.

Following October 1979, monetary aggregates became the chief intermediate targets. The principal operating target became nonborrowed reserves. Through control over reserves available, the Federal Reserve could, over time, influence movements in M1, M2, and other monetary aggregates. Short-run adjustments outside the control mechanism could still occur through depository institutions' use of the discount window. Borrowings from the Federal Reserve would permit short-run fluctuations from the targetted monetary growth path. The operating policy was designed to reduce sharp movements in the federal funds rate when depository institutions found themselves short of reserves.

## *Improved Control*

To strengthen the Federal Reserve's ability to maintain control over monetary aggregates and credit conditions, several institutional changes have been made. The Monetary Control Act of 1980 called for improved control through reduction in the Federal Reserve float. Through the Federal Reserve's pricing and payments policies, the volatile influence on the monetary base from the float has been significantly reduced (*see* Chapter 14).

The 1984 return from a lagged reserve accounting system to contemporaneous reserve accounting has tightened the relationship between changes in reserves and the money supply. Under this renewed system, a change in reservable deposits will immediately force depository institutions to acquire the required reserves. Under the lagged system, reserves were not required until two weeks into the future.

In addition, the Federal Reserve has moved to acquire more timely information. The Monetary Control Act of 1980 requires systematic reporting to the Federal Reserve from all depository institutions. Accurate information improves on the ability to formulate and adjust economic policy. Starting in the late 1970s, monetary aggregates have been continually redefined to better measure the effects of increased availability of new forms of deposit accounts. With substantial changes in the financial marketplace, the monetary authority has been adjusting to keep abreast of the innovations and improve on its ability to manage a changing economy.

## MONETARY POLICY INTO THE 1980s

Monetary policy embarked into the decade of the 1980s with a shift toward more monetarist targeting and a strong commitment to reduce inflation from the double-digit rates of the late 1970s. Attention focused on M1, and the FOMC tried to reduce the rate of monetary expansion. The annual rate of growth for M1 was reduced from over 8 percent in the late 1970s to 6.4 percent in 1981. The reduction in monetary growth was followed by two rapid recessions. Rapidly rising prices had been curtailed. For 1982 and 1983 the annual increase in the CPI-U was less than 4 percent.

Unfortunately, rising prices were not the only problem at the start of the 1980s. In the second recession civilian unemployment peaked at a post-1930s high of 10.7 percent in December 1982. The ongoing deregulation of financial markets brought continuing institutional changes that clouded economic conditions. International payments and banking contributed to uncertainty in financial sectors, and the federal government's budget deficit brought increasing concern.

In 1983 the nominal value of the federal budget deficit rose to the all-time high of $195 billion (almost 6 percent of GNP). The deficit is expected to continue through the rest of the decade in the range of $200 billion per year.[8] The net interest burden of the federal debt had doubled from 1960 through 1983 to 2.6 percent of GNP. In addition to increased borrowing, the total size of the government had risen from 18.5 percent of GNP in 1960 to almost 25 percent by 1983.[9]

Federal budget deficits are a concern of monetary policy in that they may induce another round of price increases. Although deficit spending does not, by itself, add to the rate of growth in the money supply, large deficits may induce a response by the Federal Reserve that does.

Substantial additional borrowing by the federal government places upward pressure on interest rates. Although the federal funds rate did fall from over 19 percent in 1981, by 1983 it hovered in the 8.5–10 percent range, despite substantial reductions in price increases. Persistently high interest rates brought increasing pressure for a more expansionary monetary policy.

High interest rates brought some relief through foreign financial capital inflows. The decline in domestic price increases and attractive, low-risk financial investment opportunities generated a significant rise in the dollar's foreign exchange value. Measured against 17 other major currencies, the United States dollar's value increased almost 39 percent from 1980 through 1983.[10] Foreign financial capital inflows were sufficiently strong to bid up the dollar's value despite a rising balance of trade deficit. The increase in the dollar's foreign exchange value helped forestall domestic price increases by making foreign goods cheaper. However, the dollar's appreciation contributed to international banking problems.

World financial markets expanded dramatically during the 1970s. Strong evidence for substantial economic growth induced a significant increase in foreign borrowing, and banks rushed into the field. The gross external debt of non-OPEC developing countries rose steadily from $110 billion in 1973 to $555 billion by 1982. Of this debt $282.7 was due to foreign banks.[11]

Foreign lending exposed domestic banks to substantial risk. The nine largest United States banks' loans to non-OPEC countries amounted to al-

---

[8]*Economic Report of the President* (February 1984): 36.

[9]*Ibid,* 29.

[10]*International Economic Conditions* (Federal Reserve Bank of St. Louis, January 1984): 2, 5.

[11]Teeters, N. and H. Terrell, "The Role of Banks in the International Financial System," *Federal Reserve Bulletin* (September 1983): 665.

most 11 percent of their total assets, or over 220 percent of their bank capital.[12] This exposure also permeated throughout the financial system as smaller banks participated in the lending through syndications. The world recession of 1980–1982 threatened repayment. Since the debt was primarily denominated in dollars, the rising value of the dollar added to the burden.

As a supervisor of banks the Federal Reserve became concerned over possible default on foreign loan payments with the strong possibility of increased bank failures. The Federal Reserve became active in the rescheduling of Mexico's foreign debt and responded with institutional changes to monitor the problem. Tighter supervision over foreign exposure was instituted, as were additional reporting requirements.

The international banking problems added pressure for monetary expansion. By easing monetary restraint, the more readily available dollars would facilitate debt repayment.

The monetary authority faced many conflicting forces in the early 1980s. The movement in M1 relative to its target ranges is shown in Figure 23.6. The significant deviations are the result of the operating target employed, the conflicting economic forces, and changes in institutional factors resulting from deregulation. The most significant change during the early 1980s was a shift in targets.

## De-emphasis of M1

Following October 1979, the Federal Reserve focused on monetary aggregates as intermediate targets. The operating target used was nonborrowed reserves. Changes in borrowings from the Federal Reserve and altered monetary portfolio decisions by the public will reduce the relationship between changes in nonborrowed reserves and various definitions of the money supply. Borrowings alter the monetary base, and the public's monetary portfolio decisions affect the money multipliers.

A nonborrowed reserves target will result in some short-run fluctuations in the money supplies. Some of these movements are evident in Figure 23.6. While targeting monetary aggregates, the Federal Reserve has adopted the view that temporary shifts in the money supply create few difficulties. It is the longer-term growth path that is important. Institutional changes in late 1982 brought the longer-term relationship between nonborrowed reserves and M1 into question.

The Garn–St. Germain Depository Institutions Act of 1982 authorized depository institutions to offer MMDAs, starting in December 1982. These accounts are part of the M2 definition of the money supply and proved to be an extremely attractive form of deposit. With the new deposit form likely to attract substantial funds, it was no longer clear what relationship would

---

[12] *Ibid,* 667.

*Figure 23.6*
**M1: Actual versus Target Range, 1982–1983**

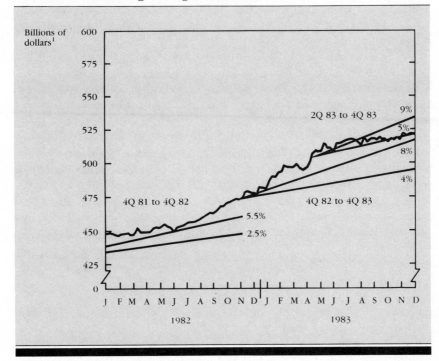

[1]Monthly averages of daily figures, seasonally adjusted.

*Source: Economic Report of the President* (February 1984): 196.

exist between nonborrowed reserves, M1 and M2. Targets on monetary aggregates may no longer prove consistent.

If the MMDA deposits resulted from transfers out of transactions deposits, M2 would increase in relation to M1. In addition, since nonpersonal time deposits have a zero reserve requirement, a shift into M2 money would enable banks to extend more loans. Foreseeing control difficulties with the monetary aggregate M1, the Federal Reserve moved in February 1983 to reduce M1 to the status of a "monitoring target" (an indicator). A target range, given in Figure 23.6, would still be specified. However, policy would not directly adjust in response to M1's movements relative to the target range. M2 still retained its status as an intermediate target, and its growth remained within the target range.

From 1983 the economy was undergoing a recovery. From the bottom of the recession in December 1982 through May 1983, M1 and M2 grew at annual rates of 15.3 and 17.6 percent. This growth was not entirely the result of changes in money multipliers. Over the same period the monetary base increased at an annual rate of 10.6 percent. The slight increase in M2 in relation to M1 indicates that some of the MMDA deposits may have come from transactions deposits. However, the majority came from shifts within M2, primarily from savings deposits and money market mutual funds. These shifts do not alter money multipliers or change the relationship between M1 and M2.

M1 has been de-emphasized for monetary control status. Yet, it still retains considerable importance. Data on M1 are available more rapidly than for M2. The public continues to monitor changes in M1 in attempts to discern the direction of monetary policy and changes in economic conditions.

The Federal Reserve is continuing its search for improved monetary control mechanisms. In 1983 the FOMC added a target range for a broader monetary aggregate, nonfinancial domestic debt. In addition, the money supply definitions will continue to change. M2 has been strongly influenced by MMDAs and money market mutual funds. This has reduced its usefulness since the late 1970s, and the de-emphasis of M1 indicates that the Federal Reserve places reduced value in that monetary aggregate.


## SUMMARY

The basic decisions concerning the conduct of monetary policy are made by the FOMC. These decisions are contained in FOMC directives, which serve to guide the actual conduct of open market operations. The directives indicate the desired adjustments during the four to six weeks between meetings of the FOMC and monetary policy is generally conducted in a series of short-term adjustments through these directives.

There are two basic conflicts in the conduct of monetary policy. These are the debate between the use of fixed rules or allowing the authorities to pursue discretionary monetary policy and the conflict over the use of interest rates or monetary aggregates as guides to monetary policy adjustments. Fixed rules for the rate of growth in monetary aggregates generally are favored by monetarists to avoid the possible destabilizing effects of continual policy adjustments. Others consider discretionary policies desirable to allow the monetary authority to adjust to changing economic conditions.

The conflict between the use of interest rates or some monetary aggregate as an operating target for monetary policy stems from differing views as to how the economy functions and considerations over the stability of the demand for money relative to stability in the product market. From the Accord between the United States Treasury and the Federal Reserve in 1951 through 1979, interest rates were the key variable in the actual day-to-day conduct of monetary policy. However, changing market conditions have brought about changes in the conduct of monetary policy. Rising prices and the effects of inflationary expectations in the late 1960s pushed the monetary authority toward a greater consideration of monetary aggregates in the actual conduct of short-term monetary policy.

The current conduct of monetary policy essentially is a set of compromises. Annual rates of growth for monetary aggregates are set as targets to establish a form of a long-term rule, with discretionary policy dominating the adjustments during the annual period. The most recent adjustment in the conduct of monetary policy is a move away from a primary consideration of interest rates toward the more monetarist operating target of bank reserves. Interest rates, however, remain as a side constraint and still influence the actual conduct of monetary policy.

The Federal Reserve does not have a good record of achievement in stabilizing the economy, and economists do not have a good record of supplying viable monetary policy guidelines to the authorities. Historically, it seems that there is no economic situation that the authorities cannot make worse, but it is easy to be critical when you have the clear vision of hindsight. It is to be hoped that the periods of monetary experimentation that we have witnessed will end with the authorities being better able to cope with at least the major fluctuations in the economy.

## Key Terms

| | |
|---|---|
| recognition lag | indicator |
| implementation lag | free reserves |
| impact lag | the Accord |
| target variable | balance of payments |
| operating target | Operation Twist |
| intermediate target | side constraint |

## Questions

1. Explain how the lag between actual changes in economic conditions and the impact of a policy change might cause discretionary monetary policy to have a destabilizing effect on the economy.

2. Interest rates have been observed to decline substantially, and the actual rate of change in prices has been reduced by less than the drop in interest rates. Is this a decline in the real rate of interest? What information do you have (or require) to determine this change? Explain. With the drop in interest rates and prices, would you expect output to be rising or falling? Explain.

3. Explain why a rise in short-term interest rates in the United States will act to increase the foreign exchange value of the dollar. How would this increase affect the ability of foreign countries to repay their debt when the debt is in dollars and the interest rate variable? Explain.

**4.** Explain how changing economic conditions have altered the Federal Reserve's use of operating targets.

**5.** Given current economic conditions, what directive would you give to the manager for domestic operations of the system open market account?

## Additional Readings

Bowsher, Norman N. "Rise and Fall of Interest Rates." *Review* 62 Federal Reserve Bank of St. Louis (August/September 1980): 16–23.

*A discussion of interest rate changes and their relationship to actual monetary policy in the last half of the 1970s.*

Brunner, Karl (ed.). *Targets and Indicators of Monetary Policy.* San Francisco: Chandler Publishing Co., 1969.

*The proceedings of a conference sponsored by the American Bankers Association on what would indicate to policymakers that a particular policy should be followed, and what would reveal that a monetary policy was having the desired effect.*

Clarke, Stephen, V. O. "Perspectives on the United States External Position Since World War II." *Quarterly Review* (Federal Reserve Bank of New York, Summer 1980): 21–38.

*A historical overview of the United States international payments problems and the international role of the dollar.*

Davis, Richard G. "The Monetary Base as an Intermediate Target for Monetary Policy." *Quarterly Review* (Federal Reserve Bank of New York, Winter 1979–1980): 3–10.

*A discussion of the usefulness of the monetary base in the conduct of monetary policy with some empirical evidence.*

*Economic Report of the President* (Washington, D.C.: United States Government Printing Office, February 1984).

*An annual report that gives a broad overview of economic activity and policy over the past few years. The* Report *generally contains insight into both micro- and macroeconomic problems facing the economy.*

Judd, J. P. "Deregulated Deposit Rates and Monetary Policy." *Economic Review* (Federal Reserve Bank of San Francisco, Fall 1983): 27–44.

*An examination of the effectiveness of M1 targeting since the removal of interest-rate ceilings on deposits. The evidence suggests that M2 has become less controllable, and the M1 relationships evidence greater stability.*

Koch, Albert R. "An Approach to Monetary Policy Formulation." *Business Review* (Federal Reserve Bank of Philadelphia, February 1965): 3–9, 12–15.

*This article is purported to be the first clear public statement from within the Federal Reserve of its "myopic" day-to-day monetary operations guided by interest rates.*

Maisel, Sherman. *Managing the Dollar.* New York: W. W. Norton, 1973.

*An insider's view of the making of monetary policy by a former member of the Board of Governors of the Federal Reserve.*

***acceptance*** A draft that the drawee has agreed to pay. *6*

***Accord*** An agreement reached in March 1951 between the Federal Reserve and the United States Treasury that enabled the Federal Reserve to pursue an active monetary policy rather than maintain pegged interest rates. *19*

***adaptive expectations*** Expectations of changes in a variable that adjust to observed changes in that variable. *16*

***advance*** The usual form of loan made by the Federal Reserve directly to eligible financial institutions, secured by eligible paper rather than by exchanging ownership of the paper as in a discount. *13*

***adverse clearings*** A net decline in deposits at the end of a business day that results when cash withdrawals and check payments exceed receipts. *9*

***aggregation*** The combination of a large set of information into one (or more) summary measures. *3*

***anticipated income*** Part of the theory of bank management that contributions to liquidity are obtained from loan payment flows. *9*

***anticipated rate of change in prices (Ṗ)*** The rate of change in the general price level that individuals expect to occur over the following time period. *5*

***arbitrage*** The simultaneous purchase and sale of an item in two separated markets for a guaranteed gain due to a price discrepancy. *4*

***asked price*** The price at which a dealer will sell, and a customer will buy, a credit instrument in the secondary market. *6*

***asset demand (for money)*** The demand for money as a form of wealth holding as part of a portfolio selection. *16*

***assignment*** The transfer of rights under a contract to another party. *6*

***attrition*** The amount of a maturing issue of a credit instrument that is paid off in cash. This is usually associated with United States Treasury securities. *7*

***auction*** A sale in which the goods are sold to the highest bidder. Treasury bills are auctioned in the primary market. *7*

***automatic transfer service accounts (ATS)*** Accounts in commercial banks that are a combination of an interest-bearing savings account and a deposit account used in payments. These accounts have an automatic provision for the transfer of funds from the savings account to the deposit account whenever a check is presented for payment. These accounts are included in M1. *1*

***balance of international payments*** The relationship between the supply of a currency by residents of a country to purchase foreign goods, services, and financial assets relative to the demand by foreign residents for purchases with that currency at a given foreign exchange rate. *3*

**bank capital**  The residual account on a bank's balance sheet. It is equal to the difference between total assets and total liabilities. This net worth represents the equity claims of the bank's owners.  *8*

**bankers' acceptance**  A bank draft after the bank has accepted the obligation to pay.  *6*

**bank failure**  The placing of a bank in receivership by the chartering agency.  *10*

**bank-holding company**  A separate organization that owns or has a controlling interest in one or more banks. It can be a one-bank or a multibank holding company.  *10*

**bank merger**  The combining of two or more banks into one operation.  *10*

**Bank of the United States**  There have been two of these. The first was a private bank, chartered by the federal government from 1791 to 1811, which performed some of the functions of a central bank. The second was a private bank, chartered by the federal government from 1816 to 1836. It performed functions similar to those of the first Bank of the United States.  *13*

**bank suspension**  The closing of a bank to the general public by the supervisory agency other than for a general bank holiday.  *10*

**bid price**  The price at which a dealer purchases, and a customer sells, a credit instrument in the secondary market.  *6*

**bimetallism**  A monetary system where a unit of money is defined as a specified weight of either of two metals, and either of the two metals is used for redemption of the monetary unit.  *4*

**Board of Governors of the Federal Reserve**  The supervisors of the Federal Reserve System. The Board consists of seven members, each appointed by the president of the United States for a fourteen-year term, staggered in such a way that one member is appointed every two years. The Board sets reserve requirements, approves discount rate changes, and constitutes a majority on the Federal Open Market Committee.  *13*

**bond**  A negotiable credit instrument that is a promise made by a corporation, public or private, to pay a specified amount of money.  *6*

**branch banking**  A bank operating at more than one site. This is a means of expanding a bank's activities geographically. Bank branching is prohibited in many states and severely restricted in others.  *10*

**broker**  An intermediary or middleman in a secondary market that brings buyers and sellers together.  *6*

**Bretton Woods system**  The modified gold exchange standard used for international payments with pegged foreign exchange rates. The system lasted from after World War II until 1973.  *4*

**Cambridge Equation**  An equation used to analyze the money market with the demand for money a proportion *(k)* of nominal income. This equation, $M = kPy$, originated in Cambridge, England.  *16*

**cash in process of collection**  The asset of the Federal Reserve that represents the value of the checks presented to banks for payment that have not yet been paid by the bank on which they are drawn. This is part of the Federal Reserve's float.  *9*

**central bank**  The bank that acts as the fiscal agent for the government and as a lender of last resort for financial institutions (primarily banks) suffering liquidity problems. In addition, a central bank may act to control a paper standard by altering the monetary base or reserve requirements, and may regulate and control banking activity.  *13*

**certificate of deposit**  An account where funds are placed at a specified time to be withdrawn at a specified time; may be negotiable or nonnegotiable.  *8*

**check**  A sight bank draft used to make payments with funds held in demand deposits.  *1*

**checking account**  An account in a commercial bank that is transferable by means of a check, usually referred to as a demand deposit.  *1*

**check clearance**  The process of transferring funds through the financial system to make payment of a check.  *9*

**classical region**  When the demand for real money balances is perfectly inelastic with respect to the real interest rate. The *lm* curve is vertical in this region, and the results of the Keynesian model are the same as those for the neoclassical system.  *22*

**clearinghouse**  An arrangement for check clearing by many banks at a single location.  *9*

***coin*** An officially certified weight and purity of metal that circulates as a means of exchange.

 ***full-bodied*** A coin that contains a market value of metal equal to the face value of the coin.

 ***token*** A coin containing a value of metal less than the face value of the coin. *1*

***commercial bank*** A financial intermediary chartered to operate as a bank that specializes in commercial and consumer loans, and has demand and other forms of deposit as liabilities. *8*

***commercial loan theory of banking*** (also known as the *Real Bills doctrine*) The theory that banks could best solve their portfolio problem by investing primarily in short-term, self-liquidating commercial paper. *9*

***commercial paper*** Short-term promissory notes, issued by banks, corporations, and finance companies. *6*

***commodity standard*** A monetary system where the unit of money is defined as a given quantity of a commodity (or commodities) and that commodity is used for redemption of the monetary unit. *4*

***comparative advantage*** The ability to produce a good or a service at a lower opportunity cost than others in the market. *2*

***competitive bid*** In the primary market for Treasury bills, a bid to buy a specified number of Treasury bills at a specified price. *7*

***composite commodity standard*** A monetary system in which the unit of money is defined as a set of commodities in fixed proportions, and the fixed basket of commodities is used for redemption of the monetary unit. *4*

***Comptroller of the Currency*** An office of the United States Treasury that charters, supervises, and examines national banks. *10*

***consumer price index (CPI)*** A price index that measures the average price of a basket of goods and services consumed by the average consumer. *3*

***contractual savings institution*** Savings institutions that receive funds on a regular, contracted basis such as insurance companies and pension funds. *11*

***convenience and needs*** A criterion that must be met to qualify for a national bank charter, membership in the Federal Reserve, or insurance from the FDIC. The requirement is that a new bank must demonstrate that the needs of the community are not being met by existing banks. *10*

***correspondent banking*** An arrangement whereby banks hold deposit balances with each other for use in check clearance and as compensation for services provided. *9*

***coupon rate of interest*** The percentage of the face value of a bond or a note that is to be paid to the holder annually. The payment may be made annually or more frequently. Also called the *contractual rate*. *6*

***credit conditions*** Conditions in the money market, usually referring to interest rates. *21*

***credit instrument*** A contract giving written evidence of the extension of credit and the existence of debt. *6*

***credit market*** A market for the borrowing and lending of a good, service, or financial asset. *5*

***credit unions*** Nonprofit, cooperative financial institutions that pool the savings of their members and lend to other members. These institutions also house share draft accounts. *11*

***Crime of '73*** Reference by the silver producers to the United States Congress's 1873 decision to establish a gold standard at the pre–Civil War mint price. *4*

***crowding-out*** The reduction in the use of goods, services, or funds in one sector that results from an increase in demand in another sector of the economy, usually associated with the impact of increased government expenditure. *18*

***currency*** Any form of the circulating medium of exchange that physically passes hand-to-hand in exchange, for example, Federal Reserve notes. *1*

***dealers*** Intermediaries who make the market for financial instruments by buying and selling on their own accounts. *6*

***default risk*** The risk that a borrower will not repay, nor will be able to make the interest payments on, a loan. *8*

**defensive open market operations** The purchase or sale of securities by the Federal Reserve, designed to stabilize economic conditions by offsetting factors deemed temporary or seasonal in nature. *14*

**deferred availability cash items** The liability of the Federal Reserve that represents the value of checks it has received for clearing that have yet to be paid to the presenting bank. This is part of the Federal Reserve's float. *9*

**deflation** A continuous decline in the average price of goods and services. *3*

**demand deposit** A deposit placed in a commercial bank (and some mutual savings banks) that is payable on demand and transferable by check. *8*

**demand deposits adjusted** Total demand deposits in commercial banks less interbank deposits, deposits of foreign commercial banks, and demand deposits of the United States Treasury and its agencies. *1*

**demonstration effect** The effect on economic activity of changes in the discount rate that result from interpreting a discount rate change as an indication of a change in monetary policy. *13*

**depository institution** A financial institution that houses transactions accounts. Under the Depository Institutions Deregulation and Monetary Control Act of 1980, depository institutions include the thrift institutions and commercial banks. *11*

**Depository Institutions Deregulation and Monetary Control Act of 1980** An act of Congress that, among other things, extends the Federal Reserve's powers over reserve requirements to all depository institutions, opens the discount window to all depository institutions, and calls for the phasing out of interest-rate ceilings on deposits. *10*

**discount** A Federal Reserve loan made to an eligible institution by the discount purchase of eligible paper, as defined in Regulation A of the Federal Reserve Code. *13*

**discounting** The process of converting a future value to a present value by dividing the future value by a discount factor, for example, $V_0 = V_1/(1 + R)$. *5*

**discount rate** The rate charged by the Federal Reserve District Banks on loans to eligible financial institutions. One of the tools of monetary policy. *13*

**discount sale** The sale of a credit instrument for less than par or face value. *6*

**discretionary monetary policy** Altering monetary policy in the short run in response to changes in economic conditions. *19*

**disintermediation** The process of taking funds out of financial intermediaries and using the funds to acquire credit instruments directly on the primary or secondary markets. *10*

**double coincidence of wants** Finding someone who has what you want and at the same time wants what you have to trade to the extent that an exchange can be made. *2*

**draft** A negotiable credit instrument where one party (the drawer) orders another party (the drawee) to pay a certain sum of money to a third party (the payee). Also called a *bill of exchange*. *6*

**drawer** The signer of a draft who orders that a payment be made. *6*

**drawee** The party named on a draft as being ordered to make a payment. *6*

**dual banking system** A banking system like that in the United States with two different types of bank charters (state and national). *10*

**dynamic open market operations** The purchase or sale of securities by the Federal Reserve, designed to alter the general level of economic activity. *14*

**economic growth** An increase over time in the level of real output per person. This is one of the ultimate goals of economic policy. *3*

**Edge Act Corporations** Subsidiary corporations set up by United States commercial banks under the supervision of the Federal Reserve or the Comptroller of the Currency for the purpose of performing most activities that are performed by foreign banking institutions. The Edge Act of 1919 is an amendment to the original Federal Reserve Act. *10*

**elasticity** The percentage change in some variable divided by the corresponding percentage change in another variable. *22*

**Employment Act of 1946** An act of Congress, stating that it was the responsibility of government, with the assistance of the private sector, to promote maximum employment, production, and purchasing power. *3*

**entry** The ability to start an operation in an existing industry. Entry is induced by anticipated profits and provides competition for existing firms. *10*

**equation of exchange** A definitional relationship between the financial sector and measures of output. $MV = Py$. *3*

**Eurodollar deposits** Dollar-denominated deposits in financial institutions outside the United States. Overnight Eurodollars held by United States residents are included in M2. *1*

**exchange** In the market for Treasury notes and bonds when the holders are offered and accept new issues to replace maturing issues. *7*

**exchange rate (foreign)** The price of a currency in terms of a foreign currency. *3*

**expected rate of return** The rate of interest or rate of return that on average is expected to be earned from an investment. *9*

**expectations theory** A theory that explains the term structure of interest rates based on what investors expect for short-term interest rates in the future. This theory assumes that short- and long-term credit instruments are good substitutes. *7*

**Federal Deposit Insurance Corporation (FDIC)** A federal regulatory authority, which began operating in 1934, that provides insurance protection for small deposits (i.e., those $100,000 or less) and supervises banks. *10*

**federal funds** Short-term (generally overnight) funds borrowed and lent between financial institutions where the funds borrowed (usually deposits held at Federal Reserve District Banks) would not be subject to reserve requirements if borrowed by a member bank of the Federal Reserve System. *8*

**Federal Home Loan Bank Board** A committee of three members, appointed by the president of the United States, to regulate the members of the Federal Home Loan Bank System. Membership in the system is open to savings and loan associations, mutual savings banks, and life insurance companies. The board also operates the Federal Savings and Loan Insurance Corporation (FSLIC) and the Federal Home Loan Mortgage Corporation (Freddy Mac). *11*

**Federal Open Market Committee (FOMC)** The committee of the Federal Reserve that directs open market operations. The committee consists of the seven members of the Board of Governors of the Federal Reserve and five presidents of Federal Reserve District Banks. *13*

**Federal Open Market Committee directives** The written or verbal instructions of the FOMC to the systems open market account managers for the conduct of open market operations. *13*

**The Federal Reserve** The central bank of the United States, established by Congress in 1913. All national banks must join the Federal Reserve System, but state banks have the option. *13*

**Federal Reserve credit** The primary source of monetary base. This is the total amount of credit extended by the Federal Reserve through the purchase of securities, through loans extended, and through the float. *14*

**Federal Reserve note** Paper currency issued by, and an obligation of, the Federal Reserve. *1*

**fiat money** A paper money that is put into circulation by government decree and functions as money so long as the public accepts it as such. *4*

**fiduciary issue** A nonredeemable paper money that circulates alongside a redeemable money; the quantity of nonredeemable money issued is entrusted to government. *4*

**finance company** A financial institution, having liabilities consisting of loans from banks or loans acquired by issuing paper in the open market and specializing in consumer, mortgage, or business loans, especially on accounts receivable. *11*

**financial futures** A contract to buy or sell a standardized credit instrument at a specified market-determined price during a specified month in the future. *9*

**financial intermediary** A financial institution that accepts funds from parties who desire to give up their current use, and uses these funds to make loans to, or buy securities from, those who wish to acquire the current use of additional funds. *8*

**financial market** A market for the borrowing and lending of funds. *5*

**fiscal agent of the government** The organization that borrows, lends, and disburses funds on behalf of the government. In the United States this function has been performed by the Federal Reserve since 1914. *7* *fiscal policy*   The use of government expenditure and taxation policy to improve or stabilize general economic activity.   *18*

*float*   Federal Reserve credit, extended through the check-clearing process. The float is equal to the difference between the Federal Reserve balance sheet items: cash in process of collection (CIPC) and deferred availability cash items (DACI).   *14*

*floating exchange rate*   A foreign exchange rate that is allowed to adjust freely and automatically in response to market forces.   *3*

*flow variable*   A variable that can be measured only over a period of time (as opposed to a point in time), for example, income, labor services, and output.   *3*

*foreign exchange market intervention*   The official purchase or sale of one currency for a foreign currency to avoid unsettled conditions in the foreign exchange markets.   *14*

*fractional reserve system*   A monetary system, where financial intermediaries hold only a fraction of their deposit liabilities in the form of primary reserves.   *12*

*free reserves*   The total of nonborrowed reserves in commercial banks less required reserves.   *23*

*frictional unemployment*   Unemployment that occurs when workers are between jobs and searching for better alternatives.   *16*

*full-bodied money*   Money that contains a market value of the commodity used as the monetary standard equal to the face value of that money. See *coin*.   *4*

*full employment*   The state of affairs in the labor market that exists when the number of people who want to work at the going real wage is equal to the number who have or are offered jobs. The economy is generally considered to have full employment when unemployment has fallen to some specified percentage, say, 4 to 7 percent.   *3*

*Full Employment and Balanced Growth Act of 1978 (Humphrey-Hawkins Act)*   An amendment to the Employment Act of 1946 that specifies in greater detail the economic concerns of government policy.   *3*

*fundamental problem of financial intermediation*   The arranging of the assets and liabilities of a financial intermediary in such a way as to achieve an optimum among profitability, liquidity, and safety within the legal constraints imposed by the regulatory agencies.   *8*

*gold exchange standard*   A monetary system that links a nonredeemable paper money in a country without a monetary gold stock to the money in a country on a gold standard.   *4*

*gold certificate account*   An asset of the Federal Reserve that represents the amount of the gold stock "monetized" by the United States Treasury's issue of gold certificates.   *14*

*gold standard*   A monometallic system using a specified weight and purity of gold to define and redeem the monetary unit.   *4*

*gold stock*   The total amount of gold held by the United States Treasury, valued at the official price.   *14*

*government expenditure*   A flow; the demand for goods and services from the government sector.   *18*

*Gresham's law*   The commodity (or commodities) in which the money supply is redeemable will always flow to where its (their) value is the highest. For metallic standards, this law becomes: monetary metal will always flow to where its value is the highest.   *4*

*Gross National Product (GNP)*   The market value of all final goods and services produced over a period of time, usually a year.   *3*

*Gurley-Shaw hypothesis*   The hypothesis that, as long as reserve requirements were only imposed on commercial banks, the activity of nonbank financial intermediaries would offset the authorities' abilities to exercise monetary control.   *12*

*human wealth*   The amount of capital embodied in a human being. This results from investment in education, training, and other forms of self-improvement.   *16*

*hyperinflation*   A situation in which the general price level is rising very rapidly. The word usually is reserved for reference to cases where prices are rising at rates in excess of 50 percent per month.   *2*

***impact lag***  The time lag between the implementation of a policy change and the realization of its effects on economic activity.  *23*

***implementation lag***  The time lag between the ecognition of a change in economic conditions and an actual change in policy designed to alleviate the recognized problem.  *23*

***indexation***  The automatic adjustment of monetary amounts in response to a change in some index, usually a price index.  *3*

***index number problem***  The problem of separating the product of two sets of numbers into two components. This problem arises in calculating and interpreting price indexes where a change in nominal value has to be separated into a price change and a real quantity change.  *3*

***indicator***  An economic variable that is used to discern changes in economic conditions.  *23*

***inflation***  A continuous rise in the average price of goods and services.  *3*

***interbank deposits***  Deposits held by a bank in another (a correspondent) bank.  *9*

***interest rate***  The annual percentage rate of return for borrowing and lending.  *5*

***interest risk***  The risk of receiving a capital gain or loss because of interest rate changes during the period that a financial instrument is held.  *8*

***intermediate target***  A goal used to guide and adjust operating targets over a short period of time.  *23*

***internal rate of return***  The yield on a capital good; the rate of interest that equates the present value of the expected net revenues to the price of the capital good.  *18*

***inventory***  Goods that are held for future sale or use in production. This is a form of investment. Unintended inventory accumulations or decreases serve as signals for adjustments in the product market.  *18*

***investment***  The use of currently produced goods and services to produce goods and services in the future. Investment is a flow that adds to the existing capital stock.  *18*

***investment company***  A company that raises funds to acquire a diversified portfolio of existing financial instruments by selling stock or shares of ownership in the portfolio.  *11*

***investment multiplier***  The quantity [1/(1 − the marginal propensity to consume)] that a change in real investment is multiplied by to yield the change in real income.  *20*

**is** *curve*  A curve that passes through the pairs of real rates of interest and real levels of output that represent equilibrium in the product market.  *20*

***Keynesian economics***  A system of economics devised by the disciples of John Maynard Keynes. Although there are many forms of Keynesian economics, it is generally characterized by the notion that aggregate supply is produced to meet aggregate demand.  *15*

***legal tender***  Currency, which when offered in payment, establishes certain legal rights related to debts.  *1*

***lender of last resort***  A traditional function of a central bank to serve as a lender to commercial banks suffering liquidity problems.  *13*

***liability management***  The active adjustment of a financial institution's liabilities to help solve its portfolio problems.  *9*

***liquidity***  A property possessed by assets that can be sold immediately for cash without a loss in nominal value.  *7*

***liquidity premium theory***  A theory to explain the term structure of interest rates, where a premium is added to longer-term interest rates to account for the loss of liquidity in longer-term loans.  *7*

***liquidity trap***  The condition that would exist if the demand for real money balances was perfectly elastic with respect to the interest rate. If this occurred, the *lm* curve would be horizontal.  *21*

**lm** *curve*  A curve that passes through the pairs of real rates of interest and real levels of output that represent equilibrium in the money market.  *21*

***loan participation***  An arrangement for the extension of a loan to a customer with another correspondent financial institution.  *9*

***macroeconomic model***  A set of assumptions that represent how an aggregate economy functions. These models are used to predict the results of policy changes.  *15*

**maker**  The signer of a promissory note who promises to make payment.  *6*

**managed float**  Allowing the foreign exchange rate to adjust in response to market conditions, with official intervention to maintain orderly adjustments.  *23*

**managed liabilities**  Part of bank management in which access to liquidity is maintained through markets where managers can directly and immediately increase or decrease the amount borrowed.  *9*

**marginal product of labor**  The additional output that results from the employment of an additional unit of labor, holding all other inputs constant.  *17*

**marginal propensity to consume**  The change in current real consumption per unit change in real income (real disposable income when there are taxes).  *18*

**market segmentation theory**  A theory to explain the term structure of interest rates based on the belief that there is only limited substitutability between long- and short-term credit instruments.  *7*

**medium of exchange**  Whatever is used as a means of payment for purchases or as a means of payment for debts.  *2*

**member bank**  A commercial bank that has joined the Federal Reserve System. This is required of all national banks, but is optional for state chartered banks.  *10*

**modern quantity theory of money**  A theory of the demand for money devised by Milton Friedman, in which the demand for money is seen as a special topic in the theory of capital.  *15*

**monetarism**  A view of economic activity, based on the belief that the money supply is the predominant influence in the determination of aggregate nominal income, that excess money balances are disposed of through increased expenditure on goods and services as well as on credit instruments, that the private sector is inherently stable, and that the allocative details of aggregate demand between sectors of the economy are irrelevant for short-run changes in money income.  *15*

**monetary base**  The set of assets available to the public that, if held by depository institutions, could be used to satisfy the Federal Reserve's requirements for holding primary reserves.  *12*

**monetary policy**  The use of the instruments available to the monetary authority to improve or stabilize general economic conditions. These instruments are open market operations, reserve requirements, the discount rate, and moral suasion.  *13*

**monetary rule**  A fixed rule for money supply changes that is not altered each time output or employment deviates from anticipated levels.  *19*

**monetary standard**  The system used to determine what, if anything, will be used for redemption of the monetary unit. Monetary standards are either commodity or paper standards.  *4*

**money**  Anything that is commonly accepted as a means of payment for goods and services or in the discharge of debts.  *2*

**M1**  Narrowly defined money, equal to the sum of currency in the hands of the nonbank public, adjusted demand deposits, NOW and ATS deposits at depository institutions, credit union share draft accounts, demand deposits at mutual savings banks, and traveler's checks issued by nonbank companies.  *1*

**M2**  Broadly defined money, equal to M1 plus highly liquid short-term assets held as liabilities of depository institutions. In addition to M1, M2 includes savings and small (less than $100,000) time deposits, money market deposit accounts, overnight Eurodollars and repurchase accounts, and deposits in general purpose and broker-dealer money market mutual funds.  *1*

**money illusion**  The erroneous perception of values by which decisions are made based on nominal or money units rather than on real values.  *17*

**Money Market Deposit Accounts**  Authorized by the Garn–St. Germain Act of 1982, these accounts require a minimum initial and average maintained balance of $2500 and pay unregulated interest rates, but have restricted transactions features. Deposits in these accounts are included in M2.  *1*

**money market mutual fund**  An open-end investment company, in which the funds held in common are used to acquire existing credit instruments. While there are many different mutual funds that acquire highly varied asset portfolios, the funds are generally transferable to third parties with check-like instruments and are included in M2.  *1*

**money multiplier** A combination of ratios of desired holdings of monetary assets, determined by the portfolio decisions of members of the public and financial intermediaries, that, when multiplied by the monetary base, gives the money supply in its various forms. *12*

**monometallism** A monetary system, in which a unit of money is defined as a specified weight of one metal and that metal is used for redemption of the monetary unit. *4*

**moral suasion** An attempt to exhort a desired form of behavior. This is also referred to as *jawboning* and is considered to be one of the monetary tools available to the monetary authority. *13*

**multiple expansion of deposits** The process under a fractional reserve system whereby, through a series of deposits and loans, a given monetary base is converted into a larger supply of money. This process is represented by the various money multipliers. *12*

**multiplier effect** The result of induced consumption demand through which a change in demand (usually investment or government) generates an even larger increase in output. *20*

**mutual savings bank** A thrift institution in which any excess in receipts over operating expenses is kept in a surplus account or distributed to depositors. *11*

**national bank** A bank chartered by the Comptroller of the Currency. *10*

**natural rate of interest** The real rate of interest that equilibrates the product market. *18*

**natural rate of unemployment** The rate of unemployment that would exist if the rate of inflation was correctly anticipated and individuals adjusted their nominal wage to compensate for the anticipated price changes. *17*

**near banks** Thrift institutions. *11*

**negotiable credit instrument** A contract for the extension of credit that meets the formal requirements of Section 3 of the Uniform Commercial Code, transfer of which is referred to as a negotiation rather than an assignment. *6*

**Negotiable Order of Withdrawal Account (NOW)** A transactions account, held in savings and loan associations, mutual savings banks, and commercial banks, that is transferable with a checklike instrument called a *negotiable order of withdrawal*. Deposits in these accounts may earn explicit interest. *1*

**net borrowed reserves** The total amount of required reserves for commercial banks less the amount of total reserves held net of the amount of reserves borrowed from the Federal Reserve when required reserves exceed nonborrowed reserves. *23*

**net exports** The value of goods exported by a country, less the value of imported goods. This net amount is part of the demand for aggregate output. *18*

**nominal income (Y)** The sum of all payments for the use of factors of production (land, labor, and capital), during a period of time, in current dollars. *3*

**nominal rate of interest** The interest rate used to determine the number of money units (as opposed to units of real purchasing power) to be paid on a loan. Nominal interest rates are the observable rates. *5*

**nominal variable** A measure of economic activity in terms of values for the period in which the variable is measured. These are the economic variables that can be directly observed. *3*

**noncompetitive bid** In the primary market for Treasury bills, a bid to buy a specified number of Treasury bills at the average price in the competitive auction. *7*

**nonnegotiable credit instrument** A contract giving evidence of the extension of credit that may be assigned but not negotiated. *6*

**nonpersonal time deposit** Time deposits held by a depositor other than a natural person. These are subject to reserve requirements under the Monetary Control Act of 1980. *9*

**normative economics** The area of economics devoted to the decision of what should or ought to be achieved. *3*

**open market account managers** Those who carry out the day-to-day business of open market operations after the instructions of the FOMC. There are two managers: one for domestic operations; one for international operations. Both are vice-presidents of the New York Federal Reserve District Bank. *13*

**open market operations**  The purchase or sale of United States Treasury or federal government agency securities by the Federal Reserve under the direction of the FOMC. This is the primary instrument of monetary control used by the Federal Reserve. *13*

**operating target**  A desired goal used to guide the actual day-to-day conduct of open market operations. *23*

**Operation Twist**  A major attempt at discretionary debt management, whereby the Federal Reserve and the Treasury attempted to lower long-term interest rates and raise short-term interest rates in the early 1960s. *7*

**opportunity cost**  The value of the benefits forgone by not undertaking the next best alternative. *2*

**paper standard**  A monetary system where the quantity of money is controlled by some monetary authority without regard to its redeemability in a standard commodity. *4*

**pass-through reserves**  A nonmember financial institution's reserves that are maintained indirectly with a Federal Reserve bank by holding them through an approved institution. *1*

**pegged exchange rate**  The setting of the foreign exchange rate for a currency at a specified number of units of another currency, where the foreign exchange rate can be adjusted to a different peg by government action. *4*

**Phillips curve**  A statistical relationship, originally found by A. W. Phillips, between the level of unemployment and the rate of change in money wages. This curve has come to be associated with the relationship between the rate of unemployment and the rate of change in the general price level. *21*

**pieces of eight**  A Spanish silver dollar that could be cut into eight pieces (bits, each worth about 12½ cents) used for making change. *1*

**Pigou effect**  The direct effect of monetary policy on the product market and the *is* curve through changes in real money balances. This is also referred to as the *real balance effect*. *22*

**point of effective demand**  The point in a Keynesian model at which the product market is in equilibrium and the current level of output can, and will, be sustained. *20*

**portfolio diversification**  Acquiring a set of highly varied assets in an attempt to reduce risk while maintaining a desired rate of return. *9*

**positive economics**  The description of what is, was, or will be the results of a specific economic action. *3*

**present value**  The translation of the value of a payment at some time in the future into its equivalent number of units today through the use of interest rates. *5*

**price index**  A measure of the average level of the prices of a set of goods and services. *3*

**primary market**  The market for the initial sale of a credit instrument where new credit is being extended. *6*

**primary reserves**  A financial intermediary's holding of cash items that can be used to satisfy legal reserve requirements. These generally have included vault cash and deposits held with Federal Reserve District Banks. *8*

**product market**  The market for all goods and services. *19*

**profitability**  The expected rate of return to the asset's owners. This is a concern in the fundamental problem of financial intermediation. *8*

**quantity theory of money**  An explanation of what will be the results, direct or indirect, of changes in the money supply on economic activity. *3*

**rational expectations**  A theory that assumes that individuals formulate their expectations on all available and relevant information and on a knowledge of how economic variables interact in some appropriate model of economic behavior. *16*

**real balance effect (Pigou effect)**  The direct effect of changes in real money balances on aggregate demand that causes shifts in the *is* curve. *22*

**real income (y)**  The purchasing power of nominal income. Real income is measured holding prices constant, $y = Y/P$. *3*

**real interest rate (r)**  An interest rate expressed in terms of the anticipated ability to purchase goods and services as the result of lending and borrowing activity. *5*

**real variable** A measure of economic activity adjusted for price changes (or, in the case of interest rates, anticipated price changes) that effectively yields a measure in quantity units. *3*

**real wage (w)** The rate of pay per period (per hour, day, or year) for the use of labor services in constant dollar units, $w = W/P$. *3*

**recognition lag** The time lag between a change in economic conditions and that change actually being discerned by policymakers. *23*

**redeemability** The ability to exchange a monetary unit for a specified amount of a commodity or commodities. *4*

**Regulation Q** The Federal Reserve's regulation that sets interest-rate ceilings payable on deposits. The regulation, however, has been used collectively to refer to interest-rate ceilings regardless of the regulatory agency imposing them. The Monetary Control Act of 1980 calls for the phasing out of these regulations by 1986. *9*

**relative price** The number of units of a good that must be forgone to acquire another good. *2*

**repurchase/resale agreement** The sale/purchase of a security with an agreement or contract to repurchase/resell the security at a specified point in time. *8*

**Reserve City bank** Any bank with demand deposits totaling $400 million or more. *9*

**reserve requirement** A legal requirement for a financial intermediary to hold specified cash assets equal to a set percentage of certain liabilities. *9*

**safety** The concern in the fundamental problem of financial intermediation over the amount of risk to which deposits and owners' financial investments are subject. *8*

**saving** A flow, the act of forgoing current consumption. *18*

**savings and loan association** A thrift institution designed to operate primarily in the mortgage market. *11*

**savings deposit** A longer-term deposit with a financial intermediary that bears interest and has no stipulated date of maturity. *8*

**secondary market** A market for the sale of previously sold credit instruments that alters the ownership of existing credit. *6*

**secondary reserves** Highly liquid, short-term assets held by financial intermediaries that can be sold immediately for cash to replenish primary reserves. *8*

**selective credit controls** Constraints that may be imposed to influence the flow of credit in specific credit markets. These selective controls include margin requirements for loans of stock purchases and reserve requirements that may be imposed on specific liabilities. *16*

**share account** A savings type of account in a credit union that actually represents a share in ownership and carries voting rights. *11*

**share draft account** A transactions account held in a credit union that is transferable by a checklike instrument called a share draft. *1*

**shiftability** A property possessed by assets with a well-developed secondary market where the ownership of the assets can be shifted easily to other parties through sales. *7*

**shiftable assets** A theory of bank management in which assets with well-developed secondary markets are used to maintain liquidity. *9*

**side constraint** A condition placed on the conduct of monetary policy that requires a change in the conduct of monetary policy only when an adjustment outside some specified limits occurs. *23*

**solvency** Having sufficient assets, given enough time, to pay off the concerns liabilities; having a positive net worth. *8*

**Special Drawing Right (SDR)** A reserve asset for use in international payments created by the International Monetary Fund (IMF) in the early 1970s and allocated to its members. *14*

**Special Drawing Rights Certificate Account** An asset of the Federal Reserve that represents the amount of SDRs "monetized" by the United States Treasury's issue of SDR certificates. *14*

**specialization** Producing relatively more of one good or performing primarily one act in the process of producing goods and services. *2*

**stabilization policy** The use of monetary or fiscal policy to offset fluctuations in economic conditions. *20*

**state bank**  A bank chartered by a state banking agency.  *10*

**stock variable**  The measure of some economic activity at a point in time (the money supply, the capital stock, or the labor force).  *3*

**store of value**  The property of holding value for a period of time. This is a property necessary for something to function as money.  *2*

**structural unemployment**  Unemployment that results from a low-marginal product in some workers, perhaps as a result of a shift in demand away from products that intensively used the skills possessed by the workers.  *17*

**subscription**  A form of auction for Treasury notes and bonds in which the notes and bonds are all sold at par, and a bid is for an amount to be purchased.  *7*

**Super Negotiable Order of Withdrawal accounts (Super NOW)**  Accounts authorized by the Garn–St. Germain Act of 1982. These transactions deposits require a minimum initial and average maintained balance of $2500, have unrestricted transactions features, and pay unregulated interest rates. Deposits in these accounts are included in M1.  *1*

**supply-side economics**  The theories that base the determination of aggregate output on economic activity in the input markets rather than a response to aggregate demand.  *17*

**swap network**  A set of reciprocal currency arrangements used to acquire foreign exchange for intervention in the foreign exchange markets.  *14*

**symmetalism**  A composite commodity standard that uses a set of metals in fixed proportion for redemption of the monetary unit.  *4*

**target**  A desired goal. Various targets are used to guide the conduct of monetary policy.  *15*

**tax and loan account**  An asset of the United States Treasury, held as a deposit in a private financial institution, that is used to minimize the Treasury's monetary impact. Most of these deposits are held in the form of interest-earning tax and loan note accounts.  *14*

**taxation**  The means of financing government expenditure that directly reduces disposable income. This is a supply of goods for purposes other than current consumption.  *18*

**technical solvency**  Being sufficiently liquid to pay bills when they become due. When applied to a commercial bank, it means being sufficiently liquid to be able to pay in cash for any withdrawal from demand deposits.  *8*

**term structure of interest rates**  The relationship that exists between short-term and long-term interest rates in the markets for credit instruments with similar risk.  *7*

**thrift institutions**  Financial intermediaries whose principal source of funds is the savings of the public. Thrift institutions (also called *near banks*) are the credit unions, mutual savings banks, and the savings and loan associations.  *11*

**time deposit**  An interest-bearing account with financial intermediaries that have a specified date of maturity ranging upward from 30 days.  *8*

**transactions account**  An account held with a financial intermediary that is transferable immediately through use of a checklike instrument. Transactions accounts include demand deposits, ATS accounts, NOW accounts, and share draft accounts.  *1*

**transactions costs**  The costs involved in the process of making exchanges and undertaking contracts. These costs include the costs of finding a double coincidence of wants and the costs of bargaining and obtaining information.  *2*

**transactions demand (for money)**  The demand for money that is determined by the intended purchases of goods and services.  *16*

**Treasury bill**  A short-term (one year or less) promissory note, issued by the United States Treasury, secured by "the full faith and credit of the United States." They are sold at a discount, initially through a primary market organized through the Federal Reserve. They have no coupon payments.  *7*

**Treasury bill rate**  The percentage discounted from the par value of a Treasury bill in its sale, based on a 360-day year. This rate is used to express the price of a Treasury bill.  *7*

**Treasury bond**  A long-term (five years or more) promissory note, issued by the United States Treasury, secured by "the full faith and credit of the United States." They are sold initially through a primary market organized through the Federal Reserve. The coupon rate of interest paid on a Treasury bond is subject to legal constraints. Prices of Treasury bonds are expressed in 32nds.  *7*

***Treasury General Account***  The United States Treasury deposits held at Federal Reserve District Banks. This account is drawn on for payments made by the United States Treasury.  *14*

***Treasury note***  A medium-term (1–10 years) promissory note issued by the United States Treasury, secured by "the full faith and credit of the United States." They are sold initially through a primary market organized through the Federal Reserve. The coupon rate of interest paid on a Treasury note is not subject to legal constraint. Prices of Treasury notes are expressed in 32nds.  *7*

***unemployed***  An individual is unemployed when the individual does not currently have a job and is actively seeking employment at the going wage rate.  *3*

***unit banking***  A limitation on banking activity that prevents banks from operating at more than one site (it prohibits branching). Unit banking has dominated the Midwest.  *10*

***unit of account***  A specific measure in which to express prices and values. This is one of the functions of money.  *2*

***velocity of circulation***  The average number of times the money stock is spent buying goods and services over a particular period, usually a year. $V = Py/M$.  *3*

***wampum***  Blue, black, and white beads, usually strung on thread, used by North American Indians and some early immigrants as a medium of exchange. Wampum was also used as jewelry and in some religious and ceremonial functions.  *1*

***yield curve***  The relationship that exists between the nominal rates of interest at a particular point in time for securities with similar risk and their terms to maturity.  *7*

***yield to maturity***  The rate of return that would be earned by holding a credit instrument to maturity.  *6*

# INDEX

acceptance, 127–128, 350, 593
acceptance fee, 128
accommodating transaction, 570
Accord, 476–477, 567, 568, 593
account, unit of, 21, 27–28, 34
adjustable rate loans, 220–221
advances, 326–327, 593
adverse clearings, 221, 593
Africa, 26
aggregate demand, 375, 376, 377, 409,
    438, 488–489, 490, 491–496,
    497, 542
  elasticity of, 536, 537–539
  excess, 520–524
  expected, 487, 489
aggregate output, 41–45, 64, 375, 386,
    410, 430–433, 438, 498
  composition of, 41, 437–457
aggregate production, 410
  neoclassical, 430–433
aggregate supply, 489
aggregation, 38–39, 593
aggregation problem, 417
agio phenomenon, 88
agricultural lending, 260
Alchian, Armen A., 35
Anderson, Leonall C., 470, 485
Anthony, Susan B., 8
arbitrage, 68, 593
Aronson, J. Richard, 141
Aristophanes, 69
asked price, 132, 138–139,
    148–149, 593

asset demand for money, 395–403,
    507–510, 593
asset portfolios, 164, 167, 170–177,
    220, 524
assets, highly liquid, 164, 508
attrition, 150, 593
auction, 145–150
Automatic Transfer Service (ATS)
    accounts, 11, 12, 13, 164, 168,
    178, 190, 291, 294, 302

Baer, Herbert, 187
balanced budget, 453
balance of payments, 59–60, 476, 478,
    593
  accounts, 570–571, 572
  deficit, 570–571
  surplus, 570–571
balances at other banks, 171, 172
Balbach, Anatol B., 312, 367
bank asset management, 170–177,
    206–215
bank audit, 252
bank borrowings, 182–183
bank capital, 178, 183–186, 594
bank charters, 181, 184, 229, 234, 316
bank draft, 127
bankers' acceptances, 128, 221, 350,
    594
  yield, 151
bank examination, 252, 316
bank failure, 228, 245, 247–248, 249,
    255, 594

bank holding companies, 236, 239–241, 278
Bank Holding Company Act, 236, 240, 241, 594
Banking Act of 1863, 229, 234, 316
Banking Act of 1933, 178, 229, 240, 253
Banking Act of 1935, 178, 235, 317, 322
banking regulation, 227–256
banking supervision, 229–230
Bank Merger Act, 244, 245
bank mergers, 244–245, 255, 594
bank note issue, 180–181
bank notes, 179, 180–181, 245
Bank of North America, 163
Bank of Pennsylvania, 163
Bank of Sweden, 316
Bank of the United States, 229, 316
bank panics, 302
bank, pass-through, 194
bank related business, 165–166, 278
bank reserves, 172
Bank for Cooperatives, 260, 280
bank suspensions, 245–249, 594
Banque Commerciale pour l'Europe du Nord, 184
barbelling assets, 214
Barnard, Billings D., 18
barter, 4, 25, 27
Baumol, William, 387, 406
bearer, 123
Bentham, Jeremy, 485
bid price, 132, 138–139, 148–149, 209
bill of exchange, 124, 127–128
bill of lading, 128
bills only policy, 568–569
bimetallism, 68, 81–86, 90, 92
  breakdown, 83–86
bits, 6
Bloomsbury Set, 377
Board of Governors, 192, 229, 318, 320, 322, 323, 344, 469, 557, 594
bonds, 149–150, 396, 397–400, 594
  long-term, 149–150
Boorman, John T., 160, 224, 256, 473
Bowsher, Norman N., 306, 590
branch banking, 235–238, 594
brassage, 70

Breit, William, 399
Bretton Woods System, 79–81, 570, 575–576, 594
Brewer, Elijah, 224, 256, 339, 359, 367
brokers and dealers, 132, 138–140, 221, 594
brokers' commission, 138–140, 278
Bronfenbrenner, Martin, 526
Brown, Weir M., 435
Brown, William W., 119
Brunner, Karl, 35, 380, 383, 590
  biography, 380–381
built-in stabilizers, 546
Bundy, James M., 224, 242
Bureau of Engraving, 9
Bureau of Labor Statistics, 42–43
Burger, Albert E., 312, 367
Burgon, John William, 69
Byzantine Empire, 68

Cacy, J. A., 193, 292
caisse populaire, 263
Cajori, Florian, 7
callable bonds, 126
Cambridge equation, 386–387, 388, 393, 394, 402, 594
Cambridge k, 386, 387, 388, 391, 393, 395, 401–402
capital
  international flows, 569–576
  demand for, 442, 444
  expected rate of return, 442
  price of, 445
  supply of, 444–446
capital stock, 410, 411, 432, 441, 444–446, 482, 495, 496, 520
  growth, 482
  utilization, 410, 411
Carlozzi, Nicholas, 65
Carlson, Keith M., 406, 485
cash items in process of collection, 171, 172, 190, 197, 202ff., 346, 594
central banking, 315–339, 594
  before 1913, 316
certificates of deposit (CDs), 182, 215, 218, 221, 222, 325, 594
check, 6, 10, 171, 172, 178, 180, 197–204, 295, 594

check clearance, 171, 172, 173, 180, 195–204, 233, 264, 317, 351, 352, 594

checking accounts, 11, 12, 13, 164, 195–196

CHIPS, 200

Clarke, Stephen V. O., 590

classical economists, 374

classical region on *lm* curve, 542–543

clearing balances, 347

clearinghouses, 180, 198–200, 594

clipping, 8

closed-end investment companies, 260, 279

coin, 27, 166, 344, 348, 353, 595

full-bodied, 4, 68, 94, 595, 598

clad, 6, 8

subsidiary, 6

token, 4, 6, 85–86, 88, 94, 595

Coinage Act of 1792, 4, 7, 81, 83

COLA clauses, 56, 466–467

Colander, Donald C., 89

collateral trust bonds, 127

commercial and industrial loans, 169, 171, 174, 176, 205, 248, 278

commercial bank

as intermediary, 163–186, 595

assets, 143, 170–177

liabilities, 177–183, 215–220

management, 166–169, 189–223

commercial banking business, 168–186

Commercial Loan Theory of Banking, 205, 326, 595

commercial paper, 126, 127, 129, 277, 327, 569

yield, 129–130, 151

commodity money, 67

commodity prices and interest rates, 114–117

commodity standards, 67–92, 364, 595

common bond, 263

comparative advantage, 23–24, 30–32, 259, 595

compensating balances, 179

competitive bid, 145–147, 595

composite commodity standard, 68, 90–92, 595

Comptroller of the Currency, 173, 181, 227, 229, 245, 252, 255, 316, 317, 595

Confederacy, 86

Consumer expenditure survey, 43

consumer lending, 169, 260, 264, 278

Consumer Price Index (CPI), 42–43, 47, 425, 466, 567, 568, 580, 595

Consumer Savings Bank of Worcester, 266

consumption

function, 491–493

induced, 493, 531

nominal, 438, 487

real, 438, 439, 475, 488

contemporaneous reserves, 195–196

contractual savings institutions, 260, 261, 271–277, 595

convenience and needs, 235, 255, 595

cooperative banks, 267

Cooperative Central Bank of Massachusetts, 267

Copernicus, 69

core deposits, 248

corporate bond, 127, 174–175, 273

corporate equities, 273, 274, 276

correspondent banking, 172, 197–198, 202, 207, 228, 595

Council of Economic Advisors, 65

coupon issue yield equivalent, 147

coupon rate, 130, 595

CPI-U, 42–43, 551, 584

CPI-W, 42–43

creative financing, 272

credit cards, 166, 177, 279, 305

credit crunch, 310

credit instruments, 121–161, 164, 511, 595

classification, 125

definition, 121–122

negotiable, 122, 123–128

non-negotiable, 122, 123, 175

types, 122–128

credit instrument markets, 131–140, 165, 210

credit investigation, 166

credit markets, 595

allocation through, 100–104

credit market interaction, 150–152, 210
credit union, 13, 168, 194, 260, 261, 263–264, 265, 303, 595
credit union liquidity facility, 194, 264
Crime of '73, 88, 595
Cross, S. Y., 365
crowding out, 451, 457, 475, 531–532, 539, 595
  complete, 451, 543
  partial, 475, 532
currency, 6, 10, 170, 181, 305–306, 311, 362–363, 389, 595
currency and coin service, 233
currency in circulation, 292, 348, 353, 362–363
currency in the hands of the nonbank public, 11–12, 288, 292, 293, 297

Darby, Michael R., 119
Davenport, John A., 563
Davis, Richard G., 590
dealers, 132, 164, 209, 595
deferred availability cash items, 202ff., 346, 351, 596
deficit spending, 105
deflation, 54, 596
debenture bonds, 127, 277
Defoe, Daniel, 264
demand deposits, 163ff., 178–179, 248, 263, 285–288, 291, 302, 305, 596
  adjusted, 11, 12
demand for labor, 411–419
  aggregate, 416–419, 430
  the firm, 411–416
demand for money, 386–388, 395, 401–402, 405, 464
demonstration effect, 330, 596
Department of Housing and Urban Development (HUD), 282
deposit insurance, 229–230, 245, 249–253
Deposit Insurance National Bank, 252
depository institution, 10, 261, 291, 308, 325, 596
Depository Institutions Deregulation and Monetary Control Act of 1980, 10, 169, 172, 180, 182, 183, 190, 191, 193, 194, 202, 231, 233, 250, 255, 259, 261, 263, 264, 266, 267, 269, 303, 308, 310, 322, 324, 326, 352, 584, 596
deposits at the Federal Reserve, 171, 292, 311, 325, 344, 347
  nonmember institutions, 347
deposits, multiple expansion, 285–311
Desjardins, Alphonse, 263
dirty float, 364
discounting, 113, 183, 326–332
  access to window, 183, 327–328
  and monetary policy, 329–332, 404, 450
  and the monetary base, 328–329, 343
discount rate, 218, 269, 320, 326–332, 344
discount sales, 129–130, 596
discount window, 183, 233, 269, 310
discounts
  adjustments, 327
  and borrowing from the Federal Reserve, 183, 221, 269, 327, 596
  defensive, 330
  emergency credit, 183, 327
  seasonal, 183, 327
disintermediation, 254, 310, 596
diversification, 165
dollar
  origin of, 5
  symbol, 7
double coincidence of wants, 25, 32, 596
draft, 10, 124, 127–128, 596
Drucker, Peter F., 274
dual banking, 229, 596
due-on-sale, 271–272

Eastburn, David P., 340
economic growth, 58, 596
economic models, 372–379, 488
Edge Act and Agreement Corporations, 175, 243–244, 596
Einzig, Paul, 18
elastic currency, 317, 326
elasticity, 537–543, 596
Electronic Funds Transfer Act, 201
electronic money, 200, 201

employment, 371, 372, 374
  maximum, 52–53
Employment Act of 1946, 51–52, 448,
  530, 534, 596
entry into banking, 228, 234–235
equation of exchange, 40, 49, 111,
  385–386, 388, 394, 597
equilibrium
  Keynesian, 492, 515–516
  long-run, 529
equipment trust certificates, 127
equities, 395, 396, 400
equity capital, 166, 400
Eurodollar borrowing, 183, 221
Eurodollar reserve requirement, 192,
  193
Eurodollars, 183, 184–185, 324
  overnight, 11, 14–15, 183, 303,
  304
Euromarks, 185
European American Bank and Trust,
  248
Euro Swiss Francs, 185
Euroyen, 185
excess reserves, 292, 304, 323–324,
  325, 363
excess reserve ratio (e), 294
exchange
  medium of, 21, 26–27, 30, 189
  theory of, 22–25
exchange rate, 59, 74, 75, 476, 477,
  597
  factors affecting, 478–480
  fixed, 79–81
  floating, 60, 364, 598
  pegged, 79–81
Exchange Stabilization Fund, 364
exit from banking, 245–249
expectations, 402–403, 428–430,
  443, 466–468
  adaptive, 428–430, 552, 553, 593
  inflationary, 428
  rational, 403, 428–430, 468, 473,
  553, 602
expected rate of return, 166, 397–
  401, 442, 546
exports, 438
Export-Trading Company Act of 1982,
  128

factors, 240, 260, 277–278
factors of production, 53, 376, 409,
  431
Fair Labor Standards Act of 1938, 425
Farmers Exchange Bank, 245
farm loans, 177
federal agency securities, 350
Federal Credit Union Act, 263
Federal Deposit Insurance Corporation
  (FDIC), 227, 229–230, 235, 242,
  244, 249–253, 255, 256, 265,
  267, 597
federal funds, 172, 173, 174, 175, 182,
  248, 597
  market, 172, 218–220, 347, 578
  rate, 173, 219, 220, 325, 331, 337
Federal Home Loan Bank, 191, 253,
  260, 281
  Board, 237, 269, 310, 597
  System, 265, 267, 269
  districts, 270
Federal Home Loan Mortgage Corporation (Freddy Mac), 260, 270, 281
Federal Home Loan Regional Banks,
  269
Federal Housing Administration (FHA),
  281
Federal Intermediate Credit Banks,
  260, 281
Federal Land Banks, 260, 281
Federal National Mortgage Association
  (Fanny Mae), 177, 260, 278, 281,
  282
Federal Open Market Committee
  (FOMC), 318, 332–338, 344, 469,
  557, 558, 563, 578, 579
  chairman, 318
  directives, 332, 336–338, 364, 558,
  579, 597
  October 1979 directive, 337–338,
  583–584
Federal Reserve Act, 316–317
Federal Reserve
  as regulator, 227, 229, 371
  as supervisor, 229, 252, 255, 371
  balance sheet, 346–348, 365
  capital, 231, 355
  check clearing, 199, 200–204
  control, 306, 318–320, 343, 391

ownership, 317–318
pricing of services, 233, 347
structure, 317–320, 321
Federal Reserve credit, 350–353, 597
Federal Reserve District Banks, 8, 170–172, 179, 194, 200–204, 218, 219, 231, 263, 269, 292, 317–319, 326, 328, 344, 346
Federal Reserve loans, 351
Federal Reserve Notes, 9, 346, 348, 597
Federal Reserve Notes Outstanding, 344, 350
Federal Reserve stock, 175
Federal Reserve System, 8, 16, 92, 158, 249, 265, 317, 321, 325, 597
Federal Savings and Loan Insurance Corporation (FSLIC), 267, 270
Feige, Edgar L., 313, 406
fiat money, 86, 597
fiduciary issue, 86, 597
finance companies, 240, 260, 261, 277–279, 597
  business and commercial, 260, 277–278
  personal, 260, 278–279
financial futures, 215, 216–217, 597
financial intermediation, 163–186, 597
financial intermediation as a business, 165–166
financial markets, 104–105, 597
fineness, 67, 82
first Bank of the United States, 229, 316
fiscal agent of the government, 145, 316, 317, 597
fiscalism, 379
fiscal policy, 431–432, 433, 462, 546, 598
  and interest rates, 450–455
  Keynesian, 500, 530–534, 540, 549
  neoclassical, 448–457
Fisher, Irving, 101, 108, 110–111, 119, 385
Fisher, Irving Norton, 111
Flannery, Mark J., 224
float, 204, 349, 351–353, 598
flow variable, 40, 598

foreign exchange, 59–62, 166, 364, 478
  and monetary policy, 61–62
  market intervention, 364–366, 598
foreign-official accounts, 355
foreign trade, 476–477
Franklin National Bank, 246, 247–248
free banking, 234
free coinage, 70, 81–82
free gold, 353
free reserves, 566, 598
Friedman, Benjamin M., 485
Friedman, Milton, 18, 90, 181, 324, 388, 389, 395, 406, 428, 473, 506
  biography, 398–399
Friedman, Rose, 399
Frisch, Ragnar, 110
full employment, 371, 374, 446, 462, 598
  defined, 422
Full Employment and Balanced Growth Act of 1978 (Humphrey-Hawkins), 52, 54, 58, 320, 371, 448, 461, 530, 534, 558, 583, 598
fundamental problem of financial intermediation, 166–168, 598
futures, 215, 216–217, 597

Garcia, F. L., 237
Garcia, G., 187
Garn-St Germain Depository Institutions Act of 1982, 11, 12, 14, 169, 180, 184, 193, 207, 237, 253, 259, 261, 272, 280, 303, 326, 586
General Motors, 273
Gilbert, R. Alton, 192, 232, 368
GNP deflator, 44, 109, 390, 567
gold, 27, 70, 356–357, 570
  official price, 70, 72, 73, 75, 354
gold certificates, 346, 349, 354, 355
gold exchange standard, 77–81, 598
Gold Reserve Act of 1934, 357
gold rush, 75
gold standard, 68–77, 90, 364, 598
  Keynes' views, 378
  problems, 75–76
gold stock, 349, 350, 598
gold tranche, 570
government agencies, 261, 280

government expenditure, 360–364, 446, 449, 450–452, 456, 474, 493–494, 530–532, 541, 598
  deficit financed, 362
  financed by new currency, 362–363
  financed by taxes, 361–362
  nominal, 438, 487
  real, 438, 450–452
  state and local, 494
government finance and the money supply, 363–364
Government National Mortgage Association (Ginny Mae), 217, 260, 282
government regulation, 260
government sponsored agencies, 261, 280
Gramley, Lyle E., 435
Great Depression, 168, 228, 234, 246, 265, 399, 487, 567
greenback, 8, 86–88
Gregory, Peter, 425
Gresham, Sir Thomas, 69
Gresham's Law, 68, 69, 83, 89, 92, 598
Gross National Income, 41–44
Gross National Product (GNP), 41–44, 48, 362, 371, 386, 392, 598
growth, 58, 428, 482
guinea, 22, 89
Gurley, John G., 307, 308, 312
Gurley-Shaw Hypothesis, 307–311, 520, 598
Gutmann, Peter M., 313

Haberler, Gottfried, 544
Hafer, R. W., 303
Hagan, Donald G., 253
Hamilton, Alexander, 83
Hamilton, Earl G., 224
Hansen, Alvin, 379
Havrilesky, Thomas M., 160, 224, 256, 473
Hayek, Friedrich A., 88
hedging, 216
Henderson D., 368
Henry VIII, 69, 89
Hicks, John R., 498, 501, 513
HUD, 282
Huber, Victor, 263

human capital, 395, 396, 401, 598
Humphrey, David, 224
Hurley, Evelyn H., 141
hyperinflation, 30, 598

impact lag, 559, 599
implementation lag, 559, 599
imports, 438, 493
income
  nominal, 47–48, 389, 403, 438, 461
  real, 47–48, 438, 448, 461, 491–493
incomes policy, 33
indexation, 55–57, 553, 599
index number problem, 46, 599
indicators, 565–566, 587, 599
inflation, 54–58, 76, 220–221, 273, 427, 599
  and monetary policy, 465
  demand-pull, 522
  Keynesian, 520–524
instability and is-lm curves, 499–500
insurance companies, 261, 271, 274–276
  casualty and property, 260, 274–276
interbank deposits, 12, 197, 599
interconvertibility, 70, 71, 82, 90, 94
Inter-District Settlement Fund, 202
interest equalization tax, 575
interest payments, 128–131, 164
interest rate, 54, 99–119, 371, 372, 379, 388, 549, 599
  and commodity prices, 114–117
  anticipated real, 108
  as market prices, 100–104
  expected, 154–155
  market, 449, 464, 479, 511, 518
  nominal, 106–109, 117, 131–134, 464, 472–474
  normal, 509–510
  real, 100, 106–109, 117, 437, 438, 440, 449, 455, 472–474, 479, 495, 496, 505, 602
  target ranges, 337–338
  term structure, 152–159
interest rate policy, 371, 505
interest rate target, 471–472, 474, 548, 560–566, 578

interest risk, 164, 208, 213, 599
intermediate target, 547, 564–565, 583, 599
internal rate of return, 442–443, 495, 599
international banking, 242–244, 585
International Banking Act, 242, 243, 244
International Banking Facilities, 244
International Monetary Fund (IMF), 79
international payments, 60–61, 73–74, 75, 79–81, 357, 493–494, 569–574
interstate banking, 236–237, 242
inventory accumulation, 446–447, 490, 599
inventory changes, 455, 490
investment, 104, 438, 549, 599
  desired, 495–496
  nominal, 487
  real, 438, 439, 441–446, 475, 488
investments, 442
investment banker, 132
investment companies, 260, 261, 279–280, 599
investment demand, 441–446, 499
investment multiplier, 493, 546
*is* curve, 497–500, 515–516, 531, 532, 536, 537, 538, 540, 543, 544, 547, 562, 565, 599

Jáchymov, 5
jaw-boning, 322
Jefferson, Thomas, 83
Jester, John J., 65
Joachimsthal, 5
Johnson, Harry G., 383
Johnson, Walter L., 502
Johnston, Robert, 243
Jones, Marcos J., 187
Jordan, Jerry L., 470, 485
Judd, J. P., 590

Kamerschen, David R., 502
Kane, Edward J., 340
Kantor, Brian, 403
Karnosky, Denis S., 485
Keynesian critique of neoclassical theory, 420–421
Keynesian economists, 539

Keynesian model, 374, 383
Keynesian policy, 376, 379, 561–562
Keynesian system, 487–554, 599
Keynesian theory, 379, 487–524, 557
Keynes, John Maynard, 374, 375, 383, 386, 487, 499, 501, 507, 508, 529, 544, 549
  biography, 377–378
Keynes, John Neville, 377
Key, Sidney J., 242, 244, 257
King, Marvyn, 65
Klein, Benjamin, 93, 187
Klein, Lawrence, 409
Kock, Albert, 590
Kroos, Herman E., 84, 93
Kubarych, Roger L., 224

labor, 409–432
labor contracts, 424, 524
labor force, growth of, 465
labor market, 374, 409, 411–433, 451, 455
  equilibrium, 422
  neoclassical, 374
labor productivity, 412–415
laddering of maturities, 214
lags, 547, 559
Laidler, David E. W., 526
Landy, Laurie, 257
Lang, Richard W., 160, 368
Laurent, Robert D., 313
legal solvency, 168
legal tender, 9–10, 91, 599
Leijonhufvud, Axel, 488
lender of last resort, 183, 315, 319, 599
Lerner, Abba P., 379, 555
LeRoy, Stephen F., 547
letter of credit, 128
Ley, Harold, 111
liability management, 177, 206, 215–220, 221–222, 254, 599
Liesner, Thelma, 65
life insurance companies, 260, 272–274, 275
limping standard, 84–86
Lindsey, David E., 547
liquidity, 166, 168, 186, 207, 222, 304, 599
  defined, 143

liquidity preference, 508–510
liquidity premium theory, 156–157
liquidity trap, 509–510, 513, 514, 539, 540, 541, 599
*lm* curve, 512–522, 531, 532, 536, 538, 540, 543, 547, 562, 565, 599
loan participations, 207, 599
loans, 164, 173
loan sharks, 279
loanable funds, 104–105
loans on security purchases, 177
lock-in, 164, 222
Los Angeles Times, 29
Louis Philippe, 85
Lovati, Jean M., 192
Luckett, Dudley M., 187
Lucas, Charles M., 187
Lucas, Robert E., 555

macroeconomic models, 38, 373–379, 599
Ma Duan Lin, 69
Maisel, Sherman, 591
Malkiel, Burton G., 160
managed float, 600
Manufacturers' Hanover Trust, 332
marginal propensity to consume (mpc), 440, 491, 531, 600
marginal propensity to save (mps), 440
margin requirements, 177
market, central, 25
market interaction, 37–38, 63
market segmentation theory, 157–158
Marshall, Alfred, 377, 386
Maryland Savings-Share Insurance Corporation, 267
matched sale/purchase agreement, 345
matching assets and liabilities, 215
Maxwell, James A., 141
Mayer, Thomas, 381, 382, 383, 458, 526, 536
McCallum, Bennett T., 403, 429
McElhatten, Rose, 435
McFadden Act, 235, 236, 242
McNiel, Charles R., 257
medium of exchange, 21, 26–27, 30, 189
Melton, William C., 225

Meltzer, Allan H., 35
merchandise trade, balance of, 478
Merris, Randall C., 224
Mexico's foreign debt, 586
microeconomic models, 38, 373
Middle East, 580
milling, 8
Mill, John Stuart, 3
minimum wage, 425
Minsky, Hyman P., 340
Mint, 8, 29
mint ratio, 82–86
Modern Quantity Theory, 394–404, 600
Modigliani, Franco, 555
monetarism, 379–383, 583–584, 600
and *is-lm* curves, 544
monetarists, 462, 471, 520, 579, 588
monetary aggregates, 300, 308, 338, 578–583, 588
target ranges, 337–338, 560–566
monetary authorities, 371
monetary base, 291–294, 296, 315, 343–366, 371, 600
alternative measures, 348
sources, 349
statistics, 349
composition of, 292, 349
monetary control, 308–311, 344–345, 352, 366
Monetary Control Act (see Depository Institutions Deregulation and Monetary Control Act)
monetary management, 322–338
monetary policy, 53–54, 58, 63, 322–338, 366, 388, 433, 450, 549, 557–588, 600
in the 1950s, 568–573
in the 1960s, 573–579
in the 1970s, 579–584
in the 1980s, 584–588
and foreign exchange, 365–366, 480–481
and Keynes, 549
conflicts, 558
discretionary, 481–483, 558, 559, 596
Keynesian, 534–543
neoclassical, 461–484

monetary policy instruments, 322–338
monetary rule, 382, 481–483, 600
monetary standards, 67–96, 600
monetary targets, 468–472, 482
  defined, 469
monetary theory, 37–65, 371–383
  Keynesian, 505–525
  neoclassical, 374, 461–484
monetized gold, 354
money changers, 163
money creation, 285–307
money, definition, 22, 32
money illusion, 421, 600
money market, 386–387, 451, 455
  equilibrium, 403–404, 511–515, 524, 534
  instability, 548, 562–563
  Keynesian, 505–524
  neoclassical, 374, 385–405
money market deposit accounts, 11, 14, 179, 180–181, 190–191, 280, 302, 305, 311, 586, 587, 588, 600
money market mutual funds, 11, 15, 254, 260, 280, 303, 305, 324, 600
money multipliers, 297, 298, 299, 301–307, 315, 344, 511, 601
money, quantity of, 4, 9, 16, 37–65, 79, 91, 94–96, 385
money supply 1 (M1), 11–13, 16, 40, 49, 50, 164, 169, 181, 189, 263, 280, 288, 290, 293, 297–298, 299, 301, 302–303, 308, 311, 344, 363, 391, 392, 471, 560, 576, 578, 584, 587, 600
money supply 2 (M2), 13–15, 16, 41, 49, 50, 181, 185, 280, 290, 293, 299–301, 302–303, 308, 311, 344, 363, 390, 391, 392, 471, 560, 565, 576, 578, 584, 586, 587, 600
  consolidation components, 15, 303
money supply, 40–49, 94–96, 315, 332–335, 371, 372, 385–404, 410, 461, 469, 505–506, 511, 541
  components, 11–15, 300, 301
  definitions, 10–15, 302–303
  determinants, 298
  real, 509, 511–519
  target ranges, 337, 471, 548, 558

monitoring target, 587
monometallism, 68–77, 92, 601
Morris, Robert, 163
moral suasion, 322, 344, 601
Morgenstern, Oskar, 65
mortgage
  bonds, 127
  brokers, 278
  companies, 260, 261, 273, 277, 278
  markets, 260, 266, 270, 272, 281, 282
multiple expansion of deposits, 285–311, 601
multiplier effect
  money, 285–311
  investment/government expenditure, 491–493, 494, 531, 541, 601
municipal bonds, 126
municipal securities, 126, 166
munis, 126
Munn, Glenn G., 237
Muth, John F., 403
mutual funds, 11, 15, 254, 279–280
mutual savings banks, 194, 253, 260, 264–266, 601

naive quantity theory, 388–394
National Bank Act, 180, 229
national banking laws, 180–181, 229
national banks, 180–181, 184–185, 228, 230, 235, 316, 601
National Credit Union Administration's Central Liquidity Facility, 194
National Credit Union Association, 253
natural person, 191
natural rate of interest, 446–447, 457, 601
natural rate of unemployment, 427–428, 434, 446, 483, 552
near bank, 271, 601
negotiable instrument, 122, 123–128, 601
negotiable order of withdrawal (NOW) account, 6, 11, 12, 163, 168, 178, 181, 190, 254, 263, 265, 266, 267, 290, 291, 294, 302, 601
neoclassical
  model, 374
  system, 385–483

neoclassical *(continued)*
   theory, 379, 383, 557
   policy, 376, 561
neoclassical synthesis, 520
net borrowed reserves, 566, 601
net exports, 601
   nominal, 438
   real, 438, 488, 493–494
neutral money, 390–391
New York Clearing House Association, 198–199, 200
New York Safety Fund Act, 249
nickel, 6
NINOW accounts, 295
Nixon, Richard M., 580
nominal interest rates and prices, 114–117
nominal output, 49–51, 389, 461
nominal variable, 40, 601
nonbank financial intermediaries, 13, 177, 259–282, 288–291, 307–311
   and multiple expansion, 288–291
   classification, 260
noncompetitive bid, 145–147, 601
non-negotiable instruments, 122, 123, 175, 601
nonpersonal time deposits, 191, 290, 292, 293, 295, 304, 601
normative economics, 51–52, 64, 372, 601
normative goals, 52, 468, 530
North Carolina Savings Guarantee Corporation, 267
notes, retired, 8

off-shore banking, 14–15
Ohio Deposit Guarantee Fund, 267
oil prices, 580
open account time deposits, 14, 182
open-end investment company, 260, 279
open market account managers, 332, 471, 476, 601
open market operations, 332–338, 343, 345, 404, 450, 471–472, 511, 564, 602
   and the New York Fed, 332, 333–335, 336
   defensive, 344, 345, 596

dynamic, 345
   purchases, 332–334, 474
   sales, 334–335
operating targets, 564, 578, 586, 602
Operation Twist, 157–158, 574–575, 577
opportunity cost, 23, 100, 332, 602
Oresme, 69
overnight repurchase account, 11, 14, 182–183, 302, 304
Oxford Provident Building Association, 267

Pagano, Penny, 29
paper, nonredeemable, 8
paper currency, 8, 90
paper gold, 81, 355
paper standard, 91–92, 602
partial equilibrium analysis, 38
participation certificates, 126
pass-through accounts, 194, 263, 344
pass-through bank, 194
Patinkin, Don, 501
payment, means of, 22
penny shortage, 87
pension funds, 260, 261, 271, 273–274, 276–277
People's Republic of China, 56
peso, 7
Philadelphia National Bank, 245
Philippines, 77–79
Phillips, A. W., 523
Phillips curve, 522–524, 602
   stability of, 550–553
picayune, 6
pieces of eight, 602
Pierce, Douglas K., 406
Pierce, James L., 485
Pigou, Arthur Cecil, 386, 544
Pigou effect, 544, 602
Pinsky, Neil, 244
pledging, 175
point of effective demand, 491, 602
Poole, William, 485
portfolio choice, 206–222, 301–307
portfolio diversification, 170–177, 209–212, 602
portfolio management, 166, 189–223, 271, 346

general rules, 213–215
portfolio ratios, 301–307
positive economics, 51, 372, 602
pound, British, 74, 79–81, 89
precautionary demand for money, 507
present value, 112–114, 602
price, relative, 27–28, 31, 54
price changes, 109–112, 390, 431, 514–515
  in Keynesian system, 377–378, 536
  in neoclassical system, 374, 466–468
price index, 39, 41–48, 417, 420, 602
price level
  constant, 482, 535–536
  general, 30–32, 40, 55, 71, 375, 386, 395–397, 400, 419, 432, 479
  Keynesian, 520–524
  stable, 461, 520
price of money, 394, 395
price stability
  domestic, 54–58, 71–73, 75, 461, 482
  international, 73–74
price takers, 413
prices, anticipated rate of change in, 106–109, 396, 797, 429, 463, 482, 506, 593
primary market, 132, 602
primary reserves, 172, 174, 190–195, 214, 221, 222, 223, 602
prime rate, 214, 220
problem bank, 252
Producer Price Index (PPI), 44, 75–76
production function, 375–376, 410, 411, 431, 432
productivity of labor, 412, 413, 415, 432
product market, 602
  equilibrium, 438–457, 489–491
  Keynesian, 487–500
  neoclassical, 437–457
  stability of, 498–500
profitability, 165, 166, 177, 222, 602
promissory note, 124, 126–127
proviso clause, 579
Pryor, Frederic L., 35
Puerto Rico, 425

quantity theories, 62–63, 602
  modern, 394–404
  naive, 62, 71

Ransom, Roger L., 399
Rasche, Robert H., 160
rate of return, expected, 208–209
ratio of currency to deposits, 295ff.
real, 6
real balance effect, 544–545, 602
real bill, 205, 350
real bills doctrine, 205
real estate loans, 169, 174, 177
real income, 448, 479, 480, 602
real money balances, 395–403, 516–519, 524, 525, 542
  demand for, 395–403, 464, 506–510, 511, 512–514
real output, 386, 461
real variable, 40, 603
Rechter, Denise M., 257
recognition lag, 559, 603
redeemability, 67, 68, 92, 603
Redlich, Fritz, 181
red-lining, 214
Regulation A, 326
Regulation D, 190, 195–196
Regulation E, 201
Regulation G, 177
regulation of Banks, 227–256
Regulation Q, 184, 243, 253–255, 603
Regulation T, 177
Regulation U, 177
Regulation Z, 228
repurchase agreement, 175, 182–183, 345, 603
rescheduling foreign debt, 586
reserve assets, official, 570, 573
reserve position management, 195–196
reserve ratio, 288, 294
reserve requirements, 172, 190–196, 231, 233, 292–293, 316, 318, 322–326, 348, 405, 603
  after the Monetary Control Act of 1980, 193, 195–196
  before the Monetary Control Act of 1980, 191–192
  California, 191
  Illinois, 191

reserve requirements *(continued)*
  New York, 192
reserves
  against private deposits (RPDs), 581
  for transactions accounts, 190–195,
    292, 293, 298
  fractional, 285, 598
  nonborrowed, 469, 586
  of depository institutions, 190–195,
    285–288, 291, 318, 344
  official, 80
  of near banks, 288–291
  required, 190–195, 322–326, 348
Resler, David H., 312
Resumption, 70, 89
Reynolds, LLoyd G., 241, 257
risk
  default, 164, 165, 167, 208, 213, 595
  interest, 164, 208, 213
Robbins, Sidney, 160
Robertson, Dennis, 386
Robinson, Joan, 379
Roos, Charles, 110
rules *versus* authorities, 481, 559–560

safe deposit boxes, 166, 180
safety, 166, 167, 603
sales finance companies, 260, 279
Sampson, S., 368
Samuelson, Paul A., 93, 502
Santoni, Gary J., 119
Sargent, Thomas J., 435
saving, 438, 439–441, 446, 473, 474–
  475, 603
savings, 439
savings account, 11, 13–14, 177, 179–
  181, 248, 264, 265, 267, 290, 302,
  305, 440, 603
savings and loan association, 168, 169,
  194, 260, 261, 264, 266–271,
  289, 290, 603
  classification, 268
savings bank, 264–266
savings deposit (see savings account)
Say, Jean Baptiste, 375
scarcity, 99
Schroeder, Frederck J., 225
Schwartz, Anna J., 18, 90, 181, 324,
  388, 389, 399, 406

Scitovsky, Tibor, 544
search behavior, 426–427, 523
secondary market, 132, 135–140, 176,
  603
secondary reserves, 174–175, 603
second Bank of the United States, 229,
  316
Securities and Exchange Commission,
  127
securities, safe keeping, 233
security holdings, 164, 171, 173–175
security prices, 132–135
security resale agreements, 173
seigniorage, 70
selected short term assets (SSTA), 11,
  13, 299, 301, 311
selective credit controls, 433, 603
self-liquidating commercial paper, 205
serial bond, 126
share draft accounts, 6, 11, 13, 164,
  168, 190, 261, 264, 291, 303, 603
Shaw, Edward S., 307, 308, 312
shiftability, 132, 143, 603
shiftable assets, 206, 221, 603
Shiller, Robert J., 119
shinplasters, 88
short-term assets in M2, 11, 13, 299,
  301, 311
Siegel, Jeremy J., 119
sight draft, 127
silver certificate, 8, 353
Simpson, Thomas D., 18
Sinkey, Joseph F. Jr., 245, 252, 257
Smithsonian Agreement, 575
Smith, Warren L., 502
Smith, Wayne J., 187
Smith, W. Stephen, 257
Social Security System, 260, 276
solvency, 168, 603
Spanish silver dollar, 4, 82, 84–85
Special Drawing Rights (SDR), 81, 355,
  570, 603
Special Drawing Rights Certificate
  account, 346, 355, 603
specialization, 23–24, 169, 603
speculation, 216
speculative demand for money, 508–
  510
spread, 137–140

stabilization policy, 546–549, 603
state and local securities, 126, 175
state banking agencies, 229
Stein, Jerome L., 380, 383
sterilization, 364–365
Stigler, George J., 228
St. Louis Fed, 469–470
stock variable, 40, 604
stone money, 26
store of value, 21, 28–30, 34, 604
subordinate debentures, 127, 183
super negotiable order of withdrawal
    accounts (S-NOW), 11, 12, 178,
    179, 190, 302, 604
supply creates its own demand, 375,
    409
supply of labor, aggregate, 420–421
supply side, 54, 409–434, 437, 604
surplus spending, 105
swap network, 365, 366, 604
symetallism, 68, 90–91, 604
System Open Market Account, 332
Systems Manager for Foreign Opera-
    tions, 476–477


target ranges, 580, 581, 582
targets, 54, 548, 564–565, 576, 578–
    579, 604
Tatom, John A., 368
Tavlas, George S., 485
tax and loan accounts, 179, 358–359,
    362, 581, 604
taxation, 361–362, 446, 494, 532–
    534, 604
  nominal, 438
  real, 438, 452–453
tax exempt, 126
technical solvency, 168, 174, 604
technology, 410, 411, 432
Teeters, N.H., 257, 585
Teigen, Ronald L., 502
Tennessee Valley Authority, 126
Terrell, H., 257, 585
term bond, 126
term insurance, 272
term structure of interest rates, 152–
    159, 400, 604
  expectations, 153–156, 597

liquidity premium, 156–157, 599
  market segmentation, 157–158, 600
thaler, 5
theories of banking, 204–206
Thompson, Thomas D., 485
Thornton, Henry, 485
Thorp, Adrian W., 187
thrift institutions, 169, 181, 260, 261,
    262–271, 302, 308, 604
Thurston, Thom B., 187
tight money, 310
time certificates of deposit (CDs), 182
time deposits, 177, 182, 264, 265, 305,
    604
  small, 11, 13–14, 215, 302
time draft, 127
time preference, 102–103
Tobin, James, 382, 406, 506, 526, 555
  biography, 519–520
trade draft, 127
trade-off, unemployment and inflation,
    522–524, 550–553
transactions accounts, 11, 12, 163–
    164, 169, 179, 215, 261, 291, 292,
    293, 294–297, 308, 604
  net, 190, 193
transactions costs, 23–25, 135–140,
    164, 304, 387, 604
transactions demand for money, 387–
    388, 397, 403, 507, 604
transfer agent, 280
transfer payments, 452
travelers' checks, 11, 12, 166, 295, 303
Treasury bill rate, 147, 221, 254, 578,
    604
Treasury bills, 124, 144, 209, 217, 304,
    568, 604
  primary market, 145–148
  secondary market, 148–149
  yield, 109, 146–148, 151, 331
Treasury bonds, 126, 144, 149–150,
    217, 604
  market for, 149–150
Treasury cash holdings, 349, 355, 358
Treasury cash management, 358–360
Treasury currency outstanding, 349,
    353
Treasury General Account, 346, 354,
    355, 358, 605

Treasury notes, 126, 144, 149–150, 217, 304, 605
  market for, 149–150
Treasury securities, 171, 173, 327
  exchange, 149–150
  subscription, 149–150
trust accounts, 166
truth in lending, 228
Tullock, Gordon, 93

underground economy, 305–306
underwriter, 132, 166
unemployment compensation, 424
unemployment, 605
  frictional, 427, 598
  in Keynesian system, 377, 522–524
  natural rate, 427–428, 434, 446, 483, 552
  neoclassical, 422–428, 434, 465–468
  rates, 427–428, 487, 577
  structural, 427, 520, 604
Uniform Commercial Code, 123
unit banking, 236, 237–238, 605
United Auto Workers, 273
United States Bureau of Engraving, 9
United States Bureau of Labor Statistics, 42–43
United States Mint, 8, 29
United States note, 8, 353
United States Treasury, 8, 16, 29, 84, 344
  monetary activity of, 16, 344
United States Treasury and Agency Securities, 124–126, 142–159, 152–153, 173, 175, 222, 276
unit of account, 21, 27–28, 34, 70, 605
U.S.S.R., 184
usury laws, 278

value of marginal product, 413–414
value, store of, 21, 28–30
variable rate loans, 220–221
vault cash, 170–171, 172, 191, 195–196, 221, 292, 347
velocity of circulation, 40, 49, 50, 163, 385, 388, 391–392, 394, 402, 404, 410, 455, 605
  stability, 391–392

Veterans' Administration, 281
Voluntary Credit Restraint Program, 322

wage
  market clearing, 423–424
  minimum, 424–425
  nominal, 63, 274, 375, 412, 413, 414, 417, 420, 421, 430, 465, 466
  real, 54, 75, 375, 412, 413, 414, 415, 417, 418, 421, 427, 430, 446, 451, 463, 465, 466, 474, 483, 603
  rigid, 423–425, 430
wage and price controls, 33
wage and price flexibility, 374, 377, 446, 462–465
wage bargains, 481
wage contracts, 468
Wallich, Henry C., 470, 563
Wall Street, 4
Walras, Leon, 38
wampum, 4, 605
Washington, George, 22
wealth, 395–401
  forms, 395, 396–401
  rates of return, 396–401
wealth effect, 545
Weimar Republic, 30
Whalen, E. L., 526
Wholesale Price Index (see Producer Price Index)
Wicksell, Knut, 458
Willes, Mark H., 435
Wilson, Charles, 273
Winningham, Scott, 193, 253, 292
wire transfer service, 166, 233
Witte, James G., 442, 458
Woodbury, Levi, 84
World War II, 215, 231, 476, 506, 566, 568

Yang, Jai-Hoon, 57
Yap Islands, 26
Yeager, Leland B., 406
yield curves, 152–159, 605
yield to maturity, 129–131, 605

Zurich, gnomes of, 4
Zwick, Burton, 141